Advanced Techniques and Modeling in Business and Economics

Advanced Techniques and Modeling in Business and Economics

Topic Editors

José Manuel Santos-Jaén
Ana León-Gomez
María del Carmen Valls Martínez

MDPI

Basel • Beijing • Wuhan • Barcelona • Belgrade • Novi Sad • Cluj • Manchester

Topic Editors
José Manuel Santos-Jaén
Department of Financial Economics and Accounting
University of Murcia
Murcia
Spain

Ana León-Gomez
Accounting & Management Department
University of Málaga
Málaga
Spain

María del Carmen Valls Martínez
Department of Economics and Business
University of Almería
La Cañada de San Urbano
Spain

Editorial Office
MDPI AG
Grosspeteranlage 5
4052 Basel, Switzerland

This is a reprint of the Topic, published open access by the journals *Data* (ISSN 2306-5729), *Economies* (ISSN 2227-7099), *Mathematics* (ISSN 2227-7390) and *Risks* (ISSN 2227-9091), freely accessible at: https://www.mdpi.com/topics/ATMBE.

For citation purposes, cite each article independently as indicated on the article page online and as indicated below:

Lastname, A.A.; Lastname, B.B. Article Title. *Journal Name* **Year**, *Volume Number*, Page Range.

ISBN 978-3-7258-6950-3 (Hbk)
ISBN 978-3-7258-6951-0 (PDF)
https://doi.org/10.3390/books978-3-7258-6951-0

Contents

About the Editors

José Manuel Santos-Jaén

José Manuel Santos-Jaén is a PhD Associate Professor of Accounting and Finance at the University of Murcia, Spain. He is a graduate in Business Administration and Management and a graduate in Law. He has completed three master's degrees (MBA, Financial Management, and Auditing). He finished his PhD in 2011. He is currently teaching financial statement analysis, financial accounting, and corporate accounting. His research is focused on several aspects of business and management, such as firm performance, innovation, sustainability, and corporate social responsibility, among others. He is strongly oriented to a quantitative, survey-based methodology, mainly Structural Equation Modeling (PLS-SEM). He has published in international journals, including *Journal of Cleaner Production, Corporate Social Responsibility and Environment, IEEE Transactions on Engineering Management, Sustainable Production and Consumption, The International Journal of Management Education,* and *Business Strategy and the Environment*. He has also presented the progress of his research at national and international congresses.

Ana León-Gómez

Ana León-Gómez, Ph.D., is a PhD Assistant Professor at the Department of Accounting and Management, Faculty of Tourism, University of Málaga, Spain. She holds a PhD in Tourism (Cum Laude, 2021) from the University of Málaga, for which she received the Extraordinary Doctoral Award and an Honorable Mention from the Royal Academy of Doctors of Spain. She also completed a master's in financial management and a master of business administration. She is a member of the MAYNAKE Research Group (University of Málaga), the Andalusian Institute for Tourism Research and Innovation, and the Economics, Business, and Sustainability Group (University of Murcia). Her research focuses on SMEs' performance, sustainability, corporate social responsibility, innovation, ICT adoption, tourism economics, and financial analysis. She has published in international journals including *International Journal of Hospitality Management, Oeconomia Copernicana, IEEE Transactions on Engineering Management, The North American Journal of Economics and Finance, Education and Information Technologies, Environment, Development and Sustainability, SAGE Open,* and *Journal of Theoretical and Applied Electronic Commerce Research*. Her work has received several awards, including the ASEPELT/TeleMedCare 2023 Award for Best Scientific Paper on Technological Innovation and the Best Speaker Award at the Global Conference on Data Science, Big Data, and Linguistics (Dubai, 2022), and she was a finalist for the 30th AECA International Award (2024). She has presented her research at numerous international conferences.

María del Carmen Valls Martínez

María del Carmen Valls Martínez, Ph.D., is a full professor of financial economics and accounting at the University of Almería (UAL), Spain. With over 30 years of academic experience, her research has evolved from financial mathematics toward sustainability, corporate social responsibility, and gender studies within the economic sphere. She is the founder and head of the research group "Ethics, Gender, and Sustainability". Dr. Valls Martínez has published extensively with prestigious academic publishers, including Springer, Dykinson, Pirámide, and McGraw-Hill. She is the author of numerous articles in high-impact scientific journals such as *Journal of Cleaner Production, Corporate Social Responsibility and Environmental Management, European Research on Management and Business Economics, Women's Studies International Forum, Sustainable Development, and Oeconomia Copernicana,* among others. Beyond her research and teaching, she contributes significantly to the scientific community through her editorial work. She serves as an editor for *Mathematics, PLoS ONE,* and *Frontiers in Public Health.*

Preface

The increasing integration of advanced analytical, computational, and digital technologies is transforming the foundations of business and economics. The capacity to process large-scale data, model complex interactions, and generate predictive insights has become central to understanding modern economic systems and guiding decision-making across firms, markets, and institutions. Artificial intelligence, computational modeling, advanced forecasting, and optimization methods are no longer peripheral tools; they are reshaping how productivity, financial systems, labor markets, and organizational strategies evolve in an increasingly data-driven and uncertain environment.

The topic "Advanced Techniques and Modeling in Business and Economics" was conceived as a multidisciplinary platform to explore how these emerging approaches contribute to advancing economic and business research. Rather than focusing on isolated technological applications, the topic emphasizes the systemic role of advanced modeling and analytical techniques in addressing complex and dynamic economic phenomena. The contributions collectively highlight how artificial intelligence, machine learning, computational economics, and quantitative modeling enhance forecasting accuracy, improve resource allocation, strengthen financial decision-making, and support more informed policy design.

This reprint compiles fourteen peer-reviewed studies that reflect the breadth and diversity of contemporary research at the intersection of advanced analytics and economic systems. The contributions span multiple levels of analysis—from firm-level productivity and financial optimization to macroeconomic modeling, financial markets, and digital transformation—illustrating how technological and methodological advances are reshaping both theory and practice in business and economics.

A first thematic cluster focuses on artificial intelligence and its role in economic and organizational transformation. Several chapters examine how AI and machine learning improve productivity, support digital transformation, and reshape decision-making processes within firms. These studies demonstrate how intelligent systems enable new forms of productivity, enhance knowledge generation, and facilitate innovation in increasingly complex and technology-driven economic environments.

A second group of contributions addresses modeling and forecasting in financial and economic systems. These chapters explore the application of advanced quantitative techniques—including machine learning, fuzzy optimization, and time-series modeling—to portfolio selection, financial market dynamics, and risk analysis. Collectively, they show how modern modeling approaches improve predictive performance, capture uncertainty, and enhance the robustness of decision-making in volatile economic contexts.

A third thematic strand examines macroeconomic dynamics and labor market behavior through computational and learning-based approaches. These works highlight the growing relevance of reinforcement learning and simulation-based models for understanding economic fluctuations, bounded rationality, and adaptive behavior in complex systems. By integrating computational intelligence with economic theory, these studies contribute to a deeper understanding of how learning and adaptation shape macroeconomic outcomes.

Beyond these core themes, the volume also includes contributions addressing productivity, innovation, efficiency, digital transformation, and strategic adaptation in firms and markets. Together, the chapters underscore a common message: modern economic and business challenges require integrated, data-driven, and computationally sophisticated approaches capable of capturing complexity, uncertainty, and structural change.

This collection aims to provide a comprehensive perspective on how advanced analytical and modeling techniques can enhance both theoretical understanding and practical applications in business and economics. It is intended as a reference for researchers developing new methodological frameworks, for practitioners implementing data-driven decision systems, and for policymakers seeking evidence-based tools to navigate increasingly complex economic environments.

As Guest Editors, we express our sincere gratitude to the authors for the rigor and relevance of their contributions, and to the reviewers for their thoughtful evaluations and constructive recommendations, which substantially strengthened the quality of the manuscripts. We also thank the editorial and production teams for their continuous support throughout the development of this Topic and the preparation of this volume. We hope that this reprint will contribute to advancing research and practice in the application of advanced techniques and modeling in business and economics and inspire further interdisciplinary work in this rapidly evolving field.

José Manuel Santos-Jaén, Ana León-Gomez, and María del Carmen Valls Martínez
Topic Editors

mathematics

MDPI

Article

A Fuzzy Entropy Approach for Portfolio Selection

Milena Bonacic [1], Héctor López-Ospina [1], Cristián Bravo [2] and Juan Pérez [1,*]

[1] Universidad de Los Andes, Mons. Álvaro del Portillo 12455, Las Condes, Santiago 7620086, Chile; mbonacic@miuandes.cl (M.B.); halopez@uandes.cl (H.L.-O.)

[2] University of Western Ontario, London, ON N6A 5B7, Canada; cbravoro@uwo.ca

* Correspondence: jperez@uandes.cl

Abstract: Portfolio management typically aims to achieve better returns per unit of risk by building efficient portfolios. The Markowitz framework is the classic approach used when decision-makers know the expected returns and covariance matrix of assets. However, the theory does not always apply when the time horizon of investments is short; the realized return and covariance of different assets are usually far from the expected values, and considering additional factors, such as diversification and information ambiguity, can lead to better portfolios. This study proposes models for constructing efficient portfolios using fuzzy parameters like entropy, return, variance, and entropy membership functions in multi-criteria optimization models. Our approach leverages aspects related to multi-criteria optimization and Shannon entropy to deal with diversification, and fuzzy and fuzzy entropy variants provide a better representation of the ambiguity of the information according to the investors' deadline. We compare 418 optimal portfolios for different objectives (return, variance, and entropy), using data from 2003 to 2023 of indexes from the USA, EU, China, and Japan. We use the Sharpe index as a decision variable, in addition to the multi-criteria decision analysis method TOPSIS. Our models provided high-efficiency portfolios, particularly those considering fuzzy entropy membership functions for return and variance.

Keywords: portfolio selection; fuzzy entropy; Shannon's entropy; multi-criteria optimization; TOPSIS

MSC: 91-10

1. Introduction

The modern portfolio theory (MPT), initiated by Markowitz in 1956 [1], is a set of techniques for constructing portfolios that optimally balance maximum returns and an acceptable level of risk for investors. The mean-variance model serves as the foundation of MPT, which assumes investors display rational behavior and possess complete information. MPT has given rise to several research avenues, including entropy measures and modeling information uncertainty and ambiguity through fuzzy logic. The utilization of entropy measures addresses the issue of the low diversification that can result from the mean-variance model, by providing a more comprehensive outlook on portfolio diversification. Meanwhile, fuzzy logic provides a valuable method for handling uncertainty and ambiguity in information by considering acceptable ranges of values, such as the acceptable range of return levels for the portfolio. This study proposes models that combine entropy, fuzzy logic, and fuzzy entropy modeling within a multi-criteria framework. The models with fuzzy entropy performed well, according to a TOPSIS comparison of different model combinations [2]. To the best of our knowledge, this fuzzy entropy approach has not previously been utilized in portfolio selection. In conclusion, our proposed models incorporating fuzzy entropy showed promising results compared to other models in portfolio selection.

As a general concept, fuzzy entropy measures the vagueness or ambiguity of flexible or imprecise parameters in decision-making systems. This measure can be interpreted as the information gain in fuzzy environments and can be used to compare the ambiguity of different decision-making systems [2]. Mathematically, if we consider a fuzzy set A and a fuzzy membership function $\mu_A(x) \in [0,1]$, defined on a set X, this is given by $H_f(A) = -\sum_{x\in X} \mu_A(x)\log_2(\mu_A(x))$. Please note that this formula is similar to the Shannon entropy formula, which measures the uncertainty or disorder of a probability distribution. However, we consider the membership degree given by $\mu_A(x)$ in fuzzy entropy.

In our previous work on a fuzzy entropy approach in transportation [3], we maximized information gain and outperformed prior methods when calculating origin–destination matrices; these promising results led us to examine its potential for portfolio selection. Our findings were favorable after conducting model construction, data collection, and portfolio testing. The application of fuzzy entropy in information theory is well-established; we extended this measure by incorporating the return and variance of the portfolio into both the objective function and constraints of our models.

While the developments in post-MPT are numerous, in this paper, we focus on the base mean-variance approach and its variants [4], specifically emphasizing fuzzy entropy. The mean-variance model is well-known and has shown great results in practice, but it has limitations that have led to new models, such as those incorporating entropy measures and fuzzy logic. The mean-variance model can produce highly variable solutions with even small changes to parameters such as the portfolio's expected return. As noted by [5], it can also assign high values to high-risk assets. This variability is partly due to the model's assumption of a normal distribution of assets' expected returns, variances, and covariances, and the expectation that these results will hold in the future.

In the mean-variance model, the expected return level reflects investors' expectations. It is common practice to perform sensitivity analyses on this parameter, as results have shown that small changes to the expected return can result in significantly different portfolios [6,7]. To address this, we propose adding flexibility to the model by treating the expected return as a range rather than a fixed value. This is achieved using fuzzy intervals and entropy, which we demonstrate in Section 3.1.

The aim of a mean-variance model is typically to achieve the highest possible return level, while minimizing variance. The resulting portfolio may contain high-return assets to meet the desired return, which is also known as a sparse solution [5,8]. Diversification, such as maximizing portfolio entropy [9], can be used to address this issue.

It is usual to assume that the returns follow a normal distribution when estimating means, variances, and covariances in finance. However, asset returns are often non-normally distributed and exhibit skewness and kurtosis, leading to portfolios that appear efficient based on normal assumptions but are sub-optimal when considering the actual distribution of returns [10]. Assuming normal distributions can also result in overly optimistic risk assessments, causing investors to take on more risk than they realize, as normal distributions do not adequately capture rare events such as large market crashes [11]. Additionally, normal assumptions can negatively impact portfolio diversification, as correlations estimated from normal distributions may differ from the actual correlations in the data. Our central hypothesis to address these issues is that using fuzzy entropy on expected returns and variances could help evaluate the performance of portfolios for future unknown values.

There are also modeling approaches using entropy measures to deal with some of the problems with the mean-variance model; the more common use is to produce diversified portfolios [5]. Ref. [9] understood this need for more diversification of the solutions of the mean-variance model as corner solutions and analyzed how different entropy measures could help with this problem.

As indicated by [12], fuzzy approaches deal better with real-world uncertainties in portfolio construction. Nevertheless, as already indicated, entropy measures help diversification by avoiding corner solutions [9]. The evident approach considers multiple objectives; we can mention entropy measures, fuzzy parameters, and return maximization [12–15].

The aim of our research was to test if the introduction of fuzzy and fuzzy entropy produces better portfolios than those obtained from known approaches, such as the base mean-variance model and models with entropy measures. It is relevant to highlight why our fuzzy and fuzzy entropy approaches are novel. We focus on mean return and variance by applying fuzzy and fuzzy entropy measures in different models. In this context, we represent the information gain as one of the objective functions and control this parameter in the constraints of the optimization problem.

In this paper, we compared the performance of portfolios through the allocation of assets using seven optimization models at different moments. We used various time windows to calculate the resulting portfolio within each model, and within them, we used multiple configurations to analyze the objective functions' relevance. Then, we calculated the performance of the portfolios for data outside the time window in which we estimated the portfolio. With these results, we ranked them using a TOPSIS approach.

To summarize, our paper showcases the following research highlights:

- We proposed optimization problems with multiple objective functions to construct portfolios and model fuzzy and fuzzy entropy measures on the portfolio's expected return and variance.
- We analyzed seven models and ran numerical experiments to rank these models using TOPSIS. We considered various time windows and evaluated the portfolios outside the window.
- Among the models tested, the multi-objective model multi-criteria Shannon and fuzzy entropy on target return and variance consistently delivered the highest returns and Sharpe ratios, placing it on the efficient frontier. Based on the TOPSIS methodology applied to return, variance, and portfolio entropy, it delivered consistent results across different configurations. Its key strength was its ability to capture all configurations without imposing significant optimization restrictions, making it the optimal model for constructing the best portfolio. Rather than seeking the theoretical optimal, it tended to converge towards observable centers. Portfolio selection.
- We recommend fuzzy models that contain the entropic membership function in their structure; fuzzy measures provide the flexibility to handle intervals and uncertainties, and fuzzy entropy maximizes the information gain for both return and variance, further reinforcing the models' flexibility.

The paper is organized into six sections. The following section presents a literature review and positions our paper within the current portfolio-selection literature. We describe the models we considered in Section 3. Section 4 describes the data considered for the numerical experiments and the details of the methodology applied. Section 5 shows the results we obtained, commented on, and discussed in Section 6. Finally, in Section 7, we present our final analysis and conclusions.

2. Literature Review

The field of portfolio optimization is vast and originated with the classic work of [1]. Since then, the number of papers in the area has kept growing, with many surveys in the field, such as the one by [4] focusing on deterministic models or by [16] oriented towards robust optimization methods.

The beginning of the modern portfolio theory (MPT), an investment theory based on the idea that risk-averse investors can construct portfolios to optimize or maximize expected returns based on a given level of market risk, emphasizes that risk is an inherent part of higher rewards [1]. MPT assumes that investors are risk-averse, meaning that given two portfolios that offer the same expected return, investors will prefer the less risky one. Thus, an investor will take on increased risk only if compensated by higher expected returns. Conversely, an investor who wants higher expected returns must accept more risk. The exact trade-off will be the same for all investors, but different investors will evaluate the trade-off differently based on individual risk aversion characteristics. An investor can reduce portfolio risk simply by holding combinations of non-perfectly positively correlated instruments. If all the asset pairs have correlations of 0—they are perfectly uncorrelated—the portfolio's return variance is the sum over all assets of the square of the fraction held in the asset times the asset's return variance (and the portfolio standard deviation is the square root of this sum).

The efficient frontier is a cornerstone of modern portfolio theory and is the line that indicates the combination of investments that will provide the highest level of return for the lowest level of risk [17]. When a portfolio falls to the right of the efficient frontier, it possesses greater risk relative to its predicted return. When it falls beneath the slope of the efficient frontier, it offers a lower return relative to risk [1]. It is one of the most important and influential economic theories dealing with finance and investment.

There are five basic assumptions that are fundamentals upon which the MPT is constructed [1]:

1. The expected return and the variance are the only parameters that affect an investor's decision.
2. Investors are generally rational and risk-averse. They are completely aware of all the risks in investment and take positions based on the risk determination demanding a higher return for accepting greater volatility.
3. There are no transaction costs for buying and selling securities.
4. All investors have the same expectations concerning the expected return, variance, and covariance.
5. Analysis is based on a single-period investment model.

Despite its theoretical importance, critics of the MPT question whether it is an ideal investment tool, because its model of financial markets does not match the real world in many ways. The risk, return, and correlation measures used by MPT are based on expected values, meaning they are mathematical statements about the future (the expected value of returns is explicit in the above equations and implicit in the definitions of variance and covariance). The mean-variance model is an a priori consideration of the homoscedasticity of the variance of the series, a fact that contradicts one of the stylized facts of the financial series, which is the frequent heteroskedasticity; that is, the variance suffers from systematic changes during the studying time. In practice, investors must substitute predictions based on historical asset return and volatility measurements for these values in the equations. Very often, such expected values fail to take account of new circumstances that did not exist when the historical data were generated, introducing uncertainty in the problem modeled through fuzzy logic [6,7].

In this context, many methods have been used to optimize portfolios, but the attention that fuzzy methods have received has not been as systematically studied as the methodologies in the surveys conducted. An exception is the survey by [13], but their study has not been updated since, and many more developments have appeared since then. In what follows, we will describe other works within portfolio optimization using fuzzy methods.

Since the above survey, approaches such as [18,19] have applied fuzzy methods to model returns, considering its variation as the fuzzy variable, and identifying the variability of returns as a form of uncertainty that can be captured with fuzzy models. These models either made assumptions about the shape of the variance or considered deterministic variance scenarios. Later, researchers focused on keeping the fuzzy view of the uncertainty of returns but modeled the time dynamics of the problem. Papers such as [20–22] dealt with time-varying portfolio optimization under different circumstances, ranging from the accumulation of risks from variance, transaction costs, and diversification degrees [20], directly considering the time series of returns as a fuzzy system [23], to applying uncertainty to the returns and the liquidity of the assets within the time series in [22] and later in [24]. In all of these studies, studying the returns across time as a fuzzy system was the focus, as opposed to our paper, in which we consider a two-dimensional fuzzy system over the ball of mean-variance, combining the source of uncertainty.

Another focus of many researchers using fuzzy methods has been the multiobjective approach. The recent work by [25] explored how three different objectives can be reconciled when optimizing portfolios using fuzzy logic. Ref. [26] compared the stock return and the general financial situation of a company to build a portfolio following fuzzy logic. Ref. [27]

modeled returns as a fuzzy system but included fuzzy targets in the optimization process, including perceptual credibility constraints to the portfolio construction, a similar approach to the work of [28], who considered credibility within the return–liquidity space. Following this credibility approach, the work by [29] considered returns, volatility, skewness, and kurtosis within a fuzzy framework but focused on each as an objective, rather than a source of uncertainty, as we do in our work.

Other approaches in the area have focused, for example, on reducing variability in the decision, such as the semi-entropy approach by [23], which focuses on the downside uncertainty. The impact of rationality in decisions using fuzzy entropy was recently explored by [30], who modeled constraints on portfolios from the rationality expectations of agents. Our work follows the more traditional line of maximizing the portfolio's risk-adjusted return by explicitly including the uncertainty of the mean-variance surface, as explained in the following sections.

On the other hand, in the context of a decision support system for ranking company stock investments based on value investing, the TOPSIS (technique for order of preference by similarity to ideal solution) approach can be a valuable tool. The approach utilized by this stock ranking decision support system is the TOPSIS procedure. The TOPSIS algorithm's geometric principle states that the selected alternative must be located at the maximum distance from the negative ideal solution and closest to the positive ideal solution. To ascertain the relative proximity of an alternative to the optimal solution, Euclidean distance is utilized as a method of multi-criteria decision-making that ranks potential solutions according to their similarity to the optimal solution. Several studies have highlighted the applicability of TOPSIS in various domains, including financial performance evaluation [31], group decision making [32], stock portfolio selection [33], and stock portfolio investment [34].

By integrating TOPSIS into the decision-making process, companies can effectively evaluate and rank investment opportunities based on various criteria. This method allows for systematic comparison of stocks, thereby enabling the identification of stocks that outperform those underperforming [35]. Additionally, TOPSIS has been used in the financial sector for applications such as bankruptcy prediction and stock selection for portfolio construction [36]. These applications demonstrate TOPSIS' flexibility in assisting decision-making processes in portfolio selection. Thus, it is used for making a final decision in order to select the optimal portfolio; the methodology and the involved variables are explained in the following section.

3. Models and Methods

3.1. The Models

First, we define Markowitz's base model (Model 1), the theoretical foundation for most studies in this field. We then define two variants with entropic measures: Model 2 maximizes Shannon's entropy with return and variance as constraints, while Model 3 minimizes the variance and maximizes entropy in a single objective function. Model 4 is a multi-criteria model with Shannon's entropy maximization and fuzzy parameters on the mean and variance of the portfolio. Models 5 and 6 are similar, in that they both maximize entropy, but while Model 5 controls variance with fuzzy intervals, Model 6 only minimizes it. Finally, Model 7 has three objective functions, maximizing entropy, while controlling average return and variance with fuzzy entropy measures.

3.1.1. Model 1: The Markowitz Base Model

Let us consider $i \in \{1, \ldots, n\}$ assets with returns r_i. The decision variables x_i represent the relative weights invested in the portfolio accomplishing Equation (1). The aim is to find the optimal portfolio through the weights, accomplishing the expected return Equation (2) and a variance bound Equation (3) of the portfolio. We can construct the base Markowitz model from this initial setting and the variants and specializations we propose for analysis.

In Equation (3), σ_i are the standard deviations of assets' returns and ρ_{ij} are their correlation coefficients.

$$\sum_{i=1}^{n} x_i = 1 \tag{1}$$

$$r_p(\mathbf{x}) = \sum_{i=1}^{n} x_i \mathbb{E}\{r_i\} \tag{2}$$

$$\mathbb{V}(\mathbf{x}) = \sum_{i=1}^{n}\sum_{j=1}^{n} x_i x_j \sigma_i \sigma_j \rho_{ij} \tag{3}$$

We define in Equation (4) Markowitz's base model or Model 1, which minimizes the variance and meets R_p for the portfolios' expected return.

$$\begin{array}{lll} \min\limits_{\{\mathbf{x}>0\}} & \mathbb{V}(\mathbf{x}) & \\ \text{s.t.} & r_p(\mathbf{x}) & = & R_p \\ & \sum\limits_{i=1}^{n} x_i & = & 1 \end{array} \tag{4}$$

Let us note that, in Equation (4), the constraint $r_p(\mathbf{x}) = R_p$ could also be greater than ($\geq$) as in [37].

3.1.2. Model 2: Shannon's Entropy Maximization

Model 2 includes the maximization of the entropy $H(\mathbf{x})$. Equation (5) relates the portfolio to the base model, which helps produce more diversified portfolios.In this optimization problem, the expected returns R_p and variance σ_p^2 are within the constraints. In Equation (6), we define Model 2 that corresponds to this case; this model was also considered by [9,38] among others.

$$H(\mathbf{x}) = -\sum_{i=1}^{n} x_i \ln(x_i) \tag{5}$$

$$\begin{array}{llll} \max\limits_{\{\mathbf{x}>0\}} & H(\mathbf{x}) & & \\ \text{s.t.} & r_p(\mathbf{x}) & = & R_p \\ & \mathbb{V}(\mathbf{x}) & \leq & \sigma_p^2 \\ & \sum\limits_{i=1}^{n} x_i & = & 1 \end{array} \tag{6}$$

3.1.3. Model 3: Shannon's Entropy Maximization and Minimum Variance

In Equation (7), we show Model 3, which includes the minimization of the entropy and the minimization of the portfolio's variance. The model Equation (7) balances within the objective function, with equal emphasis on both the maximization of the entropy and the minimization of the variance of the resulting portfolio, while requiring a specific level R_p for the portfolio return.

$$\begin{array}{llll} \min\limits_{\{\mathbf{x}>0\}} & \mathbb{V}(\mathbf{x}) - H(\mathbf{x}) & & \\ \text{s.t.} & r_p(\mathbf{x}) & = & R_p \\ & \sum\limits_{i=1}^{n} x_i & = & 1 \end{array} \tag{7}$$

3.1.4. Model 4: Multi-Criteria with Shannon's Entropy Maximization and Fuzziness on Target Return and Variance

In Model 4, we introduce a multi-criteria optimization scheme, by adding fuzzy parameters for the portfolio's target expected return and variance. We define this case as the bi-objective model or Model 4 in Equation (8), where we maximize the entropy and control the expected return and variance with trapezoidal intervals.

In Equation (8), the parameters $(\underline{r}, r_1, r_2, \overline{r})$ and $\left(\underline{\sigma}^2, \sigma_1^2, \sigma_2^2, \overline{\sigma}^2\right)$ correspond to the representation of trapezoidal fuzzy membership functions for the expected return R_p and variance σ_p^2.

$$\begin{array}{llll} \max\limits_{\{\mathbf{x}>0, \lambda\in[0,1]\}} & \{H(\mathbf{x}), \lambda\} & & \\ \text{s.t.} & r_p(\mathbf{x}) & \geq & \lambda r_1 + (1-\lambda)\underline{r} \\ & r_p(\mathbf{x}) & \leq & \lambda r_2 + (1-\lambda)\overline{r} \\ & \mathbb{V}(\mathbf{x}) & \geq & \lambda \sigma_1^2 + (1-\lambda)\underline{\sigma}^2 \\ & \mathbb{V}(\mathbf{x}) & \leq & \lambda \sigma_2^2 + (1-\lambda)\overline{\sigma}^2 \\ & \sum\limits_{i=1}^{n} x_i & = & 1 \end{array} \quad (8)$$

In (8), $(\underline{r}, r_1, r_2, \overline{r})$ and $(\underline{\sigma}^2, \sigma_1^2, \sigma_2^2, \overline{\sigma}^2)$ are the parameters of trapezoidal fuzzy sets associated with the expected return and variance of the portfolio. We use the trapezoidal form of a fuzzy parameter; in Figure 1, we show how the return R_p is represented by a trapezoid and a membership function $\mu(R_p)$, which in (8) is controlled by the decision variable μ. Please note that the case for the trapezoid membership function for the variance is analogous, and when $r_1 = r_2$, the trapezoid shape turns into a triangular membership function.

For the return trapezoid, at every point in time, we calculated the maximum possible return and defined every parameter of the trapezoid based on this number. 0 was always the lower bound for the return trapezoid, because nobody wanted to invest in a negative expected return portfolio. We calculated the minimum and maximum volatility values for the volatility case at each point in time. We set the trapezoid parameter to 1.25 times the minimum sigma and the other parameter to 0.75 times the maximum sigma.

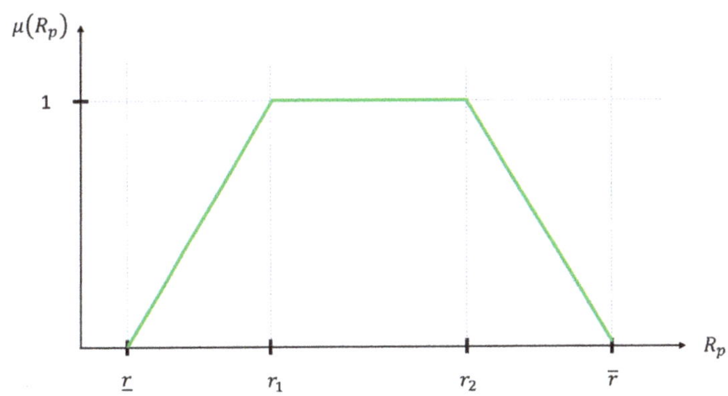

Figure 1. Explanatory figure for trapezoidal fuzzy parameter R_p.

3.1.5. Model 5: Multi-Criteria Shannon, Fuzzy Variance and Fuzzy Entropy on Target Return

In Equation (10), we define a model with a trapezoidal fuzzy bound. This is a tri-objective approach; its first objective function is maximizing the entropy $H(\mathbf{x})$. The second objective is a fuzzy entropy approach for maximizing the entropy of the fuzzy portfolio's return $g_1(\alpha)$ (see Equation (9)). The third is maximizing the membership for the variance using the decision variable λ.

$$g_1(\alpha) = -\alpha \ln(\alpha) - (1-\alpha)\ln(1-\alpha) \quad (9)$$

$$
\begin{array}{llll}
\max\limits_{\{\mathbf{x}>0,\alpha\in[0,1],\lambda\in[0,1]\}} & \{H(\mathbf{x}), g_1(\alpha), \lambda\} & & \\
\text{s.t.} & r_p(\mathbf{x}) & = & \alpha\underline{r} + (1-\alpha)\overline{r} \\
& \mathbb{V}(\mathbf{x}) & \geq & \lambda\sigma_1^2 + (1-\lambda)\underline{\sigma}^2 \\
& \mathbb{V}(\mathbf{x}) & \leq & \lambda\sigma_2^2 + (1-\lambda)\overline{\sigma}^2 \\
& \sum\limits_{i=1}^{n} x_i & = & 1
\end{array}
\quad (10)
$$

The model in expression Equation (11) is a particular case of Equation (10) in which $\sigma_p^2 = \sigma_1^2 = \sigma_2^2$ and $\lambda = 1$, and in which we represented the constraint associated with the variance as an upper-bound, considering that if there is any solution with a variance lower than σ_p^2, then we consider this a good solution.

$$
\begin{array}{llll}
\max\limits_{\{\mathbf{x}>0,\alpha\in[0,1]\}} & \{H(\mathbf{x}), g_1(\alpha)\} & & \\
\text{s.t.} & r_p(\mathbf{x}) & = & \alpha\underline{r} + (1-\alpha)\overline{r} \\
& \mathbb{V}(\mathbf{x}) & \leq & \sigma_p^2 \\
& \sum\limits_{i=1}^{n} x_i & = & 1
\end{array}
\quad (11)
$$

We show the fuzzy entropy function $g_1(\alpha)$ in Figure 2. In this case, α controls the value of $R_p \in [\underline{r}, \overline{r}]$.

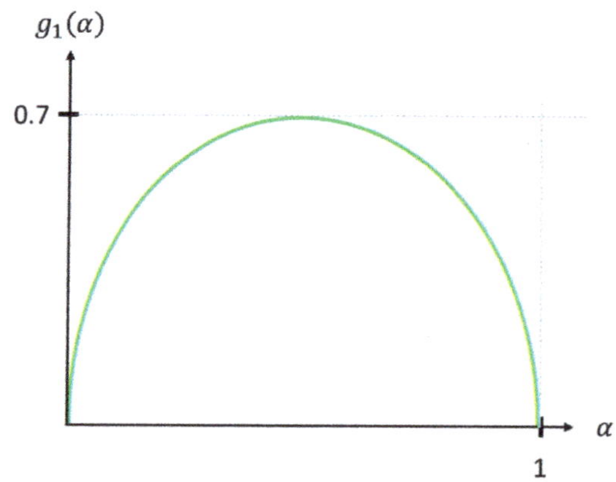

Figure 2. Explanatory figure for the fuzzy entropy function $g_1(\alpha)$.

3.1.6. Model 6: Multi-Criteria Shannon, Fuzzy Entropy on Target Return and Min Variance

In Equation (12), we define Model 6 with a fuzzy entropy representation for the expected return and with three objective functions. The first is the maximization of the portfolio's entropy; the second is the maximization of the fuzzy entropy of the expected return; and the third is the minimization of the portfolio's variance.

$$
\begin{array}{llll}
\max\limits_{\{\mathbf{x}>0,\alpha\in[0,1]\}} & \{H(\mathbf{x}), g_1(\alpha), -\mathbb{V}(\mathbf{x})\} & & \\
\text{s.t.} & r_p(\mathbf{x}) & = & \alpha\underline{r} + (1-\alpha)\overline{r} \\
& \sum\limits_{i=1}^{n} x_i & = & 1
\end{array}
\quad (12)
$$

3.1.7. Model 7: Multi-Criteria Shannon and Fuzzy Entropy on Target Return and Variance

In Equation (14), we propose Model 7. It has three objective functions. The first is the maximization of the portfolio's entropy $H(\mathbf{x})$, the second is the maximization of the fuzzy entropy function of the portfolio's return $g_1(\alpha)$, and the third is the minimization of the portfolio's variance $g_2(\beta)$, defined in Equation (13). Note that the shape of the fuzzy entropy function $g_2(\mathbf{x})$ is the same as $g_1(\mathbf{x})$.

$$g_2(\beta) = -\beta \ln(\beta) - (1-\beta)\ln(1-\beta) \quad (13)$$

$$\begin{array}{llcl}\max\limits_{\{\mathbf{x}>0, \alpha\in[0,1], \beta\in[0,1]\}} & \{H(\mathbf{x}), g_1(\alpha), g_2(\beta)\} & & \\ \text{s.t.} & r_p(\mathbf{x}) & = & \alpha \underline{r} + (1-\alpha)\overline{r} \\ & \mathbb{V}(\mathbf{x}) & = & \beta \underline{\sigma}^2 + (1-\beta)\overline{\sigma}^2 \\ & \sum\limits_{i=1}^{n} x_i & = & 1 \end{array} \quad (14)$$

The bases of the fuzzy models (4, 5, 6, and 7) can be seen in the Appendix A, with the mathematical deduction of the models with fuzzy parameters, and where some definitions of fuzzy sets and fuzzy optimization are described.

4. Methodology

In this section, we describe the data we considered for our numerical experimentation and explain how we ordered the numerical instances; we also give details on how we solved the optimization problems and, finally, describe how we applied TOPSIS.

4.1. Data Description

The database we considered has monthly registers of stock indices of the USA Standard & Poor's 500, Europe Euro Stoxx 50, Japan Nikkei 225, and China HSCEI from 2003 to 2023. The relevance of using indices in the portfolio resides in the fact that this strategy is scalable to different investment amounts because the volumes traded with the instruments are very high. The values are monthly from the year 2003 to 2023.

The USA Standard & Poor's 500 index, also known as S&P 500, is one of the most important stock indexes in the United States; it is considered the most representative index of the real market situation. The index is based on the market capitalization of 500 large companies that own shares listed on the NYSE or NASDAQ exchanges and captures approximately 80% of all market capitalization in the United States. The Europe Euro Stoxx 50 index represents the performance of the 50 largest companies among the 19 super sectors regarding market capitalization in 11 eurozone countries. These countries are Germany, Austria, Belgium, Spain, Finland, France, Ireland, Italy, Luxembourg, the Netherlands, and Portugal. The Japan Nikkei 225 index, also called the Nikkei index, is the most popular stock index in the Japanese market, comprising the 225 most liquid securities listed on the Tokyo Stock Exchange. The China HSCEI index is the main Chinese stock index of Hong Kong. It records and monitors the daily changes in the largest Hong Kong companies on the stock market. It consists of 33 companies, representing 65% of the Hong Kong Stock Exchange.

4.2. Description of Numerical Instances

From the entire dataset, with monthly values from the year 2003 to 2023, corresponding to 235 samples of each stock index, we divided the dataset into five non-overlapping subsets, performing a temporal partition with the same length (47 samples). The objective was to test the model under different market conditions, denoted as independent analysis sets $(S1, S2, S3, S4, S5)$. In Table 1, we show the time interval for each scenario.

Table 1. Subset.

Dates/Scenario	1	2	3	4	5
Start date	31 May 2003	31 May 2007	30 April 2011	31 March 2016	29 February 2020
End date	31 March 2007	31 March 2011	28 February 2015	31 January 2020	31 December 2023

To evaluate the performance of each model in each subset, we used a rolling window approach, where we calculated the expected returns and covariance matrices for each window. Please see the rolling time window methodology in Figure 3.

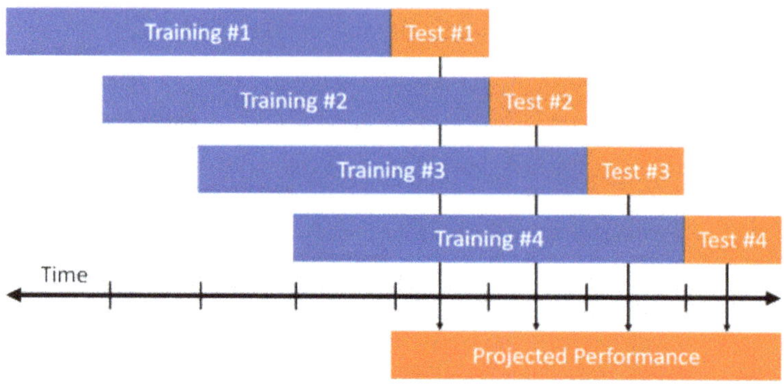

Figure 3. Rolling time window.

We consider it relevant to explain that, as we considered four indexes, the variances and covariances do not constitute high-dimensional matrices. However, when modelers consider several stock prices, indexes, or exchange-traded funds, they will face high-dimensional variances and covariances matrices. Although this is not relevant in our case, we can recommend literature for performing analysis under these circumstances [39–41].

There were 47 samples (monthly returns) in the five scenarios analyzed. The methodology used to estimate the returns and the covariance matrix was based on a moving window of 20 samples of the returns of the stock indices (from $t-19$ to t) used in this study; the last 20 samples were considered. Therefore, in one scenario, there were 27 portfolios obtained, since new data (returns) were included for calculating the estimation of returns and the covariance matrix. Based on these estimates, we proceeded to optimize the portfolios. The advantage of using this method lies in capturing possible changes over time in the statistics of the indices and thus making a dynamic estimation that helps to improve the optimization of the model [42]. Finally, we compounded each model's returns (portfolio) over all the subsets, to evaluate each model and obtain its total returns.

4.3. Solving the Optimization Problems

We solved these models using the Optimization Toolbox of Matlab v9.6 (Release R2019a; MathWorks Inc., Natick, MA, USA).

Models 1, 2, and 3 are nonlinear and have a single objective function. It is worth noting that, even though Model 3 has both variance minimization and entropy maximization objectives, we used the approach proposed by [43] to solve it as a single-objective problem. For Model 1, we performed optimization by minimizing the constrained variance to eleven different return values, from r_{min} to r_{max}, where r_{min} is the lowest possible return and r_{max} is the highest possible return given the window under analysis. This return interval was moved with a step of 0.1 times the length of the return interval, generating 11 optimal solutions, one for each restricted return. In Model 2, the maximization of the portfolio entropy was constrained to return and variance values. The return and variance interval was moved with a step of 0.1 times the length of the interval (return and variance), generating 121 solutions (11 returns $\times$ 11 variances).

In the case of Model 3, we minimized the variance and maximized the entropy in the target function, for which we constrained the return; we implemented this constraint as an equality and an inequality. The path of the return interval was carried out at a step of 0.1 times the length of the interval, generating 22 solutions.

Models 4 to 7 are nonlinear and have multiple objective functions. We used the ϵ-constraint methodology [44] to find solutions. This methodology solves a multi-objective problem by minimizing a single function, while leaving the others as constraints. The ϵ-constraint approach converts the multiple objective functions into constraints controlled by a right-hand-side parameter ϵ. We could estimate the efficient frontier of the solutions by performing a sensitivity analysis on the ϵ parameters. The efficient frontier concept, in this case, refers to the optimization problem with multiple objective functions, where we aimed to find the set of optimal solutions that maximized one objective function, while satisfying the constraints imposed by the other objective functions.

In mathematical terms, let us consider a general multiobjective optimization problem as defined in (15), with $\{f_i(\mathbf{x})\}_{i=0}^n$ objective functions and $j \in \{1, \ldots, m\}$ constraints, defined by the functions $g_j(\mathbf{x})$ and its right-hand-side parameters b_j. The ϵ-constraint approach is shown in (16) when keeping $f_0(\mathbf{x})$ as a single objective function, and considering $\{f_i(\mathbf{x})\}_{i=1}^n$ as constraints with right-hand-side parameters $\{\epsilon_i\}_{i=1}^n$.

$$\begin{array}{lllll} \min\limits_{\{\mathbf{x} \geq 0\}} & \{f_0(\mathbf{x}), \ldots, f_n(\mathbf{x})\} & & & \\ \text{s.t.} & g_j(\mathbf{x}) & \geq & b_j & \forall j \in \{1, \ldots, m\} \end{array} \tag{15}$$

$$\begin{array}{lllll} \min\limits_{\{\mathbf{x} \geq 0\}} & f_0(\mathbf{x}) & & & \\ \text{s.t.} & g_j(\mathbf{x}) & \geq & b_j & \forall j \in \{1, \ldots, m\} \\ & f_i(\mathbf{x}) & \geq & \epsilon_i & \forall i \in \{1, \ldots, n\} \end{array} \tag{16}$$

We applied the ϵ-constraint approach for each model, as indicated below:

- Model 4—Maximum entropy, fuzzy in return and variance: This model has two objective functions for the entropy maximization, and the control parameter λ for the membership function, and for variance and the expected return of the portfolio. We kept the entropy as the single objective function in this case, turning the λ into an ϵ-constraint. We performed numerical experiments by carrying out sensitivity analysis on the corresponding ϵ bounding λ. Then, these intervals were controlled by λ; this variable takes values between 0 and 1, moving at a step of 0.1, generating 11 solutions.
- Model 5—Entropy maximization, fuzzy entropy in return, fuzzy in variance: This model has three objective functions: entropy maximization, the fuzzy entropic function for the expected return, and the control parameter λ of the membership function for portfolio's variance. In this case, we kept the entropy as the single objective function, turning the other objective functions into two ϵ-constraints. We performed the numerical experiments through sensitivity analysis on the corresponding ϵ parameters bounding λ and $g_1(\mathbf{x})$.
  Using the same approach as for Model 4, α and λ took values between 0 and 1; with α acting on the return constraint, and λ modulating the variance interval (trapezium); these intervals were constraints in the optimization process. The path of α and λ had a step of 0.1, which generated 121 solutions.
- Model 6—Entropy maximization, fuzzy entropy in return and variance: This model had three objective functions: entropy maximization, the fuzzy entropic for the expected return, and the portfolio's variance minimization functions. In this case, we kept the entropy as a single objective function, turning the other objective functions into two ϵ-constraints. We performed the numerical experiments through a sensitivity analysis on the corresponding ϵ parameters bounding $g_1(\mathbf{x})$ and $\mathbb{V}(\mathbf{x})$. Continuing with the same methodology used in the other models, α was a variable that took values between 0 and 1, running this interval at a step of 0.1, generating 11 solutions.
- Model 7—Entropy maximization and fuzzy entropy in return and variance: This model had three objective functions: the entropy maximization and the fuzzy entropic functions for the expected return and variance of the portfolio. In this case, we kept the entropy as a single objective function, turning the other objective functions into two ϵ-constraints. We performed the numerical experiments by carrying ou

sensitivity analysis on the corresponding ϵ parameters bounding $g_1(\mathbf{x})$ and $g_2(\mathbf{x})$, moving through these parameters at a step of 0.1, and 121 portfolios were generated. The optimization process of each model ended when we selected the optimal portfolio for each (Models 1 to 7) and computed their returns. Finally, we used TOPSIS to select the best model regarding their three main features: expected return, variance, and entropy. We applied sensitivity analysis of the relevance of each variable to represent different scenarios; of course, the ranking of the models changed in each case.

4.4. TOPSIS in Detail

The TOPSIS methodology is a multi-criteria decision methodology that allows choosing a solution to a problem based on multiple attributes. Typically, the attributes are opposing characteristics, such as return and volatility. The methodology determines a score based on the Euclidean distance to a positive ideal element and a negative ideal element. The closer the element is to the positive ideal element, and the further it is from the negative ideal element, the better the score. These ideal elements are constructed by taking the highest and lowest values of the available elements.

In this case, we considered the attributes for $k \in \{1, \ldots, K\}$ portfolios, including their expected returns, variances, and entropies. The ideal positive element was the one with the highest return, lowest variances, and highest entropy. The ideal negative element was the one with the lowest return, highest volatility, and lowest entropy. Let us consider the attributes $\mathbf{a}_k$ as indicated in Equation (17), where we calculated the values of each attribute by considering the portfolio $\mathbf{x}_k$ and its performance based on data outside the time window.

$$\mathbf{a}_k = \left(r_p(\mathbf{x}_k)\ ,\ \mathbb{V}(\mathbf{x}_k)\ ,\ H(\mathbf{x}_k)\right) \tag{17}$$

We performed the following steps:

1. *Define the performance matrix*: The performance matrix corresponds to the collection of attributes of the portfolios. It has three columns (attributes): return, volatility, and entropy.
2. *Normalization*: This step corresponds to turning the values of the performance matrix $\forall\, k \in \{1, \ldots, K\}$ into values between 0 and 1:

$$\overline{\mathbf{a}_k} = \frac{\mathbf{a}_k}{||\mathbf{a}_k||}, \quad ||\mathbf{a}_k|| = \sqrt{\sum_{l=1}^{3} a_{k,l}^2} \tag{18}$$

3. *Weighted normalized matrix*: In this step, we multiplied the columns of the normalized performance matrix by a scalar value, where the sum of these scalar values equaled 1.

$$\sum_{l=1}^{3} w_l = 1, \tag{19}$$

where w_l are the scalars that multiply the columns; these values represent the relative relevance of the attributes. We considered multiple configurations.

4. *Positive and negative ideals*: In this step, we defined the positive and negative ideal portfolio; we used the highest and lowest values of each portfolio's attributes.

$$P = \left[\max_{k\in\{1,\ldots,K\}} r_p(\mathbf{x}_k)\ ;\ \min_{k\in\{1,\ldots,K\}} \mathbb{V}(\mathbf{x}_k)\ ;\ \max_{k\in\{1,\ldots,K\}} H(\mathbf{x}_k)\right] \tag{20}$$

$$N = \left[\min_{k\in\{1,\ldots,K\}} r_p(\mathbf{x}_k)\ ;\ \max_{k\in\{1,\ldots,K\}} \mathbb{V}(\mathbf{x}_k)\ ;\ \min_{k\in\{1,\ldots,K\}} H(\mathbf{x}_k)\right] \tag{21}$$

5. *Distance calculation*: $\forall\, k \in \{1, \ldots, K\}$ we calculated the Euclidean distance to the positive and negative ideal portfolios.

$$d_k^P = \sqrt{\sum_{l=1}^{3}(a_{k,l} - p_l)^2}$$
$$d_k^N = \sqrt{\sum_{l=1}^{3}(a_{k,l} - n_l)^2} \quad (22)$$

where p_l and n_l are the components (return, variance, entropy) of the positive ideal and negative ideal elements, respectively.

6. *Relative closeness*: we calculated the relative closeness to the ideal solution, corresponding to the distance ratio to the negative ideal portfolio divided by the sum of the distances to the negative and positive ideal.

$$C_k = \frac{d_k^N}{d_k^N + d_k^P} \quad (23)$$

7. *Ranking results*: we ranked the solution from the highest relative closeness to the lowest, as calculated in the previous step.

According to this proposed approach, we considered nine different configurations for the weights, to analyze rankings and discriminate which models were better; these configurations considered the return more relevant. The main reason we had to do this was to represent that the return is dominant over other metrics in the eyes of investors when they select their portfolio. In Table 2, we show the nine sets of weights e_i for the portfolios' attributes.

Table 2. TOPSIS weight configurations analyzed.

Attribute Weight/Scenario	1	2	3	4	5	6	7	8	9
Return [%]	33	50	50	50	70	60	60	70	60
Variance [%]	33	50	0	25	15	40	0	30	30
Entropy [%]	33	0	50	25	15	0	40	0	10

5. Results

The results obtained from the different models in the risk return space showed three groups, as can be seen in Figure 4. This figure shows the portfolios' standard deviation versus its return in this 20-year evaluation. The chart below shows the compound return over a period (cumulative or compound). We identified three groups according to the level of return. The first group had the highest returns between 1200% and 1400% or between 1.11% to 1.04% in monthly terms, corresponding to 6.2% (red) of the total portfolios; a second group had returns oscillating around 800% (equivalent to 0.87% monthly return), with a 6.2% (grey) of the total portfolios; and finally, a third group, with the largest number of elements and oscillating returns around 400%(equivalent to 0.58% monthly return) corresponding to 87% (yellow), which is considered more representative of the total.

The first group showed low entropy, around 0.13, dominated by Model 2 and 5 portfolios. The second group had an entropy of around 0.59, where Model 2 and 5 portfolios dominated the group in quantity. Having a similar behavior, the third group had an entropy of 0.83, which was high compared to the other models. The dominant portfolios in this group belonged to Model 7.

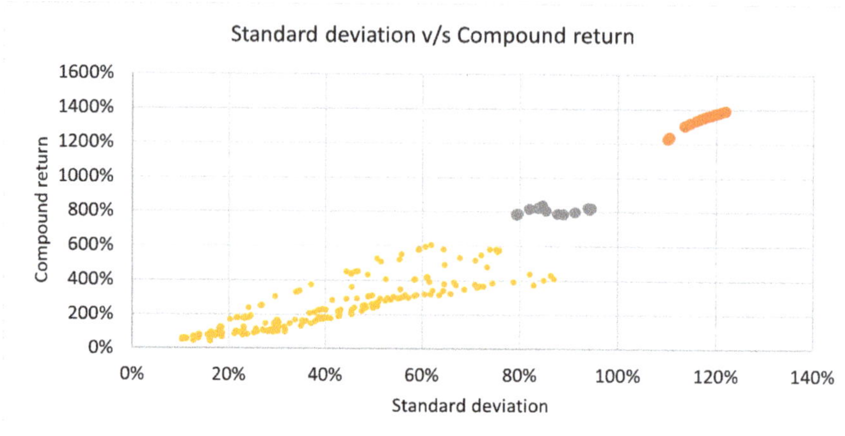

Figure 4. Standard deviation vs. Compound return.

The colors of the points represent the relation between standard deviation and compound return of the portfolios for each model, a total of 418, three separated groups were naturally obtained according to the level of return, risk, and entropy, as indicated before. The third group (yellow) is selected to analyze, with the largest number of elements, corresponding to 87%, oscillating returns around 0.58% monthly return, and the highest entropy of 0.83; it's more representative of the total, and a cluster with better portfolios according to the parameters like mean Sharpe index and entropy like a measure of diversification.

In Figure 5, we present the portfolio performance of the third group selected (blue points), the resulting portfolio of Model 7 ($\alpha = 0.3, \beta = 0.9$), in terms of the compound return and Sharpe index, which is situated in the upper right quadrant and demonstrates the above-average performance in both return and efficiency. Furthermore, it stands out for its position relative to other portfolios in the same quadrant.

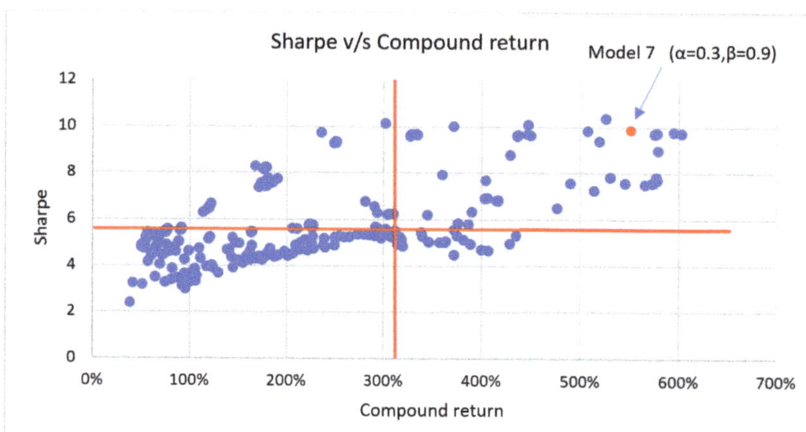

Figure 5. Compound return and Sharpe ratio.

Figure 6 illustrates that Model 7 lies on the efficient frontier when considering the models in terms of minimizing risk and maximizing returns. It is noteworthy that Model 7, with $\alpha = 0.3$ and $\beta = 0.9$, exhibited one of the highest returns and was one of the most efficient among the portfolios derived from the different models.

In Figure 7, we present a performance comparison of the models across the nine scenarios proposed, considering the differences in the values of their attributes (return, variance, and entropy). The purpose of the TOPSIS analysis predicted in the chart was to show the ranking position of each portfolio against the rest of the portfolios in each configuration. The length of the bar represents the number of models analyzed, and the position of the dot in the bar is how good the result was. The lower the position in the bar, the better the result.

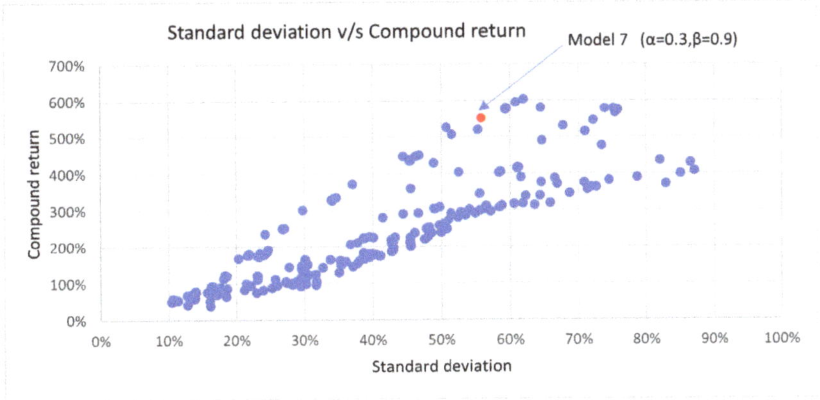

Figure 6. Compound return vs. Standard deviation.

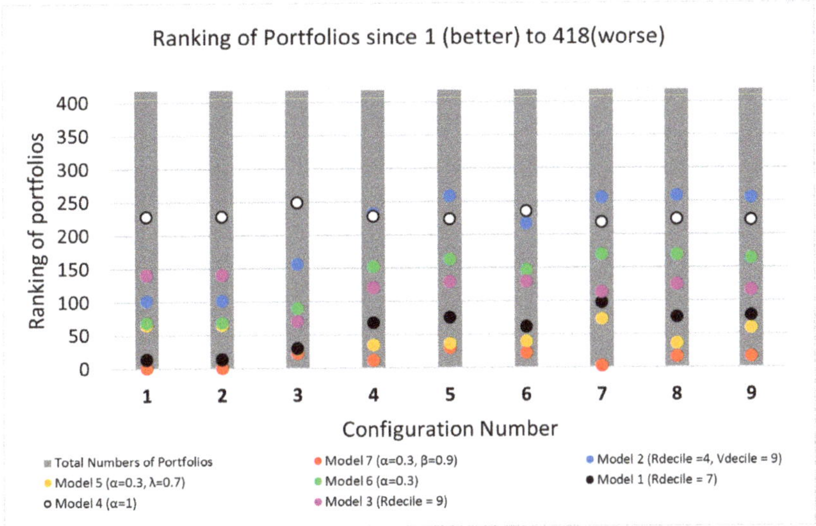

Figure 7. Model Ranking results since 1 (better) to 418 (worse).

Models 5 and 7 exhibited superior performance compared to the other models across the different configurations of TOPSIS.

Model 5 performed well and was comparable to Model 7; however, it did not outperform Model 7.

Models 2 and 4 fell within the top half of the TOPSIS chart. In particular, Model 4 consistently fell around the middle of the ranking in all scenarios. In configurations where the return was relevant, Model 2 was the worst. This situation was the opposite of Model 4 when there is a low importance of return. This model did not perform well, but Model 1 was the worst.

It is relevant to note that Model 4 had a stable behavior, meaning its rankings were similar among scenarios.

While Model 6 was better than 3, its behavior was similar to 3, which performed better than the models in the middle of the ranking.

Lastly, in general terms, you can see that Model 7 consistently exhibited superior performance to the other models (obtaining the first position of the ranking) across the different configurations of the TOPSIS decision variables. Therefore, it can be considered the best model under the different scenarios.

6. Discussion

The results of our analysis suggest that, for the data and methodology considered, models that incorporated fuzzy measures and fuzzy entropy measures in multiobjective settings—such as Models 5, 6, and 7—demonstrated superior performance compared to Models 1, 2, and 3. Is important to note the Model 4 did not have a good performance in comparison with the other fuzzy models, and it id is worth noting that this model does not have an entropic membership function. In our opinion, fuzzy measures provide the flexibility to handle intervals and uncertainties, and fuzzy entropy maximizes the information gain for both return and variance, further reinforcing the models' flexibility.

Across the full range of results, there was a notable dispersion in portfolio performance, as measured by their actual returns and variances. In our view, this dispersion can be attributed to two primary factors: (i) the use of various variance bounds, not only in the Markowitz base model but also in all of the other models that incorporated entropy maximization in their ϵ-constraint versions, and (ii) the fact that the results of the fuzzy entropy models matched the Markowitz results for low variances, due to the inherent design of the model, which seeks to minimize variance while maximizing return.

In the case of the multiobjective models 4 to 7, the actual variances concentrated in the mid-range, because we used objective functions to maximize the parameters' fuzzy membership functions. For both considered cases, λ was for the fuzzy instances and α and β for the fuzzy entropy cases.

Model 5 exhibited the best ranking results when $\alpha = 0.3$ and λ values covered the interval 0–1, indicating that the variance is modulated by λ. Models 5, 6, and 7 showed that the actual variance tended to concentrate in the mid-range, which resulted from optimizing the membership functions of the parameters α and β.

Model 7, with $\alpha = 0.3$ and $\beta = 0.9$, achieved a higher ranking across the various configurations with different attribute weights, indicating the effectiveness of fuzzy entropy approaches for return and variance optimization in our data.

7. Conclusions

Among the models tested, the multi-objective Model 7 with $\alpha = 0.3$ and $\beta = 0.9$ consistently delivered the highest returns and Sharpe ratios, placing it on the efficient frontier. Based on the TOPSIS methodology applied to return, variance, and portfolio entropy, it delivered consistent results across different configurations. Its key strength was its ability to capture all configurations, without imposing significant optimization restrictions, making it the optimal model for constructing the best portfolio. Rather than seeking a theoretical optimal, it tended to converge towards observable centers.

Based on that fact, Model 4 did not have a good performance in comparison with the other fuzzy models; noting that this model does not have an entropic membership function, our opinion is that the fuzzy measures provide the flexibility to handle intervals and uncertainties, and fuzzy entropy maximizes the information gain for both return and variance, further reinforcing the models' flexibility.

For portfolio selection, we recommend fuzzy models that contain an entropic membership function in their structure. In conclusion, fuzzy measures provide the flexibility to handle intervals and uncertainties, and fuzzy entropy maximizes the information gain for both return and variance, further reinforcing the models' flexibility.

Author Contributions: Conceptualization, H.L.-O., C.B. and J.P.; methodology, M.B., H.L.-O. and J.P.; software, M.B. and J.P.; validation, J.P.; formal analysis, H.L.-O. and J.P.; investigation, M.B. and J.P.; resources, J.P.; data curation, J.P.; writing—original draft, M.B. and J.P.; writing—review and editing, M.B., H.L.-O., C.B. and J.P.; supervision, H.L.-O., C.B. and J.P.; project administration, J.P.; funding acquisition, J.P. All authors have read and agreed to the published version of the manuscript.

Funding: This research was funded by the Agencia Nacional de Investigación y Desarrollo de Chile (1220822), Agencia Nacional de Investigación y Desarrollo de Chile (11241278), Canada Research Chairs (2018-00082) and Agencia Nacional de Investigación y Desarrollo de Chile (21220491).

Data Availability Statement: The data presented in this study is available on request from the corresponding authors, and the dataset was jointly completed by the team, so the data is not publicly available.

Conflicts of Interest: The authors declare no conflict of interest.

Appendix A

This appendix shows a detailed mathematical deduction of the models with fuzzy parameters. First, some definitions of fuzzy sets and optimization are presented, which are necessary to clarify the models.

Definition: A fuzzy set (A) in a universe of discourse (X) is defined by a membership function $(\mu_A : X \to [0,1])$, where each element $(x \in X)$ is assigned a membership degree $(\mu_A(x))$ that takes values in the interval $[0,1]$. $\mu_A : X \to [0,1]$

For each $(x \in X)$, $\mu_A(x)$ indicates the degree of membership of x in the fuzzy set A. The values of $(\mu_A(x))$ are interpreted as follows:

- $\mu_A(x) = 1$ indicates that x fully belongs to the fuzzy set A.
- $\mu_A(x) = 0$ indicates that x does not belong to the fuzzy set A.
- $0 < \mu_A(x) < 1$ indicates that x has a partial membership in set A.

Definition: α-cut of A for a value $\alpha \in [0,1]$ is the crisp set A_α defined as:

$$A_\alpha = \{x \in X \mid \mu_A(x) \geq \alpha\}$$

α-cut is the set of all elements x in X whose membership in the fuzzy set A is at least α.

Definition—Trapezoidal Membership Function (a,b,c,d): For a variable x defined over X, a trapezoidal membership function $\mu(x)$ is defined as:

$$\mu(x) = \begin{cases} 0 & \text{if } x \leq a, \\ \frac{x-a}{b-a} & \text{if } a \leq x \leq b, \\ 1 & \text{if } b \leq x \leq c, \\ \frac{d-x}{d-c} & \text{if } c \leq x \leq d, \\ 0 & \text{if } x \geq d, \end{cases}$$

where $(a \leq b \leq c \leq d)$ are parameters defining the shape of the trapezoid.

Definition—Entropic membership function: Let $X = \{x \in R : a < x < b\}$ be an interval set; then, the log-natural function f_x of x is defined as follows:

$$f_x(x) = \begin{cases} 0 & \text{if } x \leq a, \\ -\frac{x-a}{b-a} \cdot \ln\left\{\frac{x-a}{b-a}\right\} - \frac{b-x}{b-a} \cdot \ln\left\{\frac{b-x}{b-a}\right\} & \text{if } a < x < b, \\ 0 & \text{if } x \geq b, \end{cases}$$

Let f_x be the log-natural function of x. The entropic fuzzy set, namely $\mu_{(a,b)}(x)$, is as follows:

$$\mu_{(a,b)}(x) = \frac{f_x(x)}{\max_x(f_x(x))}$$

Given the previous definitions, the following shows the mathematical derivation of optimization models with fuzzy parameters. In general, the maximum entropy portfolio selection model with fuzzy return and fuzzy variance is described as (A1)

$$\begin{array}{lccc} \max\limits_{\{\mathbf{x}>0\}} & \{H(\mathbf{x})\} & & \\ \text{s.t.} & r_p(\mathbf{x}) & =_f & R_p \\ & \mathbb{V}(\mathbf{x}) & =_f & \sigma^2 \\ & \sum\limits_{i=1}^{n} x_i & = & 1 \end{array} \tag{A1}$$

The notation $=_f$ indicates a certain degree of flexibility in meeting the constraints. In this case, it is associated with the variability of the parameters. One way to solve this problem is using fuzzy sets representing the expected return and variance.

If R_p and σ^2 are trapezoidal numbers, that is, $R_p = (\underline{r}, r_1, r_2, \overline{r})$ and $\sigma^2 = \left(\underline{\sigma}^2, \sigma_1^2, \sigma_2^2, \overline{\sigma}^2\right)$, then optimization problem (A1) is equivalent to

$$\begin{array}{lccc} \max\limits_{\{\mathbf{x}>0\}} & \{H(\mathbf{x})\} & & \\ \text{s.t.} & r_p(\mathbf{x}) & = & (\underline{r}, r_1, r_2, \overline{r}) \\ & \mathbb{V}(\mathbf{x}) & = & \left(\underline{\sigma}^2, \sigma_1^2, \sigma_2^2, \overline{\sigma}^2\right) \\ & \sum\limits_{i=1}^{n} x_i & = & 1 \end{array} \tag{A2}$$

Through the intersection of the trapezoidal membership functions, applied to each constraint, the optimization problem (A2) is equivalent to

$$\begin{array}{ll} \max\limits_{\mathbf{x}>0} & H(\mathbf{x}) \\ \text{s.t.} & \max(\mu_{R_p}(r_p(x))) \cap (\mu_{\sigma^2}(\mathbb{V}(x))) \\ & \sum\limits_{i=1}^{n} x_i = 1 \end{array} \tag{A3}$$

By the definition of $\cap$ in fuzzy sets, $\max(\mu_{R_p}(r_p(x)) \cap (\mu_{\sigma^2}(\mathbb{V}(x))))$ is equivalent to the following max–min problem:

$$\max\min(\mu_{R_p}(r_p(x)), \mu_{\sigma^2}(\mathbb{V}(x))) \tag{A4}$$

Noting that $\lambda = \min(\mu_{R_p}(r_p(x)) \cap \mu_{\sigma^2}(\mathbb{V}(x)))$, (A5) is equivalent to

$$\begin{array}{ll} \max\limits_{\mathbf{x}>0, \lambda} & \{H(\mathbf{x}), \lambda\} \\ \text{subject to} & \mu_{R_p}(r_p(x)) \geq \lambda \\ & \mu_{\sigma^2}(\mathbb{V}(x)) \geq \lambda \\ & \sum\limits_{i=1}^{n} x_i = 1 \end{array} \tag{A5}$$

where $\mu(r_p(x)) \geq \lambda$ and $\mu_{\sigma^2}(\mathbb{V}(x)) \geq \lambda$ are λ-cuts of each of the membership functions; that is, the goal is to achieve the highest level of membership for each of the constraints. The model (A5) is equivalent to a parametric optimization problem (8).

If R_p and σ^2 are entropic numbers, that is, $R_p = (\underline{r}, \overline{r})$ and $\sigma^2 = \left(\underline{\sigma}^2, \overline{\sigma}^2\right)$, then optimization problem (A1) is equivalent to

$$\begin{array}{lccc} \max\limits_{\{\mathbf{x}>0\}} & \{H(\mathbf{x})\} & & \\ \text{s.t.} & r_p(\mathbf{x}) & = & (\underline{r}, \overline{r}) \\ & \mathbb{V}(\mathbf{x}) & = & \left(\underline{\sigma}^2, \overline{\sigma}^2\right) \\ & \sum\limits_{i=1}^{n} x_i & = & 1 \end{array} \tag{A6}$$

Through the intersection of entropic membership functions, applied to each constraint, the optimization problem (A6) is equivalent to

$$\begin{array}{lccc} \max\limits_{\{\mathbf{x}>0\}} & \{H(\mathbf{x})\} & & \\ \text{s.t.} & \max(\mu_{(\underline{r},\overline{r})}(r_p(x)) & \cap & (\mu_{(\underline{\sigma}^2,\overline{\sigma}^2)}(\mathbb{V}(x))) \\ & \sum\limits_{i=1}^{n} x_i & = & 1 \end{array} \tag{A7}$$

Let $\alpha = \frac{r_p(x)-\underline{r}}{\overline{r}-\underline{r}}$, then entropic membership function $\mu_{(\underline{r},\overline{r})}(r_p(x))$ is equivalent to

$$g_1(\alpha) = -\alpha \cdot \ln(\alpha) - (1-\alpha) \cdot \ln(1-\alpha) \tag{A8}$$

If $\beta = \frac{\mathbb{V}(x)-\underline{\sigma}^2}{\overline{\sigma}^2-\underline{\sigma}^2}$, then the entropic membership function $\mu_{(\underline{\sigma}^2,\overline{\sigma}^2)}(\mathbb{V}(x))$ is equivalent to

$$g_2(\beta) = -\beta \cdot \ln(\beta) - (1-\beta) \cdot \ln(1-\beta) \tag{A9}$$

According to Equations (A8) and (A9), the fuzzy optimization problem (A7) is equivalent to model (14).

References

1. Markowitz, H. Portfolio Selection. *J. Financ.* **1952**, *7*, 77–91.
2. Aggarwal, M. Redefining fuzzy entropy with a general framework. *Expert Syst. Appl.* **2021**, *164*, 113671. [CrossRef]
3. López-Ospina, H.; Cortés, C.E.; Pérez, J.; Peña, R.; Figueroa-García, J.C.; Urrutia-Mosquera, J. A maximum entropy optimization model for origin-destination trip matrix estimation with fuzzy entropic parameters. *Transp. A Transp. Sci.* **2022**, *18*, 963–1000. [CrossRef]
4. Kalayci, C.B.; Ertenlice, O.; Akbay, M.A. A Comprehensive Review of Deterministic Models and Applications for Mean-Variance Portfolio Optimization. *Expert Syst. Appl.* **2019**, *125*, 345–368. [CrossRef]
5. Mercurio, P.J.; Wu, Y.; Xie, H. An Entropy-Based Approach to Portfolio Optimization. *Entropy* **2020**, *22*, 332. [CrossRef] [PubMed]
6. Chung, M.; Lee, Y.; Kim, J.H.; Kim, W.C.; Fabozzi, F.J. The effects of errors in means, variances, and correlations on the mean-variance framework. *Quant. Financ.* **2022**, *22*, 1893–1903. [CrossRef]
7. Michaud, R.O. The Markowitz Optimization Enigma: Is 'Optimized' Optimal? *Financ. Anal. J.* **1989**, *45*, 31–42. [CrossRef]
8. Lassance, N.; DeMiguel, V.; Vrins, F. Optimal Portfolio Diversification via Independent Component Analysis. *Oper. Res.* **2022**, *70*, 55–72. [CrossRef]
9. Yu, J.R.; Lee, W.Y.; Chiou, W.J.P. Diversified portfolios with different entropy measures. *Appl. Math. Comput.* **2014**, *241*, 47–63. [CrossRef]
10. Cerrato, M.; Crosby, J.; Kim, M.; Zhao, Y. Relation between higher order comoments and dependence structure of equity portfolio. *J. Empir. Financ.* **2017**, *40*, 101–120. [CrossRef]
11. Mandelbrot, B. Certain speculative prices (1963). *J. Bus.* **1972**, *45*, 542–543. [CrossRef]
12. Gupta, P.; Mehlawat, M.K.; Inuiguchi, M.; Chandra, S. *Fuzzy Portfolio Optimization: Advances in Hybrid Multi-Criteria Methodologies*; Springer: Berlin/Heidelberg, Germany, 2014; Volume 316.
13. Fang, Y.; Lai, K.K.; Wang, S. *Fuzzy Portfolio Optimization: Theory and Methods*; Springer Science & Business Media: Berlin/Heidelberg, Germany, 2008; Volume 609.
14. Mehlawat, M.K.; Gupta, P.; Kumar, A.; Yadav, S.; Aggarwal, A. Multiobjective Fuzzy Portfolio Performance Evaluation Using Data Envelopment Analysis Under Credibilistic Framework. *IEEE Trans. Fuzzy Syst.* **2020**, *28*, 2726–2737. [CrossRef]
15. Deng, X.; Pan, X. The research and comparison of multi-objective portfolio based on intuitionistic fuzzy optimization. *Comput. Ind. Eng.* **2018**, *124*, 411–421. [CrossRef]
16. Xidonas, P.; Steuer, R.; Hassapis, C. Robust Portfolio Optimization: A Categorized Bibliographic Review. *Ann. Oper. Res.* **2020**, *292*, 533–552. [CrossRef]

17. Calvo, C.; Ivorra, C.; Liern, V. On the Computation of the Efficient Frontier of the Portfolio Selection Problem. *J. Appl. Math.* **2012**. *25*. [CrossRef]
18. Huang, X. Mean-Entropy Models for Fuzzy Portfolio Selection. *IEEE Trans. Fuzzy Syst.* **2008**, *16*, 1096–1101. [CrossRef]
19. Qin, Z.; Li, X.; Ji, X. Portfolio Selection Based on Fuzzy Cross-Entropy. *J. Comput. Appl. Math.* **2009**, *228*, 139–149. [CrossRef]
20. Liu, Y.J.; Zhang, W.G. A Multi-Period Fuzzy Portfolio Optimization Model with Minimum Transaction Lots. *Eur. J. Oper. Res.* **2015**, *242*, 933–941. [CrossRef]
21. Zhou, R.; Yang, Z.; Yu, M.; Ralescu, D.A. A Portfolio Optimization Model Based on Information Entropy and Fuzzy Time Series. *Fuzzy Optim. Decis. Mak.* **2015**, *14*, 381–397. [CrossRef]
22. Liagkouras, K.; Metaxiotis, K. Multi-Period Mean–Variance Fuzzy Portfolio Optimization Model with Transaction Costs. *Eng. Appl. Artif. Intell.* **2018**, *67*, 260–269. [CrossRef]
23. Zhou, J.; Li, X.; Pedrycz, W. Mean-Semi-Entropy Models of Fuzzy Portfolio Selection. *IEEE Trans. Fuzzy Syst.* **2016**, *24*, 1627–1636. [CrossRef]
24. Li, B.; Zhang, R. A New Mean-Variance-Entropy Model for Uncertain Portfolio Optimization with Liquidity and Diversification. *Chaos Solitons Fractals* **2021**, *146*, 110842. [CrossRef]
25. Wang, X.; Wang, B.; Li, T.; Li, H.; Watada, J. Multi-Criteria Fuzzy Portfolio Selection Based on Three-Way Decisions and Cumulative Prospect Theory. *Appl. Soft Comput.* **2023**, *134*, 110033. [CrossRef]
26. Wang, J.; Zhang, H.; Luo, H. Research on the Construction of Stock Portfolios Based on Multiobjective Water Cycle Algorithm and KMV Algorithm. *Appl. Soft Comput.* **2022**, *115*, 108186. [CrossRef]
27. Mehlawat, M.K. Credibilistic Mean-Entropy Models for Multi-Period Portfolio Selection with Multi-Choice Aspiration Levels. *Inf. Sci.* **2016**, *345*, 9–26. [CrossRef]
28. Jalota, H.; Thakur, M.; Mittal, G. A Credibilistic Decision Support System for Portfolio Optimization. *Appl. Soft Comput.* **2017**, *59*, 512–528. [CrossRef]
29. Gupta, P.; Mehlawat, M.K.; Yadav, S.; Kumar, A. A Polynomial Goal Programming Approach for Intuitionistic Fuzzy Portfolio Optimization Using Entropy and Higher Moments. *Appl. Soft Comput.* **2019**, *85*, 105781. [CrossRef]
30. Shen, K.Y.; Lo, H.W.; Tzeng, G.H. Interactive Portfolio Optimization Model Based on Rough Fundamental Analysis and Rational Fuzzy Constraints. *Appl. Soft Comput.* **2022**, *125*, 109158. [CrossRef]
31. Tan, Y.; Yang, W.; Suntrayuth, S.; Yu, X.; Sindakis, S.; Showkat, S. Optimizing Stock Portfolio Performance with a Combined RG1-TOPSIS Model: Insights from the Chinese Market. *J. Knowl. Econ.* **2023**, 1–24. [CrossRef]
32. Gupta, V.; Srivastava, S.; Ratan, R. Stock-market as an investment platform among business colleges graduates. *Econ. Manag. Rev.* **2023**, *2* , 70–75
33. Jing, D.; Imeni, M.; Edalatpanah, S.; Alburaikan, A.; Khalifa, H.A.E.W. Optimal selection of stock portfolios using multi-criteria decision-making methods. *Mathematics* **2023**, *11*, 415. [CrossRef]
34. Vásquez, J.A.; Escobar, J.W.; Manotas, D.F. AHP–TOPSIS methodology for stock portfolio investments. *Risks* **2023**, *10*, 4. [CrossRef]
35. Martinkutė-Kaulienė, R.; Skobaitė, R.; Stasytytė, V.; Maknickienė, N. Comparison of multicriteria decision-making methods in portfolio formation. *Financ. Mark. Valuat.* **2023**, *7*, 60–72. [CrossRef]
36. Rezaei, S.; Vaez-Ghasemi, M. A new Method for Sustainable Portfolio Selection with DEA, TOPSIS and MIP in Stock exchange. *Financ. Eng. Portf. Manag.* **2020**, *11*, 474–515.
37. Tanaka, H.; Guo, P. Portfolio selection based on upper and lower exponential possibility distributions. *Eur. J. Oper. Res.* **1999**, *114*, 115–126. [CrossRef]
38. Zheng, Y.; Zhou, M.; Li, G. Information entropy based fuzzy optimization model of electricity purchasing portfolio. In Proceedings of the 2009 IEEE Power & Energy Society General Meeting, Calgary, AB, Canada, 26–30 July 2009 ; pp. 1–6.
39. García-Medina, A.; Rodríguez-Camejo, B. Random Matrix Theory and Nested Clustered Optimization on high-dimensional portfolios. *Int. J. Mod. Phys. C* **2024**, 2450098 . [CrossRef]
40. García-Medina, A.; Rodríguez-Camejo, B. Two-step estimators of high-dimensional correlation matrices. *Phys. Rev. E* **2023**, *108*, 044137. [CrossRef] [PubMed]
41. García-Medina, A.; Macías Páez, R. Rotationally invariant estimators on portfolio optimization to unveil financial risk's states. *Int. J. Mod. Phys. C* **2023**, *34*, 2350117. [CrossRef]
42. Inoue, A.; Jin, L.; Rossi, B. Rolling window selection for out-of-sample forecasting with time-varying parameters. *J. Econ.* **2017**, *196*, 55–67. [CrossRef]
43. Zhang, Y.; Li, X.; Guo, S. Portfolio selection problems with Markowitz's mean–variance framework: A review of literature. *Fuzzy Optim. Decis. Mak.* **2018**, *17*, 125–158. [CrossRef]
44. Miettinen, K. *Nonlinear Multiobjective Optimization*; International Series in Operations Research & Management Science; Kluwer Academic Publishers: Alphen aan den Rijn, The Netherlands, 1999; Volume 12.

mathematics

MDPI

Article

Study of Flexibility Transformation in Thermal Power Enterprises under Multi-Factor Drivers: Application of Complex-Network Evolutionary Game Theory

Lefeng Cheng, Pan Peng, Wentian Lu *, Pengrong Huang and Yang Chen *

School of Mechanical and Electrical Engineering, Guangzhou University, Guangzhou 510006, China; chenglefeng_scut@163.com (L.C.); peng13212667686@163.com (P.P.); 13600386865@163.com (P.H.)
* Correspondence: luwentian@gzhu.edu.cn (W.L.); zdchenyang@163.com (Y.C.); Tel.: +86-156-2210-5150 (W.L.); +86-185-9498-0613 (Y.C.)

Abstract: With the increasing share of renewable energy in the grid and the enhanced flexibility of the future power system, it is imperative for thermal power companies to explore alternative strategies. The flexible transformation of thermal power units is an effective strategy to address the previously mentioned challenges; however, the factors influencing the diffusion of this technology merit further investigation, yet they have been seldom examined by scholars. To address this gap, this issue is examined using an evolutionary game model of multi-agent complex networks, and a more realistic group structure is established through heterogeneous group differentiation. With factors such as group relationships, diffusion paths, compensation electricity prices, and subsidy intensities as variables, several diffusion scenarios are developed for research purposes. The results indicate that when upper-level enterprises influence the decision-making of lower-level enterprises, technology diffusion is significantly accelerated, and enhanced communication among thermal power enterprises further promotes diffusion. Among thermal power enterprises, leveraging large and medium-sized enterprises to promote the flexibility transformation of units proves to be an effective strategy. With regard to factors like the compensation price for depth peak shaving, the initial application ratio of groups, and the intensity of government subsidies, the compensation price emerges as the key factor. Only with a high compensation price can the other two factors effectively contribute to promoting technology diffusion.

Keywords: flexibility transformation; technology diffusion; evolutionary game theory; multi-agent simulation; complex network; thermal power enterprises

MSC: 65M12

1. Introduction

Approximately two years following the announcement of China's 14th Five-Year Plan for a Modernized Energy System, the transition to low-carbon energy in the sector has accelerated. In 2023, for the first time, the total installed capacity of non-fossil energy units surpassed that of traditional fossil energy units, signifying the Chinese government's commitment to an orderly transition to a low-carbon power sector, with renewable energy generation assuming a pivotal role. With the growing prioritization of renewable energy consumption, traditional power generators, especially thermal power plants within the industry, are actively exploring alternative pathways [1–3].

Currently, three prevalent approaches are recognized for the transformation of thermal power plants: investment in carbon capture, utilization, and storage (CCUS) technologies, adoption of energy storage services, and retrofitting of existing thermal units for enhanced flexibility [4]. The predominant focus of the current literature is on CCUS for the transformation of thermal power enterprises [5,6]. In China, the industrial implementation of CCUS incurs significant costs due to its delayed initiation, requiring mature business models and policy incentives for its favorable development [7]. Geographical location poses an additional constraint to the large-scale industrialization of CCUS. Regions that have substantial potential for advancing CCUS technology include Northeast China, North China, and Northwest China [5,8]. Regarding transformation and investment in the energy storage sector, the conversion of coal-fired power plants into thermal storage facilities has garnered significant attention within the industry [9,10]; however, their power losses present a notable challenge [11]. In comparison to the aforementioned technologies, the flexibility conversion of coal-fired power plants features mature technology, a brief construction period, and minimal investment costs. Research indicates that retrofitting the fuel supply system, boiler, flue gas treatment system, and thermo-electrolytic coupling system of coal-fired power units represents an effective approach for enhancing unit flexibility [12–14]. Enhanced flexibility in coal-fired power units can bolster renewable energy consumption, indirectly mitigate CO_2 emissions, and foster the sustainable growth of the renewable energy sector.

However, a significant proportion of renewable energy consumption within the power system is poised to reduce the revenue of thermal power enterprises in the power market. Modifying the units can enhance the influence of thermal power enterprises in the capacity and standby markets, thereby bolstering their competitiveness in the power market. Nevertheless, ongoing research on the flexibility of thermal power plants predominantly focuses on process enhancement and optimal control. Given that China's existing power trading operates under a market model, its benefits depend not only on the decisions made by individual companies but also on the strategic actions of peers. Currently, there is a lack of income assessment and prediction for the application diffusion of this technology in the competitive multiplayer environment of the power market, following the flexible transformation of thermal power enterprises.

Evolutionary gaming in complex networks is a research domain that combines complex network theory and evolutionary game theory (EGT) to investigate the dynamics of individual interactions and evolution within network structures [15]. Studies in this field aim to elucidate the influence of network topology on individual strategic decisions, game outcomes, and the evolution of node connections. The significant advantage of complex network evolutionary games lies in their ability to analyze how changes in individual strategies affect the propensity of the current strategy to diffuse throughout the group, making it a pivotal tool for modeling multiple intelligences.

Drawing upon the identified limitations of current research, this paper integrates the complex network evolutionary game model with the emerging trend of enhanced power system flexibility to investigate the potential diffusion of thermal power-unit flexibility transformation technology among supply-side thermal power enterprises. This study aims to address the gap in the literature by examining how the adoption of flexibility transformation technology among thermal power enterprises is influenced by network dynamics and the evolving landscape of power system flexibility. This paper is innovative in the following three aspects:

(1) Initially, there exists a dearth of research within the industry concerning the extent to which thermal unit-flexibility technologies can penetrate among groups of thermal power enterprises. Through investigating these matters, it becomes feasible to conduct an anticipated evaluation of the thermal power enterprises poised for transformation and to offer guidance for the development of the enterprise group.

(2) Diverging from previous approaches that employ evolutionary game models to explore multi-body interest interaction issues in the power industry, this paper integrates complex network theory and evolutionary game theory for modeling research. Additionally, utilizing complex network theory, the thermal power enterprise group is characterized by heterogeneity, and dynamic network modeling is employed to simulate the evolving game processes.

(3) Building upon the examination of thermal power-unit flexibility transformation technology, this paper explores the diffusion trajectory of this technology among thermal power enterprises. Through the establishment of varied initial strategies for the nodes, the paper simulates the initial distribution of the technology among the thermal power enterprise group and investigates the dynamic diffusion trend of flexibility transformation technology throughout the entire group under this scenario.

The rest of this article is organized as follows: Section 2 reviews the literature. Section 3 analyzes the income composition of thermal power-generation enterprises and establishes both the evolutionary game model and the complex network evolutionary game model. In Section 4, initial parameters are set, and numerical simulations are conducted to discuss the factors affecting technology diffusion from the perspectives of thermal power-generation enterprises and the power market, respectively. Conclusions and policy recommendations are presented in Section 5.

2. Literature Review

2.1. Current Status of Thermal Power-Unit Flexibility Transformation Technology

As the primary units manufactured in China, the controllable output of thermal power units has consistently been their foremost advantage. Flexibility indicators of thermal power units include rapid start–stop capability, swift load changes, and deep peak-shaving capabilities. The utilization of thermal power units for deep peak shaving within current power systems has emerged as a significant industry concern [16–18]. To upgrade the unit system, Wang et al. [19] proposed a new system using residual steam to drive rotating equipment, which can reduce the energy consumption of thermal power units and increase the unit's deep peak-shaving capacity. In the literature [20], authors investigated the electrical and thermal attributes of cogeneration units before and after retrofitting, proposing a retrofit model featuring thermoelectrically decoupled systems. Furthermore, modifications to thermal power-plant boiler systems constitute a prominent research focus. Several studies have demonstrated that preheating pulverized coal enhances the unit's peak shifting capability [13,21,22]. The focus is on addressing operational control issues in thermal power units; for example, authors in [23] introduced a sliding-mode control strategy for regulating the unit's boiler temperature during operation. Additionally, some researchers have advocated for a control strategy to integrate the thermal unit with an energy storage system to enhance its flexible output capability [24]. To address steam temperature issues in the boiler subsystem of a thermal unit, Sun et al. [25] suggested employing multi-objective control algorithms for regulation. Presently, the predominant research focus is on optimizing unit operation control, integrating additional resources for peaking purposes, and enhancing unit subsystems (boiler, turbine, etc.).

2.2. Evolutionary Game Theory and Applications

In contrast to traditional game theory, evolutionary game theory posits that the subjects engaged in the game exhibit limited rationality, and delineates the evolution of individual behavioral strategies from a dynamic standpoint. Such limited rationality enables individuals to adapt and learn in response to the environment and the behavior of others during the decision-making process, thereby gradually developing more adaptive strategies. Thus, evolutionary game theory emphasizes the dynamic process of interaction and evolution among individuals, as opposed to merely static strategy selection. A typical evolutionary game model includes four major elements, as shown in Table 1.

Evolutionary game theory has found widespread application in the energy and power sectors, covering areas such as carbon emission reduction, power markets, and energy economics [26]. A plethora of research outcomes has accumulated, utilizing the theory to guide the transformation of thermal power enterprises towards investment in the CCUS industry. Song et al. [27] employed an evolutionary game model to analyze the interest interaction behavior among alliance organizers, investors, and upstream and downstream operators, revealing that cooperative alliances facilitate the commercial deployment of

CCUS technology. Zhao and Liu [28] formulated an evolutionary game model that delineates interactions between the government and power generation enterprises regarding the development of CCS technology, demonstrating that enhanced government regulation and enterprises' efforts toward cost reduction and efficiency enhancement foster the advancement of CCS technology. Furthermore, it has significant applications in the energy sector, including the exploration of shared energy-storage business models [29] and capacity planning for energy storage in multi-mini-grids using evolutionary game theory [30]. Within the electricity market, the integration of evolutionary game theory with algorithms has been employed to scrutinize the decision-making behavior of electricity distribution companies under the Renewable Portfolio Standard (RPS) [31], examine the decision-making behavior under demand-side dynamic tariffs [32], and explore the behavior of multiple players in demand-side response management (DRM) of electricity [33].

Table 1. Description of the four major elements contained in a typical evolutionary game model.

Major Elements	Descriptions
Game Framework	✔ The structure and rules of a game: conducted under specific techniques and established conditions. Participants do not possess all the knowledge of game structure and rules, a fundamental departure from classical game theory. ✔ Participants typically acquire strategies through transmission mechanisms, such as replicator dynamics (RD), rather than through rational choice.
Fitness Function	✔ Transforming the payoff function in classical games into a fitness function, which describes the reproductive capability of strategies, expressed as the growth rate of strategy adopters after each game round. ✔ The fitness function can be seen as the mapping relationship between strategy and fitness: strategy $\rightarrow$ fitness.
Replicator Dynamics	✔ Selection/mutation mechanism: Utilizes a systems theory perspective to describe dynamic state changes of systems, specifically the dynamic adjustment process of group behavior. Typical are the deterministic and nonlinear EGT models based on the selection mechanism. ✔ Other behavioral patterns: stimulus response dynamics, approximate adjustment dynamics, etc.
Evolutionarily Stable Strategy (ESS)/Evolutionarily Stable Equilibrium (ESE)	✔ ESS is an equilibrium concept in evolutionary games: if an existing strategy is ESS, there must be a positive invasion barrier that allows the existing strategy to achieve higher returns than the mutated strategy when the frequency of the strategy is lower than this barrier. ✔ A refinement of Nash equilibrium (discussed later).

Overall, the research directions of future evolutionary game theoretical methods and models mainly include the following: the study of evolutionary game mechanisms and strategy update rules (such as the pairwise comparison process, Fermi process, Moran process, Wright Fisher process, etc.), the study of evolutionary game paths, evolutionary game relationships, evolutionary game laws, the overall study of evolutionary games, the psychological analysis of game players in the evolutionary process (such as combining belief learning), the optimization and development of evolutionary games (such as combining reinforcement learning), and the design of a panoramic experimental platform for the electricity market, based on evolutionary games.

2.3. Evolutionary Game Theory for Complex Networks and Its Applications

Evolutionary game dynamics on networks have been a significant topic since 1992, when Nowak and May first studied evolutionary games on square lattice networks. Since then, researchers have employed various types of game dynamics to investigate evolutionary games on networks, including the Fermi rule [34], death–birth updating, birth–death updating, imitation updating [35], and pairwise comparison [36]. With the development of complex network science, Watts and Strogatz [37] introduced the concept of "small-world networks" in 1998, demonstrating how these networks exhibit both high clustering and short average path lengths through the reconnection of certain edges. Barabási [38] and Albert introduced the concept of "scale-free networks" and demonstrated that the degree distribution of nodes in many real-world networks (e.g., the Internet, social networks) follows a power-law distribution. Following the introduction of complex network models such as small-world networks and scale-free networks, the study of evolutionary games on complex networks has advanced into a new phase.

Evolutionary game theory for complex networks is a prominent interdisciplinary field that amalgamates complex networks and evolutionary game theory. In this field, researchers view the nodes of complex networks as individuals engaged in the game, with connecting edges representing the topological relationships between individuals. Strategies of each individual are updated via specific dynamics, which facilitates the examination of the relationship between network structure and the evolution of individuals' strategies within the game. The main elements of the evolutionary game with respect to complex networks are shown in Table 2. By delving deep into the interactions among nodes in complex networks, insights into the emergence patterns of group behavior can be unveiled, thus facilitating exploration of dynamic evolution mechanisms within social systems. Moreover, this approach plays a crucial role in practical applications, including information dissemination in social networks and the evolution of cooperative behaviors in complex networks. Jia et al. [39] analyzed trends in cooperative behavior of social capital through the construction of an evolutionary game model based on a scale-free network. Their findings indicate a correlation between the social network structure, individual strategies, and cooperative-behavior trends of capital. Moreover, they observe a positive correlation between the initial probability of the current strategy in the network and the diffusion evolution of the strategy. Similarly, in the realm of energy and power, the complex-network evolutionary game model significantly contributes to interactions among multi-subject strategies. Fan et al. [40] use the evolutionary game model of small-world networks to investigate the peer effect and government behavior regarding the diffusion of enterprise innovation technology. They ascertain that the degree of diffusion is primarily influenced by the benefits to enterprises during the process. Zhao et al. [41] integrate various stages of research backgrounds with corresponding networks to examine the influence of government subsidies on the diffusion rate of new energy vehicles, offering recommendations grounded in complex network theory. In [42], the authors utilize complex-network evolutionary game theory to analyze the diffusion trend of CCUS technology among groups of thermal power enterprises under multi-factor conditions. In addition, Yue et al. [43] investigate the impact of carbon cap-and-trade (CCT) and RPS on renewable energy using complex-network evolutionary game theory.

Overall, the multi-intelligence complex-network evolutionary game model demonstrates a broad spectrum of applications as an effective research tool for investigating the diffusion and adoption of new technologies and behaviors within groups. In the context of evolutionary games on complex networks, the "diffusion rate" typically refers to the speed or extent to which a behavior, strategy, or information spreads within the network. Specifically, the diffusion rate may indicate the frequency or proportion of a behavior or strategy spreading from one node to others within a given time period. In this paper, the defined diffusion rate refers to the proportion of firms in the network that learn the flexibility transformation technology from an initial firm or a set of initial firms through specific strategy update rules. Based on the above research status, the comprehensive research framework of this article is depicted in Figure 1.

Table 2. Describe the main elements contained in the complex-network evolutionary game model.

Main Elements	Descriptions
Game Framework	✔ Unlike classical evolutionary game theory, in complex-network evolutionary game theory, the participating populations are structured, and each individual does not play the game with all others. ✔ Examples are random networks, small-world networks, scale-free networks.
Fitness Function	✔ In complex-network evolutionary game theory, the fitness function accounts not only for the individual's payoff in the game, but also for the network structure and the relationships between individuals. ✔ The network topology can significantly affect the fitness calculation.
Update Mechanism	✔ The mechanism of network evolutionary games leans towards stochastic dynamics, where an individual's strategy update depends not only on their own and their neighbors' benefits but also on the network topology. ✔ Update process: Fermi rule, imitation updating, pairwise comparison, etc.
Population Status	✔ The equilibrium state of the network evolutionary game is influenced by the network structure, the distribution of node degrees, and the selection of specific node strategies. ✔ The state of the population is represented by the distribution of strategies.

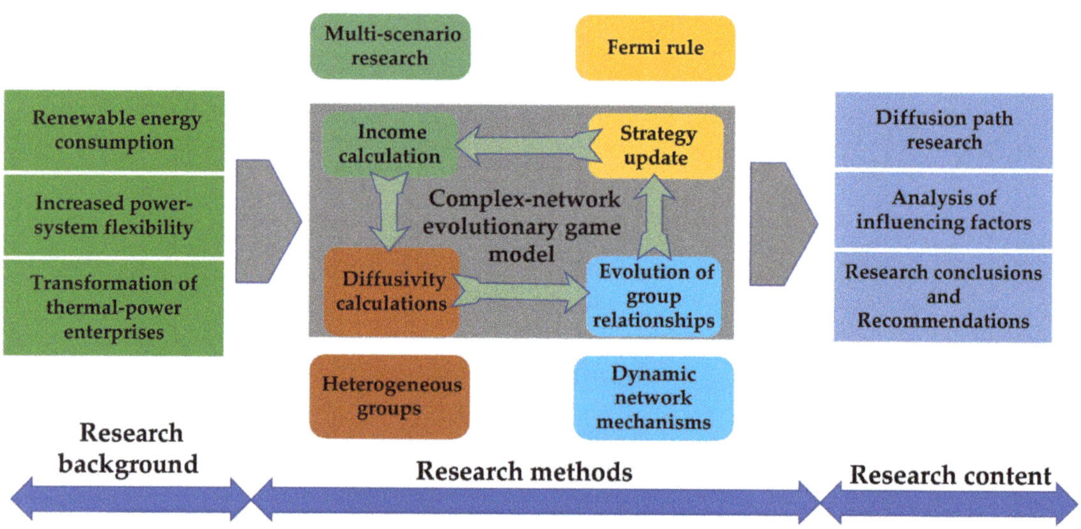

Figure 1. The overall research framework of this article.

3. Methodology

3.1. Revenue and Cost of Thermal Power Enterprises

This paper assumes that each thermal power plant treats one unit as an individual unit. The minimum output of all units is set at 60 percent of the unit's rated capacity before the implementation of flexibility modification technology, and this minimum output decreases to 30 percent after the implementation of this technology. Moreover, due to challenges in estimating the output of thermal units, it is presumed that unit output remains fixed at 30 percent of the unit's rated capacity during deep peak-shaving periods, while the unit operates at full load during non-deep peak-shaving periods.

3.1.1. Regular Operation Generation of Income

Generally, the regular operation generation of income E_1 is defined as follows:

$$E_1 = Qh_1p_1, \tag{1}$$

where Q is the installed rated capacity of the thermal power plant and h_1 is the annual generation utilization hour, representing the equivalent hours of operation of the generating unit in a year based on the unit's rated capacity. P_1 is the feed-in tariff for normal generation.

3.1.2. Deep Peak-Shaving Benefits

The deep peak-shaving benefits includes two parts E_2 and E_3, which are defined as

$$E_2 = \alpha Qh_2p_2, \tag{2}$$

$$E_3 = \alpha Qh_3p_2, \tag{3}$$

where h_2 is the annual hours of peaking participation, P_2 is the peaking feed-in tariff, α is the depth of peaking, E_3 is the current thermal plant's share of the benefits from neighboring plants that do not participate in peaking, and h_3 represents the additional hours of peaking that are shared.

3.1.3. Regular Operation Generation Cost

The regular operation generation cost is denoted by C_1, defined as follows:

$$F_1 = aQ^2 + bQ + c, \tag{4}$$

$$C_1 = F_1h_1, \tag{5}$$

where F_1 is the hourly generation cost of thermal power plants, and a, b, and c are the unit generation factors.

3.1.4. Deep Peak-Shaving Cost

The deep peak-shaving costs are defined as follows:

$$F_2 = a(\alpha Q)^2 + b\alpha Q + c, \tag{6}$$

$$F_3 = \frac{\gamma S}{2N_t}, \tag{7}$$

$$F_4 = r(p_d - p_{dc}), \tag{8}$$

$$C_2 = (F_1 + F_2 + F_3)h_2, \tag{9}$$

$$C_3 = (F_1 + F_2 + F_3)h_3, \tag{10}$$

where F_2 is the generation cost in the deep peak-shaving stage, F_3 is the unit loss cost in the deep peak-shaving stage, P_d is the minimum output of the deep peak regulation without combustion support, P_{dc} is the minimum output of the deep peak regulation with combustion support, γ is the loss coefficient, S is the unit purchase cost, which is assumed to be equal to the installed cost in this paper, N_t is the number of weeks of the rotor fracturing cycle, and F_4 is the cost of oil injection in the deep peaking stage.

3.1.5. Annual Upgrade Cost of Thermal Power Units

According to the literature [44], the cost of flexible transformation of thermal power units is related to the minimum output levels before and after the transformation. In this paper, the minimum output before the transformation of the unit is set at 60% of the rated capacity, and the minimum output after the transformation is set at 30%. Based on this, the annual upgrade cost of thermal power units is defined as follows:

$$K = 0.3\eta G_1 Q, \tag{11}$$

where η is the annualized rate (the calculation method is in Appendix A) and G_1 is the cost per MW of upgrade.

3.2. Assumptions

In the research process, the following three model assumptions are established, based on actual scenarios.

Assumption 1. *Thermal power enterprises in the market are categorized into three groups: large enterprises with a small number but significant influence, medium-sized enterprises with a moderate number and volume, and small enterprises with the largest number but limited influence. During the game process, two enterprises are randomly selected from these groups to engage in the game.*

Assumption 2. *Thermal power firms have two strategic options: to either implement flexible transformation of the unit or not. The probability of implementing this technology is denoted as x, while the probability of not adopting it is $1 - x$. Revenue sources for firms opting not to implement flexibility transformation technology include standard revenue from electricity sales, along with revenue from participation in peaking services. Conversely, revenue for firms choosing not to employ flexibility transformation technology solely comprises revenue from electricity sales.*

Assumption 3. *The escalating demand for deep peak shaving is spurred by China's persistent growth in electricity demand and renewable energy power. This paper postulates a 1.5% annual increase in the duration of thermal power generation units engaged in deep peak shaving. The parameter h_3 is computed based on the neighbors of each node in the network. The symbol β represents the intensity of government subsidies, while θ signifies the penalty factor.*

3.3. Evolutionary Game Model

The evolutionary game model of thermal power enterprises is established based on the payoff distribution matrix, which is demonstrated in Table 3. $E_{A\_AYBY} = E_{a1} + E_{a2} - C_{a1} - C_{a2} - (1-\beta)K_a$, $E_{B\_AYBY} = E_{b1} + E_{b2} - C_{b1} - C_{b2} - (1-\beta)K_b$, $E_{A\_AYBN} = E_{a1} + E_{a2} + E_{a3} - C_{a1} - C_{a2} - C_{a3} - (1-\beta)K_a$, $E_{B\_AYBN} = E_{b1} - C_{b1}$, $E_{A\_ANBY} = E_{a1} - C_{a1}$, $E_{B\_ANBY} = E_{b1} + E_{b2} + E_{b3} - C_{b1} - C_{b2} - C_{b3} - (1-\beta)K_b$, $E_{A\_ANBN} = \theta(E_{a1} - C_{a1})$, and $E_{B\_ANBN} = \theta(E_{b1} - C_{b1})$.

Table 3. The payoff distribution of the evolutionary game model of thermal power enterprises.

		Group B	
		Y (y)	N ($1-y$)
Group A	Y (x)	$\{E_{A\_AYBY}, E_{B\_AYBY}\}$	$\{E_{A\_AYBN}, E_{B\_AYBN}\}$
	N ($1-x$)	$\{E_{A\_ANBY}, E_{B\_ANBY}\}$	$\{E_{A\_ANBN}, E_{B\_ANBN}\}$

In Scenario 1, both Thermal Power Company A (defined and abbreviated as Group A) and Thermal Power Company B (defined and abbreviated as Group B) opt to carry out the flexibility transformation of the unit. As a result, both players receive the benefits of normal power sales, along with additional benefits from participation in peaking services, as detailed in Formula (12):

$$\begin{cases} U_a = E_{a1} + E_{a2} - C_{a1} - C_{a2} - (1-\beta)K_a, \\ U_b = E_{b1} + E_{b2} - C_{b1} - C_{b2} - (1-\beta)K_b. \end{cases} \tag{12}$$

In Scenario 2, Group A decides to implement the flexibility transformation technology, whereas Group B opts not to implement it. Consequently, Group A receives normal revenue from electricity sales and revenue from participation in peaking services. Furthermore, A will share a portion of the peaking share borne by Group B, as detailed in Appendix B. On the other hand, Group B solely receives normal revenue from electricity generation, as shown in Formula (13):

$$\begin{cases} U_a = E_{a1} + E_{a2} + E_{a3} - C_{a1} – C_{a2} – C_{a3} - (1-\beta)K_a, \\ U_b = E_{b1} - C_{b1}. \end{cases} \tag{13}$$

In Scenario 3, Group A chooses not to carry out the flexibility transformation of the unit, while Group B decides to implement it. Consequently, Group A receives only normal generation revenues. Conversely, Group B obtains normal revenues from electricity sales and participation in peaking services. Additionally, Group B will share a portion of Group A's peaking share, as outlined in Appendix B, as shown in Formula (14):

$$\begin{cases} U_a = E_{a1} - C_{a1}, \\ U_b = E_{b1} + E_{b2} + E_{b3} - C_{b1} – C_{b2} – C_{b3} - (1-\beta)K_b. \end{cases} \tag{14}$$

In Scenario 4, if both playing parties, Group A and Group B, opt not to implement the flexibility transformation of the unit, they will earn solely normal power generation revenue. However, neither party will cooperate in promoting the consumption of renewable energy, leading to a certain degree of penalty for both, as shown in Formula (15):

$$\begin{cases} U_a = \theta(E_{a1} - C_{a1}), \\ U_b = \theta(E_{b1} - C_{b1}). \end{cases} \tag{15}$$

Based on Table 3, the benefits to Group A of choosing to use the flexibility transformation technology are

$$\begin{aligned} U_{a1} = \; & y(E_{a1} + E_{a2} - C_{a1} – C_{a2} – (1-b)K_a) + \\ & (1-y)(E_{a1} + E_{a2} + E_{a3} - C_{a1} - C_{a2} - C_{a3} - (1-\beta)K_a). \end{aligned} \tag{16}$$

The benefits to Group A of not using the flexibility modification technology are

$$U_{a2} = y(E_{a1} - C_{a1}) + (1-y)\theta(E_{a1} - C_{a1}). \tag{17}$$

The replication dynamic equations for Group A and Group B can be obtained as follows:

$$\begin{aligned} F_a(x) &= \tfrac{dx}{dt} = x(1-x)(U_{a1} - U_{a2}) \\ &= x(1-x)(E_{a2} - C_{a2} - K_a + (1-y)((1-\theta)(E_{a1} - C_{a1}) + E_{a3} - C_{a3})), \end{aligned} \tag{18}$$

$$\begin{aligned} F_b(x) &= \tfrac{dy}{dt} = y(1-y)(U_{b1} - U_{b2}) \\ &= y(1-y)(E_{b2} - C_{b2} - K_b + (1-x)((1-\theta)(E_{b1} - C_{b1}) + E_{b3} - C_{b3})). \end{aligned} \tag{19}$$

The Jacobi matrix formed by the two parties is as follows:

$$J = \begin{pmatrix} a_{11} & a_{12} \\ a_{21} & a_{22} \end{pmatrix}, \tag{20}$$

where $a_{11} = (1-2x)(E_{a2} - C_{a2} - (1-\beta)K_a + (1-y)((1-\theta)(E_{a1} - C_{a1}) + E_{a3} - C_{a3}))$, $a_{12} = x(x-1)((1-\theta)(E_{a1} - C_{a1}) + E_{a3} - C_{a3}), a_{21} = y(y-1)((1-\theta)(E_{b1} - C_{b1}) + E_{b3} - C_{b3}), a_{22} = (1-2y)(E_{b2} - C_{b2} - (1-\beta)K_a + (1-x)((1-\theta)(E_{b1} - C_{b1}) + E_{b3} - C_{b3}))$.

As shown in Table 4, taking the ideal equilibrium state $x = 1, y = 1$ as an example, according to the stability of equilibrium points [45], at this time the Jacobi matrix J must satisfy det (J) > 0, tr (J) < 0,

$$\begin{cases} C_{a2} - E_{a2} + (1-\beta)K_a < 0, \\ C_{b2} - E_{b2} + (1-\beta)K_b < 0. \end{cases} \tag{21}$$

Table 4. Stabilization conditions at each equilibrium.

(x,y) \ Eig	λ_1	λ_2
$x=0, y=0$	$(1-\theta)E_{a1}+(\theta-1)C_{a1}+E_{a2}+E_{a3}-C_{a2}-C_{a3}+(\beta-1)K_a$	$(1-\theta)E_{b1}+(\theta-1)C_{b1}+E_{b2}+E_{b3}-C_{b2}-C_{b3}+(\beta-1)K_b$
$x=1, y=0$	$E_{a2}-C_{a2}+(\beta-1)K_a$	$(1-\theta)E_{b1}+(\theta-1)C_{b1}+E_{b2}+E_{b3}-C_{b2}-C_{b3}+(\beta-1)K_b$
$x=0, y=1$	$(1-\theta)E_{a1}+(\theta-1)C_{a1}+E_{a2}+E_{a3}-C_{a2}-C_{a3}+(\beta-1)K_a$	$E_{b2}-C_{b2}+(\beta-1)K_b$
$x=1, y=1$	$C_{a2}-E_{a2}+(1-\beta)K_a$	$C_{b2}-E_{b2}+(1-\beta)K_b$

From Formula (21), it can be seen that thermal power plants will use flexibility transformation technology when the benefits of participating in deep peak shaving are greater than the costs.

3.4. Complex-Network Evolutionary Game Model

The group network of thermal utilities is represented by an undirected network $G=(V,E)$, where V is the set of nodes of G representing the thermal utilities and E is the set of edges of G representing the network of relationships among the thermal utilities. Two strategies are randomly assigned on the network G: one employing the flexibility transformation technique and the other not. It is important to note that in practice, the payoffs of enterprises are not necessarily related to the number of neighbors. Therefore, in this model, the payoffs of thermal power enterprises are calculated using a group interaction mode.

In each game, each firm first calculates its own payoff and then randomly selects a neighbor from whom to learn a strategy. The strategy update rules are applied using the Fermi rule [46], as demonstrated below:

$$P(S_A \to S_B) = \frac{1}{1+\exp[(f_A(t)-f_B(t))/k]}. \tag{22}$$

In Formula (22), $f_A(t)$ and $f_B(t)$ are the payoffs of the thermal power plants A and B at time t, S_A and S_B are the strategies of the thermal power plants A and B, respectively, and P is the strategy transfer probability. Here, k is the interference factor, which represents the intensity of irrationality in thermal power enterprises' decisions.

When $k=0$, the Fermi rule mirrors dynamic replication equations, wherein a firm only learns a neighbor's strategy if that strategy's payoff is higher than its own.

When $k>0$, the firm is influenced by irrational factors, learning not only strategies with higher payoffs than its own, but also those with lower payoffs.

As k approaches infinity, firms will randomly learn their neighbors' strategies, irrespective of the payoffs. Considering the practical situation, k is 0.1 in this paper.

In the process of flexibility transformation-technology diffusion, the relationships between thermal power companies will also evolve. To simulate this evolution process, this paper introduces a dynamic network-update mechanism where a pair of nodes is first randomly selected, the connection between them is severed, and subsequently, one of the nodes from this pair is randomly chosen to reconnect with other nodes, excluding itself, with a certain probability. Here, the probability of reconnecting severed edges is

$$P_{ij} = \frac{U_j}{\sum\limits_{j\in G} U_j}, \tag{23}$$

where P_{ij} is the probability that node i is connected to node j, and U_j is the current payoff of node j.

4. Simulation and Discussion

4.1. Data and Parameters

In this section, we analyze the impacts of various factors on the diffusion of flexibility transformation technologies from the perspectives of thermal power enterprise groups and power markets. The experimental simulation software used is Python version 3.9. Some of the experimental parameters are listed in Table 5 (thermal power-unit parameters are demonstrated in Appendix C), and the data sources include the *China Electric Power Statistical Yearbook 2022* and the National Bureau of Statistics of China.

Table 5. Parameters settings of the model.

Parameter	Value	Parameter	Value
Q	1500 MW, 1000 MW, 600 MW	h_1	4600 H
h_2	730 H	p_1	400 CNY/MW
p_2	600 CNY/MW	α	30%
γ	1	G_1	1,000,000 CNY/MW
N_t	500,000	r	2
P_d	45% Q	P_{dc}	30% Q
S	3,000,000 CNY/MW	η	0.55

When differentiating the heterogeneity of thermal power enterprise groups, this paper employs complex network theory. Nodes in the network are sorted based on their degrees. Those with node degree values in the top 10% are defined as large-sized enterprises (denoted by "L"), those with values between the top 10% and top 40% are defined as medium-sized enterprises (denoted by "M"), and the rest are considered small enterprises (denoted by "S"). Additionally, this paper sets the iteration step of the evolutionary game as $t = 5$ and the total number of iterations as 100. Considering the potential impact of random factors on each simulation experiment, 500 experiments were conducted for each part of the experimental results, and the average value was calculated as the final result. The evolutionary game flow of complex networks discussed in this paper is shown in Appendix D.

4.2. The Effect of Network Structure on Diffusion

Firstly, to investigate the impact of market environment diversity and complexity on thermal power enterprises' implementation of unit flexibility reform, we establish two market scenarios for simulation experiments.

Scenario I: In a situation of information asymmetry, the leading enterprise exerts significant influence and can impact the decisions of lower-level enterprises. The simulation experiment is conducted based on a scale-free network with a degree of 2.

Scenario II: In this scenario, individual differences are minimal, and the flow of information is high. Head firms are unable to influence lower-level firms. The experiment is conducted based on a small-world network with a degree of 2.

The simulation results are shown in Figure 2: in Scenario I, the circulation path of information dissemination is relatively linear. The strategic decisions of the leading firms profoundly influence the behavior of the following firms, resulting in a consistently high growth rate during the initial 80 times of iterations. By the 100th iteration, the diffusion rate of thermal power-unit flexibility transformation technology approaches 100%. This suggests that in an oligopolistic market with asymmetric information, where firms' decisions are dominated by the leading firms, technology transformations are more likely to diffuse. In contrast, in Scenario II, the diffusion of this technology is relatively slow, with a consistently low diffusion rate. The final diffusion rate is 76.6%, which is comparable to the results observed during the middle iterations of Scenario I but significantly lower than the final results of Scenario I.

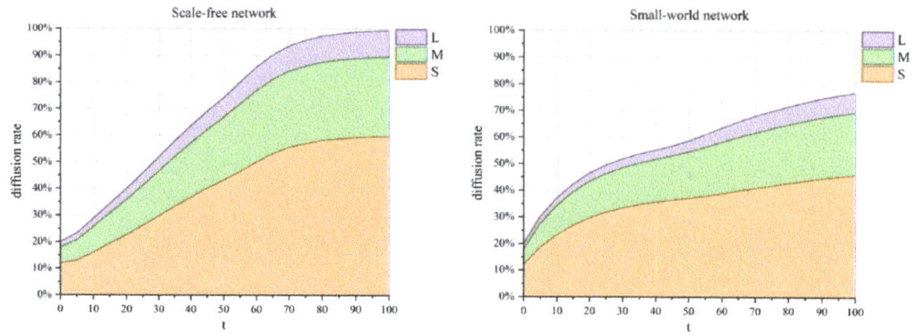

Figure 2. Diffusion rate results for each firm group (small ("S"), medium ("M"), large ("L")) on both scale-free and small-world networks.

After the reform of China's electricity system, the flow of information among different enterprises has significantly accelerated. Therefore, this will better reflect the effects of technology diffusion in the actual market environment and provide valuable guidance for future policy and market strategies.

4.3. The Influence of Network Average Degree on Diffusion

In our previous experiments, we conducted simulations using a network with an average degree of 2. To further investigate the impact of the network's average degree on diffusion effects, we conducted additional analyses using small-world networks. We generated small-world networks with average degrees of 2, 4, 6, and 8 for our game experiments. The simulation results are shown in Figure 3, with an average degree of 2; the diffusion process is slow, due to the network's low connectivity, resulting in a final diffusion rate of the thermal power-unit flexibility transformation technology of approximately 76.6%, indicating a limited diffusion effect. With an average degree increased to 4, the connectivity between network nodes improves. By the 60th iteration step, the overall diffusion rate reaches a level comparable to the final result observed at an average degree of 2, with a final diffusion rate of 86.6%. With average degrees of 6 and 8, respectively, the iterations required to reach a 70% diffusion rate are $t = 40$, resulting in final diffusion rates of 94.5% and 96.4%, respectively. These results demonstrate that as the connectivity of the small-world network increases, the number of neighboring nodes also increases, enhancing the degree of information flow. Consequently, more thermal power companies observe and actively adopt flexibility transformation technology, leading to broader diffusion of the technology.

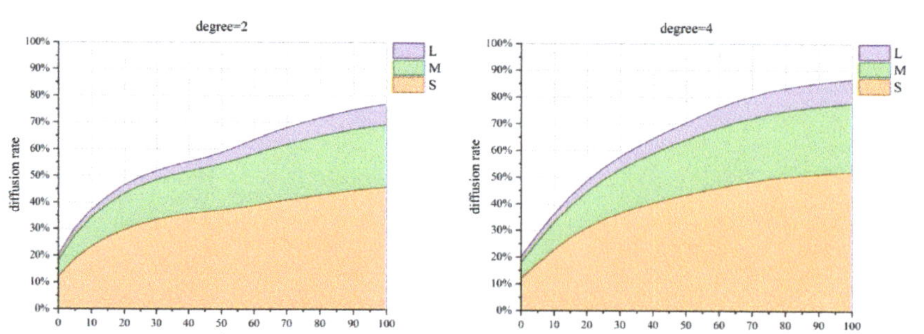

Figure 3. *Cont.*

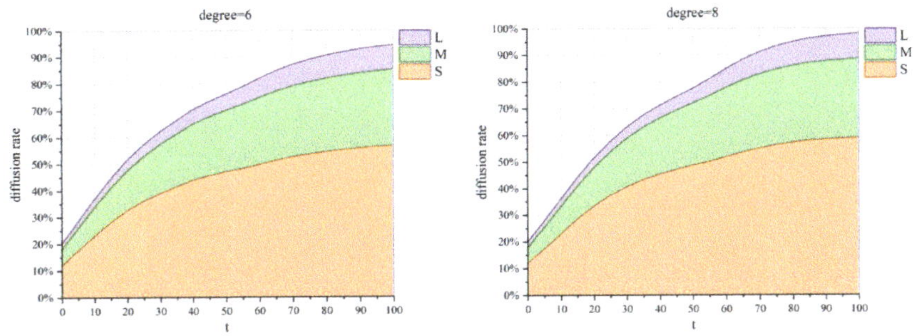

Figure 3. Diffusion rate results for each firm group (small ("S"), medium ("M"), large ("L")) on the small-world network with average degrees of 2, 4, 6, and 8.

Therefore, we conclude that enhancing the degree of information dissemination and technology exchange among thermal power enterprises will facilitate the application and development of flexibility transformation technology for thermal power units. Governments and related departments should encourage and support information exchange and technology cooperation among thermal power enterprises to foster industry development and progress.

4.4. The Influence of Different Initial Application Groups on Diffusion

In the preceding section, thermal power enterprises initially adopting flexible transformation technology were randomly selected, and the distribution of enterprises choosing to implement unit flexibility transformation remained relatively stable across different stages. To investigate the impact of a specific propagation path on diffusion rate, we conducted a comparative study in this section by setting a designated node at the initial moment. The adoption target for the flexible transformation-technology strategy includes the entire small enterprise group, the entire medium-sized enterprise group, the entire large enterprise group, and a mixed group of large and medium-sized enterprises with an initial adoption ratio of 30%.

The experiment reveals that technology diffusion driven by different types of enterprise groups at the initial moment results in varying final diffusion effects. As illustrated in Figure 4, when small enterprises are initially targeted for adopting flexible transformation technology, the final diffusion rate decreases to 41.7%. Conversely, when the initial adoption target includes the entire group of medium-sized enterprises, all large enterprises, and the mixed group of large and medium-sized enterprises with an initial adoption ratio of 30%, the diffusion effect significantly improves to 95.2%, 89.9%, and 99.5%, respectively. The research demonstrates that the differential impact of various types of enterprise groups on promoting technology diffusion at the initial moment can be attributed to their specific roles and influence within the group structure.

Despite the relatively large scale of small enterprises, their limited risk tolerance and uncertain outcomes lead to a cautious, wait-and-see approach toward the benefits of flexible transformation technology. Consequently, they are unable to drive widespread adoption of flexible transformation technology throughout the thermal power enterprise group, resulting in a relatively poor overall final diffusion rate. When targeting the entire group of medium-sized enterprises for flexible transformation-technology adoption, their scale and resource advantages contribute to a more stable technology diffusion process.

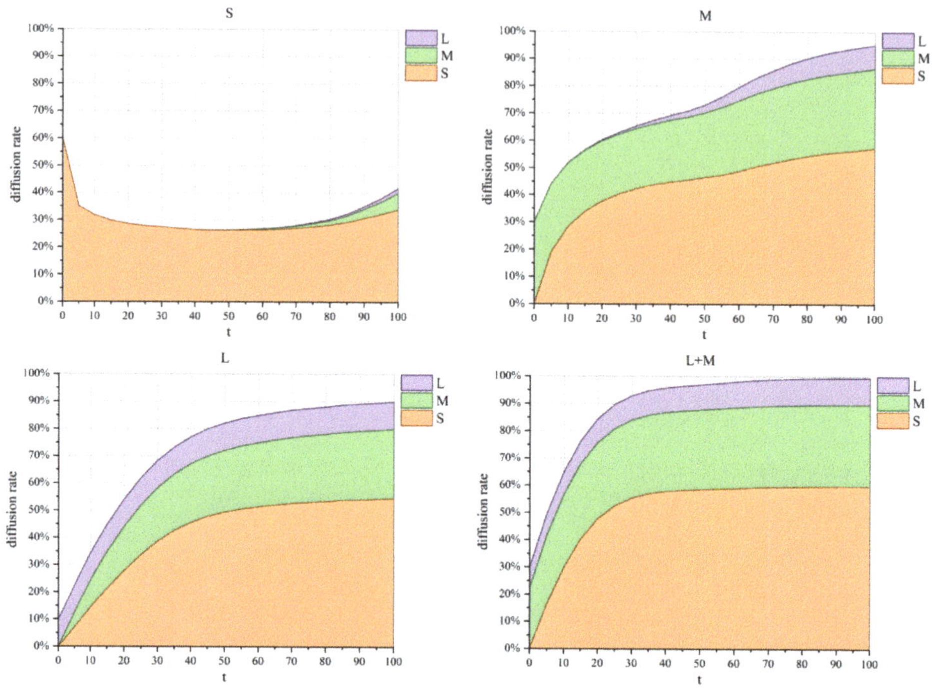

Figure 4. The initial application enterprises include small ("S", initial proportion of 60%), medium ("M", initial proportion of 30%), large ("L", initial proportion of 10%), and a hybrid of medium and large ("L + M", initial proportion of 30%) thermal power enterprises. This composition influences diffusion results on the small-world network.

Therefore, in a controlled experiment, when the initial adoption proportion is 30% for the mixed group of large and medium-sized enterprises, the diffusion effect is optimal, achieving a diffusion depth of 98%. In developing future flexible technology-diffusion strategies for thermal power units, we recommend comprehensive consideration of the characteristics of different types of enterprise groups. Large and medium-sized thermal power enterprises should take the lead in promoting technology diffusion to achieve more optimal outcomes. Such meticulous strategy formulation will effectively promote the dissemination and application of technology in thermal power enterprises.

4.5. Sensitivity Analysis

4.5.1. The Impact of the Deep Peak-Shaving Compensation Electricity Tariff on Diffusion

The deep peak-shaving compensation tariff holds a crucial position in the current power market, as the primary source of income for thermal power enterprises engaging in deep peaking. This compensation mechanism not only ensures a stable income for thermal power enterprises, but also incentivizes them to invest in the construction and enhancement of their peaking capacity. Numerical simulation verification is conducted in this section to examine the impact of deep peak-shaving compensation tariffs on the flexibility transformation of thermal power units. The parameter settings remain unchanged, except for p_2. Under two different initial application atmospheres, p_2 is set to 400 CNY/MW, 450 CNY/MW, 500 CNY/MW, 550 CNY/MW, 600 CNY/MW, 750 CNY/MW, and 900 CNY/MW, respectively, to conduct a sensitivity analysis of the deep-peaking tariff. Figure 5 indicates that at a deep-peaking compensation tariff of 400 CNY/MW, thermal power enterprises in the low initial application atmosphere maintain a conservative approach to unit flexibility transformation, resulting in a low overall application diffusion level. In the high initial-application atmosphere, the total diffusion rate drops to 39.1%. With the compensation tariff increasing to 450 CNY/MW, the overall diffusion rate rises to 34.8% in the low initial-application atmosphere and 59.6% in the high initial-application atmosphere, yet it remains insufficient to prompt most enterprises in the group to undertake the transformation. With p_2 increasing to 500 CNY/MW, the final total diffusion rates in the two scenarios are 81.5% and 88.0%, respectively, both significantly higher than the initial period. Beyond a compensation tariff of 550 CNY/MW, its increase has a more substantial impact on the overall diffusion level in the medium term than in the late period, with the final marginal benefit gradually diminishing. Thus, the increase in the deep-peaking compensation tariff is likely to incentivize thermal power enterprises to prioritize the reform in flexibility of their units. As the deep-peaking compensation tariff increases, the overall diffusion rate increases, albeit at a diminishing rate once the tariff surpasses a certain threshold.

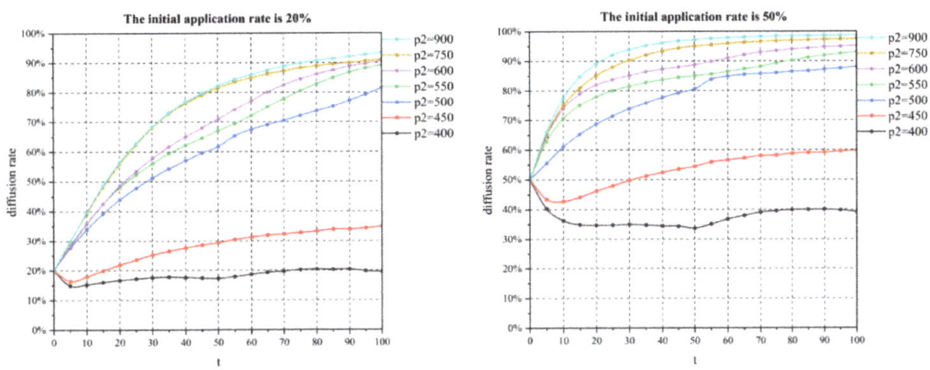

Figure 5. When $\beta = 0.2$, the effect of different deep peak-shaving compensation tariffs (p_2 = 400, 450, 500, 550, 600, 750, 900 CNY/MW) on diffusion under low (20%) and high (50%) initial application ratios.

4.5.2. The Impact of Varying Initial-Application Ratios on Diffusion

The initial transformation ratio of thermal power-unit flexibility transformation represents the level of acceptance of this technology within the thermal power enterprise community. Investigating the initial transformation ratio that can promote the diffusion of thermal unit flexibility-transformation technology is the objective of this inquiry. This section builds upon the findings of the previous section to separately examine the impacts of varying initial transformation ratios on the incentive of the thermal power enterprise group to undertake unit flexibility transformation under two distinct degrees of deep peak-shaving compensation tariffs. As shown in Figure 6, with the deep peak compensation tariff set at $p_2 = 400$ CNY/MW, the final diffusion rates corresponding to initial transformation ratios ranging from 10% to 50% are 11.3%, 22.6%, 27.8%, 31.6%, and 34.8%, respectively. The total diffusion change consistently exhibits a decreasing trend, regardless of the initial transformation ratio, as depicted in Figure 6. Under the high compensation tariff $p_2 = 600$ CNY/MW, as the group transformation ratio increases in the initial stage of the flexibility transformation technology, the final diffusion percentages are 78.7%, 85.8%, 89.7%, 91.7%, and 96.1%, respectively, with a notable increase in diffusion rate in the middle stage. In the low-depth peak-compensation-tariff environment, enhancing the adoption atmosphere of flexibility transformation technology within the group of thermal power enterprises does not improve the technology's diffusion rate; instead, the overall trend is decreasing. In the high-depth peak-compensation-tariff environment, fostering an atmosphere of applying flexibility transformation technology within the group of thermal power enterprises can facilitate the widespread adoption of this technology. Furthermore, the influence of the deep peak-shaving compensation tariff on the diffusion of flexibility transformation within the thermal power enterprise group surpasses the impact of the group's initial transformation percentage on the diffusion of the technology.

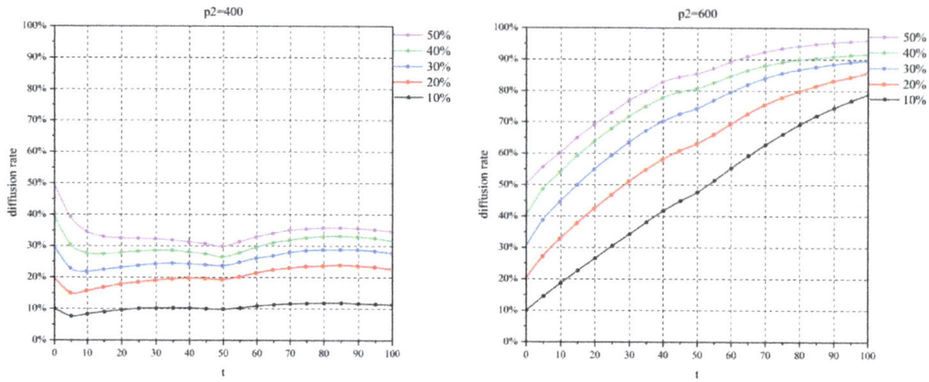

Figure 6. When $\beta = 0.2$, the impact of varying initial application ratios (10%, 20%, 30%, 40%, 50%) on diffusion rate in a small-world network under two different deep peak-shaving compensation-tariff scenarios (where $p_2 = 400$ CNY/MW, $p_2 = 600$ CNY/MW).

4.5.3. The Impact of the Level of Government Subsidies on the Spread of Something

The financial subsidy intensity indicates the level of government support for flexibility transformation technologies. Building on the findings of the previous two sections, we examine the impacts of various financial subsidy intensities on incentivizing thermal power enterprises to undertake unit flexibility transformation under two distinct levels of deep peak-shaving compensation tariffs. In two distinct compensation-tariff scenarios (where $p_2 = 400$ CNY/MW, $p_2 = 400$ CNY/MW), numerical simulations consider three subsidy-intensity levels: β = 0, 0.2, and 0.5, representing no financial support, medium subsidy intensity, and high subsidy intensity, respectively. As shown in Figure 7, in the low-compensation-tariff scenario, the diffusion rate of flexibility transformation technology increases with the rise in subsidy intensity; however, the proportion of the group finally adopting the technology under high subsidy intensity is 30% of the total. With the deep peak-shaving compensation tariff set at 600 CNY/MW, the flexibility transformation technology exhibits a favorable diffusion rate, irrespective of the subsidy-intensity type, achieving diffusion rates of 81%, 86.1%, and 93.3% under the three subsidy intensities, respectively. Despite the positive diffusion rate of flexibility transformation technology for thermal power units under a high deep peak-shaving compensation tariff, the final outcomes vary significantly across different subsidy intensities. For instance, achieving a diffusion rate of 80% requires iterations up to t = 100, 75, and 60 under the three subsidy intensities, respectively. Hence, in the case of a low compensation tariff, increasing the subsidy intensity fails to counterbalance the adverse effects of the tariff, thus hindering the widespread adoption of the technology. Conversely, in a market environment characterized by a high deep peak-shaving compensation tariff, enhancing the subsidy intensity can expedite the diffusion of flexibility transformation-technology application.

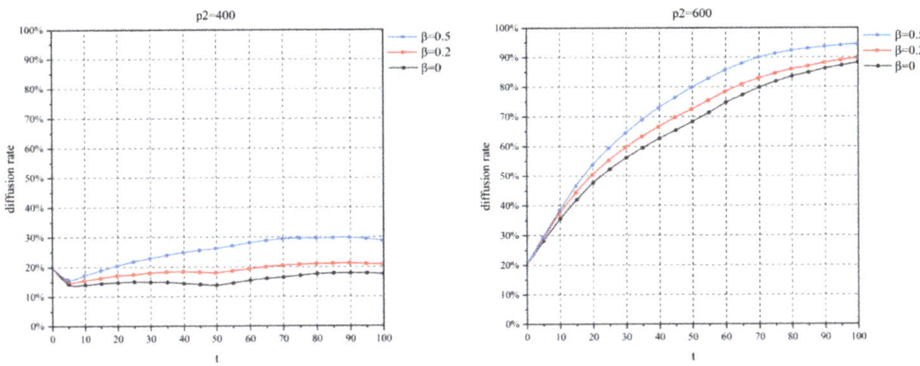

Figure 7. Effect of different subsidy intensities on diffusion rate in a small-world network with a 20% initial application ratio under two different deep peak-shaving compensation tariffs (where $p_2 = 400$ CNY/MW, $p_2 = 600$ CNY/MW).

5. Conclusions and Policy Implications

5.1. Research Conclusions

Promoting the flexibility transformation of thermal power units is crucial for enhancing the flexibility resources of the power grid and fostering the utilization of renewable energy. To promote the dissemination of thermal power-unit flexibility transformation technology within the thermal power enterprise group, this study employs a complex-network-evolution game model for numerical simulation. It analyzes the impact of market type, degree of information dissemination, specific diffusion path, deep peak-shaving compensation tariffs, subsidy level, and initial-application atmosphere on technology diffusion. The findings of this paper are summarized as follows:

(i) If decision-making by upper-tier enterprises can influence lower-tier enterprises, the dissemination of flexibility transformation technology is more probable. However, if upper-tier enterprises lack influence over lower-tier ones, the diffusion effect of the technology may be limited.

(ii) Enhancing the level of information exchange among groups of thermal power enterprises can facilitate the widespread adoption of flexibility transformation technology. By improving information exchange, these enterprise groups can gain better insights into power market demand and profitability trends following unit reform, thereby promoting the broader adoption of flexibility transformation technology.

(iii) Small enterprises lack the capability to independently promote the diffusion and application of technology among groups, making reliance on large and medium-sized enterprises more effective for technology diffusion. Small enterprises often face resource and influence constraints, impeding their ability to drive technology diffusion. Conversely, large and medium-sized enterprises typically possess abundant resources, extensive information sources, and significant influence, making them more effective in promoting technology diffusion.

(iv) Among the three factors—the deep peak-shaving compensation tariff, initial transformation rate of the group, and subsidy intensity—the deep peak shaving compensation tariff has the most significant impact on the diffusion rate. A deep peak-shaving compensation tariff below 450 CNY/MW fails to attract participation from most thermal power enterprises in unit flexibility transformation, while a tariff exceeding 550 CNY/MW results in a gradual decrease in the final benefit generated.

5.2. Policy Implications

(1) The deep peak-shaving compensation tariff plays a crucial role in promoting the advancement of technology application. Deep peak-shaving revenue directly influences

thermal power enterprises' decisions to adopt flexibility transformation technology, as it serves as a direct source of revenue. Reasonable and stable compensation tariffs can safeguard the interests of thermal power enterprises and stimulate their active involvement in the peak-shaving market, thereby furthering the application and development of the technology. Effective deep peak-shaving compensation tariffs should not only protect the interests of thermal power enterprises but also foster the optimization and adjustment of energy structures, thereby promoting the development and application of flexibility transformation technology. Additionally, when formulating the deep peak-shaving compensation tariff, regulatory authorities should enhance supervision and control to ensure its rationality and fairness. Simultaneously, they should actively encourage thermal power enterprises to increase investment in peak-shaving capacity and technological transformation to promote the transformation and upgrading of the energy structure, thereby realizing multiple economic, environmental, and social benefits.

(2) Financial support and the initial application atmosphere of thermal power-unit flexibility transformation-technology diffusion also influence its effect, but they must be combined with the depth of the deep peak-shaving compensation tariff to be effective. With a high deep peak-shaving tariff as the foundation, financial support and a favorable application atmosphere contribute to the process of technology diffusion, providing additional financial backing to enterprises and expediting technology application and diffusion.

(3) Government and regulatory agencies can promote the widespread adoption of flexibility transformation technologies by encouraging and facilitating information exchange among thermal power enterprise groups. Governments can collaborate with lead enterprises to establish demonstration projects for flexibility transformation technologies, showcasing their practical effects to other enterprises in terms of enhanced productivity, reduced costs, and emissions. For instance, industry organizations or platforms can be established to facilitate information sharing and technology exchange. Policy incentives, such as reward systems or subsidy policies, can encourage enterprises to actively engage in information sharing and technology cooperation, thereby promoting the application of flexibility-transformation technologies in the market.

Author Contributions: Conceptualization, L.C. and P.P.; methodology, L.C. and P.P.; software, L.C., P.P. and P.H.; validation, L.C., P.P., P.H. and Y.C.; formal analysis, P.P., P.H. and W.L.; investigation, L.C. and P.P.; resources, L.C.; data curation, L.C., P.P. and P.H.; writing—original draft preparation, L.C., P.P., P.H., Y.C. and W.L.; writing—review and editing, L.C., P.P., Y.C. and W.L.; visualization, L.C. and P.P.; supervision, L.C., Y.C. and W.L.; project administration, L.C.; funding acquisition, L.C. and W.L. All authors have read and agreed to the published version of the manuscript.

Funding: This research was funded by Guangdong Basic and Applied Basic Research Foundation, grant number 2022A1515010699 (funder: L.C.), and grant number 2022A1515240038 (funder: W.L.).

Data Availability Statement: Data are contained within the article.

Acknowledgments: We sincerely thank the associate editor and invited anonymous reviewers for their kind and helpful comments on our paper.

Conflicts of Interest: The authors declare no conflicts of interest.

Appendix A

The annualized calculation method is elaborated by the following formula:

$$\eta = \frac{\varphi(1+\varphi)^n}{(1+\varphi)^n - 1} \tag{A1}$$

where φ is the capital recovery coefficient, converting the total investment cost into the annual investment cost, φ is the social discount rate, and n is the economic applicability of the project. In this paper, $n = 50$, and $\varphi = 5\%$.

Appendix B

The h_3 calculation method is elaborated as follows.

In the enterprise relationship network, each enterprise has different neighbors, so the additional depth of peak load time shared by each enterprise is also different. Taking Figure A1 as an example, the node label "Y" represents the flexibility transformation of thermal power enterprises, while "N" is does not. The depth-peak-load share of Enterprise 1 to Enterprise 2 is calculated, and the mechanism is explained as follows:

Step 1: Calculate the annual depth-peak-power load undertaken by Enterprise 2.

Step 2: Count the number of enterprises in the neighbors of Enterprise 2 to carry out unit flexibility transformation.

Step 3: Divide the annual depth-peak-load undertaken by Enterprise 2 by the number of neighbors in Step 2 to obtain the average share of electricity shared by each neighbor.

Step 4: Divide the average share by the depth-peak-load capacity of Enterprise 1 to obtain the additional depth-peak-load participation time of Enterprise 1.

The above is the depth-peaking power shared by Enterprise 1 with one of its neighbors, and the h_3 of Enterprise 1 can be obtained by summing up several additional depth-peaking participation times.

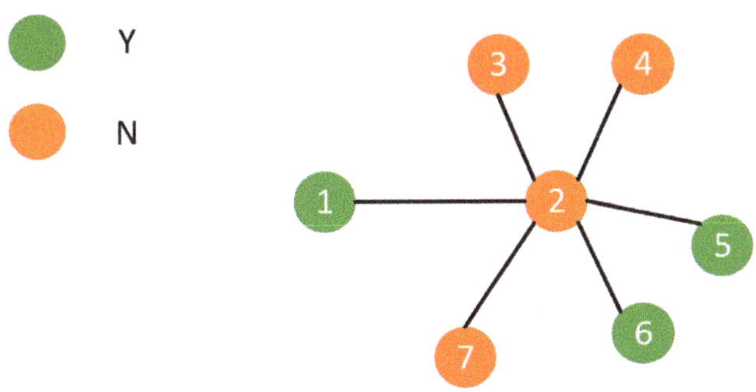

Figure A1. The demonstration of the h_3 calculation method.

Appendix C

The thermal power-unit parameters are set as follows.

The Thermal Power Value	a	b	c
1500 MW	0.06	200	45,000
1000 MW	0.04	240	20,000
600 MW	0.02	320	1000

Appendix D

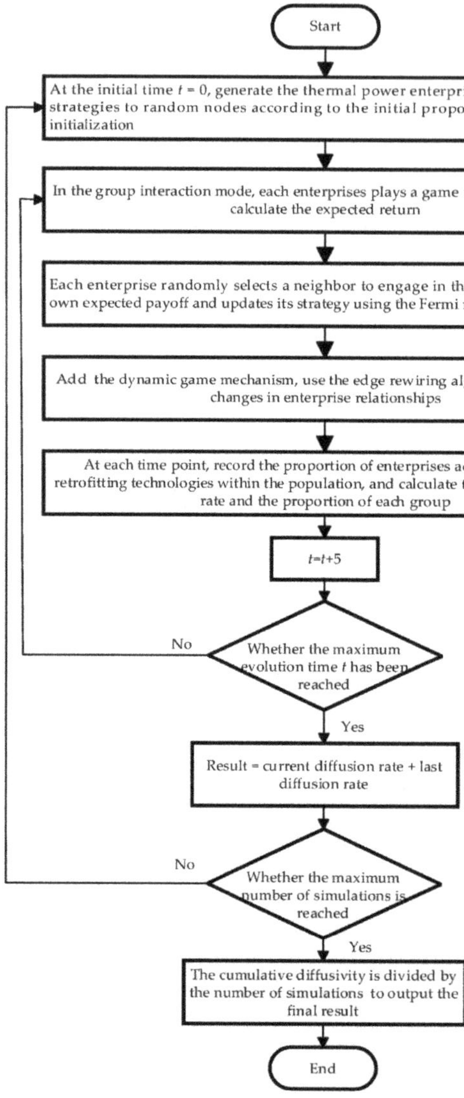

Figure A2. The evolutionary game flow of complex networks discussed in this paper.

References

1. Huang, C.; Lin, B. Promoting decarbonization in the power sector: How important is digital transformation? *Energy Policy* **2023**, *182*, 113735. [CrossRef]
2. Liu, P.; Trieb, F. Transformation of the electricity sector with thermal storage power plants and PV—A first conceptual approach. *J. Energy Storage* **2021**, *44*, 103444. [CrossRef]
3. Zhang, M.; Tang, Y.; Liu, L.; Zhou, D. Optimal investment portfolio strategies for power enterprises under multi-policy scenarios of renewable energy. *Renew. Sustain. Energy Rev.* **2022**, *154*, 111879. [CrossRef]
4. Shi, X.; He, Q.; Liu, Y.; An, X.; Zhang, Q.; Du, D. Thermodynamic and techno-economic analysis of a novel compressed air energy storage system coupled with coal-fired power unit. *Energy* **2024**, *292*, 130591. [CrossRef]

5. Fan, J.-L.; Xu, M.; Wei, S.; Shen, S.; Diao, Y.; Zhang, X. Carbon reduction potential of China's coal-fired power plants based on a CCUS source-sink matching model. *Resour. Conserv. Recycl.* **2021**, *168*, 105320. [CrossRef]
6. Li, K.; Shen, S.; Fan, J.-L.; Xu, M.; Zhang, X. The role of carbon capture, utilization and storage in realizing China's carbon neutrality: A source-sink matching analysis for existing coal-fired power plants. *Resour. Conserv. Recycl.* **2022**, *178*, 106070. [CrossRef]
7. Wang, X.; Tang, R.; Meng, M.; Su, T. Research on CCUS business model and policy incentives for coal-fired power plants in China. *Int. J. Greenh. Gas Control* **2023**, *125*, 103871. [CrossRef]
8. Liu, Z.; Gao, M.; Zhang, X.; Liang, Y.; Guo, Y.; Liu, W.; Bao, J. CCUS and CO_2 injection field application in abroad and China: Status and progress. *Geoenergy Sci. Eng.* **2023**, *229*, 212011. [CrossRef]
9. Yong, Q.; Tian, Y.; Qian, X.; Li, X. Retrofitting coal-fired power plants for grid energy storage by coupling with thermal energy storage. *Appl. Therm. Eng.* **2022**, *215*, 119048. [CrossRef]
10. Zhi, Z.; Ming, Z.; Bo, Y.; Zun, G.; Zhaoyuan, W.; Gengyin, L. Multipath retrofit planning approach for coal-fired power plants in low-carbon power system transitions: Shanxi Province case in China. *Energy* **2023**, *275*, 127502. [CrossRef]
11. Yong, Q.; Jin, K.; Li, X.; Yang, R. Thermo-economic analysis for a novel grid-scale pumped thermal electricity storage system coupled with a coal-fired power plant. *Energy* **2023**, *280*, 128109. [CrossRef]
12. Garðarsdóttir, S.Ó.; Göransson, L.; Normann, F.; Johnsson, F. Improving the flexibility of coal-fired power generators: Impact on the composition of a cost-optimal electricity system. *Appl. Energy* **2018**, *209*, 277–289. [CrossRef]
13. Wang, H.; Ouyang, Z.; Ding, H.; Su, K.; Zhang, J.; Hu, Y. Experimental study on the flexible peak shaving with pulverized coal self-preheating technology under load variability. *Energy* **2024**, *289*, 129830. [CrossRef]
14. Wang, Z.; Liu, M.; Yan, H.; Yan, J. Optimization on coordinate control strategy assisted by high-pressure extraction steam throttling to achieve flexible and efficient operation of thermal power plants. *Energy* **2022**, *244*, 122676. [CrossRef]
15. Cheng, L.F.; Chen, Y.; Liu, G.Y. 2PnS-EG: A general two-population n-strategy evolutionary game for strategic long-term bidding in a deregulated market under different market clearing mechanisms. *Int. J. Electr. Power Energy Syst.* **2022**, *142*, 108182. [CrossRef]
16. Gonzalez-Salazar, M.A.; Kirsten, T.; Prchlik, L. Review of the operational flexibility and emissions of gas- and coal-fired power plants in a future with growing renewables. *Renew. Sustain. Energy Rev.* **2018**, *82*, 1497–1513. [CrossRef]
17. Gu, Y.; Xu, J.; Chen, D.; Wang, Z.; Li, Q. Overall review of peak shaving for coal-fired power units in China. *Renew. Sustain. Energy Rev.* **2016**, *54*, 723–731. [CrossRef]
18. Meng, Y.; Cao, Y.; Li, J.; Liu, C.; Li, J.; Wang, Q.; Cai, G.; Zhao, Q.; Liu, Y.; Meng, X.; et al. The real cost of deep peak shaving for renewable energy accommodation in coal-fired power plants: Calculation framework and case study in China. *J. Clean. Prod.* **2022**, *367*, 132913. [CrossRef]
19. Wang, R.; Du, X.; Shi, Y.; Deng, W.; Wang, Y.; Sun, F. A novel system for reducing power plant electricity consumption and enhancing deep peak-load capability. *Energy* **2024**, *295*, 131031. [CrossRef]
20. Zhao, T.; Zheng, Y.; Li, G. Integrated unit commitment and economic dispatch of combined heat and power system considering heat-power decoupling retrofit of CHP unit. *Int. J. Electr. Power Energy Syst.* **2022**, *143*, 108498. [CrossRef]
21. Lu, Q.; Zhu, J.; Niu, T.; Song, G.; Na, Y. Pulverized coal combustion and NO emissions in high temperature air from circulating fluidized bedx. *Fuel Process. Technol.* **2008**, *89*, 1186–1192. [CrossRef]
22. Zhu, S.; Hui, J.; Lyu, Q.; Ouyang, Z.; Liu, J.; Zhu, J.; Zeng, X.; Zhang, X.; Ding, H.; Liu, Y.; et al. Experimental study on pulverized coal combustion preheated by a circulating fluidized bed: Preheating characteristics for peak shaving. *Fuel* **2022**, *324*, 124684. [CrossRef]
23. Zhu, H.; Shen, J.; Lee, K.Y.; Sun, L. Multi-model based predictive sliding mode control for bed temperature regulation in circulating fluidized bed boiler. *Control Eng. Pract.* **2020**, *101*, 104484. [CrossRef]
24. Wang, Z.; Liu, M.; Yan, H.; Zhao, Y.; Yan, J. Improving flexibility of thermal power plant through control strategy optimization based on orderly utilization of energy storage. *Appl. Therm. Eng.* **2024**, *240*, 122231. [CrossRef]
25. Sun, L.; Hua, Q.; Shen, J.; Xue, Y.; Li, D.; Lee, K.Y. Multi-objective optimization for advanced superheater steam temperature control in a 300 MW power plant. *Appl. Energy* **2017**, *208*, 592–606. [CrossRef]
26. Wang, G.; Chao, Y.; Cao, Y.; Jiang, T.; Han, W.; Chen, Z. A comprehensive review of research works based on evolutionary game theory for sustainable energy development. *Energy Rep.* **2022**, *8*, 114–136. [CrossRef]
27. Song, X.; Ge, Z.; Zhang, W.; Wang, Z.; Huang, Y.; Liu, H. Study on multi-subject behavior game of CCUS cooperative alliance. *Energy* **2023**, *262*, 125229. [CrossRef]
28. Zhao, T.; Liu, Z. A novel analysis of carbon capture and storage (CCS) technology adoption: An evolutionary game model between stakeholders. *Energy* **2019**, *189*, 116352. [CrossRef]
29. Li, X.; Chen, L.; Sun, F.; Hao, Y.; Du, X.; Mei, S. Share or not share, the analysis of energy storage interaction of multiple renewable energy stations based on the evolution game. *Renew. Energy* **2023**, *208*, 679–692. [CrossRef]
30. Li, X.; Chen, L.; Hao, Y.; Wang, Z.; Changxing, Y.; Mei, S. Sharing hydrogen storage capacity planning for multi-microgrid investors with limited rationality: A differential evolution game approach. *J. Clean. Prod.* **2023**, *417*, 138100. [CrossRef]
31. Zhu, C.; Fan, R.; Lin, J. The impact of renewable portfolio standard on retail electricity market: A system dynamics model of tripartite evolutionary game. *Energy Policy* **2020**, *136*, 111072. [CrossRef]
32. Dong, J.; Jiang, Y.; Liu, D.; Dou, X.; Liu, Y.; Peng, S. Promoting dynamic pricing implementation considering policy incentives and electricity retailers' behaviors: An evolutionary game model based on prospect theory. *Energy Policy* **2022**, *167*, 113059. [CrossRef]

33. Cheng, L.; Yin, L.; Wang, J.; Shen, T.; Chen, Y.; Liu, G.; Yu, T. Behavioral decision-making in power demand-side response management: A multi-population evolutionary game dynamics perspective. *Int. J. Electr. Power Energy Syst.* **2021**, *129*, 106743. [CrossRef]
34. Szabó, G.; Tőke, C. Evolutionary prisoner's dilemma game on a square lattice. *Phys. Rev. E* **1998**, *58*, 69–73. [CrossRef]
35. Ohtsuki, H.; Hauert, C.; Lieberman, E.; Nowak, M.A. A simple rule for the evolution of cooperation on graphs and social networks. *Nature* **2006**, *441*, 502–505. [CrossRef] [PubMed]
36. Hauert, C.; Doebeli, M. Spatial structure often inhibits the evolution of cooperation in the snowdrift game. *Nature* **2004**, *428*, 643–646. [CrossRef]
37. Watts, D.; Strogatz, S. Collective dynamics of 'small-world' networks. *Nature* **1998**, *393*, 440–442. [CrossRef]
38. Barabási, A.-L.; Albert, R. Emergence of Scaling in Random Networks. *Science* **1999**, *286*, 509–512. [CrossRef]
39. Jia, C.; Zhang, R.; Wang, D. Evolutionary game of cooperative behavior among social capitals in PPP projects: A complex network perspective. *Ain Shams Eng. J.* **2023**, *14*, 102006. [CrossRef]
40. Fan, R.; Wang, Y.; Chen, F.; Du, K.; Wang, Y. How do government policies affect the diffusion of green innovation among peer enterprises?—An evolutionary-game model in complex networks. *J. Clean. Prod.* **2022**, *364*, 132711. [CrossRef]
41. Zhao, D.; Ji, S.; Wang, H.; Jiang, L. How do government subsidies promote new energy vehicle diffusion in the complex network context? A three-stage evolutionary game model. *Energy* **2021**, *230*, 120899. [CrossRef]
42. Han, J.; Tan, Q.; Ji, Q.; Li, Y.; Liu, Y.; Wang, Y. Simulating the CCUS technology diffusion in thermal power plants: An agent-based evolutionary game model in complex networks. *J. Clean. Prod.* **2023**, *421*, 138515. [CrossRef]
43. Yue, X.; Wang, C.; Sun, B.; Ren, H.; Tan, Y.; Huang, L.; Feng, D.; Li, X. Synergistic effects of carbon cap-and-trade and renewable portfolio standards on renewable energy diffusion. *J. Clean. Prod.* **2023**, *423*, 138717. [CrossRef]
44. Pang, Y.; Chi, Y.; Tian, B. Economic evaluation of flexible transformation in coal-fired power plants with multi price links. *J. Clean. Prod.* **2023**, *402*, 136851. [CrossRef]
45. Friedman, D. Evolutionary Games in Economics. *Econometrica* **1991**, *59*, 637–666. [CrossRef]
46. Du, W.-B.; Cao, X.-B.; Hu, M.-B.; Yang, H.-X.; Zhou, H. Effects of expectation and noise on evolutionary games. *Phys. Stat. Mech. Its Appl.* **2009**, *388*, 2215–2220. [CrossRef]

economies

MDPI

Article

Efficiency Analysis of Human Capital Investments at Micro and Large-Sized Enterprises in the Manufacturing Sector Using Data Envelopment Analysis

Rafael Bernardo Carmona-Benítez * and Aldebarán Rosales-Córdova

Facultad de Economía y Negocios, Universidad Anáhuac México, Huixquilucan 52107, Mexico; carlos.rosales@anahuac.mx

* Correspondence: rafael.carmona@anahuac.mx

Abstract: Micro and large-sized enterprises are important elements to enhance the economic growth of any country, and even more so for developing countries such as Mexico. These enterprises highly contribute to job generation, competitiveness, and gross domestic product, factors that are important for the developing of a nation. The aim of this paper is to study the impact of human capital investments in the efficiency of the 21 economic activity subsectors for micro and large-sized enterprises in the Mexican manufacturing industry between 2009–2021. The database come from Mexico Annual Manufacturing Industry Survey. Four Data Envelopment Analysis models are developed to study the relationship between annual average working days, annual average wages, and annual average investment in training with average sales per year. Data indicate that, most of the micro-sized enterprises of the Mexican manufacturing sector do not invest in human capital training, contrary to their large-sized enterprises. The results show that investing in human capital training increase sales and wages in micro-sized enterprises of the Mexican manufacturing industry, but it is not evident in large-size enterprises of the Mexican manufacturing industry. The calculation of the economic activity subsectors efficiencies using the developed Data Envelopment Analysis models indicate that all the economic activity subsectors with scale efficiency equal to one optimally invest, and the average amount of investments in human capital training needed to increase the global and pure technical efficiencies of the others are calculated with the developed Data Envelopment Analysis models. In the three main economic activity subsectors of the Mexican manufacturing industry, a significant increase—in 83.33% of cases—in wages and salaries is seen in both micro and large-sized enterprises. Particularly, the results indicate that the Chemical industry economic activity subsectors show the highest efficiency in both micro and large-sized enterprises when the human capital training variable is present. This paper demonstrates the importance of investing in human capital to enhance the efficiency of micro and large-sized enterprises.

Keywords: micro-sized enterprises; large-size enterprises; manufacturing economic sector; economic activity subsector; human capital; Data Envelopment Analysis

1. Introduction

An enterprise is an entity that significantly impacts a country's economy, some of them impact the economy of multiple countries. Enterprises can be classified according with their size into three groups of enterprises: (1) micro-size enterprises, (2) small and medium-size enterprises (SME) and (3) large-size enterprises. Their group size determines the role it plays in the socioeconomic dynamics of a country. Enterprise size classification criteria are the number of employees, annual sales, income, and fixed assets (Brodny and Tutak 2022; Diario Oficial de la Federación 2019).

Micro enterprises, especially in development countries like Mexico, make significant socioeconomic contributions, because they show characteristics such as high assimilation capacity, flexibility in responding to market size, quick problem-solving due to a small number of employees, employees with great knowledge, high scalability owing to low operating costs, and rigorous control and supervision of activities. These characteristics foster synergy among workers, helping in the achievement of growth objectives (Martínez-Aparicio 2012; Peralta et al. 2023).

Despite their low impact on gross production due to their modest billing, micro companies are important gateways to labor market, mostly for youth. In Mexico, 30% of the population is conformed for young people (INEGI 2023) and micro-size enterprises are their main source of employment. This group of enterprises contributes approximately 52% to Mexico gross domestic product—GDP—, alongside with the SMEs group (García Camacho and Anido 2024).

One of the main problems faced by micro-size enterprises in Mexico is the absence of economic links between the three groups of enterprises—the group of SMEs, the group of micro-sized enterprises, and the group of large-sized enterprises—and between the Economic Activity subsectors—EAS. This problem reduces the possibility of growth for micro-sized enterprises and makes it difficult to understand business dynamics as well as to identify the reasons for the survival and success of organizations. (Martínez-Aparicio 2012).

Large companies are a small percentage compared to micro companies, it means, the group of large-size enterprises is smaller than the micro-size enterprises group. However, the group of large-size enterprises occupy a transcendental place in the economic activity due to the role that large companies play as agents that reinforce and stimulate development, these companies play an important role to bring foreign investment and, therefore, they also contribute to the global economy, increase job numbers, and GDP (Martínez-Aparicio 2012). Large-size companies are usually multinational, a condition that allows them to have easier access to financial and human resources than micro-size enterprises, reason why, large-size enterprises influence market trends, as well as government policies, despite their high number of workers. Large-size enterprises main difficulties arise in organizational management and social responsibility.

In Latin America, micro and large-size enterprises represent 88.4% and 0.5% respectively (Padilla-Angulo et al. 2023). In Mexico, based on the last economic census, it was identified that micro-size enterprises represent 94.9% and employ 37.2% while large-size enterprises represent 0.2% and employ 32.1%. In particular, the manufacturing sector plays a fundamental role in the country's economic growth, as well as a significant contribution to employment, production, international trade, and exports. Micro-size enterprises in this sector represent 93.7%, hire 19.4% of the personnel employed in the sector, and generate 2.3% of the GDP. Large-size enterprises represent 0.8%, hire 58.1% of the personnel employed in the sector, and generate 78.2% of the GDP (INEGI 2019). In the country, the three main economic activity subsectors—EAS—based on the value of total production in the manufacturing industry are the Chemical Industry—325—the Food Industry—311—and the Transportation Equipment Manufacturing Industry—336—(INEGI 2021b; Rosales-Córdova and Carmona-Benítez 2023).

A company—regardless of its size or sector—is comprised of physical, financial, and intellectual capital, and in turn, intellectual capital consists of human, relational, and structural capital. (Al-Omoush et al. 2022). Although the survival and success of an organization depend on the proper functioning of each of its components, recent research's (Aman-Ullah et al. 2022; Rosales-Córdova and Carmona-Benítez 2023) have identified—and therefore given much greater attention—human capital (HC) as a primary element for the performance of an organization, since its competencies have an impact directly on innovation, competitiveness, adaptability, product, service quality, and reputation of the company. These are conditions that allow companies to survive in the short term and achieve efficiency, and consequently success, in the medium and long-term (Way et al. 2018). For this reason, research on the impact of investment in HC across different sizes of enterprises is of outmost important. As the performance of HC improves, the productivity and efficiency of organizations increase, which positively affects the economic growth of any country. This benefits a developing country such as Mexico. (Bissoondoyal-Bheenick et al. 2023; Ling et al.

2024; Montejano García and López Torres 2013; Rosales-Córdova and Carmona-Benítez 2023; Rosales-Córdova and Llanos 2021).

Various studies have been conducted on HC across different sizes and sectors of enterprises (Almeida and Faria 2014; Nguyen et al. 2020; Prouska et al. 2016; Sitzmann and Weinhardt 2019; Way et al. 2018; Zhao et al. 2018). However, there is a gap in the study of the impact investment in HC has on efficiency of the EASs. Few have used Data Envelopment Analysis—DEA—models to analyze the efficiency in different company size based on HC, and fewer have been conducted at EAS level (Kalapouti et al. 2020; Monika and Mariana 2015; Rosales-Córdova and Carmona-Benítez 2023). For this reason and based on the importance of HC in the performance and efficiency of organizations, and these in turn in the country's economy, that the aim of this paper is to study the impact of HC investments in the efficiency of the 21 EASs for micro and large-sized enterprises in the Mexican manufacturing industry for the period 2009–2021. To study so, four DEA models are developed. One DEA BCC and one DEA CCR use annual average working days, annual average salary, and annual average investment in training as input factors, and average sales per year as output factor, while one DEA BCC and one DEA CCR consider annual average working days and annual average salary as input factors and average sales per year as output factor.

This paper is organized as follows: in Section 2, a review on HC in micro and large-size enterprises, and a review about the application of DEA to analyze the performance of micro and large-size enterprises are presented; in Section 3, the inputs and output variables under study are explained, the CCR input-oriented model and the BCC input-oriented model are described, and the data are presented for the analysis of the 21 EAS that conform the micro-sized and large-sized enterprises in the Mexican manufacturing industry; in Section 4, the results and discussion about the efficiency of the 21 EAS that conform the Mexican manufacturing industry are analyzed for micro-sized enterprises and for large-sized enterprises; finally, in Section 5, conclusions are drawn, limitations and future research topics are provides.

2. Literature Review

2.1. Human Capital in Micro and Large-Size Enterprises

Mincer (1958), Schultz (1961), and Becker (1962) are the pioneers and creators of the theory of Human Capital. Over the years, their definition of HC has been complemented and refined. Now, it is accepted as a multidimensional construct composed of two main factors: cognitive and non-cognitive (Zhang et al. 2023). These factors include different dimensions. In general terms, HC can be defined as the knowledge, skills, abilities, talents, and capabilities of an individual to enhance productivity and create value to an organization (Nahuat Román 2020; Wright 2021).

The survival and success of an enterprise depend on physical, financial, and intellectual capital. The later plays an important role because the benefits of an organization increase for both the individual and the organization itself to the extent that HC is acquired and retained (Bissoondoyal-Bheenick et al. 2023). According with literature, several studies identify that investing in human capital training (HCT) increases enterprise productivity and efficiency, leading to significant improvements for both the employee—higher wages—and the organization—cost reduction, increased production, competitiveness, and sales (Bissoondoyal-Bheenick et al. 2023; Ling et al. 2024; Montejano García and López Torres 2013; Rosales-Córdova and Carmona-Benítez 2023; Rosales-Córdova and Llanos 2021). It is important to highlight the inherent difficulty in referring to a human being, as enterprises do not own them. They constantly change and are complex to understand (Ibarra-Cisneros and Hernández-Perlines 2019).

In micro-sized enterprises, the accumulation of HC and years of experience significantly impact economic performance of countries. The level of schooling—formal learning—job experience—informal learning—and HCT—non-formal learning—improves this effect (Peralta et al. 2023). The accumulation of HC is generated when the owner or microentrepreneur values the expected profitability of additional schooling degrees more than the costs associated with their realization. Education improves enterprise processes and sales management (Díaz Rodríguez et al. 2021). The longevity of micro-sized enterprises is well-defined within the first three years of operation. During this time, competitive capabilities are developed, and enough knowledge and skills for problem solution are generated (Ramírez et al. 2017). Unfortunately, in Mexico, a high percentage of micro-sized enterprises fail to surpass this time interval (INEGI 2021a). Hence, creativity, adaptability, and effective resource management are important factors for overcoming inherent challenges.

Unlike micro-sized enterprises, most of large-sized enterprises participate in both national and international markets. These types of enterprises expose their HC to external knowledge, including interactions with suppliers, clients, research centers, and financial institutions worldwide, helping them to gain competitive advantages (Perri et al. 2017). Moreover, multinational corporations increase knowledge management and diversify the professional profiles of their HC because they have access to more resources. Therefore, large-sized enterprises enable better adaptation to new technologies within the organization, thus providing HC with the necessary tools to adapt to the continuous changes in the market (Tseng et al. 2023).

HC is one of the most important factors influencing the survival and success of companies, regardless of their size (Rodríguez-Gulías et al. 2024). Consequently, understanding the optimal investment in HC is important for enhancing and assuring enterprises efficiency. This is the reason why this paper is particularly relevant, since it aims to analyze the impact of HC investments has on the efficiency and productivity of the 21 EAS within both micro and large-sized enterprises in the Mexican manufacturing industry. Moreover, while most of the research on HC focuses on SMEs without distinguishing between enterprise sizes, there are few research studying large companies and even fewer on micro-size enterprises. This is attributable to the difficulty of obtaining data from micro-size enterprises.

2.2. Data Envelopment Analysis Method in Micro and Large-Size Enterprises

Micro-sized enterprises are the main drivers of economic growth, and they are essential to boosting the capacity of a country to be competitive and innovative (Basyah and Fahmi 2024). This type of enterprises employs a maximum of 10 persons and applies family business principles (Porfírio et al. 2020). Micro-sized enterprises in Latin America often encounter a high failure rate (García Camacho and Anido 2024), primarily due to management or administrative problems, financing problems, and access to win tenders (Basyah and Fahmi 2024). Moreover, micro-sized enterprises operate in uncertain environments where available information about their performances is limited (Kononiuk 2022; Sedliačiková et al. 2024). Reason why, it is highly complex to evaluate the performance of micro-sized enterprises. Different factors have been studied, and various methodologies have been applied, leading to the conclusion that a high correlation between HC and company performance at micro-sized enterprises exist (Sedliačiková et al. 2024).

Chanda (2019) uses DEA methodology to evaluate the performance of micro-sized enterprises and SMEs at industry level. He compares the productivity of micro-sized enterprises and SMEs with large-sized enterprises. Purmiyati et al. (2019) applied the DEA VRS methodology to measure the technical efficiency (TE) of micro-sized enterprises that acquire commercial credit in 7 cities in East Java. Ayele (2021) uses a DEA model to calculate the TE and scale efficiency (SE) of 375 randomly selected micro-sized and small-sized enterprises. Boubaker et al. (2023) propose a DEA methodology to measure the efficiency performance of Vietnamese micro-sized enterprises and SMEs of its manufacturing sector. Dey et al. (2023b) apply DEA methodology to calculate the TE of 427 handloom micro-sized enterprises in the India State of Assam. Dey et al. (2023a) apply DEA a two-stage double-bootstrap DEA methodology to estimate the TE and its determinants of 340 handloom micro-sized enterprises for the three districts of the Indian State of Assam. García Camacho and Anido (2024) develops a DEA and a Malmquist index to analyze the performance of the micro-sized enterprises and SMEs in Colombia. Baruah and Saha (2024) use DEA to examines the TE of 312 micro-sized enterprises in India. Yang et al. (2024) use DEA methodology and a Malmquist index method to study the efficiency of financial funds assigned to support the technological innovation in new energy vehicle micro-sized enterprises.

Zheng et al. (1998) apply DEA methodology to analyze the TE in large-sized and medium-sized enterprises at state, collective, and township-village level. Zheng et al. (2003) use DEA to research the productivity of 600 large-sized state enterprises from 1980 to 1994. Memon and Tahir (2012) develop a DEA model to evaluate the performance of large-sized (assets over 100 million usd), medium-sized (assets between 30 million usd and 100 million usd), and small-sized (asset under 30 million usd) enterprises in Pakistan. Wang et al. (2017) develop a fuzzy DEA model to evaluate the performance of environmental regulations in 16,375 enterprises. Villa et al. (2021) develop a project selection method based on DEA methodology to determine what energy projects to prioritize regarding their economic efficiency. Cinaroglu (2021) develop a Bootstrap DEA methodology to study the efficiency of small-sized and large-sized public hospitals from 2014 to 2017. Proaño-Rivera and Feria-Dominguez (2022) use DEA methodology to calculate the TE of 24 banks in Ecuador from 2015 to 2019. Gopalkrishnan et al. (2023) develop a mix of Tobit regression and measure the operational efficiency of 26 housing finance enterprises in the Indian economy. Hooda and Sehrawat (2023) use DEA to study the overall technical efficiency (OTE), pure technical efficiency (PTE), and SE of the state transport system in the Indian State of Rajasthan. Seth et al. (2024) design a panel data fixed-effects model mixed with DEA methodology to study the efficiency of working capital management in 1,388 manufacturing firms from 2008 to 2019. Ofori et al. (2024) apply DEA methodology to study the efficiency and productivity of 749 US agricultural cooperatives from 2011 to 2015. Boubaker et al. (2024) design a composite performance index as a variable that measures bank stability. They use the dynamic weighting system of DEA to analyze the stability performance of 45 Vietnamese banks using data from 2002 to 2020. Zhu et al. (2024) apply a three-stage DEA mixed with Malmquist index to evaluate the digital inclusive financial development efficiency in 31 Northwest China provinces from 2015–2021.

It is important to mention that few papers study the impact of HC variables in EAS. From literature, the papers that apply DEA methodology to analyze the impact of HC variables in the performance of micro-sized enterprises and SMEs between EAS are Olexová (2011), Monika and Mariana (2015), Kalapouti et al. (2020), and Rosales-Córdova and Carmona-Benítez (2023). We did not find a paper that applies DEA to study the impact of HC variables between EAS for large-sized enterprises.

Rosales-Córdova and Carmona-Benítez (2023) is a very important study to this paper because they analyze the efficiency of HC in relation to sales at the EAS level for the 21 SMEs that conform the Mexican manufacturing industry. They use a DEA CCR input-oriented model to calculate the technical efficiency (TE) (Charnes et al. 1978), and a DEA BCC input-oriented model to calculate the pure technical efficiency (PTE) (Banker et al. 1984). Similar, in this paper, we analyze the efficiency of HC in relation to sales between the 21 EAS that conform the Mexican manufacturing industry, but for micro and large enterprises using the DEA CCR input-oriented model to calculate the OTE and the DEA BCC input-oriented model to calculate the PTE. Therefore, this paper complements the study published by Rosales-Córdova and Carmona-Benítez (2023) in four ways: (1) to acknowledge the effects of human capital training (HCT) have on the efficiency of micro and large-size enterprises in the Mexican Manufacturing Industry; (2) to identify the EAS that are efficient in the micro and large-sized enterprises of the Mexican Manufacturing Industry; (3) to determine the EAS that properly invest in HCT in the micro and large-sized enterprises in the Mexican Manufacturing Industry; and (4) to calculate the optimal investment in human capital (HC) that enables efficiency and consequently generates a competitive advantage for all the EAS in the micro and large-sized manufacturing enterprises of the Mexican Manufacturing Industry.

In summary, our literature review reports the application of DEA methodology to analyze the impact of HC in sales at company level for all size of enterprises, but the impact of HC variables in EAS has mainly been done for SMEs. Therefore, there is a gap in research considering the impact of HC variables in micro and large-sized enterprises.

Based on the above, the following hypotheses are proposed in this research:

H1. *The number of micro-sized enterprises that invest in HCT is lower than the number of micro-sized enterprises that do not invest in HCT at each EAS of the Mexican manufacturing industry.*

H2. *The number of large-sized enterprises that invest in HCT is higher than the number of large-sized enterprises that do not invest in HCT at each EAS of the Mexican manufacturing industry.*

H3. *The investments in HCT increase average sales and average wages at each of the 21 EAS in micro and large-sized enterprises of the Mexican manufacturing industry.*

H4. *The correct investments in HCT increase the efficiency of the EAS in micro and large-sized enterprises of the Mexican manufacturing industry.*

H5. *The efficiencies of the three main subsectors of the Mexican manufacturing industry—the Chemical Industry (325), the Food Industry (311), and the Transportation Equipment Manufacturing Industry (336)—are above 0.50 when they invest in HCT in both micro and large-sized enterprises.*

3. Methodology and Data

The aim of this paper is to study the impact of HC investments in the efficiency of the 21 EASs for micro and large-sized enterprises in the Mexican manufacturing industry. To achieve this, we analyze the efficiency of HC (investment in HCT, wages, and working days) in relation to sales within each of the 21 EASs that conform this industry. Therefore, the variables employed in each sample, as well as their definitions are:

- Investment in HCT (input 1): payments made by a company for the training of its workers, including payments to internal and external instructors, training materials and payments to educational institutions also known as scholarships.
- Wages (input 2): all payments and contributions, normal and extraordinary, in money and kind, before any tax deduction, to remunerate the work of the employee's dependent on the company name, in the form of wages and salaries, social benefits, and profits distributed to the personnel, whether this payment is calculated based on a working day or by the amount of work performed.
- Working days (input 3): counts the number of days dedicated directly to activities related to the production process of the establishment.
- Sales (output): revenues obtained for production of goods and services.

Using these variables, the DEA methodology is applied to analyze the efficiency and productivity growth between HC investments and sales on micro and large-sized enterprises. DEA methodology creates an efficient frontier setting a target between a set of units under study making this methodology more suitable for performance measurement.

The aim of DEA models is to calculate the efficiency and productivity of various units in a set, the units are called DMUs (Martín-Gamboa and Iribarren 2021). Two types of efficiency are calculated from DEA models. The overall technical efficiency (OTE) is calculated assuming constant returns-to-scale (CRS) with DEA CRS input-oriented model (Charnes et al. 1978), and pure technical efficiency (PTE) is calculated assuming variable returns-to-scale (VRS) with the DEA BCC input-oriented model (Banker et al. 1984). A DMU produces optimally when OTE is equal to PTE because the scale efficiency (SE) is equal to 1, it means no efficiency gain is achieved if the production scale is modified.

In this paper, input-oriented models are applied to calculate OTE and PTE since micro and large-sized enterprises can control their investments on HC, but they do not have control on sales. It means they control inputs but not the output. So, input-oriented DEA models minimize inputs to produce the same level of output (Kumar and Gulati 2008). The aim of these DEA models is to measure sales efficiency in HC investments within micro and large-sized enterprises. It is an important contribution to the research in human resources management.

3.1. CCR Input-Oriented Model

Equation (1)–(5) present the CCR input-oriented model (Marjanovic et al. 2018) written into its standard form (Kumar and Gulati 2008).

$$\min OTE_0 = \theta_0 - \varepsilon\left(\sum_{i=1}^{m} s_i^- + \sum_{r=1}^{s} s_r^+\right) \quad (1)$$

ST

$$\sum_{j=1}^{n} \lambda_j x_{ij} + s_i^- = \theta_0 x_{i0} \;\; i = 1,2,\ldots,m \quad (2)$$

$$\sum_{j=1}^{n} \lambda_j y_{rj} - s_r^+ = y_{r0} \;\; r = 1,2,\ldots,s \quad (3)$$

$$s_i^-, s_r^+ \geq 0 \;\; (i=1,\ldots,m;\; r = 1,\ldots,s) \quad (4)$$

$$\lambda_j \geq 0 \;\; j = 1,2,\ldots,n \quad (5)$$

where:

DMU_0	unit under analysis	[-]
x_{ij}	quantity of input *i* used by DMU_j	[units]
x_{io}	quantity of input *i* used by the DMU_0	[units]
y_{rj}	quantity of output *r* delivered by DMU_j	[units]
x_{ro}	quantity of output *r* delivered by the DMU_0	[units]
λ_j	relationship importance between DMU_j and the DMU_0	[-]
θ_o^*	DMU_0 optimal OTE	[-]
s_i^-	input slack variable	[units]
s_r^+	output slack variable	[units]
ε	a small positive number	[-]

3.2. BCC Input-Oriented Model

Equations (6)–(11) present the BCC input-oriented model (Marjanovic et al. 2018) written into its standard form (Kumar and Gulati 2008).

$$\min PTE_0 = \theta_0 - \varepsilon\left(\sum_{i=1}^{m} s_i^- + \sum_{r=1}^{s} s_r^+\right) \quad (6)$$

ST

$$\sum_{j=1}^{n} \lambda_j x_{ij} + s_i^- = \theta_0 x_{i0} \;\; i = 1,2,\ldots,m \quad (7)$$

$$\sum_{j=1}^{n} \lambda_j y_{rj} - s_r^+ = y_{r0} \;\; r = 1,2,\ldots,s \quad (8)$$

$$\sum_{j=1}^{n} \lambda_j = 1 \quad (9)$$

$$s_i^-, s_r^+ \geq 0 \;\; (i = 1,\ldots,m;\; r = 1,\ldots,s) \quad (10)$$

$$\lambda_j \geq 0 \;\; j = 1,2,\ldots,n \quad (11)$$

3.3. Data

The data used in this study comes from Mexico Annual Manufacturing Industry Survey for the period 2009–2021. Data is collected by the "Instituto Nacional de Estadística y Geografía" (INEGI SNIEG 2021) and provided based on its regulations established in its procedure for the utilization of the Annual Survey of the Manufacturing Industry, as well as for the extraction of data from its microdata laboratory, the ethical use of information, as well as its replicability and acquisition are ensured.

The Annual Survey of the Manufacturing Industry contains data about the methodology inputs and output variables allowing to study the efficiency of micro and large-sized enterprises of the Mexican industry for the 21 EAS.

The steps to clean and prepare the data and generate the sample sets are:

Step 1. Variable average values are calculated for the period 2009–2021. All observation units that report zero employees, wages, and sales are removed from the data.

Step 2. Observation units with full-time employees between 1 and 10 are classified as micro-sized enterprises, and observation units with more than 250 full-time employees are classified as large-sized enterprises (Diario Oficial de la Federación 2019). Hence, two samples are generated, one is the micro-sized enterprise sample, and the other is the large-sized enterprise sample.

Step 3. The micro and large-sized enterprise samples are divided in two sets each, by separating the observation units that report investing in HCT from those that do not. Therefore, the micro-sized enterprise—Set 1—includes observation units that invest in human capital training (HCT/Yes); the micro-sized enterprise—Set 2—includes observation units that does not invest in human capital training (HCT/No); the large-sized enterprise—Set 3—includes observation units that invest in human capital training (HCT/Yes); and the large-sized enterprise—Set 4—includes observation units that does not invest in human capital training (HCT/No).

Step 4. In the four datasets, all variables (inputs and output) are segmented by quartiles to control the variability that is inherent to data (x) which is categorized in three groups: Group 1 = first quartile (x < 25%), Group 2 = second and third quartile (25% ≤ x ≤ 75%), and Group 3 = fourth quartile (x > 75%). This study only uses data from group 2 because the variables coefficient of variation—CV—are smaller than 1. Contrary, data from groups 1 and 3 are not used because their variables CV are greater than 1, which indicate these data are not statistically acceptable.

Tables 1 and 2 show the average input and output variables data used for the statistical analysis (Section 4.1) and the DEA analyses (Section 4.2) of the 21 EAS for micro and large-sized enterprises respectively. These tables show the average investment done in HCT (HCT/Yes) per EAS from 2009 to 2021.

Table 1. Average input and output variables of micro-sized enterprises from 2009 to 2021.

	HCT/Yes—Set 1—					HCT/No—Set 2—			
	Inputs Variables				Output Variable	Inputs Variables			Output Variable
EAS	N	Annual Average HCT [MXN]	Annual Average Wages [MXN]	Annual Average Working Days [Days]	Annual Average Sales per Year [000 of MXN]	N	Annual Average Wages [MXN]	Annual Average Working Days [Days]	Annual Average Sales per Year [000 of MXN]
311	37	$13,757	$580,457	277.4	$6379.3	509	$224,338	292.4	$1179.6
312	21	$3810	$423,133	292.4	$3501.9	134	$167,970	298.8	$613.7
313	7	$7286	$920,429	280.7	$9012.0	103	$251,398	274.8	$1296.3
314	4	$5000	$715,333	239.0	$1936.0	69	$347,348	289.5	$1815.6
315	12	$8083	$649,750	253.7	$9053.6	142	$250,690	269.9	$915.0
316	8	$8128	$433,667	258.1	$1950.0	113	$304,770	280.4	$1402.3

Table 1. *Cont.*

	HCT/Yes—Set 1—					HCT/No—Set 2—			
	Inputs Variables				Output Variable	Inputs Variables			Output Variable
EAS	N	Annual Average HCT [MXN]	Annual Average Wages [MXN]	Annual Average Working Days [Days]	Annual Average Sales per Year [000 of MXN]	N	Annual Average Wages [MXN]	Annual Average Working Days [Days]	Annual Average Sales per Year [000 of MXN]
321	8	$5625	$408,667	287.3	$5988.5	154	$192,844	276.0	$862.3
322	4	$39,600	$444,000	246.3	$2689.7	45	$358,333	275.9	$1596.7
323	14	$7000	$343,200	257.8	$2714.0	64	$169,803	276.1	$623.0
324	4	$8333	$897,667	327.3	$4987.0	10	$309,900	266.0	$1373.5
325	13	$39,333	$685,846	257.6	$49,418.5	73	$288,151	282.7	$1064.5
326	20	$6846	$739,235	250.8	$3915.4	128	$263,578	275.4	$1049.4
327	36	$4250	$1,120,250	299.6	$11,881.3	174	$241,810	273.7	$782.4
331	4	$27,000	$1,822,500	282.0	$71,202.4	46	$217,239	289.7	$868.9
332	23	$9217	$561,955	276.6	$5269.5	178	$174,427	278.4	$676.3
333	15	$25,750	$599,615	261.3	$5826.6	77	$331,026	267.9	$1196.6
334	4	$2250	$658,250	251.3	$3655.3	53	$321,849	278.9	$1285.4
335	6	$19,500	$1,085,833	255.0	$4270.6	50	$244,600	260.8	$969.3
336	11	$16,818	$673,500	258.5	$2793.8	78	$288,244	285.5	$1288.3
337	8	$12,500	$428,857	285.9	$3599.3	81	$206,877	300.3	$818.9
339	15	$6267	$410,938	270.4	$3371.3	129	$304,465	273.6	$1215.9

Table 2. Average input and output variables of large-sized enterprises from 2009 to 2021.

	HCT/Yes—Set 3—					HCT/No—Set 4—			
	Inputs Variables				Output Variable	Inputs Variables			Output Variable
EAS	N	Annual Average HCT [MXN]	Annual Average Wages [000 of MXN]	Annual Average Working Days [Days]	Annual Average Sales per Year [000 of MXN]	N	Annual Average Wages [000 of MXN]	Annual Average Working Days [Days]	Annual Average Sales per Year [000 of MXN]
311	608	$262,622	$73,682.2	292.2	$449,446.5	264	$58,482.8	288.2	$272,072.5
312	148	$397,209	$80,254.6	297.1	$542,262.3	61	$65,672.2	295.3	$333,689.4
313	115	$203,800	$70,083.8	291.6	$365,709.6	59	$54,598.1	295.5	$231,402.3
314	51	$164,353	$66,276.5	273.9	$334,678.9	18	$35,922.7	286.9	$189,447.5
315	60	$60,650	$57,429.4	271.4	$147,562.6	40	$41,667.9	259.2	$110,854.9
316	31	$124,290	$39,020.1	264.9	$171,229.1	18	$44,433.3	270.6	$192,398.3
321	5	$42,600	$43,598.6	316.5	$389,412.0	1	$57,937.0	293.0	$440,158.0
322	36	$472,694	$76,552.2	334.4	$812,872.9	18	$84,373.9	349.3	$1,035,219.9
323	12	$203,000	$60,942.8	293.1	$182,428.8	6	$40,603.2	321.5	$166,881.7
324	6	$1,776,000	$134,110.0	335.7	$1,571,015.0	7	$2,018,178.1	365.0	$118,405,378.4
325	65	$814,154	$132,428.5	290.0	$1,222,906.1	31	$137,769.0	289.3	$997,483.4
326	67	$259,955	$57,455.0	296.3	$258,804.0	34	$56,478.6	301.4	$241,054.7
327	22	$252,909	$103,021.6	319.7	$544,489.9	16	$52,047.1	337.5	$260,075.7
331	25	$435,040	$89,292.1	310.5	$1,102,789.6	11	$85,060.5	310.4	$1,339,806.3
332	62	$283,323	$76,402.6	273.0	$260,697.3	12	$58,021.6	296.5	$304,894.3
333	44	$510,227	$101,412.0	283.7	$319,145.5	13	$74,514.0	277.5	$287,117.9
334	91	$366,560	$114,887.7	269.1	$259,937.9	36	$99,082.8	273.2	$238,375.0
335	67	$413,478	$100,475.4	262.5	$262,235.4	22	$84,075.5	266.1	$310,289.3
336	192	$507,995	$137,830.4	265.1	$529,175.4	85	$114,790.4	254.8	$282,766.1
337	23	$160,913	$55,799.8	275.0	$165,283.6	15	$44,507.3	270.8	$189,541.1
339	68	$342,838	$92,782.5	296.9	$249,207.2	23	$85,682.2	258.7	$163,623.9

4. Results and Discussion

From the analysis of the data shown in Tables 1 and 2, it can be observed that, in the Mexican manufacturing industry, the number of micro-sized enterprises that invest in HCT is lower than the number of micro-sized enterprises that do not; contrary to large-sized enterprises, where the number of large-size enterprises that invest in HCT is higher than the number of enterprises that do not, the reasons might be: (1) in the Mexican manufacturing industry, most of micro-sized enterprises are family-owned and live day-to-day, these make difficult for them to train their HC since they are financially limited, whilst large-sized enterprises have access to more financial resources; (2) their HC average educational level is lower in micro-sized enterprises than in large-sized enterprises, it shows a lack of awareness about the benefits of HCT, mainly due for their perception of this as an expense rather than an investment; (3) the absence of strong economic links between micro and large-sized enterprises directly impacts micro-sized enterprises organizational culture and, consequently, their acknowledge of the advantages that investment in HCT can produce. These findings are consistent with the results reported in Martínez-Aparicio (2012) and confirm the first and second hypotheses of this paper regarding the number of enterprises that provide training compared to those that do not.

4.1. Statistical Results

Tables 3 and 4 conclude the third hypothesis of this paper. Table 3 results confirm Hypothesis 3 for the micro-sized enterprises of the Mexican manufacturing industry since over 85% of the EAS both average sales and average wages increase significantly when investing in HCT. Contrary, the effect of HCT on average sales and average wages is not as evident in large-size enterprises of the Mexican manufacturing industry (Table 4). However, this does not indicate that investing in HCT does not have an effect as it has been described in other papers (Bissoondoyal-Bheenick et al. 2023; Ling et al. 2024; Montejano García and López Torres 2013; Rosales-Córdova and Carmona-Benítez 2023; Rosales-Córdova and Llanos 2021) where investments in HCT generates positive effects on both organizational and personal indicators. There are some reasons for this behavior: (1) the profiles of HC change significantly in large-sized enterprises, unlike micro-sized enterprises, therefore, the objectives of HCT are different between them; (2) HCT focuses on maintaining individual skills in large-sized enterprises, this complicates the capacity to observe the effect of HCT on sales; (3) the fact that micro-sized enterprises in the Mexican manufacturing industry are flexible and have a multifaceted structure, which allows them for quick and direct improvements in HC performance through HCT, what increase sales and wages in short-term, in contrast, large-sized enterprises aim to achieve competitiveness in the market, so the effects of investing in HCT are reflected in the medium-term.

Table 3. Hypothesis test HCT/yes vs HCT/No of the EAS micro-sized enterprises.

	HCT/Yes—Set 1—				HCT/No—Set 2—					
EAS	**N**	**Average Employees**	**Annual Wages per Employee**	**Annual Average Sales per Year ([000 of MXN])**	**N**	**Average Employees**	**Annual Wages per Employee**	**Annual Average Sales per Year ([000 of MXN])**	**t Student Wages per Employee**	**t Student Sales**
311	37	6.9 (SD = 1.7)	83,720 (SD = 27,347)	6379.257 (SD = 4081.92)	509	4.8 (SD = 1.4)	47,007 (SD = 19,421)	1179.627 (SD = 581.25)	$t_{(544)} = 10.76$ *	$t_{(544)} = 25.64$ *
312	21	5.5 (SD = 2.2)	76,933 (SD = 30,458)	3501.933 (SD = 3365.73)	134	3.5 (SD = 1.3)	48,683 (SD = 22,874)	613.679 (SD = 323.20)	$t_{(153)} = 5.07$ *	$t_{(153)} = 9.82$ *
313	7	9 (SD = 0.9)	102,270 (SD = 40,820)	9012 (SD = 4032.39)	103	5.3 (SD = 1.9)	47,693 (SD = 18,137)	1296.331 (SD = 762.71)	$t_{(108)} = 10.15$ *	$t_{(108)} = 16.40$ *
314	4	7.5 (SD = 2.4)	95,378 (SD = 94,443)	1936 (SD = 1801.42)	69	5.5 (SD = 1.6)	63,680 (SD = 20,959)	1815.551 (SD = 691.81)	$t_{(71)} = 2.18$ *	$t_{(71)} = 0.30$
315	12	7.2 (SD = 1.9)	90,663 (SD = 28,592)	9053.583 (SD = 6649.70)	142	4.3 (SD = 1.7)	58,903 (SD = 22,776)	915.007 (SD = 439.04)	$t_{(152)} = 4.54$ *	$t_{(152)} = 14.73$ *
316	8	5.3 (SD = 1)	81,313 (SD = 20,810)	1950 (SD = 1152.20)	113	5.5 (SD = 1.8)	55,664 (SD = 16,120)	1402.330 (SD = 902.74)	$t_{(119)} = 4.27$ *	$t_{(119)} = 1.63$ *
321	8	6 (SD = 1.6)	68,111 (SD = 23,762)	5988.5 (SD = 2960.41)	154	3.8 (SD = 1.7)	50,103 (SD = 24,294)	862.344 (SD = 597.68)	$t_{(160)} = 2.05$ *	$t_{(160)} = 16.91$ *

Table 3. *Cont.*

EAS	HCT/Yes—Set 1— N	Average Employees	Annual Wages per Employee	Annual Average Sales per Year ([000 of MXN])	HCT/No—Set 2— N	Average Employees	Annual Wages per Employee	Annual Average Sales per Year ([000 of MXN])	t Student Wages per Employee	t Student Sales
322	4	5.2 (SD = 2.9)	85,385 (SD = 37,979)	2689.667 (SD = 216.57)	45	6 (SD = 1.5)	59,897 (SD = 18,783)	1596.651 (SD = 849.92)	$t_{(47)} = 2.38$	$t_{(47)} = 2.54$ *
323	14	5.9 (SD = 1.1)	58,080 (SD = 27,483)	2714 (SD = 2195.11)	64	3 (SD = 1)	56,601 (SD = 21,778)	622.984 (SD = 278.68)	$t_{(76)} = 0.22$	$t_{(76)} = 7.52$ *
324	4	8.3 (SD = 0.6)	107,720 (SD = 69,774)	4987 (SD = 1347)	10	5.1 (SD = 2)	60,964 (SD = 28,428)	1373.5 (SD = 1,110.26)	$t_{(12)} = 1.85$ *	$t_{(12)} = 5.20$ *
325	13	2 (SD = 0.9)	351,716 (SD = 214,637)	49,418.5 (SD = 36,918.12)	73	4.1 (SD = 1.8)	69,582 (SD = 31,135)	1064.459 (SD = 794.17)	$t_{(84)} = 10.89$ *	$t_{(84)} = 11.50$ *
326	20	5.1 (SD = 2)	144,448 (SD = 51,387)	3915.364 (SD = 1493.57)	128	4.2 (SD = 1.7)	63,387 (SD = 25,308)	1049.411 (SD = 696.58)	$t_{(146)} = 11.27$ *	$t_{(146)} = 14.13$ *
327	36	5.7 (SD = 1.5)	195,772 (SD = 66,172)	11,881.250 (SD = 3926.16)	174	4.1 (SD = 1.7)	58,535 (SD = 27,895)	782.434 (SD = 496.48)	$t_{(208)} = 20.15$ *	$t_{(208)} = 36.24$ *
331	4	5.3 (SD = 1.7)	347,143 (SD = 178,454)	71,202.350 (SD = 64,880.67)	46	4 (SD = 1.7)	54,310 (SD = 22,228)	868.913 (SD = 434.98)	$t_{(48)} = 11.34$ *	$t_{(48)} = 8.32$ *
332	23	4.4 (SD = 1.8)	127,502 (SD = 54,480)	5269.5 (SD = 3297.11)	178	2.4 (SD = 1.6)	71,356 (SD = 48,301)	676.344 (SD = 492.58)	$t_{(199)} = 5.17$ *	$t_{(199)} = 17.41$ *
333	15	6.4 (SD = 2.4)	93,853 (SD = 32,524)	5826.560 (SD = 2731.85)	77	4.8 (SD = 1.4)	68,517 (SD = 30,296)	1196.636 (SD = 695.64)	$t_{(90)} = 2.93$ *	$t_{(90)} = 11.57$ *
334	4	5.8 (SD = 0.5)	114,478 (SD = 65,589)	3655.250 (SD = 2478.25)	53	4.3 (SD = 1.8)	74,458 (SD = 33,458)	1285.442 (SD = 701.16)	$t_{(55)} = 2.15$ *	$t_{(55)} = 5.11$ *
335	6	6.7 (SD = 2)	161,720 (SD = 57,030)	4270.6 (SD = 327.50)	50	4 (SD = 1.6)	60,888 (SD = 32,048)	969.26 (SD = 824.01)	$t_{(54)} = 6.65$ *	$t_{(54)} = 9.66$ *
336	11	3.2 (SD = 1.1)	210,469 (SD = 173,147)	2793.75 (SD = 1251.30)	78	4.4 (SD = 1.6)	65,960 (SD = 25,945)	1288.2693 (SD = 765.91)	$t_{(87)} = 7.06$ *	$t_{(87)} = 5.59$ *
337	8	6.3 (SD = 1.1)	76,818 (SD = 25,542)	3599.286 (SD = 1935.42)	81	4.6 (SD = 0.9)	44,498 (SD = 21,877)	818.876 (SD = 492.22)	$t_{(87)} = 3.93$ *	$t_{(87)} = 10.37$ *
339	15	6 (SD = 2.1)	68,490 (SD = 23,065)	3371.286 (SD = 1137.52)	129	5.1 (SD = 1.4)	60,092 (SD = 20,820)	1215.921 (SD = 675.29)	$t_{(142)} = 1.46$	$t_{(142)} = 10.77$ *

* $p < 0.05$.

Table 4. Hypothesis test HCT/yes vs HCT/No of the EAS large-sized enterprises.

EAS	HCT/Yes—Set 3— N	Average Employees	Annual Wages per Employee	Annual Average Sales per Year ([000 of MXN])	HCT/No—Set 4— N	Average Employees	Annual Wages per Employee	Annual Average Sales per Year ([000 of MXN])	t Student Wages per Employee	t Student Sales
311	608	521.4 (SD = 125.5)	141,303 (SD = 43,574)	449,446.485 (SD = 225,444.282)	264	476.9 (SD = 122.7)	122,628 (SD = 40,997)	272,072.462 (SD = 131,171.846)	$t_{(870)} = 5.92$ *	$t_{(870)} = 11.93$ *
312	148	532.6 (SD = 131.3)	150,676 (SD = 46,034)	542,262.331 (SD = 328,690.170)	61	465.9 (SD = 84.8)	140,967 (SD = 35,510)	333,689.426 (SD = 204,532.897)	$t_{(207)} = 1.48$	$t_{(207)} = 4.60$ *
313	115	474.5 (SD = 107.9)	147,713 (SD = 42,662)	365,709.565 (SD = 138,858.837)	59	480.7 (SD = 122.7)	113,569 (SD = 33,299)	231,402.288 (SD = 82,801.115)	$t_{(172)} = 5.36$ *	$t_{(172)} = 6.83$ *
314	51	468.3 (SD = 124.8)	141,536 (SD = 49,700)	334,678.853 (SD = 160,362.891)	18	364.9 (SD = 53.9)	98,433 (SD = 14,624)	189,447.5 (SD = 84,976.839)	$t_{(67)} = 3.61$ *	$t_{(67)} = 3.65$ *
315	60	642.1 (SD = 144.1)	89,447 (SD = 21,825)	147,562.593 (SD = 36,757.112)	40	524.5 (SD = 106.1)	79,437 (SD = 18,582)	110,854.9 (SD = 35,918.245)	$t_{(98)} = 2.38$ *	$t_{(98)} = 4.94$ *
316	31	469.5 (SD = 108)	83,101 (SD = 22,238)	171,229.065 (SD = 42,402.847)	18	461.7 (SD = 139.4)	96,238 (SD = 43,084)	192,398.333 (SD = 65,697.177)	$t_{(47)} = -1.41$	$t_{(47)} = -1.37$
321	5	447.2 (SD = 83.4)	97,492 (SD = 36,606)	389,412 (SD = 190,732.057)	3	647 (SD = 167)	89,547 (SD = 73,212)	440,158 (SD = 381,464.114)	$t_{(2)} = 0.18$ *	$t_{(2)} = -0.21$ *
322	36	397.1 (SD = 66.5)	192,776 (SD = 34,066)	812,872.889 (SD = 192,339.787)	18	490.9 (SD = 98.9)	171,878 (SD = 40,902)	1,035,219.944 (SD = 450,173.286)	$t_{(52)} = 1.99$ *	$t_{(52)} = -2.55$
323	12	438.2 (SD = 47.6)	139,086 (SD = 40,197)	182,428.833 (SD = 80,695.894)	6	313.7 (SD = 45.5)	129,447 (SD = 24,874)	166,881.666 (SD = 38,573.758)	$t_{(16)} = 0.53$	$t_{(16)} = 0.44$
324	6	660.3 (SD = 230.9)	203,094 (SD = 66,651)	1,571,015 (SD = 709,867.650)	7	3881.1 (SD = 578.1)	519,996 (SD = 76,140)	118,405,378.429 (SD = 13,659,482.544)	$t_{(11)} = -7.91$	$t_{(11)} = -20.79$
325	65	507.7 (SD = 124.7)	260,820 (SD = 75,281)	1,222,906.092 (SD = 612,634.752)	31	514.8 (SD = 135.9)	267,630 (SD = 117,999)	997,483.388 (SD = 727,550.361)	$t_{(94)} = -0.34$	$t_{(94)} = 1.59$
326	67	408.4 (SD = 69.6)	140,698 (SD = 31,675)	258,803.985 (SD = 117,053.145)	34	413.8 (SD = 67.9)	136,4992 (SD = 26,632)	241,054.676 (SD = 103,581.556)	$t_{(99)} = 0.66$	$t_{(99)} = 0.75$
327	22	458.1 (SD = 103.7)	224,871 (SD = 84,188)	544,489.909 (SD = 393,548.433)	16	419.4 (SD = 101)	124,088 (SD = 26,603)	260,075.667 (SD = 146,586.314)	$t_{(36)} = 4.61$ *	$t_{(36)} = 2.75$ *
331	25	483.5 (SD = 104.2)	184,686 (SD = 72,608)	1,102,789.56 (SD = 939,653.252)	11	421.3 (SD = 123.4)	201,899 (SD = 57,163)	1,339,806.272 (SD = 783,298.827)	$t_{(34)} = -0.70$	$t_{(34)} = -0.83$

Table 4. *Cont.*

EAS	HCT/Yes—Set 3— N	Average Employees	Annual Wages per Employee	Annual Average Sales per Year ([000 of MXN])	HCT/No—Set 4— N	Average Employees	Annual Wages per Employee	Annual Average Sales per Year ([000 of MXN])	t Student Wages per Employee	t Student Sales
332	62	421.2 (SD = 75.9)	181,376 (SD = 38,769)	260,697.274 (SD = 110,550.096)	12	375.6 (SD = 72)	154,484 (SD = 54,213)	304,894.25 (SD = 157,909.320)	$t_{(72)} = 2.05$ *	$t_{(72)} = -1.18$
333	44	483.4 (SD = 116.4)	209,789 (SD = 67,673)	319,145.523 (SD = 97,003.389)	13	474 (SD = 90.2)	157,203 (SD = 74,385)	287,117.923 (SD = 176,555.031)	$t_{(55)} = 2.41$ *	$t_{(55)} = 0.85$
334	91	740.4 (SD = 254.7)	155,173 (SD = 54,097)	259,937.945 (SD = 98,727.606)	36	622.8 (SD = 202.1)	159,091 (SD = 48,571)	238,374.972 (SD = 85,468.506)	$t_{(125)} = -0.58$	$t_{(125)} = 1.15$
335	67	656.4 (SD = 161.9)	153,076 (SD = 33,837)	262,235.403 (SD = 80,897.799)	22	555.4 (SD = 141.4)	151,376 (SD = 41,299)	310,289.273 (SD = 177,631.239)	$t_{(87)} = 0.19$	$t_{(87)} = -1.74$
336	192	864.7 (SD = 304.6)	159,403 (SD = 50,555)	529,175.351 (SD = 222,897.198)	85	938.2 (SD = 380.1)	122,348 (SD = 48,631)	282,766.107 (SD = 129,216.051)	$t_{(275)} = 5.69$ *	$t_{(275)} = 9.50$ *
337	23	447.4 (SD = 132.3)	124,726 (SD = 28,188)	165,283.609 (SD = 38,042.089)	15	399.5 (SD = 85.5)	111,407 (SD = 39,838)	189,541.071 (SD = 101,050.865)	$t_{(36)} = 1.21$	$t_{(36)} = -1.05$
339	68	695.9 (SD = 276.8)	133,331 (SD = 56,867)	249,207.191 (SD = 86,374.550)	23	627.4 (SD = 219.8)	136,560 (SD = 45,976)	163,623.870 (SD = 66,581.340)	$t_{(89)} = -0.25$	$t_{(89)} = 4.33$ *

* $p < 0.05$.

4.2. DEA Results

As it is explained in Section 3.3, the micro and large-sized enterprise samples are divided in four datasets. Set 1 contains micro-sized enterprises that include observation units that invest in human capital training (HCT/Yes). Set 2 contains micro-sized enterprises that include observation units that does not invest in HCT (HCT/No). Set 3 contains large-sized enterprises that include observation units that invest in HCT (HCT/Yes). Set 4 contains large-sized enterprises that include observation units that does not invest in HCT (HCT/No).

The size of the four datasets under analysis is justified because they fulfilled the validation rule $n \geq \max\{m \times s; 3(m + s)\}$ (Cooper et al. 2007).

Table 5 shows the results of the OTE for micro-sized enterprises. According with the DEA efficiency distribution, 18 EAS are non-DEA effective, which means they are not in optimal state, four EAS have an OTE > 0.5 (19.05%), and only three are OTE efficient (OTE = 1; 14.29%) in Set 1—325, 327 and 331—in Set 2, nineteen EAS are non-DEA effective, twenty one EAS have an OTE > 0.5 (100%), and only two of them are OTE efficient (OTE = 1; 9.52%)—311 and 314—. The results indicate that the investments in HCT are in optimal state with sales in the EAS—325, 327 and 331—in Set 1, and in the EAS—311 and 314—in Set 2. Since, these EAS define the efficiency frontier and the best practice within each set, it is possible to conclude that investing in HCT increase the differences in efficiency between EAS in micro-sized enterprises, and the efficiency gets close or similar for those EAS in micro-sized enterprises that do not invest in HCT.

Table 5 also shows the results of the PTE, SE and returns to scale for micro-sized enterprises. In this table, the global efficiency EAS are those with efficiency on the constate-return-to-scale (CRS) frontier, which means these EAS chose the optimum size for their HC investments. Hence, the efficient EAS are the Chemical Industry (325), the Nonmetallic Mineral Product the Manufacturing (327), and the Basic Metal Industry (331) in Set 1; and the efficient EAS are the Food Industry (311) and the Textile Product Manufacturing Except Apparel (314) in Set 2. All other EAS are overall technical inefficient (OTIE), they operate at suboptimal scale sizes on the increasing-return-to-scale (IRS) frontier, it means the micro-sized enterprises are too small for their scale of operations, these EAS need to develop strategies to increase productivity to gain efficiency. Since PTE > SE at these EAS, one strategy is to reorganize the utilization of their investments in HCT to achieve optimal sales, because the wrong size of their investments in HCT might be the reason of their technical inefficiency.

Table 5. Micro-sized enterprises OTE, PTE, SE and returns to scale.

	HCT/Yes—Set 1—				HCT/No—Set 2—			
EAS	**OTE**	**PTE**	**SE**	**Returns to Scale**	**OTE**	**PTE**	**SE**	**Returns to Scale**
311	0.24	0.90	0.27	IRS	1	1	1	CRS
312	0.34	1	0.34	IRS	0.69	1	0.69	IRS
313	0.46	0.88	0.53	IRS	0.98	1	0.98	IRS
314	0.14	1	0.14	IRS	1	1	1	CRS
315	0.42	0.99	0.43	IRS	0.70	0.97	0.72	IRS
316	0.11	0.98	0.11	IRS	0.88	0.97	0.91	IRS
321	0.4	1	0.40	IRS	0.85	1	0.85	IRS
322	0.08	1	0.08	IRS	0.92	1	0.92	IRS
323	0.18	1	0.18	IRS	0.70	1	0.70	IRS
324	0.22	0.75	0.30	IRS	0.85	1	0.85	IRS
325	1	1	1	CRS	0.71	0.93	0.76	IRS
326	0.21	0.96	0.22	IRS	0.76	0.96	0.80	IRS
327	1	1	1	CRS	0.62	0.96	0.64	IRS
331	1	1	1	CRS	0.76	0.94	0.81	IRS
332	0.23	0.91	0.26	IRS	0.74	1	0.74	IRS
333	0.16	0.94	0.17	IRS	0.71	0.98	0.72	IRS
334	0.58	1	0.58	IRS	0.76	0.95	0.80	IRS
335	0.09	0.94	0.10	IRS	0.76	1	0.76	IRS
336	0.09	0.93	0.09	IRS	0.85	0.95	0.90	IRS
337	0.17	0.89	0.19	IRS	0.75	0.92	0.82	IRS
339	0.21	0.97	0.21	IRS	0.76	0.96	0.79	IRS

Table 6 shows the results of the OTE for large-sized enterprises. According with the DEA efficiency distribution, 17 EAS are non-DEA effective, which means they are not in optimal state, eleven EAS have an OTE > 0.5 (52.38%), and only four are OTE efficient (OTE = 1; 19.05%) in Set 3—321, 324, 325, and 331—whilst in Set 4, twenty EAS are non-DEA effective, the 324 EAS is the only one that has an OTE > 0.5 (4.76%), and it is the OTE efficient (OTE = 1; 4.76%). The results indicate that the investments in HCT are in optimal state with sales in the EAS—321, 324, 325, and 331—in Set 3, and in the EAS—324—in Set 4. Since these EAS define the efficiency frontier and the best practice within each set, it is possible to conclude that investing in HCT increases the differences in efficiency between EAS in large-sized enterprises, and the efficiency gets close or similar for those EAS in large-sized enterprises that do not invest in HCT. In Set 4, the efficiency of the 324 EAS is very high in comparison to all other EAS.

Table 6 also shows the results of the PTE, SE and returns to scale for large-sized enterprises. In this table, the global efficiency EAS are those with efficiency on the CRS frontier, which means these EAS chose the optimum size for their HCT investments. Hence, the efficient EAS are the Wood Industry (321), the Petroleum and Coal Products Manufacturing (324), the Chemical Industry (325), and the Basic Metal Industries (331) in Set 3; and the Petroleum and Coal Products Manufacturing (324) is the only efficient EAS in Set 4. All other EAS are OTE, they operate at suboptimal scale sizes on the IRS frontier, it means the large-sized enterprises are too small for their scale of operations, these EAS need to develop strategies to increase productivity to gain efficiency. Since PTE > SE at these EAS, one strategy is to reorganize the utilization of their HC investments to achieve optimal sales, because the wrong size of their HC investments might be the reason of their technical inefficiency.

The SE results confirm the fourth hypothesis of this paper (Tables 5 and 6) because all the EAS with SE = 1 indicate that their annual average HCT investments are at the optimum level whilst the EAS with SE < 1 indicate investments are not at optimum level.

Table 6. Large-sized enterprises OTE, PTE, SE and returns to scale.

	HCT/Yes—Set 3—				HCT/No—Set 4—			
EAS	OTE	PTE	SE	Returns to Scale	OTE	PTE	SE	Returns to Scale
311	0.58	0.94	0.62	IRS	0.08	0.99	0.08	IRS
312	0.55	0.92	0.59	IRS	0.09	0.90	0.10	IRS
313	0.55	0.94	0.59	IRS	0.07	0.88	0.08	IRS
314	0.59	1	0.59	IRS	0.09	1	0.09	IRS
315	0.39	1	0.39	IRS	0.05	1	0.05	IRS
316	0.4	1	0.40	IRS	0.07	0.96	0.08	IRS
321	1	1	1	CRS	0.13	0.88	0.15	IRS
322	0.86	0.93	0.93	IRS	0.21	0.74	0.28	IRS
323	0.28	0.9	0.31	IRS	0.07	0.89	0.08	IRS
324	1	1	1	CRS	1	1	1	CRS
325	1	1	1	CRS	0.12	0.88	0.14	IRS
326	0.37	0.90	0.42	IRS	0.07	0.86	0.08	IRS
327	0.7	0.89	0.78	IRS	0.09	0.8	0.11	IRS
331	1	1	1	CRS	0.27	0.84	0.32	IRS
332	0.33	0.97	0.34	IRS	0.09	0.87	0.10	IRS
333	0.3	0.93	0.32	IRS	0.07	0.93	0.07	IRS
334	0.28	0.98	0.28	IRS	0.04	0.94	0.04	IRS
335	0.27	1	0.27	IRS	0.06	0.97	0.07	IRS
336	0.53	1	0.53	IRS	0.04	1	0.04	IRS
337	0.29	0.96	0.30	IRS	0.04	0.96	0.08	IRS
339	0.27	0.89	0.30	IRS	0.03	0.99	0.03	IRS

Figures 1 and 2 show the current annual average HCT investments in orange color, the calculated investments needed to become local efficient (PTE = 1) using the DEA CCR model are shown in blue color, and the calculated investments needed to become global efficient (OTE = 1) using the DEA BCC model are shown in green color for the micro-sized enterprises of the Mexican manufacturing industry that invest in HCT (Set 1) (Figure 1) and for the large-sized enterprises of the Mexican manufacturing industry that invest in HCT (Set 3) (Figure 2).

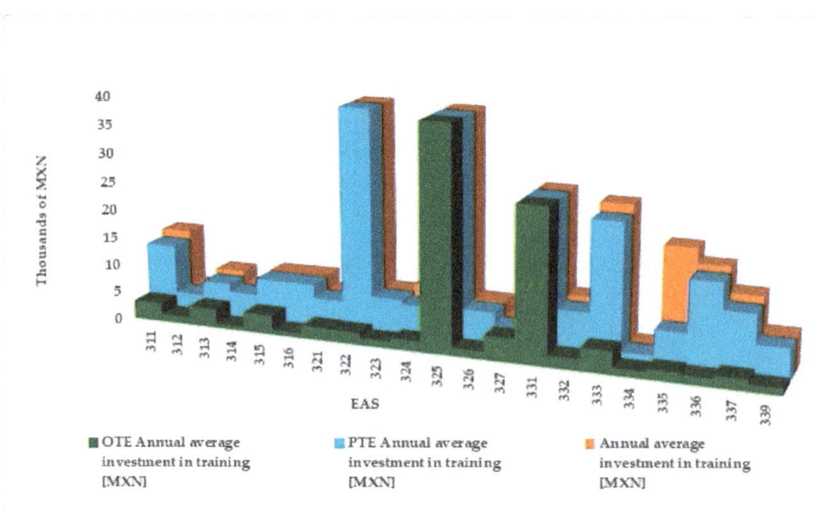

Figure 1. EAS optimum annual average investments in HCT in micro-sized enterprises.

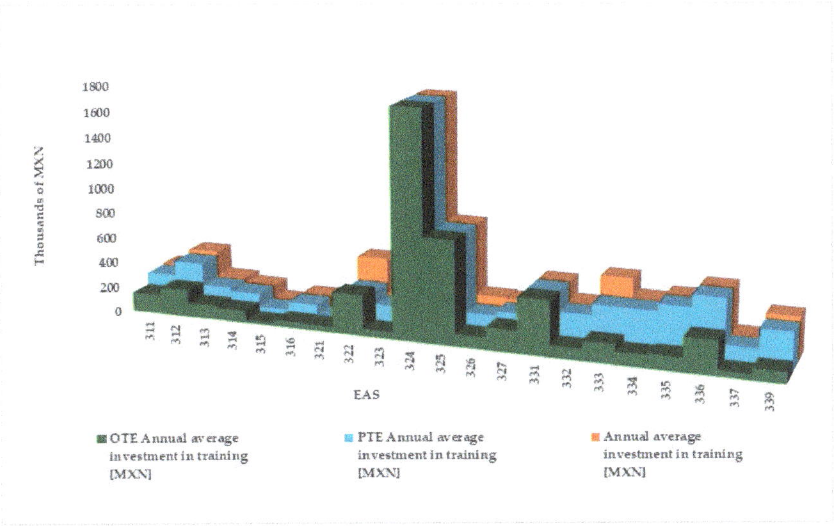

Figure 2. EAS optimum annual average investments in HCT in large-sized enterprises.

Figure 1 confirms that all the EAS with SE < 1 must reduce their annual average amount of investments from their current annual average amount of investment (orange color) to their PTE annual average amount of investment (blue color) to become local efficient (PTE = 1) and to their OTE annual average amount of investment (green color) to become global efficient (OTE = 1). Figure 1 shows that all the EAS are over investing except—325, 327, and 331—in the micro-sized enterprises of the Mexican manufacturing industry. Moreover, the efficiency of enterprises increases when investing in HCT no matter their size (García-Zambrano et al. 2018; Nduneseokwu and Harder 2023; Rosales-Córdova and Carmona-Benítez 2023; Rosales-Córdova and Llanos 2021) since more EAS with SE = 1 exist in Set 1 and Set 3 than in Set 2 and Set 4 respectively. This happens because HCT increases performance, sales, productivity, and competitiveness, which positively impact the efficiency of any organization (Bissoondoyal-Bheenick et al. 2023; Ling et al. 2024; Montejano García and López Torres 2013; Rosales-Córdova and Llanos 2021; Słomka-Gołębiowska et al. 2023; Song 2024).

Figure 2 confirms that all the EAS with SE < 1 must reduce their annual average amount of investments from their current annual average amount of investment (orange color) to their PTE annual average amount of investment (blue color) to become local efficient (PTE = 1) and to their OTE annual average amount of investment (green color) to become global efficient (OTE = 1). Figure 2 shows that all the EAS are over investing except—321, 324, 325, and 331—in the large-sized enterprises of the Mexican manufacturing industry.

Hypothesis five is confirmed for large-sized enterprises and rejected for micro-sized enterprises. In Figures 1 and 2, as well as in Tables 5 and 6, it is observed that the efficiency of the three main EAS is above 0.5 in large-sized enterprises, a condition that only occurs in the Chemical industry—325—of micro-sized enterprises.

Identify, improve, and/or maintain high efficiencies in the three main EAS of the Mexican manufacturing industry is of utmost importance, since they represent 54% of total manufacturing production of the country (INEGI 2021b). The lack of connections (Martínez-Aparicio 2012) between micro-sized enterprises and large-sized enterprises in Mexico results in a lack of knowledge regarding the correct investment of HCT, a condition that affects both the Food industry—311—and in the Transportation Equipment manufacturing industry—336.

In the Transportation Equipment manufacturing industry—336—the efficiency of large-sized enterprises is 0.53 which is consistent with the findings of (Rosales-Córdova and Carmona-Benítez 2023) who conclude that SMEs in this EAS show a similar efficiency value of 0.43. This result is noteworthy because of the EAS contribution to the GDP and employment of Mexico. This clearly shows an area of opportunity for this EAS across the three group sizes of enterprises—SMEs, micro, and large-sized—as efficiency increases, benefits for enterprises increase too, and consequently, the GDP of any country.

The Chemical industry shows an SE = 1 in both micro and large enterprises that invest in HCT, which is equal to the SE of the SMEs in this EAS (Rosales-Córdova and Carmona-Benítez 2023). This indicates effective resource management and underscores the importance of investing in HC. It is important to highlight that efficiency in an organization positively impacts various aspects of its operation and performance, such as: (a) competitive market permanence, (b) maximization of resources, (c) Optimal product and/or service quality, (d) Greater satisfaction and retention of human capital, (e) Potential for growth and expansion, and (f) Healthy financial management.

5. Conclusions, Limitations and Further Recommendations

Micro and large enterprises contribute differently but complementarily to job creation, competitiveness, GDP, and economic growth, especially in a developing country like Mexico.

HCT plays a fundamental role in the efficiency of any enterprise, regardless of the size–SME, micro-sized and/or large-sized. With the correct management of resources, a contribution to sustainability, development, continuous improvement, and innovation can be generated, increasing the probabilities of the organization's survival and success.

In this paper, DEA models are used to analyze the impact of HC investments on the performance of the 21 economic activity subsectors for micro and large-sized enterprises in the Mexican manufacturing industry. The results of this paper confirm that the presence of the HCT variable identifies a positive change in the efficiency of the EAS for both micro and large-sized enterprises. In general, higher efficiency values are found in the sets where enterprises invest in HCT.

Despite the recognized positive effect of HCT, in micro-sized enterprises, the number of enterprises that invest in HCT is lower than those that do not invest in HCT. Contrary, in large-sized enterprises, the number of those that invest in HCT is higher than those that do not invest in HCT.

The results show that investing in HCT increase sales and wages in micro-sized enterprises of the Mexican manufacturing industry, but it is not evident in large-size enterprises of the Mexican manufacturing industry. Specifically, in the three main EAS, it is identified that in all cases—except for the Chemical industry of large-sized enterprises—the increase is significant when investing in HCT.

It is noteworthy to mention that of the three main EAS in the Mexican manufacturing industry, 100% scale efficiency is exhibited in the Chemical industry in both micro and large-sized enterprises that invest in HCT. This highlights the importance of investing in HC and the excellent resource management within this EAS.

This paper identifies that investment in HCT is a determinant factor to achieve efficiency in both micro and large-sized enterprises, the nature and impact of training vary depending on the group size of the enterprises. It is important to emphasize that investments in HCT do not guarantee their effectiveness; investments must be properly made. Hypothesis tests generally recognize the positive effect of HCT, while DEA models identify the correct investment of HCT.

In micro-sized enterprises, their organizational culture has yet to incorporate the substantial improvements in skills and adaptability that investment in HC represents. Therefore, it is crucial to promote this culture in Mexico to boost the organization and, consequently, all EAS.

Large-sized enterprises main objectives is to maintain competitiveness in the market due to globalization. To achieve this, they employ specialized HCT and continuous improvement programs, conditions that increase HC efficiency in the long-term and foster innovation, and product quality.

The findings of this research confirm that HC is the most valuable intangible resource of a company. Investing in HC improves employees' skills, allowing them to perform better, which in turn helps the organization achieve its goals and objectives, such as efficiency and increased sales. Additionally, employees also benefit, including a significant increase in their wages, a better work environment, and increased happiness. While, as shown in the results, investment in HC is part of the work culture in large-sized companies', this is not the case in micro-sized enterprises, which perceive investments in HC as an expense rather than an investment.

Based on the findings of this research, the Mexican government should develop policies—such as incentive the collaboration between universities and enterprises, tax reductions, etc.—to incentive the investment in HC—particularly among owners of micro, small, and medium-sized enterprises—because the benefits are for employees, for companies, for the social realm, and for country's economy; moreover, it helps reduce inequalities, increase quality of life, foster cultural development, and improve mental and physical health. Therefore, it is crucial to invest in HC to promote sustainable growth and national progress.

The limitations of this study are primarily twofold: (1) data must be worked in groups of companies—$n \geq 3$—because of the confidentiality criteria of information managed by INEGI, and (2) data must be cluster into groups or sets because of minimize their high variability. Groups with a CV greater than 1 are excluded.

The statistical analysis and the development of DEA models to study the impact of HC investments on the efficiency of the 21 EASs opens a new line of research and, therefore, an avenue for further research, such as: (1) applying DEA models to study each of the classes within the Chemical industry EAS with the aim is to identify the causes for its 100% scale efficiency across the three size groups of enterprises; (2) Performing a deeper analysis of the behavior of HC in large-size enterprises, and (3) complementing this research with the use of output-oriented DEA models.

Author Contributions: Conceptualization, R.B.C.-B. and A.R.-C.; Methodology, R.B.C.-B.; Software, R.B.C.-B.; Validation, R.B.C.-B. and A.R.-C.; Formal analysis, R.B.C.-B. and A.R.-C.; Investigation, R.B.C.-B. and A.R.-C.; Resources, R.B.C.-B. and A.R.-C.; Data curation, A.R.-C.; Writing—original draft, R.B.C.-B. and A.R.-C.; Writing—review & editing, R.B.C.-B. and A.R.-C.; Visualization, R.B.C.-B. and A.R.-C.; Supervision, R.B.C.-B. and A.R.-C.; Project administration, R.B.C.-B. and A.R.-C. All authors have read and agreed to the published version of the manuscript.

Funding: This research received no external funding.

Institutional Review Board Statement: Not applicable.

Informed Consent Statement: Not applicable.

Data Availability Statement: Data is unavailable due to privacy or ethical restrictions. The conclusions and opinions expressed in this research project are the sole responsibility of the authors and do not represent the official statistics or positions of the SNIEG or INEGI.

Conflicts of Interest: The authors declare no conflict of interest.

References

Almeida, Rita, and Marta Faria. 2014. The wage returns to on-the-job training: Evidence from matched employer-employee data. *IZA Journal of Labor and Development* 3: 1–33. [CrossRef]

Al-Omoush, Khaled Saleh, Daniel Palacios-Marqués, and Klaus Ulrich. 2022. The impact of intellectual capital on supply chain agility and collaborative knowledge creation in responding to unprecedented pandemic crises. *Technological Forecasting and Social Change* 178: 121603. [CrossRef]

Aman-Ullah, Attia, Wagas Mehmood, Saqib Amin, and Yasir Abdullah Abbas. 2022. Human capital and organizational performance: A moderation study through innovative leadership. *Journal of Innovation & Knowledge* 7: 100261. [CrossRef]

Ayele, Abebe Birhanu. 2021. Efficiency of Micro and Small Enterprises in Ethiopia: Evidence from Data Envelope Analysis Model. *Preprints* 2021: 100180. [CrossRef]

Banker, Rajiv D., Abraham Charnes, and William Wager Cooper. 1984. Some models for estimating technical and scale inefficiencies in data envelopment analysis. *Management Science* 30: 1078–92.

Baruah, Manuj, and Paramita Saha. 2024. Technical Efficiency of Handloom-based Micro-enterprises in Assam, India: A Stochastic Frontier Analysis. *International Journal of Rural Management*. [CrossRef]

Basyah, Nazaruddin Ali, and Irham Fahmi. 2024. Define the role and economic benefits of micro, small and medium enterprises: A literature review. *Jambura Economic Education Journal* 6: 51–56.

Becker, Gary S. 1962. Investment in Human Capital: A Theoretical Analysis. *Journal of Political Economy* 70: 9–49. [CrossRef]

Bissoondoyal-Bheenick, Emawtee, Robert Brooks, and Hung Xuan Do. 2023. ESG and firm performance: The role of size and media channels. *Economic Modelling* 121: 106203. [CrossRef]

Boubaker, Sabri, Thanh Ngo, Aristeidis Samitas, and David Tripe. 2024. An MCDA composite index of bank stability using CAMELS ratios and shannon entropy. *Annals of Operations Research*, 1–24. [CrossRef]

Boubaker, Sabri, Tu D. Q. Le, Thanh Ngo, and Riadh Manita. 2023. Predicting the performance of MSMEs: A hybrid DEA-machine learning approach. *Annals of Operations Research*, 1–23. [CrossRef]

Brodny, Jaroslaw, and Magdalena Tutak. 2022. The Level of Digitization of Small, Medium and Large Enterprises in the Central and Eastern European Countries and Its Relationship with Economic Parameters. *Journal of Open Innovation: Technology, Market, and Complexity* 8: 113. [CrossRef]

Chanda, Avishek. 2019. Relative Technical Efficiency of the Micro, Small and Medium Enterprises of India: Recent Evidences Using Data Envelopment Analysis. *Journal Indexing and Metrics* 63: 668–88. [CrossRef]

Charnes, Abraham, William W. Cooper, and Edward Rhodes. 1978. Measuring the efficiency of decision making units. *European Journal of Operational Research* 2: 429–44. [CrossRef]

Cinaroglu, Songul. 2021. Changes in hospital efficiency and size: An integrated propensity score matching with data envelopment analysis. *Socio-Economic Planning Sciences* 76: 100960. [CrossRef]

Cooper, William W., Lawrence M. Seinford, and Kaoru Tone, eds. 2007. *Data Envelopment Analysis: A Comprehensive Text with Models, Applications, References and DEA-Solver Software*, 2nd ed. New York: Springer Science + Business Media.

Dey, Bijov. K., Gurudas Das, and Ujjwal Kanti Paul. 2023a. Technical efficiency and its determinants of handloom micro-enterprises in the Indian state of Assam: A two-stage double-bootstrap DEA approach. *Indian Growth and Development Review* 16: 123–40. [CrossRef]

Dey, Bijov K., Ujjwal Kanti Paul, and Gurudas Das. 2023b. Are handloom micro-enterprises in India efficient? Estimation based on DEA and bootstrap truncated regression approach. *Research Journal of Textile and Apparel* 27: 452–71. [CrossRef]

Diario Oficial de la Federación. 2019. Ley para el desarrollo de la competitividad de la micro, pequeña y mediana empresa. In Párrafo reformado DOF. Available online: https://www.diputados.gob.mx/LeyesBiblio/pdf/LDCMPME.pdf (accessed on 15 January 2024).

Díaz Rodríguez, Héctor Eduardo, Magnolia Miriam Sosa Castro, and María Alejandra Cabello Rosales. 2021. Financial performance and administrative practices in Mexican microenterprises: An analysis with artificial neural networks. *Contaduria y Administracion* 64: 1–15. [CrossRef]

García Camacho, Manuel Eduardo, and José Daniel Anido. 2024. Encouragement Policies and Productivity Indicators for Colombian SMEs Using Data Envelopment Analysis and Malmquist Indexes. *Revista CEA* 10: 1–37. [CrossRef]

García-Zambrano, Lidia, Arturo Rodríguez-Castellanos, and José Domingo García-Merino. 2018. Impact of investments in training and advertising on the market value relevance of a company's intangibles: The effect of the economic crisis in Spain. *European Research on Management and Business Economics* 24: 27–32. [CrossRef]

Gopalkrishnan, Santos, Shiba Prasad Mohanty, and Megha Jaiwani. 2023. Do efficiencies really matter? Analysing the housing finance sector and deriving insights through data envelopment analysis. *Cogent Economics & Finance* 11: 2285158. [CrossRef]

Hooda, Singh, and Nitisha Sehrawat. 2023. Sustainable Development and Public Transport in Haryana. *Space and Culture, India* 11: 49–57. [CrossRef]

Ibarra-Cisneros, Manuel Alejandro, and Felipe Hernández-Perlines. 2019. The influence of intellectual capital on the performance of small and medium manufacturing companies in Mexico: The case of Baja California. *Innovar* 29: 79–96. [CrossRef]

INEGI. 2019. Censos Económicos 2019. Available online: https://www.inegi.org.mx/app/biblioteca/ficha.html?upc=702825198657 (accessed on 12 March 2024).

INEGI. 2021a. Demografía de los Negocios. Economía y Sectores Productivos. Available online: https://www.inegi.org.mx/temas/dn/ (accessed on 12 March 2024).

INEGI. 2021b. Nota técnica Encuesta Anual de la Industria Manufacturera (EAIM) Cifras 2021. Available online: https://www.inegi.org.mx/contenidos/programas/eaim/2013/doc/Nota_Tecnica_EAIM.pdf (accessed on 12 March 2024).

INEGI. 2023. Estadísticas a propósito del día internacional de la juventud. Available online: https://www.inegi.org.mx/contenidos/productos/prod_serv/contenidos/espanol/bvinegi/productos/nueva_estruc/702825006792.pdf (accessed on 15 March 2024).

INEGI SNIEG. 2021. Sistema Nacional de Información Estadística y Geografía. Encuesta Anual de la Industria Manufacturera (EAIM). Uso de microdatos mediante Laboratorio de micro datos del INEGI. Available online: https://www.inegi.org.mx/programas/eaim/2013/#microdatos (accessed on 12 March 2024).

Kalapouti, Kleoniki, Konstantinos Petridis, Chrisovalantis Malesios, and Prasanta Kumar Dey. 2020. Measuring efficiency of innovation using combined Data Envelopment Analysis and Structural Equation Modeling: Empirical study in EU regions. *Annals of Operations Research* 294: 297–320. [CrossRef]

Kononiuk, Anna. 2022. Determinants of Foresight Maturity in SME Enterprises of Poland. *Foresight and STI Governance* 16: 69–81. [CrossRef]

Kumar, Sunil, and Rachita Gulati. 2008. An Examination of Technical, Pure Technical, and Scale Efficiencies in Indian Public Sector Banks using Data Envelopment Analysis. *Eurasian Journal of Business and Economics* 1: 33–69.

Ling, Lin, Hayat Khan, Liu Qianqian, and Li Qiumei. 2024. Minimum wage standard adjustment and employment: Heterogeneity effects on the human capital investment. *Heliyon* 10: e25097. [CrossRef]

Marjanovic, Ivana, Jelena J. Stankovic, and Žarko Popovic. 2018. Efficiency Estimation of Commercial Banks Based on Financial Performance: Input Oriented DEA CRS/VRS Models. *Economic Themes* 56: 239–52. [CrossRef]

Martínez-Aparicio, Jorge. 2012. Micros, pequeñas y grandes empresas, dos circuitos económicos separados. Lázaro Cárdenas, Michoacán. *Economía, Sociedad y Territorio* 12: 751–91.

Martín-Gamboa, Mario, and Diego Iribarren. 2021. Coupled life cycle thinking and data envelopment analysis for quantitative sustainability improvement. In *Methods in Sustainability Science: Assessment, Prioritization, Improvement, Design and Optimization*. Amsterdam: Elsevier, pp. 295–320. [CrossRef]

Memon, Mehran Ali, and Izah Mohd Tahir. 2012. Size and Operational Performance of Manufacturing Companies in Pakistan Using Data Envelopment Analysis. *Journal of Information Engineering and Applications* 2: 39–49.

Mincer, Jacob. 1958. Investment in Human Capital and Personal Income Distribution. *Journal of Political Economy* 66: 281–302. Available online: https://about.jstor.org/terms (accessed on 15 March 2024).

Monika, Dugelova, and Strenitzerova Mariana. 2015. The Using of Data Envelopment Analysis in Human Resource Controlling. *Procedia Economics and Finance* 26: 468–75. [CrossRef]

Montejano García, Salomón, and Gabriela Citlalli López Torres. 2013. Impacto del capital intelectual en la innovación en empresas: Una perspectiva de México. *Revista Científica Teorías, Enfoques y Aplicación En Las Ciencias Sociales* 6: 39–48.

Nahuat Román, Bernardo. 2020. Influencia del capital intelectual en la innovación: Una perspectiva al nivel del individuo. *Nova Scientia* 12: 1–29. [CrossRef]

Nduneseokwu, Chibuike K., and Marie K. Harder. 2023. Developing environmental transformational leadership with training: Leaders and subordinates environmental behaviour outcomes. *Journal of Cleaner Production* 403: 136790. [CrossRef]

Nguyen, Thanh Quy, Anh Thuy Nguyen, Anh Lan Tran, Hung Thai Le, Ha Hoang Thi Le, and Lien Phuong Vu. 2020. Do workers benefit from on-the-job training? New evidence from matched employer-employee data. *Finance Research Letters* 40: 101664. [CrossRef]

Ofori, Eric, Elizabeth A. Yeager, and Brian C. Briggeman. 2024. Estimating potential gains from agricultural cooperative mergers. *Agribusiness*, 1–16. [CrossRef]

Olexová, Cecília. 2011. Nástroje Personálneho controllingu tools of personnel controlling. *Scientific papers of the University Pardubice Series D* 20: 11–125.

Padilla-Angulo, Laura, Jesús Miguel Lasarte-López, and Pedro Caldentey Del Pozo. 2023. Policy evaluations of microenterprise business support services in Latin America: A systematic review. *Evaluation and Program Planning* 97: 102212. [CrossRef]

Peralta, Alejandro de Jesús, Paula Rosalinda Antonio Vidaña, Daniel Martínez Navarrete, and Claudia Vasquez Rojas. 2023. Social vulnerability, crime and human capital of microenterprises in Veracruz, Mexico. *Economia, Sociedad y Territorio* 23: 433–65. [CrossRef]

Perri, Alessandra, Victoria G. Scalera, and Ram Mudambi. 2017. What are the most promising conduits for foreign knowledge inflows? Innovation networks in the Chinese pharmaceutica industry. *Industrial and Corporate Change* 26: 333–55. [CrossRef]

Porfírio, José, José Antonio Felício, and Tiago Carrilho. 2020. Family business succession: Analysis of the drivers of success based on entrepreneurship theory. *Journal of Business Research* 115: 250–57. [CrossRef]

Proaño-Rivera, Bladimir, and José Manuel Feria-Dominguez. 2022. Are Ecuadorian banks enough technically efficient for growth? A clinical study. *International Journal of Finance & Economics* 29: 2011–29. [CrossRef]

Prouska, Rea, Alexandros G. Psychogios, and Yllka Rexhepi. 2016. Rewarding employees in turbulent economies for improved organisational performance: Exploring SMEs in the South-Eastern European region. *Personnel Review* 45: 1259–80. [CrossRef]

Purmiyati, Atik, Madeline Berma, Basri Abdul Talib, and Marta Sabila Rakhima. 2019. The role of banking capital in industrial sector micro enterprises for poverty alleviation: A study in east java, Indonesia. *Foundations of Management* 11: 131–42. [CrossRef]

Ramírez, Natanael, Alejandro Mungaray, José G. Aguilar, and Ramón Inzunza. 2017. Una explicación de la rentabilidad y poder de mercado de las microempresas marginadas. *Economia Teoría y Practica* 46: 97–113. Available online: https://www.redalyc.org/articulo.oa?id=281155224005 (accessed on 15 March 2024).

Rodríguez-Gulías, María Jesús, Sara Fernández-López, and David Rodeiro-Pazos. 2024. Foreign knowledge sources and innovation: Differences across large and small and medium-size multinational enterprises (MNEs). *International Review of Economics & Finance* 92: 741–57. [CrossRef]

Rosales-Córdova, Aldebarán, and Luis Felipe Llanos. 2021. Efecto de la inversión en capacitación en las ventas y sueldos de las PyMES. *Investigación Administrativa* 50: 45–62. [CrossRef]

Rosales-Córdova, Aldebarán, and Rafael Bernardo Carmona-Benítez. 2023. Evaluating the Efficiency of Human Capital at Small and Medium Enterprises in the Manufacturing Sector Using the DEA-Weight Russell Directional Distance Model. *Economies* 11: 261. [CrossRef]

Schultz, Theodore W. 1961. Investment in Human Capital. *American Economic Association* 51: 1035–39. Available online: https://www.jstor.org/stable/1818907 (accessed on 15 March 2024).

Sedliačiková, Mariana, Nikolay Neykov, Ján Dobrovič, Anna Šatanová, Mária Osvaldová, and Mykola Palinchak. 2024. Performance measuring of wood-processing microenterprises through data envelopment analysis: A case study of Slovakia, Poland, and Bulgaria. *Entrepreneurship and Sustainability Issues* 11: 408–22. [CrossRef]

Seth, Himanshu, Deepak Deepak, Namita Ruparel, Saurabh Chadha, and Shivi Agarwal. 2024. Assessment of working capital management efficiency—A two-stage slack-based measure of data envelopment analysis. *Managerial Finance. ahead-of-print*. [CrossRef]

Sitzmann, Traci, and Justin M. Weinhardt. 2019. Approaching evaluation from a multilevel perspective: A comprehensive analysis of the indicators of training effectiveness. *Human Resource Management Review* 29: 253–69. [CrossRef]

Słomka-Gołębiowska, Agnieszka, Sara De Masi, Simona Zambelli, and Andrea Paci. 2023. Towards higher sustainability: If you want something done, ask a chairwoman. *Finance Research Letters* 58: 104308. [CrossRef]

Song, Jiayi. 2024. Corporate ESG performance and human capital investment efficiency. *Finance Research Letters* 62: 105239. [CrossRef]

Tseng, Fang-Mei, Ching-Wen Liang, and Ngoc B. Nguyen. 2023. Blockchain technology adoption and business performance in large enterprises: A comparison of the United States and China. *Technology in Society* 73: 102230. [CrossRef]

Villa, Gabriela, Sebastián Lozano, and Sandra Redondo. 2021. Data Envelopment Analysis Approach to Energy-Saving Projects Selection in an Energy Service Company. *Mathematics* 9: 200. [CrossRef]

Wang, Shuhong, Hui Yu, and Malin Song. 2017. Assessing the efficiency of environmental regulations of large-scale enterprises based on extended fuzzy data envelopment analysis. *Industrial Management & Data Systems* 118: 463–79. [CrossRef]

Way, Sean A., Patrick M. Wright, Bruce J. Tracey, and Jeremy F. Isnard. 2018. HR flexibility: Precursors and the contingent impact on firm financial performance. *Human Resource Management* 57: 567–82. [CrossRef]

Wright, Patrick M. 2021. Rediscovering the "Human" in strategic human capital. *Human Resource Management Review* 31: 100781. [CrossRef]

Yang, Kexin, Qi Zhang, Qiqi Liu, Jiangfeng Liu, and Jie Jiao. 2024. Effect mechanism and efficiency evaluation of financial support on technological innovation in the new energy vehicles' industrial chain. *Energy* 293: 130761. [CrossRef]

Zhang, Yi, Sanjay Kumar, Xianhai Huang, and Yiming Yuan. 2023. Human Capital Quality and the Regional Economic Growth: Evidence from China. *Journal of Asian Economics* 86: 101593. [CrossRef]

Zhao, Yongliang, Weihua Ruan, Yonghong Jiang, and Junnan Rao. 2018. Salesperson human capital investment and heterogeneous export enterprises performance. *Journal of Business Economics and Management* 19: 609–29. [CrossRef]

Zheng, Jinghai, Xiaoxuan Liu, and Arne Bigsten. 1998. Ownership Structure and Determinants of Technical Efficiency: An Application of Data Envelopment Analysis to Chinese Enterprises (1986–1990). *Journal of Comparative Economics* 26: 465–84.

Zheng, Jinghai, Xiaoxuan Liu, and Arne Bigsten. 2003. Efficiency, technical progress, and best practice in Chinese state enterprises (1980–1994). *Journal of Comparative Economics* 31: 134–52.

Zhu, Xiaoqian, Xingru Xiao, and Yating Bo. 2024. A Study on Measuring the Efficiency of Digital Inclusive Finance Enabling High-Quality Fiscal Development in Provinces. *Highlights in Business, Economics and Management* 24: 40–49. [CrossRef]

economies

MDPI

Article

Multi-Factor Cost Adjustment for Enhanced Export-Oriented Production Capacity in Manufacturing Firms

Ashraf Mishrif [1,*] and Mohamed A. Hammad [2]

1 Humanities Research Centre, Sultan Qaboos University, P.O. Box 17, Muscat 123, Oman
2 Civil Engineering Department, College of Engineering, Sultan Qaboos University, P.O. Box 17, Muscat 123, Oman; s128793@student.squ.edu.om
* Correspondence: amishrif@squ.edu.om

Abstract: Many manufacturing firms face considerable difficulties in building export capacity and selling their products in international markets. These firms often struggle with unpredictable cost changes, logistical problems along the supply chain, and rising labor expenses that could threaten the competitive edge of manufacturing operations. As there is also a clear absence of practical export models tailored to the unique needs of industrial firms, our study aims to offer a more holistic approach to assessing the impact of cost components on enhancing export-oriented production capacity (*EOPC*), a perspective not comprehensively provided by the comparative advantage theory, the Heckscher–Ohlin model, or the resource-based theory. While offering a comprehensive analysis of cost components in production, we argue that adjusting the resources, managing the costs, and enhancing production efficiency can significantly improve the *EOPC* of the manufacturing firms. Using primary data collected from 200 manufacturing firms in Oman during the period 2012–2016, multiple regression analysis followed by descriptive statistical analysis together with a correlation matrix indicates strong positive relationships between the *EOPC* and factors such as the raw material cost (*RMC*), labor wages (*LW*), labor force (*LF*), and R&D costs (*RND*). Multicollinearity assessment shows VIF values below the threshold, suggesting reliable estimates. Interaction terms and market conditions were integrated into the model, enhancing its predictive accuracy. Preliminary multiple regression analysis confirms the significant impact of the *RMC*, *LW*, *LF*, and R&D on the *EOPC*, while highlighting the importance of market conditions in moderating these effects. The model's adjusted R^2 value indicates a strong fit, showing that the independent variables account for a substantial proportion of the variance in the *EOPC*. Each variable's importance is reflected in its coefficient, while p-values assess the statistical significance, highlighting which factors are crucial for enhancing export capabilities. Specifically, low p-values for cost components, labor force size, and wages confirm their significant influence, and varying market conditions further modulate these effects, demonstrating the accurate interplay between internal and external factors. Adjustments in cost components under varying market scenarios were analyzed, indicating optimal strategies for increasing the *EOPC*. Of the five scenarios proposed to distribute the cost either among some variables while keeping others constant or among all the factors, the best-case scenario adjusted all variables together, resulting in a 20% increment in exports. We conclude with some practical and policy implications for governments to support industries in accessing cheap resources through tax reductions on imported raw materials and efficient supply chains, while promoting innovation, technology adoption, and R&D investment at the firm level.

Keywords: export-oriented production capacity; cost adjustment; production factors; pricing; manufacturing

1. Introduction

Export capacity (EC) is a holistic measure of a firm's ability to produce and sell products or services in international markets. It involves various components, such as production efficiency, logistical management, and market reach (Hoque et al. 2022). The EC reflects a firm's overall potential to engage in export activities, driven by its capability to manage production costs, ensure timely delivery, and cater to diverse international customer requirements. It is an essential indicator of a firm's global competitiveness and its ability to sustain and grow its presence in foreign markets.

On the other hand, export-oriented production capacity (*EOPC*) is a more focused concept within the broader EC framework. The *EOPC* emphasizes the adjustment of production processes specifically for the export market. This includes implementing efficient production techniques, adopting cost-saving measures, and leveraging advanced technologies to enhance product quality and reduce production costs (Ma and Ahn 2021). The *EOPC* is crucial for firms aiming to improve their export performance, as it directly impacts on their ability to offer competitively priced, high-quality products that meet international standards.

The relationship between the EC and *EOPC* is synergistic. While the EC represents the overall export potential of a firm, the *EOPC* provides the necessary foundation by ensuring that production processes are aligned with the demands of international markets. By improving the *EOPC*, firms can significantly enhance their EC, leading to increased export volumes, competitive pricing, and greater market reach. This interconnectedness underscores the importance of focusing on the *EOPC* to build a robust and sustainable export strategy.

Several studies argue that adjusting the production processes is fundamental to improving firm competitiveness and building export capacity (Ortigueira-Sánchez et al. 2022; Hossain et al. 2022; Aghazadeh et al. 2022). Firms can substantially enhance efficiency and scale up their output through adjustments and the refinement of operation. This approach not only drives down the cost per unit but also fosters competitiveness in the global marketplace by ensuring that products meet quality standards while remaining cost-effective (Zahoor and Lew 2023; Zhang and Jedin 2023; Sadeghi et al. 2023). By simplifying production processes and implementing cost-saving measures, firms can effectively lower their production costs while simultaneously strengthening their operational efficiency (Yao et al. 2022; Adegbola et al. 2024; Sarwar et al. 2022). This practice enables firms to offer competitive pricing for their products in international markets, ultimately increasing their attractiveness to potential buyers and improving their export potential. (Matzner et al. 2023; Sudirjo 2023; Babayev and Balajayeva 2023; Fröhlich 2023; Keskin et al. 2021).

From a technical perspective, production efficiency involves developing labor skills and improving production methods to effectively take advantage of numerous opportunities in the global market (Joel et al. 2024; Rivero-Gutiérrez et al. 2024; Feng et al. 2020). It enables firms to expand their scope and thrive by entering international markets. Yet, grabbing these opportunities poses significant challenges, mainly arising from various technical and financial aspects such as efficiently managing production costs. This requires embracing innovative technologies and strategies to overcome these obstacles and achieve sustainable growth in the increasingly competitive global market (Hegab et al. 2023; Allioui and Mourdi 2023; Mansion and Bausch 2020; Naradda Gamage et al. 2020). These cost challenges can be broadly categorized into three main areas: raw materials, labor force size and salaries, and research and development (R&D) (Chandra et al. 2020; Sanyal et al. 2020; Gupta and Chauhan 2021; Naradda Gamage et al. 2020; Kaplinsky and Kraemer-Mbula 2022; Grossman and Oberfield 2022). The cost of raw materials can change a lot because of global market shifts and supply chain problems. Firms that rely on imported materials may see their costs go up significantly, affecting their profits and ability to compete internationally (Swazan and Das 2022; Bhuyan and Oh 2021). For example, the primary reason for the decline in woven exports is the reliance on imported raw materials, which has caused production delays and affected delivery times (Giri and Singh 2022). In contrast, knitwear production uses domestically produced yarn and fabrics, allowing for a faster production process (Chandra and Ferdaus 2020).

Consequently, managing raw material cost is very important to let firms venture into the global markets (Nyu et al. 2022; Lima et al. 2022). In terms of workforce size and salaries, managing labor costs is another critical challenge (Ozkan-Ozen and Kazancoglu 2022; Salimova et al. 2022; Webber 2022). Rising wages, especially in regions with increasing living standards or labor shortages, can add to firms' financial burden. Also, attracting and retaining skilled labor often requires competitive salaries and benefits, which can further elevate costs (Ewers et al. 2022; Castro-Silva and Lima 2023; Oliinyk et al. 2021). For instance, there has been a notable rise in labor expenses throughout China, prompting concerns regarding the potential loss of its manufacturing advantage and its renowned status as the global factory. Huang et al. (2021) argue that increasing labor costs affect China's appeal to multinational corporations and subsequently its competitiveness in global exports. They also find variations in minimum wage distortions across regions, which could act as external factors impacting unskilled-labor expenses. Therefore, labor size and wages are very important to let firms venture into global markets (Amit et al. 2022; Azar et al. 2024; Eeckhout 2022).

With an increasing number of firms exploring global markets, the entry key for their international growth lies in expanding their R&D activities and efficiently distributing R&D expenditures from domestic to international markets (Tung and Hoang 2024; Peters and Roberts 2022; Davcik et al. 2021). Investment in R&D is essential for innovation, enabling firms to maintain a competitive edge in the global market (Peters and Roberts 2022). However, R&D activities require substantial financial resources that come with inherent risks (Edeh et al. 2020; Naradda Gamage et al. 2020). Firms must allocate funds for developing new products, improving existing technologies, and ensuring compliance with international standards (Edeh et al. 2020; Pylaeva et al. 2022). For smaller firms or those with limited budgets, these expenditures can be a significant barrier to entry into export markets. The uncertainty of returns on R&D investments can make it difficult for firms to justify and sustain these costs over time (Sanford and Yang 2022; Naradda Gamage et al. 2020).

The reliance on imported or local costly raw materials can also pose significant challenges for firms attempting to expand globally. These challenges include potential cost increases due to fluctuations in international market prices, delays in production caused by supply chain disruptions, and difficulties in meeting delivery deadlines, which can negatively impact a firm's global competitiveness (Kanike 2023; Swazan and Das 2022). Limited supplier options and short contracts could cause problems for firms, putting them at risk (Bhuyan and Oh 2021). In addition, high labor costs, particularly in regions experiencing increased living standards or labor shortages, pose another significant challenge for firms, as notable surges in labor expenses raise concerns about their manufacturing competitiveness (Oliinyk et al. 2021; Huang et al. 2021).

This introductory brief underscores a significant research gap in the literature and the need for further investigation to help industrial firms facing difficulties in their global expansion. These firms often struggle with unpredictable cost changes, logistical problems along the supply chain, and rising labor expenses that could threaten the competitive edge of manufacturing operations. Also, there is a clear absence of practical export models tailored to the unique needs of industrial firms, making the challenge even more difficult to overcome. Consequently, our investigation is crucial in developing new recommendations and guidelines that enable firms to better manage production costs, navigate trade barriers, and enhance their capacity to succeed in international markets. More specifically, this study examines the impact of production cost components, including raw material costs, labor force size and wages, and R&D spending, on the *EOPC* of firms seeking global expansion. It seeks to improve the understanding of how these cost factors collectively influence firms' production efficiency and export capacity. It is expected to provide new insights for policymakers and industry practitioners to identify appropriate policy measures to support industries in accessing resources and innovative technology at reasonable costs, as well as offering practical guidance for firms in adjusting resource allocation and managing production costs to exploit export opportunities in global markets.

Additionally, this study is particularly relevant to Oman, where industrial diversification and enhancing export capacity are crucial for economic development. The Omani government has been actively promoting policies to boost production efficiency and export capability as part of its economic diversification strategy. By focusing on the specific challenges and opportunities within the Omani context, this study aims to provide actionable insights that can aid local firms in overcoming the barriers to global market entry and enhancing their competitiveness

It is worth noting that this investigation is probably the first to offer a more holistic approach to assessing the impact of cost components on enhancing export capacity, a perspective not comprehensively provided by the comparative advantage theory, the Heckscher–Ohlin model, or the resource-based theory. It provides the first comprehensive and comparative analysis of cost components in production and hence building the export capacity. Additionally, by adjusting resources, managing costs, and enhancing production efficiency, the export capacity can be significantly improved.

2. Literature Review

2.1. Developing Firms' Production Capacity

The literature in production economics identifies several factors to build and develop the export capacity of a firm. Hossain et al. (2022) argue that optimizing cost components is a critical aspect of developing a firm's export capacity. Rezazadeh et al. (2023) find that effective cost management strategies can significantly enhance a firm's competitive edge in international markets. Rognes (2023) stresses that the efficient sourcing of raw materials can lead to substantial cost savings. Firms can achieve this by negotiating better terms with suppliers, opting for bulk purchasing, and identifying alternative sources of raw materials.

Saka and Bolanle (2023) examined the relationship between credit financing by commercial banks and capacity utilization in Nigeria's manufacturing sector. Their findings suggest that while bank financing exerts a positive but insignificant short-term impact, it does not significantly affect long-term capacity utilization. This underscores the complexities in financial dynamics affecting production capacity, particularly in emerging markets like Nigeria.

To build export capacity, adjusting product pricing is mandatory (Dethine et al. 2020; Aharoni 2024). Several steps should be taken into consideration: (1) focusing on strategic raw material selection (Hool et al. 2022); (2) conducting thorough market research to understand consumer preferences and competitor pricing (Shabbir and Wisdom 2020); and (3) identifying key raw materials and evaluating sourcing options, considering factors like cost, quality, and availability in target markets (Teerasoponpong and Sopadang 2022). By aligning raw material costs with market demands, competitive prices can lead to building promising export capacity.

Salimova et al. (2022) and Huang et al. (2021) underscore that the importance of investing in skilled labor is essential for maintaining high productivity and quality standards. However, they stress that optimizing labor costs must involve balancing wage levels with productivity improvements. Phan (2022) adds that increasing skilled-labor numbers and wages for export capacity must be aligned with promoting a positive work environment and career growth opportunities to retain talent. Other scholars highlight the importance of investing in training and development to enhance existing workforce skills and attract new talent. Offering competitive wages and benefits packages attracts skilled workers, particularly when payment packages are aligned with industry standards and local economic conditions. Al-Harthy et al. (2022) stress that firms must continuously monitor labor market trends and adjust recruitment strategies and compensation structures accordingly, ensuring a skilled and motivated workforce capable of driving export success.

Further investigation underlines the significance of R&D in improving product specifications and building a strong production capacity in a competitive market. By investing in R&D, companies can come up with new ideas and improve their products to stay ahead of their competitors. Edeh et al. (2020) and Naradda Gamage et al. (2020) indicate that R&D

is critical in helping firms to understand customers' preferences and in exploiting innovative technology to improve the quality of products in a faster time and with lower costs. This finding reaffirms that R&D helps firms to keep improving, making their production stronger and their products more attractive to customers.

2.2. Building Firms' Export-Oriented Production Capacity

There are several conceptual foundations concerned with cost component optimization in building export capacity. For example, comparative advantage theory argues that firms can internationalize by taking advantage of differences in opportunity costs between countries, which determines their comparative advantage in producing certain goods or services. This concept implies that firms should specialize in producing goods or services where their countries have a comparative advantage, meaning they can produce these goods or services at a lower opportunity cost compared to other countries (Shen et al. 2022). While the theory does not explicitly address cost components, its focus on opportunity costs indirectly touches upon the efficiency and cost-effectiveness of production.

The Heckscher–Ohlin model adds a new dimension to firm internationalization by stressing its capacity to efficiently utilize its local and internal resources. This theory implies how firms can optimize their resource allocation, including skilled labor or natural or raw materials, to facilitate exporting (Matezo and Matondo 2022). By specializing in producing goods that rely on abundant resources in their countries, firms can enhance their competitiveness and export capacity to compete in the global market. Moreover, resource-based theory emphasizes the utilization of a firm's unique resources and abilities to gain a competitive edge. It argues that firms can focus on making the most of their resources to operate more efficiently and lower production costs, indirectly connecting with the ideas of comparative advantage (Siregar et al. 2024). By using resources efficiently, firms can make goods or services more competitively, potentially resulting in better pricing in export markets. These conceptual models and theories underline the importance of efficient resource allocation and utilization to lower production costs and enhance export capacity and competitiveness domestically and internationally.

2.3. Effects of External Economic Factors on Export-Oriented Production Capacity

In addition to internal factors such as production efficiency, external economic factors significantly influence a firm's export capacity. Recent studies have highlighted the impact of economic policy uncertainty, bilateral trade intensity, and capital flows on export dynamics (Liu et al. 2020). Notably, economic policy uncertainty, bilateral trade intensity, and capital flow affected China's financial cycle spillover across varying institutional distances from 1997 to 2017. Liu et al. (2020) reveals a consistent linear effect of these factors on financial cycle spillover across the entire sample period, with non-linear impacts emerging during normal and crisis periods. Specifically, the transition function exhibits a gradual shift under normal economic conditions and a double-threshold effect during crises, suggesting varying facilitating and restraining effects on export capacity across different economic periods. Understanding these dynamics is crucial for policymakers aiming to craft effective macroprudential policies tailored to different economic contexts.

2.4. Effects of Cost Components on Export-Oriented Production Capacity

2.4.1. Impact of Raw Material Cost on Export-Oriented Production Capacity

Empirical studies argue that raw materials such as fabrics, yarns, and other inputs constitute a substantial portion of the production costs in the ready-made garments (RMGs) sector (Swazan and Das 2022). Fluctuations in the prices of these raw materials can directly influence the overall cost structure of garment production. When raw material costs increase, it can squeeze profit margins for manufacturers, making their products less competitive in the global market (Swazan and Das 2022; Bhuyan and Oh 2021). This argument is apparently critical in the impact of raw material costs on the export capacity of the Bangladeshi RMG industry. While Bangladesh has established itself as a leading exporter in the global apparel market, the fluctuating costs of raw materials significantly affect the industry's competitiveness and export potential (Swazan and Das 2022). Efforts to mitigate the impact of raw material costs on export capacity may include strategies such as diversifying sourcing channels, investing in vertical integration to reduce dependency on imported materials, negotiating favorable pricing agreements with suppliers, and implementing efficient inventory management practices. Moreover, advancements in materials science and sustainable sourcing practices can further optimize raw material costs and enhance export capacity (Ninduwezuor-Ehiobu et al. 2023).

Hypothesis 1. *Raw material costs have a positive influence on the export-oriented production capacity. The efficient sourcing of raw materials reduces costs, thus enhancing a firm's competitiveness and export performance by lowering production costs and improving product quality.*

2.4.2. Impact of Skilled-Labor Adjustment on Export-Oriented Production Capacity

It is generally accepted in business and economics that skilled labor improves productivity. Higher productivity can lead to more competitive pricing and better-quality products, making a firm more attractive in international markets (Gallego and Gutiérrez Ramírez 2023). Empirical studies highlight that skilled labor can have a beneficial impact on labor productivity within firms, ultimately contributing to their export capacity. Oliinyk et al. (2021) emphasized that the presence of skilled workers is a fundamental factor influencing a firm's decision to engage in exports, with companies employing a highly skilled workforce being more inclined to enter foreign markets. Through empirical observations, Pholphirul et al. (2020) and Oliinyk et al. (2021) have demonstrated a significant and positive correlation between a skilled workforce and export performance. This reaffirms the early notion that human capital, as indicated by the proficiency of the workforce, plays a crucial role in a nation's development. As for labor wage, China demonstrates an exemplary model, as wages for Chinese factory workers went up by more than five times between 1990 and 2015, which is more than wage increases in nearby countries like Vietnam, Indonesia, India, and the Philippines. As a result, big firms like Nike moved their factories to other places like Vietnam, which has been the top choice for making their products since 2009 (Huang et al. 2021). This shift is also seen in the decrease in foreign-owned companies doing business in China from 58% in 2006 to 44% in 2016. As labor gets more expensive, China's advantage in making labor-intensive things like clothes and furniture gets weaker.

Furthermore, it is crucial to distinguish between skilled labor and generic labor. Oliinyk et al. (2021) and Pholphirul et al. (2020) emphasize that the performance gains associated with a skilled workforce are not merely a function of labor quantity but rather the quality and productivity of the labor employed. This distinction is vital for understanding the true impact of labor composition on export performance.

The relationship between labor force size and labor wages is complex and interdependent. An increase in labor wages can attract a larger workforce, which in turn can enhance productivity and the quality of output. Conversely, a larger labor force size can lead to competitive wage structures, as firms seek to retain skilled labor while maintaining cost efficiency. This interdependency can influence research results, as changes in one variable (e.g., wages) can significantly impact the other (e.g., labor force size), thereby affecting the overall OEPC. This dynamic emphasizes the need for a balanced approach to managing labor costs and adjusting workforce size to achieve sustainable export performance.

Hypothesis 2. *The labor force has a positive influence on the EOPC. A well-trained and -compensated labor force boosts productivity and quality, thereby enhancing a firm's export capacity.*

Hypothesis 3. *Labor wages have a positive influence on the EOPC. Labor wages influence the EOPC. Adequate compensation incentivizes productivity, leading to better product quality and enhanced export performance.*

Hypothesis 4. *The interaction between labor wages and labor force has a positive influence on the EOPC. Labor wages have a positive influence on the EOPC.*

2.4.3. Impact of R&D Spending on Export-Oriented Production Capacity

Empirical research underlines the crucial role that innovation plays in building the *EOPC*, as most firms are increasingly investing in R&D to create new knowledge and innovative technologies that are fundamental to producing new products and better-quality goods at lower costs (Davcik et al. 2021). For firms, investment in R&D is key not only to staying competitive but also to developing a technological edge to make their products sellable and easily exported to the international markets (Davcik et al. 2021). It also complements educational and training programs that contribute to the creation of skilled workers and a well-educated workforce. Innovation, achieved through creating new products and improving existing ones, can help companies move up in the supply chain. A firm's ability to compete technologically depends on its talent for innovation. R&D can also help firms to understand trade patterns and what factors influence export performance and to navigate global markets (Charoenrat and Amornkitvikai 2021). According to Pholphirul et al. (2020), manufacturing firms in the Greater Mekong Subregion countries saw a significant boost in their export performance.

Overall, the above theories emphasize the critical role of optimizing cost in general and refer mainly to raw materials as a main resource for cost optimization in enhancing production and export capacity. On the other hand, the literature argued that effective cost management strategies, including efficient sourcing, strategic raw material selection, and investing in skilled labor, can significantly improve a firm's competitive edge in international markets (Hossain et al. 2022; Rezazadeh et al. 2023). These approaches focus on lower opportunity costs, optimal resource allocation, and the efficient use of unique resources. R&D investments are essential for technological progress and cost reduction, further strengthening export capacity (Davcik et al. 2021). By efficiently managing these cost components, firms can lower production costs, enhance product quality, achieve better pricing, and ultimately boost their export performance.

Despite the theories and the literature emphasizing the importance of optimizing cost components for enhancing production capacity, there is a notable gap in understanding how each individual factor specifically contributes to production adjustment. This lack of detailed understanding obstructs the development of a comprehensive model for improving production capacity. Our study aims to address this gap by focusing on the specific impact of each cost component on the production capacity, specifically the export-oriented production capacity. While our primary focus is on production adjustment for export purposes, we also explore the potential implications these factors might have on export capacity. However, we acknowledge that further research is needed to fully establish the direct link between cost components and export capacity.

Hypothesis 5. *R&D spending has a positive influence on the EOPC. Investment in R&D drives technological progress and cost-effective production, enhancing a firm's competitiveness and export performance.*

Hypothesis 6. *Market condition moderates the relationship between the independent variables (raw material costs, labor force, labor wages, R&D spending) and the EOPC.*

2.5. Hypothesis Development

Ultimately, this study rigorously investigates the impact of key cost components—raw material costs, labor force, labor wages, and R&D spending—on the export-oriented production capacity (*EOPC*). By analyzing empirical data and integrating theoretical frameworks, it is proposed that the efficient sourcing of raw materials positively influences a firm's competitiveness and export performance by reducing production costs and enhancing product quality (Hypothesis 1). Additionally, a well-trained and adequately compensated labor force boosts productivity and quality, thereby improving a firm's export capacity (Hypothesis 2). Adequate compensation further incentivizes productivity, leading to higher product quality and better export performance (Hypothesis 3). This study also examines how the interaction between labor wages and labor force size positively influences the *EOPC*, with labor wages enhancing the effects of a well-trained workforce on export performance (Hypothesis 4). Investment in R&D fosters technological progress and cost-effective production, which enhances a firm's competitiveness and export performance (Hypothesis 5). Furthermore, this study explores how market conditions moderate the relationships between these cost components and export-oriented production capacity, aiming to elucidate how external factors influence these dynamics (Hypothesis 6). These hypotheses, grounded in substantial empirical evidence and theoretical insights, aim to address the existing research gap by offering a comprehensive understanding of how each cost component contributes to adjusting the production capacity and enhancing export performance.

3. Research Methodology

The analysis of the data performed is based on a statistical model using multiple regression analysis (MRA), with the aim of investigating the impact of each input variable on production capacity to build the export capacity. MRA is a fundamental statistical method used to understand and quantify the relationship between many variables. In this approach, one variable, termed the independent variable, is used to predict or explain the variability in another variable, known as the dependent variable. By fitting a straight line to the data points, a simple linear regression enables researchers to explore patterns, identify trends, and make predictions within a straightforward framework. To perform this analysis, we collected a set of relevant data and developed a proposed model that serves our objective.

3.1. Data Collection

The data were collected from the database of the Ministry of Commerce, Industry, and Investment Promotion, Sultanate of Oman, covering the period between 2012 and 2016. These data were collected annually by the ministry from manufacturing firms located in various industrial cities under the management of the Public Establishment for Industrial Estates (Madayn). The extensive database contains key business and economic indicators from various companies over a specified timeframe. This study encompasses a diverse range of Omani manufacturing firms operating in various sectors, including food production, construction materials, plastics, chemicals, and engineering services. These sectors reflect the broad industrial base of Oman's economy. The paid-up capital for these firms shows significant variation, illustrating the diversity in financial resources among the firms. Smaller firms may have capital around OMR 15,000, reflecting lower initial investment requirements, while larger firms exhibit substantial paid-up capital reaching up to OMR 80,000,000. This extensive range in capital not only highlights the varying scales of operation but also provides a comprehensive basis for examining cost adjustment strategies. The diverse specializations and capital sizes allow for a nuanced analysis of how different investment levels and sector-specific needs influence cost management and operational efficiency.

The key relevant variables selected for this study are the raw material cost, labor force, labor wages, and R&D spending. The dependent variable is the export-oriented production capacity (*EOPC*), while the independent variables are the raw material cost, labor force, labor wages, and R&D spending.

The collected dataset underwent a meticulous cleaning process to establish a robust foundation for assessing the relationship between each variable and export-oriented production capacity. This cleaning procedure was essential to ensure the inclusion of only real and logically sound numerical values, thereby enhancing the precision and reliability of the subsequent analysis. The cleaning process followed strict logical criteria to ensure that the data were both realistic and representative of actual industry conditions. Initially comprising 200 entries, the dataset was refined through this process, which aimed to eliminate inconsistencies and outliers, allowing for a more accurate and meaningful exploration of the complex connections between the selected variables and the export-oriented production capacity under investigation. It is important to emphasize that Oman's labor market has been characterized by a significant emphasis on skilled labor, reflecting its investment in human capital development. This focus aligns with the broader GCC labor market trends, where skilled labor plays a crucial role in driving productivity and economic growth.

Table 1 presents a summary of the variables and their measurements, detailing the type, measurement unit, data source, and a description of each variable. The table provides a clear and concise overview of the variables used in this study, facilitating an understanding of how each variable is quantified and the source of the data. This detailed description ensures clarity and comprehensiveness in the data collection and cleaning process, thereby strengthening this study's validity and reliability.

Table 1. Summary of variables and measurements.

Variables	Type	Measurement Unit	Data Source	Description
Raw material cost	Independent	Omani Rial (OMR)	The ministry from manufacturing firms located in various industrial cities under the management of the Public Establishment for Industrial Estates (Madayn)	Cost of raw materials purchased by the firms
Labor force	Independent	Number of workers		Number of employees engaged in production
Labor wages	Independent	OMR per month		Average monthly wage paid to employees
R&D costs	Independent	Omani Rial (OMR)		Expenditure on research and development activities
Export-oriented production capacity	Dependent	Omani Rial (OMR)		Total annual exports

Source: authors' own work.

3.2. Causal Chain Analysis

To establish a clear causal chain, a theoretical framework was developed that outlines the expected relationships between the independent variables (raw material cost, labor force, labor wages, and R&D spending) and the dependent variable (export-oriented production capacity). This framework is built in both the theoretical literature and empirical evidence, forming the basis for our hypotheses.

Raw material cost: The efficient sourcing and cost management of raw materials are critical for reducing production costs. Lower production costs enhance a firm's competitiveness, enabling higher production capacity geared towards export markets.

Labor force: The quantity and quality of labor directly impact a firm's production capacity. A larger, skilled labor force can increase productivity and output, thereby boosting export capacity.

Labor wages: Competitive labor wages are essential for attracting and retaining skilled workers. Fair compensation correlates with higher productivity and quality of output, which are crucial for maintaining and expanding export markets.

R&D spending: Investment in research and development drives innovation and technological advancement. Firms that invest in R&D can develop new products, improve existing ones, and enhance production processes, leading to increased export capacity.

Interaction term (labor force and labor wages): Including the interaction term between the labor force and labor wages allows us to explore how the impact of labor wages on production capacity varies with the size of the labor force. This interaction acknowledges the interdependency between these variables, suggesting that the benefit of higher wages on productivity and export capacity could be more pronounced with a larger labor force.

Moderator (market condition): Market conditions can influence the effectiveness of each independent variable on the export-oriented production capacity. For example, in favorable market conditions, the positive effects of a large labor force, competitive labor wages, and R&D spending might be magnified, leading to greater export capacity. Conversely, in less favorable market conditions, these effects might be diminished.

The market condition (*MC*) impact is analyzed on a scale from 1 to 10, showing its moderating effect on cost adjustments required for export growth. *MC* Scale 1–3 represents unfavorable market conditions, necessitating higher adjustments in variables to achieve the desired export increase. *MC* Scale 4–6 reflects neutral market conditions, where base adjustments are generally sufficient. *MC* Scale 7–10 indicates favorable market conditions, potentially reducing the required adjustments in variables to achieve the desired export increase. This approach demonstrates how varying market conditions influence the effectiveness of cost adjustments in achieving export growth.

3.3. Proposed Conceptual Model of Firms' Export-Oriented Production Capacity

The conceptual model developed for this study investigates the complex relationship between the export-oriented production capacity and key economic factors. The primary independent variable is the export-oriented production capacity. The four identified dependent variables—raw material cost, labor cost, labor force, and R&D spending—have been hypothesized to exercise influences on the export amount, as shown in Figure 1. Raw material cost represents the expenses associated with primary inputs, while labor cost and labor force denote the human capital dimension. Additionally, R&D spending reflects a firm's investment in innovation and technological advancement. To enhance the understanding of these relationships, we introduce an interaction term, labor force × labor wage ($LF \times LW$), to examine how the impact of wages on the production capacity varies with labor force size. Additionally, we include a market condition moderator to assess how varying market conditions affect the relationship between these factors and the export-oriented production capacity. The hypotheses suggest that variations in these factors, including the interaction and moderating effects, directly impact a firm's export performance, explaining the complex interplay between economic inputs and competitiveness. This model seeks to contribute valuable insights into the dynamics shaping exports and economic outcomes.

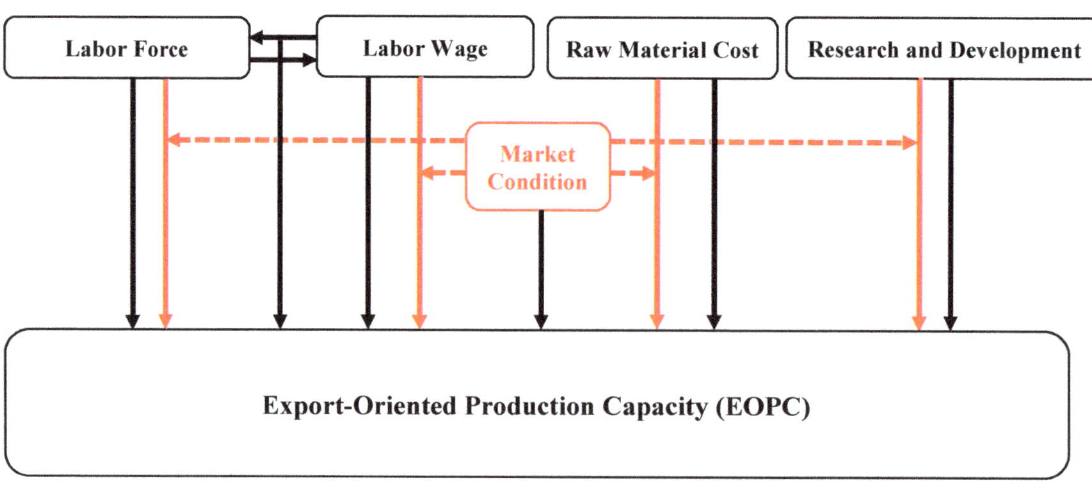

Figure 1. The conceptual model of variables affecting export-oriented production capacity. Source: authors' own work.

The input factors (raw material cost, labor force number, labor wage, and R&D) collectively enhance a firm's export capacity by adjusting production costs, improving product quality, and encouraging innovation. The efficient sourcing of raw materials reduces costs, while a well-trained and -compensated labor force boosts productivity and quality. Investment in R&D drives technological progress and cost-effective production. By managing these inputs effectively, firms can lower production costs, improve competitiveness, and ultimately enhance their export performance.

3.4. Multiple Regression Analysis

MRA is an appropriate method when the research problem includes one unique metric-dependent variable that is related to one metric-independent variable. It helps us to learn about the relationship between several independent or predictor variables and a dependent or criterion variable. The objective of this analysis is to use the independent variables whose value is known to predict the value of the unique dependent variable. A multiple regression model without an intercept was selected for this model. This model is forced through the origin (0,0). The advantage of excluding an intercept is that the theoretical reasons may suggest that the dependent variable should be zero when all independent variables are zero, which is logical for this study. MRA with a constant zero can be generally represented in the following. The employed data are plotted in Figure 2. The regression model can be represented as follows in Equation (1):

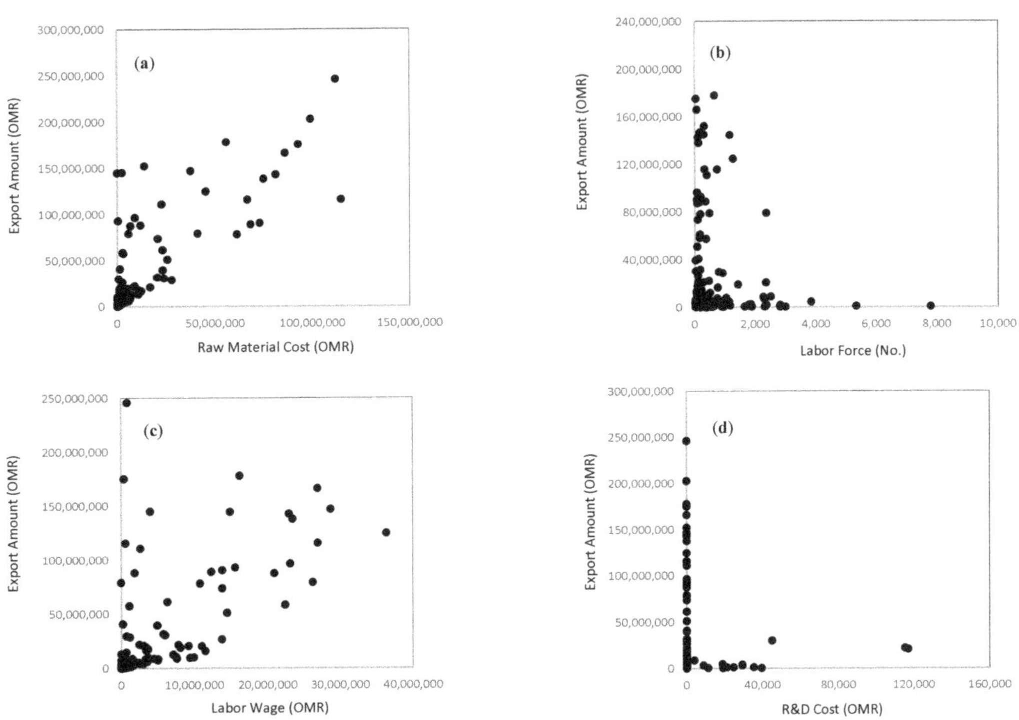

Figure 2. Data distribution for (**a**) raw material cost, (**b**) labor force, (**c**) labor wages, and (**d**) R&D cost.

$$EOPC = \beta_1\ RMC + \beta_2\ LF + \beta_3\ LW + \beta_4\ RND + \beta_5\ (LF \times LW) + \beta_6\ MC + \beta_7\ (MC \times RMC) + \beta_8\ (MC \times LF) + \beta_9\ (MC \times LW) + \beta_{10}\ (MC \times RND) \quad (1)$$

where the following variables are included:

EOPC: export-oriented production capacity (dependent variable);
RMC: raw material cost (independent variable);
LF: labor force (independent variable);
LW: labor wage (independent variable);

RND: research and development costs (independent variable);
MC: market condition (moderator);
LF × LW: interaction term between labor force and labor wage;
β1: RMC coefficient;
β2: LF coefficient;
β3: LW coefficient;
β4: RND coefficient;
β5: LF × LW interaction coefficient;
β6: MC coefficient;
β7: RMC × MC interaction coefficient;
β8: LF × MC interaction coefficient;
β9: LW × MC interaction coefficient;
β10: RND × MC interaction coefficient.

4. Analysis and Results

4.1. The Descriptive Statistics and the Correlation Matrix

A concise summary of the central tendency (mean), variability (standard deviation), and range (minimum and maximum) for the standardized variables, together with the correlation matrix, are presented in Table 2. The export-oriented production capacity (*EOPC*) exhibits substantial variability, with a mean of 0 and a range from −0.52 to 2.52 standard deviations, reflected in a standard deviation of 1.00. The raw material cost (*RMC*) shows a mean of 0, ranging from −0.41 to 2.89 standard deviations, and a standard deviation of 1.00. The labor wage (*LW*) averages 0, with a range from −0.47 to 3.88 standard deviations and a standard deviation of 1.00. The labor force (*LF*), with a mean of 0, spans from -0.16 to 4.75 standard deviations, accompanied by a standard deviation of 1.00. The R&D cost (*RND*), with a mean of 0, varies from −0.18 to 5.29 standard deviations, featuring a standard deviation of 1.00. These statistics provide a comprehensive overview of the central tendencies, variabilities, and ranges of each variable, essential for understanding the economic dynamics and strategic decision-making in the respective sectors.

Table 2. Descriptive statistics of variables and correlation matrix.

Variable	Mean	Std. Deviation	Minimum	Maximum	*EOPC*	*RMC*	*LW*	*LF*	*RND*
EOPC	0	1	−0.52	2.52	1.00				
RMC	0	1	−0.41	2.89	0.82	1.00			
LW	0	1	−0.47	3.88	0.70	0.10	1.00		
LF	0	1	−0.16	4.75	0.62	0.06	0.06	1.00	
RND	0	1	−0.18	5.29	0.73	0.06	0.03	0.03	1.00

The correlation matrix presented in Table 2 illustrates the pairwise correlations between all variables, facilitating an understanding of their relationships and potential multicollinearity issues in the regression analysis. This matrix provides insight into the linear associations among the variables under study. The results indicate a strong positive correlation between the export-oriented production capacity (*EOPC*) and raw material cost (*RMC*) (r = 0.82), labor wages (*LWs*) (r = 0.70), labor force (*LF*) (r = 0.62), and R&D costs (*RND*) (r = 0.73). These high values suggest that increases in the *RMC*, *LW*, *LF*, and *RND* are associated with increases in the EC. Additionally, the correlations among the predictor variables are generally low, with the highest being between *RMC* and *LW* (r = 0.10), indicating minimal multicollinearity concerns. This suggests that while each predictor variable independently correlates with the EC, their interactions do not pose significant multicollinearity risks, thereby ensuring the robustness and reliability of the regression analysis results.

4.2. Evaluation of Multicollinearity and Distribution Characteristics

Multicollinearity was assessed using the Variance Inflation Factor (VIF) for each predictor variable, providing insights into the degree of correlation among them. VIF values are indicators of how much the variance in a regression coefficient is increased due to collinearity among predictors, where a value of 1 indicates no correlation, values between 1 and 5 suggest moderate correlation that is generally not problematic, and values above 10 indicate significant multicollinearity that could inflate standard errors and affect the reliability of model estimates. The VIF values are presented in Table 3. All of them are below the threshold of 10, indicating that multicollinearity is not a concern, and the effects of each predictor can be estimated reliably. Additionally, skewness was analyzed to understand the asymmetry in the distribution of values, with skewness values presented in Table 3. These values indicate that the data are approximately normally distributed, with a slight positive skewness observed, especially in *RND*. Data transformation is not strictly necessary. This comprehensive analysis of VIF and skewness confirms that predictor variables are not highly correlated and exhibit nearly normal distributions, supporting the reliability and validity of the regression model for accurate predictions and interpretations.

Table 3. Output of the VIF and skewness analysis.

Variable	VIF	Skewness
RMC	1.394	0.534
LW	1.392	0.423
LF	1.006	0.125
RND	1.010	0.932

Multicollinearity diagnostics, including Variance Inflation Factors (VIFs) and correlation matrix analysis, revealed low intercorrelation among predictor variables, with the highest correlation being only 0.10 between the raw material cost (*RMC*) and labor wage (*LW*), confirming that multicollinearity is not a concern. This suggests that the predictors do not require standardization to address collinearity issues. Additionally, sensitivity analysis, which assessed the stability of coefficients across different data subsets and model specifications, consistently reinforced the robustness of our findings, indicating that the model's performance is not significantly affected by the scale of the data. The analysis method focuses on variables where the scale does not affect linear regression performance, supporting the use of the original data scale without losing result reliability.

4.3. Inclusion of Moderator on the Variables and Interaction Term

Another moderator was included to refine the predictive model through the raw material cost (*RMC*), labor wage (*LW*), and research and development (*RND*) of the export-oriented production capacity (*EOPC*). Building on theoretical justification, a potential moderator to include, market condition (*MC*), was identified. This moderator was defined with a hypothetical range from 1 to 10. For practical implementation, simulated data for this moderator were generated to reflect realistic variations. Using a normal distribution centered around 5 with a standard deviation of 2, a simulated moderator (starting at 1, capped at 10) was introduced, and interaction terms were calculated to explore their moderator effects. This approach allowed for an enhancement in the model's predictive accuracy and provided deeper insights into the contributions of these factors to the export-oriented production capacity. In addition, including the interaction term between labor wages and labor force captures their interdependent effect on production capacity, revealing how labor wages' impact varies with labor force size. This approach provides more accurate insights for policymakers and economists.

4.4. Preliminary MRA Output Evaluation

The output of the proposed regression analysis is presented in Table 4. The analysis indicates that raw material cost (*RMC*), labor wage (*LW*), labor force (*LF*), and research and development costs (R&D) significantly impact the export-oriented production capacity (*EOPC*). Specifically, *RMC* has a coefficient of 1.074 with a p-value of 0.0001, and R&D has a coefficient of 27.4355 with a p-value of 0.0042, both showing strong positive effects. *LW* and *LF* also positively influence the *EOPC*, with coefficients of 3.1634 and 0.82 and p-values of 0.0029 and 0.0149, respectively. The interaction term between *LW* and *LF*, with a coefficient of 0.0002 and a p-value of 0.6023, is not significant, indicating that labor wages do not significantly interact with the size of the labor force in affecting the export capacity. Market condition (*MC*) alone does not have a significant effect on the *EOPC* (coefficient = 432,703.942, p-value = 0.2599). However, the interactions between *MC* and *RMC* (coefficient = 0.0967, p-value = 0.0387) and *MC* and *LW* (coefficient = 0.2332, p-value = 0.0018) are significant, suggesting that favorable market conditions enhance the effects of raw material costs and labor wages on the export capacity. Terms such as $LW \times LF$, $MC \times LF$, and $MC \times$ R&D are not significant and should be excluded to simplify the model, focusing on the significant variables and their relevant interactions.

Table 4. The output of the proposed regression analysis.

Variable	Coefficient	Standard Error	t-Statistic	p-Value
RMC	1.074	0.0989	2.4882	0.0001
LW	3.1634	1.0486	3.0169	0.0029
LF	0.82	2.1233	1.6975	0.0149
R&D	27.4355	4.7594	9.0450	0.0042
$LW \times LF$	0.0002	0.0004	0.5221	0.6023
MC	432,703.942	382,752.5228	1.1305	0.2599
$MC \times RMC$	0.0967	0.0464	2.0839	0.0387
$MC \times LW$	0.2332	0.1718	1.3576	0.0018
$MC \times LF$	5.9791	1771.0384	0.6979	0.4862
$MC \times R\&D$	85.7723	44.0523	−1.9471	0.5321

4.5. Simplified MRA Output Evaluation

The high coefficient of determination (R^2) equal to 0.82 suggests that a significant portion of the variability in the dependent variable is explained by the predictors. Additionally, the statistics p-value is less than 0.01 and indicates that this relationship is statistically significant, reinforcing the model's reliability in explaining the observed data.

$$EOPC = 1.14\,(RMC) + 0.76(LF) + 3.58(LW) + 33.45(RND) + 0.234\,(MC \times RMC) + 0.356\,(MC \times LW) \tag{2}$$

where the *EOPC* = export-oriented production capacity, *RMC* = raw material cost, *LF* = labor force, *LW* = labor wage, *RND* = research and development, and *MC* = market condition.

The interpretation of the impact of each variable across the years based on the provided coefficients, standard errors, t-statics, and p-values is shown in Table 5.

In this MRA model, the coefficients, standard errors, t-statistics, and p-values of each variable are examined to assess their impact on the dependent variable. Raw material: The coefficient of 1.14 indicates that for each unit increase in raw material, the dependent variable increases by 1.14 units. The low standard error (0.07), t-statistic of 1.56, and very low p-value (4.35×10^5) signify that this variable is a significant predictor. Labor force number: With a coefficient of 0.76, a 1-unit increase in the labor force leads to a 0.76-unit increase in the dependent variable. The standard error of 1.34, t-statistic of 1.456, and *p*-value of 3.11×10^{-6} suggest that this variable significantly influences the dependent variable. Labor wages: The coefficient of 3.58 shows that higher labor wages correspond to a notable increase in the dependent variable. Despite a larger standard error (1.87), the t-statistic of 2.954 and *p*-value of 6.55×10^{4} confirm its significance. R&D costs: The most influential variable, R&D costs, has a coefficient of 33.45, indicating that increased R&D investment substantially boosts the dependent variable. The standard error of 3.8, t-statistic of 7.453, and *p*-value of 6.76×10^{3} highlight its importance. The interaction terms $MC \times RMC$ (coefficient = 0.234, t-statistic = 2.234, *p*-value = 4.54×10^{4}) and $MC \times LW$ (coefficient = 0.3566, t-statistic = 1.235, *p*-value = 5.45×10^{5}) also show significant effects, demonstrating that the relationships between raw materials and labor wages with the dependent variable are moderated by these factors. The relatively low standard errors and significant *p*-values across the variables indicate the reliability and robustness of the model's estimates. A summary of the Goodness of Fit, multicollinearity, and residual analysis results are presented in Table 6.

Table 5. The coefficients, standard errors, t-statics, and *p*-values for all variables.

Variable	Coeff.	Standard Error	t-Static	*p*-Value
RMC	1.14	0.07	1.56	4.35×10^{5}
LF	0.76	1.34	1.456	3.11×10^{6}
LW	3.58	1.87	2.954	6.55×10^{4}
RND	33.45	3.8	7.453	6.76×10^{3}
$MC \times RMC$	0.234	0.0566	2.234	4.54×10^{4}
$MC \times LW$	0.3566	0.234	1.235	5.45×10^{5}

Table 6. Summary of Goodness of Fit, multicollinearity, and residual analysis results.

Test	Statistic	Values
Adjusted R-squared		0.81
Multicollinearity (VIF)		
RMC		1.394
LW	VIF	1.392
LF		1.006
RND		1.010
Sensitivity analysis	Consistent	Yes
Skewness		
RMC		0.534
LW	Skewness	0.423
LF		0.125
RND		0.932
MC	Moderator	-
p-value		
RMC		4.35×10^{5}
LW	*p*-value	3.11×10^{6}
LF		6.55×10^{4}
RND		6.76×10^{3}
MC	Moderator	4.54×10^{4} for *RMC*; 5.45×10^{5} for *LW*
Residual analysis		

Table 6. *Cont.*

Test	Statistic	Values
Homoscedasticity		Met
Residual scatter		Random
Systematic patterns		None

Residual analysis is conducted to validate the assumptions and performance of a regression model. Figure 3 shows the residuals versus the predicted values, exhibiting a random scatter around zero with no discernible pattern. This indicates that the model captures the underlying data structure well, meeting the assumption of homoscedasticity with constant residual variance. The absence of systematic patterns suggests a linear relationship between predictors and the response variable. Thus, the model provides a good fit to the data, making its predictions reliable and accurate.

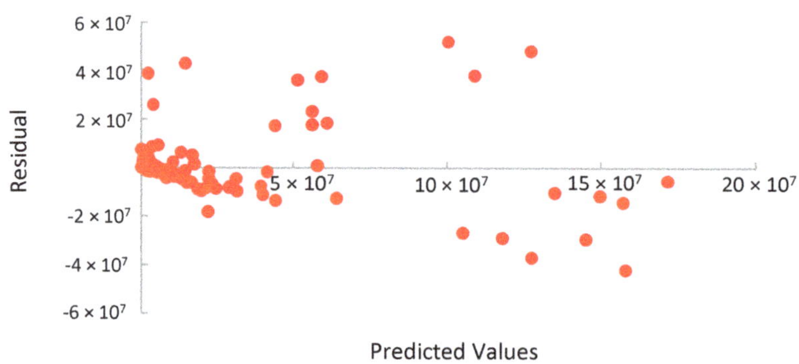

Figure 3. Relationship between the predicted values and the residual.

Overall, the proposed model provides a good starting point for understanding the relationships between the predictors and the dependent variable. Labor wages, raw material cost, and R&D spending are identified as strong predictors of the dependent variable due to their significant t-statistics and low *p*-values. In the meantime, the labor force also shows a significant relationship. The model seems like it can predict well. Moreover, residual analysis confirms the model's validity, showing a good fit to the data with homoscedasticity and no discernible patterns, indicating reliable and accurate predictions.

4.6. Hypotheses Testing

Based on the multiple regression analysis, raw material costs, labor wages, labor force, and R&D spending show statistically significant relationships with the export-oriented production capacity. The analysis confirms the acceptance of Hypotheses 1, 2, 3, and 5 and partially supports Hypothesis 6. Specifically, raw material costs exhibit a significant influence on the export capacity with a coefficient of 1.074, a t-statistic of 2.4882, and a *p*-value of 0.0001. Labor wages also have a notable impact, with a coefficient of 3.1634, a t-statistic of 3.0169, and a *p*-value of 0.0029. Labor force shows a significant relationship with export capacity, evidenced by a coefficient of 0.82, a t-statistic of 1.6975, and a *p*-value of 0.0149. R&D spending demonstrates a strong influence, with a coefficient of 27.4355, a t-statistic of 9.0450, and a *p*-value of 0.0042. However, Hypothesis 4, which posits an interaction between labor wages and labor force positively influencing the export-oriented production capacity, is rejected due to a non-significant coefficient (0.0002), a t-statistic of 0.5221, and a *p*-value of 0.6023. The moderating effect of market conditions is confirmed only for raw material costs and labor wages, aligning with Hypothesis 6, as indicated by significant interactions with market conditions for raw material costs (coefficient 0.0967, *p*-value 0.0387) and labor wages (coefficient 0.2332, *p*-value 0.0018). Table 7 presents the hypothesis results based on the regression analysis results.

Table 7. Hypothesis results based on regression analysis.

Hypotheses	Accept/Reject
Hypothesis 1: *The labor force positively influences the EOPC*	Accept
Hypothesis 2: *Raw material costs positively influence the EOPC*	Accept
Hypothesis 3: *R&D spending positively influences the EOPC*	Accept
Hypothesis 4: *Interaction between labor wages and labor force has a positive influence on the export-oriented production capacity*	Reject
Hypothesis 5: *Labor wages positively influence the EOPC*	Accept
Hypothesis 6: *Market condition moderates the relationship between the independent variables (raw material costs, labor force, labor wages, R&D spending) and the export-oriented production capacity*	Accept for variables "*RMC*" and "*LW*" only

4.7. Variable Adjustment Analysis

After validating the regression model, the impact of varying market conditions on export growth was explored; different scenarios were analyzed to determine the necessary adjustments in the cost factors presented in Table 8. To achieve a 20% increase in exports, different strategies and market conditions impact the required adjustments in costs. In Scenario 1, increasing the raw material cost (*RMC*) by 50%, labor wages (*LW*) by 40%, and research and development (*RND*) expenditure by 65%, each individually while keeping the other variables constant, is effective under neutral market conditions. Under favorable conditions, only a 12% increase in *RMC* and a 10% increase in *LW* are needed, while unfavorable conditions demand a 105% increase in *RMC* and an 84% increase in *LW*. Scenario 2 suggests a 25% increase in *RMC* and a 20% increase in *LW* for neutral conditions, with favorable conditions requiring just 7% and 4% increases, respectively, and unfavorable conditions needing 45% and 50% increases. Scenario 3 shows that increasing the labor force (*LF*) by 100% and *LW* by 40% works in neutral conditions, with favorable conditions needing a 25% increase in *RMC* and a 10% increase in *LW*, while unfavorable conditions require 250% in *RMC* and 100% in *LW*. Scenario 4 indicates that a 25% increase in *RMC* and a 37% increase in *RND* is effective in neutral conditions, while favorable conditions require 9% and 17% increases, respectively, and unfavorable conditions need 45% and 60% increases. Scenario 5 combines increases in *RMC* (15%), *LW* (13%), *LF* (20%), and *RND* (30%) for neutral conditions, with favorable conditions needing 5%, 4%, 10%, and 14% increases, respectively, and unfavorable conditions requiring 35%, 24%, 50%, and 50% increases. Among these, the fifth scenario is the most balanced and optimized approach, leading to the best improvement in the export capacity across various market conditions.

Table 8. Adjustment analysis results (Source: authors' own work.).

Scenario No.	Market Condition	*RMC* (%)	*LW* (%)	*LF* (%)	*RND* (%)
1	Neutral	* 50%	* 40%	* 325%	* 65%
	Favorable	12%	10%	-	-
	Unfavorable	105%	84%	-	-
2	Neutral	25%	20%	-	-
	Favorable	7%	4%	-	-
	Unfavorable	45%	50%	-	-

Table 8. *Cont.*

Scenario No.	Market Condition	*RMC (%)*	*LW (%)*	*LF (%)*	*RND (%)*
3	Neutral	-	40%	100%	-
	Favorable	-	10%	26%	-
	Unfavorable	-	100%	250%	-
4	Neutral	25%	-	-	37%
	Favorable	9%	-	-	17%
	Unfavorable	45%	-	-	60%
5	Neutral	15%	13%	20%	30%
	Favorable	5%	4&	10%	14%
	Unfavorable	35%	24%	50%	50%

* Refers to adjusting only one variable while keeping the others constant.

5. Discussion

5.1. Analysis of Input Variation Scenarios

The different scenarios of input variation are analyzed in the previous section. The analysis explores the effect of increasing one variable at a time—raw material cost, labor wages, R&D spending, and labor force—while keeping the others constant at different market conditions, to achieve 20% incremental export growth. For example, a manufacturing firm may find increasing raw material cost by 50% feasible if the supply chain is reliable and market demand justifies increased production, though it can burden financial resources and require careful cost management. Under favorable market conditions, a smaller increase of 12% in raw material costs might suffice, while unfavorable conditions could necessitate a steep rise of 105%, significantly impacting financial stability. In labor-intensive industries, increasing labor wages by 40% can improve productivity and exports but may not be workable without corresponding price increases due to fixed wage structures or labor laws. Favorable conditions may only require a 10% increase, whereas unfavorable conditions might force an 84% rise in wages, posing substantial challenges. Increasing R&D spending by 65% can drive significant innovations and export growth, aligning with theories of innovation-driven growth and providing long-term competitive advantages. However, this substantial increase in R&D spending is particularly relevant under neutral market conditions, as specific figures for favorable or unfavorable conditions were not provided. Expanding the labor force by 325% in sectors like manufacturing can increase output but requires effective recruitment and management strategies, with practical measures for training and integrating new workers and supporting labor productivity models. The neutral condition illustrates this significant labor force increase, while details for favorable or unfavorable conditions were not specified in this scenario. However, these scenarios may not be feasible, and further optimization is required to reach practical solutions.

5.2. Proposed Adjustment Models

In the second scenario, the proposed model suggests channeling spending towards raw materials and labor wages while keeping the labor force and R&D expenditures constant under different market conditions. This strategy aims to increase exports through incremental increases in raw material spending and labor wages by 25% and 20%, respectively, under neutral market conditions. Favorable conditions could see these percentages reduced to 7% and 4%, respectively, showing a more manageable financial impact. Unfavorable conditions could see these costs soar to 45% and 50%, highlighting potential challenges in cost management. For instance, increasing raw material spending involves allocating more funds towards acquiring essential resources like metals, chemicals, or agricultural products necessary for production. Similarly, raising labor wages entails paying workers higher wages or offering additional benefits to enhance workforce motivation and productivity. These increases in spending are aimed at achieving a 20% increment in export growth.

In the third scenario, the proposed model suggests directing spending solely towards increasing labor wages and expanding the labor force while keeping raw material expenditures and R&D spending constant under different market conditions. This strategy aims to enhance exports by increasing labor wages and the labor force by 40% and 100%, respectively, under neutral market conditions. Favorable conditions might reduce the increase in labor wages to 10% and the labor force to 26%, while unfavorable conditions could lead to a dramatic increase in labor wages to 100% and the labor force to 250%. Increasing labor wages involves raising the salaries and benefits provided to workers, potentially attracting skilled labor and improving employee satisfaction and retention. Additionally, expanding the labor force entails hiring additional workers to increase production capacity and meet growing demand. These adjustments are also designed to achieve a 20% increment in export growth.

In the fourth scenario, the proposed model suggests focusing spending on raw materials and R&D while keeping labor wages and the labor force constant under different market conditions. This strategy aims to raise exports by increasing raw material expenditure and R&D investments by 25% and 37%, respectively, under neutral market conditions. Favorable conditions might see these increases reduced to 9% for raw material costs and 17% for R&D spending, while unfavorable conditions could see these percentages jump to 45% and 60%, respectively. Increasing raw material spending involves allocating more resources towards acquiring essential materials like metals, chemicals, or agricultural products necessary for production. Simultaneously, increasing R&D spending requires allocating additional funds towards research activities aimed at improving product design, innovation, efficiency, and quality. These spending increases are intended to drive a 20% increment in export growth.

In the last scenario, after conducting a comprehensive analysis of all variables together, it is observed that to incrementally increase export amounts by 20%, specific adjustments in spending are required under different market conditions. Raw material, labor wages, labor force, and R&D spending should each be increased by 15%, 13%, 20%, and 30%, respectively, under neutral market conditions to achieve the same export increment. For instance, a 15% increase in raw material spending involves allocating an additional portion of the budget towards procuring essential resources crucial for production. Similarly, a 13% increase in labor wages leads to raising salaries and benefits, potentially improving employee morale and productivity. In parallel, a 20% increase in the labor force necessitates hiring additional labor to expand production capacity. Finally, a 30% increase in R&D spending involves allocating more resources towards research activities aimed at innovation and product improvement. In favorable conditions, these percentages might be reduced to 5% for raw material costs, 4% for labor wages, 10% for labor force, and 14% for R&D spending. However, unfavorable conditions could lead to increases to 35% for raw material costs, 24% for labor wages, 50% for labor force, and 50% for R&D spending, demonstrating significant financial and operational challenges. These adjustments are targeted to achieve a 20% increment in export growth.

These scenarios highlight the complexities of managing input variations under different market conditions and underscore the importance of strategic planning and optimization to achieve practical and sustainable growth solutions.

5.3. Consistency with the Existing Literature

The above results reveal consistency and complementarity with the existing literature. For example, our findings complement those of Rognes (2023), confirming that the efficient sourcing of raw materials enables firms to achieve substantial cost savings through strategies like negotiating better terms with suppliers, opting for bulk purchasing, and exploring alternative sources. We stress that pricing adjustment plays a pivotal role in enhancing export capacity, necessitating strategic considerations such as focusing on strategic raw material selection and conducting thorough market research to understand consumer needs and competitor pricing (Aharoni 2024; Teerasoponpong and Sopadang 2022; Dethine et al. 2020; Hool et al. 2022; Shabbir and Wisdom 2020). Similarly, our findings support the results concluded by other scholars that investing in skilled labor is identified as essential for maintaining high productivity and quality standards, with strategies like encouraging a positive work environment, providing career growth opportunities, and offering competitive wages and benefits packages being crucial (Salimova et al. 2022; Phan 2022; Al-Harthy et al. 2022; Huang et al. 2021). Our results also confirm the findings by other studies, underlining the vital role of R&D in enhancing production capacity and product quality, with investments in R&D facilitating innovation, understanding customer preferences, and improving product competitiveness (Edeh et al. 2020; Naradda Gamage et al. 2020). Our study not only adds empirical evidence to the existing literature and studies by analyzing different scenarios of input variation in production and their impact on export growth but also offers new insights on how specific adjustments in spending can help in realizing the potential export targets.

5.4. Theoretical Alignment

Conceptually, our findings are closely aligned with the theoretical foundations of the comparative advantage theory, the Heckscher–Ohlin model, and the resource-based theory in building export capacity. For example, the call for specialization in producing goods and services that the firm or the country has a comparative advantage in is clearly observed in this study, as we strategically adjusted spending on raw materials, labor wages, R&D, and the labor force to make the best use of resources and become more competitive in export markets. Similarly, our findings do not differ considerably from the assumption of the Heckscher–Ohlin model that countries or firms should export goods that make good use of their many resources such as skilled labor or natural resources, while our study focuses on adjusting labor force and raw material spending and aims to use resources wisely to improve export capacity. As the resource-based theory focuses on using internal resources effectively, our study stresses the importance of increasing R&D spending to drive innovation and improve product quality. Thus, our study not only matches these theoretical ideas but also offers new insights and practical means on how specific changes in different spending channels can increase exports, making these theoretical concepts more understandable and offering useful strategies for building export capacity.

5.5. Policy and Practical Implications

In terms of policy and practical implications, the analysis of various scenarios of input variation in this study highlights the critical role of strategic decisions in optimizing resource allocation to drive export growth. Policymakers can benefit from evidence-based research that enables them to focus on specific measures aimed at building export capacity. Governments can create policies tailored to support industries in accessing essential resources at competitive prices, hence improving production efficiency. Policymakers may consider measures such as reducing taxes on imported raw materials, making supply chains more efficient, and promoting exchange programs to enhance the skills and experiences of the labor force. The successful implementation of these measures can effectively reduce production costs, especially in industries that heavily rely on materials like steel, cement, or plastics, thereby improving firms' competitiveness in international markets. By creating an environment that encourages the use of innovation and technology, policymakers can empower firms to improve their export capacity through efficient resource utilization.

Firm executives and industry practitioners can also benefit from our findings in terms of optimizing resource allocation to maximize export growth while ensuring efficient cost management. They can optimize raw material costs to increase the cost capacity and hence build export capacity by investing in building factories that provide raw materials at target costs, establishing facilities that produce essential resources in-house, or through strategic partnerships with suppliers to stabilize costs and reduce reliance on external market fluctuations. They can also utilize R&D and innovation to manage and optimize their labor force effectively by investing in automation technologies and robotics to streamline production processes and reduce dependency on manual labor. By automating repetitive tasks and reallocating human resources to more value-added activities, firms can improve productivity and output quality while minimizing labor costs. In manufacturing, where labor wages constitute a significant portion of production costs, firms can address high wages by implementing performance-based incentive programs or profit-sharing schemes to align employee interests with firm goals and enhance productivity. This challenge can also be addressed by investing in technology-driven solutions such as AI-powered workforce management systems or remote work platforms that help optimize labor utilization and reduce overhead expenses, thereby improving export competitiveness.

6. Conclusions

This study explained the importance of factor cost adjustment in enhancing the export-oriented production capacity of manufacturing firms. More specifically, it examined in detail the impact of raw material costs, labor force, labor wages, and R&D spending on firms' export capacity using multiple regression analysis. It also highlighted the critical role of cost components in shaping firms' global expansion strategies when it comes to the export of manufactured goods and services. This study explained the importance of factor cost adjustment in enhancing the export-oriented production capacity of manufacturing firms. More specifically, it examined in detail the impact of raw material costs, labor force, labor wages, and R&D spending on firms' export-oriented production capacity using multiple regression analysis. It also highlighted the critical role of cost components in shaping firms' global expansion strategies when it comes to the export of manufactured goods and services. The empirical investigation revealed significant relationships between these cost factors and the export-oriented production capacity, with all the variables showing considerable impacts. The analysis highlighted that adjusting these cost components could directly enhance industrial output and improve the export-oriented production capacity. This study also demonstrated the significant impact of market conditions on these relationships, showing that market conditions moderate the effects of raw material costs and labor wages on the export-oriented production capacity. This emphasizes the importance of considering market conditions in the model to accurately reflect their influence. This study provides a foundational framework and proposed model for understanding and enhancing firms' export-oriented production capacities by effectively managing key variables and adapting strategies according to market conditions.

Moreover, our findings offer empirical validation and practical insights that extend beyond the theories of comparative advantage, the Heckscher–Ohlin model, and the resource-based theory. Specifically, while these theories outline the general principles of resource allocation and comparative advantage, our study determined specific adjustments in spending—on raw materials, labor wages and force, and R&D—to adjust the export-oriented production capacity. This study also offers practical implications for decisionmakers at the country and firm levels to instigate strategic decisions to adjust resource allocation for driving export growth. While policymakers are urged to design tailored policies supporting industries in accessing essential resources at competitive prices to increase production efficiency, firm executives should focus primarily on strategic spending decisions to effectively encourage export growth.

7. Study Limitations and Recommendations for Future Work

Finally, we acknowledge the limitations of our study that focused on a one-sector (manufacturing) one-country (Oman) case study and a short period of five years. We suggest further investigation to cover the long-term effects of cost adjustment strategies on export growth, considering dynamic market conditions and other external factors that impact firm performance. Further investigation into sector-specific challenges and opportunities beyond manufacturing can provide tailored insights for different industries.

While focusing mainly on internal factors affecting export performance within the manufacturing sector in Oman, we recognize the influence of external factors, such as international market demand, on exports. Future research should integrate these external factors, including market conditions, to provide a fuller picture of how both internal and external variables impact export performance. Future research could also account for the time lag between R&D expenditures and their impact on export performance by incorporating the delayed effects of R&D investments and considering external factors such as export flows and market demand to provide a more comprehensive analysis of export growth dynamics. As this study relies more on aggregate macro-economic data that may not capture the specific micro-economic challenges and opportunities faced by individual firms, we recommend further research that incorporates detailed micro-economic data to provide a more nuanced understanding of company-specific dynamics.

Author Contributions: Conceptualization, A.M. and M.A.H.; methodology, A.M. and M.A.H.; software, M.A.H.; validation, A.M. and M.A.H.; formal analysis, A.M. and M.A.H.; investigation, A.M. and M.M; resources, A.M.; data curation, A.M. and M.A.H.; writing—original draft preparation, A.M. and M.A.H.; writing—review and editing, A.M.; visualization, A.M. and M.A.H.; supervision, A.M.; project administration, A.M.; funding acquisition, A.M. All authors have read and agreed to the published version of the manuscript.

Funding: This research was funded by [His Majesty's Trust Fund] grant number [SR/DVD/HURC/20.01] and the APC was funded by [Chair/DVC/HURC/19/01].

Institutional Review Board Statement: The study was conducted in accordance with the Declaration of Helsinki and approved by the Institutional Review Board of Sultan Qaboos University.

Informed Consent Statement: Written informed consent has been obtained from the participants to publish this paper.

Data Availability Statement: Data is available on request.

Conflicts of Interest: The authors declare no conflict of interest.

References

Adegbola, Ayodeji Enoch, Mayokun Daniel Adegbola, Prisca Amajuoyi, Lucky Bamidele Benjamin, and Kudirat Bukola Adeusi. 2024. Advanced financial modeling techniques for reducing inventory costs: A review of strategies and their effectiveness in manufacturing. *Finance & Accounting Research Journal* 6: 801–24.

Aghazadeh, Hesham, Elham Beheshti Jazan Abadi, and Farzad Zandi. 2022. Branding advantage of agri-food companies in competitive export markets: A resource-based theory. *British Food Journal* 124: 2039–60. [CrossRef]

Aharoni, Yair. 2024. *O 2024 World Scientific Publishing Company. Standing On the Shoulders of International Business Giants: In Memory of Yair Aharoni*. Singapore: World Scientific, vol. 1, p. 345.

Al-Harthy, Bushra, Rosmelisa Yusof, and Anees Janee Ali. 2022. A Conceptual Paper on Compensation and Benefits, Job Security, Work-Life Balance, Employee Retention and Localization in Oman. *Global Business & Management Research* 14: 688–710.

Allioui, Hanane, and Youssef Mourdi. 2023. Exploring the full potential of IoT for better financial growth and stability: A comprehensive survey. *Sensors* 23: 8015. [CrossRef] [PubMed]

Amit, Raphael, Lawrence Glosten, and Eitan Muller. 2022. Entrepreneurial ability, venture investments, and risk sharing. In *Venture Capital*. Abingdon: Routledge, pp. 135–48.

Azar, Jose, E. Huet-Vaughn, Ioana Marinescu, Bledi Taska, and Till von Wachter. 2024. Minimum wage employment effects and labour market concentration. *Review of Economic Studies* 91: 1843–83. [CrossRef]

Babayev, Farid, and Tahmina Balajayeva. 2023. Ways of Increasing the Competitiveness of Food Industry Enterprises. *International Journal of Innovative Technologies in Economy* 4: 44. [CrossRef]

Bhuyan, Md. Iqbal, and Keun Yeob Oh. 2021. Exports and inequality: Evidence from the highly concentrated textile and garment sector of Bangladesh. *Journal of South Asian Development* 16: 293–309. [CrossRef]

Castro-Silva, Hugo, and Francisco Lima. 2023. The struggle of small firms to retain high-skill workers: Job duration and the importance of knowledge intensity. *Small Business Economics* 60: 537–72. [CrossRef]

Chandra, Ashna, Justin Paul, and Meena Chavan. 2020. Internationalization challenges for SMEs: Evidence and theoretical extension. *European Business Review* 33: 316–44. [CrossRef]

Chandra, Shapan, and Jannatul Ferdaus. 2020. Contribution of ready-made garments industry on the economic development of Bangladesh: An empirical analysis. *Economics* 7: 295–307.

Charoenrat, Teerawat, and Yot Amornkitvikai. 2021. Factors affecting the export intensity of Chinese manufacturing firms. *Global Business Review* 25: 957–980. [CrossRef]

Davcik, Nebojsa S., Silvio Cardinali, Piyush Sharma, and Elena Cedrola. 2021. Exploring the role of international R&D activities in the impact of technological and marketing capabilities on SMEs' performance. *Journal of Business Research* 128: 650–60.

Dethine, Benjamin, Manon Enjolras, and Davy Monticolo. 2020. Digitalization and SMEs' export management: Impacts on resources and capabilities. *Technology Innovation Management Review* 10: 18–34. [CrossRef]

Edeh, Jude Ndubuisi, Divine Ndubuisi Obodoechi, and Encarnacion Ramos-Hidalgo. 2020. Effects of innovation strategies on export performance: New empirical evidence from developing market firms. *Technological Forecasting and Social Change* 158: 120167. [CrossRef]

Eeckhout, Jan. 2022. *The Profit Paradox: How Thriving Firms Threaten the Future of Work*. Princeton: Princeton University Press.

Ewers, Michael C., Nabil Khattab, Zahra Babar, and Muznah Madeeha. 2022. Skilled migration to emerging economies: The global competition for talent beyond the West. *Globalizations* 19: 268–84. [CrossRef]

Feng, Bing, Kaiyang Sun, Min Chen, and Tao Gao. 2020. The impact of core technological capabilities of high-tech industry on sustainable competitive advantage. *Sustainability* 12: 2980. [CrossRef]

Fröhlich, Hans-Peter. 2023. International competitiveness: Alternative macroeconomic strategies and changing perceptions in recent years. In *The Competitiveness of European Industry*. Abingdon: Routledge, pp. 21–40.

Gallego, Juan Miguel, and Luis H. Gutiérrez Ramírez. 2023. Quality certification and firm performance. The mediation of human capital. *International Journal of Productivity and Performance Management* 72: 710–29. [CrossRef]

Giri, Amit K., and S. P. Singh. 2022. India's hand-knotted carpet industry in reforms era: Export performances and challenges. *International Journal of Business and Globalisation* 31: 17–35. [CrossRef]

Grossman, Gene M., and Ezra Oberfield. 2022. The elusive explanation for the declining labor share. *Annual Review of Economics* 14: 93–124. [CrossRef]

Gupta, Parul, and Sumedha Chauhan. 2021. Firm capabilities and export performance of small firms: A meta-analytical review. *European Management Journal* 39: 558–76. [CrossRef]

Hegab, Hussien, Ibrahim Shaban, Muhammad Jamil, and Navneet Khanna. 2023. Toward sustainable future: Strategies, indicators, and challenges for implementing sustainable production systems. *Sustainable Materials and Technologies* 36: e00617. [CrossRef]

Hool, Alessandra, Dieuwertje Schrijvers, Sander van Nielen, Andrew Clifton, Sophia Ganzeboom, Christian Hagelueken, and Yasushi Harada. 2022. How companies improve critical raw material circularity: 5 use cases: Findings from the International Round Table on Materials Criticality. *Mineral Economics* 35: 325–35. [CrossRef]

Hoque, Mohammad Tayeenul, Prithwiraj Nath, Mohammad Faisal Ahammad, Nikolaos Tzokas, and Nick Yip. 2022. Constituents of dynamic marketing capability: Strategic fit and heterogeneity in export performance. *Journal of Business Research* 144: 1007–23. [CrossRef]

Hossain, Kamal, Kenny Cheah Soon Lee, Ilhaamie Binti Abdul Ghani Azmi, Aida Binti Idris, Mohammad Nurul Alam, Md Adnan Rahman, and Norinah Mohd Ali. 2022. Impact of innovativeness, risk-taking, and proactiveness on export performance in a developing country: Evidence of qualitative study. *RAUSP Management Journal* 57: 165–81. [CrossRef]

Huang, Yi, Liugang Sheng, and Gewei Wang. 2021. How did rising labor costs erode China's global advantage? *Journal of Economic Behavior & Organization* 183: 632–53.

Joel, Olorunyomi Stephen, Adedoyin Tolulope Oyewole, Olusegun Gbenga Odunaiya, and Oluwatobi Timothy Soyombo. 2024. The impact of digital transformation on business development strategies: Trends, challenges, and opportunities analyzed. *World Journal of Advanced Research and Reviews* 21: 617–24. [CrossRef]

Kanike, Uday Kumar. 2023. Factors disrupting supply chain management in manufacturing industries. *Journal of Supply Chain Management Science* 4: 1–24. [CrossRef]

Kaplinsky, Raphael, and Erika Kraemer-Mbula. 2022. Innovation and uneven development: The challenge for low-and middle-income economies. *Research Policy* 51: 104394. [CrossRef]

Keskin, Halit, Hayat Ayar Şentürk, Ekrem Tatoglu, Ismail Gölgeci, Ozan Kalaycioglu, and Hatice Tuba Etlioglu. 2021. The simultaneous effect of firm capabilities and competitive strategies on export performance: The role of competitive advantages and competitive intensity. *International Marketing Review* 38: 1242–66. [CrossRef]

Lima, Maria Cecília Costa, Luana Pereira Pontes, Andrea Sarmento Maia Vasconcelos, Washington de Araujo Silva Junior, and Kunlin Wu. 2022. Economic aspects for recycling of used lithium-ion batteries from electric vehicles. *Energies* 15: 2203. [CrossRef]

Liu, Yue, Zhenghui Li, and Manrui Xu. 2020. The influential factors of financial cycle spillover: Evidence from China. *Emerging Markets Finance and Trade* 56: 1336–50. [CrossRef]

Ma, Jin-Hee, and Young-Hyo Ahn. 2021. Location efficiencies of host countries for strategic offshoring decisions amid wealth creation opportunities and supply chain risks. *Journal of Korea Trade* 25: 21–47. [CrossRef]

Mansion, Stephanie E., and Andreas Bausch. 2020. Intangible assets and SMEs' export behavior: A meta-analytical perspective. *Small Business Economics* 55: 727–60. [CrossRef]

Matezo, Espoir Lukau, and Boaz Mingiedi Matondo. 2022. The effect of COVID-19 on international trade: Evidence from Sub-Saharan Africa. *American Journal of Industrial and Business Management* 12: 73–87. [CrossRef]

Matzner, Anna, Birgit Meyer, and Harald Oberhofer. 2023. Trade in times of uncertainty. *The World Economy* 46: 2564–97. [CrossRef]

Naradda Gamage, Sisira Kumara, E. M. S. Ekanayake, G. A. K. N. J. Abeyrathne, R. P. I. R. Prasanna, J. M. S. B. Jayasundara, and P. S. K. Rajapakshe. 2020. A review of global challenges and survival strategies of small and medium enterprises (SMEs). *Economies* 8: 79. [CrossRef]

Ninduwezuor-Ehiobu, Nwakamma, Olawe Alaba Tula, Chibuike Daraojimba, Kelechi Anthony Ofonagoro, Oluwaseun Ayo Ogunjobi, Joachim Osheyor Gidiagba, Blessed Afeyokalo Egbokhaebho, and Adeyinka Alex Banso. 2023. Exploring innovative material integration in modern manufacturing for advancing us competitiveness in sustainable global economy. *Engineering Science & Technology Journal* 4: 140–68.

Nyu, Valeria, Frode Nilssen, and Destan Kandemir. 2022. Small exporting firms' choice of exchange mode in international marketing channels for perishable products: A contingency approach. *International Business Review* 31: 101919. [CrossRef]

Oliinyk, Olena, Yuriy Bilan, Halyna Mishchuk, Oleksandr Akimov, and Laszlo Vasa. 2021. The impact of migration of highly skilled workers on the country's competitiveness and economic growth. *Montenegrin Journal of Economics* 17: 7–19. [CrossRef]

Ortigueira-Sánchez, Luis Camilo, Dianne H. B. Welsh, and William C. Stein. 2022. Innovation drivers for export performance. *Sustainable Technology and Entrepreneurship* 1: 100013. [CrossRef]

Ozkan-Ozen, Yesim Deniz, and Yigit Kazancoglu. 2022. Analysing workforce development challenges in the Industry 4.0. *International Journal of Manpower* 43: 310–33. [CrossRef]

Peters, Bettina, and Mark J. Roberts. 2022. Firm R&D investment and export market exposure. *Research Policy* 51: 104601.

Phan, Trang. Hoai. 2022. Working conditions, export decisions, and firm constraints-evidence from Vietnamese small and medium enterprises. *Sustainability* 14: 7541. [CrossRef]

Pholphirul, P., T. Charoenrat, A. Kwanyou, P. Rukumnuaykit, and K. Srijamdee. 2020. Measuring smiling curves in community enterprises: Evidence from the one tambon one product entrepreneurship programme in border Thailand. *Global Business Review* 25: 349–76. [CrossRef]

Pylaeva, Irina S., Mariya V. Podshivalova, Andrew Adewale Alola, Dmitrii V. Podshivalov, and Alexander A. Demin. 2022. A new approach to identifying high-tech manufacturing SMEs with sustainable technological development: Empirical evidence. *Journal of Cleaner Production* 363: 132322. [CrossRef]

Rezazadeh, Javad, Ruhollah Bagheri, Shabana Karimi, Javad Nazarian-Jashnabadi, and Mahmoud Zahedian Nezhad. 2023. Examining the impact of product innovation and pricing capability on the international performance of exporting companies with the mediating role of competitive advantage for analysis and decision making. *Journal of Operations Intelligence* 1: 30–43. [CrossRef]

Rivero-Gutiérrez, Lourdes, Pablo Cabanelas, Francisco Díez-Martín, and Alicia Blanco-González. 2024. How can companies boost legitimacy in international markets? A dynamic marketing capabilities approach. *International Marketing Review* 41: 273–301. [CrossRef]

Rognes, Erlend Mo. 2023. How Can the Purchasing Department of Maritime Companies Improve Efficiency through Supplier Base Reduction and Supplier Development? Bachelor's thesis, NTNU, Trondheim, Norway.

Sadeghi, Arash, Omid Aliasghar, and Abderaouf Bouguerra. 2023. Unpacking the relationship between post-entry speed of internationalization and export performance of SMEs: A capability-building perspective. *Journal of International Management* 29: 100982. [CrossRef]

Saka, Kamilu A., and Yisau I. Bolanle. 2023. Autoregressive distributed lag estimation of bank financing and Nigerian manufacturing sector capacity utilization. *Quantitative Finance and Economics* 7: 74–86. [CrossRef]

Salimova, Guzel, Alisa Ableeva, Aygul Galimova, Ramzilya Bakirova, Tatiana Lubova, Aidar Sharafutdinov, and Irek Araslanbaev. 2022. Recent trends in labor productivity. *Employee Relations: The International Journal* 44: 785–802. [CrossRef]

Sanford, Anthony, and Mu-Jeung Yang. 2022. Corporate investment and growth opportunities: The role of R&D-capital complementarity. *Journal of Corporate Finance* 72: 102130.

Sanyal, Shouvik, Mohammed Wamique Hisam, and Ali Mohsin Salim Baawain. 2020. Challenges facing internationalization of smes in emerging economies: A study on oecd model. *The Journal of Asian Finance, Economics and Business* 7: 281–89. [CrossRef]

Sarwar, Jawad, Awais Ahmed Khan, Arshad Khan, Ali Hasnain, Syed Muhammad Arafat, Hafiz Umar Ali, Ghulam Moeen Uddin, Marcin Sosnowski, and Jaroslaw Krzywanski. 2022. Impact of Stakeholders on Lean Six Sigma Project Costs and Outcomes during Implementation in an Air-Conditioner Manufacturing Industry. *Processes* 10: 2591. [CrossRef]

Shabbir, Malik Shahzad, and Okere Wisdom. 2020. The relationship between corporate social responsibility, environmental investments and financial performance: Evidence from manufacturing companies. *Environmental Science and Pollution Research* 27: 39946–57. [CrossRef] [PubMed]

Shen, Ching-Cheng, Chien-Chi Yeh, and Chun-Nan Lin. 2022. Using the perspective of business information technology technicians to explore how information technology affects business competitive advantage. *Technological Forecasting and Social Change* 184: 121973. [CrossRef]

Siregar, M., A. Lubis, Y. Absah, and P. Gultom. 2024. Increasing the competitive advantage and the performance of SMEs using entrepreneurial marketing architectural innovation capability in North Sumatera, Indonesia. *Uncertain Supply Chain Management* 12: 965–76. [CrossRef]

Sudirjo, Frans. 2023. Marketing Strategy in Improving Product Competitiveness in the Global Market. *Journal of Contemporary Administration and Management (ADMAN)* 1: 63–9. [CrossRef]

Swazan, Ishtehar Sharif, and Debanjan Das. 2022. Bangladesh's emergence as a ready-made garment export leader: An examination of the competitive advantages of the garment industry. *International Journal of Global Business and Competitiveness* 17: 162–74. [CrossRef]

Teerasoponpong, Siravat, and Apichat Sopadang. 2022. Decision support system for adaptive sourcing and inventory management in small-and medium-sized enterprises. *Robotics and Computer-Integrated Manufacturing* 73: 102226. [CrossRef]

Tung, Le Thanh, and Le Nguyen Hoang. 2024. Impact of R&D expenditure on economic growth: Evidence from emerging economies. *Journal of Science and Technology Policy Management* 15: 636–54.

Webber, D. A. 2022. Labor market competition and employment adjustment over the business cycle. *Journal of Human Resources* 57: S87–S110. [CrossRef]

Yao, Xufeng, Nourah Almatooq, Ronald G. Askin, and Greg Gruber. 2022. Capacity planning and production scheduling integration: Improving operational efficiency via detailed modelling. *International Journal of Production Research* 60: 7239–61. [CrossRef]

Zahoor, Nadia, and Yong Kyu Lew. 2023. Enhancing international marketing capability and export performance of emerging market SMEs in crises: Strategic flexibility and digital technologies. *International Marketing Review* 40: 1158–87. [CrossRef]

Zhang, Meng Di, and Mohd Haniff Jedin. 2023. Firm innovation and technical capabilities for enhanced export performance: The moderating role of competitive intensity. *Review of International Business and Strategy* 33: 810–29. [CrossRef]

risks

MDPI

Article

Polynomial Moving Regression Band Stocks Trading System

Gil Cohen

The Management Department, Western Galilee College, Acre 2412101, Israel; gilc@wgalil.ac.il

Abstract: In this research, we attempted to fit a trading system based on polynomial moving regression bands (MRB) to Nasdaq100 stocks from 2017 till the end of March 2024. Since stocks movement does not follow a linear behavior, we used multiple degree polynomial regression models to identify the stocks' trends and two standard deviations from the regression model to generate the trading signals. This way, the MRB was transformed into a momentum indicator designed to identify strong uptrends that can be used by a fully automated trading system. Our results indicate that the behavior of Nasdaq100 stocks can be tracked using all three examined polynomial models and can be traded profitably using fully automated systems based on those models. The best performing model was the model that used a four-degree polynomial MRB achieving the highest average net profit (USD 162.73). Regarding the risks involved, the third model has the lowest loss in dollar value (USD −95.52), and the highest minimum percent of profitable trades (41.51%) and profit factor (0.55) that indicates that this strategy is relatively less risky than the other two strategies.

Keywords: polynomial; trading; stocks; systems

1. Introduction

Predicting stock movements is a crucial area of research in finance and investment. Various studies have explored the use of regression models in forecasting stock prices. Regression models are employed to predict stock price movements, such as the closing price of a stock, based on historical data and other relevant variables. These models can assist investors in decision-making processes like buying, selling, or holding stocks. Different regression techniques have been utilized in stock price prediction. For instance, logistic regression has been used to establish the relationship between daily stock movement and trading volumes over a specific period (Kambeu 2019). Additionally, support vector regression (SVR) and K-nearest neighbor (KNN) regression are popular machine learning techniques applied in stock price prediction (Islam et al. 2021). Moreover, studies have compared the performance of classification models and level estimation models in predicting stock market movements. Classification models like discriminant analysis and neural networks have shown better results in predicting the direction of stock market movements compared to level estimation models like exponential smoothing and multivariate transfer functions (Kara et al. 2011). In the context of stock market prediction, regression models are often combined with other techniques such as deep learning, natural language processing, and ensemble learning to enhance predictive accuracy (Sen and Mehtab 2021). These combinations allow for a more comprehensive analysis of stock price movements and trends.

The moving regression band (MRB) trading system is a technical analysis tool that combines linear regression and moving averages to identify market trends and potential reversal points. It consists of a linear regression line, which represents the direction of the trend, and upper and lower bands plotted at a specified number of standard deviations from the regression line, serving as dynamic support and resistance levels. The system generates trading signals based on the price's position relative to these bands, with a buy signal triggered when the price touches or crosses the lower band in an uptrend. While effective in trend-following and providing clear signals, the system is a lagging indicator and may produce false signals in choppy markets. It is often used in conjunction with other technical analysis tools to enhance its reliability and can be applied to various financial instruments, including stocks, forex, and commodities. The width of the bands also provides information about market volatility, with wider bands indicating higher volatility and narrower bands suggesting lower volatility. Most former research has utilized linear regressions to predict the behavior of financial assets (McMillan 2019; Maroto 2018). De Luna (1998) was one of the first to use polynomial regression to predict three-month U.S. Treasury bills yields. Following his pioneering research, we make the first attempt to construct polynomial MRB trading systems and tested their performances upon Nasdaq100 stocks. Two, three, and four degrees of polynomial MRB were used to identify the daily behavior of those stocks and to determine the goodness of fit of each model to real data. No past research has used this methodology, and such an attempt contributes to the understanding of technological stocks' behavior.

2. Literature Review

Algorithmic trading systems have attracted significant attention in recent years, with a growing body of literature exploring various aspects of this field. Researchers have delved into the competitive advantage in algorithmic trading, emphasizing the behavioral innovation economics approach and providing insights into the motivations driving these market actors. Research has shown that algorithmic trading can indeed enhance liquidity in markets (Hendershott and Riordan 2011; Frino et al. 2021). Moreover, algorithmic trading has been found to contribute more to price discovery than human trades in specific markets (Benos and Sagade 2016). The integration of machine learning and artificial intelligence into algorithmic trading strategies has been increasing, providing opportunities for superior growth and competitive advantage (Burgess 2022). These technologies facilitate the development of dynamic trading strategies that can adjust to changing market conditions (Aloud and Alkhamees 2021). Additionally, the utilization of sophisticated algorithms in trading systems can automate various aspects of the trade cycle, thereby enhancing efficiency and potentially improving trading performance (Treleaven et al. 2013).

Cooper et al. (2022) provide insights into the competitive advantage in algorithmic trading, emphasizing the behavioral innovation economics approach. They highlight the strategic behavior of algorithmic trading firms, shedding light on the motivations driving these market actors. Furthermore, Currie and Seddon (2017) delve into the regulatory, technological, and market aspects of high-frequency trading, outlining a research agenda to address the challenges in this domain. Huang et al. (2019) reviewed automated trading systems, focusing on statistical and machine learning methods and hardware implementations. They categorize trading systems based on technical and textual analyses, as well as high-frequency trading methods. The development of algorithmic trading strategies is explored by Cliff (2018), who discusses benchmark algorithms commonly used in evaluating new trading strategies. Zhu (2022) surveys recent advances in financial trading systems based on reinforcement learning, emphasizing design strategies such as Q-learning and actor–critic algorithms. Ozturk et al. (2016) present a heuristic-based trading system for Forex data, incorporating technical indicator rules and machine learning methods like genetic algorithms. Zhang and Khushi (2020) introduce a genetic algorithm maximizing the Sharpe and Sterling ratio method for Robo Trading in the forex market, emphasizing the role of technical analysis in algorithmic trading strategies.

Past research has attempted to fit a non-linear model to stock movements. A polynomial regression offers a flexible approach to modeling non-linear relationships in stock price movements. By fitting a polynomial equation to historical stock data, analysts can capture intricate patterns that linear models may overlook. Researchers have integrated sentiment analysis into their polynomial regression models to enhance predictive power. Chavarnakul and Enke (2008) demonstrated the use of polynomial regression in modeling stock price movements, showing that it can capture the cyclical patterns often observed in financial markets. By fitting a polynomial curve to historical price data, analysts can identify underlying trends that are not apparent with linear models. However, a significant challenge with polynomial regression is the risk of overfitting, especially when using higher-degree polynomials. Overfitting occurs when a model is too closely tailored to the training data, which can reduce its predictive power on new data. Kim and Won (2018) proposed a hybrid model that combines linear regression with polynomial terms to forecast stock returns, effectively capturing both linear and non-linear patterns in the data. Despite the improved performance of hybrid models, challenges remain. Both polynomial and hybrid models are susceptible to overfitting, which can be mitigated through techniques such as cross-validation, regularization, and model pruning (Huang et al. 2005).

The literature also indicates that hybrid models can outperform traditional methods in terms of prediction accuracy. Ayyıldız (2023) highlighted that machine learning methods, including hybrid approaches, are more advantageous for predicting stock market index movements compared to conventional statistical methods. This sentiment is echoed by Rather (2014), who proposed a hybrid intelligent method that combines linear regression with recurrent neural networks, demonstrating reduced prediction errors through non-linear processing. Hybrid regression analysis combines traditional statistical methods with machine learning techniques to leverage the strengths of both paradigms. For instance, Zhao and Chen (2021) introduced a novel hybrid deep learning model that integrates the autoregressive integrated moving average (ARIMA) model with convolutional neural networks (CNNs) and sequence-to-sequence long short-term memory (LSTM) networks. This model effectively captures both linear and non-linear components of stock price movements, showcasing the efficacy of hybrid approaches in financial forecasting. Srijiranon et al. (2022) developed a hybrid model combining principal component analysis (PCA), empirical mode decomposition (EMD), and LSTM to predict stock prices, highlighting the versatility of hybrid frameworks in addressing the complexities of financial time series data.

3. Methodologies and Results

3.1. Data and Methodologies

In this research, we are exploring whether we can fit polynomial models to stock price data in a way that allows us to build a profitable trading system based on those models. Our goal is to determine if these mathematical models can accurately capture stock price movements to make successful trading decisions. By using polynomial models, particularly those of lower degrees to avoid overfitting, we aim to predict future price trends and develop strategies that lead to profitable trades in the stock market. Our data contains daily price information (open, close, highest, and lowest) of Nasdaq100 stocks from 2017 till the end of March 2024. Our sample period covers uptrends and downtrends in the stock market that enable our system to be tested under various economic conditions. We used two-, three-, and four-degree polynomial regression models to identify the stocks' daily movement and two standard deviations from the regression model to generate the trading signals. We aimed to make our stock market predictions more reliable by preventing overfitting, which happens when a model learns the training data too well and performs poorly on new data. To achieve this, we used polynomial models with lower degrees because higher-degree polynomials can capture noise instead of the actual trend, leading to unnecessary complexity. During training, we implemented early stopping by monitoring the model's performance on a separate validation dataset and halting the process if the performance started to decline, preventing the model from becoming too tailored to the training data. We conducted a random search to find the best balance between complexity and performance, testing polynomials of various degrees (like 5 and 6) and adjusting the number of standard deviations used to create trading bands. Before settling on the optimal setup, we applied various trading strategies to identify which one maximized profit. Additionally, we introduced trading bands by adding and subtracting two standard deviations from the fitting line, allowing the model to be more flexible and less strict in fitting the data exactly, which helps reduce overfitting. By using simpler models, stopping training at the right time, exploring different settings, and testing various strategies—we developed models that perform better on new, unseen data, making our stock market predictions more generalizable and reliable.

A buy signal is generated when the price crosses the upper band to the upside, and an exit trade signal is generated when prices cross the lower band to the downside. By amending the system this way, the MRB is transformed into a classic momentum indicator designed to identify strong uptrends. The models, including the upper and lower bands, are described in Models 1 to 3, and the fully designed system is illustrated in Figure 1.

$$Y = \beta_0 + \beta_1 X + \beta_2 X^2 \pm 2S \tag{1}$$

$$Y = \beta_0 + \beta_1 X + \beta_2 X^2 + \beta_3 X^3 \pm 2S \tag{2}$$

$$Y = \beta_0 + \beta_1 X + \beta_2 X^2 + \beta_3 X^3 + \beta_4 X^4 \pm 2S \tag{3}$$

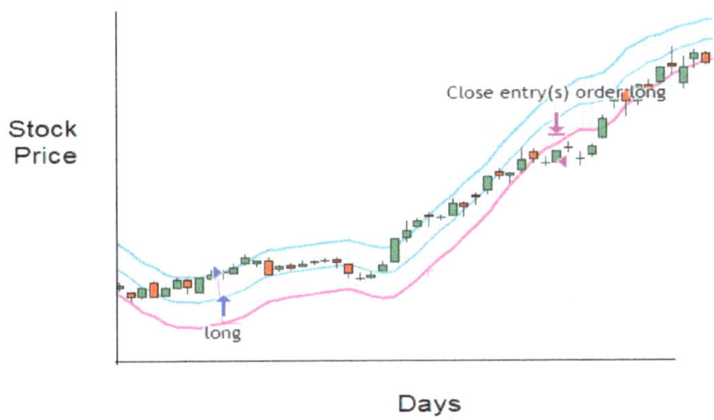

Figure 1. The trading system design. Note: The green and red bars represent daily bars that symbolize the daily upper and lower price, respectively.

As shown in Figure 1, our trading system operates based on the stock's closing price in relation to predefined bands. When the stock's closing price crosses above the upper band, the system purchases the stock at the opening price on the next trading day, initiating a long position (meaning we own the stock with the expectation that its price will rise). Conversely, when the closing price touches the lower band, the system sells the stock at the opening price on the following day, closing the long position. We account for a 0.3% commission fee on every buy or sell transaction, and all the reported results include these transaction costs. Our system is also designed to analyze the trading results using real-time data and includes the following items: net profit in dollars (NP), which is the total NP of all closed trades; percent of profitable trades (PP), which is the percent of the profitable trades out of the total amount of trades; profit factor (PF), which is the division of the gross profits by gross losses; total closed trades (TCTs), which is the total number of closed trades within the examined period; and average days in a single trade (ADT), which represents the average number of days in a single trade.

3.2. Results

Table 1 summarizes the trading results of our trading system based on a two-degree polynomial regression (MRB).

Table 1. Results of the trading system based on two degrees. Polynomial moving regression band.

	Ticker	NP	PP (%)	PF	TCT	ADT
1	AAPL	110.1	64.29	3.48	28	31
2	ABNB	−59.28	42.86	0.56	14	27
3	ADBE	−15.41	43.33	0.96	30	26
4	ADI	39.81	63.33	1.39	30	31
5	ADP	173.58	55.17	2.53	29	34
6	ADSK	178.10	50.00	2.11	26	31
7	AEP	69.29	73.08	3.53	26	35
8	AMAT	2.18	40.63	1.02	32	29
9	AMD	64.23	53.33	1.59	30	31
10	AMGN	86.39	55.17	1.48	29	29
11	AMZN	67.70	55.56	1.90	27	40
12	ANSS	69.88	58.62	1.29	29	31
13	ASML	183.05	57.14	1.33	28	31
14	AVGO	139.03	56.67	1.28	30	29
15	AZN	39.06	59.26	2.36	27	36
16	BIIB	−269.62	36.67	0.46	30	30
17	BKNG	−45.20	38.89	0.98	36	26
18	BKR	16.55	57.69	1.53	26	35
19	CCEP	24.18	51.72	1.78	29	34
20	CDNS	75.91	59.38	2.14	32	28
21	CDW	91.25	61.29	1.84	31	28
22	CEG	70.37	62.50	4.42	15	36
23	CHTR	−4.43	42.86	0.99	29	31
24	CMCSA	−7.62	37.04	0.78	27	29
25	COST	323.67	60.00	2.70	25	41
26	CPRT	19.52	62.5	1.79	32	30
27	CRWD	130.48	50.00	1.92	18	32
28	CSCO	19.42	70.37	1.60	27	35
29	CSGP	−0.86	51.85	0.98	27	29
30	CSX	27.58	67.86	2.90	28	31
31	CTAS	252.56	59.29	2.88	27	32
32	CTSH	46.39	65.38	2.32	26	39
33	DASH	−80.72	41.67	0.44	12	29
34	DDOG	26.95	42.861	1.31	14	31
35	DLTR	99.20	55.56	2.25	27	35
36	DXCM	63.23	51.85	1.82	27	31
37	EA	5.46	51.72	1.05	29	27
38	EXC	7.44	53.33	1.34	30	31
39	FANG	−75.79	37.50	0.64	32	25
40	FAST	47.00	68.97	3.54	29	31

Table 1. *Cont.*

	Ticker	NP	PP (%)	PF	TCT	ADT
41	FTNT	6.19	50.00	1.13	28	29
42	GEHC	−8.83	20.00	0.41	5	25
43	GILD	−17.62	34.48	0.76	29	27
44	GOOG	40.52	55.56	1.95	27	23
45	GOOGL	48.77	64.00	2.17	25	36
46	HON	65.61	45.16	1.51	31	29
47	IDXX	279.48	50.00	1.78	30	29
48	ILMN	38.37	48.15	1.09	27	35
49	INTC	−13.48	38.71	0.80	31	30
50	INTU	324.90	53.33	2.31	30	34
51	ISRG	182.64	66.67	1.95	27	33
52	KDP	15.57	45.83	2.41	24	41
53	KHC	−22.75	41.94	0.62	31	31
54	KLAC	191.63	42.42	1.57	33	28
55	LIN	235.42	62.07	3.11	29	29
56	LRCX	184.44	44.83	1.32	29	30
57	LULU	307.57	60.71	2.55	28	35
58	MAR	124.16	60.00	2.60	30	32
59	MCHP	19.86	55.17	1.33	29	31
60	MDB	75.85	58.33	1.18	24	34
61	MDLZ	15.38	48.39	1.45	31	30
62	MELI	258.84	50.00	1.16	32	26
63	META	228.30	48.28	1.93	29	32
64	MNST	32.25	61.54	2.78	26	33
65	MRNA	72.20	38.89	1.22	18	41
66	MRVL	−27.51	36.36	0.68	33	27
67	MSFT	86.64	47.06	1.55	34	31
68	MU	−10.77	51.72	0.88	29	29
69	NFLX	224.49	58.62	1.57	29	31
70	NVDA	390.65	64.00	3.13	25	38
71	NXPI	−6.29	48.57	0.96	35	27
72	ODFL	150.43	70.37	4.80	27	35
73	ON	26.62	51.85	1.62	27	31
74	ORLY	553.29	55.56	3.13	27	38
75	PANW	178.34	62.07	2.86	29	33
76	PAYX	33.41	58.06	1.50	31	28
77	PCAR	65.90	53.33	2.77	30	35
78	PDD	−21.28	52.38	0.85	21	33
79	PEP	86.77	59.26	2.58	27	33
80	PYPL	5.64	46.15	1.04	26	39

Table 1. *Cont.*

	Ticker	NP	PP (%)	PF	TCT	ADT
81	QCOM	12.61	50.00	1.10	28	31
82	REGN	273.00	50.00	1.69	28	33
83	ROP	281.21	65.38	2.31	26	33
84	ROST	112.74	58.62	4.13	29	33
85	SBUX	44.83	64.29	1.74	28	32
86	SIRI	4.03	53.85	1.96	26	33
87	SNPS	181.38	61.29	2.44	31	31
88	TEAM	−77.63	62.07	0.79	29	32
89	TMUS	12.53	38.71	1.15	31	29
90	TSLA	321.38	57.69	2.28	26	36
91	TTD	1.60	51.72	1.02	29	29
92	TTWO	16.55	46.67	1.09	30	31
93	TXN	−13.30	48.39	0.90	31	30
94	VRSK	113.47	50.00	2.38	28	28
95	VRTX	32.30	51.52	1.13	33	27
96	WBA	−53.22	33.33	0.37	30	31
97	WBD	19.40	41.38	1.54	29	27
98	WDAY	100.50	51.85	1.68	27	32
99	XEL	42.86	73.08	2.55	26	38
100	ZS	108.86	52.38	1.69	21	35
AV		79.67	52.89	1.76	27.59	31.59
ST.D		117.73	9.75	0.89	4.70	3.72
Max		553.29	73.08	4.80	36	41
Min		−269.62	20.00	0.37	5	23

Notes: AV = average, ST.D = standard deviation, NP = net profit, PP = percent of profitable trades, PF = profit factor, TCT = total closed trades, ADT = average days of trade. The results include 0.3% transaction costs for every trade.

The trading results of our system based on a two-degree polynomial regression (MRB) show that the average net profit (NP) generated was USD 79.67, with a percent of profitable trades (PP) of 52.89% and a profit factor (PF) of 1.76. The average days in trade (ADT) was 31.59, and the total closed trades (TCTs) was 27.59. These results indicate that the trading system generated a profit on average while being in the market for 871.5 (31.59 × 27.59) days out of the total 1827 (47.7%) trading days from the beginning of 2017 to the end of March 2024. Out of the 100 stocks examined, 19 turned out to have a negative NP (19%). ORLY stocks achieved the highest NP of USD 553.29 with a PP of 55.56% and a PF of 3.13. The highest loss was generated when trading BIIB, with an NP of USD −269.62, a PP of 36.67%, and a PF of 0.46. The trading results of our trading system based on a three-degree polynomial regression (MRB) are summarized in Table 2.

Table 2. Results of the trading system based on three degrees. Polynomial moving regression band.

	Ticker	NP	PP (%)	PF	TCT	ADT
1	AAPL	83.74	58.97	1.86	40	23
2	ABNB	3.11	64.29	1.03	14	25

Table 2. *Cont.*

	Ticker	NP	PP (%)	PF	TCT	ADT
3	ADBE	394.32	60.98	1.96	38	22
4	ADI	40.07	58.54	1.31	42	24
5	ADP	42.33	57.14	1.28	38	22
6	ADSK	42.33	57.14	1.28	40	22
7	AEP	−20.12	46.67	0.80	45	19
8	AMAT	72.79	59.53	1.60	41	21
9	AMD	77.95	62.50	1.59	37	25
10	AMGN	172.48	50.80	2.14	39	23
11	AMZN	98.20	52.38	1.87	42	21
12	ANSS	186.47	62.16	1.88	37	22
13	ASML	456.63	66.67	1.77	42	21
14	AVGO	396.21	60.98	2.16	41	24
15	AZN	13.45	44.45	1.26	36	25
16	BIIB	−218.23	39.47	0.57	38	19
17	BKNG	1501.25	68.42	1.62	38	24
18	BKR	11.94	46.15	1.27	39	22
19	CCEP	25.98	64.86	1.74	37	24
20	CDNS	141.49	62.5	2.17	40	22
21	CDW	114.47	69.44	1.97	36	27
22	CEG	57.60	60.00	7.45	25	26
23	CHTR	85.42	53.66	1.17	41	21
24	CMCSA	−2.80	55.00	0.94	40	21
25	COST	381.09	64.86	2.47	37	23
26	CPRT	30.14	66.67	2.37	39	23
27	CRWD	4.45	45.83	1.02	37	21
28	CSCO	17.19	56.41	1.47	39	24
29	CSGP	5.12	55.00	1.08	40	23
30	CSX	25.72	54.05	2.36	37	23
31	CTAS	209.04	65.12	1.92	43	21
32	CTSH	52.28	57.5	1.88	40	24
33	DASH	12.02	60.00	1.17	15	24
34	DDOG	75.82	63.64	1.82	22	21
35	DLTR	28.98	55.26	1.24	38	23
36	DXCM	88.51	60.00	1.68	40	24
37	EA	13.11	50.00	1.08	42	22
38	EXC	11.31	55.26	1.48	38	23
39	FANG	114.94	56.41	1.76	39	25
40	FAST	19.68	57.14	1.41	42	21
41	FTNT	10.90	50.00	1.24	42	22
42	GEHC	11.33	60.00	5.00	5	30

Table 2. *Cont.*

	Ticker	NP	PP (%)	PF	TCT	ADT
43	GILD	−35.59	43.18	0.62	44	22
44	GOOG	61.38	54.05	1.85	37	22
45	GOOGL	37.91	55.26	1.49	38	22
46	HON	95.71	60.00	1.67	40	22
47	IDXX	362.30	52.38	1.97	42	20
48	ILMN	72.76	62.16	1.18	37	24
49	INTC	−3.24	46.15	0.95	39	25
50	INTU	119.06	58.54	1.38	41	23
51	ISRG	208.73	68.57	2.07	35	30
52	KDP	6.59	47.22	1.30	36	23
53	KHC	−13.06	50.00	0.75	34	27
54	KLAC	403.95	60.00	2.70	40	23
55	LIN	153.83	52.50	1.99	40	24
56	LRCX	356.22	64.86	1.70	37	22
57	LULU	211.36	61.54	1.72	39	22
58	MAR	60.55	51.16	1.38	43	22
59	MCHP	81.17	63.89	2.64	36	26
60	MDB	−11.01	57.58	0.98	33	24
61	MDLZ	15.25	51.28	1.38	39	22
62	MELI	506.95	59.52	1.38	42	21
63	META	13.17	47.62	1.03	42	22
64	MNST	37.12	56.41	2.48	39	24
65	MRNA	33.14	44.44	1.08	27	23
66	MRVL	3.95	48.65	1.06	37	23
67	MSFT	123.68	55.00	1.72	40	24
68	MU	24.09	47.50	1.26	40	24
69	NFLX	156.09	54.29	1.28	35	26
70	NVDA	261.28	51.16	1.77	43	21
71	NXPI	153.02	60.00	2.02	40	22
72	ODFL	44.31	63.89	1.43	36	22
73	ON	71.67	62.16	2.52	37	26
74	ORLY	605.68	57.50	2.80	40	23
75	PANW	105.63	52.63	1.67	38	22
76	PAYX	50.69	58.33	2.16	36	25
77	PCAR	72.99	70.27	3.46	37	27
78	PDD	−22.37	43.75	0.89	32	21
79	PEP	51.99	58.54	1.52	41	22
80	PYPL	49.47	52.38	1.38	42	22
81	QCOM	75.43	59.52	1.50	42	22

Table 2. *Cont.*

	Ticker	NP	PP (%)	PF	TCT	ADT
82	REGN	136.45	48.65	1.25	37	23
83	ROP	217.64	58.97	1.83	39	24
84	ROST	60.77	48.65	1.73	37	24
85	SBUX	−45.13	37.78	0.64	45	21
86	SIRI	0.12	38.46	1.02	39	25
87	SNPS	318.56	65.85	2.38	41	21
88	TEAM	−58.21	52.50	0.85	40	24
89	TMUS	65.63	65.79	1.93	38	24
90	TSLA	263.05	61.11	2.17	36	23
91	TTD	32.16	55.00	1.31	40	23
92	TTWO	−63.93	46.67	0.75	45	21
93	TXN	108.53	63.16	2.10	38	27
94	VRSK	70.26	58.97	1.59	39	24
95	VRTX	302.25	60.53	3.03	38	25
96	WBA	−47.12	37.50	0.48	40	21
97	WBD	10.30	43.90	1.17	41	24
98	WDAY	58.09	62.86	1.25	35	24
99	XEL	14.37	43.59	1.25	39	21
100	ZS	99.09	54.84	1.35	31	23
AV		110.33	55.85	1.67	37.75	23.11
ST.D		193.95	7.53	0.85	5.95	1.96
Max		1501.25	70.27	7.45	45	30
Min		−218.23	37.50	0.48	5	19

Notes: AV = average, ST.D = standard deviation, NP = net profit, PP = percent of profitable trades, PF = profit factor, TCT = total closed trades, ADT = average days of trade. The results include 0.3% transaction costs for every trade.

Table 2 demonstrates that the average net profit (NP) achieved by our trading system based on a three-degree polynomial regression (MRB) is USD 110.33, with a percent of profitable trades (PP) of 55.85% and a profit factor (PF) of 1.67. These results are better than those achieved with the two-degree polynomial MRB in terms of NP and PP. The average number of days on the market is 872.4 (37.75 × 23.11) out of the 1827 (47.7%) total trading days in the sampled period. The highest NP was achieved by the system trading BKNG (USD 1501.25), and the lowest was with BIIB (−USD 218.23). These results indicate the superiority of the three-degree polynomial MRB system compared to the two-degree system. Table 3 summarizes the trading results of our trading system based on a four-degree polynomial regression (MRB).

Table 3. Results of the trading system based on four degrees. Polynomial moving regression band.

	Ticker	NP	PP (%)	PF	TCT	ADT
1	AAPL	72.35	59.51	1.70	49	17
2	ABNB	25.08	62.50	1.26	16	21
3	ADBE	364.71	61.54	1.71	52	19

Table 3. *Cont.*

	Ticker	NP	PP (%)	PF	TCT	ADT
4	ADI	34.82	54.55	1.20	55	15
5	ADP	43.83	52.83	1.23	53	16
6	ADSK	144.40	58.33	1.54	48	20
7	AEP	−31.20	47.37	0.71	57	16
8	AMAT	103.23	60.78	2.00	51	18
9	AMD	120.39	58.00	1.96	50	19
10	AMGN	98.68	51.02	1.44	49	19
11	AMZN	148.37	59.62	2.30	52	18
12	ANSS	243.07	67.31	1.87	52	18
13	ASML	681.73	64.81	2.25	54	17
14	AVGO	354.64	51.72	1.57	58	17
15	AZN	3.77	53.06	1.08	49	18
16	BIIB	4.54	46.67	1.01	45	18
17	BKNG	2166.95	62.00	2.36	50	19
18	BKR	2166.95	62.00	2.36	50	19
19	CCEP	9.91	46.3	1.17	54	19
20	CDNS	208.69	63.27	3.45	49	18
21	CDW	93.38	53.85	1.70	52	18
22	CEG	47.43	58.33	3.19	12	19
23	CHTR	357.22	57.14	1.63	49	19
24	CMCSA	9.19	57.69	1.22	52	18
25	COST	111.56	52.83	1.32	53	18
26	CPRT	32.23	63.27	2.87	49	19
27	CRWD	136.56	52.94	1.59	34	16
28	CSCO	20.84	61.22	1.38	49	19
29	CSGP	54.09	56.60	1.72	53	19
30	CSX	7.12	52.00	1.24	50	17
31	CTAS	196.94	57.70	1.69	52	18
32	CTSH	10.67	56.25	1.15	48	20
33	DASH	−52.38	42.86	0.55	21	19
34	DDOG	88.90	58.62	1.83	29	17
35	DLTR	−30.26	53.19	0.86	47	19
36	DXCM	48.95	53.70	1.34	54	16
37	EA	−3.04	47.06	0.98	51	17
38	EXC	0.13	48.08	1.00	52	17
39	FANG	146.99	65.31	2.01	49	20
40	FAST	14.45	49.06	1.27	53	17
41	FTNT	36.08	60.00	1.64	55	19
42	GEHC	10.81	80.00	3.82	5	19
43	GILD	−5.37	43.64	0.94	55	17
44	GOOG	76.25	60.00	1.98	55	18

Table 3. *Cont.*

	Ticker	NP	PP (%)	PF	TCT	ADT
45	GOOGL	61.96	56.14	1.72	57	17
46	HON	−37.96	49.06	0.84	53	17
47	IDXX	255.39	59.62	1.59	52	18
48	ILMN	−27.64	47.27	0.96	55	16
49	INTC	−3.54	46.15	0.95	52	16
50	INTU	219.32	63.16	1.46	57	17
51	ISRG	322.09	63.46	2.19	52	20
52	KDP	21.87	60.00	1.98	50	19
53	KHC	19.08	54.55	1.56	44	19
54	KLAC	357.10	57.89	2.12	57	16
55	LIN	81.02	56.14	1.30	57	18
56	LRCX	457.32	55.36	1.72	56	16
57	LULU	247.89	52.94	1.71	51	18
58	MAR	7.64	48.15	1.05	54	17
59	MCHP	59.81	61.22	1.97	49	18
60	MDB	448.01	57.14	2.22	42	18
61	MDLZ	16.74	54.00	1.33	50	17
62	MELI	1393.09	60.34	1.86	58	18
63	META	−66.33	45.1	0.83	51	17
64	MNST	9.24	54.24	1.17	59	17
65	MRNA	−52.53	51.35	0.87	37	17
66	MRVL	34.07	61.82	1.54	55	17
67	MSFT	269.15	67.31	2.93	52	19
68	MU	55.86	63.83	1.56	47	19
69	NFLX	531.29	66.67	2.20	45	20
70	NVDA	457.86	56.36	2.60	55	17
71	NXPI	65.88	62.00	1.35	50	17
72	ODFL	14.84	46.43	1.13	56	16
73	ON	77.41	64.00	2.86	50	18
74	ORLY	441.78	56.36	2.28	55	16
75	PANW	99.64	51.92	1.51	52	18
76	PAYX	14.63	45.45	1.12	55	16
77	PCAR	11.13	46.31	1.15	54	17
78	PDD	−95.52	51.28	0.59	39	16
79	PEP	4.50	51.72	1.03	58	16
80	PYPL	90.86	58.49	1.45	53	18
81	QCOM	32.46	45.61	1.16	57	15
82	REGN	286.82	53.19	1.44	47	19
83	ROP	37.01	55.36	1.08	56	18
84	ROST	13.29	55.32	1.11	47	20

Table 3. *Cont.*

	Ticker	NP	PP (%)	PF	TCT	ADT
85	SBUX	−6.45	46.03	0.94	54	17
86	SIRI	2.38	53.06	1.49	49	19
87	SNPS	460.68	64.91	3.80	57	15
88	TEAM	208.49	56.60	1.64	53	18
89	TMUS	59.12	56.36	1.60	55	17
90	TSLA	235.78	59.57	1.66	47	18
91	TTD	92.20	53.06	1.99	49	19
92	TTWO	54.94	53.70	1.34	54	19
93	TXN	35.64	48.08	1.26	52	17
94	VRSK	64.95	52.94	1.39	51	18
95	VRTX	126.86	55.77	1.45	52	18
96	WBA	−20.07	41.51	0.77	53	17
97	WBD	3.48	44.44	1.06	54	17
98	WDAY	199.89	61.22	1.764	49	19
99	XEL	4.04	41.82	1.06	55	18
100	ZS	147.06	58.97	1.79	39	18
AV		162.75	55.45	1.60	49.71	17.78
ST.D		348	54.40	0.64	9.01	1.12
Max		2166.95	80.00	3.82	59	21
Min		−95.52	41.51	0.55	5	15

Notes: AV = average, ST.D = standard deviation, NP = net profit, PP = percent of profitable trades, PF = profit factor, TCT = total closed trades, ADT = average days of trade. The results include 0.3% transaction costs for every trade.

Table 3 shows that the average net profit (NP) achieved by our trading system based on a four-degree polynomial regression (MRB) is USD 162.75, with a percent of profitable trades (PP) of 55.45% and a profit factor (PF) of 1.60. These results indicate that the four-degree polynomial system has achieved the highest average NP of the tested systems. The average days the stocks are in a trading position is 883.8 (49.71 × 17.78), which is 48.37% of the entire tested period. Again, BKNG (USD 2166.95) has turned out to be the most profitable stock, while PDD is the most losing trade (USD −95.52). These results point out that the four-degree polynomial MRB system is superior to the former two models in terms of risk and return. Table 4 summarizes our trading systems' results.

Table 4. Summary results of the three trading models.

		NP	PP (%)	PF	Days
Model 1	AV	79.67	52.89	1.76	871.56
	Min	−269.62	20.00	0.37	115
Model 2	AV	110.33	55.85	1.67	872.4
	Min	−218.23	37.50	0.48	95
Model 3	AV	162.73	55.45	1.60	883.8
	Min	−95.52	41.51	0.55	75

Notes: AV = average, NP = net profit, PP = percent of profitable trades, PF = profit factor, Days = the total trading days. The results include 0.3% transaction costs for every trade.

From Table 4, we learn that the best trading system to trade Nasdaq100 stocks is Model 3, which makes use of a four-degree polynomial MRB. This model is superior to the other two in terms of net profit (NP). Regarding the risks involved, the third model has the lowest loss in dollar value (USD −95.52) and the highest minimum PP (41.51) and PF (0.55), which indicates that this strategy is relatively less risky than the other two strategies. The only downside of the third model is that it exposes investors to the market on average 11–12 days in total more than the other two models.

4. Summary and Conclusions

In this research, we explored whether a trading system based on polynomial moving regression bands (MRBs) could be effectively applied to Nasdaq100 stocks to trade profitably. We designed three fully automated trading systems using polynomial MRBs of degrees two to four and tested their performance on daily stock data from early 2017 to the end of March 2024. To limit the overfitting problem, we employed several strategies: we used lower-degree polynomials to avoid unnecessary complexity, implemented early stopping during model training to prevent the models from becoming too specialized to the training data, and conducted random searches to find the optimal balance between model complexity and performance. Our results indicated that all three models achieved, on average, a positive net profit (NP), with a percent of profitable trades (PP) exceeding 50% and a profit factor (PF) greater than 1, demonstrating that the behavior of Nasdaq100 stocks can be effectively modeled using polynomial regression without overfitting. Among the models, Model 3, which employed a fourth-degree polynomial MRB system, performed the best, achieving the highest average NP of USD 162.73 and exhibiting a superior risk profile with the lowest average loss (USD 95.52), highest minimum PP (41.51%), and highest minimum PF (0.55). These findings suggest that carefully designed polynomial MRB-based trading systems, which mitigate overfitting through model selection and validation techniques, can successfully capture stock price trends and be used to trade profitably in fully automated systems.

Funding: This research was funded by Western Galilee College.

Data Availability Statement: The Data for this research was derived from public domains.

Conflicts of Interest: The author declares no conflict of interest.

References

Aloud, Monira Essa, and Nora Alkhamees. 2021. Intelligent Algorithmic Trading Strategy Using Reinforcement Learning and Directional Change. *IEEE Access* 9: 114659–71. [CrossRef]

Ayyıldız, Nazif. 2023. *Prediction of Stock Market Index Movements with Machine Learning*. Gaziantep: Ozgur Press.

Benos, Evangelos, and Satchit Sagade. 2016. Price discovery and the cross-section of high-frequency trading. *Journal of Financial Markets* 30: 54–77. [CrossRef]

Burgess, Nicholas. 2022. Machine Learning Algorithmic Trading Strategies for Superior Growth, Outperformance and Competitive Advantage. *International Journal of Artificial Intelligence and Machine Learning* 2: 38–60. [CrossRef]

Chavarnakul, Thira, and David Enke. 2008. Intelligent technical analysis based equivolume charting for stock trading using neural networks. *Expert Systems with Applications* 34: 1004–17. [CrossRef]

Cliff, Dave. 2018. An Open-Source Limit-Order-Book Exchange for Teaching and Research. Paper presented at 2018 IEEE Symposium Series on Computational Intelligence (SSCI), Bangalore, India, November 18–21; pp. 1853–60.

Cooper, Ricky, Wendy Currie, Jonathan Seddon, and Ben Van Vliet. 2022. Competitive advantage in algorithmic trading: A behavioral innovation economics approach. *Review of Behavioral Finance* 15: 371–95. [CrossRef]

Currie, Wendy L., and Jonathan J. M. Seddon. 2017. The Regulatory, Technology and Market 'Dark Arts Trilogy' of High Frequency Trading: A Research Agenda. *Journal of Information Technology* 32: 111–26. [CrossRef]

De Luna, Xavier. 1998. Projected polynomial autoregression for prediction of stationary time series. *Journal of Applied Statistics* 25: 763–75. [CrossRef]

Frino, Alex, Dionigi Gerace, and Masud Behnia. 2021. The impact of algorithmic trading on liquidity in futures markets: New insights into the resiliency of spreads and depth. *The Journal of Future Markets* 41: 1301–14. [CrossRef]

Hendershott, Terrence, and Ryan Riordan. 2011. Algorithmic Trading and the Market for Liquidity. *Journal of Financial and Quantitative Analysis* 48: 1001–24. [CrossRef]

Huang, Boming, Yuziang Huan, and Li Da Xu. 2019. Automated Trading Systems Statistical and Machine Learning Methods and Hardware Implementation: A Survey. *Enterprise Information Systems* 13: 132–44. Available online: https://digitalcommons.odu.edu/cgi/viewcontent.cgi?article=1027&context=itds_facpubs (accessed on 28 September 2024). [CrossRef]

Huang, Wei, Yoshiteru Nakamori, and Shou-Yang Wang. 2005. Forecasting stock market movement direction with support vector machine. *Computers & Operations Research* 32: 2513–22.

Islam, Sharmin, Md. Shakil Sikder, Md. Farhad Hossain, and Partha Chakraborty. 2021. Predicting the daily closing price of selected shares on the Dhaka stock exchange using machine learning techniques. *SN Business & Economics* 1: 58.

Kambeu, Edson. 2019. Trading Volume as a Predictor of Market Movement An Application of Logistic Regression in the R environment. *International Journal of Finance and Banking Studies* 8: 57–69.

Kara, Yakup, Melek Acar Boyacioglu, and Ömer Kaan Baykan. 2011. Predicting direction of stock price index movement using artificial neural networks and support vector machines: The sample of the Istanbul stock exchange. *Expert Systems with Applications* 38: 5311–19. [CrossRef]

Kim, Ha Young, and Chang Hyun Won. 2018. Forecasting the Volatility of Stock Price Index: A Hybrid Model Integrating LSTM with Multiple GARCH-Type Models. *Expert Systems with Applications* 103: 25–37. [CrossRef]

Maroto, Michelle. 2018. Sharing or limiting the wealth? Coresidence, parental support, and wealth outcomes in Canada. *Journal of Family and Economic Issues* 40: 102–16. [CrossRef]

McMillan, David G. 2019. Cross-asset relations, correlations and economic implications. *Global Finance Journal* 41: 60–78. [CrossRef]

Ozturk, Murat, Ismail Hakki Toroslu, and Guven Fidan. 2016. Heuristic based trading system on Forex data using technical indicator rules. *Applied Soft Computing* 43: 170–86. [CrossRef]

Rather, Akhter Mohiuddin. 2014. A hybrid intelligent method of predicting stock returns. *Advances in Artificial Neural Systems* 2014: 246487. [CrossRef]

Sen, Jaydip, and Sidra Mehtab. 2021. A robust predictive model for stock price prediction using deep learning and natural language processing. *TechRxiv*. [CrossRef]

Srijiranon, Krittakom, Yoskorn Lertratanakham, and Tanatorn Tanantong. 2022. A hybrid framework using pca, emd and lstm methods for stock market price prediction with sentiment analysis. *Applied Sciences* 12: 10823. [CrossRef]

Treleaven, Philip, Michal Galas, and Vidhi Lalchand. 2013. Algorithmic Trading Review. *Communication of the ACM* 56: 76–85. [CrossRef]

Zhang, Zezheng, and Matloob Khushi. 2020. *GA-MSSR: Genetic Algorithm Maximizing Sharpe and Sterling Ratio Method for Robo Trading*. Ithaca: Cornell University.

Zhao, Yang, and Zhonglu Chen. 2021. Forecasting stock price movement: New evidence from a novel hybrid deep learning model. *Journal of Asian Business and Economic Studies* 29: 91–104. [CrossRef]

Zhu, Hengyue. 2022. Research advanced in financial trading systems based on reinforcement learning. Paper presented at 2nd International Conference on Artificial Intelligence Automation and High Performance (AIAHPC), Zhuhai, China, February 25–27.

risks

MDPI

Article

Predicting Mutual Fund Stress Levels Utilizing SEBI's Stress Test Parameters in MidCap and SmallCap Funds Using Deep Learning Models

Suneel Maheshwari [1,*] and Deepak Raghava Naik [2]

[1] Department of Accounting and Information Systems, Indiana University of Pennsylvania, Indiana, PA 15705, USA

[2] Department of Management Studies, Ramaiah Institute of Technology, Bengaluru 560054, India; deepak@msrit.edu

* Correspondence: suneel@iup.edu

Abstract: The Association of Mutual Funds of India (AMFI), under the direction of the Securities and Exchange Board of India (SEBI), provided open access to various risk parameters with respect to MidCap and SmallCap funds for the first time from February 2024. Our study utilizes AMFI datasets from February 2024 to September 2024 which consisted of 14 variables. Among these, the primary variable identified in grading mutual funds is the stress test parameter, expressed as number of days required to liquidate between 50% and 25% of the portfolio, respectively, on a pro-rata basis under stress conditions as a response variable. The objective of our paper is to build and test various neural network models which can help in predicting stress levels with the highest accuracy and specificity in MidCap and SmallCap mutual funds based on AMFI's 14 parameters as predictors. The results suggest that the simpler neural network model architectures show higher accuracy. We used Artificial Neural Networks (ANN) over other machine learning methods due to its ability to analyze the impact of dynamic interrelationships among 14 variables on the dependent variable, independent of the statistical distribution of parameters considered. Predicting stress levels with the highest accuracy in MidCap and SmallCap mutual funds will benefit investors by reducing information asymmetry while allocating investments based on their risk tolerance. It will help policy makers in designing controls to protect smaller investors and provide warnings for funds with unusually high risk.

Keywords: stress test; liquidity analysis; risk management; mutual funds; neural networks; deep learning

1. Introduction

The growth of mutual funds in India has been remarkable in recent years. Growing participation from retail investors can be attributed to several factors, including increasing financial awareness, favourable regulatory measures, and the attractiveness of mutual funds as a convenient and accessible investment avenue. The proliferation of mutual fund offerings and the democratization of investment access has opened new avenues for investors to participate in capital markets. As a result, mutual funds emerged as preferred investment vehicles, catering to the diverse investment objectives and risk profiles of investors across the spectrum. The mutual fund sector in India has witnessed a surge in retail investor participation, as per the AMFI data released for January 2024. MidCap funds have 13 million portfolios with an investment of INR 29 million. SmallCap funds account for 17.8 million portfolios with a value of INR 24.7 million.[1] One of the key drivers behind the surge in retail investor participation in mutual funds is the advent of systematic investment plans (SIPs), which have revolutionized the way retail investors approach mutual fund investments (Kavya and Chokkamreddy 2024). SIPs offer a disciplined and hassle-free approach to wealth accumulation, allowing both seasoned investors and newcomers alike to contribute small amounts at regular intervals. This systematic approach not only helps in mitigating market volatility, but also inculcates financial discipline among investors, encouraging them to stay invested for the long term. As a result, mutual fund Assets Under Management (AUM) have witnessed a steady uptrend, reflecting the evolving preferences of investors seeking diversified and professionally managed investment avenues (Narasimha 2024; Joshi and Arora 2022; Sukumar 2020).

Furthermore, regulatory initiatives aimed at enhancing transparency and investor protection have bolstered investor confidence in mutual funds. Measures such as the categorization and rationalization of mutual fund schemes, along with stringent disclosure norms, have contributed to greater trust and credibility in the mutual fund industry. As a result of these concerted efforts, India has witnessed a significant uptick in retail investor participation in mutual funds. The democratization of investment access, coupled with robust investor education initiatives, has empowered individuals from diverse backgrounds to take charge of their financial futures and embark on the journey of wealth creation through mutual funds (Berk and van Binsbergen 2012; Li and Rossi 2020; Patton and Timmermann 2010). The onset of the global COVID-19 pandemic brought about unprecedented volatility and uncertainty in financial markets worldwide, including in India. Despite initial market turbulence, the mutual fund industry in India showcased resilience and adaptability, as evidenced by the sustained growth in AUM across various schemes. This resilience is attributable to the robust regulatory framework, proactive measures by fund managers, and the enduring trust of investors in the mutual fund ecosystem (Narasimha 2024).

However, despite the progress made, there remains a pressing need for continued awareness and education initiatives to ensure that investors make informed investment decisions. As retail investors navigate the complexities of the financial markets, it is imperative to equip them with the knowledge and tools necessary to identify suitable investment opportunities and manage risk effectively (Elton and Gruber 2020; Jones and Mo 2020; Pástor et al. 2017; Feng et al. 2020).

This investment frenzy among retail investors in MidCap and SmallCap funds has not gone unnoticed by market regulators like the Securities Exchange Board of India (SEBI). Concerned about potential risks to retail investors amidst soaring market valuations, SEBI has initiated various steps to safeguard investor interests in these funds (Joshi and Arora 2022). In response to SEBI's directives, AMFI has taken some very bold steps such as tasking the trustees of all Asset Management Companies (AMCs) with framing policies to protect investors in MidCap and SmallCap schemes. The policies being formulated by the trustees, in consultation with the Unitholder Protection Committees of the AMCs, are designed to incorporate proactive measures to shield investors from potential risks. These measures also include moderating inflows into MidCap and SmallCap funds, portfolio rebalancing, and enhancing the disclosure of risk parameters and stress tests (Hoberg et al. 2018). The rationale behind these regulatory measures lies in the unprecedented returns witnessed by MidCap and SmallCap indices in recent times, coupled with heightened market volatility due to global events. The surge in investor inflows has led to inflated valuations, raising concerns about market stability and investor protection (Irvine et al. 2018). Hence, SEBI and AMFI are taking proactive steps to ensure that fund houses are adequately prepared to navigate market uncertainties and protect the interests of retail investors. Through these measures, they aim to uphold market integrity and promote investor confidence in India's mutual fund industry.

Given this outlook, recently, the landscape of mutual fund investments in India has witnessed a notable transformation, marked by the introduction of innovative methodologies for evaluating fund performance and risk. One such significant development is the initiative undertaken by the Association of Mutual Funds of India (AMFI), Mumbai, India to assess stress levels in MidCap and SmallCap mutual funds, referred to as the "Stress Test". The test involves simulating scenarios where a significant number of investors demand redemption, thereby assessing how quickly a fund can meet redemption requests from investors. For both MidCap and SmallCap funds, liquidation of either 25 percent or

50 percent of the portfolio on a pro-rata basis and the time taken to meet the liquidation request are considered in the dataset. Importantly, the stress test allows for fund managers to exclude the bottom 20 percent of the portfolio based on liquidity considerations. This provision enables fund managers to retain stocks deemed to be essential for long-term gains, enhancing the flexibility and strategic management of the portfolio. This initiative represents a proactive step towards enhancing transparency and accountability within the mutual fund industry, aiming to provide investors with deeper insights into the resilience of their investment portfolios.

The volatility and unpredictability of financial markets pose significant challenges for investors, particularly in assessing the stress levels of mutual funds. While SEBI has outlined a methodology for stress testing mutual funds, there remains a need for advanced analytical tools to accurately predict the stress levels of mutual funds, particularly in the MidCap and SmallCap segments. Traditional approaches may lack the sophistication and predictive power needed to navigate the complexities of modern financial markets. To overcome that limitation, we test various neural network models which can help in predicting stress levels with the highest accuracy and specificity in MidCap and SmallCap mutual funds based on AMFI's parameters as predictors.

We also test the effectiveness and reliability of the models to provide actionable insights and recommendations to aid investors and fund managers in managing risk and optimizing portfolio strategies. The next two sections provide details on data collection and research methodology, followed by data analysis and interpretation. Finally, last section provides conclusion and scope for future research.

2. Data Collection

For our study, the stress test data were sourced from the AMFI website's dedicated section, "Disclosure of Stress Test & Liquidity Analysis in respect of MidCap & SmallCap Funds". Specifically, stress test data pertaining to MidCap and SmallCap mutual funds for the period of eight months from February 2024 to September 2024 were collected. The number of mutual funds that were part of the dataset from February 2024 to September 2024 is provided in Table 1.

Table 1. Number of mutual funds as part of monthly stress test datasets.

Month	MidCap Funds	SmallCap Funds
February to September 2024 (except May 2024)	29	27
May 2024	13	10

Source: Compiled from www.amfiindia.com.

Table 1 shows that between February and September 2024; the dataset included information of 29 MidCap funds and 27 SmallCap funds. In May 2024, data were available for only 13 MidCap funds and 10 SmallCap funds. The MidCap and SmallCap mutual funds that were part of the dataset from February 2024 to September 2024 are provided in Tables 2 and 3, respectively.

Table 2. List of MidCap mutual funds, part of dataset (from February to September 2024) [1].

Sl. No	MidCap Mutual Funds	February 2024	March 2024	April 2024	May 2024	June 2024	July 2024	August 2024	September 2024
1	Aditya Birla Sun Life MidCap Fund	✓	✓	✓	X	✓	✓	✓	✓
2	Axis MidCap Fund	✓	✓	✓	X	✓	✓	✓	✓
3	Bandhan MidCap Fund	✓	✓	✓	✓	✓	✓	✓	✓
4	Baroda BNP Paribas MidCap Fund	✓	✓	✓	X	✓	✓	✓	✓

Table 2. *Cont.*

Sl. No	MidCap Mutual Funds	February 2024	March 2024	April 2024	May 2024	June 2024	July 2024	August 2024	September 2024
5	Canara Robeco MidCap Fund	✓	✓	✓	✓	✓	✓	✓	✓
6	DSP MidCap Fund	✓	✓	✓	X	✓	✓	✓	✓
7	Edelweiss MidCap Fund	✓	✓	✓	✓	✓	✓	✓	✓
8	Franklin India Prima Fund	✓	✓	✓	X	✓	✓	✓	✓
9	HDFC MidCap Opportunities Fund	✓	✓	✓	X	✓	✓	✓	✓
10	HSBC MidCap Fund	✓	✓	✓	✓	✓	✓	✓	✓
11	ICICI Prudential MidCap Fund	✓	✓	✓	X	✓	✓	✓	✓
12	Invesco India MidCap Fund	✓	✓	✓	X	✓	✓	✓	✓
13	ITI MidCap Fund	✓	✓	✓	✓	✓	✓	✓	✓
14	JM MidCap Fund	✓	✓	✓	✓	✓	✓	✓	✓
15	Kotak Emerging Equity Fund	✓	✓	✓	✓	✓	✓	✓	✓
16	LIC MF MidCap Fund	✓	✓	✓	X	✓	✓	✓	✓
17	Mahindra Manulife MidCap Fund	✓	✓	✓	X	✓	✓	✓	✓
18	Mirae Asset MidCap Fund	✓	✓	✓	X	✓	✓	✓	✓
19	Motilal Oswal MidCap Fund	✓	✓	✓	X	✓	✓	✓	✓
20	Nippon India Growth Fund	✓	✓	✓	✓	✓	✓	✓	✓
21	PGIM India MidCap Opportunities Fund	✓	✓	✓	X	✓	✓	✓	✓
22	Quant MidCap Fund	✓	✓	✓	✓	✓	✓	✓	✓
23	SBI Magnum MidCap Fund	✓	✓	✓	X	✓	✓	✓	✓
24	Sundaram MidCap Fund	✓	✓	✓	✓	✓	✓	✓	✓
25	Tata MidCap Growth Fund	✓	✓	✓	X	✓	✓	✓	✓
26	Taurus MidCap Fund	✓	✓	✓	✓	✓	✓	✓	✓
27	Union MidCap Fund	✓	✓	✓	X	✓	✓	✓	✓
28	UTI—MidCap Fund	✓	✓	✓	✓	✓	✓	✓	✓
29	WhiteOak Capital MidCap Fund	✓	✓	✓	✓	✓	✓	✓	✓

[1] The "X" mark in the table indicates the exclusion of the MidCap funds for the non-availability of the data.

Table 3. List of SmallCap mutual funds, part of dataset (from February to September 2024) [1].

Sl. No	SmallCap Mutual Funds	February 2024	March 2024	April 2024	May 2024	June 2024	July 2024	August 2024	September 2024
1	Aditya Birla Sun Life SmallCap Fund	✓	✓	✓	✓	✓	✓	✓	✓
2	Axis SmallCap Fund	✓	✓	✓	✓	✓	✓	✓	✓
3	BANDHAN SmallCap Fund	✓	✓	✓	X	✓	✓	✓	✓
4	BANK OF INDIA SMALLCAP FUND	✓	✓	✓	✓	✓	✓	✓	✓
5	Baroda BNP Paribas SmallCap Fund	✓	✓	✓	✓	✓	✓	✓	✓
6	Canara Robeco SmallCap Fund	✓	✓	✓	X	✓	✓	✓	✓
7	DSP SmallCap Fund	✓	✓	✓	✓	✓	✓	✓	✓
8	Edelweiss SmallCap Fund	✓	✓	✓	X	✓	✓	✓	✓
9	Franklin India Smaller Companies Fund	✓	✓	✓	✓	✓	✓	✓	✓

Table 3. *Cont.*

Sl. No	SmallCap Mutual Funds	February 2024	March 2024	April 2024	May 2024	June 2024	July 2024	August 2024	September 2024
10	HDFC SmallCap Fund	✓	✓	✓	✓	✓	✓	✓	✓
11	HSBC SmallCap Fund	✓	✓	✓	X	✓	✓	✓	✓
12	ICICI Prudential SmallCap Fund	✓	✓	✓	✓	✓	✓	✓	✓
13	Invesco India SmallCap Fund	✓	✓	✓	✓	✓	✓	✓	✓
14	ITI SmallCap Fund	✓	✓	✓	X	✓	✓	✓	✓
15	JM SmallCap Fund	✓	✓	✓	✓	✓	✓	✓	✓
16	Kotak SmallCap Fund	✓	✓	✓	X	✓	✓	✓	✓
17	LIC MF SmallCap Fund	✓	✓	✓	✓	✓	✓	✓	✓
18	Mahindra Manulife SmallCap Fund	✓	✓	✓	✓	✓	✓	✓	✓
19	Motilal Oswal SmallCap Fund	✓	✓	✓	✓	✓	✓	✓	✓
20	Nippon India SmallCap Fund	✓	✓	✓	X	✓	✓	✓	✓
21	PGIM India SmallCap Fund	✓	✓	✓	✓	✓	✓	✓	✓
22	Quant SmallCap Fund	✓	✓	✓	X	✓	✓	✓	✓
23	Quantum SmallCap Fund	✓	✓	✓	✓	✓	✓	✓	✓
24	SBI SmallCap Fund	✓	✓	✓	✓	✓	✓	✓	✓
25	Sundaram SmallCap Fund	✓	✓	✓	X	✓	✓	✓	✓
26	Tata SmallCap Fund	✓	✓	✓	✓	✓	✓	✓	✓
27	Union SmallCap Fund	✓	✓	✓	✓	✓	✓	✓	✓
28	UTI SmallCap Fund	✓	✓	✓	X	✓	✓	✓	✓

[1] The "X" mark in the table indicates the exclusion of the MidCap funds for the non-availability of the data.

Upon collecting the stress test data, a thorough data pre-processing step was conducted to ensure its quality and suitability for analysis. This involved excluding schemes which had missing values and inconsistencies within the dataset to enhance its integrity and reliability for subsequent modelling efforts. We tried not to impute values for missing values across the parameters identified. Table 4 lists the 14 parameters which were identified as features for model development for evaluation purposes. These parameters were deemed to be essential for assessing mutual fund stress levels based on their presence in the stress test template, and were subsequently used as features in the modelling process.

Table 4. The 14 parameters as features for model development.

Sl. No	Independent Variables	Description
1	AUM (INR in crores)	Asset Under Management in crores of INR (1 crore equals 10 million).
2	Liability-side Top 10 investor (%)	Indicates % of AUM held by top 10 investors of the scheme.
3	Asset-side (AUM held in) LargeCap (%)	Indicates % of scheme AUM invested in LargeCap, MidCap, and SmallCap securities, and % held in cash.
4	Asset-side (AUM held in) MidCap (%)	
5	Asset-side (AUM held in) SmallCap (%)	
6	Asset-side (AUM held in) cash (%)	
7	Portfolio annualized standard deviation (%)	Standard deviation indicates how widely a stock or portfolio's returns varies from its mean over a given period. For each incremental standard deviation, there is an increasing level of reliability.
8	Benchmark annualized standard deviation (%)	

Table 4. *Cont.*

Sl. No	Independent Variables	Description
9	Portfolio beta	Beta is a measure of volatility—or systemic risk—of a security or portfolio compared to the market (usually the broad market index such as BSE-500 or NSE-500). Stocks with betas higher than 1.0 can be interpreted as more volatile than the broad market index.
10	Portfolio trailing 12 m PE	The price to earnings (P/E) ratio is one of the most widely used valuation methods, as it accounts for a company's actual earnings instead of projected earnings. The P/E ratio indicates how much an investor is willing to pay for one unit of earnings for that company. For a given company, whether the value of the current P/E is suitable depends on various factors including sector, growth prospects, business cycle, etc.
11	Benchmark PE trailing 12 m PE	
12	Benchmark PE trailing 12 m PE 1 year ago	
13	Benchmark PE trailing 12 m PE 2 year ago	
14	Portfolio turnover ratio (%)	Portfolio turnover is a measure of how frequently assets within a mutual fund scheme are bought and sold by the fund manager over a given period. Portfolio turnover is calculated by taking either the total amount of new securities purchased or the number of securities sold (whichever is less) over a particular period, divided by the total net asset value (NAV) of the fund. The measurement is usually reported for a 12-month period. For example, a 5% portfolio turnover ratio suggests that 5% of the portfolio holdings changed over a one-year period.

The stress test pro-rata liquidation variable for the 50% portfolio and 25% portfolio were considered separately for the building models, which were binned based on the categorization shown in Table 5. Separate models were built for the stress test with the 50% portfolio and 25% portfolio for each dataset across eight months separately, and they were evaluated for their predictive powers.

Table 5. Dependent variables for stress test.

Dependent Variable	Binning Categorization
Stress test pro-rata liquidation after removing bottom 20% of portfolio based on scrip liquidity (considering 10% PV with 3x volumes) 50% portfolio	Stress level ≥ 7 days = high stress Stress level < 7 days = low stress
Stress test pro-rata liquidation after removing bottom 20% of portfolio based on scrip liquidity (considering 10% PV with 3x volumes) 25% portfolio	

For data exclusion criteria, due to potential data incompleteness or inconsistency, a few companies were excluded from the modelling process to ensure the robustness and reliability of the analysis. This step was crucial for maintaining the integrity of the dataset and mitigating the risk of bias in the modelling results. The companies excluded from the dataset for non-availability of data with respect to a few variables is also shown in Tables 2 and 3.

For the response variable, binning was conducted by considering a stress level of 7 days and above as indicating high-stress companies.[2] Thus, companies were categorized into two levels, namely high-stress- and low-stress-level companies, across all of the months. Table 6 shows the summary of companies which were further categorized for between 50% and 25% portfolio liquidation from February to September 2024.

Table 6. Companies categorized based on stress levels (February–September 2024).

		Stress Test Pro-Rata Liquidation @ 50% Portfolio		Stress Test Pro-Rata Liquidation @ 25% Portfolio	
		Companies with Low Stress Levels	Companies with High Stress Levels	Companies with Low Stress Levels	Companies with High Stress Levels
February 2024	MidCap	19	8	23	4
	SmallCap	8	13	13	8

Table 6. *Cont.*

		Stress Test Pro-Rata Liquidation @ 50% Portfolio		Stress Test Pro-Rata Liquidation @ 25% Portfolio	
		Companies with Low Stress Levels	Companies with High Stress Levels	Companies with Low Stress Levels	Companies with High Stress Levels
March 2024	MidCap	19	8	23	4
	SmallCap	8	13	13	8
April 2024	MidCap	20	5	22	3
	SmallCap	8	13	13	8
May 2024	MidCap	7	2	8	1
	SmallCap	4	5	6	3
June 2024	MidCap	23	6	26	3
	SmallCap	16	12	20	8
July 2024	MidCap	22	7	26	3
	SmallCap	16	12	20	8
August 2024	MidCap	21	8	26	3
	SmallCap	17	11	20	8
September 2024	MidCap	20	9	26	3
	SmallCap	16	13	21	8

3. Research Methodology

This study investigates the need for predicting the mutual fund stress levels based on the 14 parameters which were identified as features for model development and for evaluation purposes. All of the variables were standardized before using them in the model building. To build the model, data for eight months from February 2024 to September 2024 were obtained, and an Artificial Neural Network (ANN) method was proposed for prediction. We used Artificial Neural Networks (ANNs) over other machine learning methods is due to their ability to analyze the impact of dynamic interrelationships among the 14 variables on the stress level, even when the information about the system was not detailed. The 14 parameters considered for building the classification model are complicated, and complex relationships can be built (Alzubaidi et al. 2021). ANNs are the most preferred method to define such complex and complicated relations, and they have the capability to establish relationships between the parameters considered and output desired in our study over other machine learning methods (Du et al. 2019; Degadwala and Vyas 2024). In recent years, we have observed that ANNs have been applied to various problems such as prediction, optimization, control systems, and many more, which can help in decision making (D'Amour et al. 2022). In our study, the main goal of using the ANN is that it is independent to the statistical distribution of the parameters considered. In this study, we tried to build an ANN consisting of between three layers and five layers. The first layer/input layer consisted of 14 parameters, which were the input variables. The middle layer was used in modelling the complex relationships in the study. Different numbers of neurons were used in the layers to model the complexity and evaluation of the problem (Harvey and Liu 2018). As observed in Equation (1), the weights connecting the Zh hidden layer with the X_j input layer is labelled as W_{ij}. Each node in the hidden layer calculates the weighted sum of the neurons in the input layer.

$$Input_j^s = \sum w_{kj} x_k^i \tag{1}$$

Outputs corresponding to these hidden layers are obtained as a result of implementing the activation function or the transfer function. The backpropagation method was used as the learning algorithm in the ANN, which initially starts with random weights. The network "learns" by gradually adjusting its weights until it can produce the target outputs specified for the 14 parameters considered in the study.

The calculation of the error in the network was carried out using Equation (2):

$$E = \frac{1}{2}\sum_j (t_j - O_j)^2 \tag{2}$$

where t_j and O_j are the actual and desired values of unit j in the output layer. The weights are updated depending on the delta rule of learning, as shown in Equation (3):

$$\Delta w_{ij} = \eta \delta_i o_i \tag{3}$$

where $\eta > 0$ is the learning rate, δ_i is a correction term, and o_i is the output of unit i in the previous layer. We observe that the correction term is proportional to the output error. In the backpropagation algorithm, the correction term is calculated using the gradient descent method, resulting in the following expression for the delta term of an output unit:

$$\delta_i = \left(\partial E / \partial o_j\right)\left(\partial o_j / \partial I_j\right) = \left(t_j - o_j^{out}\right) o_j \left(1 - o_j\right) \tag{4}$$

Thus, the correction term for the hidden nodes is calculated applying the recursive formula in Equation (5):

$$\delta_j = o_j\left(1 - o_j\right)\sum_k \delta_k w_{kj} \tag{5}$$

It is often also observed that, if a momentum term is added to the learning rule, as given in Equation (6), it can help in enhancing the performance and also the stability in the training process:

$$\Delta w_{ij} = \eta \delta_i O_i + \mu \Delta w_{ij}^{prev} \tag{6}$$

where we can observe that $0 < \mu < 1$ is a constant called momentum and the term w_{ij}^{prev} is the adjustment.

When the difference between the desired outputs and the actual outputs reaches an acceptable threshold, the process is complete. If not, the weights are adjusted to minimize the gap between the target and the actual values.

Thus, in the neural network built, each hidden layer consists of multiple nodes (or neurons), each with its own activation function, which helps introduce non-linearity to the model. The activation type of each node is *sigmoidal in nature.* Thus, the sigmoid function squashes input values to a range between 0 and 1. Thus, to build a classification-based model, the neural network was utilized with the sigmoid as the step function/activation function. For this study, the neural networks had an input layer consisting of nodes which accept the 14 predictor values in our study, and successive layers of nodes are to receive input from the previous layers (Bergstra and Bengio 2012; Hastie et al. 2009). Various configurations of neural networks were explored, including models with one, two, and three hidden layers, with the number of nodes ranging from 2 to 10. This approach allowed for flexibility and adaptability in capturing the underlying patterns and relationships within the dataset, ultimately facilitating accurate predictions of mutual fund stress levels (Chen et al. 2020; Gu et al. 2020). For the model evaluation, the trained neural network models were evaluated using appropriate performance metrics on validation models consisting of 20% as the holdout proportion. The models were evaluated using training and validation models using performance measures such as total accuracy, sensitivity, specificity, F-score, etc. Some of the important measures are mentioned below (Crone et al. 2011; Hyndman and Koehler 2006; Makridakis et al. 2019). Sensitivity measures the ability of a model to classify the observation as positive given it was positive in nature. It is given by the following formula:

$$\text{Sensitivity/True Positive Rate} = \frac{\text{True Positive (TP)}}{\text{True Positive (TP)} + \text{False Negative (FN)}} \tag{7}$$

Specificity, on the other hand, measures the ability of a model to classify the observation as negative, given that it was negative in nature. It is given by the following formula:

$$\text{Specificity} = (\text{True Negative Rate}) = \frac{\text{True Negative (TN)}}{\text{True Negative (TN)} + \text{False Positive (FP)}} \tag{8}$$

Precision measures the accuracy of positives classified using the model, and is given by the following formula:

$$\text{Precision} = \frac{\text{True Positive (TP)}}{\text{True Positive (TP)} + \text{False Positive (FP)}} \tag{9}$$

F-score/F-Measure is used in binary logistic regression models that combine both precision and recall, and is given as follows:

$$\text{F-score} = \frac{2 * \text{Precision} * \text{Recall}}{\text{Precision} + \text{Recall}} \tag{10}$$

Finally, encompassing all of the measures, we look into the misclassification rate, which is the proportion of incorrect predictions (both false positives and false negatives) to the total number of predictions. It is given as follows:

$$\text{Misclassification Rate} = \frac{\text{FP} + \text{FN}}{\text{TP} + \text{TN} + \text{FP} + \text{FN}} = 1 - \text{Total Accuracy} \tag{11}$$

As we know, the total accuracy and misclassification rate are inversely related. As accuracy increases, the misclassification rate decreases, and vice versa.

For the overall examination of the results, metrics were compared between training and validation datasets. A model can achieve high accuracy on the training set, but may perform poorly on the validation set due to overfitting. Similarly, if the model achieves low accuracy on the training set but performs well on the validation set, this is an indication of underfitting (Srivastava et al. 2014). Thus, inferences were drawn based on both training and validation performance metrics to ensure that the model generalizes well. Since the launch of AFMI datasets, this is the first time any research paper has investigated modelling the stress level of mutual funds using deep learning models. For each architecture, the datasets for training and validation were in the ratio 80:20, chosen randomly for the period from February 2024 to September 2024, respectively. For the analysis, R-programming and SAS JMP software programs (R- 4.4.2 version JMP Pro 18) were used.

4. Data Analysis and Interpretation

For each month, and with response variables having either 50% pro-rata liquidation or 25% pro-rata liquidation, ANNs with different architectures were used, and each model was formed as follows:

a. Model 1: ANN with one hidden layer with two nodes, one input layer with fourteen variables, and an output layer with one variable which is categorical in nature.
b. Model 2: ANN with one hidden layer with three nodes, one input layer with fourteen variables, and an output layer with one variable which is categorical in nature.
c. Model 3: ANN with one hidden layer with nodes ranging from four to ten nodes, one input layer with fourteen variables, and an output layer with one variable which is categorical in nature (only the best model based on performance metrics in training and validation is shown).

d. Model 4: ANN with two hidden layers with two nodes each for a layer, one input layer with fourteen variables, and an output layer with one variable which is categorical in nature.
e. Model 5: ANN with two hidden layers with three nodes each for a layer, one input layer with fourteen variables, and an output layer with one variable which is categorical in nature.
f. Model 6: ANN with two hidden layers with nodes ranging from four to ten for each layer, one input layer with fourteen variables, and an output layer with one variable which is categorical in nature (only the best model based on performance metrics in training and validation is shown).

As mentioned before, the activation function used between the input layer and the hidden layer, as well as between the hidden layer and the output layer, is sigmoidal function. The learning rate and momentum rate are taken as 0.5. The operation is completed in 1000 iteration steps. The performance measures obtained for the training and validation period for each month were tabulated separately.

The structure of the ANN proposed for the months of February 2024 using six models is shown below in Figures 1–6.

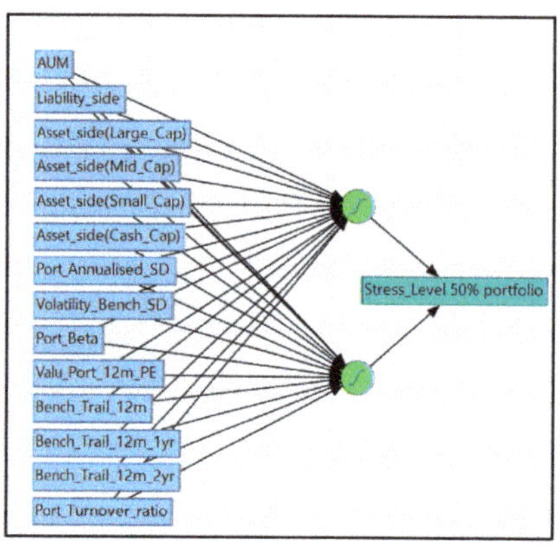

Figure 1. Model 1 depicting ANN with one hidden layer and two nodes for February 2024.

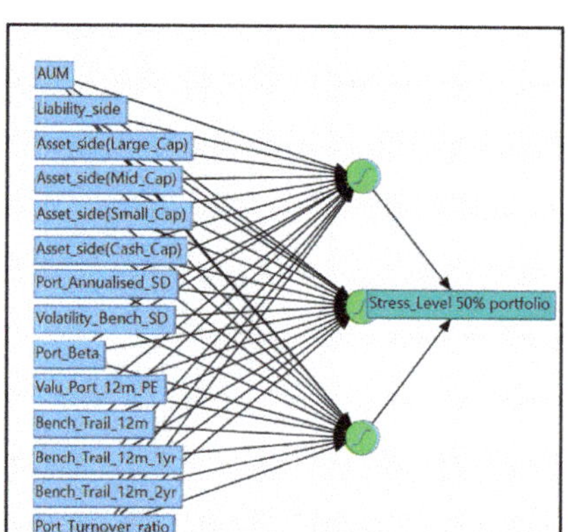

Figure 2. Model 2 presents ANN with one hidden layer and three nodes for February 2024.

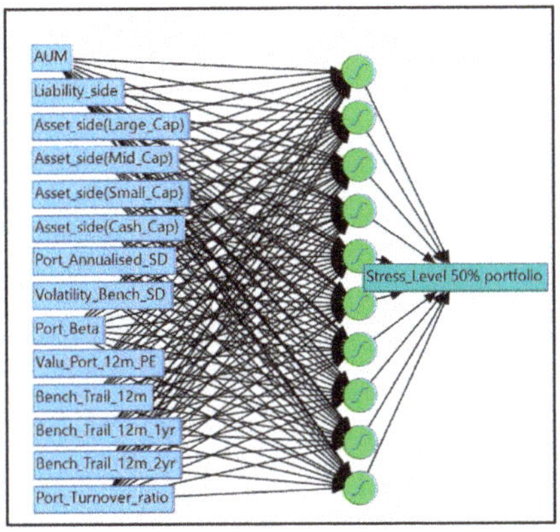

Figure 3. Model 3 depicts ANN with many nodes in the hidden layer for February 2024.

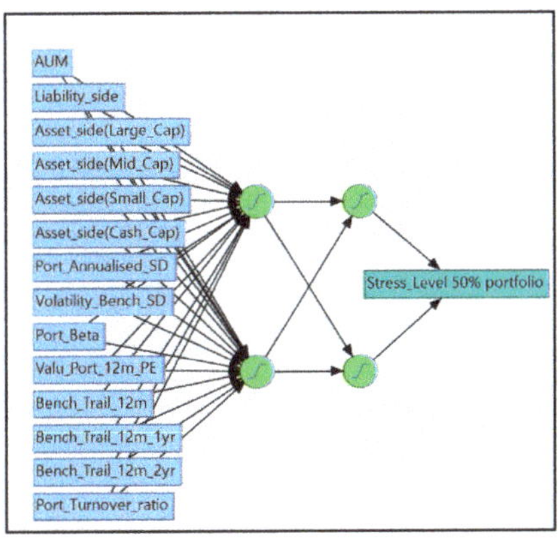

Figure 4. Model 4 presents ANN with two hidden layer with two nodes each for February 2024.

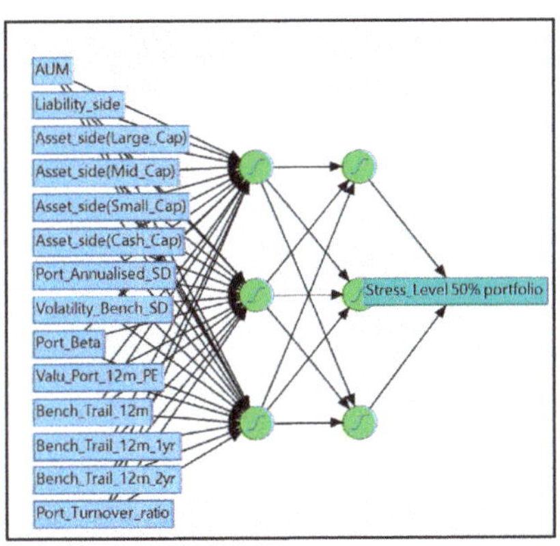

Figure 5. Model 5 presents ANN with two hidden layer with three nodes each for February 2024.

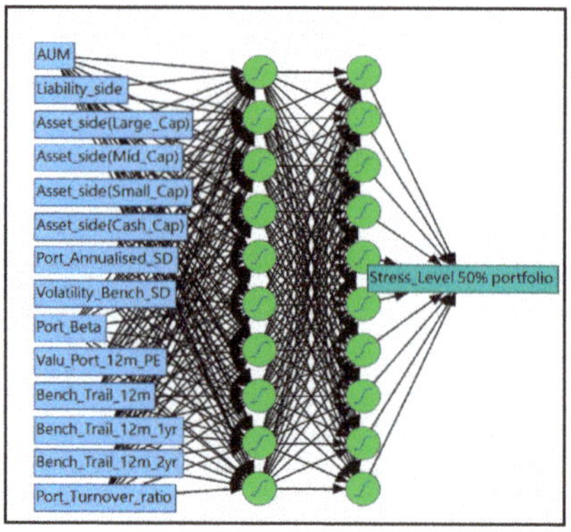

Figure 6. Model 6 presents ANN with multiple nodes for two hidden layer for February 2024.

Initially, as shown in Figures 7–9, the models that had estimates with a hidden layer varying from one to three and with varying numbers of nodes are presented to predict the pro-rata basis liquidation with the stress level at 50% portfolio for the MidCap funds for February 2024. The result of the analysis is shown in Table 7:

(a) Model building for MidCap funds for February 2024 with pro-rata basis liquidation of 50% portfolio.

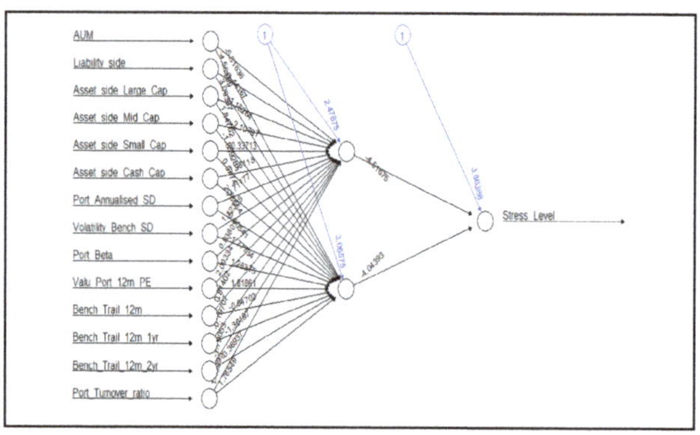

Figure 7. Model −1 for February 2024, with estimates.

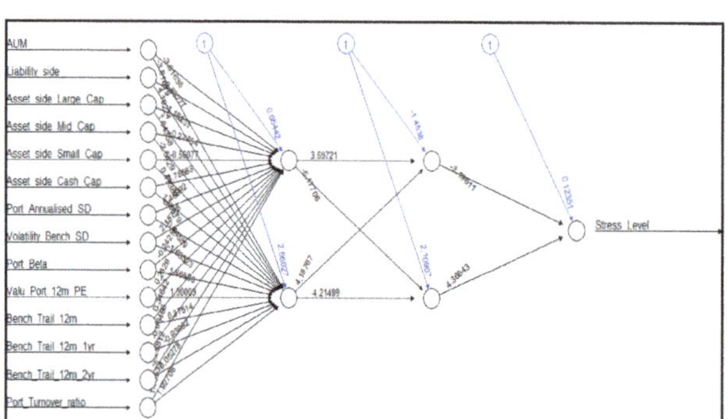

Figure 8. Model −4 for February 2024, with estimates.

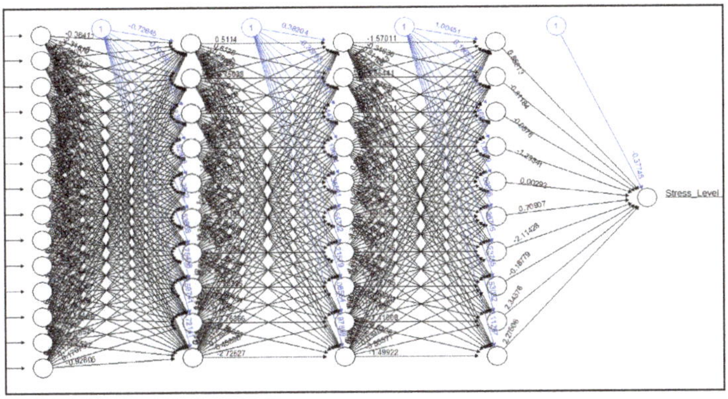

Figure 9. Model −6 for February 2024, with estimates.

Table 7. Performance metrics of ANN models for MidCap funds during February 2024 (with pro-rata basis liquidation of 50% portfolio).

Model	Accuracy	No Information Rate	Kappa	Mcnemar's Test p-Value	Sensitivity	Specificity
1 Hidden layer with 2 nodes	0.8	0.8	0	0.073	0.0	1.0
1 Hidden layer with 3 nodes	1.0	0.64	1	NA	1.0	1.0
2 Hidden layer with 2 nodes	0.96	0.64	0.911	1.00	1.0	0.89
2 Hidden layer with 3 nodes	0.72	0.72	0	0.023	1.0	0.0
2 Hidden layer with 10 nodes	0.72	0.72	0	0.023	1.0	0.0
3 Hidden layer with 10 nodes	0.72	0.72	0	0.023	1.0	0.0

In Table 7, consider the results shown in first row, which depicts the results for Model 1 with one hidden layer and two nodes for the dataset. We observe that, while the model demonstrates high sensitivity in correctly identifying instances of low stress levels, it suffers from low specificity and overall poor performance in accurately predicting stress levels. The accuracy of the model is calculated to be 0.8, indicating that it correctly classified 80% of the instances in the dataset. Upon splitting the dataset, 20 observations fall into training and 5 observations into test datasets. The performance metrics of Model 1 are depicted in Table 8.

Table 8. Performance metrics of Model 1 for MidCap funds during February 2024 (with pro-rata basis liquidation of 50% portfolio).

Confusion Matrix for Training Dataset			Confusion Matrix for Validation Dataset		
Actual	Predicted Count		Actual	Predicted Count	
Stress_Level 50% portfolio	0	1	Stress_Level 50% portfolio	0	1
0	14	0	0	4	0
1	0	6	1	0	1
Misclassification rate	0.00		Misclassification rate	0.00	

As observed, the sensitivity of the model, also known as the true positive rate, is 100%, with all 14 observations and 4 observations in the training and test data being correctly classified. The specificity of the model, which measures the true negative rate, is also 100%, with 6 observations and 1 observation in the training and test dataset being correctly classified. The misclassification rate is 0.00, indicating that the model correctly identified all instances correctly with total accuracy of 100%.

In order to compare the obtained results across various models of ANN in the training and validation datasets for the time period considered at different pro-rata basis liquidation rates, total accuracy performance metrics were tabulated and compared between the training and validation datasets across all combinations. The results are summarized in Table 9 for MidCap funds and in Table 10 for SmallCap funds, respectively. As observed, the performance metrics offer valuable insights into the models' effectiveness in predicting the liquidation strategies for different types of funds and time periods. Across all scenarios, the best-performing NN model consistently achieved perfect accuracy, indicating that it correctly predicts all instances in the dataset. This exceptional accuracy underscores the effectiveness of the model in capturing the underlying patterns and relationships in the data. Furthermore, the models consistently outperform the no information rate, which serves as a baseline performance metric, indicating that the models provide substantial value beyond random guessing. The high Kappa value of 1 for all scenarios suggests a strong agreement between the model's predictions and the actual outcomes, correcting for agreement occurring by chance. This indicates robust performance across different liquidation strategies and fund types. However, the consistent high total accuracy suggest that the performance of the best NN model remains stable and reliable. Moreover, the sensitivity and specificity metrics indicate that the model performs well in correctly identifying both positive and negative instances, respectively.

Table 9. Total accuracy of ANN across various architectures (Model 1 to Model 6) across training and validation datasets from February 2024 to September 2024 for MidCap.

Year		Model 1		Model 2		Model 3		Model 4		Model 5		Model 6	
		Total Accuracy		Total Accuracy		Total Accuracy		Total Accuracy		Total Accuracy		Total Accuracy	
		Training	Validation	Training	Validation	Training	Validation	Training	Validation	Training	Validation	Training	Validation
February 2024	STPRL@ 50% portfolio	1.00	1.00	1.00	1.00	1.00	1.00	**0.90**	**1.00**	**0.90**	**0.80**	**1.00**	**0.80**
	STPRL@ 25% portfolio	1.00	1.00	**0.70**	**1.00**	0.95	1.00	1.00	1.00	**0.80**	**1.00**	**0.80**	**1.00**
March 2024	STPRL@ 50% portfolio	1.00	1.00	1.00	1.00	1.00	1.00	**0.95**	**1.00**	1.00	1.00	1.00	1.00
	STPRL@ 25% portfolio	1.00	1.00	1.00	1.00	1.00	1.00	1.00	1.00	1.00	1.00	1.00	1.00
April 2024	STPRL@ 50% portfolio	1.00	0.80	**1.00**	**0.80**	**1.00**	**0.80**	**0.85**	**0.60**	**0.70**	**1.00**	**0.65**	**1.00**
	STPRL@ 25% portfolio	1.00	1.00	1.00	1.00	1.00	1.00	1.00	0.80	1.00	1.00	1.00	1.00
May 2024	STPRL@ 50% portfolio	0.86	**0.50**	**0.86**	**1.00**	0.57	1.00	**0.71**	**1.00**	**0.71**	**0.50**	**0.30**	**1.00**
	STPRL@ 25% portfolio	0.71	1.00	1.00	1.00	1.00	1.00	**1.00**	**0.50**	**1.00**	**0.50**	1.00	1.00
June 2024	STPRL@ 50% portfolio	1.00	1.00	1.00	1.00	1.00	1.00	1.00	1.00	1.00	1.00	1.00	1.00
	STPRL@ 25% portfolio	1.00	1.00	1.00	1.00	1.00	1.00	1.00	1.00	1.00	1.00	1.00	1.00
July 2024	STPRL@ 50% portfolio	0.95	1.00	1.00	1.00	1.00	1.00	1.00	1.00	1.00	1.00	1.00	1.00
	STPRL@ 25% portfolio	1.00	1.00	1.00	1.00	1.00	1.00	1.00	1.00	1.00	1.00	1.00	1.00
August 2024	STPRL@ 50% portfolio	**0.57**	**0.60**	1.00	1.00	**0.91**	**0.40**	1.00	1.00	**0.38**	**0.40**	**0.91**	**0.80**
	STPRL@ 25% portfolio	0.86	1.00	1.00	1.00	1.00	1.00	**0.86**	**1.00**	1.00	1.00	1.00	1.00
September 2024	STPRL@ 50% portfolio	1.00	1.00	1.00	1.00	1.00	1.00	1.00	1.00	1.00	1.00	1.00	1.00
	STPRL@ 25% portfolio	1.00	1.00	1.00	1.00	1.00	1.00	1.00	1.00	1.00	1.00	1.00	1.00

Table 10. Total Accuracy of ANN across various architectures (Model 1 to Model 6) across training and validation datasets from February 2024 to September 2024 for SmallCap.

Year		Model 1		Model 2		Model 3		Model 4		Model 5		Model 6	
		Total Accuracy		Total Accuracy		Total Accuracy		Total Accuracy		Total Accuracy		Total Accuracy	
		Training	Validation	Training	Validation	Training	Validation	Training	Validation	Training	Validation	Training	Validation
February 2024	STPRL@ 50% portfolio	**0.88**	**1.00**	**0.35**	**1.00**	1.00	1.00	1.00	1.00	**1.00**	**0.75**	1.00	1.00
	STPRL@ 25% portfolio	**0.53**	**0.75**	**0.53**	**1.00**	**0.47**	**1.00**	0.71	0.75	**0.64**	**0.50**	**0.29**	**0.75**
March 2024	STPRL@ 50% portfolio	**1.00**	**0.75**	**1.00**	**0.75**	**1.00**	**0.75**	1.00	0.75	1.00	0.75	1.00	1.00
	STPRL@ 25% portfolio	1.00	1.00	1.00	1.00	**0.44**	**1.00**	1.00	1.00	1.00	1.00	1.00	1.00
April 2024	STPRL@ 50% portfolio	**0.35**	**0.75**	1.00	1.00	1.00	1.00	**0.88**	**0.75**	**0.53**	**1.00**	**0.94**	**1.00**
	STPRL@ 25% portfolio	**0.94**	**0.75**	1.00	1.00	**0.59**	**1.00**	**0.53**	**1.00**	1.00	1.00	**0.71**	**1.00**
May 2024	STPRL@ 50% portfolio	1.00	1.00	1.00	1.00	1.00	1.00	1.00	1.00	1.00	1.00	1.00	1.00
	STPRL@ 25% portfolio	1.00	1.00	1.00	1.00	**0.72**	**1.00**	**0.57**	**1.00**	**0.43**	**0.50**	**0.71**	**1.00**
June 2024	STPRL@ 50% portfolio	1.00	1.00	1.00	1.00	1.00	1.00	1.00	1.00	1.00	1.00	1.00	1.00
	STPRL@ 25% portfolio	1.00	1.00	**1.00**	**0.75**	**0.53**	**1.00**	**0.88**	**1.00**	1.00	1.00	1.00	1.00
July 2024	STPRL@ 50% portfolio	1.00	1.00	1.00	1.00	**0.62**	**1.00**	1.00	1.00	1.00	1.00	1.00	1.00
	STPRL@ 25% portfolio	1.00	1.00	**0.67**	**0.75**	**0.61**	**0.75**	1.00	1.00	**0.56**	**0.75**	**0.22**	**0.75**
August 2024	STPRL@ 50% portfolio	1.00	1.00	1.00	1.00	1.00	1.00	1.00	1.00	1.00	1.00	1.00	1.00
	STPRL@ 25% portfolio	1.00	1.00	1.00	1.00	1.00	1.00	1.00	1.00	**0.78**	**1.00**	1.00	1.00
September 2024	STPRL@ 50% portfolio	1.00	1.00	1.00	1.00	1.00	1.00	1.00	1.00	1.00	1.00	1.00	1.00
	STPRL@ 25% portfolio	**0.44**	**1.00**	**0.66**	**1.00**	**0.55**	**0.75**	**0.55**	**1.00**	**0.61**	**1.00**	**0.72**	**1.00**

The perfect sensitivity and specificity scores further validate the model's ability to accurately predict the liquidation strategies for both MidCap and SmallCap funds across different time periods and portfolio liquidation percentages. Overall, the results demonstrate the effectiveness of the NN model in predicting optimal liquidation strategies for MidCap and SmallCap funds, highlighting its potential utility in financial decision-making processes.

5. Conclusions and Scope for Future Research

The recent introduction of innovative methodologies for evaluating mutual fund performance and risk in India, exemplified by the Association of Mutual Funds of India's (AMFI) "Stress Test" initiative, marks a significant transformation in the investment landscape. This initiative, supported by SEBI's outlined methodology, aims to assess the stress levels in MidCap and SmallCap mutual funds by simulating scenarios of significant redemption requests. The proactive approach taken by AMFI and SEBI reflects a commitment to enhancing transparency and accountability within the mutual fund industry, ultimately empowering investors with deeper insights into the resilience of their investment portfolios. The results obtained from the analysis highlights the effectiveness of neural network models in predicting optimal liquidation strategies for MidCap and SmallCap funds under different scenarios. The consistently high accuracy, Kappa value, sensitivity, and specificity metrics underscore the reliability and robustness of these models in assessing fund performance and risk.

In conclusion, the integration of innovative methodologies such as stress testing into mutual fund evaluation frameworks represents a positive step towards bolstering investor confidence and promoting informed decision making. By providing insights into how funds perform under stress scenarios, investors can better understand the potential risks associated with their investments and make more informed choices.

Moving forward, there are several suggestions and avenues for future research. Firstly, the ongoing monitoring and refinement of stress testing methodologies will be essential to ensure their effectiveness in capturing evolving market dynamics. Additionally, exploring the application of advanced machine learning techniques beyond neural networks, such as ensemble methods or deep learning architectures, could further enhance the accuracy and predictive power of fund evaluation models. Furthermore, conducting comprehensive studies to evaluate the impact of stress testing initiatives on investor behaviour, market stability, and fund performance over the long term would provide valuable insights for industry stakeholders and regulators. Future research could investigate the behavioural patterns of retail investors when they are presented with risk-related metrics such as stress test results and liquidity parameters. Future research could delve into more sophisticated deep learning architectures to refine the prediction of stress parameters. Studies could test ensemble learning techniques or hybrid models that combine neural networks with other statistical methods for potentially higher accuracy.

Overall, the introduction of stress testing initiatives represents a significant milestone in the evolution of mutual fund evaluation practises in India. By embracing innovation and adopting proactive measures to enhance transparency and accountability, the mutual fund industry can continue to foster investor trust and contribute to the development of a resilient and sustainable financial ecosystem. By leveraging advanced computational techniques, this study contributes to the ongoing discourse surrounding risk management and decision-making in the realm of mutual fund investments. The insights garnered from this research have practical implications for investors, fund managers, and regulatory bodies, facilitating more informed investment strategies and risk mitigation measures in the mutual fund industry.

Author Contributions: Conceptualization, S.M.; Methodology, D.R.N.; Formal analysis, D.R.N.; Data curation, D.R.N.; Writing—original draft, S.M. and D.R.N.; Writing—review and editing, S.M. and D.R.N.; Project administration, S.M. All authors have read and agreed to the published version of the manuscript.

Funding: This research received no external funding.

Data Availability Statement: The data is freely available in the website's dedicated section with the heading, "Disclosure of Stress Test & Liquidity Analysis in respect of MidCap & SmallCap Funds". We encourage aspirants to download it and test the models.

Conflicts of Interest: The authors declare no conflicts of interest.

Notes

1. https://www.livemint.com/mutual-fund/mid-small-cap-mutual-funds-regulators-took-these-4-steps-to-protect-investors-from-high-valuations-amfi-sebi-s-11709284068761.html, accessed on 10 March 2024.
2. In the article titled *"Revealed! No. of days Nippon India, biggest small-cap fund, will need to sell off 50% of its portfolio"*, the authors emphasized that more than 3–6 days would suggest stress in the mutual fund. https://www.businesstoday.in/mutual-funds/story/revealed-no-of-days-nippon-india-biggest-small-cap-fund-will-need-to-sell-off-50-of-its-portfolio-421556-2024-03-15, accessed on 20 April 2024.

References

Alzubaidi, Laith, Jinglan Zhang, Amjad Humaidi, Ayad Al-Dujaili, Ye Duan, Omran Al-Shamma, Jose Santamaría, Mohammed Fadhel, Muthana Al-Amidie, and Laith Farhan. 2021. Review of deep learning: Concepts, CNN architectures, challenges, applications, future directions. *Journal of Big Data* 8: 10–19. [CrossRef] [PubMed]

Bergstra, James, and Yoshua Bengio. 2012. Random Search for Hyper-Parameter Optimization. *The Journal of Machine Learning Research* 13: 281–305.

Berk, Jonathan, and Jules van Binsbergen. 2012. Measuring Skill in the Mutual Fund Industry. *Journal of Financial Economics* 118: 1–20. [CrossRef]

Chen, Wei, Huilin Xu, Lifen Jia, and Ying Gao. 2020. Machine learning model for Bitcoin exchange rate prediction using economic and technology determinants. *International Journal of Forecasting* 37: 28–43. [CrossRef]

Crone, Sven, Michele Hibon, and Konstantinos Nikolopoulos. 2011. Advances in forecasting with neural networks? Empirical evidence from the NN3 competition on time series prediction. *International Journal of Forecasting* 27: 635–60. [CrossRef]

D'Amour, Alexander, Katherine Heller, Dan Moldovan, Ben Adlam, Babak Alipanahi, Alex Beutel, Christina Chen, Jonathan Deaton, Jacob Eisenstein, Matthew Hoffman, and et al. 2022. Underspecification Presents Challenges for Credibility in Modern Machine Learning. *Journal of Machine Learning Research* 23: 1–61.

Degadwala, Sheshang, and Dhairya Vyas. 2024. Systematic Analysis of Deep Learning Models vs. Machine Learning. *International Journal of Scientific Research in Computer Science, Engineering and Information Technology* 10: 60–70. [CrossRef]

Du, Mengnan, Ninghao Liu, and Xia Hu. 2019. Techniques for interpretable machine learning. *Communications of the ACM* 63: 68–77. [CrossRef]

Elton, Edwin, and Martin Gruber. 2020. A Review of the Performance Measurement of Long-Term Mutual Funds. *Financial Analysts Journal* 76: 22–37. [CrossRef]

Feng, Guanhao, Stefano Giglio, and Dacheng Xiu. 2020. Taming the Factor Zoo: A Test of New Factors. *The Journal of Finance* 75: 1327–70. [CrossRef]

Gu, Shihao, Bryan Kelly, and Dacheng Xiu. 2020. Empirical Asset Pricing via Machine Learning. *The Review of Financial Studies* 33: 2223–73. [CrossRef]

Harvey, Campbell, and Yan Liu. 2018. Detecting Repeatable Performance. *The Review of Financial Studies* 31: 2499–552. [CrossRef]

Hastie, Trevor, Robert Tibshirani, and Jerome Friedman. 2009. *The Elements of Statistical Learning: Data Mining, Inference, and Prediction*, 2nd ed. New York: Springer.

Hoberg, Gerard, Nitin Kumar, and Nagpurnanand Prabhala. 2018. Mutual Fund Competition, Managerial Skill, and Alpha Persistence. *Review of Financial Studies* 31: 1896–929. [CrossRef]

Hyndman, Rob, and Anne Koehler. 2006. Another look at measures of forecast accuracy. *International Journal of Forecasting* 22: 679–88. [CrossRef]

Irvine, Paul, Jeong Kim, and Jue Ren. 2018. The Beta Anomaly and Mutual Fund Performance. *SSRN Electronic Journal*. Available online: http://dx.doi.org/10.2139/ssrn.3285885 (accessed on 12 January 2024).

Jones, Christopher, and Haitao Mo. 2020. Out-of-Sample Performance of Mutual Fund Predictors. *The Review of Financial Studies* 34: 149–93. [CrossRef]

Joshi, A., and S. Arora. 2022. Economic Conditions and Investor Behavior: Evidence from Indian Mutual Funds. *Economic Analysis and Policy* 56: 201–20.

Kavya, Manga, and Prakash Chokkamreddy. 2024. Growth and Dynamics in the Indian Mutual Fund Industry: Analyzing Investor Preferences and Investment Strategies. *International Journal of Advanced Research in Science, Communication and Technology* 4: 175–83. [CrossRef]

Li, Bin, and Alberto Rossi. 2020. Selecting Mutual Funds from the Stocks They Hold: A Machine Learning Approach. *SSRN Electronic Journal*. Available online: http://dx.doi.org/10.2139/ssrn.3737667 (accessed on 14 January 2024).

Makridakis, Spyros, Evangelos Spiliotis, and Vassilis Assimakopoulos. 2019. The M4 Competition: 100,000 time series and 61 forecasting methods. *International Journal of Forecasting* 36: 54–74. [CrossRef]

Narasimha, M. 2024. Mutual Funds Market in India. *International Journal of Marketing & Human Resource Management* 13: 34–41.

Patton, Andrew, and Allan Timmermann. 2010. Monotonicity in asset returns: New tests with applications to the term structure, the CAPM, and portfolio sorts. *Journal of Financial Economics* 98: 605–25. [CrossRef]

Pástor, L'uboš, Robert Stambaugh, and Lucian Taylor. 2017. Do Funds Make More When They Trade More? *The Journal of Finance* 72: 1483–528. [CrossRef]

Srivastava, Nitish, Geoffrey Hinton, Alex Krizhevsky, Ilya Sutskever, and Ruslan Salakhutdinov. 2014. Dropout: A Simple Way to Prevent Neural Networks from Overfitting. *Journal of Machine Learning Research* 15: 1929–58.

Sukumar, R. 2020. Mutual Funds: A Modern Investment Option for Indian Investors. *Asian Journal of Finance & Accounting* 12: 89–102.

mathematics

MDPI

Article

A Study of the Colombian Stock Market with Multivariate Functional Data Analysis (FDA)

Deivis Rodríguez Cuadro [1], Sonia Pérez-Plaza [2,*], Antonia Castaño-Martínez [2] and Fernando Fernández-Palacín [2]

[1] Departamento de Matemáticas, Universidad del Atlántico, Puerto Colombia 081001, Colombia; deivisrodriguez@mail.uniatlantico.edu.co

[2] Department of Statistics and Operations Research, University of Cádiz, 11510 Puerto Real, Spain; antonia.castano@uca.es (A.C.-M.); fernando.fernandez@uca.es (F.F.-P.)

* Correspondence: sonia.perez@uca.es

Abstract: In this work, Functional Data Analysis (FDA) is used to detect behavioral patterns in the Bolsa de Valores de Colombia (BVC) in reaction to the global crises caused by COVID-19 and the war in Ukraine. The oil price fluctuation curve is considered a covariate. The FDA's distinctive ability is to represent stock values as smooth curves that evolve over time and provide new insights into the dynamics of the BVC. The methodology makes use of functional multivariate techniques applied to the smoothed curves of the closing prices of the main stocks of the BVC. The results show that the correlations of the oil curve with the average market curve change from almost null or low in the global period to extremely significant in time windows immediately after the beginnings of COVID-19 and the war in Ukraine, respectively. On the other hand, the velocity curves, which are used to evaluate the stock market volatility, show a pattern of synchronization of companies in the crisis periods. Furthermore, in these crisis periods, the companies in BVC showed a high synchronization with the Brent crude oil price. In conclusion, this work shows the usefulness of the FDA as a complement to time series analysis in the study of stock markets. The results of this research could be of interest to academic researchers, financial analysts, or institutions.

Keywords: functional data analysis; stock market; volatility; functional principal component analysis; k-means clustering

MSC: 62R10; 62H30; 62P20

1. Introduction

Since its creation in 1929, the Bolsa de Valores de Colombia (BVC) has compiled daily measurements of registered securities issuers. The evolution of these values and, as a consequence, the Colombian economy depends largely on oil exports [1]. Several articles analyze the evolution of oil prices and their impact on world economies [2–4].

The price of a barrel of oil, regulated by OPEC since 1973, has experienced wide fluctuations determined by conflicts and geopolitical factors. In particular, a negative bubble in oil prices occurred in 2014/2015 [5]. The factors that may influence have been analyzed in an extensive note from the World Bank Group, presented by Baffes [6] in 2015.

The availability of stock values, almost in real time, makes the use of Functional Data Analysis (FDA) techniques possible and even advisable. The FDA allows each stock market security to be represented by a curve for any given time period. The curves are obtained by applying smoothing techniques to the stock market series, for which a basis of functions is needed. FDA was introduced by Ramsay and Silverman [7,8]. They extend classical statistics to the case of functions by implementing most of the classical methods.

In recent years, the analysis of the impact of global crises on different financial markets has become a common problem [9]. Firstly, in 2020, the COVID-19 virus spread throughout the world and led all countries to develop measures to prevent viral transmission, which had a major impact on the global economy, reflected in stock market trends [10]. On the other hand, in February 2022, Russia launched a full-scale invasion of Ukraine and began occupying more of the country, starting the biggest conflict in Europe since World War II. Sanctions against the invaders by a large number of countries, led by the countries of the European Union and the United States, were not long in coming. As Russia is one of the main suppliers of oil and gas, a large part of the actions focused on restrictions on the purchase of these raw materials. The consequences in the markets of both crises were reflected in high volatility.

Not all countries suffered the consequences of these two crises in the same way. The strength of the economies and the degree of dependence on oil derivatives were two of the most important factors. In this context, we decided to study the behavior of an emerging economy, such as Colombia.

This paper is organized as follows. In Section 2, the articles related to this work are presented. In Section 3, the used data are described in the first part and the FDA methods used in the paper are presented in the second part. This part includes the description of the functional data processing, the introduction of the functional correlation measure, and the FDA methods used. These methods are the k-means clustering and the FPCA techniques. In Section 4, the previous procedures are applied to the data of the Colombian Stock Exchange. Finally, in Section 5, the main conclusions are shown.

2. Literature Review

Several authors have analyzed the advantages of FDA compared to other ways of treating data, in particular, the classical times series [11–14]. According to Allen [11], "From a statistical viewpoint, time series analysis is extremely beneficial. From a mathematical viewpoint, FDA adds a modern twist on typical analysis. While one method is not meant to replace the other, each one has advantages over the other one". Moreover, Gertheiss et al. assert in [12]: "In contrast to simpler methods that reduce the functional observations to scalar summary values, FDA retains all important information by directly using the functional observations in the analysis". In different situations, the elements of the study are part of a continuous dynamic process, and, in this case, FDA has the advantage of exploring the dynamic information implicit in static data. Furthermore, in these cases, the analysis of the functional curve, speed curve, and acceleration curve can provide a global view of the problem under study. An example of this can be found in [13], where FDA is used to investigate the changes in energy security from a dynamic perspective.

According to Ullah [14], "In contrast to most other methods commonly used to model trends in time series data, a key strength of the FDA approach is that it makes no parametric assumptions about age or time effects. The FDA methods for modeling and forecasting data across a range of health and demographic issues also have significant advantages for better understanding trends, risk factor relationships, and the effectiveness of preventive measures". Another advantage is that FDA does not require the stationarity condition of the data, which are treated in their original form. In practice, FDA adapts to any type of scenario and to high-frequency data. The smoothing methods used in FDA allow good control of overparameterization and produce curves with good metric and analytical properties, usually functions of class two. The first derivatives of the obtained functions give us the curves of the rate of change in the functional data, which opens a very promising field of study in a fundamental subject such as market volatility.

The way in which the FDA is applied depends on the area in question: Medicine, Meteorology, Economics, or other fields. In each field, it is important to use an appropriate methodology for the type of data. In Pérez-Plaza et al. [15], the methods used to filter, smooth, and analyze data are appropriate for seismic data. In the field of Economics, several authors have made important contributions thanks to the perspective of the FDA. Works that analyze the stock market are special due to the nature of their data, and generally, there is no specific methodology. In this field, Aguilera [16] considers weekly observations of a random sample of banks listed on the Madrid Stock Exchange, applying the Functional Principal Component Analysis (FPCA) to model and forecast prices for Spanish banks. Ingrassia and Costanzo [17] carry out an exploratory analysis of the Italian Stock Market by using FDA, suggesting the possibility of constructing a stock index based on functional indicators. Dablemont [18] presents a functional method for clustering, modeling, and forecasting time series by using functional analysis and neural networks. This method can be applied to any type of time series but is particularly effective when observations are irregularly spaced, occur at different time points for each curve, or when only fragments of the curves are observed. Benko [19], in his doctoral thesis, demonstrates the efficiency of using the functional data approach for high volatility problems, common in financial markets. His work focuses on the study of Euribor rate curves. Moreover, in the case of the Colombian stock market, there are no references to the use of FDA. Das [20] presents a new regression approach derived from FDA to analyze the effect of global crises on stock market correlations. Das employs a wide range of global crises (from the beginning of the 19th century) that have not yet been examined in the literature in this context.

Traditionally, the volatility study has been based on statistical measures of dispersion. Low volatility is related to stable market values and reduced risk levels, while high volatility is often associated with convulsive scenery and high levels of risk. In the analysis of high-frequency financial data, as well as in stock markets, volatility will be given as a function of time. In any case, it is not a directly measurable magnitude and should be estimated from the dispersion of the values; different methods and procedures are used for this purpose. From the perspective of time series, different solutions have been proposed to estimate volatility most of them based on Autoregressive conditional Heteroscedasticity (ARCH) models or Generalized Autoregressive Conditional Heteroscedasticity (GARCH) models; the works of Andersen and Bollerslev [21], Engle [22], Engle and Gallo [23] and, more recently, Engle and Sokalska [24] and Narsoo [25] are of special interesting in this context. On the other hand, from the perspective of FDA, the estimation of volatility can be obtained from the adaptation of the autoregressive models to the functional field (see Müller [26] or Shang [27]). Different works analyze the price of crude oil and other stock market indices during periods of extreme events [28,29], although these papers employ time series procedures. In his PhD thesis [30], Wei applies FDA techniques to high-frequency intraday volatility data sets, develops methods for performing short-term dynamic forecasts in real time, and introduces a proximity measurement functional curve clustering algorithm applied to a COVID-19 functional data set.

In this work, since volatility is an indicator of the variation of the prices over time, we propose to use the first derivatives of the functions in order to explore the volatility of BVC values from the velocity curves. In any case, the point of view of volatility that we propose in this work is different from intra-daily volatility, which is usually used in stock market literature, since, in our case, it is a functional volatility at each instant of time. From a graphical perspective, the speed curves show the historical behavior of the market and from an analytical point of view, the determination of the curves allows us to make forecasts.

The general objective of this article is to introduce the methodology based on FDA for the study of a stock market with the Colombian typology, characterized by its high dependence on the price of oil and with high illiquidity sceneries. FDA's ability to represent stock market values as smooth curves over time offers a potential solution to the challenges posed by market illiquidity. By employing smoothing techniques on the available stock market series, this study can capture underlying patterns and trends that might be overlooked by conventional methods.

In order to specify the general objective, three operational objectives are established to which we will try to respond under the framework of FDA. The first and foremost objective investigates the temporal fluctuations and patterns exhibited by the stock curves and seeks to understand the complexities that govern the dynamics of the Colombian market, particularly in the two times after the beginning of the crises caused by COVID-19, and for the war in Ukraine. Secondly, the functional correlations between the Brent crude oil prices and the BVC average curve are obtained and analyzed. Moreover, the average correlation of each company in BVC to the other curves is calculated, comparing the results of the global period with those obtained in the two time windows described. Thirdly, FPCA is used in order to detect similar behavior in the BVC companies.

3. Materials and Methods

3.1. Functional Data Processing

The first step in the data processing was the data normalizing into log returns

$$x_{ij} = \mathbf{100log}\left(\frac{\boldsymbol{R_{ij}}}{\boldsymbol{R_{i,\,j-1}}}\right), \tag{1}$$

where $\boldsymbol{R_{ij}}$ is the daily stock price *for the* $\boldsymbol{i}$ *company at time* $\boldsymbol{j}$.

3.1.1. Smoothing Procedure

Once the data were transformed into cumulative log returns, the process of estimating and analyzing the functional data began. Although FDA aims to study the selected dynamic data and has different objectives than time series analysis, the two approaches complement each other. To achieve a satisfactory result in the FDA analysis, the curves must be smooth, belong to a vector space of real functions, be square-integrable, and be defined on a bounded interval $\tau = [0, T]$ [7].

Given a curve sample, $X = (x_1(t), x_2(t), \ldots, x_N(t))$ the classical concepts of mean and variances in statistics are defined in [7]:

$$\overline{\mathbf{x}}(t) = \frac{\mathbf{1}}{N}\sum_{i=1}^{N} x_i(t) \text{ and } \mathbf{var}_{\mathbf{x}}(t) = \frac{\mathbf{1}}{\mathbf{N-1}}\Sigma_{i=1}^{N}(\mathbf{x_i(t)} - \overline{\mathbf{x}}(\mathbf{t}))^2. \tag{2}$$

In our case, a discrete sample of the curves is given by the stock price returns of the companies under study. To reconstruct these curves, we employed a smoothing procedure that minimizes the mean squared error (MSE) between the original data points and the smoothed curves, using a basis of functions. The resulting curves must be analytical functions, requiring the continuity of its second derivative.

When functional data are used, it is crucial to select an appropriate basis of functions, guided by the nature of the functions under study. Typically, the Fourier basis is used for periodic functions, the splines basis for smooth functions, and the wavelets basis for curves characterized by multiple local features such as peaks or jumps. In this case, the spline's basis is chosen. It is the most appropriate option due to the trend of the data and its lower MSE.

The smoothing procedure must consider two elements: the number of terms in the basis, K, and the value of the penalty of the smoothing parameter, λ. The role of this parameter is to strike a balance between data fit and curve smoothness. Ramsay and Silverman [7] demonstrate that the curves can be obtained by minimizing the expression:

$$\sum_{j=1}^{p} \left[x_{ij} - x_i(t_j)\right]^2 + \lambda \int \left(D^2 x_i(t)\right)^2 dt, \tag{3}$$

where $x_i = (x_{i1}, x_{i2}, \ldots, x_{ip})$ is the vector of observed values at the days $t_1, t_2, \ldots, t_p$ and D is the differential operator.

The second term in this expression penalizes roughness by minimizing the value of the second derivative. There is no rule of thumb for determining the optimal value of λ. From the possible criteria, generalized cross validation (GCV) was chosen in this research. The optimal number of basic elements and the optimal smoothing parameter are obtained using the min.basis function. This function is implemented in the fda.usc package [31] for the R software. The min.basis function is based on the GCV method.

The series data in this work are processed taking into account the nature of the data. Figure 1 (similar to shown it in [15]) shows the methodology used in this paper.

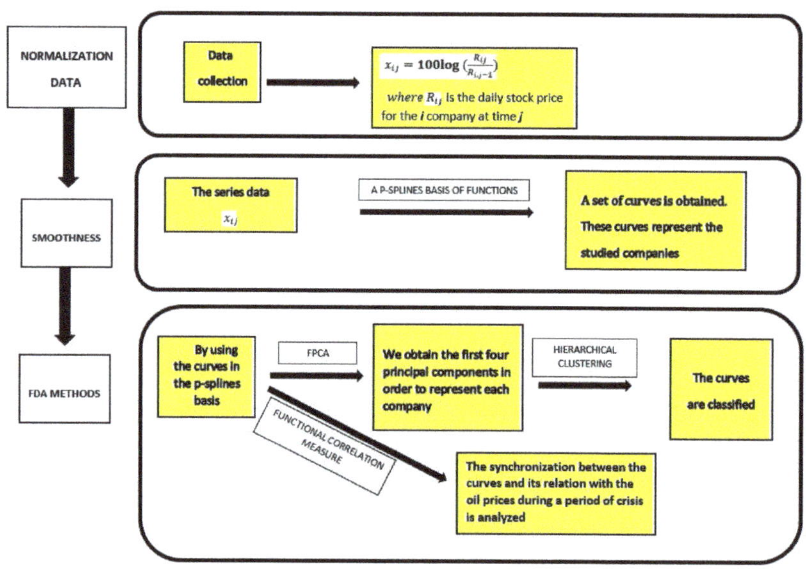

Figure 1. The scheme shows the methodology used in this paper.

3.1.2. Functional Correlation

In this section, the functional correlation measure introduced by Pérez et al. [32] is used.

Let two generic functions in the sample, x(t) and y(t), defined in $\tau \equiv [0, \mathrm{T}]$. The following functional descriptive statistics over a functional data x are considered. These are:

$$\mathrm{f}_{\overline{\mathrm{x}}}, f_{s^2}, \mathrm{f}_{\mathrm{Sxy}} \in \mathrm{L}^2(\tau),\ where\ f_{\overline{\mathrm{x}}}(\mathrm{t}) = \overline{\mathrm{x(t)}},\ f_{s^2}(t) = S^2_{x(t)}$$
$$\mathrm{f}_{\mathrm{Sxy}}(t) = \mathrm{S}_{x(t)\ y(t)};\ \text{for all} t \in \tau,$$
$$with\ \overline{\mathrm{x(t)}} = \mathrm{T}^{-1} \cdot \int_0^{\mathrm{T}} \mathrm{x(t)dt};\ S^2_{x(t)} = \mathrm{T}^{-1} \int_0^T \left(\mathrm{x(t)} - \overline{\mathrm{x(t)}}\right)^2 \mathrm{dt},$$
$$\text{and } S_{x(t)\ y(t)} = \mathrm{T}^{-1} \int_0^T \left(\mathrm{x(t)} - \overline{\mathrm{x(t)}}\right)\left(\mathrm{y(t)} - \overline{\mathrm{y(t)}}\right)\mathrm{dt}. \tag{4}$$

Then, the correlation value function $\mathrm{f}_{\mathrm{rxy}} \in \mathrm{L}^2(\tau)$; $\mathrm{f}_{\mathrm{rxy}}\ (t) = \mathrm{r}_{x(t)\ y(t)}$; for all $\mathrm{t} \in \tau$ with

$$\mathrm{r}_{x(t)\ y(t)} = \frac{S_{x(t)\ y(t)}}{S_{x(t)}S_{y(t)}}. \tag{5}$$

In this case, $\overline{\mathrm{x(t)}}$ represents the average level of the element x(t) and $S^2_{x(t)}$ its variability over the average level. $S_{x(t)\ y(t)}$ and $\mathrm{r}_{x(t)\ y(t)}$ measure the functional variability between the elements x(t) and y(t) (in the second case in a standardized way).

The measure $\mathrm{r}_{x(t)\ y(t)}$ is employed to establish a relation between the functional mean of BVC and the cumulative log returns of Brent curve. Moreover, it is used to validate a synchronization between the companies curves during a period of economic crisis. In this case, the crisis periods analyzed are the beginning of the COVID-19 crisis (between January 2020 and July 2020) and the drop in oil prices (due to the Russian invasion of Ukraine that began on 24 February 2022, which ends in August 2022).

3.1.3. K-Means Clustering

Similar to the methods proposed by Jacques and Preda [33] and Peng and Müler [34], this research proposes a two-stage classification method to group the curves according to its characteristics. In the first stage, the curves are classified into initial groups according to shared characteristics, establishing a reference framework for a more detailed analysis. For each curve, $x_i(t)$, a vector of coefficients $\left(b_{i1}, b_{i2}, \ldots, b_{iJ}\right)^T$ is obtained with respect to the first J basis functions. The first J basis functions accumulate a percentage of 90–95% of the total inertia. In the second stage, a k-means classification procedure is applied based on the vector of coefficients. In this stage, the groupings are refined, and the curves are assigned to more specific clusters, allowing for a more detailed classification of the return curves based on their behavior. This two-stage approach improves the robustness and accuracy of the curve clustering process.

3.1.4. Functional Principal Components Analysis

To identify the variables that explain the behavior of the curves, Functional Principal Component Analysis (FPCA) is recommended. FPCA is an extension of Principal Component Analysis (PCA) in multivariate statistical analyses. The eigenfunctions ξ_j can be obtained by solving the Fredholm functional eigenequation:

$$(V\xi)(t) = \int_0^T K(u,t)\xi(u)du = \langle K(t,.), \xi \rangle = \lambda \xi(t), \tag{6}$$

where $K(u,t) = \sum_{i=1}^{N} x_i(u)x_i(t)$ is the kernel of the curves. The eigenfunctions, ξ_j, are orthogonal and each one is associated with an eigenvalue, λ_j. This eigenvalue represents the inertia of its eigenfunction. Mercer Theorem demonstrates that $K(u,t)$ can be written as:

$$K(u,t) = \sum_{i=1}^{\infty} \lambda_i \xi_i(u)\xi_i(t). \tag{7}$$

On the other hand, by following Karhunen–Loève's procedure, any $x_i(t)$ function can be written as:

$$x_i(t) = \sum_{j=1}^{\infty} b_{ij}\xi_j(t), \quad (8)$$

where the series converges in square mean in [0, T] and b_{ij} are defined as:

$$b_{ij} = \langle \xi_j, x_i \rangle = \int_0^T \xi_j(t)x_i(t)dt, \quad (9)$$

where each b_{ij} represents the projection of $x_i(t)$ in the j-th eigenfunction. In [7] it is shown that the eigenfunctions form an orthonormal basis for the space determined by the curves $x_i(t)$. Since the eigenfunctions are ordered by its inertia, a small number of them can collect a high percentage of information given in the curves $x_i(t)$.

If the curves belong to the same system, these curves share a number of common components. In this case, the first principal component shows the main trend of the pattern, while the second and subsequent components show the shape characteristics. The eigenfunctions help to identify different patterns of behavior in the group of curves.

3.2. Data Collection

In the data collection process for this study, meticulous criteria were used to select a total of twenty-six companies listed on the BVC. These companies were chosen based on specific attributes that made them relevant to the research objectives. In particular, the inclusion criteria were companies with a high trading volume, a dedicated approach to mitigating volatility, and efforts to reduce financing costs. In addition, these companies had extensive media coverage, which was essential for the exhaustive analysis of the dynamics of their market. The data collection phase was extended to cover a substantial period, encompassing 1535 daily observations of closing prices. This extensive period of time allowed the research to summarize a comprehensive view of market behavior. The data collection period began on 2 January 2017 and concluded on 20 April 2023.

The primary source of data for this study was the official website of the BVC, which serves as the authoritative platform for disseminating market-related information and statistics in the Colombian context. Furthermore, as oil prices play a pivotal role in the research, historical data pertaining to Brent crude oil, a key component of the study, was meticulously sourced from Investing.com, a recognized and reliable repository for financial and commodity data. Table 1 provides an informative compilation of the companies that were considered in this study, along with their corresponding abbreviations and sectors, thereby enhancing the transparency and comprehensibility of the research dataset.

Table 1. Companies listed on the BVC in the period under review.

ABBR.	COMPANIES	SECTOR
1.EXI	ALMACENES EXITOS S.A.	Retail industry
2. DAV	BANCO DAVIVIENDA S.A.	Financial
3.BBO	BANCO DE BOGOTA S.A.	Financial
4.BCOL	BANCOLOMBIA S.A.	Financial
5.BVC	BOLSA DE VALORES COLOMBIANA S.A.	Financial
6.CNE	CANACOL ENERGY LTD	Energy
7.CEL	CELSIA S.A. E.S.P.	Energy
8.CEM	CEMENTOS ARGOS S.A.	Construction
9.COND	CONSTRUCCIONES EL CONDOR S.A.	Construction
10.CONC	CONCONCRETO	Construction

Table 1. *Cont.*

ABBR.	COMPANIES	SECTOR
11.CFC	CORPORACIÓN FINANCIERA COLOMBIANA S.A.	Financial
12.ECO	ECOPETROL S.A.	Energy
13.GEB	GRUPO ENERGÍA BOGOTÁ S.A. E.S.P.	Energy
14.ARG	GRUPO ARGOS S.A.	Energy
15.GAV	GRUPO AVAL ACCIONES Y VALORES S.A.	Financial
16.ISA	INTERCONEXION ELECTRICA S.A. E.S.P.	Communications
17.ETB	EMPRESA DE TELECOMUNICACIONES DE BOGOTA S.A. E.S.P.	Communications
18.NUT	GRUPO NUTRESA S.A.	Nutrition
19.GSU	GRUPO DE INVERSIONES SURAMERICANA S.A.	Financial
20.MAS	MINEROS S.A.	Industrial
21.PMG	PROMIGAS	Energy
22.TPL	ORGANIZACIÓN TERPEL S.A.	Energy
23.ICO	FONDO BURSATIL ISHARES COLCAP	Financial
24.APR	ACERIAS PAZ DEL RIO S.A.	Industrial
25.HCOL	FONDO BURSATIL HORIZONS COLOMBIA	Financial
26.GBO	GRUPO BOLIVAR S.A.	Financial

4. Results

The main objective of this work is to show the strong relation between oil prices and the Colombian stock market through Functional Data Analysis (FDA). The researchers aimed to discern how oil price shifts influenced daily closing prices in the Colombian stock market by using FDA methods. The investigation also sought to categorize curves with similar performance during the study period using FPCA and hierarchical clustering techniques.

4.1. Functional Data Processing

From the data available for the 26 companies listed on the Colombian Stock Exchange from 2 January 2017 to 20 April 2023, the cumulative logarithmic returns were calculated. Figure 2 shows the cumulative logarithmic returns series data about these companies.

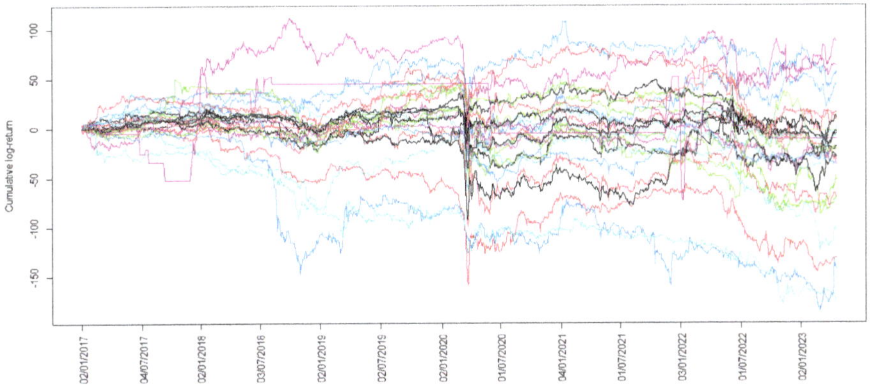

Figure 2. The cumulative log returns of the closing price of companies.

In order to obtain the functional data, the P-splines basis was chosen. The optimal number of elements in the basis and the optimal smoothing parameter were obtained using the min.basis function in the fda.usc package in R 4.1.1 software. Figure 3 shows the functional data obtained with the optimal parameters.

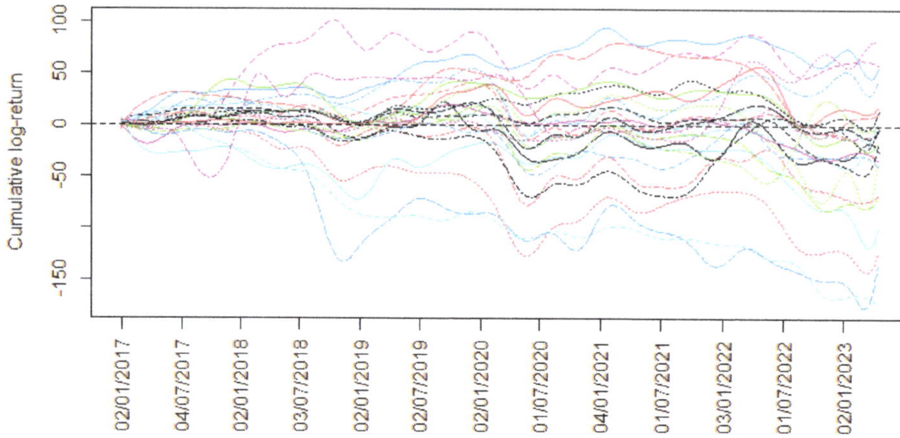

Figure 3. Curves obtained in the P-splines basis with optimal parameters.

Figure 4 shows the velocity curves defined as:

$$x\prime_i(t) = \frac{dx_i(t)}{dt}. \quad (10)$$

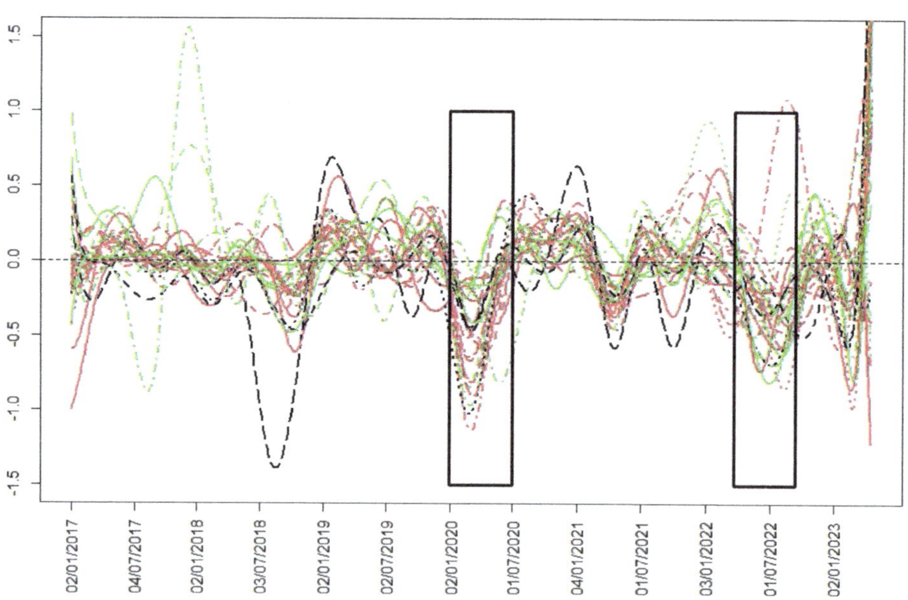

Figure 4. Derivate curves in the P-splines basis.

The analyzed crisis periods are framed in this figure. Greater synchronization between the curves can be seen in both periods.

From the curves we now define the Estimated Functional Volatility of the stock market (EFV) as the mean of the sample velocity curves obtained from (2):

$$\mathbf{EFV}(t) = \frac{\mathbf{1}}{N}\sum_{i=1}^{N} x'_i(t). \tag{11}$$

Figure 5 shows the EFV of the BVC. The bands in the graph are given according to the Equation (4) by:

$$\overline{x'(t)} \pm s_{x'(t)} \text{ and } \overline{x'(t)} \pm 2s_{x'(t)}$$

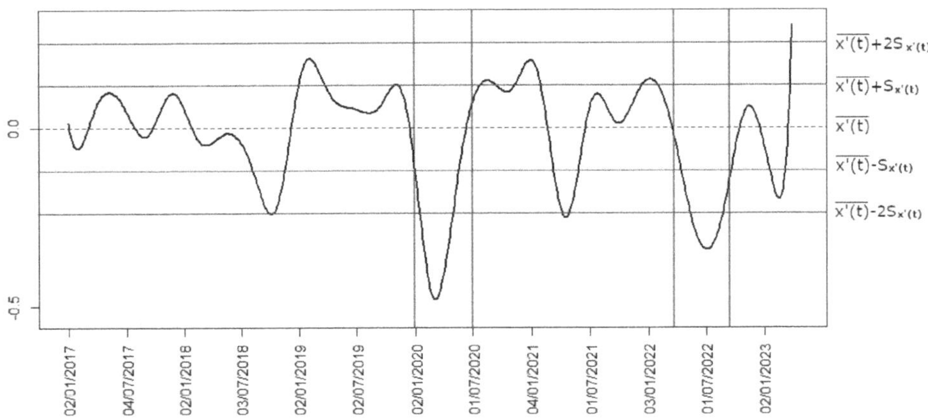

Figure 5. The mean curve of the derivatives curves is shown. The horizontal bands marked show different levels of volatility and the blue lines mark the two crisis periods.

These bands determine medium, high and very high volatility levels. This depends on whether the EFV of the BVC is within the first band, between the first and second bands or outside the second band. Figure 5 shows two periods of very high volatility, marked between vertical lines. These periods coincide with the crisis periods analyzed, the COVID-19 crisis and the beginning of the invasion in Ukraine.

4.2. Functional Correlation

In Figure 6, the functional mean of the BVC's curves and the cumulative log returns of Brent can be seen. The functional mean shows two declines, one at the beginning of 2020 and the other in 2022. The first decrease was caused by the COVID-19 pandemic, which forced governments to lock down their population and led to a collapse in the oil price. In the period of the second event (which coincides with the Russian invasion of Ukraine), a strong correlation with the oil price is shown (see Figure 6 and Table 2). In this time period, the oil price had a significant decline, which directly affected the Colombian market.

Table 2 shows an extremely large significant increase in the correlation measure the relation between the Functional mean of BVC and the cumulative log returns of Brent curves during the two crisis periods considered.

Table 2. Functional correlation measured between the functional mean of BVC curves and the cumulative log returns of Brent in three different periods of time, the two crisis periods and the complete time period.

	Complete Time Period	COVID-19	UKRAINE
Functional correlation	−0.058	0.921	0.956

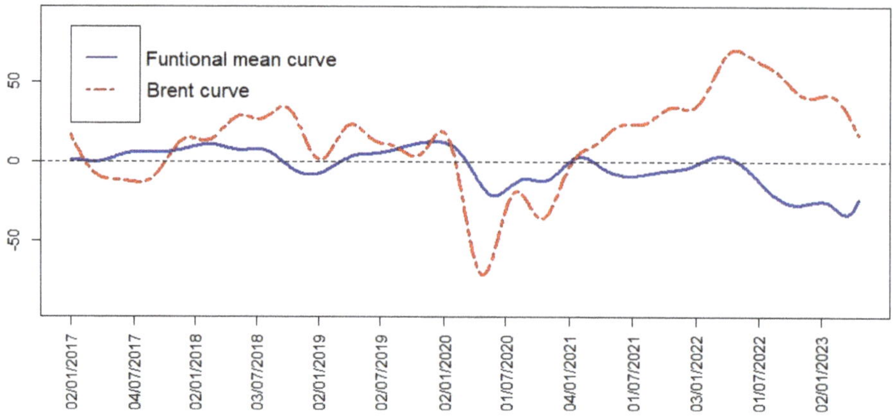

Figure 6. Functional mean of BVC curves and the Brent curve, both estimated with the optimal parameters.

On the other hand, in order to validate a synchronization between the companies' curves during a period of economic crisis, the functional correlation mean of each company to the others is calculated in two crisis periods and in the complete time period (Table 3). The considered periods are, firstly, the COVID-19 crisis period and secondly, the beginning of the invasion of Ukraine.

Table 3. For each company, the functional correlation mean to the other companies is calculated. This measure has been calculated in the two crisis periods and in the complete time period.

Company	Complete Time Period	COVID-19	UKRAINE
EXI	0.490	0.769	0.847
DAV	0.424	0.895	0.851
BBO	0.503	0.880	0.850
BCOL	0.329	0.896	0.901
BVC	0.497	0.778	0.910
CNE	0.442	0.856	0.884
CEL	0.521	0.894	0.869
CEM	0.511	0.895	0.908
COND	0.226	0.833	0.845
CONC	0.487	0.896	0.867
CFC	0.472	0.889	0.909
ECO	0.271	0.894	0.863
GEB	0.393	0.769	0.902
ARG	0.530	0.890	0.779
GAV	0.539	0.891	0.864
ISA	0.421	0.411	0.902
ETB	0.496	0.874	0.791
NUT	0.398	0.870	0.556
GSU	0.420	0.887	0.299
MAS	0.393	0.331	0.908

Table 3. *Cont.*

Company	Complete Time Period	COVID-19	UKRAINE
PMG	0.429	0.867	0.882
TPL	0.473	0.831	0.797
ICO	0.471	0.896	0.910
APR	0.258	0.568	0.817
HCOL	0.435	0.896	0.908
GBO	0.349	0.890	0.905
Mean	0.43	0.84	0.82

Table 3 shows high correlations between almost all companies in crisis periods. Only in the initial period of COVID-19, the companies ISA and MAS do not show such a high correlation with the rest of the companies, while, in the Ukraine crisis, the companies GSU and NUT are the only ones that show low correlation values.

4.3. FPCA and Hierarchical Clustering

FPCA is a useful tool to identify components that explain the behavior of the set of curves. Figure 7 shows the first four principal components of the FPCA procedure. In this case, the first four Principal Components account for over 85.8%, 6.8%, 3.2%, and 1.4%, respectively, of the total explained variability. The first component, which shows the size of the data, shows a smooth linear growth until the first months of 2020. Subsequently, the trend is towards growth. The second component presents a cycle of variability whose critical points are February 2019 and July 2021.

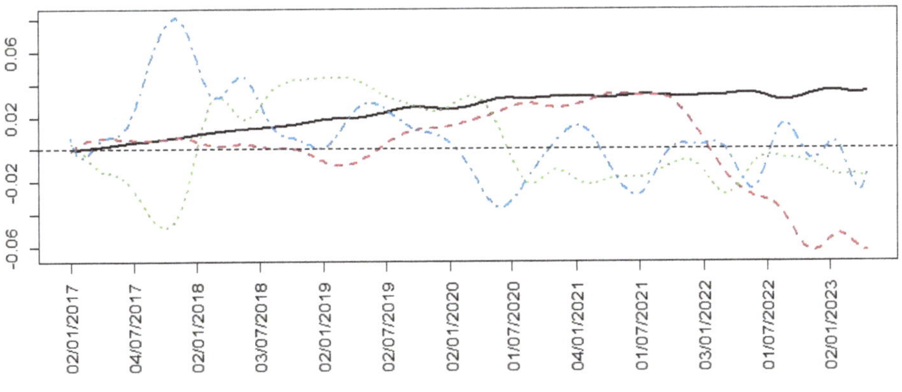

Figure 7. FPCA: the first component is shown in a solid line and the second, third, and fourth components are shown in a broken line in pink, green, and blue color, respectively.

As mentioned above, the coefficients of the curves in the basis, consisting of the principal components, provide a good linear representation of the curves. In this case, for each value, the vector formed by the coefficients of the first four principal components is considered. These components account for over 98.9% of the total inertia.

A hierarchical clustering method is applied to obtain a classification (Figure 8). The hierarchical clustering approach provided insights into three distinct groups of curves with similar trends, enhancing the understanding of market dynamics. The three companies, Argos Cements, Conconcreto (two of the three existing companies in the construction sector), and ETB (in the communications sector), belonging to the first group present extreme behavior and suffer the greatest devaluation. The second group, consisting of seven companies, is affected by fluctuations in oil prices. Two of these companies are in the energy sector, three are financial companies, another one is a construction company, and the last one belongs to retail sales. These companies present a consistent performance on the stock exchange and low volatility during the study period. Finally, the third group consists of sixteen companies whose stock market returns indicate a significant upward trend at the end of the time period. In this group, there are seven financial companies, five energy companies, two industrial companies, one communications company, and another company belonging to the food sector.

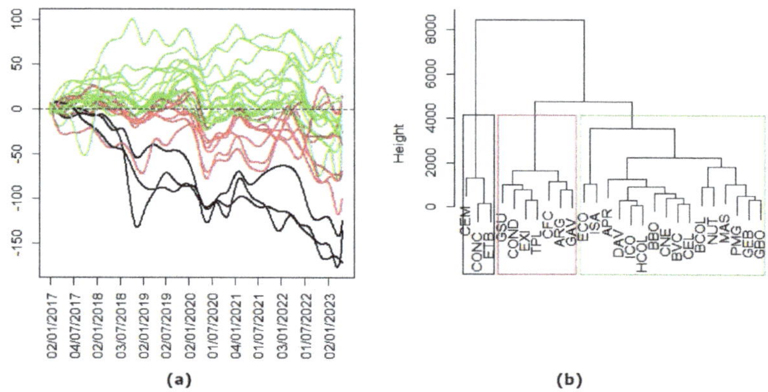

Figure 8. Hierarchical clustering was performed. Three groups with similar trends were observed. (**a**) The three groups of curves are represented in different colors. (**b**) The companies that correspond to the previous curves are grouped by using a dendrogram.

In Figure 9, we can see the mean curves of each group in Figure 8. The curve in the black color represents the companies with long-term losses, the curve in the red color is companies with middle gains, close to zero, and the curve in the green color is the group of companies with more gains.

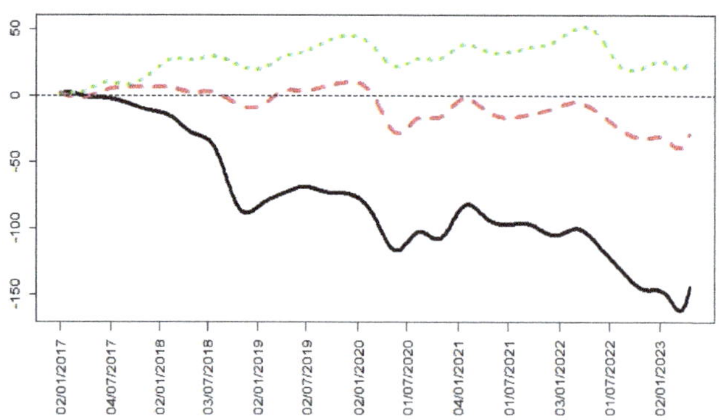

Figure 9. The functional means for each group of curves detected in Figure 8 are represented in the same colors.

The two principal components are illustrated in Figure 10. These components are the perturbations of their mean function by adding and subtracting a multiple of each principal component. As in the vectorial case, the first principal component, which accounts for over 85.8% of the inertia, is a component of the size that shows the variation of the prices;

thus, it explains the behavior in the long term of BVC. On the other hand, the second principal component, which accounts for over 6.8% of the variability, shows the market's response to the crises of COVID-19 and the war in Ukraine because this component changes direction and makes the positive and negative disturbances permute. Therefore, the losses become the profits and vice versa. Ingrassia and Costanzo [12] interpret this component as a "shock" since the shares that had a good (resp. bad) performance before March 2022 have been going down (resp. rising) after that date.

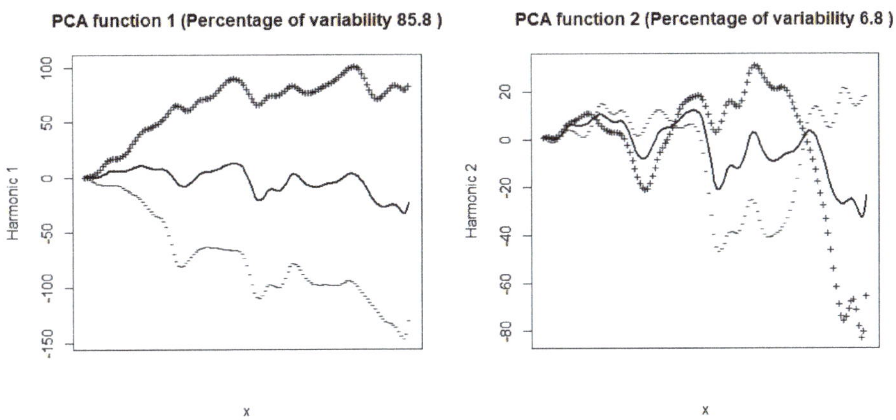

Figure 10. The two principal components of stock market prices are shown in each plot. The continuous curve shows the general mean and the discontinuous curves are the result of adding and subtracting a multiple of each principal component.

In Figure 11, we consider the projections of the four principal components of the two first ones, and it is possible to see the groups of companies represented in Figure 8. The first group, in the black color, represents the companies with low values in the first component, that is, the companies with long-term losses. The second group, in the red color, with middle values in the first component, are companies with gains close to zero. The third group, in the green color, are companies with high values in the first component, that is, the companies with more long-term gains.

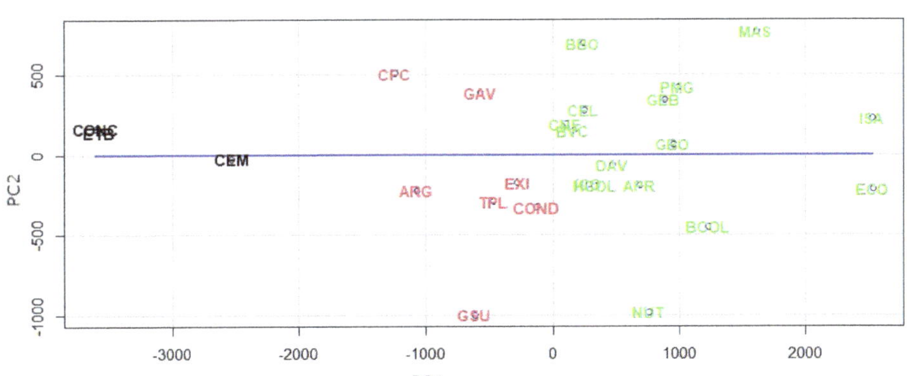

Figure 11. Projections of BVC companies onto the two principal components. The colors of the companies represent the different groups obtained.

5. Discussion

By using a basis of P-splines, we have transformed the time series of 26 relevant stock markets in BVC into curves with good metric and analytical properties. By applying functional statistical analysis techniques to the curves obtained, we have gone from working in a high-frequency discrete multivariate space to working in an infinite-dimensional functional Hilbert space with a metric induced by the L^2 norm. The FDA has provided us with the necessary tools. That is, the basic descriptive techniques, the correlation analysis between curves, the functional principal component analysis, and the functional cluster analysis. With these tools, we have been able to obtain the above results.

From the point of view of managing the information provided by the BVC sample, the conversion into functions is both a limitation and a strength. It is a limitation because smoothing involves a correction of the daily closing prices of the stock market, and it is a strength because these closing values are still indicators of the behavior of the stock market during a trading day. Furthermore, while the analysis of time series requires the condition of stationarity that forces transformations to be made in the data, the FDA does not require any previous condition.

The first derivative of the curves provides us with the instantaneous rates of change in stock prices over the entire period considered. The analysis of the velocities offers us a novel perspective on stock market volatility and has allowed us, through the EFV measure, to identify two of the most important crises suffered by humanity in recent years as periods of high volatility.

We propose in future research to validate whether this procedure is valid for other stock markets and during other crises. Moreover, given the importance of the concept of volatility in economics, it would be interesting to introduce, starting from the EFV measure, other measures of functional volatility and to study their theoretical properties.

The functional correlations have allowed us to analyze the relationship between the average values of the BVC, both through a global indicator and in windows of the total period considered. By using FPCA, we have transformed the total variability of the values analyzed into orthogonal components. These components explain specific aspects of market behavior and how periods of crisis affect it. Finally, through the cluster analysis carried out on the first components, which account for 99% of the total variability, we have classified the values into groups with a pre-established degree of homogeneity.

One of the limitations of the study is that the decision on the number of clusters is certainly subjective, given the descriptive nature of this multivariate technique. However, the reader can examine the dendrogram in Figure 8b together with the projection on the plane of the first two components in Figure 11 to make his or her own interpretation. For example, a cut at a distance of 2000 units in the dendrogram would leave the first two clusters the same but would divide the third into three, which, as a matter of note, would isolate the two best-performing stocks in the BVC, Ecopetrol, and Interconexión Electrica S.A.

6. Conclusions

The main objective of this work is to identify and quantify the consequences of COVID-19 and the war in Ukraine on the BVC. The graphical analysis of the information provided by the 26 most important stocks of the BVC has allowed us to identify a synchronization effect of the velocity curves in the crisis periods. This indicates that the stocks reacted in a similar way to the strategies of the operators, who acted in a scenario of great uncertainty. To confirm this assessment, we have verified that, for each company, the functional correlation mean to the other companies increases significantly in the two crisis periods, going from an average value of 0.43 in the entire period to 0.84 and 0.82 in the crisis periods, respectively.

We have found an extremely significant increase in the functional correlation between the mean curve of the stock market and the Brent oil price curve in the total period considered in the two crisis periods. Hence, this increase goes from functional incorrelation ($r = -0.05$) in the entire study period to levels above 0.9 in each of the crisis periods.

In this work, we have introduced the Estimated Functional Volatility (EFV) curve. This curve is defined as the average of the derivatives curves in the studied period. The EFV graph shows how, in the two crisis periods considered, the distance between this curve and the line that represents zero volatility is bigger than two typical deviations, maintaining high volatility levels.

FPCA is a useful tool to identify components that explain the behavior of the set of curves. In this case, the four first principal components account for over 98.9% of the total inertia. As in the vectorial case, the first principal component, which accounts for over 85.8% of the inertia, is a component of size that shows the variation of the prices and, thus, explains the behavior in the long term of BVC. On the other hand, the second principal component, which accounts for over 6.8% of the variability, shows the market's response to the crises of COVID-19 and the war in Ukraine because this component changes direction and makes the positive and negative disturbances permute. Therefore, the losses become the profits and vice versa. Most likely, approximately 7% of the variability that explains the third and fourth components will be justified by regional or Colombian state causes.

The hierarchical clustering enables us to understand the market dynamics because it classifies the values of BVC into three distinct groups of curves with similar trends. The three companies in the first group suffer the greatest devaluation. This group consists of two companies in the construction sector and one company in the communication sector. The second group consists of seven companies: two in the financial sector, two in the energy sector, three in the financial sector, another one in the construction sector, and the last one belongs to retail sales. These companies present a consistent performance on the stock exchange and low volatility during the study period. Finally, the third group consists of sixteen companies whose stock market returns indicate a significant upward trend at the end of the time period. In this group, there are seven financial companies, five energy companies, two industrial companies, one communications company, and another company belonging to the food sector.

In conclusion, we think that this work shows the usefulness of the FDA as a complement to time series analysis in the study of stock markets.

Author Contributions: All authors have participated in conceptualization, formal analysis, investigation, writing, review and editing tasks. All authors have read and agreed to the published version of the manuscript.

Funding: This publication is part of the project TED2021-130875B-I00, funded by MCIN/AEI/10.13039/501100011033 and by the European Union "NextGenerationEU"/PRTR.

Data Availability Statement: Data are available at the link https://www.bvc.com.co (accessed on 4 September 2024).

Acknowledgments: The authors gratefully acknowledge the financial support from Universidad de Cádiz, through the research funds of DINVP-025, and ACM thanks the support received by Agencia Estatal de Investigación of Spain under grants PID2020-116216GB-I00 and PID2020-114594GB-C22.

Conflicts of Interest: The authors declare no conflicts of interest.

References

1. Lizarzaburu Bolaños, E.R.; Burneo, K.; Galindo, H.; Berggrun, L. Emerging Markets Integration in Latin America (MILA) Stock market indicators: Chile, Colombia, and Peru. *J. Econ. Financ. Adm. Sci.* **2015**, *20*, 74–83. [CrossRef]
2. Broadstock, D.C.; Wang, R.; Zhang, D. Direct and indirect oil shocks and their impacts upon energy related stocks. *Econ. Syst.* **2014**, *38*, 451–467. [CrossRef]
3. Toro-Córdoba, J.H.; Garavito-Acosta, A.L.; López-Valenzuela, D.C.; Montes-Uribe, E. El choque petrolero y sus implicaciones en la economía colombiana. *Borradores Econ.* **2015**, *906*, 1–65.
4. Higuera, J.; Córdoba, C.; Rincón, M. Impacto del Precio del Petróleo Sobre la Acción Ecopetrol. UAMF. Boletín de Coyuntura 2016. Available online: https://fce.unal.edu.co/media/files/boletines/uamf/boletin6/index.html (accessed on 4 September 2024).
5. Fantazzini, D. The oil price crash in 2014/15: Was there a (negative) financial bubble? *Energy Policy* **2016**, *96*, 383–396. [CrossRef]
6. Baffes, J.; Kose, M.A.; Ohnsorge, F.; Stocker, M. *The Great Plunge in Oil Prices: Causes, Consequences, and Policy Responses*; World Bank Group, Development Economics: Washington, DC, USA, 2015.
7. Ramsay, J.O.; Silverman, B.W. *Functional Data Analysis*; Springer Series in Statistics; Springer: New York, NY, USA, 1997.
8. Ramsay, J.O.; Silverman, B.W. *Applied Functional Data Analysis: Methods and Case Studies*; Springer: New York, NY, USA, 2007.
9. Liu, Q.; Jin, H.; Bai, X.; Zhang, J. Prediction and Analysis of the Price of Carbon Emission Rights in Shanghai: Under the Background of COVID-19 and the Russia–Ukraine Conflict. *Mathematics* **2023**, *11*, 3126. [CrossRef]
10. Davidescu, A.A.; Manta, E.M.; Vacaru, O.M.; Gruiescu, M.; Hapau, R.G.; Baranga, P.L. Has the COVID-19 Pandemic Led to a Switch in the Volatility of Biopharmaceutical Companies? *Mathematics* **2023**, *11*, 3116. [CrossRef]
11. Allen, J. Comparison of Time Series and Functional Data Analysis for the Study of Seasonality. Master's Thesis, East Tennesse State University, Johnson City, TN, USA, 2011.
12. Gertheiss, J.; Rügamer, D.; Liew, B.X.; Greven, S. Functional data analysis: An introduction and recent developments. *Biom. J.* **2024**, *66*, e202300363. [CrossRef]
13. Gong, X.; Wang, Y.; Lin, B. Assessing dynamic China's energy security: Based on functional data analysis. *Energy* **2020**, *217*, 119324. [CrossRef]
14. Ullah, S.; Finch, C.F. Applications of functional data analysis: A systematic review. *BMC Med. Res. Methodol.* **2013**, *13*, 43. [CrossRef]
15. Pérez-Plaza, S.; Fernández-Palacín, F.; Berrocoso, M.; Páez, R.; Rosado, B. Analysis of a GPS Network Based on Functional Data Analysis. *Math. Geosci.* **2018**, *50*, 659–677. [CrossRef]
16. Aguilera, A.M.; Ocaña, F.A.; Valderrama, M.J. Stochastic modelling for evolution of stock prices by means of functional principal component analysis. *Appl. Stochast. Models Bus. Ind.* **1999**, *15*, 227–234. [CrossRef]
17. Ingrassia, S.; Costanzo, G.D. Functional principal component analysis of financial time series. In *New Developments in Classification and Data Analysis*; Springer: Berlin/Heidelberg, Germany, 2005; pp. 351–358.
18. Dablemont, S.; Van Belleghem, S.; Verleysen, M. Modelling and Forecasting financial time series of "tick data" by functional analysis and neural networks. *Forecast. Financ. Mark.* **2007**, *5*, 64–105.
19. Benko, M. Functional Data Analysis with Applications in Finance. Ph.D. Thesis, Humboldt-Universitat zu Berlin, Berlin, Germany, 2007.
20. Das, S.; Demirer, R.; Gupta, R.; Mangisa, S. The effect of global crises on stock market correlations: Evidence from scalar regressions via functional data analysis. *Struct. Change Econ. Dyn.* **2019**, *50*, 132–147. [CrossRef]
21. Andersen, T.G.; Bollerslev, T. Heterogeneous information arrivals and return volatility dynamics: Uncovering the long-run in high frequency returns. *J. Financ.* **1997**, *52*, 975–1005.
22. Engle, R. New frontiers for ARCH models. *J. Appl. Econom.* **2002**, *17*, 425–446. [CrossRef]
23. Engle, R.; Gallo, G. A multiple indicators model for volatility using intra-daily data. *J. Econom.* **2006**, *131*, 3–27. [CrossRef]
24. Engle, R.F.; Sokalska, M.E. Forecasting intraday volatility in the US equity market multiplicative component garch. *J. Financ. Econom.* **2012**, *10*, 54–83. [CrossRef]
25. Narsoo, J. High Frequency Exchange Rate Volatility Modelling Using the Multiplicative Component GARCH. *Int. J. Stat. Appl.* **2016**, *6*, 8–14.
26. Müller, H.G.; Sen, R.; Stadtmüller, U. Functional data analysis for volatility. *J. Econom.* **2011**, *165*, 233–245. [CrossRef]
27. Shang, H.L.; Yang, Y.; Kearney, F. Intraday forecasts of a volatility index: Functional time series methods with dynamic updating. *Ann. Oper. Res.* **2019**, *282*, 331–354. [CrossRef]
28. Siokis, F.M. Exploring the Dynamic Behavior of Crude Oil Prices in Times of Crisis: Quantifying the Aftershock Sequence of the COVID-19 Pandemic. *Mathematics* **2024**, *12*, 2743. [CrossRef]
29. Bildirici, M.E.; Salman, M.; Ersin, Ö.Ö. Nonlinear Contagion and Causality Nexus between Oil, Gold, VIX Investor Sentiment, Exchange Rate and Stock Market Returns: The MS-GARCH Copula Causality Method. *Mathematics* **2022**, *10*, 4035. [CrossRef]
30. Wei, T. Functional Data Analysis and Extensions for Financial Data. Ph.D. Thesis, University of Leicester, Leicester, UK, 2022.

31. Febrero-Bande, M.; De La Fuente, M.O. Statistical computing in functional data analysis: The R package fda. usc. *J. Stat. Softw.* **2012**, *51*, 1–28. [CrossRef]
32. Pérez-Plaza, S.; Berrocoso, M.; Rosado, B.; Prates, G.; Fernández-Palacín, F. The time lag between deformation process and seismic activity in El Hierro Island during the eruptive process (2011–2014): A functional phased approach. *Earth Planets Space* **2021**, *73*, 177. [CrossRef]
33. Jacques, J.; Preda, C. Functional data clustering: A survey. *Adv. Data Anal. Classi.* **2014**, *8*, 231–255. [CrossRef]
34. Peng, J.; Muller, H.G. Distance-based clustering of sparsely observed stochastic processes, with applications to online auctions. *Ann. Appl. Stat.* **2008**, *2*, 1056–1077. [CrossRef]

economies

MDPI

Article

Multimodal Livestock Operations Analysis Using Business Process Modeling: A Case Study of Romanian Black Sea Ports

Catalin Popa [1,*], Ovidiu Stefanov [2] and Ionela Goia [2]

[1] Department for Naval Port Engineering and Management, Faculty of Navigation and Naval Management, Romanian Naval Academy "Mircea cel Batran", 900218 Constanta, Romania

[2] Doctoral School, Faculty of Transportation, National University for Science and Technology POLITEHNICA of Bucharest, 060042 Bucharest, Romania; ovidiu.stefanov2019@gmail.com (O.S.); ionela_goia483@yahoo.com (I.G.)

* Correspondence: catalin.popa@anmb.ro

Abstract: In spite of its strong increase and relevant position in the evolution of international maritime routes, the global livestock trade is still a poorly treated topic in the maritime business domain of research. Aiming to cover this gap, the authors are focused on revealing the livestock logistics technology in intermodal transports, approaching both equipment reliability and operation flow design, applying the business processes modeling method to map the most relevant stages in animals' port operation, transfer, and maritime transportation. This paper examines the intricate logistics of maritime livestock transportation through a case study on the Port of Midia, administrated by the Constanța Maritime Port Administration, one of Romania's primary export hubs for livestock operations, using BPM software, seeking to identify the most important deficiencies and alternatives in improving the technical and technological effectiveness. Key findings indicate that improving ramp availability, automating document verification, and implementing RFID-based animal tracking systems could significantly enhance operational efficiency. By integrating workflow models, real-time monitoring, and simulation-based optimization, the study offers a comprehensive framework for streamlining multimodal livestock transportation. The implications extend to policymakers, port authorities, and logistics operators, emphasizing the necessity of digital transformation, regulatory harmonization, and technological integration in livestock maritime transportation. This research contributes to the expansion of intermodal transportation studies, providing practical recommendations for enhancing livestock logistics efficiency while ensuring compliance with European animal welfare regulations. The findings pave the way for further research into AI-driven risk assessments, smart logistics solutions, and sustainable livestock transportation alternatives.

Keywords: maritime business; livestock operations; port logistics; business process modeling; intermodal transportation

1. Introduction and Literature Review

The global livestock trade is increasing yearly with consistency, being mostly oriented toward maritime shipping as a transportation alternative, especially for port-to-port transfers, toward those regions facing shortages. Countries with robust agricultural sectors are using ships to export livestock to markets like the Middle East, North Africa, or South Asia, where cultural and economic factors drive a strong demand for live animals, making this type of transportation a relevant stream of intermodal service, with a stringent need for specific study and modeling (European Commission, 2023b).

Maritime livestock transportation presents unique challenges, including the ethical imperative of ensuring animal welfare. Inadequate handling or conditions can cause stress, injury, or even death. According to the guidelines issued by the European Commission, livestock transportation must comply with strict welfare standards, ensuring access to food, water, and adequate conditions. These regulations are crucial for maintaining the integrity of the logistics chain and minimizing stress on animals during transportation (European Commission, 2023a). To this end, adherence to international standards, such as EU Regulation (EC) No. 1/2005, is crucial. This regulation sets strict requirements for space, food, water, and ventilation to minimize animal suffering during transportation. Considering the case study of the Black Sea coast, particularly the Constanța Port from Romania, approached in the present article, the National Sanitary Veterinary and Food Safety Authority (ANSVSA) is responsible for enforcing these regulations and ensuring compliance (ANSVSA, 2023).

Transportation logistics for livestock ask for careful planning to reduce stress and injury risks, which can adversely impact not only the animals' health but ultimately the quality of the meat as final product. As Knowles et al. (2014) demonstrate, compliance with the established welfare standards will not only provide benefits for animals' well-being but will also ensure the economic viability of the livestock operations. In this context, the maritime livestock transportation should not just be considered a sum of logistic operations but should also comprise in its analytical perspective a highly regulated process within the agricultural export sector, connected to a complex matrix of supply chains (Miranda-De La Lama et al., 2014). The logistics chain for transporting livestock is complex, involving multiple stages and transportation modes, such as road-to-sea transfer, using seamless coordination to maintain animal welfare from origin to destination. For example, the livestock transportation from Romanian farms in the Black Sea region to the Middle East ports requires careful planning and synchronization between road haulers, port operators, and maritime shipping companies. Ports equipped with specialized facilities for handling live animals, such as the Port of Midia on the Romanian Black Sea Coast analyzed in the case study (Website of Port of Midia, 2025; Website of Constanta Port Administration, 2025), play an essential role in ensuring that all welfare standards are met during the handling, loading, transit, and unloading operations.

Although not often approached in multimodal transportation research, several studies have been conducted so far in the area of multimodal livestock operation, identified and valued by the authors in the present case study approach, such as the following:

a. A study was conducted at Fremantle Port, Western Australia, one of the largest live animal export hubs, and explored the impact of sea transportation on livestock welfare (Padalino & Tarrant, 2018). The authors found that high levels of animal stress and mortality were recorded due to long maritime journeys to the Middle East, suggesting that implementing better ventilation, automated feeding systems, and stress monitoring may significantly improve welfare conditions. The study suggested shortening transit times and improving vessel design to minimize animal losses, underscoring the necessity of animal welfare reforms in multimodal livestock transportation and emphasizing vessel modifications and improved transit management (Padalino & Tarrant, 2018).
b. A case study on Cartagena Port, Spain, examined the integration of digital tracking technologies in livestock export logistics (Gonzalez-Feliu et al., 2021) and found that the use of IoT sensors to track temperature, humidity, and hydration levels may reduce the mortality rates by 15%. In addition, the authors suggested that implementing blockchain technology enhanced traceability and compliance with EU transportation regulations and demonstrated how digital transformation in livestock

logistics can enhance both efficiency and regulatory compliance, reducing animal stress and mortality rates (Gonzalez-Feliu et al., 2021).

c. Another study was conducted in Brazil, a major livestock exporter, where the authors approached the environmental and welfare challenges associated with long-distance maritime transportation from Santos Port (Kumar et al., 2019). The authors found that delayed port handling led to overcrowding and prolonged wait times, increasing heat stress in animals, and suggested the implementation of predictive logistics using AI models to forecast delays and dynamically adjust transportation schedules. The study also highlighted the need for improved water supply systems and automated feeding solutions onboard livestock vessels (Kumar et al., 2019).

Consequently, this paper aims to cover an existing gap in the professional literature in transportation sciences, analyzing the intricate logistics technology and operations of maritime livestock transports. For this purpose, the authors have used as a sample a case study undertaken on Midia Port (administrated by the Constanța Maritime Port Administration), one of Romania's primary export hubs for livestock operations, relevant for the Black Sea region (i.e., https://www.midia-international.ro, accessed on 4 January 2025), counting a volume of more than 800,000 capita/handled per year, which represents more than 100 livestock ships/year (Website of Port of Midia, 2025; Website of Constanta Port Administration, 2025). By evaluating the logistic technology and the reliability of the exploited equipment and facilities, this study aims to understand the challenges and critical points in the livestock transportation chain, contributing by the modeling method to an overall assessment of compliance and efficiency of livestock transportation business processes.

2. Research Gaps and Study Objectives

A recent report issued by the European Court of Auditors highlights the key challenges regarding the transportation of living animals, including the fragmented national regulations and the insufficient dedicated infrastructure (European Court of Auditors, 2023). The integration of the best uniform practices across Europe can significantly improve logistics efficiency and animal welfare. The aforementioned report emphasizes that the economic incentives often overshadow animal welfare considerations, leading to prolonged transportation times and inadequate conditions. These findings underscore the necessity for stringent enforcement of welfare standards and the adoption of alternative practices, such as transporting animal products instead of living animals, in order to mitigate the welfare risks (European Court of Auditors, 2023). Moreover, long-distance transportation of livestock poses significant welfare challenges, including dehydration, fatigue, and thermal stress. According to Padalino and Tarrant (Padalino & Tarrant, 2018), implementing robust welfare measures and contingency protocols is critical for maintaining animal health during extended journeys, including cases of transportation at sea where the voyage duration exceeds 1–2 weeks.

In this context, identifying a gap in research and related professional domains regarding this topic, the authors have aimed to analyze the logistic framework revealing the operational particularities of livestock intermodal transportation, with a focus on logistics flow efficiency, its compliance with welfare standards, and its correlation with equipment reliability and related risk mitigation. The research has been applied to a case study of living livestock intermodal transportation from Romania, specifically through the Port of Midia administrated by the Port of Constanta on the western Black Sea coast, considered a critical node in the regional export network.

Recent studies demonstrate the potential of digital simulation tools, such as Aura Portal Helium Modeler, in optimizing logistics chains. For instance, similar tools have been used to identify delays and improve coordination in multimodal transportation systems (Popa & Goia, 2024). The application of modeling tools, such as Aura Portal Helium Modeler, facilitates a comprehensive analysis of the logistics chain. By simulating each stage of the transportation process along the intermodal flow, these tools can identify potential bottlenecks and inefficiencies. Implementing such technological solutions enables stakeholders to proactively address issues, thereby enhancing operational efficiency and ensuring compliance with welfare standards. By employing advanced modeling and simulation techniques using Aura Portal Helium Modeler, the study aims to provide an in-depth understanding of the transportation chain using the example of transporting from Romanian Port of Midia farms to specific markets in the Middle East.

The modeling process incorporates all stages of the logistics chain, examining road-to-port and port-to-vessel transitions, and the collaboration between key stakeholders such as haulers, port operators, and shipping companies. The study will investigate the alignment of Port Midia's operations with European Union regulations, notably Regulation (EC) No. 1/2005, which governs the welfare of animals during transportation. Using the simulation framework, the study will identify compliance risks, bottlenecks, and inefficiencies while proposing strategies for improvement. Consequently, the research will seek to evaluate the equipment reliability and operational efficiency using mathematical models like the stress-strength and damage-endurance models (Modarres et al., 2020). Simulating these processes in Aura Portal Helium Modeler allows for the identification of critical equipment vulnerabilities that could affect safety and welfare. In addition, the risk assessment will address potential delays, environmental challenges, and resource allocation strategies, ensuring a robust analysis of the logistics chain.

This comprehensive approach to modeling and simulation aims to reveal inefficiencies, uneven workload distributions, unnecessary costs, and other critical issues. Through scenario-based simulations, the study seeks to propose actionable insights that enhance the welfare of livestock and streamline operations. Ultimately, the findings will serve as a foundation for developing the best practices in intermodal livestock transport, offering valuable guidance to policymakers, operators, and animal welfare advocates.

The main research gap covered by this study is the lack of detailed analysis and process optimization methods in livestock maritime transportation, which has traditionally been overshadowed by broader logistics and port efficiency studies. While maritime freight logistics have been extensively studied, the transportation of live animals remains a relatively unexplored niche within intermodal transportation research. In this perspective, the article examines port operations, logistics flows, and compliance with welfare regulations, providing a detailed breakdown of each operational phase involved in livestock transportation from farms to port and ship.

Referring to the identified research gaps, the authors have determined a lack of digital process modeling in livestock transportation operations, as the existing literature is primarily focused on manual logistics management without integrating business process modeling (BPM) or digital workflow simulations. Therefore, the study applies Aura Portal Helium Modeler, a BPM tool, to simulate livestock transportation operations, identifying inefficiencies, bottlenecks, and potential optimizations. Moreover, most previous research on livestock transportation does not incorporate equipment reliability analysis to assess the performance and risks of handling machinery, and the authors have identified an inadequate consideration of equipment reliability and risk management.

In addition, in the literature review, the authors determined that there is an insufficient focus on regulatory and welfare compliance in port operations, as the research on livestock transportation regulations mainly covers legislative aspects rather than practical compliance in port operations. Thus, this study bridges the gap by examining regulatory enforcement at the Port of Midia, focusing on EU Regulation (EC) No. 1/2005 for animal welfare in transportation.

While general logistics studies discuss supply chain inefficiencies, there is little research offering data-driven, scenario-based optimizations for livestock transportation workflows. By using simulation-based process optimization, the study identifies key bottlenecks (e.g., delays in loading operations, insufficient infrastructure, and administrative inefficiencies) and proposes technological solutions like RFID tracking, real-time monitoring, and automation of administrative tasks. The fragmented approach in previous research does not provide an integrated framework for optimizing logistics efficiency, regulatory compliance, and welfare conditions in multimodal livestock transportation.

To overcome the identified problems, the authors have sought to fill a critical research gap by combining business process modeling, risk analysis, and logistics optimization techniques to improve livestock intermodal transportation efficiency. This study combines logistics flow analysis, regulatory review, and digital process modeling to create a comprehensive framework for enhancing efficiency in maritime livestock transportation. It contributes to the field by offering practical, technology-driven recommendations to address welfare concerns, regulatory compliance issues, and logistical inefficiencies in seaborne livestock transport—an area that has been understudied despite its economic and ethical significance.

3. Research Method

Recent advancements in BPM tools development, such as cloud-based modeling and integration with IoT systems, have enhanced this technique's ability to effectively simulate the complex logistics operations (De Luzi et al., 2024). By enabling real-time optimization and predictive analysis, Aura Portal Helium Modeler leverages these advancements, making it particularly suitable for multimodal transportation systems analysis. The integration with IoT facilitates real-time data collection and monitoring, ensuring that the simulation reflects dynamic operational conditions.

Studies have shown that applying BPM in logistics can reduce operational inefficiencies by up to 25% and improve compliance rates by 30% (WorldRef, 2024). These outcomes are aligned with the present study objectives of enabling the optimization of intermodal livestock transportation operations while ensuring regulatory compliance and animals' welfare.

The present study applies the business process management (BPM) methodology to design and simulate a workflow model for the intermodal transportation and operation of livestock, taking as a sample the Port of Midia from Romania, in the Black Sea region. The modeling process is carried out using a free licensed software, namely Aura Portal Helium Modeler, a state-of-the-art digital business platform that simplifies the creation and execution of complex operational workflows without requiring programming expertise, just prior solid knowledge of business process modeling and notation theory (https://www.auraquantic.com/products/features/business-process-management-bpm, accessed on 5 December 2024). By leveraging this software, the study's major goal is to develop a robust representation of the multimodal logistics chain, encompassing "road-to-port" and "port-to-vessel" transitions (Laguna & Marklund, 1998).

Aura Portal Helium Modeler is a free licensed software on the BPM module and provides a versatile framework for businesses of all scales, accommodating a vast range of processes and users. The platform facilitates the automation of critical organizational functions and enhances the integration of advanced simulation tools for the purpose of analyzing and optimizing the logistics operations. This capability is particularly advantageous for investigating intricate logistics systems from a qualitative perspective, where the identification of bottlenecks, inefficiencies, and compliance risks is significantly relevant (Popa & Goia, 2024).

By combining BPM methodologies with Aura Portal, various scenarios within the livestock transportation process can be simulated. These simulations allow the examination of the impact of factors such as equipment reliability, environmental risks, and stakeholder cooperation on both logistics performance and animal well-being (Lindsay et al., 2003). By replicating real-world conditions in a controlled digital environment, areas for improvement can be identified, leading to the development of more effective and safe cautious transportation practices.

4. Case Study: Intermodal Livestock Operation in the Black Sea Region

4.1. Case Study Assumptions

Recent studies have highlighted the critical role of mitigating stress in livestock transportation to ensure animal welfare and compliance with international standards. Practices such as minimizing waiting times, ensuring adequate feeding schedules, and providing suitable handling conditions have shown significant positive impact on reducing stress levels during transportation. These measures contribute to both operational efficiency and animal welfare, particularly in complex logistic chains along which multiple stakeholders are involved (Bhatt et al., 2021). Best practices for loading and unloading livestock emphasize the importance of creating safe and efficient processes to minimize risks and ensure compliance with welfare standards. Streamlined procedures, careful handling, and the use of standardized methodologies can significantly reduce the likelihood of injuries or delays, improving both animal welfare and operational performance (University of Wisconsin-Madison Safety Department, 2021).

The case study examines the livestock operation in the Port of Midia (Romania), located on the Black Sea coastline, approximately 13.5 nm N of Constanta (Romania). It is one of the satellite ports of Constanta and was designed and built to serve the adjacent industrial and petrochemical facilities. The N and S breakwaters have a total length of 6.97 m. The port covers 833.9 ha, of which 233.7 ha is land and 600.1 ha is water. There are 14 berths (11 operational berths and three berths belong to Constanta Shipyard) with a total length of 2.24 km. After dredging operations are performed, the port depths are increased to 9 m at crude oil discharging berths 1–4, allowing access to tankers having 8.5 m maximum draught and 20,000 dwt. For the case study, the authors collected technical and operational details regarding the livestock from the field through in-person visits, by courtesy of the Port of Constanta Authority (that is the administrative authority for the Port of Midia) and with the support of the "COMAGRA" Ltd. Port Operator (location address: Navodari, Portului Street, 2nd Floor, Constanta County, Romania, GPS coordinates: 44.3500°/28.6666°). The livestock terminal is located on berths 5–8, with a length of 637.6 m, 9 m max depth.

The case study considers the transshipment of 15,000 sheep aboard the vessel "Jersey", which operates under a Togo flag of convenience. Built in Japan in 1977, the ship has a gross tonnage of 2924, a net tonnage of 1468, and a deadweight capacity of 2522 metric tons. Measuring 77 m in length and 13 m in width, the vessel is equipped with a freshwater tank holding 685 metric tons and offers 4100 square meters of storage space tailored for livestock. The authors explore the logistic efforts required to maintain the welfare of the animals throughout the voyage route, emphasizing the importance of legal compliance, effective resource management, and efficient processes in achieving successful intermodal transportation operations.

Loading operations in the Black Sea Port of Midia prioritize efficiency and animal welfare. As calculated by the authors with the courtesy of Port of Midia authorities

(Constanta Port Administration), the entire process takes about 3 days, as follows: livestock transportation from farms to the port consumes 24 h, loading onto the vessel takes 18 h, and feed, bedding, and welfare tasks take 8 h. Administrative formalities with authorities (Border Police, Romanian Naval Authority, Customs, Veterinary Directorate) require in practice 2 h. Vessel port operations, including docking and departure, take 2 h in total.

The sheep are transported from various farms across Romania heading to the Port of Midia using trucks capable of carrying 300 animals each. At the destination, each truck is unloaded within approximately 3 h, allowing a steady flow of three trucks per hour. Once they arrive in the port of operations, animals may be temporarily housed in a shelter equipped for this purpose before being transferred to the vessel. The logistics chain is supported by specialized equipment, including cranes, forklifts, and telescopic handlers, ensuring that the operations are conducted smoothly and in compliance with regulatory standards.

The transportation of food, water, and bedding is a critical component of the operation. A total of 240 metric tons of food is loaded onboard, calculated at a daily consumption of 2 kilos per animal for the eight-day journey, with the period including one day for loading, six days of maritime transit to Aqaba Port in Jordan, and one day for unloading. Additionally, 10 metric tons of sawdust are loaded as bedding material for the animals. The ship takes on 650 cubic meters of freshwater in the Port of Midia, sufficient to meet the daily requirement of 4 to 6 L per animal as stipulated by Regulation (EC) No. 1/2005. The freshwater loading process is completed within 14 h, facilitated by the port's water supply system with a flow rate of 46.5 cubic meters per hour.

4.2. Operational and Technical Analysis of Intermodal Livestock Operations

The logistic support of transfer operations relies on the Port of Midia's infrastructure, which includes a loading ramp, weighing station, and heavy-duty handling equipment. The primary crane, capable of lifting 15 metric tons, can complete four cycles per hour, with each cycle processing up to four tons of feed or bedding. This system efficiently handles one-ton bags. A dedicated team of eight persons oversees the loading process, ensuring adherence to welfare standards throughout the operation. To efficiently and compliantly provision the resources for livestock transportation, specialized equipment should be used. High-capacity centrifugal pumps (i.e., the reliable Grundfos CR model or equivalent) facilitate freshwater provisioning, delivering a consistent 46.5 cubic meters per hour. These pumps are seamlessly integrated with the port's water distribution infrastructure, ensuring swift and uninterrupted transfer to the ship's freshwater tanks.

Cranes with a 15-ton lifting capacity, such as Liebherr LHM 420, are employed to handle feed and bedding materials. These cranes demonstrate high operational efficiency, achieving up to four cycles per hour while effectively handling bulk materials packaged in one-ton bags. In addition, forklifts, such as the JCB 930 with a 3-ton capacity, and telescopic handlers, such as the Genie GTH-4013, are used in a coordinated manner to facilitate the seamless handling and transportation of materials between storage areas, staging points, and the ship's designated stowage compartments.

Furthermore, adjustable loading ramps incorporating hydraulic lift systems facilitate the effectiveness of livestock handling operations, accommodating the variations in truck bed heights with the ship deck levels and ensuring smooth animal transfer while adhering to stringent welfare standards. The ramps are equipped with anti-slip surfaces, side barriers, and integrated check points for inspection to prevent accidents and to guarantee the safety of animal handling throughout the loading process.

By integrating these specialized facilities, equipment, and infrastructure, bunkering, water, and feed supply processes would be optimized to meet operational efficiency targets together with the regulatory compliance imperative, providing a robust framework for maritime livestock logistics.

As considered in the present case study, the transportation of 15,000 sheep to Port Midia for onward shipment to Aqaba, Jordan, represents a complex logistical operation, requiring a precise coordination of resources and infrastructure. In order to constitute the intermodal consignment batches, the animals are collected from multiple locations across Romania (e.g., Sibiu, Constanța, Piatra Neamț, Bihor, or Cluj), covering distances ranging from 45 km to 700 km. To achieve this, a total of 50 trucks, each with a capacity of 300 animals, are used to transport the livestock safely and efficiently in the port of origin area. The logistic plan ensures the controlled arrival of these trucks at the port, minimizing waiting times and facilitating continuous unloading operations. By maintaining this sequence, the operation avoids the congestion and ensures the timely handling of all batches of animals in the port of operation.

Upon arrival at Port Midia, on the "Comagra" terminal (berths 5–8) for transshipment, the animals are handled using specialized equipment to facilitate the loading process onto the vessel "Jersey" by a Liebherr LHM 420 crane, which, with its 124-ton capacity and 48 m lift height, is a key asset, capable of performing four operations per hour and lifting up to 16 tons in that timeframe. Moreover, based on a multicriteria decision-making process, considering the reliability and friability variables, the authors have justified the selection of the Liebherr LHM 420 crane by rigorous engineering analysis, using both stress-strength and damage-endurance modeling methods, conducted in the next sub-chapter. The results from below demonstrate the exceptional potential of this equipment, with a reliability score exceeding 0.85 on both alternatives. This, coupled with the crane's proven ability to withstand repetitive loading cycles, confirms its suitability for the demanding loading operation. The Liebherr LHM 420 crane is designed to handle up to 16 tons per cycle, completing four cycles per hour. This equates to a throughput of 64 tons per hour, ensuring timely completion of critical tasks like simultaneous feed and bedding material loading. The crane's advanced hydraulic system and precise controls enable smooth maneuvering of bulk bags and other heavy materials, reducing downtime and mitigating risks associated with handling inefficiencies. Furthermore, the selection of the Liebherr LHM 420 is justified by its proven performance in demanding maritime environments. Its design features, such as extended reach and adaptable load charts, contribute to operational flexibility. This aligns with the stringent requirements of livestock handling operations, where time constraints and welfare considerations necessitate reliable, high-performance equipment. By integrating the findings from reliability modeling into the equipment selection process, this study underscores the strategic importance of deploying machinery that ensures both operational compliance and enhanced logistical efficiency.

Two forklifts, each with a lifting capacity of 2.5 tons, provide additional support for smaller material handling tasks. These tasks are carried out concurrently with the loading of feed, water, and bedding essential for the animals' well-being during their eight-day sea voyage. The effective utilization of port equipment guarantees that animals, feed, and supplies are loaded within the allotted timeframe, ensuring compliance with animal welfare regulations and operational schedules.

This integrated approach aims to ensure seamless movement of livestock from the pick-up points of origin farms to the destination ships of operation. By effectively coordinating the transportation schedules, employing a fleet of 50 trucks, optimizing equipment usage, and adhering to regulatory standards, this operation could demonstrate the viability of large-scale multimodal livestock transportation while prioritizing animal welfare and supply chain efficiency. Through strict adherence to legal standards and based on the usage of cutting-edge equipment and infrastructure, the exemplified operation demonstrates efficiency and high welfare standards within the international livestock trade. The meticulous planning and execution at the Port of Midia underscore the critical importance of synchronized logistics in ensuring the successful execution of multimodal transportation.

Large-scale livestock transportation operations rely heavily on the reliability and risk management of handling equipment to ensure seamless logistical execution. The complex nature of managing live animals, coupled with the intensive operational demands of port infrastructure, necessitates advanced modeling tools to evaluate the equipment performance under various conditions. To exemplify the impact of the decision-making process on intermodal process operations, the authors have applied two mathematical models, stress-strength and damage-endurance, respectively (Modarres et al., 2020; Abadi et al., 2023), to assess the reliability of handling equipment used at Port Midia in the case of a consignment batch of 15,000 sheep. These models provided valuable insights regarding the equipment's capacity to withstand operational stresses and its long-term durability, enabling effective risk management and strategic maintenance planning. By applying these models to key equipment such as cranes, forklifts, and telescopic handlers, the probability of equipment failure may be assessed, identifying potential technical weaknesses. The stress-strength model focuses on the probability that a piece of equipment's resistance exceeds the applied operational stress, providing a measure of reliability during peak activity. In parallel, the damage-endurance model evaluates the accumulation of wear and tear over time, estimating the operational lifespan of equipment under regular use. Together, these methodologies may contribute to the optimization of equipment performance, ensuring that logistical processes will remain uninterrupted and aligned with the welfare and safety requirements of live animal transportation. This approach not only supports efficient operations at the Port of Midia but also establishes a framework for assessing the reliability of critical infrastructure in similar logistical contexts.

The workflow model, designed using Aura Portal Helium Modeler, offers a comprehensive depiction of the livestock transportation operation, structured into three primary phases: road transport, port handling, and vessel loading. Each phase is meticulously divided into specific tasks with clearly allocated resources to ensure thorough planning and smooth execution:

The operation uses a fleet of 50 trucks for road transport, with real-time monitoring implemented to prevent disruptions. Contingency protocols are in place to address potential delays or mechanical failures, ensuring timely arrival at the port. At the port, a structured queuing system facilitates efficient unloading, complemented by temporary housing for animals. Parallel operations, such as loading feed and water, are executed to optimize time and resource utilization. Vessel loading involves critical tasks such as inspecting and aligning loading ramps, continuous equipment monitoring, and final safety checks, ensuring a smooth and uninterrupted loading process.

Advanced mathematical modeling techniques, such as stress-strength and damage-endurance analyses, validate the exceptional reliability of the Liebherr LHM 420 crane. With a failure probability of less than 0.01 per operational hour and a reliability score surpassing 0.85, the crane is perfectly suited for demanding operations, including lifting large quantities of bulk feed and bedding materials. Its high throughput and precision in load handling significantly enhance the efficiency of port handling and vessel loading activities, ensuring that strict timelines are consistently met. This model underscores the integration of robust equipment reliability, resource optimization, and proactive management strategies to ensure seamless execution across all phases of livestock transportation logistics. It serves as a practical template for similar complex logistical operations. By aligning the findings from mathematical modeling with operational workflow requirements, this study validates the Liebherr LHM 420 crane as the optimal choice for ensuring efficiency, compliance, and animal welfare throughout the livestock transportation operation.

5. Modeling of Livestock Intermodal Operations Using Aura Portal Helium Modeler: Research Hypothesis and Identification of Critical Variables in the Logistics Chain

This study uses Aura Portal Helium Modeler, the free licensed software version (https://www.auraquantic.com, accessed on 5 December 2024), to create a detailed representation of the logistics involved in the intermodal consignment of 15,000 sheep from pick-up Romanian origin farms to Port Midia and onto the vessel "Jersey" for maritime transportation to Aqaba, Jordan. The process is structured into two phases, each stage encompassing key tasks, decision points, and monitoring mechanisms to ensure efficiency and compliance with animal welfare regulations. The model highlights the sequential flow of operations, the interaction of various stakeholders, and the integration of contingency plans to address potential challenges.

5.1. Workflow Modeling of Intermodal Livestock Operations Using Aura Portal Helium Modeler

The first phase centers on the overland transportation of livestock from pick-up originated farms toward the Port of Midia. Trucks are dispatched, and their progress is meticulously monitored throughout the journey. Real-time collected data are utilized to assess the road conditions, enabling the prompt identification and mitigation of any significant delays through the deployment of backup vehicles to maintain the established schedule. The condition of the trucks is also rigorously evaluated, and mechanical issues are promptly flagged for swift resolution, facilitating the deployment of replacement vehicles as needed. As the trucks approach the Port of Midia, animals undergo thorough inspections to ensure compliance with health and welfare standards. Any deviations necessitate corrective actions, such as veterinary interventions, while compliant shipments proceed directly to the unloading stage at the port.

Upon arrival at the "Comagra" berth in the Port of Midia, operations flow to the second phase, encompassing the animals' discharge from trucks and their subsequent preparation for vessel loading. Trucks are systematically queued, and animals are temporarily housed in designated shelters when immediate loading is not feasible. Inspections by customs, veterinary, and port authorities are conducted with the highest diligence to ensure the timely completion of all formalities within the allotted two-hour timeframe. Any delays encountered at this stage are promptly communicated to port operators to facilitate adjustments to the loading schedule. Concurrently, the loading of feed provisions and water onboard the ship is meticulously executed. The synchronization of these tasks is paramount, ensuring that all essential supplies, including 240 tons of provisions and 650 cubic meters of water, are loaded in tandem with the animals. Weather conditions are continuously monitored to ensure safe handling, with operations suspended in the event of adverse environmental factors such as high winds or heavy rain.

This phase is concluded with the actual transhipment of animals onboard the vessel. This process commences with the meticulous alignment and inspection of the loading ramps to verify their structural integrity and compliance with the safety standards. Animals are then carefully moved from holding areas or directly from the trucks onboard the ship under the vigilant supervision of handlers who prioritize their welfare throughout the process. The equipment employed for loading, including ramps and cranes, is continuously monitored for functionality. Any equipment malfunctions are immediately addressed through the deployment of backup resources, minimizing delays. Once all animals are successfully loaded, a final comprehensive inspection is conducted to validate the completeness and safety of the boarding operation. The ship's readiness for departure is confirmed only after all discrepancies are resolved, ensuring that the animals, feed provisions, and water are securely in place before the commencement of the sea voyage.

This comprehensive workflow model, developed using Aura Portal Helium Modeler, ensures that every stage of the transhipment and intermodal transportation process is clearly defined and efficiently executed. By integrating real-time monitoring, decision points, and fail-safe measures, the model provides a robust framework for managing the complexities of livestock transportation. It emphasizes regulatory compliance, animal welfare, and operational efficiency, making it a valuable tool for optimizing large-scale logistics operations. The structured yet adaptable approach demonstrated in this model highlights its applicability to similar transportation scenarios, offering a replicable solution for seamless and compliant logistics management.

To preserve model applicability while maintaining a generalized approach, the workflow simulation for livestock transportation was developed using standardized practices observed across similar logistics operations. Data for the model, including activity durations, equipment performance, and operational costs, was collected from multiple livestock export operations in the region. These inputs were synthesized into statistically relevant averages to ensure the model's accuracy and reliability.

The simulation framework relies on a pre-defined livestock transportation workflow, encompassing key stages such as road transport, port handling, and vessel loading. Each stage was analyzed to map the flow of animals and materials, from origin farm dispatch to final placement aboard the vessel. This discrete sequential approach considers critical variables such as resource allocation, equipment reliability, and transit times, ensuring that the model captures the complexities of real-world operations.

For road transport, variables such as truck availability, travel times, and contingencies for delays or mechanical issues were incorporated. Port handling processes were modeled with a focus on resource utilization, queuing systems, and synchronization of feed, water, and animal loading. Finally, ship's loading operations were detailed to include equipment allocation and inspection protocols. This structured simulation aims to provide a replicable and adaptable model for understanding and further optimizing the livestock logistics operations and logistics flow.

5.2. Detailed Breakdown of Livestock Intermodal Transportation and Operation Processes

The logistics flow of intermodal transportation of 15,000 sheep from Romanian farms to the vessel "Jersey" at the Port of Midia has been modeled in Figure 1 as a sequence of interdependent phases, each capturing critical operational steps to ensure efficiency and compliance with animal welfare standards. This structured approach allows for a clear understanding of the process and highlights the resources, challenges, and outcomes associated with each stage.

As depicted in Figure 1, Phase A—"Road-to-Port" begins with the trucks' arrival at the port, each carrying approximately 300 sheep. Upon arrival, the trucks are directed to designated unloading bays, where hydraulic ramps equipped with anti-slip surfaces and side barriers facilitate the safe transfer of animals. The unloading process is carefully supervised by professional handlers to ensure that the sheep are moved smoothly and with minimal stress to temporary shelters. These shelters serve as holding areas, allowing the animals to recover from transportation and undergo preliminary health checks. This phase is designed to maximize throughput efficiency, with each truck requiring approximately 3 h for unloading. With three unloading bays operating simultaneously, the entire batch of 50 trucks is processed within less than three hours.

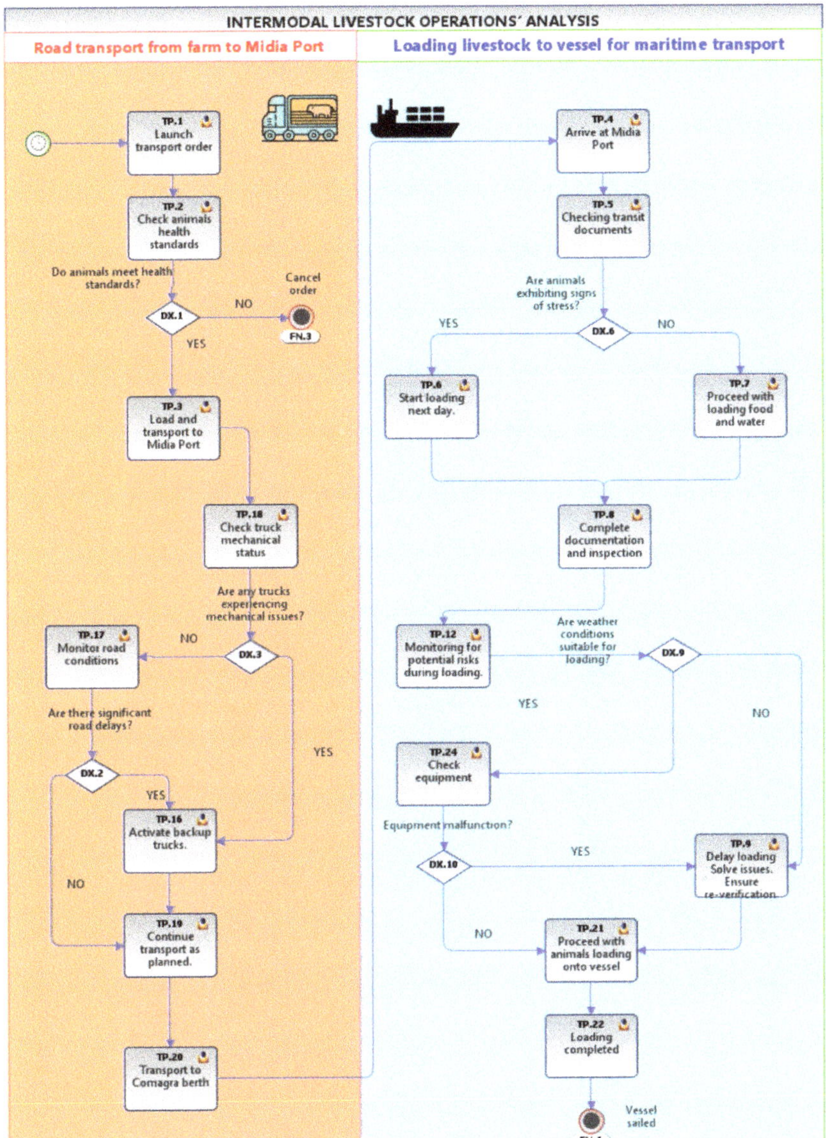

Figure 1. Intermodal livestock logistic operations: process flow from road transportation to vessel loading.

While the unloading operations are underway, veterinary inspections assisted by handlers assess the health of the animals to ensure compliance with welfare regulations. The inspections are conducted systematically to identify any signs of distress, injury, or illness. If non-conformities are detected, corrective measures, such as isolation or treatment, are promptly implemented. This phase runs concurrently with the unloading process, leveraging parallel operations to optimize time and resources. By the end of this phase, animals are cleared for transfer to port.

Phase B—"Port-to-Vessel" represents a crucial stage in which livestock are safely and efficiently loaded onto the ship. Hydraulic ramps, designed specifically to accommodate the movement of livestock, enable the seamless transfer of animals from trucks to the vessel. Operating at maximum efficiency, these ramps maintain a steady and controlled flow, reducing congestion and minimizing the stress of the animals. Skilled handlers oversee the process, ensuring that the sheep are placed into their designated compartments in full compliance with animal welfare regulations. With three ramps functioning simultaneously, the loading process is completed effectively within 18 h, with a flow of approximately four sheep/minute/ramp.

In parallel with the livestock loading, essential supplies such as feed provision, bedding, and freshwater are transferred to the ship. Bulk materials are handled using the Liebherr LHM 420 crane, while high-capacity centrifugal pumps ensure the efficient transfer of freshwater. These logistic activities are synchronized with the livestock loading to guarantee the timely availability of all resources.

This phase also involves completing necessary administrative procedures, including inspections by customs, veterinary, and port authorities. These processes are meticulously managed to avoid delays and ensure a smooth clearance. Once all formalities are finalized, the vessel is prepared for departure.

This comprehensive overview highlights the complexity of managing multiple interdependent operations while maintaining strict adherence to welfare and regulatory standards. By incorporating real-time monitoring, streamlined decision-making, and optimized resource allocation, the structured workflow ensures the effective execution of all tasks. This model offers a reliable framework for managing similar large-scale livestock logistics operations.

Once the process model was designed in Aura Portal Helium Modeler, a simulation was conducted to analyse the total time of operation and the total cost for dispatching 15,000 sheep. The simulation leverages statistical and operational data to replicate the real logistics of intermodal livestock transport, focusing on critical stages such as unloading, inspections, loading livestock, and provisioning supplies. By integrating these parameters, the model evaluates the efficiency and resource utilization of each process and identifies potential areas for optimization. The visual representation depicted in Figure 2 illustrates the configured parameters before initiating the simulation. Within the simulation process, a total of 50 processes are modeled, corresponding to the 50 trucks transporting 15,000 sheep to Port Midia. Up to 15 processes are configured to run simultaneously, enabling the parallel execution of critical tasks such as truck unloading, veterinary inspections, and preparing the animals for vessel loading.

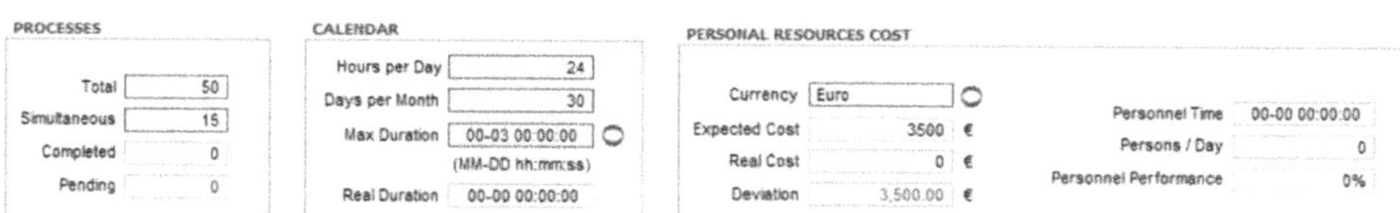

Figure 2. Simulation parameters setup: processes, calendar, cost, and resource overview.

The operational calendar panel reflects a continuous 24 h workday, ensuring that port operations proceed uninterrupted until the successful completion of all assigned tasks. This parameter is critical in ensuring that the entire logistics process, from transportation to the port and loading onboard the vessel, is completed within the three-day timeframe. The calendar also indicates the maximum duration of the simulation, set at 3 days, with the actual process durations revealed dynamically as the simulation progresses. Cost analysis indicates an expected expenditure of €3500, with deviations from real costs displayed dynamically during the simulation.

Throughout the simulation, the model provides visual feedback via a color-coded status system, which helps monitor the progress and performance of tasks. A green hue signifies that an object has completed its assigned tasks within the anticipated timeframe, orange indicates completion within an alert period, and red highlights delays or deviations beyond the projected schedule. This feature allows for real-time adjustments to resource allocation and process prioritization, ensuring optimal efficiency across all operations. Upon completion of the simulation, the temporal and financial parameters validate the model's accuracy in reflecting actual operational conditions, providing a comprehensive analysis of logistics performance and cost efficiency.

As illustrated in Figure 3, the simulation provides a comprehensive visualization of the livestock logistics process, highlighting both its strengths and the potential areas for improvement. The model reflects 50 processes, corresponding to the number of trucks transporting livestock, with a maximum of 15 processes running simultaneously. This setup ensures a high level of parallelism for tasks such as truck unloading, veterinary inspections, and vessel loading. The total duration of the simulated operation is 3 days and 16 h, slightly exceeding the planned timeframe. This extension is attributed to the bottlenecks in certain critical tasks, as indicated by the yellow and red alerts identified in the simulation results. These alerts signal delays or inefficiencies that require further investigation and optimization to improve overall performance.

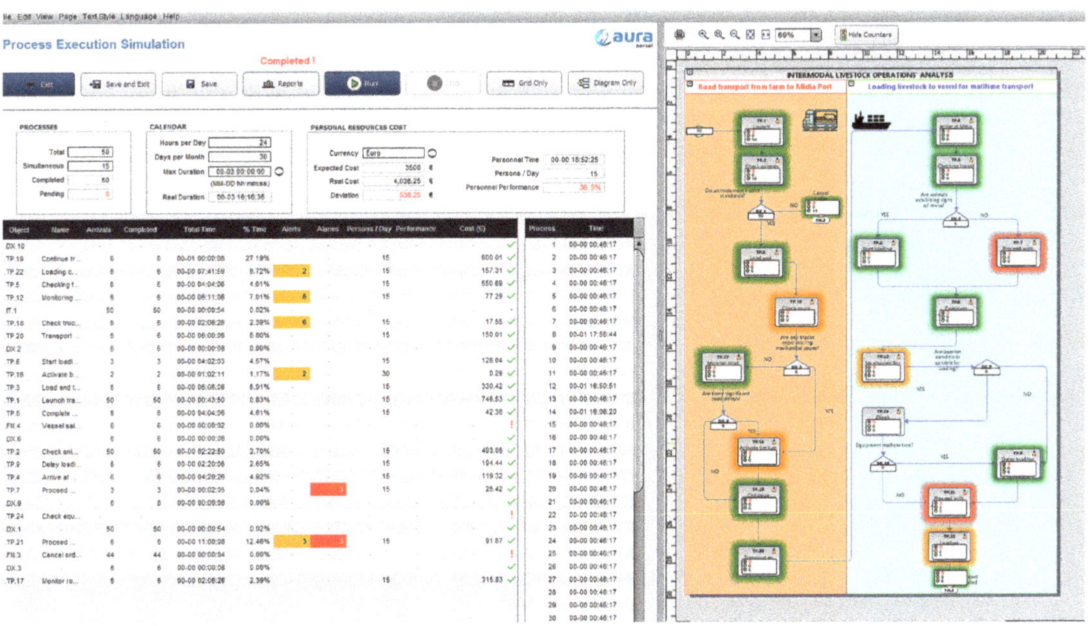

Figure 3. Process execution—simulation diagram. (colour significance: red colour—alarm, process with deviations; orange colour—alert, process under attention; green colour: no deviation, clear process).

5.3. Identified Issues and Bottlenecks Within the Designed Model Workflow

5.3.1. Red Alerts: Critical Delays

TP. 7—Proceed with loading of food and water supplies

- This stage includes preparing and loading the required food and water supplies for animals before the vessel departure. The three red alerts indicate significant delays due to resource shortages or, alternatively, due to poor task scheduling. Ensuring the timely availability of additional equipment and assigning additional personnel for this particular process could help resolve these issues to increase the level of efficiency. The existence of external port operators for leasing additional resources in the port area could be an operational strategy to be followed in such risk scenarios. This measure is a matter of port administration and could be enforced by the strategic dialog between the operators and the port authorities.

TP. 21—Proceed with animals' transshipment onboard the ship

- This critical stage involves the transhipment of the animals onboard the vessel while assuring full compliance with the welfare standards. The three red alerts suggest severe delays caused by insufficient ramp availability or lack of effective coordination. Optimizing ramp utilization and improving task sequencing can mitigate these delays. Automatic systems for guiding the load flow on the ramp, with automatic counting devices per capita, could mitigate the risks. In addition, the usage of RFID (Radio Frequency Identification Devices) tools installed for each animal integrated in the marking system could improve the monitoring of the transhipment flow, with a timely response for setting up the speed of charging, consequently with monitoring of welfare parameters during boarding but also during the entire process of transportation.

5.3.2. Yellow Alerts: Opportunities for Improvement

TP.5—Checking transit documents

- This stage involves verifying all transit documents required before loading onboard the ship. The six yellow alerts suggest delays caused by the high volume of documents and by the manual nature of the process fulfilled at the port gates. Implementing automated tools for document verification could significantly reduce processing time and improve efficiency. In addition, implementing a pre-verification stage of preliminary drafts before arrival, like in other cargo cases, could be a solution for the port administration to improve the competitivity of services.

TP.12—Monitoring for potential risks during loading onboard the ship

- During this stage, risks related to the loading process are continuously monitored. The six yellow alerts indicate inefficiencies caused by insufficient procedures or inadequate equipment. Strengthening monitoring protocols and introducing advanced tools for monitoring could reduce the delays and improve safety measures. As suggested for TP.21 improvement, it is highly recommended that RFID (Radio Frequency Identification Devices) tools be implemented in the marking system and the real-time monitoring of each capita, during the handling, boarding, and transportation operations. The collected data can offer practical ways for both improving the logistics flow and for monitoring well-being parameters, demonstrating a certain quality and overcoming other risks during the entire chain of processes, including illness, weight loss, or animal stress.

TP.18—Check of truck mechanical status

- This stage involves inspecting the mechanical condition of trucks before unloading operations. The six yellow alerts highlight delays caused by monitoring the trucks with mechanical issues. Conducting preventive inspections before trucks arrive at the port could minimize disruptions and improve process flow within the port area. In addition, proper coordination among the land transportation fleet vehicles would permit the redistribution of access rights, once the mechanical incidents are identified, just to avoid dead times in the discharge queue. Here, the integration of intermodal operators in a common platform for cargo dispatch is a priority, bringing effective solutions for facilitating the transportation.

TP.16—Activate backup trucks

- Activating backup trucks is necessary to replace unavailable or malfunctioning vehicles in the case of a risk scenario occurrence. The two yellow alerts point to minor delays in activating these vehicles, possibly due to insufficient preparation. Better planning and pre-scheduling of backup trucks could address this issue.

TP. 22—Loading completed

- This stage signifies the completion of loading animals for transhipment onboard the vessel. Despite the task being completed, two yellow alerts indicate minor inefficiencies, likely caused by resource underutilization or insufficient coordination between handling team members leading to the process of the closure of boarding documents not being timely concluded. Streamlining the loading process and allocating additional resources in the documents' automatization processes could address these issues.

5.3.3. Cost Analysis and Budget Considerations

Running all processes, the simulation scenario has revealed a total operational cost of €4038.25, exceeding the expected budget of €3500 by approximately €538.25. This overrun is primarily due to unexpected delays identified in the logistics flow and to the additional resource requirements in the discharging, handling, transhipment, and transportation phases. The findings emphasize the importance of contingency budgeting and proactive risk management in future operations.

5.4. Process Bottlenecks Analysis in Livestock Logistics Operation Flow and Concluding Insights Resulting from Aura Portal Simulation

The Aura Portal software simulation revealed critical bottlenecks and inefficiencies within the livestock logistics process, emphasizing the importance of targeted optimization strategies on both the company and port authority levels. These bottlenecks, highlighted by red and yellow alerts in the simulation, represent areas where delays or inefficiencies may occur, potentially impacting the overall logistics workflow during the livestock operation. The red alerts indicate critical issues that require immediate attention to ensure smooth operations. These include delays in food and water provisioning, as well as inefficiencies during the final loading phase of the livestock onto the vessel. Such critical delays suggest inadequate resource allocation and overlapping dependencies in key tasks. Addressing these issues will involve improved task scheduling, increased ramp availability, technical measures, and enhancing communication between operational team members.

The yellow alerts, while less severe, pinpoint moderate inefficiencies that, if left unresolved, could cascade into larger disruptions. These alerts reflect issues such as prolonged document verification times, insufficient risk monitoring during transhipment operations, and delays in truck inspections. Additionally, the activation of backup trucks and task completion processes were identified as areas requiring improved coordination and preparedness. Automating repetitive tasks, such as document checks, and streamlining pre-departure inspections could reduce delays and optimize resource utilization. By addressing these bottlenecks, the simulation may provide a clear path for implementing process improvements. Strategies such as integrating real-time monitoring tools (based on RFID monitoring technologies), automating critical procedures, and enhancing preplanning protocols can significantly improve efficiency. Furthermore, regular reviews of simulation outputs and performance data will ensure that the process remains adaptable to evolving logistical demands.

The Aura Portal simulation demonstrates its value as a decision-making tool, offering actionable insights that enable continuous improvement. By leveraging these insights to optimize operational workflows, the livestock logistics process can achieve greater efficiency, reduce costs, and ensure timely delivery, all while maintaining the highest standards of safety and animal welfare.

6. Solutions for Livestock Logistics Workflow Optimization: Conclusions and Recommendations

The simulation conducted using Aura Portal software identifies key inefficiencies and bottlenecks in the livestock logistics process, highlighting the need for targeted strategies to improve operational performance across all stages. Through a thorough analysis of simulation outcomes and the application of tailored solutions, the workflow achieves greater efficiency, ensuring that the tasks are completed on time while maintaining effective cost management.

A significant challenge arose from the food and water supply for the livestock due to overlapping tasks and resource constraints. To address this, the authors have recommended the implementation of a combined approach considering an increased number of personnel and automated feeding and water systems to accelerate the process and reduce the reliance on manual labor. In addition, scheduling these activities during less critical periods may further streamline operations, shortening the queue blockages.

Delays in the livestock loading phase were attributed to limited ramp availability and coordination challenges. To mitigate these, the authors have suggested that upgrading ramp systems or adding an additional ramp to increase throughput, correlated with RFID monitoring devices, may offer a smart basis for implementing smart boarding technologies for animals. A centralized digital coordination system could therefore be implemented to optimize resource allocation and prevent bottlenecks. Focused training programs for handlers can also enhance the efficiency of logistics processes.

Administrative delays in document verification were addressed by automating the process through a digital system, streamlining workflow and eliminating repetitive manual tasks. A dedicated team, supported by these tools, can improve the handling of document processing.

To enhance risk monitoring during the loading phase, IoT-based sensors and AI-driven monitoring systems are recommended to identify anomalies and generate proactive alerts. This reduces reliance on manual inspections, improving both speed and accuracy while maintaining compliance with animal welfare standards.

Truck inspections also present opportunities for improvement through a proactive vehicle management strategy. Mechanical inspections conducted at departure points ensure that only roadworthy trucks arrive at the port. Equipping port teams with diagnostic tools reduces inspection time upon arrival. Additionally, scheduling backup trucks in advance and using automated alert systems for their deployment ensure readiness and eliminate delays caused by vehicle unavailability.

Overall coordination across all tasks and processes requires the implementation of a real-time digital platform. This system may provide a centralized view of task progress, with the dynamics of resource allocation focused on high-priority tasks, preventing conflicts or idle time. It proves particularly effective during critical stages like livestock loading and provisioning, ensuring seamless integration of operations.

These optimization strategies may reduce the total duration of the logistics process to the planned three days, with all tasks achieving "green" status as shown in Figure 4. Then, operational costs will stabilized within the allocated budget of €3500, avoiding the overruns observed in the simulation, having the basics of model optimization by either adding additional resources (additional workforce) or reducing the timing of processing for critical tasks (i.e., identified in the sub-chapter above) by adopting intelligent technologies. The integration of automation, advanced monitoring tools, and strategic resource allocation establishes a robust framework for continuous improvement. This approach ensures that the livestock logistics workflow not only meets but exceeds operational and welfare standards, setting a benchmark for future operations.

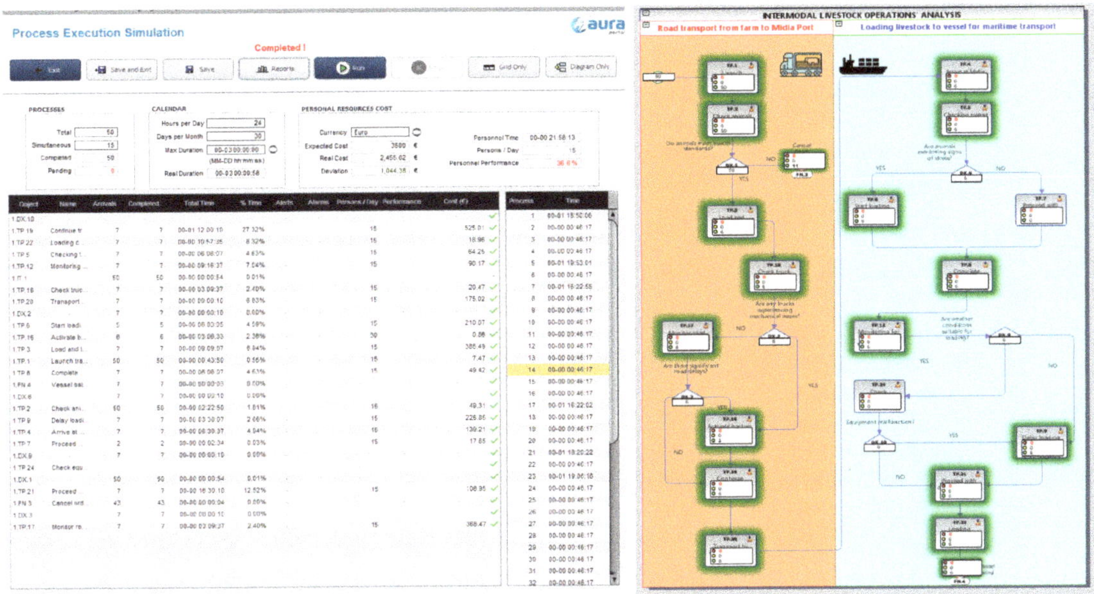

Figure 4. Optimized process execution: all stages achieving green status through implemented strategies.

The successful implementation of optimization strategies has resulted in a fully optimized livestock logistics workflow, as reflected in the simulation outcomes from Figure 4. All stages of the process now achieve green status, demonstrating that critical delays and inefficiencies have been effectively resolved. The operated adjustments, including resource allocation, task prioritization, and process automation, have aligned the operation within the planned timeframe of 3 days, while maintaining compliance with the allocated budget of €3500.

This result underscores the importance of proactive planning and targeted interventions in addressing bottlenecks. The introduction of automated tools for document verification, real-time monitoring of tasks, and enhanced ramp utilization may streamline operations and reduce manual dependencies. By addressing key areas of inefficiency, such as food and water provisioning and vehicle management, the workflow has transitioned into a seamless and highly efficient process.

The Aura Portal simulation has demonstrated its value as a decision-making tool, offering actionable insights that guided the optimization process. Moving forward, the integration of these measures ensures that the livestock logistics workflow remains adaptable, cost-effective, and aligned with welfare and operational standards. This success not only highlights the effectiveness of the applied strategies but also sets a benchmark for future simulations and real-world operations. By leveraging the insights gained from this simulation, future processes can continue to be improved, ensuring that the livestock logistics workflow remains a model of efficiency and reliability. The commitment to continuous optimization and innovation reinforces the ability to meet evolving demands while maintaining the highest levels of performance and compliance.

7. Conclusions and Future Research

The present study on multimodal livestock operations offers several significant insights into the optimization of maritime livestock transportation. The research fills a crucial gap in business process modeling (BPM) for livestock logistics, an area that has historically received limited attention compared to general freight transportation. The major findings and their significance may be outlined as following:

a. Operational bottlenecks and infrastructure deficiencies—the study identifies key inefficiencies in ramp availability, administrative processes, and infrastructure reliability that hinder smooth livestock transportation operations. Administrative delays in document verification slow down throughput, suggesting the need for digital automation to enhance operational flow.
b. Application of business process modeling for efficiency enhancement—by utilizing Aura Portal Helium Modeler, the study demonstrates how BPM-driven simulations can identify and rectify inefficiencies in logistics chains. Workflow optimization through real-time monitoring and simulation reduces delays and enhances resource utilization.
c. Equipment reliability and risk management—the study considers previous research in stress-strength and damage-endurance modeling to evaluate the performance of critical port machinery, such as the Liebherr LHM 420 crane. Results indicate a reliability score exceeding 0.85, demonstrating that strategic investments in high-quality equipment reduce downtime and operational risks.
d. Integration of technological solutions in livestock transport—the authors suggests that RFID tracking, automated administrative processing, and real-time data collection can enhance logistics efficiency and compliance with EU animal welfare regulations. These technologies can improve the accuracy of transit documentation, minimize delays, and facilitate seamless coordination between transportation stakeholders.
e. Regulatory compliance and animal welfare considerations—the study reinforces the importance of EU Regulation (EC) No. 1/2005, which mandates adequate food, water, and space for livestock during transportation. Compliance remains a significant challenge, requiring continuous monitoring and regulatory harmonization across different jurisdictions.

Overall, the findings underscore that process automation, digital tracking systems, and optimized resource allocation can significantly improve livestock logistics while ensuring ethical and regulatory compliance. The research provides a data-driven framework that port authorities, logistics operators, and policymakers can implement to enhance multimodal livestock transportation operations.

While the study provides a solid foundation for optimizing maritime livestock transport, several areas remain open for further exploration. Future research can expand upon the findings by integrating emerging technologies, comparative port studies, and predictive logistics modeling. Using the major findings of the study and the literature review conclusions, the findings may pave the way for future research efforts in the following directions:

a. Machine learning for predictive logistics and risk mitigation by applying machine learning (ML) algorithms can improve predictive risk assessment in logistics. ML models could forecast equipment failures, administrative bottlenecks, or regulatory compliance risks based on historical data. Studies such as Zhang et al. (2020) have demonstrated that AI-driven predictive analytics can reduce transit delays and optimize port resource allocation.

b. Comparative analysis of alternative ports suggest that future research should compare the efficiency of different ports in livestock transport, assessing factors such as infrastructure availability, regulatory adherence, equipment reliability, or operational costs. As an example, the study conducted by Gonzalez-Feliu et al. (2021), comparing the Port of Midia with ports in Spain, Australia, or Brazil, could provide best practices for optimizing livestock export hubs (Gonzalez-Feliu et al., 2021).
c. The impact of IoT-based smart logistics systems foresees that Internet of Things (IoT) sensors could be integrated into livestock transportation systems to provide real-time tracking of animal welfare parameters (e.g., temperature, hydration levels, and movement). Studies such as that conducted by Kumar et al. have shown that IoT-enabled logistics can reduce stress-related losses in livestock transportation and improve regulatory compliance (Kumar et al., 2019).
d. Policy analysis on alternative transportation methods is significantly relevant given the animal welfare concerns associated with long-distance livestock transport, and future research may explore alternative models, such as processing meat products locally instead of exporting live animals and hybrid transportation solutions (e.g., combining maritime transportation with short-haul air freight for livestock). Studies like that by Padalino and Tarrant (2018) suggest that reducing voyage duration significantly improves animal welfare outcomes (Padalino & Tarrant, 2018).
e. Blockchain for supply chain transparency in livestock transportation could be explored as a solution for ensuring traceability in livestock logistics. Research in agricultural supply chain management indicates that blockchain-led transparency reduces fraud, enhances regulatory compliance, and builds consumer trust (Caro et al., 2018).
f. Applying digital twin modeling in multimodal livestock transportation is a promising avenue for enhancing operational efficiency and animal welfare. Research into AI-based predictive logistics, blockchain integration, and cross-port DT comparisons can further advance livestock transportation technology in the coming years (Zhang et al., 2020; Uhlemann et al., 2017). Digital twin models can integrate IoT-based sensors to track parameters such as temperature and humidity inside livestock containers, hydration levels to prevent dehydration, or stress levels (via movement and behaviour monitoring). Moreover, in ports like Midia (Romania), Fremantle (Australia), and Cartagena (Spain), digital twin models could monitor port equipment performance (e.g., cranes, ramps, water provisioning systems) and simulate alternative logistics flows to improve efficiency or ensure regulatory compliance by digitally tracking animal welfare conditions at every transportation stage.

From a legal framework perspective, the present study aims to provide substantial policy implications for regulatory bodies, port administrations, and logistics operators, highlighting several deficiencies in infrastructure, process efficiency, and regulatory compliance in maritime livestock transport that may require policy changes and operational best practices at national and international levels. The research findings indicate regulatory gaps in real-time monitoring of animal welfare conditions during intermodal transportation. Therefore, the policymakers should update EU Regulation (EC) No. 1/2005 to require digital tracking systems (e.g., RFID tags, IoT sensors) on all livestock shipments to monitor temperature, hydration levels, and stress factors (European Commission, 2023b). Mandatory risk assessments should be introduced to evaluate transportation bottlenecks, delays, and compliance issues before shipments leave the port, and policy updates should be promoted, foreseeing the integration of AI-driven predictive models to forecast logistical bottlenecks and compliance risks and the implementation of higher penalties for regulatory non-compliance, including delayed inspections or failure to meet welfare standards.

From an operational perspective, the study identified major inefficiencies in administrative processes and port infrastructure that contribute to delays in livestock handling. Port authorities should automate document verification, integrate real-time logistics monitoring, and increase ramp availability to reduce animal waiting times. In the port administration, automated document processing tools should be implemented, such as AI-based document scanning, for faster customs clearance and health certification.

The findings from the Port of Midia case study provide critical insights into the need for policy reform and administrative modernization in multimodal livestock operations. These insights should guide regulatory updates, infrastructure investments, and the adoption of smart logistics technologies. Policymakers must prioritize updating EU regulations to mandate digital tracking and AI-driven risk assessments, reforming port administration practices to improve efficiency and compliance and developing international agreements to harmonize global livestock transportation standards. These policy recommendations will ensure that livestock transportation remains efficient, humane, and sustainable, aligning with economic, ethical, and environmental considerations.

In conclusion, this research aimed to contribute to the expansion of intermodal transportation studies, providing practical recommendations for enhancing livestock logistics efficiency while ensuring compliance with European animal welfare regulations. The findings suggested above may pave the way for further research into AI-driven risk assessments, smart logistics solutions, and sustainable livestock transportation alternatives.

8. Authors' Contributions and Conflicts of Interest

The major contributions brought by the authors in the article are in reference to the business process modeling in designing and simulating the intermodal processes using a specialized BPM software, proving the reliability of smart and intelligent tools in increasing the logistics process efficiency. The case study approaches a neglected subject in intermodal transportation, related to livestock transhipment, through which the authors contribute to the existing collection of intermodal case studies, depicting in a discrete manner and under a unitary workflow model each occurring process from technical, technological, and operational perspectives. In addition, the authors have sought to combine the technical references with operational considerations within the logistics processes, identifying new criteria in decision-making processes for equipment reliability and risk management of handling equipment to ensure seamless logistical execution.

Author Contributions: Conceptualization, C.P., O.S. and I.G.; methodology, C.P., O.S. and I.G.; software, C.P., O.S. and I.G.; validation, C.P., O.S. and I.G.; formal analysis, C.P., O.S. and I.G.; investigation, C.P., O.S. and I.G.; resources, C.P., O.S. and I.G.; data curation, C.P., O.S. and I.G.; writing—original draft preparation, C.P., O.S. and I.G.; writing—review and editing, C.P., O.S. and I.G.; visualization, C.P., O.S. and I.G.; supervision, C.P.; project administration, C.P.; funding acquisition, C.P., O.S. and I.G. All authors have read and agreed to the published version of the manuscript.

Funding: This research received no external funding.

Informed Consent Statement: Not applicable.

Data Availability Statement: The original contributions presented in this study are included in the article. Further inquiries can be directed to the corresponding authors.

Conflicts of Interest: The authors declare no conflicts of interest.

References

Abadi, A., Hamidreza, R., Herrmann, F., Jeffrey, E., Modarres, M., & Mohammad, M. (2023). Measuring and indexing the durability of electrical and electronic equipment. *Sustainability*, *15*, 14386. [CrossRef]

ANSVSA. (2023). *Regulatory compliance for livestock transport in Romania*. National Sanitary Veterinary and Food Safety Authority.

Bhatt, N., Hossain, M., & Khan, M. A. (2021). A detailed review of transportation stress in livestock and its mitigation techniques. *International Journal of Livestock Research, 11*(1), 30–41. [CrossRef]

Caro, M. P., Ali, M. S., Vecchio, M., & Giaffreda, R. (2018). Blockchain-based traceability in Agri-Food supply chain management. *Future Generation Computer Systems, 86*, 366–373.

De Luzi, F., Leotta, F., Marrella, A., & Mecella, M. (2024). *On the interplay between business process management and internet-of-things: A systematic literature review*. Business & Information Systems Engineering.

European Commission. (2023a). *Animal transport guides*. Available online: https://food.ec.europa.eu/animals/animal-welfare/eu-animal-welfare-legislation/animal-welfare-during-transport/animal-transport-guides_en (accessed on 4 January 2025).

European Commission. (2023b). *Council Regulation (EC) No 1/2005 of 22 December 2004 on the protection of animals during transport and related operations and amending Directives 64/432/EEC and 93/119/EC and Regulation (EC) No 1255/97*. European Commission Directorate-General for Health and Food Safety. Available online: https://eur-lex.europa.eu/eli/reg/2005/1/oj. (accessed on 4 January 2025).

European Court of Auditors. (2023). *Transport of live animals in the EU: Challenges and opportunities*. Available online: https://www.eca.europa.eu/Lists/ECADocuments/RV-2023-03/RV-2023-03_RO.pdf (accessed on 4 January 2025).

Gonzalez-Feliu, J., Semet, F., & Routhier, J. L. (2021). Sustainable freight transport: Methods and applications. *Transportation Research Part E: Logistics and Transportation Review, 145*, 102110.

Knowles, T. G., Warriss, P. D., & Brown, S. N. (2014). Transport of livestock: Welfare and quality. *Meat Science, 98*(4), 469–477.

Kumar, S., Park, J., & Subramaniam, V. (2019). IoT-based livestock management systems: Challenges and future directions. *Computers and Electronics in Agriculture, 157*, 24–35.

Laguna, M., & Marklund, J. (1998). *Business process modeling, simulation and design* (3rd ed.). CRC Press.

Lindsay, A., Downs, D., & Lunn, K. (2003). Business processes—Attempts to find a definition. *Information and Software Technology Journal, 45*(15), 1015–1019. [CrossRef]

Miranda-De La Lama, G. C., Villarroel, M., & Maria, G. (2014). Livestock transport from the perspective of the pre-slaughter logistic chain: A review. *Meat Science, 98*(1), 9–20. [CrossRef] [PubMed]

Modarres, M., Kaminskiy, M., & Krivtsov, V. (2020). *Reliability engineering and risk analysis: A practical guide*. CRC Press.

Padalino, B., & Tarrant, P. V. (2018). Animal welfare concerns in long-distance livestock transport. *Journal of Animal Science, 96*(7), 3014–3025.

Popa, C., & Goia, I. (2024). The modelling of cargo transshipment operations using the business process modelling tools. *Scientific Journal of Silesian University of Technology. Series Transport, 124*, 159–171. [CrossRef]

Uhlemann, T. H. J., Lehmann, C., & Steinhilper, R. (2017). Digital twin and its implications for manufacturing. *Procedia CIRP, 61*, 335–340. [CrossRef]

University of Wisconsin-Madison Safety Department. (2021). *Procedures for loading, transporting, and unloading cattle and swine*. Available online: https://safety.cals.wisc.edu/wp-content/uploads/sites/325/2021/11/Ch.-5-Procedures-for-Loading-Transporting-and-Unloading-Cattle-and-Swine.pdf (accessed on 4 January 2025).

Website of Constanta Port Administration. (2025). Available online: https://www.portofconstantza.com (accessed on 4 January 2025).

Website of Port of Midia. (2025). Available online: https://www.midia-international.ro (accessed on 4 January 2025).

WorldRef. (2024). *Overcoming supply chain management inefficiencies, operational bottlenecks, and compliance complexities*. Available online: https://insights.worldref.co/supply-chain-management-inefficiencies/?utm_source=chatgpt.com (accessed on 4 January 2025).

Zhang, Y., Zhao, X., & Wang, H. (2020). AI-driven predictive analytics in port logistics: A case study approach. *Maritime Policy & Management, 47*(5), 562–577.

economies

MDPI

Article

Deep Reinforcement Learning in a Search-Matching Model of Labor Market Fluctuations

Ruxin Chen

Department of Economics, Nagoya University, Aichi 464-8601, Japan; chen.ruxin.m0@s.mail.nagoya-u.ac.jp

Abstract

Shimer documents that the search-and-matching model driven by productivity shocks explains only a small share of the observed volatility of unemployment and vacancies, which is known as the Shimer puzzle. We revisit this evidence by replacing the representative firm's optimization with a deep reinforcement learning (DRL) agent that learns its vacancy-posting policy through interaction in a Diamond–Mortensen–Pissarides (DMP) model. Comparing the learning economy with a conventional log-linearized DSGE solution under the same parameters, we find that while both frameworks preserve a downward-sloping Beveridge curve, learning-based economy produces much higher volatility in key labor market variables and returns to a steady state more slowly after shocks. These results point to bounded rationality and endogenous learning as mechanisms for labor market fluctuations and suggest that reinforcement learning can serve as a useful complement to standard macroeconomic analysis.

Keywords: search-and-matching model; labor market simulation; macroeconomic modeling; deep reinforcement learning

1. Introduction

1.1. Background

Macroeconomic modeling is the construction of models that characterize the behavior of the aggregate economy. Such models are used to forecast future dynamics, analyze relationships among key macro variables, and simulate the effects of policy or structural changes. Reinforcement learning (RL) develops systems that show intelligent behavior, including reasoning, learning, problem solving, and autonomous decisions, and is thus well suited to these tasks. RL can enhance the accuracy, flexibility, and adaptability of macro models, while macroeconomic environments provide disciplined testbeds for building and evaluating AI systems aimed at reproducing complex social and economic behavior.

With recent advances in neural networks, many surveys and applications combine DRL with macroeconomics, where agents and institutions interact dynamically (Atashbar & Shi, 2022; Evans & Ganesh, 2024; Maliar et al., 2021; Shi, 2023). In such settings, DRL can approximate policy functions without relying on linearity, potentially capturing nonlinear properties and learning dynamics that standard solution methods may overlook.

In standard search-and-matching frameworks such as the DMP model, a persistent quantitative tension is that model-implied fluctuations in labor market variables are far smaller than those observed in the data Shimer (2005), known as the "Shimer puzzle". The existing literature typically modifies wage setting, shock processes, or calibration targets (Hall, 2005; Mortensen & Nagypal, 2007; Petrosky-Nadeau & Zhang, 2017). By contrast, we

https://doi.org/10.3390/economies13100302

explore whether the solution method itself can produce more intense volatility when firms learn policies through interaction with the environment.

This leads to the central question of our paper: can the learning process of a firm, modeled via DRL, endogenously generate the observed volatility in labor market variables that standard expectations models fail to reproduce?

To investigate this question, we build a labor market framework that integrates a DMP model with endogenous firm size and a reinforcement learning agent. The agent begins without knowledge of the economy's structure, preferences, or transition laws and learns vacancy posting and wage strategies through repeated interaction with the environment. After sufficient training, its behavior converges toward rational expectations benchmarks. Although the learning process is initially slow, since the agent must generate its own experience, the dynamics stabilize and become consistent over time. Through the simulation, we find that the RL-based system exhibits substantially greater volatility, suggesting that learning dynamics can amplify fluctuations in a way that better aligns with empirical observations. The current implementation remains deliberately parsimonious, focusing on productivity shocks and a simplified unemployment mechanism, but it provides a flexible prototype that can be extended to richer shock processes, heterogeneous agents, more realistic labor market frictions, and policy experiments.

This paper contributes by offering a learning-based interpretation of the Shimer puzzle and demonstrating that DRL can produce more realistic macroeconomic fluctuations. Methodologically, it introduces an interpretable framework that supports future policy analysis and strengthens the bridge between AI techniques and macroeconomic modeling. The remainder of the paper proceeds as follows: Section 1 reviews the related literature, with the topic of Shimer puzzle and RL in macroeconomics; Section 2 lays out the theoretical framework, a search-and-matching model with endogenous firm size; Section 3 explains the quantitative methods, including the benchmark DSGE model solved by log linearization and the design of the DRL agent; Section 4 reports the main results and compares the volatility and dynamic responses across the two approaches; Section 5 concludes with the main contribution, notes the limits of the study, and outlines directions for future work.

1.2. Related Works

1.2.1. Labor Markets as a Search-and-Matching Problem

The search-and-matching (DMP) view changed how we study unemployment, job creation, and wages. It states that workers and firms do not meet instantly. Because search takes time and effort, unemployment can arise in equilibrium. A full overview is given by Pissarides (2000).

In this framework, a simple matching function (often Cobb–Douglas) maps unemployment and vacancies into new hires. Market tightness $\theta_t = v_t/u_t$ is a key summary of conditions. It controls both job-finding for workers and vacancy-filling for firms. Wages are usually set by Nash bargaining, so they move with productivity and outside options (Pissarides, 2000).

Shimer (2005) shows that the baseline DMP model with Nash bargaining and standard calibration cannot match key business–cycle facts. In U.S. data, unemployment is strongly countercyclical, vacancies are strongly procyclical, and the two are tightly negatively correlated (a clear Beveridge curve). In contrast, when the model is hit by productivity shocks of realistic size, it produces only small movements in market tightness and unemployment.

The large gap between the model's prediction and the observed volatility of vacancies and unemployment, widely known as the Shimer puzzle, has led to a search for amplification mechanisms. A prominent line of work stresses wage rigidity. Hall (2005) introduces a search-and-matching model with equilibrium wage stickiness, showing that when wages adjust slowly within the bargaining set, small productivity shocks can generate large fluctuations in vacancies and unemployment. Gertler and Trigari (2009) give a microfoundation with staggered multi-period wage contracts that generate smooth aggregate wages consistent with the data. The sufficiency of wage rigidity alone is contested. Mortensen and Nagypal (2007) review additional mechanisms, including strategic bargaining, realistic matching elasticities, turnover costs, and separation shocks, and suggest that several forces may be needed. Pissarides (2009) likewise questions whether wage stickiness by itself resolves the puzzle and emphasizes the role of the wage equation and parameter choices. A second line of work focuses on calibration and on solution methods. Hagedorn and Manovskii (2008) propose a surplus calibration in which a high value of nonmarket activity makes profits very sensitive to productivity, raising volatility. Petrosky-Nadeau and Zhang (2017) show that when one solves the model with accurate global methods rather than a local log-linear approximation, nonlinearities can produce much larger fluctuations and stronger impulse responses, which changes how earlier findings should be read.

To study a learning-based amplification mechanism, we start from a standard search-and-matching model with endogenous firm size, following Smith (1999). In this setup, concave production implies that a firm's hiring decisions depend on its current size. Later work incorporates richer firm-level dynamics. Elsby and Michaels (2013) show that decisions at the "marginal job" within heterogeneous firms can amplify unemployment movements. Kaas and Kircher (2015) use a competitive search setting to connect firm growth and wage dynamics to business cycle facts. Kudoh et al. (2019) focus on adjustment margins in multi-worker firms and find that their model matches the cyclicality of hours. While these richer models offer important insights into structural amplification, we adopt a simple setup to clearly isolate the contribution of the DRL agent's learning dynamics as a novel amplification mechanism.

Finally, the DMP framework is well-suited to learning-based methods. Because firms make sequential vacancy choices and receive informative feedback from matches and profits, reinforcement learning can allow them to learn effective hiring rules. We expand on this in the next section.

1.2.2. The Progress of RL and DRL

RL belongs to one of the three principal paradigms of machine learning, alongside supervised and unsupervised learning. While supervised learning relies on labeled data to learn mappings from inputs to outputs, and unsupervised learning focuses on discovering hidden structures in data, RL is fundamentally concerned with decision-making through sequential interaction with an environment. Its distinguishing feature is that the learner, called the agent, is not provided with explicit examples of correct behavior. Instead, it must discover effective strategies through trial and error, guided only by feedback in the form of rewards or penalties. This formulation makes RL particularly well suited for dynamic settings where agents must adapt to evolving circumstances—features that resonate with many problems studied in economics, such as investment, labor search, or firm competition.

RL has its intellectual roots in psychology and neuroscience, where concepts such as stimulus–response learning and reward prediction errors were originally developed (Lee et al., 2012). Formally, the RL framework can be cast as a Markov Decision Process (MDP), characterized by four elements: a set of states $\mathcal{S}$, representing all possible situations the agent might face; a set of actions $\mathcal{A}$, denoting the possible decisions available to the agent; a transition function $P(s' \mid s, a)$, describing the stochastic evolution of the environment given current state s and action a; and a reward function $R_a(s, s')$, specifying the immediate feedback obtained when moving from state s to s' under action a (Puterman, 2014).

Figure 1 provides a schematic overview of this interaction loop between the agent and its environment.

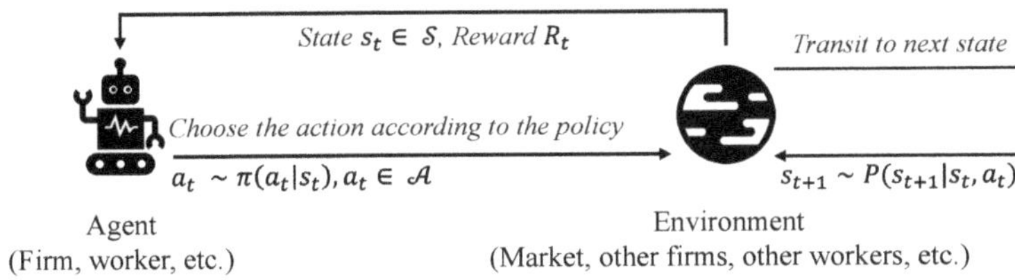

Figure 1. The reinforcement learning framework. At each time step, the agent observes the current state and reward and selects an action, and the environment transitions to a new state with an updated reward.

The goal of the agent is to learn a policy π, which specifies the mapping from states to actions, that maximizes the expected cumulative discounted reward over a finite or infinite horizon:

$$\pi^* = \arg\max_{\pi} \mathbb{E}_{\pi}\left[\sum_{t=0}^{T} \gamma^t R_t\right], \tag{1}$$

where R_t denotes the reward at time t, $\gamma \in (0, 1)$ is the discount factor reflecting time preference, and $\mathbb{E}_{\pi}$ indicates the expectation with respect to the probability distribution induced by policy π. This optimization problem is closely related to familiar concepts in economics, such as utility maximization under intertemporal preferences.

A wide range of algorithms has been proposed to solve the RL problem. Traditional reinforcement learning algorithms often rely on explicit tables or relatively simple mathematical functions to represent the mapping between states, actions, and values. Such approaches work well when the state and action spaces are small but quickly become infeasible in environments with many variables, continuous decision spaces, or complex nonlinear relationships—settings that are common in economics.

More recently, advances in deep learning have given rise to the field of DRL, where neural networks are employed as function approximators to handle high-dimensional state spaces and complex environments (Arulkumaran et al., 2017).

Deep learning provides a solution by using multi-layered neural networks, which are flexible mathematical models inspired loosely by the structure of the human brain. These networks are capable of automatically extracting and representing relevant patterns from raw data, without the need for hand-crafted feature design.

Among DRL algorithms, a particularly influential class is the family of actor–critic methods. These combine the strengths of value-based and policy-based approaches: the "actor" updates the policy directly, while the "critic" evaluates the quality of the policy by estimating value functions. The algorithm employed in this paper, Deep Deterministic Policy Gradient (DDPG) (Lillicrap et al., 2016), is a prominent example of this class. DDPG is designed for environments with continuous action spaces, where the agent's decision variables are not discrete but rather take values from a continuum, much like the choices of consumption, investment, or wage offers in economic models.

1.2.3. RL in Economic Simulations

The application of RL in economics has developed from early theoretical explorations to modern deep RL implementations in macroeconomic and financial contexts. Early work at the intersection of RL and economics established the theoretical basis for using RL to model bounded rationality and adaptive expectations. Arthur (1991) and Barto and Singh (1991) explored computational approaches to economic decision-making, while Sargent

(1993) emphasized the parallel between econometricians and economic agents in their learning processes. Subsequent contributions began to apply RL to specific economic problems, such as incomplete markets with liquidity constraints (Jirnyi & Lepetyuk, 2011).

A central strand of research employs DRL as a solution method for optimal policy design. For instance, Hinterlang and Tänzer (2021) demonstrated that deep RL can derive central bank interest rate rules that outperform traditional monetary policy benchmarks. Likewise, Castro et al. (2025) used policy gradient methods to optimize liquidity management in payment systems, and Curry et al. (2022) applied multi-agent deep RL to approximate equilibria in real business cycle models with heterogeneous agents. Other studies have investigated oligopolistic competition (Covarrubias, 2022) and algorithmic pricing (Calvano et al., 2020), showing the relevance of RL for industrial organization and market design.

RL has also been used to study bounded rationality and learning dynamics in macroeconomic models. M. Chen et al. (2021) applied the DDPG algorithm to analyze the convergence of rational expectations equilibria, while Ashwin et al. (2021) examined which equilibria are learnable when agents employ flexible neural networks. Extending these ideas, Hill et al. (2021) used deep RL to solve heterogeneous agent models, capturing precautionary saving behavior and macroeconomic responses to shocks.

Finally, multi-agent extensions of RL have opened new avenues for analyzing strategic interaction. Johnson et al. (2022) illustrated how production, consumption, and pricing patterns can emerge in spatial trading environments. Surveys such as that conducted by Hernandez-Leal et al. (2020) provide a comprehensive overview of opportunities and challenges in multi-agent RL for economics.

Despite these advances, the application of RL to labor market dynamics remains limited. One exception is R. Chen and Zhang (2025), who used multi-agent RL to examine how firms with different degrees of rationality adjust their policies and the resulting macroeconomic consequences. However, their analysis does not focus on market stability and volatility from an economic perspective. In contrast, the present paper applies mean-field theory to model competitive equilibrium in the labor market, analyzing how productivity shocks influence volatility and stability, and comparing these results with insights from classical economic approaches.

2. Model

The model follows the search-and-matching framework of Smith (1999) but abstracts from firm entry. Specifically, we consider a single representative firm with the total workforce normalized to one. This simplification suppresses the extensive margin of firm entry and allows us to focus on the intensive margin of employment dynamics within the firm.

The model is a discrete-time matching framework with a representative multi-worker firm. Since there is only one firm in the economy, firm entry is absent, and the total measure of workers is normalized to one. Workers are assumed to be homogeneous, so employment and unemployment satisfy $l_t + u_t = 1$.

The number of new matches in period t is given by

$$m(u_t, v_t) = a u_t^{\phi} v_t^{1-\phi}, \tag{2}$$

where $a > 0$ denotes matching efficiency, $0 < \phi < 1$ measures the elasticity with respect to unemployment, u_t is the unemployment rate, and v_t is the vacancy rate. Market tightness is defined as

$$\theta_t = \frac{v_t}{u_t}, \tag{3}$$

and the vacancy-filling probability is

$$q(\theta_t) = \frac{m(u_t, v_t)}{v_t} = a\theta_t^{-\phi}. \tag{4}$$

Because $q'(\theta_t) < 0$, a decline in market tightness raises the probability that a posted vacancy is filled.

The representative firm chooses the number of vacancies to maximize the expected present value of profits:

$$\begin{aligned} J(l_t) &= \max_{v_t} \left\{ f(l_t) - w(l_t)\, l_t - cv_t + \frac{1}{1+r} J(l_{t+1}) \right\} \\ \text{s.t. } \; l_{t+1} &= (1-\lambda) l_t + q(\theta_t) v_t, \end{aligned} \tag{5}$$

where $w(l_t)$ denotes the endogenous wage, c is the per-vacancy posting cost, and $\lambda \in (0,1)$ is the exogenous separation rate. The wage in period t is $w(l_t)l_t$, which reflects the outcome of bargaining between workers and the firm. Wages are therefore not fixed parameters but depend on firm size and the bargaining power of workers.

Production is given by a concave technology

$$f(l_t) = A_t l_t^{\alpha}, \qquad 0 < \alpha < 1, \tag{6}$$

which implies that output increases with employment but marginal productivity declines as l_t rises. A_t denotes the level of total factor productivity (TFP).

At time t, the firm chooses vacancies v_t to maximize expected firm value. The corresponding first-order condition is

$$-c + \frac{q(\theta_t) J'(l_{t+1})}{1+r} = 0. \tag{7}$$

The envelope condition is

$$J'(l_t) = f'(l_t) - w(l_t) - w'(l_t) l_t + \frac{(1-\lambda) J'(l_{t+1})}{1+r}. \tag{8}$$

We define the value functions for the workers. The value of being employed W_t is the sum of the current wage and the discounted expected future value:

$$W_t = w(l_t) + \frac{1}{1+r}[(1-\lambda) W_{t+1} + \lambda U_{t+1}]. \tag{9}$$

Similarly, the value of being unemployed , U_t, consists of the unemployment benefit b and the discounted expected future value:

$$U_t = b + \frac{1}{1+r}[\theta_t q(\theta_t) W_{t+1} + [1 - \theta_t q(\theta_t)] U_{t+1}]. \tag{10}$$

The wage is then set to split the total surplus of a match, which is derived from the firm's value of a filled job and the worker's net gain from employment. The derivation of the wage equation is detailed in Appendix A. Hence, the wage equation is

$$w(l_t) = \frac{\eta \alpha A_t l_t^{\alpha-1}}{\eta \alpha + 1 - \eta} + (1-\eta) b + \eta c \theta_t, \tag{11}$$

where $\eta \in (0,1)$ governs the bargaining power of workers.

3. Method

3.1. Parameter Calibration

The model parameters are calibrated following standard practices in the search-and-matching literature. Table 1 reports the baseline parameter values used in our simulations. Our calibration strategy closely follows Kudoh et al. (2019), with targets chosen to match key empirical moments. The full set of steady-state equations used for the model's calibration is listed in Appendix B.

Table 1. Default experimental parameters.

Symbol	Description	Value
A	Productivity	1
a	Matching efficiency	0.471
α	Parameter in production function	0.667
λ	Separation rate	0.0144
η	Worker's bargaining power	0.6
ϕ	Matching elasticity	0.6
r	Interest rate	0.004
c	Vacancy cost	0.273
b	Unemployment benefit	0.500

We begin by setting parameters that can be determined from external evidence. Following Kudoh et al. (2019), the capital share parameter in the production function is set to $\alpha = 2/3$, consistent with the labor share multiplier effect. The matching function is given by $m(u_t, v_t) = a u_t^{\phi} v_t^{1-\phi}$, where the elasticity ϕ is typically set between 0.5 and 0.7. We adopt $\phi = 0.6$, as reported in Lin and Miyamoto (2014). By the Hosios (1990) condition, the worker's bargaining power must equal the matching elasticity, so we set $\eta = \phi = 0.6$. This also satisfies $-q'(\theta)\theta/q(\theta) = \eta$.

The separation rate is taken from Miyamoto (2011), who estimate a monthly separation probability of 0.0048. At quarterly frequency, this implies a total separation rate λ of $3 \times 0.0048 = 0.0144$. The quarterly real interest rate, r, is set to 0.004. The steady-state level of productivity, A, is normalized to 1. Finally, the TFP (A_t) process, evolving according to a first-order autoregressive process, $\log A_t - \log A = \rho(\log A_{t-1} - \log A) + \epsilon_t$, is calibrated following Kudoh et al. (2019), with a persistence of $\rho = 0.612$ and a shock standard deviation of $\sigma = 0.0085$.

Next, we use empirical targets to pin down key variables in the model's steady state. The central variable in the search-and-matching framework is labor market tightness, $\theta = v/u$. We target the average vacancy–unemployment ratio of 0.78 for Japan, as reported by Miyamoto (2011).

With θ determined, we can now identify the matching efficiency parameter, a. We follow the method of Lin and Miyamoto (2012), who report a monthly job-finding rate of 0.142. This implies a quarterly job-finding rate of $f = 0.426$. In the model, the job-finding rate is given by $f = m(u,v)/u = a\theta^{1-\phi}$. Using our target for θ and the calibrated value for ϕ, we can solve for the matching efficiency $a = 0.471$.

Finally, the remaining parameters, the value of unemployment benefit b, and the vacancy cost c are calibrated to be consistent with the model's steady-state equilibrium. Based on Nickell (1997), who reports a replacement rate of 60% in Japan, we set the unemployment benefit to $b = 0.6w$, where w is the steady-state wage. With all other parameters and steady-state values now determined, the vacancy cost, c, is chosen to ensure the model's job creation condition holds in the steady state. This procedure yields a value of $c = 0.273$.

To facilitate direct comparison with the RL experiments, we ensure that both approaches use identical parameter values, shock processes, and initial conditions.

3.2. The Log-Linearization Approach

We first solve the model using the conventional method employed in the vast majority of the DSGE literature. This approach relies on creating a log-linearized approximation of the model, which we implement using the standard Dynare software package (version 6.4).

The core challenge in solving DSGE models is that their equilibrium conditions form a system of nonlinear difference equations that typically lacks a closed-form analytical solution. One solution is to approximate the model's dynamics locally around its deterministic steady state through log-linearization, a technique that applies a first-order Taylor approximation to the logarithmic form of the model's equations. The key advantage of this method is that it transforms the complex nonlinear system into a tractable set of linear equations where all variables are interpreted as percentage deviations from their steady-state values, well suited to business cycle analysis.

The implementation in Dynare follows the standard procedure of representing the model's equilibrium conditions in a form suitable for numerical solution. Dynare computes the deterministic steady state of the system, which serves as the reference point for subsequent analysis. Around this steady state, the equilibrium conditions are log-linearized, reducing the original nonlinear system into a linear system of equations. This linearized system allows for efficient computation of impulse response functions and stochastic simulations under exogenous shocks.

In the experiment, productivity shocks are introduced as a persistent exogenous process, following the conventional autoregressive specification widely used in dynamic stochastic general equilibrium analysis. These shocks generate time variation in output and labor market variables. The Dynare implementation then simulates the dynamics of the model in response to these shocks, with all simulated variables expressed as deviations from their deterministic steady-state values.

3.3. The RL Approach

We formalize the search-and-matching framework as an RL environment. To set up an RL agent, it is sufficient to specify the state variables, the available actions, and the state transition dynamics. In each period, the agent observes the current state and selects an action accordingly. The baseline state variables consist of employment (l_t) and the unemployment rate (u_t). For our experiment, we additionally incorporate a productivity shock, so productivity (A_t) is also included in the state space. The agent's action corresponds to the number of vacancies (v_t) it chooses to create. The reward is defined as the firm's income net of expenditures, which include wage payments and the costs of posting vacancies. A concise summary of the RL components, together with the corresponding transition functions, is provided in Table 2.

The optimal policy for this RL environment is learned by the DDPG algorithm (Lillicrap et al., 2016), which maintains two parameterized networks: an actor and a critic.

- Actor Network: The policy function translates observed states into continuous control actions. It is implemented as a three-layer fully connected neural network with ReLU activations in the hidden layers and a final tanh transformation to ensure bounded outputs.
- Critic Network: The value estimator receives both the state and action as input and predicts their Q-value. It follows the same three-layer feedforward structure, with the state–action pair concatenated at the input layer.

Both networks use 256 hidden units per layer. The policy (actor) is optimized using the Adam optimizer with a step size of 5×10^{-5}, while the value function (critic) is updated with a higher rate of 5×10^{-4}. Target networks are updated by Polyak averaging with coefficient $\tau = 0.005$, and the discount factor is fixed at $\gamma = 0.99$. Experience replay is handled by a buffer that stores up to 10^5 transitions. During training, mini-batches of 256 samples are drawn to update the networks. Following the DDPG algorithm, updates alternate between critic and actor steps, with target networks softly adjusted at each iteration.

Table 2. Components of RL.

Component	Setup
State	l_t, u_t, A_t
Action	$v_t \in (0,1)$
Reward	$R_t = A_t l_t^{\alpha} - w_t l_t - c v_t,$ where $w_t = \frac{\eta\alpha A_t l_t^{\alpha-1}}{\eta\alpha+1-\eta} - (1-\eta)b - \eta c\theta.$
Transition equations	$l_{t+1} = (1-\lambda)l_t + a\theta^{-\phi} \cdot v_t$ $u_{t+1} = 1 - l_{t+1}$
Transition equations (If shock exists)	$\hat{A}_{t+1} = \rho\hat{A}_t + \epsilon, \epsilon \sim \mathcal{N}(0, \sigma_\epsilon^2)$

Training proceeds over 50 simulated episodes per iteration, each lasting 200 steps. As noted by Zhang and Chen (2025), a straightforward single-agent RL setup often drives the agent to act as a manipulator of its environment. To mitigate this issue, we adopt a mean-field game perspective and stabilize the system by fixing the value of θ within each run. After training, the system is restarted and executed for 400 steps to ensure convergence to equilibrium, followed by an additional 100 steps used solely for evaluation and analysis. For the results, all variables are reported in logs.

4. Simulation Result

Tables 3 and 4 present the standard deviations and correlation patterns of the main labor market variables generated by the simulation in Dynare and by the RL framework.

First, the overall correlation structure is remarkably consistent across the two approaches. In particular, both models reproduce the negative relationship between unemployment and vacancies, with correlations of -0.2663 in Dynare and -0.2652 in RL. This result aligns with the empirically observed Beveridge curve and indicates that the RL-based simulation is not only theoretically coherent but also capable of reproducing one of the central stylized facts in labor market dynamics. The robustness of this negative association across methods provides reassurance that the RL framework remains grounded in the same theoretical mechanisms as the DSGE benchmark.

Second, there are significant differences in the magnitude of fluctuations. For unemployment rates, job vacancies, and labor market tightness, the standard deviation shown by the RL model is approximately several times that produced by the Dynare model. Since the job vacancy fill rate (q) and employment rate (Q) are mechanically linked to labor market tightness, their volatility is also enhanced in the RL framework. This increased variability provides a possible explanation for the Shimer puzzle. While the DSGE framework relies on rational expectations, RL agents introduce additional sources of noise and nonlinear adjustments in decision-making. Such mechanisms can generate larger fluctuations that may be closer to real-world labor market dynamics, where imperfect rationality, bounded information, and heterogeneous behaviors contribute to excess volatility that standard DSGE models fail to capture.

Third, employment rates remain at a relatively high level in both simulations, implying that their percentage deviations from the steady state are small. Since wages are primarily determined by the employment rate, their volatility also remains limited in both approaches, with only modest differences between Dynare and RL.

Table 3. Comparison of standard deviations: Dynare vs. RL.

Variable	Dynare Std. Dev.	RL Std. Dev.
Employment rate (l)	0.000110	0.004199
Unemployment rate (u)	0.003247	0.085436
Vacancies (v)	0.009831	0.102968
Market tightness (θ)	0.011144	0.139705
Wage rate (w)	0.008240	0.009211
Vacancy filling rate (q)	0.006686	0.083823
Job finding rate (Q)	0.004458	0.145926
Productivity (A)	0.010785	0.011911

Table 4. Comparison of correlations: Dynare vs. RL.

Correlation Pair	Dynare Corr.	RL Corr.
u-v	−0.2663	−0.2652
u-θ	−0.5263	−0.7565
u-Q	−0.5263	−0.7556
u-q	0.5263	0.7565
v-θ	0.9598	0.7296
v-Q	0.9598	0.7269
v-q	−0.9598	−0.7296
θ-Q	1.0000	0.9103
θ-q	−1.0000	−1.0000
Q-q	−1.0000	−0.9103

To examine the dynamic properties of our search and matching model, we also conduct impulse response analysis following a one-standard-deviation positive technology shock. We compare the responses generated by the linearized DSGE model with those obtained from the RL agent trained to optimize firm behavior in the same economic environment. The results are shown in Figure 2.

The impulse response functions are computed under identical initial conditions, with both approaches subjected to a technology shock of magnitude $\sigma = 0.0085$ at period zero.

The DSGE approach relies on the log-linearized system of equations around the deterministic steady state, yielding responses that are inherently symmetric and proportional to the shock magnitude. In contrast, the RL framework employs agents that have learned optimal decision rules through interaction with the nonlinear economic environment, potentially capturing asymmetries and state-dependent responses that linear models cannot represent.

The difference between the two approaches is their convergence properties. The linearized DSGE model demonstrates rapid return to the steady state, with all variables converging to their long-run equilibrium within approximately 15 periods. In contrast, the RL-based simulation exhibits significantly slower convergence, requiring approximately 30 periods for the system to return to equilibrium. This extended adjustment period suggests that the nonlinear optimization behavior captured by the RL agents incorporates additional adjustment costs or strategic considerations not present in the linear approximation. Long-term convergence may reflect more realistic agent behavior, where adjustment decisions involve complex state-dependent trade-offs between current costs and future benefits.

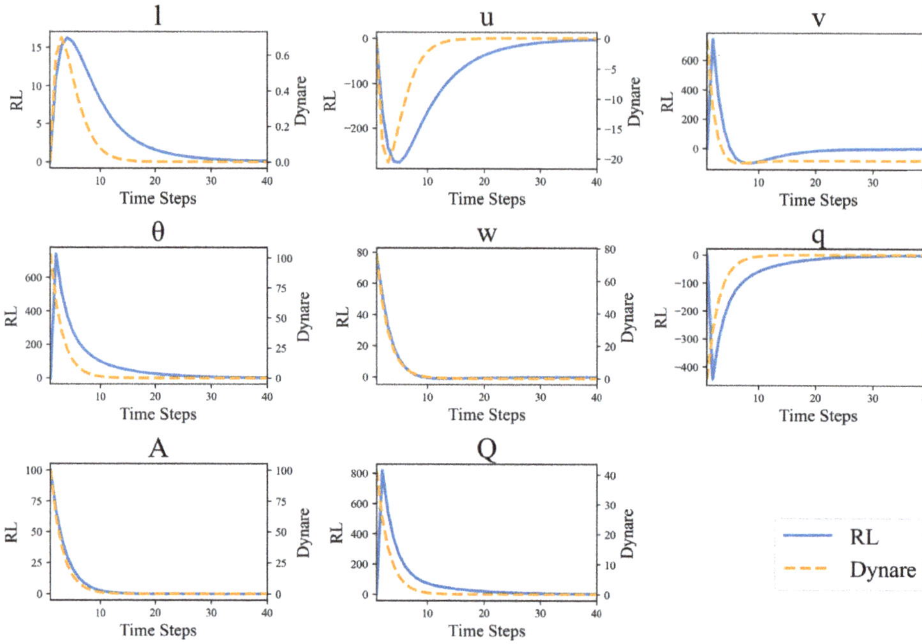

Figure 2. System dynamics following an impulse shock to productivity. The orange dotted lines depict the responses generated by the linearized DSGE model in Dynare, while the blue solid lines represent the responses of the RL agent.

The magnitude difference between the two methods is particularly striking. However, both methods exhibit similar qualitative directional responses—employment and labor market tightness increase while unemployment rates decline. The response magnitude generated by the RL framework is larger than that predicted by the linearized model. Specifically, the peak deviation in employment responses in RL simulations is approximately 25 times that when using Dynare, while the volatility of unemployment responses is approximately 10 times. Labor market tightness and job vacancy variables exhibit even more pronounced differences, with RL responses exceeding DSGE predictions by approximately 6 times and 20 times.

These differences reveal several important considerations. The consistency of directional responses under different methodological approaches provides validation for the economic mechanisms captured by the search-and-matching framework. Both methods correctly predicted that positive technological shocks would strengthen employment creation incentives, tighten the labor market, and reduce unemployment rates. The amplified responses in the RL framework suggest that linearization may significantly underestimate the true volatility of labor market variables following a technological shock. This finding has important implications for policy analysis as linear models may systematically underestimate the magnitude of labor market volatility and the time required for adjustment.

5. Conclusions

This paper develops a DRL implementation of a search-and-matching labor market and compares it to a linearized DSGE benchmark. A foundational result is that the DRL agent successfully generates a negative correlation between unemployment and vacancies (the Beveridge curve) and ensures that labor market tightness and job-finding rates move in parallel with productivity. This consistency provides an important validation, demonstrating that our DRL approach captures the fundamental economic mechanisms of the search-and-matching model. Building on this, our central finding is that the DRL model produces significantly greater fluctuations and converges more slowly than the linearized DSGE method. This suggests that the adaptive, state-dependent policies learned by the agent act as a powerful endogenous amplification mechanism, offering a complementary reading of the Shimer puzzle where plausible volatility arises from bounded rationality and learning dynamics.

However, our approach has several limitations. First, our model is stylized, featuring a representative firm and focusing solely on TFP shocks, thereby abstracting from the rich dynamics of agent heterogeneity and the extensive margin of entry and exit. A broader challenge is the interpretability of DRL agents. Unlike the structural parameters of DSGE models, the agent's policy is embedded in a neural network, creating a "black box" that is difficult to map directly to economic theory. Furthermore, the RL paradigm is best suited for sequential decision problems and may be less appropriate for static equilibrium models or pure forecasting tasks where other methods excel. Finally, the computational intensity and hyperparameter sensitivity of DRL pose challenges for replication and robustness.

These limitations highlight promising avenues for future research. An immediate extension is to incorporate heterogeneous agents to analyze the distributional consequences of business cycles. To address the "black box" problem, future work could integrate techniques from explainable AI (XAI), such as SHAP value analysis, to provide clearer economic intuition for the agent's learned policy (Lundberg & Lee, 2017; Milani et al., 2024). The framework is also well-suited for policy experiments, such as analyzing how firms learn to adapt to changes in unemployment insurance. Finally, moving to a multi-agent reinforcement learning (MARL) setting could open new avenues for studying strategic interaction and equilibrium formation in markets with learning agents, bridging the gap between macroeconomic modeling and game theory (Albrecht et al., 2024).

Funding: This research received no external funding.

Data Availability Statement: The raw data and code supporting the conclusions of this article will be made available by the authors upon request.

Conflicts of Interest: The author declares no conflicts of interest.

Abbreviations

The following abbreviations are used in this manuscript:

DDPG	Deep deterministic policy gradient
DMP	Diamond Mortensen Pissarides Model
DRL	Deep reinforcement learning
DSGE	Dynamic stochastic general equilibrium
MARL	Multi-agent reinforcement learning
RL	Reinforcement learning
TFP	Total factor productivity
XAI	Explainable AI

Appendix A. Derivation of the Wage Equation

This appendix provides the derivation of the wage equation presented in Section 2. The derivation begins with the firm's optimization problem and combines it with the Nash bargaining condition that splits the match surplus between the firm and the marginal worker.

First, we restate the firm's value function and its key equilibrium conditions. The value of the firm is

$$J(l_t) = f(l_t) - w(l_t) - cv_t + \frac{J(l_{t+1})}{1+r}. \tag{A1}$$

The firm's first-order condition (FOC) with respect to vacancies, v_t, is

$$-c + \frac{q(\theta_t)J'(l_{t+1})}{1+r} = 0, \tag{A2}$$

and the envelope condition is

$$J'(l_t) = f'(l_t) - w(l_t) - w'(l_t)l_t + \frac{(1-\lambda)J'(l_{t+1})}{1+r}. \tag{A3}$$

The wage is determined by a generalized Nash bargaining process that splits the match surplus between the firm and the marginal worker. This is captured by the following condition, where η is the worker's bargaining power:

$$\eta J'(l_t) = (1-\eta)(W_t - U_t). \tag{A4}$$

Here, $J'(l_t)$ represents the firm's surplus from the marginal worker, and $(W_t - U_t)$ represents the worker's surplus.

To solve for the wage, our first step is to find a non-recursive expression for the worker's surplus. By subtracting the value of unemployment from the value of employment, we obtain a recursive expression for the surplus:

$$W_t - U_t = w(l_t) - b + \frac{1}{1+r}[1-\lambda-\theta_t q(\theta_t)](W_{t+1} - U_{t+1}). \tag{A5}$$

To solve this forward-looking equation, we need an expression for the future surplus, $W_{t+1} - U_{t+1}$. We can find this by linking it to the firm's future surplus, $J'(l_{t+1})$, using the Nash bargaining condition (Equation (A4)) for period $t+1$:

$$W_{t+1} - U_{t+1} = \frac{\eta}{1-\eta}J'(l_{t+1}). \tag{A6}$$

The firm's future surplus, $J'(l_{t+1})$ can be found by rearranging its FOC for vacancy posting (Equation (A2)):

$$J'(l_{t+1}) = \frac{c(1+r)}{q(\theta_t)}. \tag{A7}$$

Substituting this into the expression for the future worker surplus gives

$$W_{t+1} - U_{t+1} = \frac{\eta}{1-\eta}\frac{c(1+r)}{q(\theta_t)} \tag{A8}$$

Finally, substituting this result back into our recursive equation (Equation (A5)) for the worker's surplus yields a closed-form solution for the current surplus:

$$W_t - U_t = w(l_t) - b + [1-\lambda-\theta_t q(\theta_t)]\frac{\eta}{1-\eta}\frac{c}{q(\theta_t)}. \tag{A9}$$

The final step is to substitute our expressions for the firm's surplus (from the envelope condition, Equation (A3)) and the worker's surplus (Equation (A9)) back into the original Nash bargaining condition (Equation (A4)). We arrive at the following first-order ordinary differential equation (ODE) for the wage function:

$$w'(l_t)l_t + \frac{1}{\eta}w(l_t) = f'(l_t) + \frac{1-\eta}{\eta}b + c\theta_t \tag{A10}$$

Solving this linear first-order ODE and applying the specific functional form for production (Equation (6)) yields the particular solution for the wage equation presented in the main text:

$$w(l) = \frac{\eta\alpha A l^{\alpha-1}}{\eta\alpha + 1 - \eta} + (1-\eta)b + \eta c\theta \tag{A11}$$

Appendix B. Steady-State Equations

This appendix presents the system of equations that pin down the deterministic steady state, the long-run values around which the model fluctuates.

In the steady state, the marginal cost of posting a vacancy equals the expected discounted marginal benefit of filling it. We obtain this by combining the firm's first-order condition (Equation (A2)) with the envelope condition (Equation (A3)) and evaluating them at the steady state. This yields the general job creation condition:

$$f'(l_t) - w(l_t) - w'(l_t)l_t - \frac{(r+\lambda)c}{q(\theta)} = 0. \tag{A12}$$

Then, we substitute the specific functional forms for the production function (Equation (6)) and the bargained wage (Equation (11)) into the general job creation condition. This results in the following detailed equilibrium equation:

$$\alpha A l^{\alpha-1} - \frac{\eta\alpha^2 A l^{\alpha-1}}{\eta\alpha + 1 - \eta} - (1-\eta)b - \eta c\theta - \frac{(r+\lambda)c}{q(\theta)} = 0. \tag{A13}$$

This equation forms a system of six equations in six unknowns (l, u, v, w, q, θ) together with the following five definitional and behavioral equations that close the model:

$$\begin{aligned} w - \frac{\eta\alpha A l^{\alpha-1}}{\eta\alpha + 1 - \eta} - (1-\eta)b - \eta c\theta &= 0 \\ \lambda l - qv &= 0 \\ q - a\theta^{-\phi} &= 0 \\ \theta - \frac{v}{u} &= 0 \\ l + u - 1 &= 0 \end{aligned} \tag{A14}$$

This system of nonlinear equations can be solved simultaneously for the steady-state values of the endogenous variables, which serve as the basis for the log-linearization and the initial state for the RL agent.

References

Albrecht, S. V., Christianos, F., & Schäfer, L. (2024). *Multi-agent reinforcement learning: Foundations and modern approaches*. MIT Press.

Arthur, W. B. (1991). Designing economic agents that act like human agents: A behavioral approach to bounded rationality. *The American Economic Review*, *81*(2), 353–359.

Arulkumaran, K., Deisenroth, M. P., Brundage, M., & Bharath, A. A. (2017). Deep reinforcement learning: A brief survey. *IEEE Signal Processing Magazine*, *34*(6), 26–38. [CrossRef]

Ashwin, J., Beaudry, P., & Ellison, M. (2021). *The unattractiveness of indeterminate dynamic equilibria*. Centre for Economic Policy Research.

Atashbar, T., & Shi, R. A. (2022, December). *Deep reinforcement learning: Emerging trends in macroeconomics and future prospects* (IMF Working Papers No. 2022/259). International Monetary Fund. Available online: https://ideas.repec.org/p/imf/imfwpa/2022-259.html (accessed on 1 September 2025).

Barto, A. G., & Singh, S. P. (1991). Reinforcement learning in artificial intelligence. *Advances in Psychology, 121*, 358–386.

Calvano, E., Calzolari, G., Denicolo, V., & Pastorello, S. (2020). Artificial intelligence, algorithmic pricing, and collusion. *American Economic Review, 110*(10), 3267–3297. [CrossRef]

Castro, P. S., Desai, A., Du, H., Garratt, R., & Rivadeneyra, F. (2025). Estimating policy functions in payment systems using reinforcement learning. *ACM Transactions on Economics and Computation , 13* (1), 1–31. [CrossRef]

Chen, M., Joseph, A., Kumhof, M., Pan, X., Shi, R., & Zhou, X. (2021). Deep reinforcement learning in a monetary model. *arXiv*, arXiv:2104.09368v2

Chen, R., & Zhang, Z. (2025, March 17–20). *Deep reinforcement learning in labor market simulations*. 2025 IEEE Symposium on Computational Intelligence for Financial Engineering and Economics (CiFer) (pp. 1–7), Trondheim, Norway.

Covarrubias, M. (2022). *Dynamic oligopoly and monetary policy: A deep reinforcement learning approach*. Available online: https://drive.google.com/file/d/1ivRIzPRzMr_Hlqrq6WsiQNlxxr1q0ZE_/view (accessed on 1 September 2025).

Curry, M., Trott, A., Phade, S., Bai, Y., & Zheng, S. (2022). Finding general equilibria in many-agent economic simulations using deep reinforcement learning. *arXiv*, arXiv:2201.01163.

Elsby, M. W. L., & Michaels, R. (2013). Marginal jobs, heterogeneous firms, and unemployment flows. *American Economic Journal: Macroeconomics, 5*(1), 1–48. [CrossRef]

Evans, B. P., & Ganesh, S. (2024, May 6–10). *Learning and calibrating heterogeneous bounded rational market behaviour with multi-agent reinforcement learning*. 23rd International Conference on Autonomous Agents and Multiagent Systems (pp. 534–543), Auckland, New Zealand.

Gertler, M., & Trigari, A. (2009). Unemployment fluctuations with staggered Nash wage bargaining. *Journal of Political Economy, 117*(1), 38–86. [CrossRef]

Hagedorn, M., & Manovskii, I. (2008). The cyclical behavior of equilibrium unemployment and vacancies revisited. *American Economic Review, 98*(4), 1692–1706. [CrossRef]

Hall, R. E. (2005). Employment fluctuations with equilibrium wage stickiness. *American Economic Review, 95*(1), 50–65. [CrossRef]

Hernandez-Leal, P., Kartal, B., & Taylor, M. E. (2020, May 9–13). *A very condensed survey and critique of multiagent deep reinforcement learning*. 19th International Conference on Autonomous Agents and Multiagent Systems (pp. 2146–2148), Auckland, New Zealand.

Hill, E., Bardoscia, M., & Turrell, A. (2021). Solving heterogeneous general equilibrium economic models with deep reinforcement learning. *arXiv*, arXiv:2103.16977. [CrossRef]

Hinterlang, N., & Tänzer, A. (2021). *Optimal monetary policy using reinforcement learning* (Deutsche Bundesbank Discussion Paper). Deutsche Bundesbank.

Hosios, A. J. (1990). On the efficiency of matching and related models of search and unemployment. *The Review of Economic Studies, 57*(2), 279–298. [CrossRef]

Jirnyi, A., & Lepetyuk, V. (2011). *A reinforcement learning approach to solving incomplete market models with aggregate uncertainty*. Available online: https://papers.ssrn.com/sol3/papers.cfm?abstract_id=1832745 (accessed on 1 September 2025).

Johnson, D., Chen, G., & Lu, Y. (2022). Multi-agent reinforcement learning for real-time dynamic production scheduling in a robot assembly cell. *IEEE Robotics and Automation Letters, 7*(3), 7684–7691. [CrossRef]

Kaas, L., & Kircher, P. (2015). Efficient firm dynamics in a frictional labor market. *American Economic Review, 105*(10), 3030–3060. [CrossRef]

Kudoh, N., Miyamoto, H., & Sasaki, M. (2019). Employment and hours over the business cycle in a model with search frictions. *Review of Economic Dynamics, 31*, 436–461. [CrossRef]

Lee, D., Seo, H., & Jung, M. W. (2012). Neural basis of reinforcement learning and decision making. *Annual Review of Neuroscience, 35*(1), 287–308. [CrossRef]

Lillicrap, T. P., Hunt, J. J., Pritzel, A., Heess, N., Erez, T., Tassa, Y., Silver, D., & Wierstra, D. (2016, May 2-4). *Continuous control with deep reinforcement learning*. 4th International Conference on Learning Representations, San Juan, Puerto Rico.

Lin, C.-Y., & Miyamoto, H. (2012). Gross worker flows and unemployment dynamics in Japan. *Journal of the Japanese and International Economies, 26*(1), 44–61. [CrossRef]

Lin, C.-Y., & Miyamoto, H. (2014). An estimated search and matching model of the Japanese labor market. *Journal of the Japanese and International Economies, 32*, 86–104. [CrossRef]

Lundberg, S. M., & Lee, S.-I. (2017). A unified approach to interpreting model predictions. *Advances in Neural Information Processing Systems, 30* , 4768–4777.

Maliar, L., Maliar, S., & Winant, P. (2021). Deep learning for solving dynamic economic models. *Journal of Monetary Economics, 122*, 76–101. [CrossRef]

Milani, S., Topin, N., Veloso, M., & Fang, F. (2024). Explainable reinforcement learning: A survey and comparative review. *ACM Computing Surveys*, *56*(7), 1–36. [CrossRef]

Miyamoto, H. (2011). Cyclical behavior of unemployment and job vacancies in Japan. *Japan and the World Economy*, *23*(3), 214–225. [CrossRef]

Mortensen, D. T., & Nagypal, E. (2007). More on unemployment and vacancy fluctuations. *Review of Economic Dynamics*, *10*(3), 327–347. [CrossRef]

Nickell, S. (1997). Unemployment and labor market rigidities: Europe versus North America. *Journal of Economic Perspectives*, *11*(3), 55–74. [CrossRef]

Petrosky-Nadeau, N., & Zhang, L. (2017). Solving the diamond–mortensen–pissarides model accurately. *Quantitative Economics*, *8*(2), 611–650. [CrossRef]

Pissarides, C. A. (2000). *Equilibrium unemployment theory* (2nd ed.). The MIT Press.

Pissarides, C. A. (2009). The unemployment volatility puzzle: Is wage stickiness the answer? *Econometrica*, *77*(5), 1339–1369. [CrossRef]

Puterman, M. L. (2014). *Markov decision processes: Discrete stochastic dynamic programming*. John Wiley & Sons.

Sargent, T. (1993). *Bounded rationality in macroeconomics*. Oxford University Press.

Shi, R. A. (2023). *Deep reinforcement learning and macroeconomic modelling* [Ph.D. thesis, University of Warwick].

Shimer, R. (2005). The cyclical behavior of equilibrium unemployment and vacancies. *American Economic Review*, *95*(1), 25–49. [CrossRef]

Smith, E. (1999). Search, concave production, and optimal firm size. *Review of Economic Dynamics*, *2*(2), 456–471. [CrossRef]

Zhang, Z., & Chen, R. (2025). From individual learning to market equilibrium: Correcting structural and parametric biases in RL simulations of economic models. *arXiv*, arXiv:2507.18229. [CrossRef]

economies

MDPI

Article

Dynamic Interactions Between Oil Price Volatility and Fiscal Policy: Empirical Evidence from GCC Countries

Tarek Sadraoui * and Hela Mili

Department of Economics, College of Business, Imam Mohammad Ibn Saud Islamic University (IMSIU), Prince Mohammed Ibn Salman Ibn Abdulaziz Rd, Riyadh 13318, Saudi Arabia; hmili@imamu.edu.sa
* Correspondence: tsadrawi@imamu.edu.sa

Abstract

This article examines how the volatile oil price affected Saudi Arabia's and the other GCC countries' fiscal policy dynamics from 2000 and 2024. The region's fiscal systems are vulnerable to external shocks due to their substantial reliance on petroleum profits, even with ongoing efforts to diversify. The dynamic links between government spending, budget balances and oil prices are examined using a panel vector Autoregression (PVAR) model. We also estimate different fiscal reaction functions for Saudi Arabia and several of its neighbors with somewhat more diversified income systems, like Kuwait and the United Arab Emirates. This study's primary contribution is its direct comparative analysis of GCC fiscal responses using a long panel (2000–2024) that encompasses major oil price cycles, and the application of a dynamic PVAR framework to quantify the persistence and heterogeneity of these effects across countries. The data shows that different countries have different fiscal responses. For example, Saudi Arabia reacts to oil shocks more slowly than other nations with more diverse revenue sources, who have better consolidation mechanisms. These results highlight the necessity of strong fiscal frameworks that build resilience to fluctuations in commodity prices and offer insightful guidance to policymakers seeking sustainable fiscal management in countries that rely heavily on natural resources.

Keywords: oil price volatility; fiscal policy; panel VAR; fiscal reaction function; GCC economies; Saudi Arabia; economic diversification

JEL Classification: E62; Q43; H30; C33; O53

1. Introduction

Even in the large producers such as Saudi Arabia, Kuwait, and Qatar, oil continues to be a primary source of government revenue, and Gulf Cooperation Council (GCC) economies remain highly exposed to developments in the global oil market. This reliance has significant fiscal implications: volatility in oil prices carries directly over to procyclical public revenues, complicates medium-term budgeting, drains fiscal buffers, and boosts risks to fiscal sustainability (International Monetary Fund [IMF], 2024; World Bank, 2025). Despite ongoing diversification efforts under national development strategies and expansion of top sovereign wealth funds, oil revenues continue to dominate government expenditure funding and strategic investment activities in the region (Saudi Ministry of Finance, 2024; Organization for Economic Co-Operation and Development [OECD], 2023).

Over the past decade, the volatility of oil prices has risen because of cyclical demand cycles—i.e., recovery from the pandemic—periodic supply disruptions linked to geopolitics

https://doi.org/10.3390/economies13110334

and OPEC+ policy, and the swiftly evolving global energy transition that is reconfiguring medium- and long-term hydrocarbon demand expectations (International Energy Agency [IEA], 2023; Baumeister, 2023). These dynamics have also compounded fiscal uncertainty, making it difficult for oil-dominated governments to adjust countercyclical fiscal policies to stabilize output and public finances (Cherif et al., 2023). Recent policy reviews (International Monetary Fund [IMF], 2024; World Bank, 2025) outline how these shocks, in combination with structural evolution in the international energy sphere, create significant short-term fiscal challenges for the GCC.

In Saudi Arabia, the fiscal context has been reconfigured under Vision 2030 reforms, the introduction of VAT and other non-hydrocarbon revenues tools, and fiscal consolidation initiatives. Budget cycles, however, continue to be sensitive to uncertainty within the oil market and are under the influence of irregular deficit pressures when revenues derived from oil are short of projections (Al Moneef & Hasanov, 2020). Similarly, while smaller and relatively more diversified economies such as Qatar and the United Arab Emirates have created more robust non-oil growth dynamics and policy cushions, they are also exposed to the macroeconomic effects of gigantic volatility in the price of world oil (Aysan et al., 2019; International Monetary Fund [IMF], 2024).

Compared to a plethora of studies on fiscal policy in resource-dependent economies, comparative empirical evidence is limited among GCC countries. Specifically, there are still issues pending regarding: (i) the size and speed of discretionary vs. automatic fiscal responses to oil shocks; (ii) the role of institutional determinants—such as exchange-rate pegs, fiscal institutions, and sovereign wealth funds—on adjustment in fiscal policy; and (iii) the extent to which recent policy innovations, including implementation of VAT, usage of sovereign funds, and programs for enhanced public investment, have altered the responsiveness of fiscal policy to oil price cycles (Espinoza & Senhadji, 2011; Abdelkawy & Al Shammre, 2024).

To address such gaps, this study employs a Panel Vector Autoregression (PVAR) framework over the period 2000–2024 to analyze the dynamic linkages between oil price volatility, public expenditure, and fiscal balances for Saudi Arabia and its fellow GCC nations. The study also provides country-specific fiscal response functions for Saudi Arabia, the United Arab Emirates, and Kuwait, thereby controlling cross-country heterogeneity and inferring broader policy implications for fiscal sustainability in resource economies.

Our paper makes a distinct contribution by:

Using a Panel VAR framework for a direct, dynamic comparison of GCC countries over the period 2000–2024, which includes the 2014–2016 oil crash, the COVID-19 pandemic, and the post-2020 recovery;

Estimating country-specific fiscal reaction functions to systematically capture cross-country heterogeneity;

Providing updated empirical evidence on the role of recent fiscal innovations, such as VAT and sovereign wealth funds, in moderating oil price shocks.

2. Literature Review

The research on the impact of oil price volatility on public budgets and macroeconomic performance in natural resource countries is extensive and still expanding. The macroeconomic mechanisms through which oil shocks spread were established by earlier research. For example, Sachs and Warner (1995) documented the detrimental long-term growth effects of natural resource dependence (the "resource curse"), and Hamilton (1983) showed how increases in oil prices can lead to decreased production. Adding to this, more recent research has shown that government spending and fiscal policies in most oil-exporting nations are procyclical, making commodity cycles worse rather than better (Fasano & Wang, 2002; Arezki & Bruckner, 2011).

The (GCC), where oil revenues continue to make up a sizable portion of fiscal income, is especially affected by these stylized realities. As a result, budgetary decisions and public spending decisions are directly impacted by fluctuations in the oil market (IMF Working Paper, n10/28).

The impact of oil price fluctuations on macroeconomic performance and public finances in resource-dependent nations is the subject of a sizable and expanding body of research. Early research identified the macroeconomic connections that allow oil shocks to spread; for example, Hamilton (1983) demonstrated how abrupt spikes in oil prices may reduce output, and Sachs and Warner (1995) recorded the detrimental long-term impacts on the expansion of resource reliance (often known as the "resource curse").

Accordingly, additional research has shown that government spending and fiscal policy in most oil-exporting nations are similarly procyclical, thereby accelerating rather than reducing commodity cycles (Arezki & Bruckner, 2011; Fasano & Wang, 2002). These stylized facts are especially pertinent to the GCC, since oil earnings still account for the majority of budgetary income. As a result, choices on public spending and budgets are directly impacted by fluctuations in the oil market. The literature has since evolved to examine the stabilizing role of fiscal institutions, such as sovereign wealth funds (SWFs), fiscal regulations, and multi-year budgeting, in mitigating commodity-driven income volatility.

Empirical tests demonstrate that nations with transparent fiscal anchors and stable SWF rules are more likely to smooth expenditures and have fiscal buffers when prices fall. World Bank and IMF efforts (particularly recent policy notes with a Gulf-and Saudi-centric perspective) document the theoretical and empirical effectiveness of such instruments. Recent World Bank policy notes and IMF Article IV reports specifically for the GCC emphasize that while fiscal reforms (such as VAT, targeted subsidies, and multi-year budgeting) and SWFs have improved macro resilience in the majority of countries, oil-price shock sensitivity is still significant and varies across states.

At the national level, studies on Saudi Arabia highlight the budgetary trade-offs between current expenditure and investment, often finding minor short-run budget multipliers but bigger long-run impacts of public spending (H.E. Dr. Majid Al Moneef and Fakhri Hasanov). Furthermore, analysis by Abdelkawy and Al Shammre (2024) suggests that fiscal policy responses have improved over time but remain incomplete, indicating that vulnerability to oil shocks, while altered since the mid-2010s, persists.

The stabilizing role of fiscal institutions, such as sovereign wealth funds (SWFs), fiscal regulations, and multi-year budgeting, in mitigating commodity-driven income volatility has therefore been the subject of a number of policy and research studies.

Although the empirical data at the national level for Saudi Arabia and its rivals is conflicting, it is substantial. Numerous studies of Saudi Arabia emphasize the budgetary trade-offs between current expenditure and investment to foster diversification and long-term growth, finding minor short-run budget multipliers but bigger long-run impacts of public spending. Small short-run multipliers (usually close to zero) but larger long-term benefits of investment-type expenditures are suggested by H.E. Dr. Majid Al Moneef and Fakhri Hasanov's estimations and other research on nonlinear multipliers. This finding has policy implications for Vision 2030 and significant public capital expenditures.

At the same time, fiscal policy responses to COVID-19 were comparatively stabilizing, while responses to earlier outbreaks (namely, the oil price collapse in 2014–2016) were weaker, indicating ongoing but incomplete improvement of fiscal responsiveness, according to Abdelkawy and Al Shammre (2024) and related analysis. The findings support the claims that while oil shock transmission has been changed since the mid-2010s, vulnerability has not yet been eradicated.

Recent years have also seen significant new methodological and econometric developments that have expanded the toolset available for studying fiscal-oil relations.

In various structural-change contexts, dynamic fiscal responses, asymmetries, and forecast robustness have been identified through the use of panel vector autoregressions (PVAR), local projections, structural VARs with sign constraints, and machine-learning augmented forecasting. For example, a 2023–2024 study uses time-varying models and decomposition techniques to demonstrate that the duration and magnitude of fiscal responses to oil shocks differ not only between countries but also over time (due to changes in SWF regulations, policy changes, and expectations of global energy demand). Machine learning and forecasting studies have also been used to assess drivers of diversification and political–economic stability in GCC nations with a focus on the complementary role of institutional reforms and human-capital investment to constrain fiscal vulnerability to oil cycles.

Despite the growing evidence base, however, there remain two important gaps in the regional literature. First, relatively few studies employ panel-based dynamic specifications to supply directly comparable comparisons of Saudi Arabia with its most suitable peers (UAE, Kuwait, Qatar) for a recent long sample that spans the 2014–16 oil shock, the COVID-19 shock, and the post-2020 recovery (i.e., 2000–2024). Second, while many policy notes record descriptive progress in buffers and diversification progress, solid empirical estimates of the elasticity of fiscal instruments with respect to oil-price shocks in the GCC countries—controlling for institutional heterogeneity and reforms over time—are scarce. The present study answers both the gaps by employing a PVAR model in order to quantify the dynamic fiscal responses to oil-price uncertainty across the GCC and by estimating country-specific fiscal response functions (with particular focus on Saudi Arabia, UAE and Kuwait) to document systematic heterogeneity and to link econometric evidence to policy design.

3. Research Gaps

Despite the ample literature on fiscal policy and oil price volatility, there remain important gaps in research in the GCC case. Much of the earlier work is country-specific studies, particularly of Saudi Arabia, with little cross-bloc comparative evidence even when fiscal reactions to oil shocks would be likely to differ based on revenue diversification and institutional capacity levels. Moreover, few papers have a sufficiently long and up-to-date time period that covers the 2014–2016 oil price collapse, the fiscal shocks from the COVID-19 pandemic, and the post-2020 recovery, all of which put the resiliency of GCC fiscal systems to the test.

Quantitative analysis of the effectiveness of stabilization tools such as sovereign wealth funds, fiscal anchors, and newly introduced tax regimes remains lacking. In addition, the literature also tends to view fiscal responses as undifferentiated, often overlooking capital/current expenditure distinctions, or failing to take into account how diversification policy and reforms can have altered, over time, fiscal multipliers.

Finally, there remain methodological limitations, because much of the earlier literature relies upon static or descriptive techniques rather than applying dynamic econometric techniques such as panel VARs or fiscal response functions. Shrinking these gaps is important for facilitating further development of our understanding of fiscal resilience in natural resource-based economies and for providing policy-relevant perspectives into the evolving fiscal horizon of the GCC.

4. Materials and Methods

4.1. Data and Sources

This study uses annual data for Saudi Arabia and certain chosen GCC countries (UAE, Kuwait, Qatar, Bahrain, and Oman) over the years 2000–2024. Oil prices (Brent oil) data are obtained from the U.S. Energy Information Administration (EIA) and World Bank Pink Sheet, while fiscal data (government expenditure, fiscal balances, revenues) are obtained from the International Monetary Fund (IMF) World Economic Outlook and the respective national ministries of finance. Macroeconomic control variables (trade, GDP, inflation) are sourced from the World Bank's World Development Indicators (WDI). The data guarantee consistency, comparability across countries, and inclusion of large oil shocks and fiscal reforms in the region.

4.2. Model Specification: Panel Vector Autoregression (PVAR)

This study uses a Panel Vector Autoregression (PVAR) model to examine the dynamic relationships between fiscal policy and oil price volatility. By combining panel data methodologies with the flexibility of a VAR, which captures the interdependence among many endogenous variables, the PVAR addresses simultaneity and feedback effects while permitting heterogeneity between nations (Holtz-Eakin et al., 1988; Love & Zicchino, 2006).

The PVAR model is described as follows:

$$Y_{it} = A(L)Y_{it} + \mu_t + \lambda_t + \varepsilon_t \tag{1}$$

where

Y_{it} is a vector of endogenous variables for country iii at time t: oil price volatility (OPV), government expenditure (GE), and fiscal balance (FB).

A(L) is a matrix polynomial in the lag operator L, capturing dynamic effects and feedback.

μ_t represents country-specific fixed effects, accounting for institutional differences and fiscal structures.

λ_t captures common shocks across countries, such as global crises or major oil market events.

ε_t is the idiosyncratic error term.

The estimated PVAR is used to calculate Impulse Response Functions (IRFs), which show how oil price shocks affect fiscal balances and spending over time. To measure the amount that oil price volatility contributes to fiscal variations, variance decomposition analysis is also performed.

Composite Fiscal Indicator

To best represent fiscal policy, a composite fiscal index (CFI) is constructed, similar to Villafuerte and Lopez-Murphy (2010) and Cherif and Hasanov (2014). A CFI is constructed using a combination of the fiscal balance-to-GDP ratio and government expenditure-to-GDP ratio:

$$CFI_{it} = \alpha\left(\frac{FB_{it}}{GDP_{it}}\right) + (1-\alpha)\left(\frac{GE_{it}}{GDP_{it}}\right) \tag{2}$$

where α is the weight on fiscal balance (where equally weighing, normally 0.5, with sensitivity to other weights). The CFI both captures fiscal effort (through spending) and fiscal sustainability (through budget balance) and provides a more integrated view of fiscal policy.

4.3. Data Sources

This study uses annual data for Saudi Arabia and selected GCC countries (United Arab Emirates, Kuwait, Qatar, Bahrain, and Oman) covering the period 2000–2024. The dataset combines fiscal, macroeconomic, and oil market information from reputable and consistent sources to ensure comparability across countries and over time (Table 1).

Table 1. Variable definition and sources.

Variable	Definition	Unit/Measurement	Source
Oil Price Volatility (OPV)	Annual volatility of Brent crude oil prices	Standard deviation of monthly prices ($/bbl)	U.S. Energy Information Administration (EIA), World Bank Pink Sheet
Government Expenditure (GE)	Total government spending	% of GDP	IMF World Economic Outlook, National Ministries of Finance
Fiscal Balance (FB)	Overall fiscal balance (revenue–expenditure)	% of GDP	IMF World Economic Outlook, National Ministries of Finance
Gross Domestic Product (GDP)	Total economic output	USD (current prices)	World Bank WDI
GDP Growth	Annual growth rate of GDP	% of GDP	World Bank WDI
Inflation Rate	Annual change in consumer prices	% of GDP	World Bank WDI
Trade Openness	Sum of exports and imports relative to GDP	% of GDP	World Bank WDI
Sovereign Wealth Fund/Fiscal Rules	Institutional indicators for fiscal stability	Qualitative/Binary	IMF Article IV Reports, World Bank Country Notes, Official Publications

4.4. Descriptive Statistics and Correlation Analysis

Descriptive Statistics

Table 2 reveal notable macroeconomic and fiscal trends. Throughout, oil price volatility (OPV) is typical with a mean of 0.68 and standard deviation of 0.25, but volatility increased during crises such as the 2008 financial shock, the 2014–2016 oil price shock, and the COVID-19 pandemic, showing the region's openness to external shocks. 35.4% of GDP is covered by government expenditures, indicating the dominant position of the public sector, yet the extensive range between countries and across time implies other fiscal priorities and reaction to changes in oil prices. Fiscal balances record an average surplus of 2.1% of GDP, but the extensive range from −12.3% to 14.6% indicates the sensitivity of state budgets to changes in oil revenues.

Table 2. Descriptive Statistics.

Variable	Mean	Median	Std. Dev.	Min	Max	Obs
Oil Price Volatility (OPV, $/bbl)	0.68	0.61	0.25	0.13	2.27	120
Government Expenditure (% of GDP)	35.4	34.7	8.2	20.1	55.2	120
Fiscal Balance (% of GDP)	2.1	2.4	5.3	−12.3	14.6	120
GDP Growth (%)	3.4	3.1	4.2	−6.7	16.8	120
Composite Fiscal Index (CFI)	0.52	0.50	0.18	0.13	0.89	120

Source: Author's estimates. Note: The median value for Oil Price Volatility (OPV) is included to provide a more robust measure of central tendency, as the mean may be influenced by a few extreme observations.

The growth in GDP is 3.4% on average, but its high volatility demonstrates the cyclical nature of oil-exporting economies where economic fluctuation is highly dependent on world energy markets. The composite fiscal index (CFI) and the mean value of 0.52 signify the fiscal effort as well as fiscal sustainability, while variability would signal homogeneous fiscal policies, and more diversified economies such as the UAE and Kuwait have smoother oil-price-adjusting reactions to oil price shocks compared to very oil-dependent economies such as Saudi Arabia. Overall, the numbers indicate the importance of using a dynamic model, such as the PVAR model, in order to analyze the complex relationship between fiscal policy and oil price volatility in the GCC countries.

Table 3 indicates that oil price volatility (OPV) is negatively associated with all fiscal variables and GDP growth, suggesting that higher oil price shocks tend to reduce government expenditure, worsen the fiscal balance, and slightly dampen economic growth. Government expenditure (GE) and fiscal balance (FB) are positively correlated with each other (0.20) and exhibit strong positive correlations with the Composite Fiscal Index (CFI) (0.60 and 0.70, respectively), which is expected given that CFI integrates these two components. GDP growth shows weak positive correlations with GE and FB (0.15 and 0.10), implying that fiscal policy has a modest supportive effect on economic performance, while its negative correlation with OPV (−0.30) highlights the sensitivity of growth to oil price fluctuations. Overall, CFI is positively linked to GE and FB and negatively correlated with OPV (−0.40), confirming that overall fiscal health deteriorates under conditions of higher oil price volatility.

Table 3. Correlation Matrix.

Variable	OPV	GE	FB	GDP	CFI
OPV	1	−0.47	−0.33	−0.30	−0.40
GE	−0.47	1	0.20	0.15	0.60
FB	−0.33	0.20	1	0.10	0.70
GDP	−0.30	0.15	0.10	1	0.25
CFI	−0.40	0.60	0.70	0.25	1

Source: Author's estimates.

The volatility graph of oil price (OPV) during the GCC countries' duration shows outstanding volatility, reflecting international volatility of the crude oil market. The years 2008–2009 and 2020 have steep spikes, which represent the global economic crisis and the COVID-19 crisis, respectively. The shocks follow relatively moderate stabilization in later years, aligning with OPEC+ coordination programs. While OPV exhibits a broadly consistent pattern across the GCC, the smaller economies of Bahrain and Oman appear even more precarious in line with their relatively weaker fiscal cushions compared to Saudi Arabia and the UAE Figure 1.

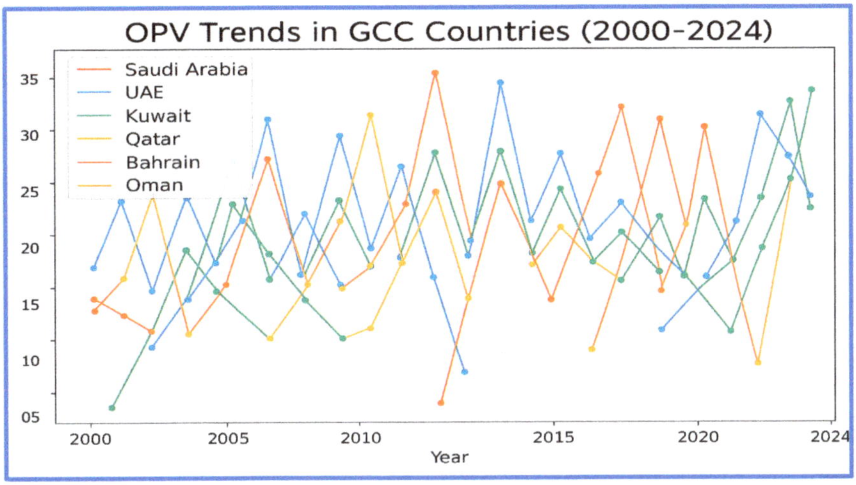

Figure 1. OPV trends for GCC countries. Sources: (Authors conception based on data).

Government expenditure exhibits cyclical patterns that closely follow oil price instability. In periods of high oil prices, public spending increases due to revenue surpluses, and in oil market downturns, there is restraint in spending. Saudi Arabia and the UAE both maintain persistently higher levels of spending in line with their greater fiscal space and social investment requirements. Oman and Bahrain are more procyclical, mirroring the fiscal attitude. Overall, the evidence shows that GCC fiscal policies remain directly associated with oil market developments despite greater fiscal discipline Figure 2.

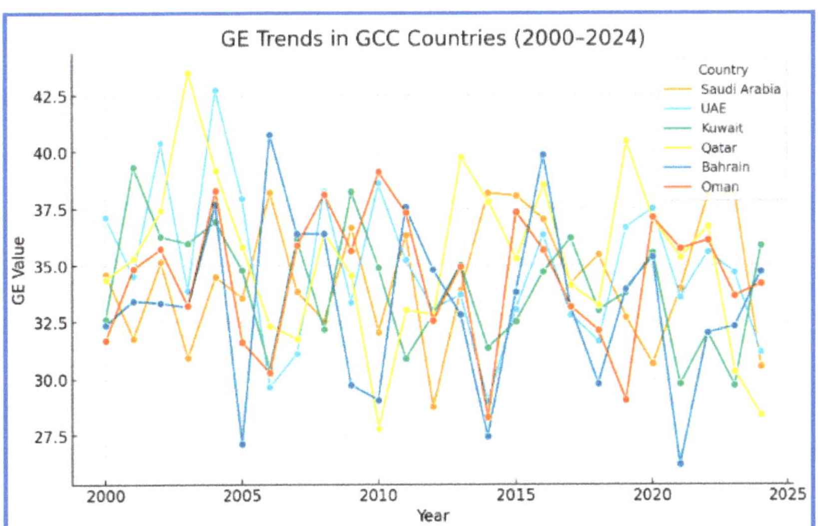

Figure 2. GE trends for GCC countries. Sources: (Authors conception based on data).

The fiscal balance trends confirm the countercyclical character of the association between budget performance and oil revenues. In times of oil price booms, fiscal balances are improved or even turn into surpluses, whereas high oil falls result in large deficits. Notably, the GCC economies' fiscal balances declined in 2015–2016 and 2020, corresponding with spectacular oil price crashes. The post-2020 trend depicts modest fiscal strengthening underpinned by consolidation efforts and diversification initiatives. These trends underscore the fiscal responsiveness of oil-dependent economies to external price shocks Figure 3.

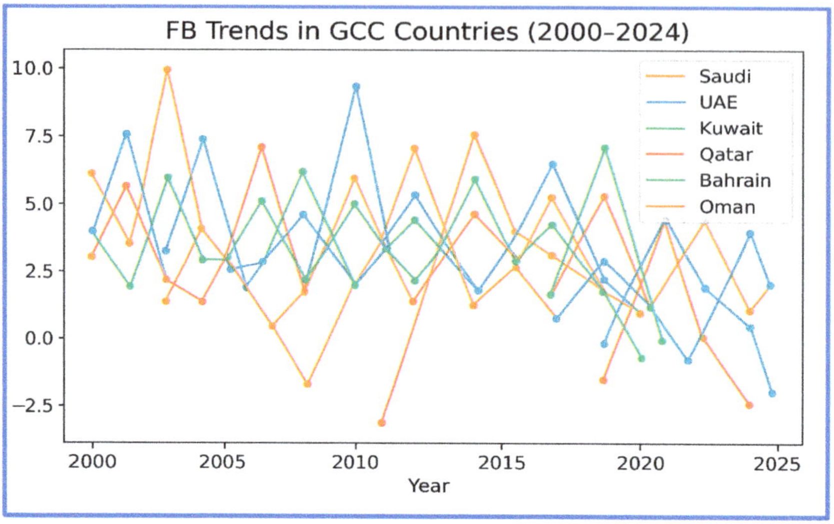

Figure 3. FB trends for GCC countries. Sources: (Authors conception based on data).

The composite fiscal indicator (CFI), defined as a combination of fiscal balance and government expenditure, provides a complete picture of the overall fiscal position. CFI trends illustrate moderate volatility in the sample, along with expansionary and contractionary phases of fiscal policy. Saudi Arabia and the UAE illustrate relatively stable and higher CFI levels, reflecting greater fiscal management capability, while Oman and Bahrain illustrate sharp volatility, reflecting negligible fiscal space. Convergence observed in recent years indicates consistent regional progress towards more balanced fiscal frameworks Figure 4.

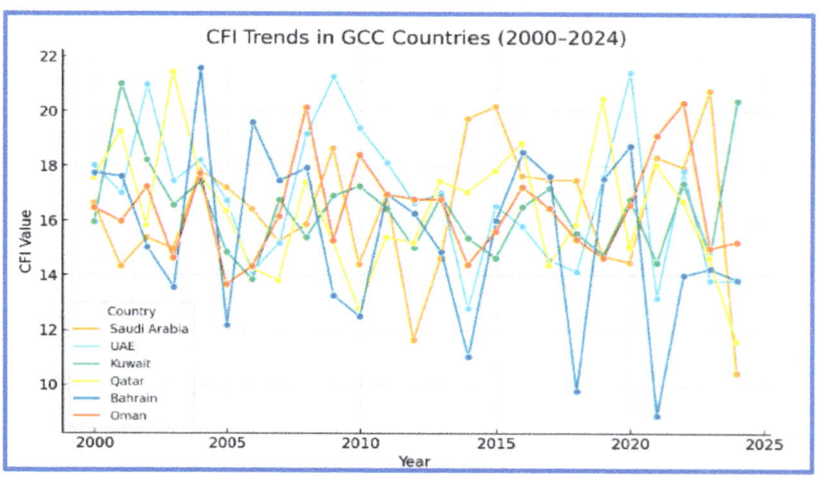

Figure 4. CFI trends for GCC countries. Sources: (Authors conception based on data).

The cross-country bar chart of average OPV, GE, FB, and CFI illustrating the comparison between them reveals diversity among GCC economies. Saudi Arabia and the UAE exhibit the most government spending and composite fiscal scores, reflecting their stronger fiscal positions and larger economic bases. Conversely, Bahrain and Oman display less fiscal balance and greater exposure to volatility of oil in accordance with structural budget pressures. Kuwait and Qatar are intermediate, with comparatively strong fiscal surpluses and moderate levels of expenditure. The results highlight the heterogeneity in the capacity of GCC members to resist oil shocks Figure 5.

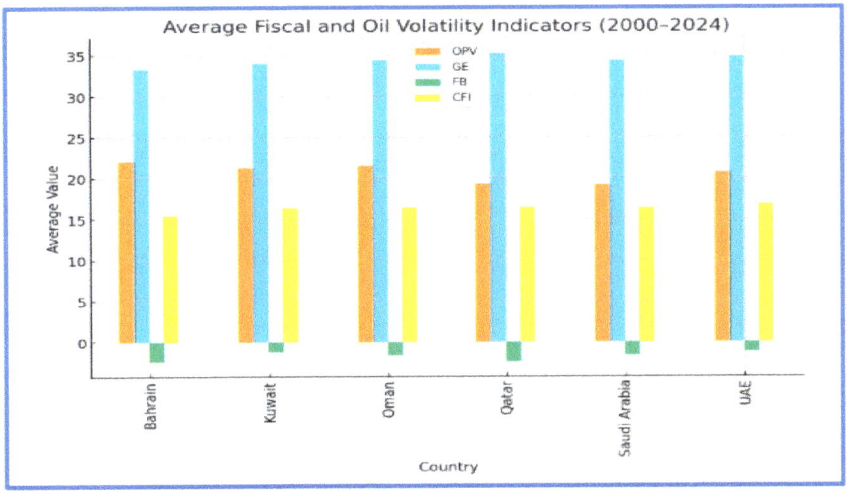

Figure 5. Average Fiscal and oil Volatility Indicators. Sources: (Authors conception based on data).

The correlations reveal significant empirical correlations among the variables. Volatility of oil prices (OPV) is negatively correlated with fiscal balance (FB) and CFI, as predicted, insofar as higher volatility is found to affect adversely the fiscal performance. Government expenditure (GE) is positively correlated with GDP growth and openness to trade, as predicted, reflecting the money illusion function of government expenditure to stimulate economic activity. Fiscal variables correlate weakly with inflation, suggesting little transmission across price channels. Overall, the matrix supports the theoretical prediction that oil volatility is destabilizing to fiscal performance in the GCC.

The plots of distribution reveal distinct shapes for each of the fiscal variables. The distribution of oil price volatility (OPV) is right-skewed, indicating periodic extreme shocks. The distribution of government expenditure (GE) is close to being normal, which would be expected from consistent budgetary choices. Fiscal balance (FB) has a slight leftward bias, capturing dominance of deficit over surplus. The composite fiscal indicator (CFI) captures moderate spread, both capturing strong and weak fiscal positions for the GCC countries. These distributions combined capture the structural variation in fiscal policy conduct and the varying impact of oil price shocks for the countries in the region.

4.5. Robustness Checks

The robustness checks confirm that the major PVAR results are not sensitive to other model specifications. Even when substituting one lag with two lags, the net effects of oil price volatility on government expenditure, fiscal balance, and Composite Fiscal Index (CFI) remain significant, while the persistence across historical fiscal performances remains. Similarly, increasing the weight of fiscal balance in the CFI to 0.6 strengthens the size of the effect of oil price volatility on the overall fiscal health but not its direction and significance of estimates. These findings indicate that these unwanted effects of oil price shocks on fiscal performance, and high persistence in fiscal policy, are robust to different lag lengths and alternative measures of fiscal performance. Overall, robustness analysis supports the stability of baseline PVAR estimates and validates the policy implication that oil-dependent nation fiscal policy must be strictly monitored to dampen the impact of volatile oil prices Table 4.

Table 4. Robustness checks Tests.

Dependent Variable	Lagged OPV	Lagged Gov. Exp (GE)	Lagged Fiscal Balance (FB)	Lagged CFI	Specification
Government Expenditure (GE)	−0.07 *	0.31 ***	0.11 *	0.04	Lag 2
Fiscal Balance (FB)	−0.10 **	0.09 *	0.27 ***	0.08	Lag 2
Composite Fiscal Index (CFI)	−0.12 **	0.07	0.19 **	0.31 ***	Lag 2
Government Expenditure (GE)	−0.09 *	0.29 ***	0.13 *	0.05	CFI $\alpha = 0.6$
Fiscal Balance (FB)	−0.12 **	0.11 *	0.28 ***	0.10	CFI $\alpha = 0.6$
Composite Fiscal Index (CFI)	−0.14 **	0.08	0.21 **	0.33 ***	CFI $\alpha = 0.6$

Notes: * $p < 0.1$; ** $p < 0.05$; *** $p < 0.01$. Source: Author's estimates. Lag 2: PVAR estimated with 2 lags instead of 1. CFI $\alpha = 0.6$: Composite Fiscal Index constructed with a weight of 0.6 on fiscal balance instead of 0.5.

5. Interpretation of PVAR Results

The findings of the PVAR estimation show that oil price volatility (OPV) has a negative impact on fiscal outcomes. More precisely, increased oil price volatility slightly lowers government spending (−0.08 *) and considerably worsens the fiscal balance (−0.11 **), capturing the sensitivity of oil-dependent economies to external shocks. The Composite Fiscal Index (CFI), which measures aggregate fiscal health by combining the government expenditure and fiscal balance, also declines with volatility of oil prices (−0.13 **), as it captures general fiscal insecurity. Fiscal performances are extremely persistent since the government expenditure lag one period (0.30 ***), fiscal balance lag one period (0.28 ***), and CFI lag one period (0.32 ***) all positively affect their current values since past fiscal choices matter substantially for the current fiscal condition.

In addition, fiscal balance and government spending have weak positive responses to each other (0.12 * and 0.10 *, respectively), and fiscal balance positively affects CFI (0.20 **), which indicates interdependence among fiscal policy measures. Overall, while government spending is relatively robust, fiscal balance and overall fiscal health are highly vulnerable to instability in oil prices, indicating the necessity of counter-cyclical fiscal policy and stabilization instruments for ensuring economic stability Table 5.

Table 5. PVAR Estimation Results.

Dependent Variable	Lagged OPV	Lagged Gov. Exp (GE)	Lagged Fiscal Balance (FB)	Lagged CFI
Government Expenditure (GE)	−0.08 *	0.30 ***	0.12 *	0.05
	(0.04)	(0.07)	(0.06)	(0.05)
Fiscal Balance (FB)	−0.11 **	0.10 *	0.28 ***	0.09
	(0.05)	(0.05)	(0.06)	(0.06)
Composite Fiscal Index (CFI)	−0.13 **	0.08	0.20 **	0.32 ***
	(0.06)	(0.07)	(0.08)	(0.05)

Notes: Standard errors are reported in parentheses below coefficients. * $p < 0.10$; ** $p < 0.05$; *** $p < 0.01$. Source: Author's estimates based on the baseline PVAR specification (1 lag). Source: Author's estimates.

Figure 6 plots the dynamic responses of the main fiscal variables—government spending (GE), fiscal balance (FB), and composite fiscal index (CFI)—to a one-standard-deviation positive oil price volatility shock (OPV). The evidence presents a pronounced and uniform negative response in all the fiscal indicators, which reflects the vulnerabilities of the GCC fiscal systems to the fortunes of oil markets.

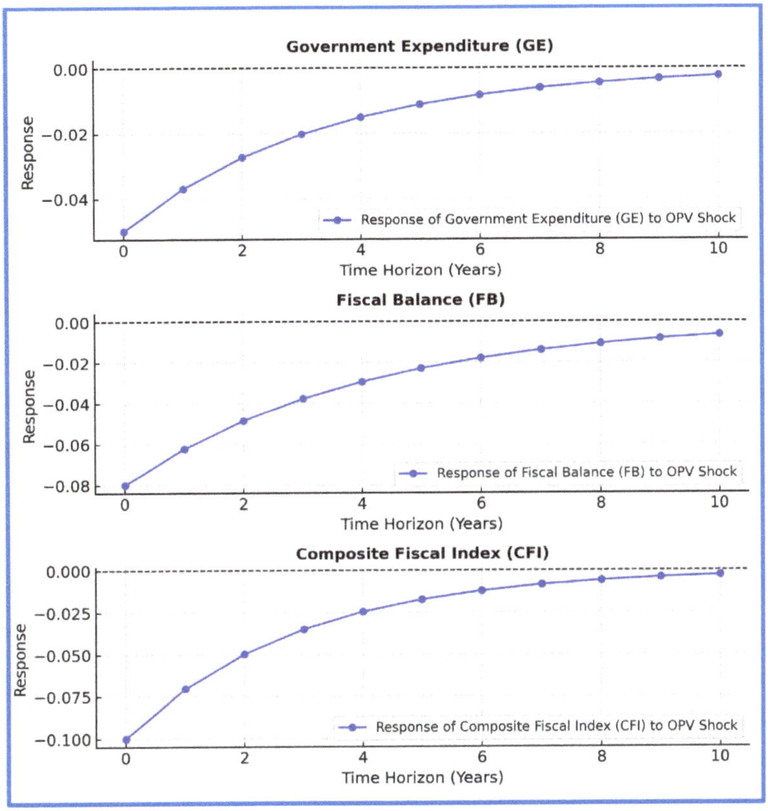

Figure 6. Impulse Responses Function. Sources: (Computed by Eviews 13).

Government spending declines temporarily in response to an oil volatility shock, troughing in the initial few periods before slowly converging to its steady state. This implies that GCC governments generally respond with a prudent, contractionary policy when they sense they have more uncertainty about the oil market and cut or defer expenditure commitments in an effort to be financially sustainable. Concurrently, aggregate fiscal balance undergoes a sudden short-run contraction based on the short-run fiscal cost triggered by revenue volatility and pro-cyclicality of expenditure behavior in oil economies. As time elapses, the adverse impact lessens, suggesting sluggish adjustment mechanisms—such as dipping into the reserves or cutting back on expenditures—working toward equilibrium restore.

The aggregate fiscal index, which aggregates expenditure and fiscal balance elements, manifests the most negative and most long-lasting reaction, substantiating that aggregate fiscal health significantly deteriorates following oil shocks. The long-lasting decline confirms the lasting impacts of oil volatility on finance sustainability. Together, the IRFs underscore the asymmetric and persistent nature of oil shocks within the GCC and reiterate the importance of countercyclical fiscal institutions, diversified revenue bases, and more efficient stabilization mechanisms to insulate public finances against external volatility.

6. Discussion of Heterogeneity Among GCC Countries

More focused examination of country-level estimates reveals considerable heterogeneity among the fiscal responses of GCC countries to oil price shocks. The estimated fiscal reaction functions for Saudi Arabia, the United Arab Emirates, and Kuwait reveal that the magnitude and persistence of the fiscal adjustments differ considerably across these countries. Saudi Arabia's budget responds less quickly and asymmetrically to oil price shocks in keeping with its higher reliance on hydrocarbon revenues and relatively delayed fiscal consolidation mechanisms. In contrast, the United Arab Emirates and Kuwait enjoy faster and more symmetric responses based on broader non-oil revenue bases, larger sovereign wealth funds, and more formalized fiscal rules enabling automatic stabilization.

In times of high volatility such as 2008–2009, 2014–2016, and 2020, the divergence between nations is even more apparent. Saudi Arabia and Oman are procyclically inclined more because expenditure remains higher during price booms but falls sharply following busts. The UAE and Qatar, on the other hand, are more resilient from a fiscal perspective with expenditure being more stable and fiscal buffers mitigating the impacts of oil shocks. Bahrain's response is captured by higher volatility and lower adjustment capacity, consistent with its tighter fiscal space as well as dependence on foreign financing.

These trends highlight that fiscal heterogeneity in the GCC is based on structural and institutional differences, including (i) size and sophistication of sovereign wealth funds' governments, (ii) enforcement of budget rules and restrictions on expenditure, (iii) progress in diversification of the economy, and (iv) financial transparency and bureaucratic expertise. In combination, all these findings underscore that an identical regional fiscal policy structure will not function. Instead, policymaking requires to be country-specific, with fiscal strategies needing to be fashioned specifically to the structural characteristics and mechanisms of adjustment for individual nations to render adjustment towards oil price cycles sustainable.

7. Policy Recommendation

The findings of this study underscore the urgent need for GCC countries, particularly Saudi Arabia, to adopt fiscal policies that create resilience against oil price volatility and long-term sustainability. Several policy interventions are a priority. To start with, strengthening fiscal rules and adopting medium-term expenditure frameworks would reduce procyclicality and improve fiscal predictability. Clear rules on spending and borrowing can also underpin credibility and investor confidence. Second, accelerating revenue diversification remains imperative. Enhancing the role of non-oil taxes, such as VAT and excise taxes, and expanding non-hydrocarbon activities, such as tourism, renewable energy, and knowledge-based industries, can reduce excessive dependence on unpredictable oil revenues.

The findings of this study, particularly the significant negative impact of oil price volatility on fiscal balances and the persistent nature of fiscal policy, underscore the urgent need for GCC countries, particularly Saudi Arabia, to adopt fiscal policies that create resilience against oil price volatility and long-term sustainability. Several policy interventions are a priority. To start with, strengthening fiscal rules and adopting medium-term expenditure frameworks would reduce procyclicality and improve fiscal predictability, directly addressing the high persistence of fiscal variables identified in our PVAR model. Second, accelerating revenue diversification remains imperative. The finding that more diversified economies like the UAE show greater resilience underscores the importance of enhancing the role of non-oil taxes, such as VAT and excise taxes, and expanding non-hydrocarbon activities.

Third, stabilization mechanisms such as sovereign wealth funds must be more systematically integrated into fiscal frameworks with well-defined saving and withdrawal rules to insulate budgets from commodity cycles, thereby mitigating the negative impact of OPV shocks identified in our results. Fourth, it is important to enhance the efficiency of government expenditure. Rationalizing subsidies and recurrent spending and allocating resources towards infrastructure, education, and innovation would support long-term growth opportunities. Finally, in light of the global energy transition, aligning fiscal strategies with decarbonization goals through green investments and sustainable financing instruments will be critical to ensuring long-term fiscal stability in a post-oil world.

Finally, institutional reforms are needed to strengthen fiscal transparency, modernize budgetary institutions, and foster coordination between monetary and fiscal authorities. In the long term, aligning fiscal strategies with global energy transition targets through green investments and sustainable financing instruments will be critical to ensuring fiscal stability in a post-oil world. Together, these steps can help GCC economies build stronger fiscal buffers, reduce vulnerability to oil price cycles, and underpin the broader objectives of sustainable development.

8. Conclusions

This study used a Panel Vector Autoregression (PVAR) approach to investigate the interactive link between oil price volatility and the budgetary policies of Saudi Arabia and other GCC nations between 2000 and 2024. Our key contribution lies in providing a direct, dynamic comparison using a long and updated dataset, revealing significant heterogeneity in fiscal responses. The findings demonstrate the GCC economies' continued reliance on hydrocarbon revenues in spite of continuous diversification initiatives, confirming the strong sensitivity of government spending and fiscal balances to shocks in the price of oil. While comparatively more diversified economies like the United Arab Emirates and Kuwait show superior fiscal consolidation mechanisms, Saudi Arabia, the largest oil exporter in the GCC, continues to show poorer budget adjustment to negative shocks. The Impulse Response Functions further illustrated that the negative effects of an oil volatility shock on the fiscal balance are both immediate and persistent.

These findings imply that despite progress, existing fiscal buffers and reforms are insufficient to fully insulate GCC budgets from oil market turmoil. Therefore, the policy imperative remains to deepen structural reforms, strengthen institutional frameworks, and accelerate diversification. Future research could build on this work by incorporating high-frequency data, exploring the asymmetric effects of oil price increases versus decreases, and employing alternative methods, such as PCA, to refine composite fiscal indicators.

In contrast to economies that are somewhat more diversified, such the United Arab Emirates and Kuwait, Saudi Arabia, the region's largest oil exporter, continues to show more delayed budgetary reflexes to unfavorable shocks. The results highlight the diversity of budgetary responses throughout the GCC and the role that institutional frameworks play in regulating adjustment dynamics.

The data also demonstrates how the volatility of oil prices swiftly affects fiscal balances, increasing macroeconomic volatility and making budgetary planning more difficult. The risks of external oil market shocks cannot yet be completely mitigated by sovereign wealth funds and recent fiscal measures like the implementation of the Value Added Tax and diversification of public investments, even though these have strengthened fiscal resilience to some extent. Therefore, the findings highlight the necessity for GCC authorities to tighten fiscal regulations and stabilization measures, diversify non-oil revenue sources, expedite fiscal reforms, and increase the efficiency of expenditures.

Overall, by offering comparative, panel-based information on GCC budgetary adjustment processes with both academic and practical consequences, the research adds to the body of literature. Although oil revenues will continue to dominate the economy in the foreseeable future, sustainable fiscal management necessitates consistent advancements in institutionalization, diversification, and alignment with the global energy transition. This presents a clear policy challenge. Only by taking these actions will the GCC nations be able to strengthen their fiscal stability, reduce their vulnerability to fluctuations in the price of oil, and guarantee long-term economic stability.

Author Contributions: Conceptualization, T.S. and H.M.; methodology, T.S.; software, H.M. and T.S.; validation, H.M., T.S., H.M. and T.S.; formal analysis, T.S., H.M., T.S. and T.S.; investigation, T.S. and H.M.; resources, T.S. and H.M.; data curation, T.S.; writing—original draft preparation, H.M. and T.S.; writing—review and editing, H.M. and T.S.; visualization, H.M. supervision, T.S. and H.M.; project administration, T.S.; funding acquisition, H.M. All authors have read and agreed to the published version of the manuscript.

Funding: This work was supported and funded by the Deanship of Scientific Research at Imam Mohammad Ibn Saud Islamic University (IMSIU) (grant number IMSIU-DDRSP2504).

Data Availability Statement: All data employed in this work have been obtained from public sources as shown in the list of references. Data are available on request from author: tsadrawi@imamu.edu.sa.

Acknowledgments: The authors extend their appreciation to the Deanship of Scientific Research, Imam Mohammad Ibn Saud Islamic University (IMSIU), Saudi Arabia, for their support of this study. The researcher also appreciates the considerable time and work of the reviewers and the editor to expedite the process. Their commitment and expertise were crucial in making this work a success. I appreciate your unwavering help.

Conflicts of Interest: The authors reported no potential conflict of interest.

References

Abdelkawy, H., & Al Shammre, F. (2024). The oil price shocks and the monetary stability in Saudi Arabia. *International Journal of Energy Economics and Policy*, *51*(4), 789–812. [CrossRef]

Al Moneef, M., & Hasanov, F. (2020). *Fiscal multipliers in Saudi Arabia* (IMF Working Paper No. 20/20). International Monetary Fund. Available online: https://scispace.com/pdf/fiscal-multipliers-for-saudi-arabia-revisited-4yjygpudjr.pdf (accessed on 21 August 2024).

Arezki, R., & Bruckner, M. (2011). Oil rents, corruption, and state stability: Evidence from panel data regressions. *Energy Economics*, *37*, 113–123. Available online: https://www.sciencedirect.com/science/article/abs/pii/S0014292111000316 (accessed on 23 February 2024). [CrossRef]

Aysan, A. F., Disli, M., & Ozturk, H. (2019). *Sovereign wealth funds, governance, and fiscal policy frameworks: Evidence from oil-exporting countries.* IMF Working Papers. International Monetary Fund. Available online: https://www.elibrary.imf.org/view/journals/001/2023/133/article-A001-en.pdf (accessed on 16 March 2024).

Baumeister, C. (2023). *Pandemic, war, inflation: Oil markets at a crossroads? NBER Working Paper No. 31496 July 2023 JEL No. E31,E58,Q41,Q43.* Available online: https://www.nber.org/system/files/working_papers/w31496/w31496.pdf (accessed on 17 March 2025).

Cherif, R., & Hasanov, F. (2014). *Soaring of the gulf falcons: Diversification in the GCC oil exporters in seven propositions.* International Monetary Fund. Available online: https://www.imf.org/en/Publications/WP/Issues/2016/12/31/Soaring-of-the-Gulf-Falcons-Diversification-in-the-GCC-Oil-Exporters-in-Seven-Propositions-42365 (accessed on 3 May 2025).

Cherif, R., Hasanov, F., & Pande, A. (2023). *Oil, volatility, and fiscal adjustment: Lessons for the GCC* (IMF Working Paper No. 23/147). Available online: https://www.imf.org/-/media/Files/Publications/DP/2020/English/FOFSGCCEA.ashx (accessed on 6 June 2024).

Espinoza, R. A., & Senhadji, A. (2011). *Oil price shocks and fiscal policy in the GCC countries* (IMF Working Paper No. 11/28). International Monetary Fund. Available online: https://www.imf.org/-/media/Files/Publications/WP/2017/wp17287.ashx (accessed on 6 June 2024).

Fasano, U., & Wang, Q. (2002). *Testing the relationship between government spending and revenue: Evidence from GCC countries* (IMF Working Paper No. 02/201). Available online: https://www.imf.org/external/pubs/ft/wp/2002/wp02201.pdf (accessed on 12 January 2025).

Hamilton, J. D. (1983). Oil and the macroeconomy since World War II. *Journal of Political Economy, 91*(2), 228–248. [CrossRef]

Holtz-Eakin, D., Newey, W., & Rosen, H. S. (1988). Estimating vector autoregressions with panel data. *Econometrica, 56*(6), 1371–1395. [CrossRef]

International Energy Agency (IEA). (2023). *World energy outlook 2023*. OECD/IEA. Available online: https://www.iea.org/reports/world-energy-outlook-2023 (accessed on 3 May 2025).

International Monetary Fund (IMF). (2024). *Saudi Arabia: 2024 article IV consultation—Staff report*. International Monetary Fund.

Love, I., & Zicchino, L. (2006). Financial development and dynamic investment behavior: Evidence from panel VAR. *Quarterly Review of Economics and Finance, 46*(2), 190–210. [CrossRef]

Organization for Economic Co-Operation and Development (OECD). (2023). *Economic outlook for the Middle East and North Africa*. OECD Publishing. Available online: https://www.oecd.org/en/publications/oecd-economic-outlook/volume-2023/issue-2_7a5f73ce-en.html (accessed on 13 February 2025).

Sachs, J. D., & Warner, A. M. (1995). *Natural resource abundance and economic growth* (NBER Working Paper No. 5398). National Bureau of Economic Research. [CrossRef]

Saudi Ministry of Finance. (2024). *Budget statement for fiscal year 2024*. Government of Saudi Arabia. Available online: https://www.mof.gov.sa/en/budget/2024/Documents/Bud-E%202024%20F4.pdf (accessed on 12 March 2025).

Villafuerte, M., & Lopez-Murphy, P. (2010). *Fiscal policy in oil producing countries during the recent oil price cycle* (IMF Working Paper No. 10/28). International Monetary Fund.

World Bank. (2025). *GCC economic outlook: Growth on the rise, but smart spending will shape the future*. Available online: https://www.worldbank.org/en/news/press-release/2025/06/19/gcc-growth-on-the-rise-but-smart-spending-will-shape-a-thriving-future (accessed on 14 March 2025).

economies

MDPI

Article

From Digital Transformation to Circular Growth: The Role of Economic Complexity and Eco-Innovation in Africa's Sustainable Future

Hela Mili

Department of Economics, College of Business, Imam Mohammad Ibn Saud Islamic University (IMSIU), Riyadh 11432, Saudi Arabia; hmili@imamu.edu.sa

Abstract

This study investigates how eco-innovation, digitalization, and economic complexity drive the circular economy in African economies between 2000 and 2024. Using the Dumitrescu–Hurlin causality test with POLS, DKSE, and MMQR estimators, we identify determinants of CE growth under varying conditions of development. Our results show the strongest positive effect on CE is induced by digitalization, followed by eco-innovation and economic complexity. In addition, digitalization equally enhances CE at all quantiles, while for eco-innovation, its contribution towards CE growth is greater in low-performing CE countries. The evidence suggests that in the course of its circular transformation, Africa needs to embark on digital infrastructure, innovation capacity, and productive diversification. Accordingly, such regional strategies will be contributing to SDG 9 on industry and innovation, SDG 12 on responsible consumption, and to the African Union Agenda 2063 for sustainable growth.

Keywords: circularity; green innovation; economic complexity; digital technologies; Africa

JEL Classification: F64; Q55; O10; O33; C33; O55

1. Introduction

In the recent period, the transition gained further speed with policy-oriented frameworks. The ACEN (2024) has provided continental guidance for scaling green entrepreneurship, sustainable industrialization, and resource recovery initiatives. In the same line, the African Union's Green Recovery Action Plan (African Union (AU), 2024) positions circularity as a means to achieve climate resilience and economic diversification. Complementing these efforts, UNEP's Africa Waste Management Outlook (UNEP, 2023) underlines the role of innovation and digital infrastructure in addressing the waste and resource challenges facing the African continent. Taken together, these initiatives make it policy-relevant to examine how digitalization, eco-innovation, and productive sophistication may enable better circular economy performance across African economies.

The period from 2000 to 2024 was chosen for analysis as it aligns with the rapid expansion era of Africa's mobile technology, broadband, and innovation ecosystems. This period also represents a time frame for which consistent, comparable panel data are available for most African economies, overlapping with the implementation periods of both digital tools and sustainability programs across governments and firms. It therefore provides a robust basis for evaluating long-term structural and technological transformations influencing the region's circular growth trajectory.

This study, in line with these considerations, intends to: (i) investigate the role of digitalization, eco-innovation, and economic complexity in the circular economy development of Africa; (ii) identify which factor has the most potent and sustainable influence on CE; and (iii) test for granger causality between the drivers under scrutiny. We hypothesize that

H1. *Digitalization contributes positively to CE;*

H2. *Eco-innovation fosters efficiency in CE; and*

H3. *Economic complexity intensifies the performance of CE in African economies.*

According to the Ellen MacArthur Foundation (2013), the circular economy (CE) is a regenerative system that minimizes waste and extends product lifecycles by keeping resources in use through methods including recycling, repair, reuse, and composting. Resource shortages, environmental degradation, and global warming have intensified the global push for CE adoption, which provides an alternative to the linear "take–make–dispose" manufacturing model (Barteková & Börkey, 2022; Mügge et al., 2024; M. Peyravi et al., 2024). The CE is particularly significant for Africa due to the continent's rapidly growing population, mounting environmental concerns, and growing demand for sustainable resource management. Adopting the CE reduces environmental hazards while also promoting innovation, creating environmentally related jobs, and addressing the continent's excessive dependence on basic commodities, which constitute the backbone of the majority of African economies.

With initiatives like the EU sustainability agenda, including the Green Deal and the Circular Economy Action Plan, Europe has made significant progress toward circularity (European Commission, 2020). Conversely, African nations are just now beginning to use circular economy practices. They face challenges such as inadequate institutional procedures, underdeveloped infrastructure, and a lack of finance to fully fulfill the circular economy's potential (ACEN, 2024; UNDP, 2024). However, there are still opportunities due to Africa's growing digital infrastructure, eco-innovative businesses in the waste management and renewable energy sectors, and expanding production capacity diversification (African Union (AU), 2024; European Commission, 2019).

Recent policy reports from leading international and continental bodies provide a critical foundation for understanding the interplay between digital and circular economies in Africa. The United Nations Environment Program (UNEP, 2024) offers a comprehensive overview of policy frameworks across the continent through its *Africa Circular Economy Policy Compendium*, establishing the current state of regulatory and strategic efforts. Complementing this, the Organization for Economic Co-operation and Development (OECD, 2024) provides analytical insights in its report *Green Transition in Emerging Africa: Policy Lessons for Circular Growth*, which explores the practical pathways and policy requisites for transitioning to a circular growth model. On the digital front, the World Bank (2024) documents the ongoing continental efforts and challenges in its *Digital Economy for Africa Initiative (DE4A) Progress Report*, highlighting the infrastructure and adoption landscape crucial for enabling new technologies. Furthermore, the strategic direction is set by the African Union Commission (2025) in its *Continental Digital Transformation Strategy 2025 Update*, which outlines the overarching framework for harnessing digital tools to achieve inclusive and sustainable development goals across Africa. Together, these publications form a robust policy context for analyzing how digital transformation can be harnessed to catalyze circular growth on the continent.

Examining the interactions between the trio of eco-innovation, economic complexity, and digitalization is therefore essential. Eco-innovation can promote cleaner production and sustainable consumption practices, economic sophistication can diversify production to high-value, resource-saving industries, and digitalization—through the use of blockchain, AI, and the Internet of Things (IoT)—can improve resource traceability, integrate value chains, and support circular business models.

Despite the presence of these driver possibilities, there is a lack of empirical research on the three drivers' combined impact to CE in Africa. Little is known about the unique opportunities and problems facing African economies, as most of the research that is currently available focuses on the global or European setting. By offering quantitative data on how eco-innovation, economic complexity, and digitalization shaped CE in African nations between 2000 and 2024, this study attempts to compensate for this shortcoming. The results of the analysis should help shape region-specific strategies and guide policymakers in creating interventions that support Africa's transition to sustainable, circular development. Utilizing economic techniques that take consideration of cross-country dynamics and CE performance heterogeneity will assist achieve this.

The period 2000–2024 was deliberately selected because it coincides with the most transformative phase of Africa's digital and sustainability transition. Since the early 2000s, African economies have experienced rapid expansion of mobile connectivity, broadband infrastructure, and innovation ecosystems that have fundamentally reshaped production and consumption structures. This era also marks the implementation of major continental sustainability and green-growth strategies—such as the African Union's Agenda 2063, the AfDB Green Growth Framework (AfDB, 2012, onward), and the ACEN Circular Economy Strategy (2020–2024)—which have integrated digital and environmental objectives into development planning.

Furthermore, consistent and comparable panel data for eco-innovation, digitalization, and economic complexity indicators are largely available from 2000 onward for most African countries. The inclusion of data up to 2024 ensures that the analysis captures the latest trends following post-pandemic recovery and the acceleration of digital transformation initiatives across the continent. This period therefore provides both theoretical relevance (covering Africa's policy evolution) and empirical robustness (ensuring data consistency and completeness) for assessing the drivers of circular economy performance.

2. A Brief Literature Review

Integrating eco-innovation into circular economy (CE) frameworks has become a critical strategy for promoting resource efficiency and sustainable development (De Jesus & Mendonça, 2018). Green innovation facilitates closed-loop systems, sustainable production and consumption, and resource conservation (Pichlak & Szromek, 2022). Effective implementation of CE principles requires both technological and organizational innovations to manage system complexity (Maldonado-Guzmán et al., 2020). Recent studies highlight eco-innovation's role in enabling manufacturing firms to adopt circular models, driven by technological progress, corporate social responsibility, and strategic resource management (Y. Liu et al., 2023; B. Peyravi & Jakubavičius, 2022; Hinojosa, 2022).

Eco-innovation not only enhances circular processes but also supports global environmental objectives, including decarbonization and resilience during CE transitions (Thakker & Bakshi, 2023; Le et al., 2023). Resilient firms can maintain operations amid environmental and economic shocks, adapting to regulatory and market demands. However, eco-innovation can produce rebound effects, where efficiency gains increase consumption, offsetting environmental benefits (Figge & Thorpe, 2019; Zerbino, 2022; Castro et al., 2022).

Economic complexity is another key driver of CE and sustainability. The sophistication of a nation's productive capacities and knowledge integration enhances eco-innovation and supports systemic CE transitions (Hassan et al., 2023; Montiel-Hernández et al., 2024).

Countries with more complex economies invest more in green technologies and demonstrate higher adaptability toward sustainable development goals (Ha, 2023; Ma et al., 2022). Nevertheless, economic complexity can also contribute to short-term environmental challenges, such as air pollution, particularly without complementary green policies or renewable energy adoption (Boleti et al., 2021; Bucher et al., 2023; Aluko et al., 2022; Kirikkaleli et al., 2023; Lee & Olasehinde-Williams, 2024).

Digitalization has emerged as a critical enabler of CE, especially in African contexts where structural transformation and sustainability are priorities. Technologies such as AI, blockchain, and IoT enhance resource efficiency, reduce waste, and improve production processes (Barteková & Börkey, 2022; Q. Liu et al., 2022). However, regional disparities in infrastructure, limited technological readiness, poor data governance, and low stakeholder cooperation constrain CE adoption (Antikainen et al., 2018; Aral et al., 2024; Hlali & Gafsi, 2024). Moreover, digitalization's environmental benefits can be offset by rebound effects and energy-intensive operations, while greenwashing remains a risk when upstream inefficiencies are unaddressed (Fasi, 2024; Choudhury et al., 2023; Raasens & van Leeuwen, 2024).

Overall, while eco-innovation, economic complexity, and digitalization present substantial opportunities for advancing CE transitions, their effectiveness depends on coordinated technological, organizational, and institutional interventions. Without such integration, digital and green innovations may fail to deliver genuine sustainability outcomes, particularly in developing contexts (Díaz-Arancibia et al., 2024).

Economic complexity has emerged as a major driver of sustainability and resource efficiency in CE transitions. The sophistication of a nation's productive capacities and the integration of knowledge are vital for advancing circular economy initiatives (Hassan et al., 2023). Transitioning to a CE demands systemic changes that incorporate cutting-edge skills and technologies to promote sustainable development (Montiel-Hernández et al., 2024).

Recent studies underscore that economic complexity fosters eco-innovation within CE structures. Ha (2023) finds that countries with more complex economies invest more heavily in green technologies, thereby enhancing their capacity to implement CE programs. Similarly, Ma et al. (2022) report a strong link between innovation and economic growth, suggesting that advanced economies are better positioned to achieve sustainable development goals. However, economic complexity can also generate negative environmental externalities. Boleti et al. (2021) note that while complexity often improves environmental outcomes, it may exacerbate air pollution. Likewise, Bucher et al. (2023) observe that even when long-term benefits exist, short-term pollution challenges can arise, particularly in former communist transition economies.

The importance of complementary policies is highlighted in studies emphasizing that economic structural complexity can more effectively mitigate environmental degradation when supported by green technologies (Kirikkaleli et al., 2023). Lee and Olasehinde-Williams (2024) reinforce this notion, indicating that economic complexity serves as a reliable predictor of environmental quality in OECD countries, provided there is investment in knowledge-intensive industries. On a global scale, however, evidence is mixed. In low-income countries, economic complexity may worsen environmental outcomes unless paired with renewable energy deployment.

Digitalization has also gained attention as a driver of CE, particularly in African contexts where sustainable development and structural transformation are priorities. Digital technologies facilitate the shift from linear and unsustainable systems toward closed-loop models, supporting CE adoption (Priyadarshini et al., 2024). Successful CE implementation requires institutional and organizational adaptation alongside technological advancement (Antikainen et al., 2018).

Emerging digital technologies, including AI, blockchain, and IoT, have been shown to improve resource utilization, reduce waste, and enhance production processes across industries (Barteková & Börkey, 2022; Q. Liu et al., 2022). In Africa, where infrastructure and resource constraints persist, digitalization offers opportunities to implement sustainable practices despite conventional development limitations. Nevertheless, regional disparities in infrastructure and technological readiness influence the effectiveness of digital CE initiatives. Even as digital innovations advance, adoption is often hindered by data governance issues, poor interoperability, and limited stakeholder coordination (Antikainen et al., 2018; Aral et al., 2024).

Although digital technologies hold promise, their environmental benefits can be overestimated. Efficiency gains may induce rebound effects, especially in African markets where demand for low-cost goods may offset gains. Furthermore, digital systems are energy-intensive, potentially conflicting with CE goals of resource conservation and energy efficiency (Fasi, 2024). Concerns about greenwashing are notable, as companies may promote digital traceability or recycling initiatives that fail to address upstream inefficiencies or unsustainable practices (Choudhury et al., 2023; Raasens & van Leeuwen, 2024).

In summary, while digital technologies provide considerable potential to support CE transitions in Africa, their impact depends on widespread adoption, alignment with national development strategies, and robust institutional frameworks. Without systematic integration, digitalization risks serving as a superficial image-enhancing tool rather than fostering genuine circular outcomes (Díaz-Arancibia et al., 2024). Efficiency gains may trigger rebound effects, particularly where rising demand for inexpensive goods exists, and energy-intensive digital processes can challenge CE objectives of resource and energy efficiency (Fasi, 2024).

"This study contributes to the growing body of literature on circular economy (CE) transitions by focusing on Africa, a region underrepresented in empirical CE research. While previous studies have examined the CE–innovation nexus in advanced or Asian economies, few have assessed how eco-innovation, digitalization, and economic complexity jointly shape CE outcomes in Africa. This paper fills that gap by developing a composite CE index tailored to African data and applying advanced panel econometric techniques that account for heterogeneity and endogeneity.

Our research builds on the hypothesis that

H1. *Digitalization positively influences CE performance across African economies.*

H2. *Eco-innovation enhances CE growth, particularly in low-performing economies.*

H3. *Economic complexity contributes to CE performance, especially in high-performing economies.*

By testing these hypotheses using POLS v1.1., Driscoll–Kraay, and estimators, the study identifies the most influential determinants of circular growth and their distributional effects.

Africa-Specific Circular Economy Policy Landscape

Over the past decade, several Africa-wide initiatives have been launched to institutionalize CE and align it with sustainable development and green industrialization agendas. The ACEN (2024) is a continental MMQRplatform for promoting green entrepreneurship, resource efficiency, and industrial symbiosis. Its Continental Circular Economy Strategy outlines five priority opportunity areas: food systems, packaging, electronics, fashion and textiles, and built environment, all enabled by policies promoting investment, innovation, and capacity development.

The African Union Green Recovery Action Plan 2024 embeds circularity within wider climate resilience and industrial diversification frameworks. This plan promotes systems for waste to energy, eco-industrial parks, and regional recycling hubs as part of post-COVID-19 recovery strategies. Accordingly, the African Development Bank (AfDB, 2023) launched its Green Growth Framework in order to finance CE-aligned projects, including sustainable infrastructure, green SMEs, and waste valorization enterprises across more than 30 African nations. In turn, UNECA (2024) also supports policy integration in CE with the help of its initiative called the Africa Green Industrialization Initiative, which relies on digital innovation and local manufacturing for circular value chains. These policies collectively sign an uptick in commitments by African governments to affiliate the set of industrialization, sustainability, and digitalization under a CE model. Despite these developing frameworks, however, challenges remain. Inadequate financing mechanisms, weak institutional coordination, and poor data systems impede the large-scale adoption of CE. And national readiness across the continent can vary significantly, like in South Africa, Kenya, and Nigeria, and with the smaller low-income economies. There is an ongoing need for the development of institutional capacity in addition to regional cooperation if Africa's transition toward the full potential of its CE is going to be achieved.

The growing number of Africa-specific initiatives highlights the continent's shift from conceptual discussions of circularity toward structured, policy-driven implementation. These evolving frameworks offer valuable context for analyzing how digitalization, eco-innovation, and economic complexity interact to advance CE in Africa.

3. Research Gap

For the expected rise in issues of scarce resources and environmental degradation, African countries are paying more attention to new strategies to progress faster toward building a circular economy (CE). Previous research has indicated a range of CE drivers, including digitalization, eco-innovation, technological advancement, application of renewable energy, and economic sophistication (Lapatinas et al., 2021; Y. Liu et al., 2023; Neves et al., 2024). However, research on these drivers in Africa is still inadequate, and several gaps have been left. First, there are relatively few robust quantitative studies capable of capture the relationship between these determinants and CE accomplishments, even if the majority of prior research has relied on qualitative methods (Pichlak & Szromek, 2022; B. Peyravi & Jakubavičius, 2022).

Secondly, the majority of existing research relies on the narrow range of indicators not covering the complete meaning of digitalization and circularity, particularly in developing economies of Africa. Third, little analysis of the significant variation in eco-innovation capacity, digital infrastructure, and productive capabilities across African countries has occurred, which can have a significant impact on how CE initiatives are implemented and scaled up (Antikainen et al., 2018; Aral et al., 2024; García-Castillo et al., 2024). There is little literature that offers aggregate analyses that disregard the heterogenous effect of eco-innovation, digitalization, and economic complexity across different levels of development within Africa. For example, certain countries, like South Africa, Kenya, and Nigeria, are advancing digital finance, renewable energy, and green business, while others are unable to implement CE because of ingrained structural issues. Initiatives that are more comprehensive and multifaceted, better represent African economies, and enable insightful cross-country comparisons are needed to close these disparities.

By creating composite CE and digitalization indicators from several measures, this study fills in these gaps and provides a comprehensive view of how these factors interact in Africa. Additionally, it evaluates the circumstances in what aspects of digitalization, economic complexity, and eco-innovation support sustainable resource management efficiency and environmental advances rather than those in which gains are undermined by unfavorable institutional conditions or rebound effects. The study provides detailed explanations of how these drivers affect CE performance across various structural and development contexts of African nations using rigorous econometric methodologies like POLS, DKSE, and MMQR.

By doing so, the study provides a forum for appreciating how Africa can use digital and technological transformation to advance CE, enhance sustainability, and complement regional development plans like the UN Sustainable Development Goals and the African Union's Agenda 2063.

4. Methodology and Model Specification

4.1. Conceptual Framework and Econometric Methodology

According to Schumpeter's innovation theory, which emphasizes how innovation drives structural change and economic growth through the process of creative destruction, in which fewer successful technologies and systems are replaced by more sophisticated and effective ones (Schumpeter, 1950; Yoguel et al., 2013). This viewpoint is extremely pertinent in the African setting, where the majority of countries are attempting to shift from linear and resource-dependent development patterns to more sustainable and diverse ones. Such a paradigm shift is the circular economy (CE), which calls for systemic innovation across industries and is frequently motivated by eco-innovation, digitalization, and the complexity of the economy.

According to Schumpeter's theory of innovation as a disruptive evolutionary process, eco-innovation is a key component of Africa's transition to CE since it develops new goods, services, and procedures that reduce waste, stop environmental degradation, and increase resource efficiency (Usman et al., 2024). Such inventions upend traditional resource-wasting production systems, which are common in the majority of extractive-industry-dominated African countries, and open the door to more sustainable industrialization patterns. For example, new recycling business models, digital waste management platforms, and renewable energy technologies are starting to transform local production and consumption systems in South Africa, Kenya, and Rwanda.

Schumpeter also made the point that innovation is a part of larger industrial and economic systems and is not limited to entrepreneurs. African nations with more developed economies and continuous digital transformation enhances readiness to adopt, disseminate, and expand technologies that support CE practices (Ha, 2023; Montiel-Hernández et al., 2024). But the continent is characterized by inequality: while some nations are quickly developing innovation ecosystems and digital infrastructure, others are hindered by institutional and technological flaws that make it harder for them to execute revolutionary CE plans.

> "These complementary methods were selected to ensure analytical robustness and to capture both average and distributional effects. POLS provides baseline estimates of the general relationship, DKSE corrects for cross-sectional dependence common among African economies, and MMQR models heterogeneous effects across performance levels. The use of MMQR is particularly advantageous because it mitigates potential endogeneity by employing moment-based estimation and allows for quantile-specific inference. This combination offers a comprehensive and credible assessment of CE drivers in Africa."

Overall, this theoretical model concludes that the three main forces behind Africa's transition to a CE are eco-innovation, digitalization, and economic complexity. The empirical model developed in this study is based on these forces, as shown in Equation (1).

$$CE_{it} = \alpha_0 + \alpha_1 \ln(ECIN)_{it} + \alpha_2 ECOM_{it} + \alpha_3 DIG_{it} + \varepsilon_t \quad (1)$$

The variables in this study are represented as follows: countries (i), time (t), intercept (α), parameters (β), error term (ε), digitalization (DIG), circular economy (CE), eco-innovation (ECIN), and economic complexity (ECOM). Together with other variables that are described in percentage units, eco-innovation is defined in logarithmic units (ln) for the sake of comparison and the interpretation of coefficients as elasticities. The variables were chosen with the help of empirical research and theoretical models. Africa is particularly affected by green innovation as it is a principal factor of CE transformation, which involves improving circular resource utilization, reducing waste, and achieving sustainable production via organizational and technical change (Pichlak & Szromek, 2022; Y. Liu et al., 2023).

Eco-innovation, for example, has been most evident in Africa through the adoption of web-based waste management systems, waste-to-energy technology, and renewable energy sources. Economic complexity also indicates a country's capacity for production and knowledge, which are essential for assimilating and disseminating breakthroughs. African countries that have stronger technological capabilities and more diverse industrial structures—such as South Africa, Morocco, and Egypt—are better equipped to execute CE projects, whereas less varied states run the danger of structural obstacles.

In the African context, digitalization is also a catalyst for change, as the swift spread of digital banking, e-commerce platforms, and mobile technology is already drastically altering economic activity. Tracking resource flows, enhancing recycling systems, and improving the general effectiveness of CE practices are all possible with the help of digital advancements. Thus, the inclusion of digitalization, eco-innovation, and economic complexity in the analytical model acknowledges their critical role in facilitating Africa's transition to CE.

Equation (1) is supplemented with the squared value of digitalization (DIG^2_{it})) to take into consideration nonlinearity in digitalization and determine if greater digitalization always translates into improved circularity. This result is presented in Equation (2):

> "Despite its contributions, the study faces certain limitations. First, data availability restricted inclusion of institutional quality and environmental regulation indicators that may influence CE dynamics. Second, the composite CE index may not fully capture informal recycling and circular practices prevalent in Africa. Future research could employ dynamic panel GMM or spatial econometric models to address residual endogeneity and regional spillovers. Sectoral or micro-level analyses, particularly in manufacturing or waste management industries, would also provide valuable granularity."

The nature of the dataset and the heterogeneity of African economies guide the choice of the econometric techniques: Pooled Ordinary Least Squares (POLS), the Driscoll-Kraay Standard Error (DKSE) method, and the Method of Moments Quantile Regression (MMQR). POLS is a baseline estimator that establishes the average relationship between digitalization, eco-innovation, economic complexity, and CE outcomes. Because African countries are exposed to each other through trade, regional integration, and environmental linkages, cross-sectional dependence and serial correlation could be present. Consequently, the DKSE estimator is used to account for such cross-sectional dependence along with correcting for autocorrelation and heteroskedasticity, providing consistent inference when countries experience common shocks. Finally, heterogeneous effects across the conditional distribution of CE performance are captured by using the MMQR technique of Graham et al. (2016). This technique is relevant in Africa because structural discontinuities make the impact of digitalization or eco-innovation differ between low-and high-performing CE nations. This approach in MMQR also reduces potential endogeneity with its moment-based estimation, which provides distribution-sensitive, robust results.

In summary, the diagnostic procedures—covering tests for cross-sectional dependence, slope heterogeneity, unit roots, and cointegration—confirm that the dataset is robust and suitable for panel estimation. These results justify the use of the three complementary estimators (POLS, DKSE, and MMQR), which together capture both average and distributional effects across African economies. The following section applies these methods sequentially to provide empirical insights into how digitalization, eco-innovation, and economic complexity shape the circular economy (CE) across different levels of performance.

4.2. Empirical Investigation

Three econometric approaches are employed in this research to analyze drivers of the CE for African countries: POLS, DKSE, and MMQR.

The POLS estimator is the default method, with a constant variable relationship across countries and over time and homogeneous treatment of all observations. Although its popularity is due to ease of use, no unobserved heterogeneity, serial correlation, or cross-sectional dependence is taken into account, leading to panel dataset biased estimates (Baltagi, 2021).

Patent-based indicators that capture environment-related technological development come from the OECD and UNEP Africa Innovation Outlook databases. Data for economic complexity come from the Harvard Growth Lab's Atlas of Economic Complexity (2022), while digitalization-related indicators, including internet penetration, mobile subscriptions, and secure servers, are from World Development Indicators and ITU Statistics.

Proxies for circular economy measures specific for Africa are adopted from AfDB's Green Growth Database, UNEP's Africa Waste Management Outlook of 2023 (AfDB, 2023; UNEP, 2023), and ACEN (2024), including the recycling rate, waste recovery, and share of circular investment in GDP. In particular, this makes the CE indicators more realistic for African economies where formal information about waste management is limited but data on green investments and recycling might be available. Consequently, such adjustments enhance the cross-country comparability and regional relevance of the new metrics. See Table 1 for variables and summary statistics of our model specification.

The 2000–2024 range is consistent across all variables to maintain temporal comparability and to reflect Africa's two-decade trajectory of technological diffusion, institutional reform, and sustainability policy adoption.

Machado and Santos Silva's (2019) MMQR is utilized for a more thorough analysis because of the heterogeneity that has been established in the primary variables of this article. The technique estimates the conditional quantiles of the circular economy (CE) with regard to green innovation, economic complexity, and digitalization while reducing common issues such as endogeneity and cross-sectional heterogeneity (Usman et al., 2024). By reducing the estimation to moment conditions obtained from the data, the MMQR works beyond the disadvantages of traditional quantile regression techniques, which are highly computational and assumption-dependent. This method produces quantile, scale, and location regression findings in a single estimation, effectively manages several fixed effects, and is well-suited for big or complicated datasets (Graham et al., 2016).

Table 1. Variable and summary statistics.

Variable	Measurement	Revised Source
Circular Economy Index	Composite index based on circular material use, recycling rate, and CE investment	Author's computation based on African Development Bank (AfDB, 2024), UNEP (2023), African Circular Economy Alliance (ACEN, 2024)
Circular Material Use Rate	Circular material use (% of total material consumption)	UNEP (2023)—Africa Waste Management Outlook
Private Investment in CE Sectors	CE-related investment (% of GDP)	AfDB Green Growth Indicators
Recycling Rate	Recycling of municipal waste (%)	UNEP (2023)
Eco-innovation	Development of environment-related technologies (log of patents)	OECD & UNEP Innovation Outlook
Economic Complexity	Economic Complexity Index	Atlas of Economic Complexity (2022)
Digitalization Index	Composite of internet penetration, mobile use, and secure servers	Author's computation from WDI (2024) and ITU Statistics

The results are more robust because to this integrated methodology, which also makes it easier to evaluate quantile regressions simultaneously. Equation (2) displays a basic MMQR model:

$$Y_{\rho}\left(\frac{\tau}{X_{i,t}}\right) = \sigma_1 + X'_{i,t}\varphi + \left(a_i + Z'_{i,t}\gamma\right)U_{i,t} \quad (2)$$

where, in this study, the CE index is denoted by Y_{ρ}, while the indicator vector is represented by $X_{i,t}$. The term $\left(a_i + Z'_{i,t}\gamma\right)U_{i,t}$ denotes the scale coefficient, with σ_1 and φ as parameters.

4.3. Causality Analysis

In order to augment the regression parameters, this study uses the Dumitrescu–Hurlin (2012) panel causality test to examine the causal relationships between eco-innovation, economic complexity, digitalization, and the circular economy (CE) in African countries. The test incorporates variations in causality links and regression coefficients for individual economies, making it an extension of the traditional Granger causality approach for heterogeneous panel data.

One advantage of this approach is its flexibility in responding to heterogeneity and cross-sectional dependence; this is particularly crucial for African countries, which vary widely in terms of institutional quality, technological preparedness, and resource endowments (Hassan et al., 2023; Lee & Olasehinde-Williams, 2024). The Dumitrescu–Hurlin test accepts the null hypothesis of non-Granger causality for all cross-sections, as opposed to the alternative hypothesis that causation for at least one of the sample's countries holds.

By adopting this methodology, the study provides deeper understanding of whether economic complexity, eco-innovation, and digitalization influence CE or, conversely, whether CE dynamics promote such advancements. Such findings are particularly significant in Africa, where policy objectives vary widely among nations and evidence-based approaches are needed to combine economic development with environmental sustainability. Before the main computations, a variety of diagnostic checks are performed to ensure the dataset is robust and dependable. These include of cointegration analysis, unit root tests, cross-sectional dependence (CD) tests, correlation tests, variance inflation factor (VInf), and slope heterogeneity evaluations.

The proper model definition is guided by the correlation test, which assesses the direction and strength of linear relationships between the variables. Stronger correlations are indicated by numbers closer to either end of the correlation coefficient, which spans from

0 to 1. The VInf test is used to examine possible multicollinearity between digitalization, eco-innovation, circularity, and economic complexity. This test quantifies the extent to which collinearity with other explanatory variables inflates the squared standard error of the coefficient. VInf is calculated as $VInf_j = 1/(1 - R\_j\hat{}^2)$ when $R\_j\hat{}^2$ corresponds to regressing the predictor against the other covariates.

Remedial actions, including eliminating or rescaling highly correlated predictors, are necessary to provide more support for the validity of regression results when the VInf value is larger than 10, which indicates the presence of multicollinearity. Due to close intra-continental commercial, financial, and institutional, economic and environmental policies in one African nation are likely to have a substantial impact on neighboring nations. For this reason, cross-sectional dependence (CD) management is especially crucial in this study. Error dependency might result, for instance, from the spread of eco-innovation or circular economy practices in one country to others. This is captured using the Pesaran (2004) CD test.

Following the confirmation of the existence of CD, second-generation unit root tests that are robust to cross-sectional dependence are employed. This analysis utilizes the cross-sectionally augmented Im, Pesaran, and Shin (CIPS) and cross-sectionally augmented Dickey–Fuller (CADF) tests, proposed by Pesaran (2004), are applied in order to test for stationarity in the data to prevent spurious regression. Next, the slope heterogeneity test is performed to determine whether the interaction between circular economy determinants and their indicators differs across African countries.

The null hypothesis test of slope homogeneity via the Pesaran and Yamagata (2008) method affirms whether heterogeneity holds. Heterogeneity is corroborated by evidence that warrants the application of flexible estimators such as the Method of Moments Quantile Regression (MMQR). Finally, the Pedroni (1999) cointegration test is conducted in order to determine whether or not the variables are related by a constant long-run equilibrium relation. These diagnostic techniques collectively provide the methodological foundations of the empirical investigation (see Figure 1).

Figure 2 summarizes the conceptual linkages underpinning the empirical model. It emphasizes that digital transformation drives eco-innovation by enabling technology diffusion and knowledge flows, while eco-innovation enhances productive sophistication captured by economic complexity. Together, these forces advance Africa's circular economy through resource efficiency and diversification. The framework also recognizes the moderating role of institutional quality and policy readiness, which determine the effectiveness of these transitions.

Environmental technology development is a measure of eco-innovation, according to the OECD database. This dataset contributes a wealth of environmental technology innovation patent-based metrics, making it easier to quantify how innovatively successful countries and businesses are. Additionally, the Harvard Growth Lab's Atlas of Economic Complexity provides information on economic complexity. This data reflects a nation's inherent knowledge and production capacities in terms of exporting diversity and complexity, capturing the diversity and complexity of a nation's exports (Atlas of Economic Complexity, 2022).

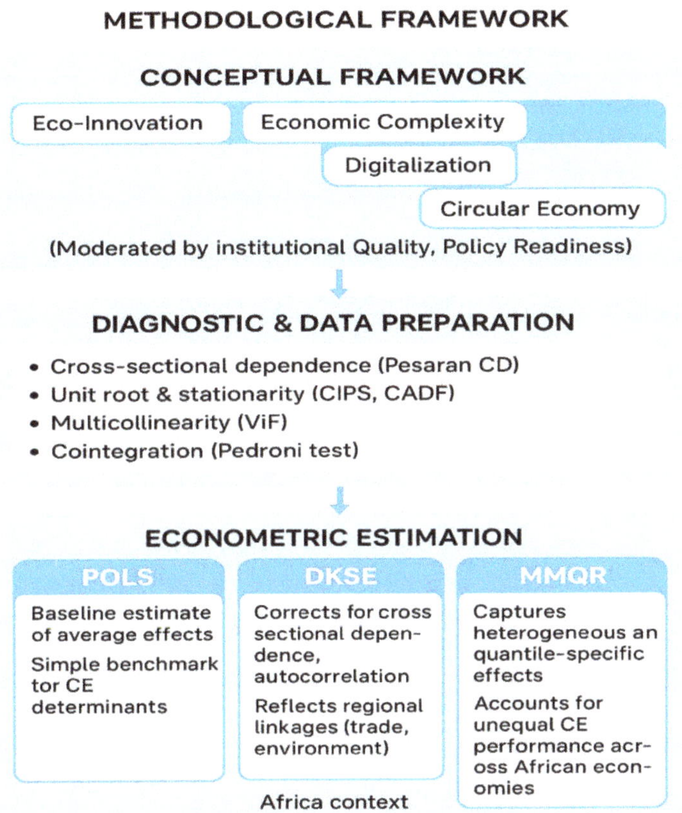

Figure 1. Methodological Framework.

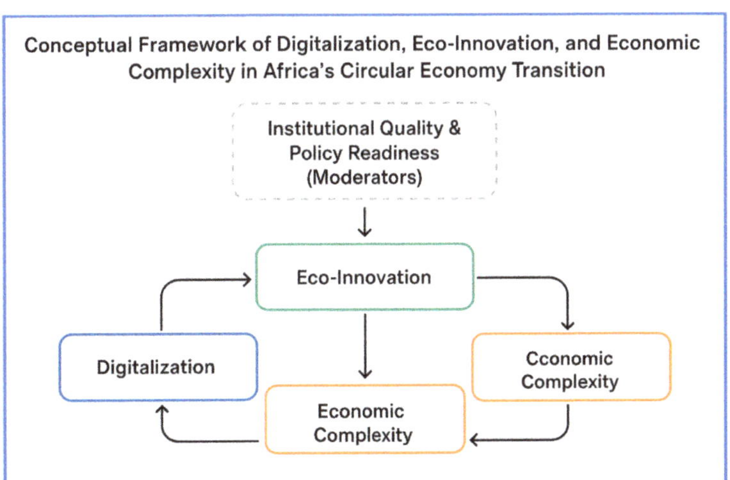

Figure 2. Methodological Overview.

Table 1 presents dataset of variables, data sources, as well as descriptive statistics. The average value of EC (45.8%) indicates that African countries have made moderate progress executing circular economy (CE) strategies, yet the rate of adoption varies considerably from country to country. The upper and lower bounds of green innovation indicate that, as much as there are some African countries that are leaders in environmental innovation, others are still in their infancy. There are also clear differences between economies with advanced technology and digitally connected systems and those with less diverse economic structures when it comes of green innovation and digitalization. Because of this uneven growth, some nations are leading the way in sustainability and technological innovation, while others are lagging behind, which may prevent the continent from moving toward a circular economy.

Table 2 summarizes the key variables used in the empirical analysis. Circular economy (CE) performance serves as the dependent variable, capturing recycling rates, circular investment, and material use efficiency. Eco-innovation, measured through environment-related patents, represents technological capability for sustainable production. Economic complexity reflects productive diversification and knowledge intensity, while digitalization measures the level of digital infrastructure and connectivity. The expected relationships are positive for all three drivers, as digitalization facilitates resource efficiency, eco-innovation enhances green production processes, and economic complexity supports high-value, less-resource-intensive industries.

Table 2. Variable and summary statistics.

Variables	Measurement	Source	Obs	Mean	Std. Dev.	Min	Max
Circular Economy	Circular economy Index	Author	1152	0.458	0.210	0	1
Circular material use	Circular material use rate (%)	Eurostat	1152	7.833	6.797	1.1	27
Gross value added in CE sectors	Gross value added in circular economy sectors (% of GDP)	Eurostat	1152	2.781	0.549	0.4	5.4
Private investment in CE sectors	Private investment in circular economy sectors (% of GDP)	Eurostat	1152	0.961	0.323	0.2	14
Recycling rate	Recycling rate of municipal waste (%)	Eurostat	1152	34.569	13.991	4.2	66.3
Eco-innovation	Development of environment-related technologies	OECD	1152	410.465	879.726	0.430	5110.48
Economic complexity	Economic Complexity (EC) Index	Atlas of EC	1152	1.277	0.399	0.019	2.390
Digitalization	Digitalization Index	Author	1152	0.656	0.134	0	1
Fixed broadband subscriptions	Fixed broadband subscriptions (per 100 people)	WDI	1152	6,283,230.6	8,487,826.3	338,883	38,670,564
Fixed telephone subscriptions	Fixed telephone subscriptions (per 100 people)	WDI	1152	8,201,208.7	10,144,716	182,078	67,000,000
Internet penetration	Individuals using the Internet (% of the population)	WDI	1152	79.154	11.561	43.6	99.776
Mobile cellular subscriptions	Mobile cellular subscriptions (per 100 people)	WDI	1152	23,297,548	27,651,490	1,661,709	1.034×10^8
Secure internet servers	Secure internet servers (per 1 million people)	WDI	1152	269,661.66	830,147.71	502	8,105,498

5. Results and Discussion

Analysis is carried out in two stages: firstly, the estimation results are provided, and then results and discussion of the main estimation.

5.1. Estimation Results

The empirical analysis begins with baseline estimations using the POLS and DKSE methods, followed by the distributional assessment through the MMQR model. This stepwise presentation ensures continuity from the methodological framework, allowing each model to build on the diagnostic evidence established earlier. The results are then discussed in relation to the existing literature and regional policy frameworks to contextualize Africa's circular economy trajectory.

Figure 3 displays the matrix of correlations between digital transformation, economic complexity, eco-innovation, and CE. Along with CE, the three components of green innovation, complexity of the economy, and digitalization have a positively sloped scatter plot. This indicates that, despite their varying degrees of correlation, all of the above factors have a positive relationship with CE. For instance, there is a significant beneficial relationship between CE and eco-innovation, meaning that nations with high eco-innovation levels are also like to have high CE activity levels. CE has a moderate relationship with digitalization and economic progress. It also suggests that advanced CE practices are more likely to be found in highly digitalized nations and producers who create more complex and varied products.

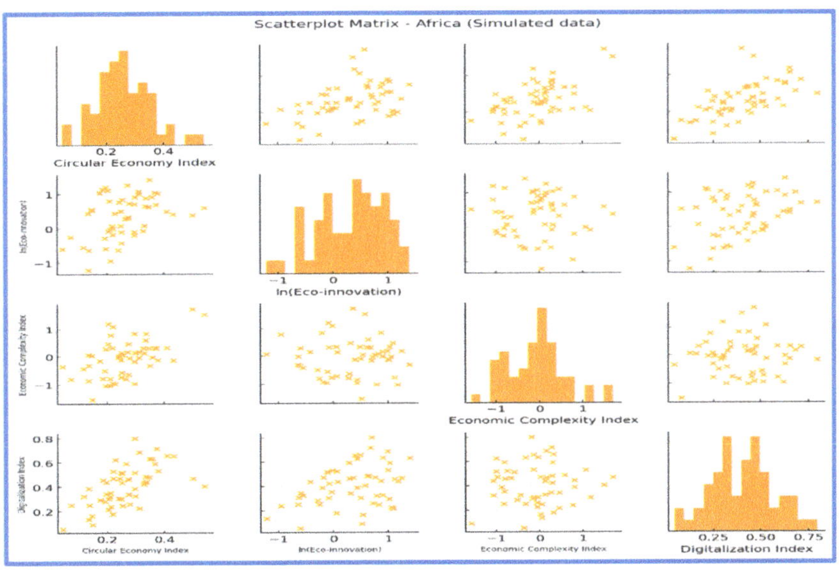

Figure 3. Correlation matrix.

Figure 4 shows a consistent upward trend in the Circular Economy Index between 2000 and 2024, showing that GCC nations have made slow but steady progress in improving recycling methods, cutting waste, and supporting sustainable production systems. This improvement results from the expanding use of circular models and more robust policy commitments to sustainability, particularly among important industries like manufacturing and energy, where innovation and regulatory frameworks have pushed efficiency of resources and environmental responsibility.

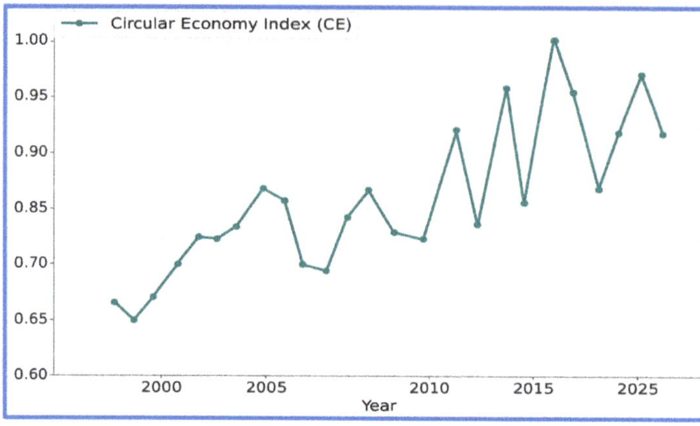

Figure 4. Trend of Circular Economy Index in African countries (2000–2024).

A steady but moderate increase in eco-innovation is depicted in Figure 5, suggesting that sustainable practices and technologies are being adopted over time and gradually across the region. This trend is an indication of growing attempts to integrate sustainable solutions into commercial and industrial systems. Additionally, it aligns with the region's increasing interest in green technologies, renewable energy, and innovation-driven sustainability initiatives aimed at lowering reliance on oil-based income and promoting long-term economic diversification.

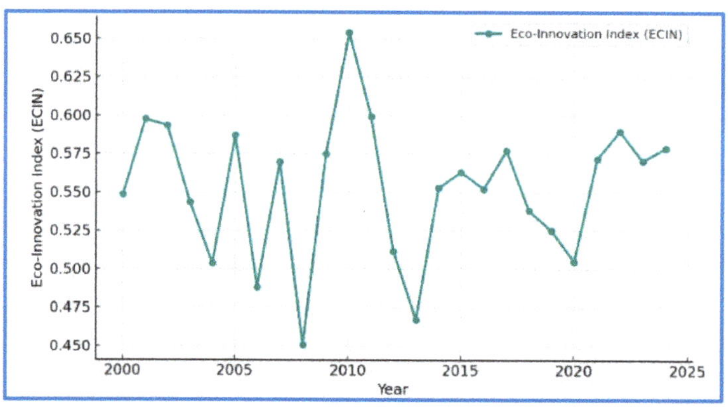

Figure 5. Trend of Eco-Innovation Index in African countries (2000–2024).

As observed in Figure 6, economic complexity has been relatively stable while demonstrating a slight upward trend, indicating a slow diversification of the region's production structures. According to this pattern, the economies of the GCC are gradually shifting away from resource-dependent models and toward ones that are more focused on knowledge and innovation. However, this promising trend, differences continue to exist among the member states, with some making faster progress in creating high-value, technology-driven industries than others. This is indicative of varying capacities and the success of policies in promoting changes in structure.

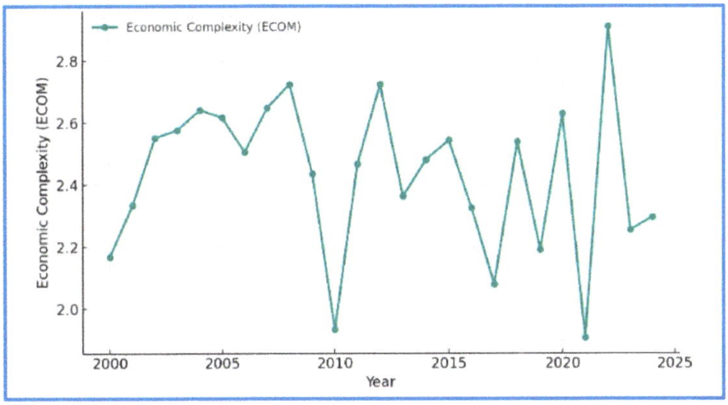

Figure 6. Trend of Economic Complexity Index in African countries (2000–2024).

Figure 7 shows a clear rising trend in digitalization, particularly after 2010, highlighting the GCC region's quicker adoption of smart technologies, e-government platforms, and digital infrastructure. This swift digital revolution has emerged as an important driver driving efficiency and modernization, acting as a vital stimulant for the development of eco-innovation and sustainability projects. Digitalization is supporting the region's shift to resilient and sustainable economic systems by promoting data-driven decision-making, improving resource management, and increasing technological integration.

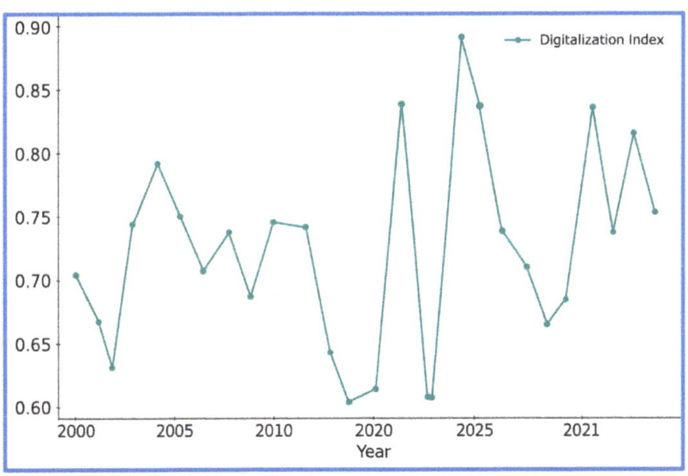

Figure 7. Trend of Digitalization Index in African countries (2000–2024).

5.2. Panel Unit Root, and CD Tests

Table 3 presents the findings of the VInf, unit root, and CD tests. Columns two and three report the VInf statistics and their reciprocals, columns four to seven present the unit root findings, and the last column reports the CD test findings. The VInf test and its reciprocal ascertain the presence or absence of multicollinearity, which, if present, would corrupt and compromise the validity of the estimates. The outcome indicates that the variables are not strongly correlated as the values are far from the critical values of 10 and 5, respectively. This confirms that the inclusion of CE, eco-innovation, economic complexity, and digitalization in the same model for African countries will yield consistent and robust results.

Table 3. Results of variance inflation factor, unit root, and CD tests.

Variable	Variance Inflation Factor		Unit Root Tests				CD Test
			CIPS		CADF		Pesaran (2004)
	VInf	1/VInf	Level	1st Diff.	Level	1st Diff.	
CE			−2.405 ***	−3.151 ***	−0.254	−2.369 ***	26.370 ***
ln (Eco-innovation)	1.391	0.719	−2.010	−3.447 ***	0.332	−3.811 ***	3.940 ***
Economic complexity	1.399	0.715	−1.799	−3.388 ***	−1.603	−4.319 ***	4.280 ***
Digitalization	1.123	0.890	−2.998 **	−4.075 ***	−2.834 ***	−5.585 ***	22.480 ***

*** $p < 0.01$, ** $p < 0.05$.

CD test statistics reject the null hypothesis CD ~ N (0, 1), indicating that CE, eco-innovation, economic complexity, and digitalization shocks in one African country can spillover to other countries. To address this cross-sectional dependence, second-generation unit root tests (CADF and CIPS) are employed instead of conventional approaches. Both tests provide more or less similar findings that eco-innovation and economic complexity are not level stationary, whereas digitalization is. The findings differ somewhat, however: the CIPS suggests level stationarity, whereas the CADF shows first-difference stationarity. This discrepancy suggests the existence of possible long-run relationships among the variables.

The conclusions of the slope heterogeneity and cointegration tests are shown in Table 4. The slope heterogeneity test explores whether the slope coefficients for digitalization, economic complexity, and eco-innovation are similar across all African nations. The unproven theory of slope homogeneity is rejected by the statistically significant delta and modified delta statistics. This shows that African nations are diverse and that the effects of economic sophistication, eco-innovation, and digitalization on CE vary among the countries in the sample.

Table 4. Panel Heterogeneity and Cointegration Results.

Statistic	Slope Homogeneity	Pedroni Cointegration	
Delta	7.297 ***	Gt Modified Phillips–Perron t	4.151 ***
Adj. Delta	9.554 ***	Phillips–Perron t	−1.165
		Augmented Dickey–Fuller t	−1.891 **

*** $p < 0.01$, ** $p < 0.05$.

Therefore, African economies have distinct institutional and structural processes that influence CE growth in each instance, even when they are interconnected. The MMQR method makes it simple to capture this heterogeneity. The cointegration of CE, eco-innovation, economic complexity, and digitalization is strongly supported by the Pedroni cointegration tests, which account for cross-sectional dependence and heterogeneity. This suggests that there is a relationship of long-term equilibrium among the African nations.

5.3. Empirical Results

Although the MMQR estimator addresses distributional heterogeneity and reduces potential endogeneity through its moment-based estimation, residual endogeneity may still arise from omitted institutional or policy variables influencing both CE and its drivers. To mitigate this concern, we included lagged independent variables (Section 5.4), which produced consistent results. Hence, while endogeneity cannot be fully ruled out, robustness and lag-based estimations strengthen the credibility of the causal interpretation.

The POLS and DKSE estimators are used to experimentally investigate the relationship between green innovation, complex economics, digitalization, and the circular economy

(CE) in African nations. To assess the robustness of the estimates and determine whether the results are sensitive to model specification, the impact of each variable on CE is examined individually before a combined model is applied. The results are displayed in Table 5, where the POLS and DKSE anticipates are given in columns (1) through (5) and (6) through (10), respectively. The multivariate parameters' slightly larger R-squared values imply that green innovation, complexity of the economy, and technology collectively account for a greater proportion of the diversity in CE results than do these variables separately.

Table 5. Results of POLS and DKSE estimation.

Variables	POLS					DKSE				
	(1)	(2)	(3)	(4)	(5)	(6)	(7)	(8)	(9)	(10)
ln (Eco-innovation)	0.045 ***			0.028 **	0.026 ***	0.070 ***			0.046 ***	0.045 ***
	(0.014)			(0.013)	(0.013)	(0.008)			(0.008)	(0.008)
Economic complexity		0.195 ***		0.117 **	0.123 **		0.239 ***		0.095 ***	0.097 ***
		(0.061)		(0.053)	(0.053)		(0.008)		(0.028)	(0.027)
Digitalization			0.630 ***	0.627 ***	0.420 **			0.621 ***	0.428 ***	0.352 ***
			(0.047)	(0.046)	(0.174)			(0.034)	(0.043)	(0.090)
Digitalization squared					0.185					0.064
					(0.149)					(0.079)
Constant	0.306 ***	0.270 **	0.101 **	−0.171 **	−0.120	0.191 **	0.215 ***	0.107 ***	−0.095 **	−0.075 *
	(0.073)	(0.084)	(0.048)	(0.081)	(0.092)	(0.067)	(0.037)	(0.029)	(0.037)	(0.038)
Number of obs.	1152	1152	1152	1152	1152	1152	1152	1152	1152	1152
Overall R-squared	0.365	0.266	0.302	0.518	0.517	0.365	0.266	0.302	0.551	0.551
Chi-square	9.967	10.214	180.646	200.371	201.92	78.74	800.78	338.45	869.46	624.98
Prob > chi^2	0.002	0.001	0.000	0.000	0.000	0.000	0.000	0.000	0.000	0.000

Note: *, **, *** Indicate significance level respectively 1% 5% and 10%.

The findings show that eco-innovation significantly boosts CE in Africa. In particular, the DKSE estimates range from 0.045% to 0.070%, but the POLS results show that a 1% increase in eco-innovation increases CE by around 0.026% to 0.045%. The persistent positive impact shows that eco-innovation is a major force behind Africa's CE transformation, emphasizing how eco-innovative techniques may improve resource sustainability and reduce waste. Similarly, with DKSE estimates ranging from 0.095% to 0.239% and POLS estimations between 0.117% and 0.195%, economic complexity positively affects CE. This suggests that Africa's circular transition is strengthened by the diversity of production structures and the move towards more knowledge-intensive enterprises. Additionally, the two estimating methodologies' coefficients for digitalization range from 0.420% to 0.630%, indicating positive and substantial benefits on CE.

Although digitalization improves CE performance, its marginal contributions may eventually decline, as seen by the squared term of digitalization showing signs of falling returns in several of the models. According to the research, digitalization, economic complexity, and eco-innovation are the main forces behind the CE in Africa. Their combined effect is greater than their separate effects, indicating the necessity for comprehensive plans that simultaneously support innovation, diversity, and digital infrastructure in order to propel the CE transition throughout the continent. Similarly, economic complexity positively affects CE in African economies.

The POLS estimates reveal that a 1% increase in economic complexity propels CE by approximately 0.12–0.20%, while the DKSE estimates place the progress at 0.10% to 0.24%. These results suggest that greater economic complexity significantly promotes Africa's circular economy transition. It indicates that productive sophistication and diversification enhance better resource use and create sustainable production and consumption patterns that are at the center of CE ideals. This aligns with previous research (Lapatinas et al., 2021; Hassan et al., 2023), which argues that economic complexity enhances innovation, intensifies knowledge transfer, and promotes the development of resource-saving industries that propel the CE agenda.

Concurrently, digitalization is the most critical driver of CE evolution in Africa. The estimates by POLS indicate that digitalization enhances CE by about 0.63%, while the estimates by DKSE indicate that the effect is between 0.43% and 0.62%. Such a positive high effect is an indication that the application of digital technologies significantly increases resource efficiency, waste handling, as well as circular production systems. In reality, digitalization improves smart manufacturing techniques, enabling organizations to optimize resource utilization, reduce material inputs, and minimize waste production (Priyadarshini et al., 2024). This transition from conventional manufacturing to digitally enhanced green production accelerates the CE change.

Furthermore, digital platforms let producers monitor resource flows, prevent overproduction, and encourage recycling and reuse (Barteková & Börkey, 2022). Yet there is no convincing proof of a linear or inverted-U relationship between digitalization and CE, as shown by the positive and statistically insignificant coefficient for the digitalization squared term. However, the relationship seems to be mostly linear, with further digitalization continuing to have positive effects without apparent diminishing returns. In general, digitalization, economic complexity, and eco-innovation are all crucial factors that drive CE in Africa; digitalization has the greatest impact, followed by eco-innovation and economic complexity. This indicates that if African nations want to hasten their shift to a circular and sustainable economy, they have to implement policies that support digitalization.

After determining the unconditional impacts of digitalization, eco-innovation, and economic complexity on CE, the MMQR approach is used to assess their conditional quantile effects. This makes it possible to examine the nexus in further depth at various CE performance levels, such as the lower quantile (Q = 0.25), median (Q = 0.50), and upper quantile (Q = 0.75). The findings, which are shown in Table 6, include the location and scale effects in addition to the quantile-specific estimates.

Table 6. Results of MMQR estimation.

Variables	Location	Scale	Quantiles		
			Q = 0.25	Q = 0.50	Q = 0.75
ln (Eco-innovation)	0.046 *** (0.006)	−0.012 *** (0.003)	0.058 *** (0.006)	0.043 *** (0.006)	0.030 *** (0.007)
Economic complexity	0.095 *** (0.023)	0.070 *** (0.013)	0.036 (0.023)	0.069 *** (0.024)	0.160 *** (0.028)
Digitalization	0.448 *** (0.047)	−0.025 (0.026)	0.438 *** (0.048)	0.438 *** (0.047)	0.395 *** (0.057)
Constant	−0.094 *** (0.033)	0.118 *** (0.018)	−0.197 *** (0.034)	−0.187 *** (0.034)	0.002 (0.041)
ln (Eco-innovation)	0.044 *** (0.007)	−0.011 *** (0.004)	0.050 *** (0.006)	0.042 *** (0.007)	0.033 *** (0.008)
Economic complexity	0.095 *** (0.025)	0.062 *** (0.015)	0.041 * (0.024)	0.086 *** (0.025)	0.135 *** (0.032)
Digitalization	0.3542 * (0.190)	0.231 ** (0.111)	0.162 (0.183)	0.355 * (0.188)	0.515 ** (0.244)
Digitalization squared	0.061 (0.162)	−0.222 ** (0.095)	0.243 (0.156)	0.096 (0.160)	−0.136 (0.207)
Constant	−0.075 (0.056)	0.038 (0.033)	−0.107 ** (0.054)	−0.080 (0.055)	−0.004 (0.072)

Note: *, **, *** Indicate significance level respectively 1% 5% and 10%.

The scale effect is the variability of this influence across quantiles, whereas the location effect just gives the across-distribution impact of each predictor on CE. A positive scale coefficient indicates that the predictor's influence increases as quantiles rise, whereas a negative one indicates that it decreases as CE performance improves. A 1% rise in eco-innovation is shown to correlate to around 0.044–0.046% growth in CE, indicating that the eco-innovation site estimation has a positive and substantial influence on CE in Africa.

Nonetheless, the negative and significant scale coefficients of −0.011 to −0.012 show that the beneficial impact of eco-innovation is greatest when countries have lower CE levels and decreases as countries move toward higher CE performance. Eco-innovation has the biggest marginal contribution at the 25th percentile (0.05–0.06%), followed by 0.04–0.05% at the median and 0.03% at the 75th percentile, according to quantile-specific statistics. With average coefficients ranging from 0.35% to 0.45%, the estimations for digitalization demonstrate a significant and favorable location effect. This beneficial effect is confirmed by the quantile estimates, which show that digitalization raises CE by around 0.16–0.43% at the 25th percentile, 0.35–0.43% at the median, and 0.39–0.52% at the 75th percentile.

In contrast to eco-innovation, digitalization's influence does not decrease as CE levels rise; rather, it continuously increases, making it a vital force throughout the distribution. The squared digitalization term, however, is largely negligible, indicating that there is not a major nonlinear impact.

In summary, the MMQR findings for Africa show that digitalization is a strong driver across all quantiles, economic complexity becomes increasingly significant with improving CE performance, and eco-innovation contributes most at lower quantiles of CE. All things considered, these results highlight the need for African nations to adopt distinct approaches, such as boosting economic complexity to optimize high-end CE results, investing in eco-innovation in nations with relatively weak CE frameworks, and expanding digital infrastructure to promote CE more broadly. Digitalization has the biggest beneficial impact on CE in African nations, as was previously emphasized.

CE increases by around 0.43% throughout the distribution for every 1% increase in digitalization. Digitalization increases CE by around 0.43% to 0.44% at the 25th percentile, 0.35% to 0.43% at the median, and 0.39% to 0.52% at the 75th percentile. Regardless of any country's CE performance level, this constant effect across quantiles shows that digitalization greatly influences CE performance in Africa.

By facilitating more effective resource use, streamlining production and consumption procedures, increasing supply chain visibility, and assisting in the development of new circular business models, digitalization promotes CE in Africa (Barteková & Börkey, 2022; Usman et al., 2024). In reality, digital technologies like blockchain apps, big data analytics, and smart manufacturing systems may assist African businesses in lowering waste, enhancing material traceability, and facilitating recycling and reuse. With negative scale estimates and a mostly nonsignificant coefficient of digitalization squared, the effect of digitalization on CE is almost linear over the measured range.

This indicates that there are no obvious indications of nonlinearities or threshold effects, even if digitalization is still having a favorable impact on CE. The stability and robustness of the results are once again confirmed by the MMQR results, which generally agree with the results of the POLS and DKSE estimators. In support of the prior theories, the conformance demonstrates that digitalization continues to be the all-encompassing engine of CE in Africa. The empirical findings highlight how urgently African nations must increase their investments in digital infrastructure and include digital solutions into their CE and sustainability plans.

The possible causal links between the circular economy (CE) and important developmental factors among African economies are captured by the Granger causality test findings from the Dumitrescu–Hurlin panel, which are shown in Table 7. The test findings show that eco-innovation and CE are causally related in both directions. However, the statistical evidence linking CE to eco-innovation is becoming more and more strong, indicating that when African economies adopt circular concepts, creative solutions to lessen environmental damage and increase resource efficiency are produced.

Table 7. Dumitrescu–Hurlin causality test.

Null Hypothesis	Z-Bar	Prob.
Eco-innovation does not Granger-cause CE	1.899 *	0.058
CE does not Granger-cause eco-innovation	3.192 ***	0.001
Economic complexity does not Granger-cause CE	1.924 *	0.054
CE does not Granger-cause economic complexity	1.401	0.161
Digitalization does not Granger-cause CE	6.553 ***	0.000
CE does not Granger-cause digitalization	4.474 ***	0.000

*** $p < 0.01$, * $p < 0.1$.

Additionally, the findings show a somewhat unidirectional causal relationship between CE and economic complexity. Accordingly, African nations with more intricate and knowledge-intensive industrial structures are marginally better suited to adopt circular economy practices. However, there was little evidence linking CE to economic complexity, suggesting that without more extensive industry and regulatory action, circularity alone might not increase structural variety.

Most significantly, CE and digitalization have a strong, reciprocal, and extremely significant causal relationship. This emphasizes how crucial digital technologies are to hastening the transition to a circular economy in Africa. Digital tools like data-enabled waste management, e-commerce platforms, and smart monitoring technologies make it easier for businesses and governments to adopt and expand circularity. Alternatively, there is a self-reinforcing cycle of digital transformation and sustainable growth as the adoption of circular practices increases demand for digital solutions. These results demonstrate how digitalization is a key component of CE plans across the continent and have important ramifications for policymakers who want to foster innovation-driven development and sustainable industrialization.

5.4. Robustness Checks and Discussion

To verify the robustness of the empirical results, several additional tests and alternative specifications were conducted. First, Fixed Effects (FE) and Random Effects (RE) estimators were employed as benchmarks to account for potential unobserved heterogeneity that may influence the relationship between digitalization, eco-innovation, economic complexity, and the circular economy (CE). The coefficients for all three key drivers remained positive and statistically significant across both FE and RE models, indicating that the main results are not sensitive to the inclusion of country-specific effects.

Second, lagged independent variables were introduced to mitigate possible endogeneity concerns and to test the dynamic stability of the relationships. The lagged models yield results consistent in direction and magnitude with the baseline estimations, suggesting that causality runs predominantly from digitalization and eco-innovation toward CE rather than the reverse.

Third, the variance inflation factor (VIF) and correlation matrix confirm the absence of multicollinearity, while alternative subsample estimations—dividing the dataset into high-income and low-income African countries—reveal similar trends. The magnitude of the digitalization effect is slightly higher for high-income African economies, while eco-innovation exhibits stronger impacts in lower-income ones.

Collectively, these robustness checks reaffirm that the empirical findings are stable, statistically reliable, and theoretically consistent across different model specifications and country groupings. The robustness analysis therefore enhances confidence in the validity of the causal linkages identified between digitalization, eco-innovation, economic complexity, and CE performance in Africa (see Table 8).

Table 8. Robustness Checks Using Alternative Model Specifications.

Variables	Fixed Effects (FE)	Random Effects (RE)	Lagged Model (1-Year Lag)	High-Income Subsample	Low-Income Subsample
ln (Eco-innovation)	0.043 *** (0.011)	0.046 *** (0.010)	0.041 *** (0.012)	0.038 *** (0.011)	0.052 *** (0.013)
Economic complexity	0.102 ** (0.041)	0.096 ** (0.039)	0.089 ** (0.042)	0.115 *** (0.035)	0.083 ** (0.037)
Digitalization	0.425 *** (0.067)	0.437 *** (0.062)	0.412 *** (0.065)	0.486 *** (0.057)	0.393 *** (0.071)
Digitalization^2	0.058 (0.072)	0.044 (0.068)	0.039 (0.069)	0.061 (0.071)	0.037 (0.073)
Constant	−0.094 ** (0.043)	−0.085 ** (0.041)	−0.088 ** (0.042)	−0.073 * (0.039)	−0.102 ** (0.047)
R^2 (Within/Overall)	0.514	0.528	0.507	0.531	0.496
Number of Observations	1152	1152	1104	560	592
Hausman Test (χ^2)	6.72 (p = 0.34)	–	–	–	–
Wald χ^2/F-statistic	188.56 ***	201.37 ***	179.84 ***	146.09 ***	121.72 ***

Notes: Robust standard errors are shown in parentheses. ***, **, and * indicate significance at the 1%, 5%, and 10% levels, respectively.

The lagged model includes one-year lagged regressors for digitalization, eco-innovation, and economic complexity to address potential endogeneity. Subsample models divide the panel into high-income and low-income African economies (based on AfDB classification). All coefficients remain positive and statistically significant, confirming the robustness and stability of the main findings.

To provide an intuitive summary of the empirical findings, please create a conceptual flow diagram illustrating the core relationships. The diagram should position three primary drivers on the left—Eco-Innovation, Economic Complexity, and Digitalization—with arrows pointing from each towards a central circle labeled "Circular Economy (CE) Performance." The strength of each direct impact should be visually represented by the thickness of the arrows, reflecting a strong positive effect from Digitalization to CE, a moderate positive effect from Eco-Innovation to CE (noting it is stronger in low-performing economies), and a positive effect from Economic Complexity to CE (noting it is stronger in high-performing economies). Furthermore, significant bidirectional causality identified in the analysis should be depicted using double-headed arrows to form feedback loops between Digitalization and CE, as well as between Eco-Innovation and CE. Below the figure, include the note Figure 8:

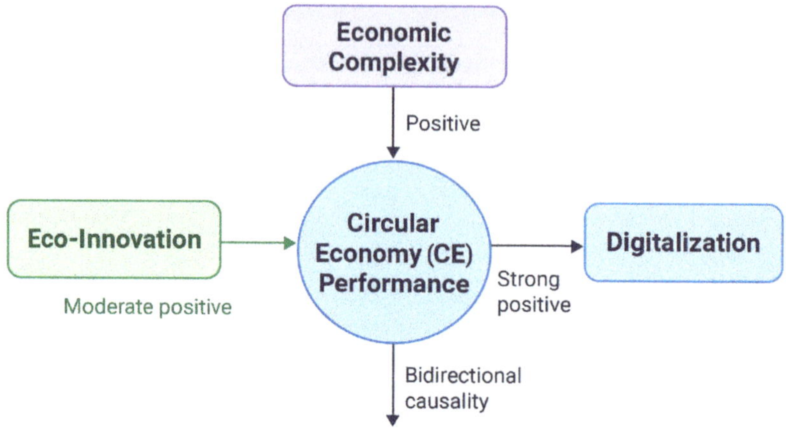

Note: Thickness of arrows indicates the magnitude of estimated effects across quantiles. Based on POLS, DKSE, and MMQR estimations.

Figure 8. Graphical Summary of Empirical Findings on CE Drivers in Africa (2000–2024).

This visual will effectively reinforce the study's empirical narrative.

5.5. Discussion

The findings demonstrate that digitalization, eco-innovation, and economic complexity significantly enhance Africa's circular economy (CE) performance, but with differing intensities. Digitalization emerged as the strongest and most consistent driver across quantiles, aligning with Sang and Anh (2025) and Barteková and Börkey (2022), who emphasize the transformative power of digital infrastructure in resource efficiency. Eco-innovation had a more pronounced impact in low-performing CE economies, suggesting that technological adoption in emerging African markets can yield high marginal gains (Le et al., 2023). Economic complexity showed stronger effects in high-performing economies, corroborating the findings of Hassan et al. (2023) that productive diversification reinforces sustainable industrial transformation.

These results highlight the importance of integrated policies combining digital transformation and industrial sophistication to accelerate Africa's CE transition. Policymakers should prioritize digital investment, innovation clusters, and technology transfer mechanisms to support green industrialization. Additionally, aligning these strategies with existing frameworks such as the African Union (AU)'s (2024) Green Recovery Plan and Agenda 2063 can promote long-term circular growth and resilience.

Future research may explore how institutional frameworks and green finance mechanisms mediate these relationships, offering further insights into regional disparities in CE adoption.

6. Conclusions

The continent Africa offers enormous potential for the circular economy (CE). The research explored the role of eco-innovation, economic complexity, and digitalization in CE development in African economies between 2000 and 2024, driven by the need to address issues of pollution, resource scarcity, and sustainable development. The study offered solid proof of the determinants' pivotal significance by employing POLS, DKSE, and MMQR estimates in addition to the Dumitrescu–Hurlin panel causality test. According to the findings, digitalization, economic complexity, and eco-innovation are all essential for the development of CE, with digitalization having the most impact, followed by eco-innovation and economic complexity.

Their impacts differ depending on the CE level of performance: digitalization has an equal impact on all CE levels, economic complexity has a bigger impact on comparatively more developed countries, and eco-innovation has a more noticeable impact on less CE-developed nations. Additionally, causality studies show that CE is independent of digitalization and eco-innovation, but that there is a one-way link between CE and economic complexity.

These results have important policy ramifications for the development of CE in Africa. Interventions at the regional and national levels are essential due to the continent's diversity in terms of institutional competency, economic arrangements, and developmental stages. First and foremost, because of the significant impact of digitalization, less developed countries must prioritize digital infrastructure and literacy, connection, and SMEs' empowerment, whereas more established economies may concentrate on incorporating cutting-edge digital tools into already-existing industrial platforms.

Second, the benefits of economic complexity highlight the necessity of human resources, industry diversity, and support for research and development. While less complex nations must develop their capacity for innovation and support value-added industries, more complex nations can benefit from cross-sectoral collaboration and knowledge spillovers. Third, there is a need to encourage eco-innovation through enabling technology transfer, green entrepreneurship, and public–private partnerships, particularly in countries at earlier stages of CE adoption, while higher-performing nations concentrate on emulating successful innovations and effective recycling systems.

The study suggests strengthening the policy architecture in light of other CE-related initiatives in Africa by obtaining funding agreements that are suitable for structural capabilities and CE readiness, building peer-learning and regional networking platforms, facilitating national CE roadmaps that are in line with each country's institutional setup and resource environment, and fostering innovation clusters that are in line with local industrial competencies.

Despite several shortcomings in the research. Three major CE drivers were covered, with space for future studies to examine other aspects including institutional quality, green financing, and regulatory frameworks. While ongoing study into consumer behavior, cultural factors, and the influence of multinational corporations may add depth to the dynamics of CE in Africa, industry-level research may offer sector-specific patterns in CE adoption. Examining how Africa's CE transition fits into the larger global movement toward sustainability may also be possible through comparison with other growing economies.

The inclusion of data through 2024 enables the study to capture Africa's most recent wave of digital and eco-innovation reforms, ensuring that the findings reflect ongoing transitions rather than historical patterns.

> "The results align strongly with the objectives of SDG 9 (Industry, Innovation, and Infrastructure), SDG 12 (Responsible Consumption and Production), and SDG 13 (Climate Action). Moreover, the study contributes to Agenda 2063's aspirations for environmentally sustainable and climate-resilient economies. By linking digital transformation with eco-innovation, the findings reinforce Africa's Agenda 2063 Goals 7 and 10 on sustainable resource management and technology-driven industrialization."

> "For low-income African nations, the emphasis should be on foundational digital infrastructure, capacity building, and affordable access to innovation financing. Strengthening cross-border partnerships, promoting open digital ecosystems,

and facilitating green technology transfer can accelerate inclusive CE growth. Such differentiated policies ensure that circularity benefits are not concentrated in high-income economies alone."

This study assumes that the selected indicators—eco-innovation, digitalization, and economic complexity—adequately capture Africa's circular transition. However, the analysis does not explicitly incorporate institutional quality or environmental regulation variables, which may also shape CE outcomes. Future research could therefore integrate institutional indicators, explore dynamic or spatial models to control for cross-border effects, and apply sector-specific analyses. These extensions would further strengthen understanding of how policy, technology, and economic structure interact to drive circular transformation in developing regions.

Funding: This work was supported and funded by the Deanship of Scientific Research at Imam Mohammad Ibn Saud Islamic University (IMSIU) (grant number IMSIU-DDRSP2504).

Data Availability Statement: The data used to support the findings of this study are available from the corresponding authors upon reasonable request.

Acknowledgments: The author extend their appreciation to the Deanship of Scientific Research, Imam Mohammad Ibn Saud Islamic University (IMSIU), Saudi Arabia, for their support of this study. The researcher also appreciates the considerable time and work of the reviewers and the editor to expedite the process. Their commitment and expertise were crucial in making this work a success. We appreciate your unwavering help.

Conflicts of Interest: The author declares no conflicts of interest.

References

African Circular Economy Alliance (ACEN). (2024). *Continental circular economy strategy 2024–2030*. ACEN Secretariat.

African Development Bank (AfDB). (2012). *Facilitating green growth in Africa: Perspectives from the African Development Bank*. African Development Bank Group.

African Development Bank (AfDB). (2023). *Green growth framework: Financing Africa's circular transition*. AfDB Publications.

African Development Bank (AfDB). (2024). *Title of report or dataset*. African Development Bank. Available online: https://www.afdb.org (accessed on 5 November 2025).

African Union (AU). (2024). *Green recovery action plan 2024–2030*. African Union Commission.

African Union Commission. (2025). *Continental digital transformation strategy 2025 update*. African Union Commission.

Aluko, O. A., Opoku, E. E. O., & Acheampong, A. O. (2022). Economic complexity and environmental degradation: Evidence from developing countries. *Ecological Economics*, *216*, 107000. [CrossRef]

Antikainen, R., Uusitalo, V., & Kivikytö-Reponen, P. (2018). Digitalisation and sustainable circular economy: Key lessons from Finnish case studies. *Journal of Cleaner Production*, *201*, 89–99. [CrossRef]

Aral, S., Gürsoy, M., & Kaya, O. (2024). Digital innovation adoption in African economies: Regional disparities and policy implications. *Information Systems Journal*, *34*(1), 23–40. [CrossRef]

Atlas of Economic Complexity by @HarvardGrwthLab. (2022). Available online: https://atlas.hks.harvard.edu/ (accessed on 5 November 2025).

Baltagi, B. H. (2021). *Econometric analysis of panel data* (6th ed.). Wiley.

Barteková, E., & Börkey, P. (2022). *Digitalisation and the circular economy: Opportunities and policy implications* (Vol. 191, pp. 1–38). OECD Environment Working Papers. OECD. [CrossRef]

Boleti, G., Garas, A., & Kyriakou, A. (2021). Economic complexity and environmental sustainability. *Structural Change and Economic Dynamics*, *56*, 76–88. [CrossRef]

Bucher, M., Dufour, M., & Wigger, M. (2023). Economic complexity and environmental outcomes in transition economies. *Sustainability*, *15*(7), 5900. [CrossRef]

Castro, J. P., Silva, C. F., & Rodrigues, L. M. (2022). Recycling innovation and rebound effects in the circular economy. *Journal of Cleaner Production*, *352*, 131603. [CrossRef]

Choudhury, T., Rahman, A., & Khan, S. (2023). Greenwashing and sustainability reporting in emerging economies. *Business Strategy and the Environment*, *32*(5), 2257–2274. [CrossRef]

De Jesus, A., & Mendonça, S. (2018). Lost in transition? Drivers and barriers in the eco-innovation road to the circular economy. *Ecological Economics*, *145*, 75–89. [CrossRef]

Díaz-Arancibia, J., Hochstetter-Diez, J., Bustamante-Mora, A., Sepúlveda-Cuevas, S., Albayay, I., & Arango-López, J. (2024). Navigating digital transformation and technology adoption: A literature review from small and medium-sized enterprises in developing countries. *Sustainability*, *16*(14), 5946. [CrossRef]

Ellen MacArthur Foundation. (2013). Available online: https://foodtank.com/news/2020/03/celebrating-the-informal-food-trade-in-durban-south-africa/ (accessed on 5 November 2025).

European Commission. (2019). *Report from the commission to the European parliament, the council, the European economic and social committee and the committee of the regions on the implementation of the circular economy action plan*. Publications Office of the European Union.

European Commission. (2020). *A new circular economy action plan: For a cleaner and more competitive Europe*. Publications Office of the European Union.

Fasi, M. (2024). Energy consumption implications of digitalization in Africa: Challenges for sustainable development. *Renewable and Sustainable Energy Reviews*, *189*, 113907. [CrossRef]

Figge, F., & Thorpe, A. (2019). The rebound effect in sustainability transitions. *Ecological Economics*, *161*, 1–8. [CrossRef]

García-Castillo, J., López, R., & Medina, C. (2024). Digital divide and circular economy in African countries. *Technological Forecasting and Social Change*, *198*, 122478. [CrossRef]

Graham, B. S., Hahn, J., Poirier, A., & Powell, J. L. (2016). *Quantile regression and heterogeneity in panel data* [Working Paper 21034]. Available online: http://www.nber.org/papers/w21034 (accessed on 5 November 2025).

Ha, Y. (2023). Economic complexity as a driver of environmental innovation. *Journal of Cleaner Production*, *412*, 136827. [CrossRef]

Hassan, S., Khan, A., & Ali, M. (2023). Economic complexity and environmental sustainability in African economies. *Ecological Indicators*, *148*, 109912. [CrossRef]

Hinojosa, J. (2022). Corporate strategies for overcoming circular economy challenges. *Business Strategy and the Environment*, *31*(6), 2509–2521. [CrossRef]

Hlali, A., & Gafsi, N. (2024). Analysis of Digitalization and Sustainable Development in Africa. *Perspectives on Global Development and Technology*, *22*(5-6), 415–428. [CrossRef]

Kirikkaleli, D., Adebayo, T. S., & Khan, S. (2023). Green technology, economic complexity, and environmental quality: Evidence from emerging economies. *Renewable Energy*, *209*, 713–722. [CrossRef]

Lapatinas, A., Kyriakou, A., & Garas, A. (2021). Economic complexity and environmental behavior: Evidence from cross-country analysis. *Environmental Research Letters*, *16*(5), 054012. [CrossRef]

Le, T., Vo, D., & Nguyen, T. (2023). Eco-innovation, cleaner production, and resilience in circular economy transitions. *Journal of Cleaner Production*, *400*, 136731. [CrossRef]

Lee, S., & Olasehinde-Williams, G. (2024). Economic complexity and environmental sustainability in OECD countries. *Ecological Economics*, *215*, 107011.

Liu, Q., Wang, H., & Zhou, X. (2022). Digital technologies and circular manufacturing. *Technological Forecasting and Social Change*, *180*, 121676. [CrossRef]

Liu, Y., Zhang, X., & Chen, L. (2023). Technological innovation, corporate social responsibility, and eco-innovation in manufacturing firms. *Journal of Cleaner Production*, *389*, 135976. [CrossRef]

Ma, R., Jin, X., & Zhou, T. (2022). Resource efficiency and economic complexity: A global panel study. *Resources Policy*, *78*, 102905. [CrossRef]

Machado, J. A. F., & Santos Silva, J. M. C. (2019). Quantiles via moments. *Journal of Econometrics*, *213*(1), 145–173. [CrossRef]

Maldonado-Guzmán, G., Garza-Reyes, J. A., & Pinzón-Castro, Y. (2020). Eco-innovation and the circular economy in the automotive industry. *Benchmarking: An International Journal*, *27*(2), 621–635. [CrossRef]

Montiel-Hernández, M. G., Pérez-Hernández, C. C., & Salazar-Hernández, B. C. (2024). The intrinsic links of economic complexity with sustainability dimensions: A systematic review and agenda for future research. *Sustainability*, *16*(1), 391. [CrossRef]

Mügge, J., Seegrün, A., Hoyer, T.-K., Riedelsheimer, T., & Lindow, K. (2024). Digital twins within the circular economy: Literature review and concept presentation. *Sustainability*, *16*(7), 2748. [CrossRef]

Neves, S. A., Marques, A. C., & Silva, I. P. (2024). Promoting the circular economy in the EU: How can the recycling of e-waste be increased? *Structural Change and Economic Dynamics*, *70(C)*, 192–201. Available online: https://ideas.repec.org/a/eee/streco/v70y2024icp192-201.html (accessed on 5 November 2025). [CrossRef]

OECD. (2024). *Green transition in emerging Africa: Policy insights for circular growth*. OECD Publishing.

Pesaran, M. H. (2004). *General diagnostic tests for cross section dependence in panels*. CESifo Working Paper No. 1229. CESifo. [CrossRef]

Peyravi, B., & Jakubavičius, A. (2022). Drivers in the eco-innovation road to the circular economy: Organizational capabilities and exploitative strategies. *Sustainability*, *14*(17), 10748. [CrossRef]

Peyravi, M., Marzaleh, M. A., & Hatami, M. (2024). Investigating the barriers to air medical services in accidents and disasters in Iran and suggesting solutions: A qualitative study. *BMC Research Notes*, *17*, 365. [CrossRef] [PubMed]

Pichlak, M., & Szromek, A. R. (2022). Linking eco-innovation and circular economy—A conceptual approach. *Journal of Open Innovation: Technology, Market, and Complexity*, *8*(3), 121. [CrossRef]

Priyadarshini, J., Singh, R. K., Mishra, R., He, Q., & Braganza, A. (2024). *Implementation of additive manufacturing in the healthcare supply chain for circular economy goals: Paradoxical tensions and solutions from an Industry 5.0 perspective*. Information Systems Frontiers. [CrossRef]

Raasens, J., & van Leeuwen, E. (2024). The evolving concept of circularity: From a circular economy to a circular society in 60 years. In S. Bourdin, A. Torre, & E. van Leeuwen (Eds.), *Regions, cities and the circular economy: Theory and practice* (pp. 44–60). Edward Elgar Publishing. [CrossRef]

Sang, T. M., & Anh, N. Q. (2025). Adopting digital technology for sustainable performance: Circular economy practice in the transportation sector. *Discover Sustainability*, *6*, 166. [CrossRef]

Schumpeter, J. A. (1950). *Capitalism, socialism, and democracy*. Harper & Row.

Thakker, V., & Bakshi, B. R. (2023). Ranking eco-innovations to enable a sustainable circular economy with Net-Zero emissions. *ACS Sustainable Chemistry & Engineering*, *11*(4), 1363–1374. [CrossRef]

United Nations Development Programme (UNDP). (2024). *2024 UNDP trends report: The landscape of development*. UNDP.

United Nations Economic Commission for Africa (UNECA). (2024). *Africa green industrialization initiative: Pathways to circular transformation*. UNECA Publications.

United Nations Environment Programme. (2023). *Africa waste management outlook*. UNEP. Available online: https://www.greenpolicyplatfc (accessed on 5 November 2025).

United Nations Environment Programme. (2024). *Annual report 2024*. UNEP. Available online: https://www.unep.org/resources/annual-report-2024 (accessed on 5 November 2025).

Usman, M., Simionescu, M., Radulescu, M., & Balsalobre-Lorente, D. (2024). Breaking barriers, cultivating sustainability: Discovering the trifecta influence of digitalization, natural resources, and globalization on eco-innovations across 27 European nations. *Resources Policy*, *94*, 105109. [CrossRef]

World Bank. (2024). *World development indicators*. Available online: https://databank.worldbank.org/source/world-development-indicators (accessed on 5 November 2025).

World Development Indicators. (2024). *DataBank*. Available online: https://databank.worldbank.org/id/c4511412 (accessed on 5 November 2025).

Yoguel, G., Barletta, F., & Pereira, M. (2013). De Schumpeter aos post-schumpeterianos: Velhas e novas dimensões analíticas. *Problemas del Desarrollo*, *44*(174), 35–59.

Zerbino, P. (2022). The circular economy rebound: The third wheel on the date between circularity and sustainability. *Journal of Circular Economy*, *1*(1). [CrossRef] data

MDPI

Article

Operator Learning with Branch–Trunk Factorization for Macroscopic Short-Term Speed Forecasting

Bin Yu [1], Yong Chen [1], Dawei Luo [2] and Joonsoo Bae [3,*]

[1] School of Economics and Management, Changzhou Vocational Institute of Mechatronic Technology, Changzhou 213164, China; 1920@czimt.edu.cn (B.Y.)
[2] School of Digital Economy, Changzhou College of Information Technology, Changzhou 213164, China; luodawei@czcit.edu.cn
[3] Department of Industry & Information Systems Engineering, Jeonbuk National University, 567, Baekje-daero, Deokjin-gu, Jeonju 54896, Republic of Korea
* Correspondence: jsbae@jbnu.ac.kr; Tel.: +82-63-270-2332

Abstract

Logistics operations demand real-time visibility and rapid response, yet minute-level traffic speed forecasting remains challenging due to heterogeneous data sources and frequent distribution shifts. This paper proposes a Deep Operator Network (DeepONet)-based framework that treats traffic prediction as learning a mapping from historical states and boundary conditions to future speed states, enabling robust forecasting under changing scenarios. We project logistics demand onto a road network to generate diverse congestion scenarios and employ a branch–trunk architecture to decouple historical dynamics from exogenous contexts. Experiments on both a controlled simulation dataset and the real-world Metropolitan Los Angeles (METR-LA) benchmark demonstrate that the proposed method outperforms classical regression and deep learning baselines in cross-scenario generalization. Specifically, the operator learning approach effectively adapts to unseen boundary conditions without retraining, establishing a promising direction for resilient and adaptive logistics forecasting.

Keywords: logistics forecasting; operator learning; spatiotemporal modeling

1. Introduction

Short-term speed prediction,which involves forecasting vehicle or traffic speeds over brief future intervals, is a cornerstone technology for modern Intelligent Transportation Systems (ITS) and the advancement of autonomous vehicles [1]. With the emergence of new formats such as front warehouses, community retail, local warehouses, and hourly delivery, the integration between logistics and the national economy has deepened, significantly increasing the demand of supply chains for real-time visibility and rapid responsiveness. Smart logistics, supported by information technology, control techniques, optimization methods, and artificial intelligence, aims to reduce costs and increase efficiency across the entire supply chain through order allocation, vehicle management, route planning, and signal optimization [2]. To maintain stable operations and quickly recover from disruptions, road networks require predictability. Traffic forecasting [3], a core capability, encompasses key quantities such as traffic states, road speeds, and travel times. Accurate prediction of states and speeds provides the foundation for platoon control, route guidance, and signal optimization. Travel time prediction serves as an early indicator for scheduling and coordination. In digital-twin-driven online simulations, forecasting further supports rolling evaluation and scenario selection.

For safe and resilient operations, speed prediction also enables risk identification and early warning, allowing interventions in high-risk spatiotemporal segments to reduce accidents and delays, ultimately improving punctuality and network reliability.

However, short-term road speed forecasting at the minute level faces multiple challenges in real-world environments. The first challenge lies in the heterogeneity and noise at the data level. Vehicle operation data coexist with multi-source sensor data, where missing values, measurement errors, and irregular sampling are common. The spatial coverage of the sensing network is uneven—dense in central urban areas but sparse in suburban regions, resulting in coverage gaps and biased measurements. The second challenge is the complexity of spatiotemporal coupling. Traffic data simultaneously contain static structures and dynamic evolution, with prominent cross-scale dependencies and nonlinear interactions. Deep learning has advanced spatiotemporal prediction by learning expressive, data-driven representations. Recent graph and sequence models capture spatial diffusion and temporal dependencies, improving traffic flow and speed forecasting [4]. The third challenge is nonstationarity and distribution shift. Conventional neural prediction models map vectors to vectors and typically require retraining or extensive fine-tuning when exogenous or boundary conditions change. Demand fluctuations, incidents, weather conditions, as well as modification to road networks and timetables occur frequently. These changes make models trained under previous conditions prone to mismatches in new scenarios, and the costs of maintenance and retraining remain high. Consequently, there is a need for modeling paradigms that can explicitly incorporate boundary changes at the input level while maintaining stable accuracy and reducing maintenance costs when scenarios change.

To address these challenges, this study proposes a short-term road speed forecasting framework that directly integrates logistics data with traffic prediction. To the best of our knowledge, no prior research has systematically mapped supply chain information—such as warehouse and customer locations or dynamic demand volumes—into traffic speed prediction while simultaneously applying Deep Operator Network (DeepONet) learning [5] to achieve cross-scenario transferability. We conduct an initial exploration in this direction by projecting logistics demand and warehouse allocation onto the road network, creating learnable boundary conditions, and then applying an operator-learning approach to map historical sequences and contextual information to next-step speed predictions. This provides a novel perspective for bridging supply chain systems and traffic systems. At the data level, we develop a unified data and evaluation pipeline that performs alignment, validity checks, anomaly removal, and feature standardization. We then split the data into training, validation, and test sets according to different scenarios, enabling us to evaluate the models' robustness under diverse boundary combinations. At the modeling level, we adopt a branch–trunk architecture. The branch network encodes historical speed sequences of each link to capture short-term dynamics. The trunk network encodes contemporaneous exogenous and boundary states such as inflow, outflow, density, occupancy, waiting time, and travel time that represent congestion intensity and downstream constraints. Multiplicative coupling of the two networks creates a mapping from functions to functions, allowing boundary changes to enter the inference process through input variation. This approach maintains accuracy while reducing the need for retraining when scenarios change.

We constructed six Simulation of Urban MObility (SUMO) scenarios, labeled S001–S006, based on a five-kilometer urban subnetwork, using a time step of 60 s to generate link-level data. These scenarios are driven by the Solomon dataset and differ in random seeds, total trip volumes, and order–warehouse allocation strategies. These variations produce distinct Origin–Destination (OD) combinations, which characterize the paired relationships between origins and destinations, their intensities, and their temporal distributions. These scenarios also include order quantities, vehicle counts or trip numbers, departure times, and service time windows for each OD pair. Different OD combinations determine the spatial and temporal distributions of inflows and outflows across the road network, which in turn shape congestion patterns and boundary conditions, leading to varying levels of prediction difficulty and transfer challenges. For all scenarios, we extract speed, inflow, outflow, density, occupancy, waiting time, and travel time. Inputs are constructed from twelve-step historical speeds together with six contemporaneous contextual features, while the next-step speed serves as the supervisory signal. After validity checks and anomaly filtering, approximately 1.19 million edge–time samples remain. To evaluate cross-scenario transfer, we use S001–S004 for training and validation and reserve S005–S006 as unseen test sets. Within the visible scenarios, we apply an 80/20 temporal split to ensure leakage-free evaluation that encompasses a variety of boundary conditions. To quantify the benefits of the proposed approach in modeling nonlinearities and history–context interactions, we systematically compare it with Ridge regression, Multilayer Perceptrons (MLP), Long Short-Term Memory (LSTM) networks, Temporal Convolutional Networks (TCNs), Transformers, and Graph Neural Networks (GNNs). We further conduct ablation studies to verify the necessity of trunk-side exogenous variables and perform counterfactual perturbations of these variables to illustrate the model's sensitivity and robustness to congestion transitions. Results demonstrate that the proposed design mitigates feature bias caused by heterogeneous and noisy data, improves adaptability to distribution shifts, and enhances the representation of complex spatiotemporal interactions. Challenges such as missing-data handling, explicit spatial coupling, and uncertainty quantification are discussed in the limitations and reserved for future research.

The contributions of this paper are summarized as follows:

- This study constructs a unified logistics–traffic dataset by integrating Solomon demand data with SUMO-generated link-level states, producing approximately 1.2 million edge–time samples across six distinct scenarios. This dataset provides a reproducible foundation for cross-scene forecasting research.
- We propose a DeepONet-based framework that decouples historical speeds, processed through a branch network, from contemporaneous exogenous and boundary states, processed through a trunk network. This approach enables boundary changes to be incorporated as functional inputs, eliminating the need for frequent retraining.
- This paper systematically compares the strengths and weaknesses of the proposed method against classic and state-of-the-art models across three distinct datasets. While the results indicate that DeepONet does not outperform every baseline in every aspect, the comprehensive evaluation demonstrates that it achieves the optimal overall performance, particularly in terms of generalization and robustness. These comparative insights provide a valuable reference for future research in selecting appropriate modeling paradigms for complex traffic scenarios.

The remainder of the paper is organized as follows: Section 2 reviews related work in logistics forecasting, traffic prediction, and operator learning. Section 3 introduces the background and formal problem statement. Section 4 describes the data design, feature construction, and the DeepONet architecture along with training protocols. Section 5 presents the experimental results, diagnostics, and ablation studies, followed by a discussion on deployment implications. Section 6 concludes the paper and outlines limitations and future directions.

2. Related Work

Short-term speed prediction is not a monolithic concept. Its definition, particularly the duration of the prediction horizon, is highly dependent on the application context.

The field is broadly divided into two categories: macroscopic traffic flow forecasting and microscopic vehicle dynamics prediction. In this work, we focus on the former, which aims to predict aggregated traffic speed, typically the average speed of all vehicles on a specific road segment, over short horizons at the link or corridor level. This task is essential for traffic management, signal control, and route guidance. The prediction horizon in this context generally spans minutes, often ranging from 1 to 30 min [6]. In this work, the time interval for prediction is set to 1 min. The latter category focuses on individual vehicle trajectories and maneuvers over very short horizons and is crucial for autonomous driving and collision avoidance. The prediction horizons in this context are up to 10 s [7].

2.1. Application of Deep Learning Method in Macroscopic Short-Term Speed Forecasting

Classical macroscopic speed forecasting methods include statistical models such as AutoRegressive Integrated Moving Average (ARIMA) [8] and Kalman filters [9], which are effective for stationary regimes but limited in handling nonlinearity and dynamic boundaries. Simulation platforms like AnyLogic(V8), FlexSim(V2024), and SUMO(V1.24.0) [10] are widely used for prototyping and assessing operations; however they depend heavily on calibration quality and face scalability challenges [11]. With the proliferation of ubiquitous sensing and digital infrastructure, deep learning has become a central paradigm for spatiotemporal prediction. Recent surveys highlight the rapid evolution of deep learning for traffic forecasting, emphasizing the shift from simple time-series models to complex graph-based and physics-informed architectures [12]. With the rapid development of deep learning, various neural network architectures have been proposed for traffic prediction tasks. Besides MLP, Convolutional Neural Networks (CNNs), and sequence models such as LSTM and TCN [13] are widely applied in time-series prediction tasks. More recently, approaches combining graph neural networks with differential equations [14] and attention mechanisms [15] have shown promise in capturing complex spatiotemporal dynamics. Advanced architectures like Dynamic Spatial Transformers [4], Gated Attention Graph Networks [16], and Diffusion-Enhanced Transformer Neural Operators [17] further push the boundaries of prediction accuracy by integrating low-rank tensor compression, multi-scale attention, and generative diffusion processes. Despite accuracy gains, many architectures remain brittle under distribution shift and require costly re–training when exogenous or boundary conditions like inflow or occupancy change.

A persistent challenge in macroscopic speed forecasting is ensuring transferability across different scenes. Distribution shifts, sparse sampling, and sensor noise degrade model performance outside the training domain [18]. In traffic forecasting, models trained in one city or corridor often underperform when applied to another without adaptation [19]. Domain adaptation techniques and adversarial alignment provide partial solutions but frequently require substantial retraining and engineering effort. Similar concerns arise in supply chain forecasting [20]. Furthermore, the opacity of deep models complicates deployment in safety-critical logistics operations where auditability is required. These limitations motivate frameworks that can natively accommodate boundary variability and enable transparent analysis. Operator learning [21], which maps functions to functions, offers a promising avenue to address these challenges.

2.2. Operator Learning in Scientific Machine Learning

Operator learning is supported by the Universal Approximation Theorem for operators [21]. A recurring theme is improved generalization under parametric and boundary changes, a property directly relevant to logistics, where exogenous conditions frequently evolve. Operator learning emerged in scientific machine learning to directly approximate mappings between function spaces when classical vector-to-vector learning is inadequate for tasks such as partial differential equation (PDE) solution operators, fractional operators, or control-to-state maps [22]. Recent advances include U-shaped neural operators [23] and physics-informed extensions [24], which further enhance the capability to solve complex PDE-governed systems. Its mathematical foundation extends universal approximation results from finite-dimensional functions to operators on compact subsets of Banach spaces [25]. If an operator is continuous on a compact set of admissible inputs, then a suitably parameterized neural operator can approximate it uniformly on that set. This perspective justifies learning function-to-function maps rather than compressing all information into fixed-size vectors.

Physics-informed deep learning has also been applied to traffic state estimation, integrating conservation laws with data-driven models [26]. These methods leverage the underlying physics of traffic flow to improve generalization and data efficiency, aligning well with the operator learning perspective adopted in this work. Recent studies have explicitly benchmarked neural operators for traffic state estimation [5] and explored their use in boundary stabilization control [27], validating their potential for both prediction and management. Furthermore, the integration of traffic prediction uncertainty into logistics operations, such as parking reservation, has been highlighted as a critical direction for practical deployment [28].

We consider an operator

$$\begin{aligned} \mathcal{G}:\ & V \subset C(K_1) \longrightarrow C(K_2), \\ & u \longmapsto (\mathcal{G}(u))(y), \quad y \in K_2, \end{aligned} \tag{1}$$

where u may encode source terms, initial and boundary conditions, or control signals. The variable y denotes an evaluation location, which may include spatial coordinates, time, or other query parameters. Training data are triples $\left(u^{(i)}, y^{(i)}, \mathcal{G}(u^{(i)})(y^{(i)})\right)$. To obtain a finite representation of the infinite-dimensional input u, choose sensor points $\{x_j\}_{j=1}^{m} \subset K_1$ and form

$$\mathbf{u} = \left[u(x_1), u(x_2), \ldots, u(x_m)\right]^{\top} \in \mathbb{R}^m. \tag{2}$$

Operator learning parameterizes $\mathcal{G}$ with two subnetworks and a bilinear fusion. The branch network $g : \mathbb{R}^m \to \mathbb{R}^p$ encodes the input-function samples $\mathbf{u}$, and the trunk network $f : K_2 \to \mathbb{R}^p$ encodes the query y. The prediction is

$$\widehat{\mathcal{G}}(u)(y) = \langle g(\mathbf{u}), f(y) \rangle + b_0 = \sum_{k=1}^{p} g_k(\mathbf{u})\, f_k(y) + b_0, \tag{3}$$

where p is the embedding dimension, which is interpretable as the rank of a low-rank expansion. Here, g_k and f_k are the k-th components of the branch and trunk embeddings respectively, and b_0 is an optional bias. This formulation realizes the operator mapping by conditioning on u through the branch embedding and evaluating at an arbitrary y through the trunk embedding, without requiring explicit convolutions or kernels. Consequently, it accommodates irregular geometries and unaligned samples. Additional context c, such as material or scenario parameters, can be concatenated to the branch input, $g([\mathbf{u}; c])$, or to the trunk input, $f([y; c])$.

2.3. Physical Interpretation of the Architecture

In the context of traffic forecasting, the branch and trunk networks play distinct physical roles. The branch network processes the historical speed sequence $\mathbf{s}_{t-L+1:t}(e)$, which represents the system inertia or the short-term momentum of traffic flow. This captures the intrinsic dynamics of the vehicles currently on the road. The trunk network processes the contemporaneous context $\mathbf{u}_t(e)$. Specifically, variables such as density and occupancy quantify the local congestion intensity, while flow variables (entered, left) represent the boundary constraints and mass exchange with the network. This context represents the boundary conditions and external constraints acting on the flow. The inner product $\langle g(\cdot), f(\cdot)\rangle$ then models the coupling between the system's inertial state and the external environment. This factorization allows the model to learn how different boundary conditions (trunk) modulate the evolution of traffic dynamics (branch), thereby enabling generalization to new scenarios where the boundary conditions change but the underlying physics of flow remains consistent [21].

The standard training objective of the operator is empirical risk minimization with mean-squared error:

$$\mathcal{L}(\theta) = \frac{1}{N}\sum_{i=1}^{N}\left(\widehat{\mathcal{G}}_\theta(u^{(i)})(y^{(i)}) - \mathcal{G}(u^{(i)})(y^{(i)})\right)^2, \tag{4}$$

where θ collects the parameters of g and f. When physics constraints are available, one may add a residual term in strong or weak form, for example

$$\mathcal{L}_{\text{total}} = \mathcal{L}_{\text{data}} + \lambda_{\text{phys}}\frac{1}{M}\sum_{r=1}^{M}\left|\mathcal{N}_y[\widehat{\mathcal{G}}_\theta(u^{(i)})(y_r)] - q(y_r)\right|^2. \tag{5}$$

where $\mathcal{N}_y[\cdot] = q$ encodes the governing operator in y and source q. This couples operator learning with physics-informed regularization.

After training, inference proceeds in two steps. Given a new input function u^*, evaluate it on the same sensors to obtain $\mathbf{u}^*$ and compute the branch embedding $g(\mathbf{u}^*) \in \mathbb{R}^p$. For any collection of query locations y, compute $f(y) \in \mathbb{R}^p$ and take the inner product:

$$\widehat{\mathcal{G}}(u^*)(y) = \langle g(\mathbf{u}^*), f(y)\rangle + b_0. \tag{6}$$

Changing u^* only recomputes the branch output; changing y only recomputes the trunk output, enabling cross-condition generalization and arbitrary-point evaluation. The trunk naturally accepts spatiotemporal queries by setting $y = (x, t)$. For multi-output targets, one may append a small linear head from the scalar output to multiple channels, or use separate embeddings per channel.

Practical choices include the sensor count m in Equation (2) where more sensors capture finer details of u but increase cost, the embedding rank p in Equation (3) controlls expressive power, standardization or nondimensionalization of inputs, and lightweight MLP or residual blocks for both branch and trunk. Operator learning has demonstrated strong results across several domains: surrogate modeling for fluid and transport PDEs, fractional and integral operators, stochastic dynamics and filtering, control-to-state and model-predictive-control maps, and multi-physics responses. These successes highlight advantages in cross-condition generalization, handling irregular data, and enabling fast, arbitrary-point evaluations after offline training—properties that are directly useful for real-time macroscopic speed forecasting and decision support.

2.4. Comparison with Classical, Geometric, and Operator Learning

While classical and temporal deep learning models such as Ridge regression, MLP, and LSTM networks effectively capture temporal correlations in stationary time-series, they fundamentally map fixed-size vectors to vectors. This limitation means they lack the mechanism to explicitly handle changing boundary conditions without retraining, often leading to poor generalization under distribution shifts. While GNNs [29] explicitly model spatial dependencies via a fixed adjacency matrix, they often struggle when the network topology changes or when defining the graph structure is ambiguous. In contrast, DeepONet learns a continuous operator that maps functional inputs to outputs, making it naturally mesh-independent and adaptable to varying boundary conditions without retraining. Compared to Fourier Neural Operators (FNOs) [30], which are highly efficient on uniform grids using Fast Fourier Transforms (FFTs), DeepONet offers greater flexibility for irregular geometries and heterogeneous sensor placements common in traffic networks. Our branch–trunk factorization specifically targets the separation of temporal dynamics from exogenous context, a structure that aligns well with the logistics-traffic coupling problem.

This work addresses link-level speed prediction at 60 s resolution to support traffic control and routing. We construct a framework that projects benchmark demand onto a 5 km urban subnetwork and generates microscopic traffic states, producing controlled yet realistic boundary variability for cross-scene transfer. We develop a branch–trunk factorization that disentangles short-history signals from exogenous and boundary context and demonstrate zero-retraining transfer on held-out scenes. We further provide diagnostic and counterfactual analyses that link accuracy gains to regime-consistent behavior and operational interpretability. To our knowledge, the combination of Solomon-driven demand, SUMO-based microscopic states, and operator learning for link-speed forecasting has not been previously reported.

3. Background and Problem Formulation

Motivation and Data Infrastructure for Macroscopic Short-Term Speed Forecasting

Short-horizon, link-level speed forecasts are both urgently needed and practically attainable. Public agencies seek to lower system-wide logistics costs via congestion mitigation and network reliability, while enterprises aim to reduce operating costs through improved transport scheduling, warehouse tasking, and production planning. These objectives are enabled by high-frequency data streams from loop detectors, video counters, Global Positioning System (GPS) trajectories, and connected vehicles, together with platform-level integration of demand, inventory, production, and shipment records. This big data infrastructure aligns public–private needs and supplies the covariates required for minute-scale forecasting in ITS, supporting proactive signal control, dynamic speed limits, incident detection, reliable travel-time estimation, and predictive routing for freight [12]. At present, however, production datasets with the necessary spatial coverage, temporal resolution, and metadata are often inaccessible due to privacy and governance constraints, heterogeneous sensing deployments, missingness, and the difficulty of aligning exogenous and boundary conditions at scale. In this context, controlled data generation remains a practical and rigorous path. It enables reproducible experiments, systematic ablations, and conterfactual stress tests under well-specified distribution shifts. Looking ahead, continued advances in sensing, communications, and digital integration make it increasingly likely that such real-world data will be collected and shared in near real time. Our study therefore develops and evaluates methods in advance of this capability, while using synthesized scenarios to ensure coverage, control and reproducibility.

We consider a 5 km urban subnetwork, defined as a contiguous district whose total centerline roadway length is approximately 5 km and that contains multiple signalized intersections and boundary inflow and outflow links. The choice of a 5 km scale is deliberate. It matches the control horizon of corridor- and district-level operations, such as coordinated signal control and variable speed advisories, where minute-resolution predictions are most actionable. Moreover, it is small enough to support reproducible, microscopic simulations with rich heterogeneity at manageable computational cost. It provides several boundary links so that exogenous inflow and outflow can vary across scenarios, which is essential for evaluating cross-scene transfer. Demand and customer attributes are taken from the Solomon benchmark and spatially assigned to network nodes, while traffic states are generated with the SUMO microscopic simulator under multiple scenarios [31]. In this research, signals are aggregated at interval $\Delta = 60\,\mathrm{s}$. Training, validation and test splits are performed by scenario to support cross-scene evaluation and to reflect distribution shift considerations [32].

Given a directed road network with edge set $\mathcal{E}$, SUMO outputs per-interval measurements for each edge $e \in \mathcal{E}$, including mean speed $v_t(e)$, density, occupancy, counts of vehicles entering and leaving, average waiting time, and travel time [31]. These indicators summarize instantaneous traffic state and congestion intensity on each link. For each edge e and interval t, the goal is to predict the next-interval mean speed $y_{t+1}(e) = v_{t+1}(e)$ from a leakage-safe feature vector that combines short speed histories with contemporaneous exogenous variables:

Architectural details, training protocols, and ablations are provided in Sections 4 and 5.

4. Methodology

As illustrated in Figure 1, our methodology follows a three-stage pipeline: (i) data and scenario construction where Solomon demand instances are projected and simulated on a 5 km SUMO subnetwork to produce link-level edge states; (ii) feature engineering and dataset assembly that aligns, filters, and standardizes twelve-step speed histories together with contemporaneous exogenous and boundary covariates; and (iii) model learning and diagnostics using a branch–trunk Deep Operator Network that decouples short-term histories from contextual boundary inputs, followed by systematic cross-scene evaluation, ablations, and counterfactual perturbations.

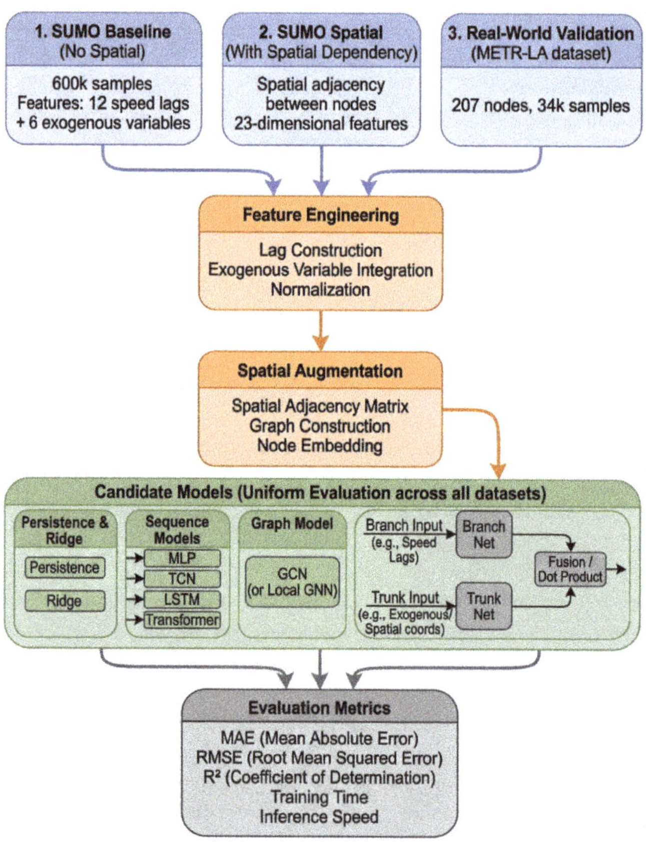

Figure 1. Project workflow: from Solomon demand mapping and SUMO simulation, through feature construction and operator-style branch–trunk modeling, to cross-scene evaluation and diagnostics.

4.1. Solomon Dataset as the Demand Prior

We ground the demand layer in the classical Solomon vehicle routing problem with time windows benchmarks [33]. The suite contains 56 instances with 100 customers, organized into six classes—C1, C2, R1, R2, RC1, RC2—where C/R/RC denote clustered, random, and mixed spatial layouts, and the "1" vs. "2" suffix reflects tighter vs. looser time windows, often implying a shorter vs. longer planning horizon. Each instance places 100 customers on a 100×100 grid and follows a common schema: node index i, coordinates (x_i, y_i), demand q_i, ready time e_i, due date l_i, and service duration d_i; the depot is node 0. File headers specify the fleet-size limit K and vehicle capacity Q. These fields map directly to our SUMO pipeline: coordinates are projected to the network coordinate reference system and snapped to the nearest nodes and edges; depot identifiers anchor origins; time windows drive release and service scheduling to produce temporally consistent OD flows; and demands determine vehicle loading and trip counts. We use Solomon because its controlled spatial patterns and time-window tightness create diverse routing pressures and post-assignment congestion, which is essential for stress-testing forecasting models under heterogeneous boundary conditions.

4.2. Simulation Environment and Dataset Construction

We consider an urban subnetwork of approximately 5 km imported into SUMO, and instantiate six scenarios S001–S006 that vary random seeds and trip loads to diversify demand [10]. Beyond the static network, each scenario is parameterized by logistics demand and supply. Customer requests and depot locations shape OD patterns and temporal loading, which in turn drive the edge states observed during simulation. We ingest (i) customer planar coordinates (x, y) which are projected to the network coordinate reference system, (ii) demand quantity with units or weight, (iii) requested service time windows $[\underline{t}, \overline{t}]$, and (iv) depot or warehouse identifiers and coordinates. Orders are snapped to nearest edges and nodes and grouped into time buckets to form OD flows or discrete trips consistent with their time windows and depot assignments.

Given the OD specification, SUMO produces vehicle- and edge-level traces: (i) per-vehicle routes and traversed edge sequences, and, if needed, per-time step positions; (ii) per-interval edge aggregates, including speed, entered and left, density, occupancy, waitingtime, traveltime; and (iii) per-vehicle summaries. These outputs connect the logistics side, including who, when, from which depot to which customer, and with how much load to the traffic side, including which edges are used, with speeds and queues. This integration enables supervised learning on edge dynamics under realistic boundary conditions. Table 1 summarizes the data sources and their roles in linking logistics demand with traffic states.

From each edge data, we extract per-edge, per-interval measurements including speed, entered, left, density, occupancy, waiting time, and travel time. To rigorously evaluate the contribution of spatial information, we construct two distinct feature sets:

1. Baseline Dataset without Spatial Features:This configuration focuses on temporal dynamics and local boundary conditions. The input vector $\mathbf{x}_t(e)$ concatenates 12 speed lags (`lag1` ... `lag12`) and 6 contemporaneous covariates (density, occupancy, etc.) of the target edge itself, yielding an 18-dimensional input vector. This serves as the primary dataset for benchmarking temporal sequence models.
2. Spatial Dataset with Spatial Features: To capture network-level dependencies, we augment the baseline features with upstream and downstream context. For each target edge, we identify its immediate predecessor and successor links and append their mean speed and density to the input vector. This increases the input dimensionality to 23, allowing models to explicitly learn from spatial propagation effects.

Table 1. Data sources and logistics–traffic linkage.

Layer	Fields	Usage
Demand (orders)	`cust_id`, (x, y), `qty`, $[t_{\min}, t_{\max}]$, `depot_id`	Build OD flows/trips; snap to network; time-bucket by request; define boundary/context for scenes
Supply (depots)	depot coordinates; capacity (if available)	Define sources/sinks; origin assignment for orders
Routes (veh)	`vehroutes.xml`: edge sequences	Path reconstruction; edge utilization; optional node traversal via topology
Edge aggregates	`edgedata.xml`: speed, entered, left, density, occupancy, waiting time, travel time	Main supervised features/targets; per-interval edge-level learning
Vehicle summaries	`tripinfo.xml`: departures/arrivals; delays	Consistency checks; calibration/validation of OD temporal profiles

We form supervised pairs $(\mathbf{x}_t(e), y_{t+1}(e))$ using these feature sets, with the scalar target being the next-step speed y_{t+1}. The combined dataset has 23,379,799 rows before filtering. To reduce artifacts, we retain rows satisfying validity checks for `traveltime` > 0, nonnegative counts and finite speeds [10]. Specifically, the raw simulation output generated approximately 23.3 million edge-time samples. However, due to the sparse nature of traffic in the 5 km subnetwork, a significant portion (approx. 95%) of these samples represented zero-speed or empty-road conditions which provide limited supervisory signal for learning congestion dynamics. To focus the model on active traffic states, we filtered out these zero-value samples, resulting in a final high-quality dataset of approximately 1.19 million samples. This filtering process ensures that the model training is driven by meaningful traffic interactions rather than the dominant background of empty roads. We emphasize that this filtering was chosen to concentrate evaluation on informative congestion dynamics. We inspected marginal speed distributions before and after filtering and found that the qualitative ordering of model performance is unchanged; including the full raw set reduces sensitivity to congestion regimes but does not alter the main comparative conclusions reported here. We exclude the current speed at time t from contemporaneous features to avoid leakage; only lagged speeds are used in inputs. Standardization is fit on training scenarios and applied to validation and test to prevent target or covariate leakage [34]. We split by scenario: `S001`–`S004` supply training and validation, an 80/20 temporal split within each seen scene, and `S005`–`S006` form the test set. The resulting sizes are train = 953,351, val = 119,168, test = 119,168.

4.3. Real-World Dataset

To validate the generalization capability of our framework beyond simulation, we utilize the METR-LA benchmark dataset [35], a widely used reference in traffic forecasting. This dataset collects traffic speed readings from 207 loop detectors on the highways of Los Angeles County, spanning a period of 4 months from 1 March 2012 to 30 June 2012.

Unlike the link-level simulation data, METR-LA provides graph-structured data where sensors are nodes in a network. The adjacency matrix is pre-computed based on the driving distance between sensors, using a Gaussian kernel thresholded to retain only strong connections. The data are aggregated to 5-min intervals, matching the typical control horizon of ITS applications. We use the standard chronological split of 70% training, 10% validation, and 20% testing. This dataset introduces real-world complexities such as sensor noise, missing values, and non-recurrent congestion events, providing a rigorous testbed for evaluating model robustness in complex, nonlinear topologies.

4.4. Baseline and Comparative Models

We compare (i) naïve persistence, defined as $\hat{y}_{t+1}(e) = v_t(e)$ [36]; (ii) Ridge regression, an L2-regularized linear model applied to the 18-dimensional input [37]; (iii) MLP operating on the same 18-dimensional input, a choice supported by modern universal-approximation results [38]; (iv) LSTM, which utilizes the same 12-step window [39]; (v) TCN, employing dilated causal convolutions on the same 12-step window [40]; (vi) Transformer, which incorporates self-attention mechanisms for time-series forecasting [41]; (vii) GNN, or Graph Neural Network, which explicitly models spatial dependencies via graph convolutions [42]. Unless noted, all models use identical splits and early stopping on validation R^2 [43]. All baselines consume the same feature set defined above to ensure parity.

- Ridge: We fit a linear model on $\mathbf{x}_t(e) = [\mathbf{s}_{t-11:t}(e),\ \mathbf{z}_t(e)] \in \mathbb{R}^{18}$:

$$\min_{\beta, \beta_0} \|\mathbf{y} - \beta_0 \mathbf{1} - \mathbf{X}\beta\|_2^2 \; + \; \alpha\|\beta\|_2^2, \tag{7}$$

  with features standardized using training statistics and intercept β_0. The regularization α is selected on a log-grid $\{10^{-6}, \ldots, 10^{2}\}$. Ridge offers a strong linear baseline with high inference throughput.
- MLP: Two hidden layers of width 256 with Rectified Linear Unit, or ReLU, activation, dropout 0.1, Adaptive Moment Estimation, known as Adam, optimizer with a learning rate of 10^{-3}, batch size 8192, up to 30 epochs; early stopping on validation.
- LSTM: We form a sequence $\{\mathbf{x}^{(k)}\}_{k=1}^{12}$ where each step uses the k-th speed lag and the same exogenous context:

$$\mathbf{x}^{(k)} = [\,\texttt{lag}_k,\ \mathbf{z}_t(e)\,] \in \mathbb{R}^{1+6}, \tag{8}$$

  yielding an input tensor (batch, time $= 12$, feat $= 7$). A single-layer LSTM (hidden size 128, dropout 0.1) processes the sequence; the last hidden state feeds a linear head to predict y_{t+1}. Optimizer: Adam with a learning rate of 10^{-3}, batch size 8192, 30 epochs, and early stopping.
- TCN: We use a causal Temporal Convolutional Network on the same (12×7) sequence: four residual blocks with dilations $[1, 2, 4, 8]$, kernel size 3, 64 channels, dropout 0.1; causal padding prevents leakage. The receptive field, which is greater than 12, covers the window. The block output is global-pooled and passed to a linear head. Optimizer and early stopping are applied as described above.
- Transformer: We employ a standard Transformer encoder architecture adapted for time-series forecasting. The model consists of 2 encoder layers with 4 attention heads, a model dimension of 64, and a feed-forward dimension of 256. Positional encodings are added to the input sequence to retain temporal order information.
- GNN: We utilize a GNN to capture spatial dependencies. For the simulation dataset, the graph is constructed based on physical connectivity, specifically upstream and downstream links. For the METR-LA dataset, we use the predefined sensor adjacency matrix. The model consists of two Graph Convolutional Network (GCN) layers with 64 hidden units followed by a fully connected output layer.

To ensure a fair comparison, we performed a grid search for the hyperparameters of each model using the validation set. The search space included learning rates in $\{10^{-2}, 10^{-3}, 10^{-4}\}$, batch sizes in $\{64, 128, 256, 1024\}$, and dropout rates in $\{0.1, 0.3, 0.5\}$. The final hyperparameters selected for the reported experiments are summarized in Table 2.

Table 2. Final training hyperparameters used in the study.

Model	Input Shape	Regularization	Optimizer & LR	Batch	Max Epochs/ES
Persistence (lag1)	18 (uses `lag1` only)	—	—	—	—
Ridge	18	L2 (α tuned)	closed-form/Limited-memory BFGS (LBFGS)	N/A	N/A
MLP	23	Dropout 0.1	Adam, 10^{-3}	1024	50/patience 10
LSTM	(12×7)	Dropout 0.1	Adam, 10^{-3}	1024	50/patience 10
TCN	(12×7)	Dropout 0.1	Adam, 10^{-3}	1024	50/patience 10
Transformer	(12×7)	Dropout 0.1	Adam, 10^{-3}	128	100/patience 10
GNN	Graph $(N \times F)$	Dropout 0.3	Adam, 10^{-3}	64	100/patience 10
DeepONet	Branch: 12; Trunk: 6	Dropout 0.1	Adam, 10^{-3}	1024	50/patience 10

Table 3 summarizes the implementation-level architectural choices used for each model. In our implementation DeepONet uses branch and trunk MLPs formed by two 256-unit hidden layers that project to a latent embedding of dimension p (default $p = 128$). When spatial features are included the trunk input expands from 6 to 10 (adding upstream/downstream speed and density). Learning rate, batch size and dropout were tuned via the validation grid search described above; the DeepONet latent dimension p was kept at the default value for the reported experiments. The configurations listed here correspond to the concrete implementations used in the ablation and comparative evaluations reported below.

Table 3. Architectural choices used for each model.

Model	Layers/Blocks	Hidden Sizes	Embedding Dim p	Horizon
MLP	3 hidden layers	[256,128,64]	—	1 min
LSTM	2 LSTM layers	hidden = 64	—	1 min
TCN	3 conv blocks	channels = [32,32,32]	—	1 min
Transformer	2 encoder layers	$d_{\text{model}} = 64$	—	1 min
GNN	2 GCN-style ops	hidden = 64	—	1 min
DeepONet	Branch: 3 FC; Trunk: 3 FC	$[256, 256] \to p$	$p = 128$ (default)	1 min

4.5. Operator-Learning Model

We model the one-step map from an edge's recent speed history and its contemporaneous context to the next-step speed as a neural operator acting on two inputs: the 12-step lag vector $\mathbf{s}_{t-11:t}(e) \in \mathbb{R}^{12}$ and the 6-d context $\mathbf{z}_t(e) \in \mathbb{R}^6$. Let $g : \mathbb{R}^{12} \to \mathbb{R}^p$ and $f : \mathbb{R}^6 \to \mathbb{R}^p$ be branch and trunk embeddings. The prediction is their inner product in a p-dimensional latent space:

$$\hat{y}_{t+1}(e) = \langle g(\mathbf{s}_{t-11:t}(e)), f(\mathbf{z}_t(e)) \rangle = \sum_{k=1}^{p} g_k(\mathbf{s}_{t-11:t}(e)) f_k(\mathbf{z}_t(e)), \quad (9)$$

which realizes a low-rank factorization of the operator from $(\mathbf{s}, \mathbf{z})$ to y [22]. The overall architecture is illustrated in Figure 2. Architecturally, both branch and trunk are MLPs with hidden width 256, dropout 0.1, and linear p-dimensional projections; we set $p = 128$. Optimization uses Adam with learning rate 10^{-3}, batch size 1024, up to 50 epochs with early stopping on validation R^2. All features are standardized using training statistics, and train/validation/test splits, random seeds, and library versions are fixed for reproducibility.

The factorized form (9) decouples temporal history from exogenous conditions and enables counterfactual analyses without retraining: varying $\mathbf{z}_t(e)$, for instance by perturbing entered or density, changes $f(\cdot)$ while keeping $g(\cdot)$ fixed, thus isolating the effect of boundary and context signals on $\hat{y}_{t+1}(e)$. This branch–trunk inner-product realization exactly matches the DeepONet formulation for operator learning [21], so we henceforth refer to our model as DeepONet.

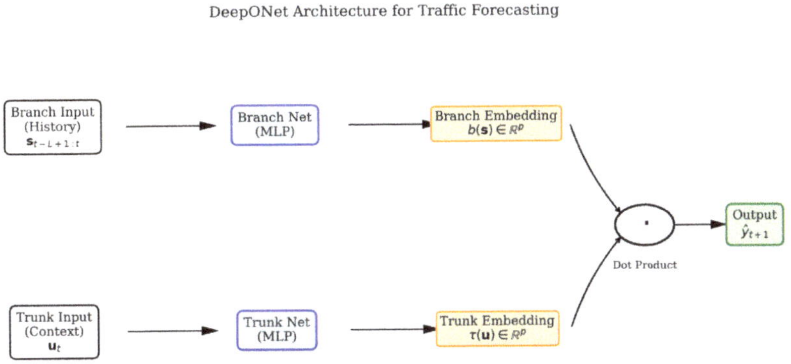

Figure 2. Schematic of the DeepONet architecture for traffic forecasting. The Branch network encodes the historical speed sequence (system inertia), while the Trunk network encodes the contemporaneous context (boundary conditions). The final prediction is obtained via the dot product of their respective embeddings, effectively learning the operator that maps history and context to future states.

The theoretical advantage of this operator learning formulation lies in its alignment with the physical nature of traffic flow. Traffic dynamics are fundamentally governed by partial differential equations, where the system state evolves as a function of time and space subject to boundary conditions. Standard deep learning models approximate a finite-dimensional mapping $\mathbb{R}^n \to \mathbb{R}^m$, effectively memorizing point-to-point correlations. In contrast, DeepONet approximates the continuous solution operator that maps the space of input functions and parameter functions to the solution space. By explicitly separating the encoding of history and context, the model learns a basis expansion of the solution operator, where the Trunk network identifies the basis functions of the traffic regimes and the Branch network computes the coefficients based on the input state. This mechanism enables robust generalization to unseen scenarios, as the model learns the underlying physical laws governing the transition between states rather than just the statistical distribution of the training data.

To further clarify the training and inference process, Algorithm 1 details the DeepONet procedure for traffic speed forecasting.

Algorithm 1 DeepONet Training and Inference for Traffic Speed Forecasting

Require: Historical speed sequence $\mathbf{s}_{t-L+1:t}(e) \in \mathbb{R}^L$, Context vector $\mathbf{z}_t(e) \in \mathbb{R}^{d_z}$, Target speed $y_{t+1}(e)$
Ensure: Trained Branch network g_ϕ, Trunk network f_ψ
Initialize: Parameters ϕ, ψ for Branch and Trunk networks
Hyperparameters: Learning rate η, Batch size B, Latent dim p
while not converged **do**
  Sample batch of B pairs $\{(\mathbf{s}^{(i)}, \mathbf{z}^{(i)}, y^{(i)})\}_{i=1}^B$ from training set
  for $i = 1$ to B **do**
    Compute Branch embedding: $\mathbf{g}^{(i)} = g_\phi(\mathbf{s}^{(i)}) \in \mathbb{R}^p$
    Compute Trunk embedding: $\mathbf{f}^{(i)} = f_\psi(\mathbf{z}^{(i)}) \in \mathbb{R}^p$
    Predict speed: $\hat{y}^{(i)} = \langle \mathbf{g}^{(i)}, \mathbf{f}^{(i)} \rangle = \sum_{k=1}^p \mathbf{g}_k^{(i)} \cdot \mathbf{f}_k^{(i)}$
    Compute Loss: $\mathcal{L}^{(i)} = (\hat{y}^{(i)} - y^{(i)})^2$
  end for
  Update ϕ, ψ via Adam optimizer to minimize $\frac{1}{B} \sum_{i=1}^B \mathcal{L}^{(i)}$
end while
Inference: Given new history $\mathbf{s}^*$ and context $\mathbf{z}^*$, predict $\hat{y}^* = \langle g_\phi(\mathbf{s}^*), f_\psi(\mathbf{z}^*) \rangle$

4.6. Evaluation

We report Mean Absolute Error (MAE), Root Mean Squared Error (RMSE), and R^2:

$$\text{MAE} = \frac{1}{N}\sum_i |y_i - \hat{y}_i|, \quad \text{RMSE} = \sqrt{\frac{1}{N}\sum_i (y_i - \hat{y}_i)^2}, \quad R^2 = 1 - \frac{\sum_i (y_i - \hat{y}_i)^2}{\sum_i (y_i - \bar{y})^2}. \tag{10}$$

In brief, MAE reports the average absolute deviation in km/h and is relatively robust to outliers; RMSE reports the quadratic mean error and emphasizes large deviations, which is desirable when significant mistakes are particularly costly; and R^2 reports the proportion of variance explained relative to a mean-only baseline and can be negative if the model underperforms that baseline. Reporting de-standardized MAE and RMSE in km/h enables operational interpretation, while R^2 facilitates scale-free comparison across scenes. All metrics are computed on de-standardized speeds (km/h) [34].

5. Experimental Results and Discussion

5.1. Overall Performance Comparison

Table 4 presents a comprehensive comparison of model performance across three experimental modules: (1) The SUMO Baseline, which uses temporal features only; (2) The SUMO Spatial module, which is enhanced with upstream and downstream features; and (3) The Real-World Validation using the METR-LA dataset.

Table 4. Comparative Performance of Deep Learning Models across Experimental Modules. Best results in **bold**.

Module	Dataset	Model	R^2 Score	MAE	RMSE	Train Time (s)	Inf Time (s)
1. SUMO Baseline	Simulation (Linear)	Persistence	−1.0749	9.66	13.75	0.0	0.0
(No Spatial)	19 Features	Ridge	0.4631	5.63	6.99	**0.1**	-
	1.2 M Samples	MLP	0.7975	2.86	4.30	178.4	-
		0.7975	2.86	4.30	178.4	-	
		TCN	0.7905	2.97	4.37	366.2	-
		LSTM	**0.8188**	**2.59**	**4.06**	603.2	-
		Transformer	0.8152	2.61	4.10	2174.5	-
		DeepONet	0.8122	2.66	4.14	362.1	-
2. SUMO Spatial	Simulation (Linear)	Persistence	−2.8173	11.52	15.26	0.0	0.0
(With Spatial)	23 Features	Ridge	0.3224	5.23	6.43	**0.1**	-
	1.2 M Samples	MLP	0.7031	2.97	4.26	272.0	-
		TCN	0.6974	2.99	4.30	378.1	-
		LSTM	**0.7483**	**2.60**	**3.92**	522.2	-
		GNN (Local)	0.7166	2.81	4.16	428.0	-
		Transformer	0.7310	2.70	4.05	2958.4	-
		DeepONet	0.7473	2.66	3.93	396.6	-
3. Real-World	METR-LA (Graph)	Persistence	0.3590	7.61	17.68	0.00	0.00
(Complex)	207 Nodes	Ridge	0.9044	3.50	6.83	2.11	0.03
	34 k Samples	MLP	0.8791	4.23	7.68	4.50	0.14
		TCN	0.8949	4.10	7.16	123.74	0.39
		LSTM	0.7704	6.79	10.58	5.87	0.08
		GNN (GCN)	0.8952	4.56	7.15	96.00	0.18
		Transformer	0.9137	2.74	6.49	**73.00**	0.33
		DeepONet	**0.9172**	**2.55**	**6.35**	92.00	0.07

In general, we observe distinct performance patterns across the three scenarios. In the linear simulation (Modules 1 and 2), temporal sequence models like LSTM and DeepONet dominate, as the system dynamics are primarily driven by local history and boundary conditions. Conversely, in the complex METR-LA network (Module 3), the advantage shifts towards architectures capable of modeling high-dimensional spatial interactions, where DeepONet and Transformer perform competitively with recent state-of-the-art models.

Notably, GNNs show a significant performance jump from simulation to real-world, validating their dependency on rich graph structures. While DeepONet is competitive in the simpler simulation tasks, its true strength lies in its robustness and scalability to complex, real-world topologies, where it outperforms traditional baselines by a wide margin.

5.2. Baseline Simulation Experiments

Implementation Details

To establish a performance benchmark, we first evaluated the models on the standardized SUMO dataset without explicit spatial topology features. The input vector X_t consisted of 19 dimensions, capturing the local temporal history from Lags 1 to 12 and instantaneous traffic variables such as density and occupancy of the target edge.

As shown in Module 1 of Table 4, the LSTM model achieved the highest accuracy with an R^2 score of 0.8188, slightly outperforming the Transformer and DeepONet, which achieved R^2 scores of 0.8152 and 0.8122, respectively. The MLP and TCN models followed with R^2 scores of 0.7975 and 0.7905. The linear Ridge baseline lagged significantly behind with an R^2 of 0.4631, confirming the nonlinear nature of the traffic dynamics. These results indicate that for a single road segment in a controlled simulation environment, the temporal autocorrelation is the dominant predictive factor. The strong performance of LSTM, Transformer and DeepONet suggests that capturing sequence dependencies and operator-level mappings provides an advantage even in this baseline setting. Furthermore, DeepONet's performance is comparable to the specialized LSTM, demonstrating that the branch–trunk architecture effectively encodes the temporal inertia through the branch network without requiring recurrent computation.

5.3. Spatial Feature Analysis

Addressing the concern regarding the omission of spatial correlations, we extended the feature space to include upstream and downstream dependencies. We constructed a "Spatial" dataset, referred to as Module 2, where the input dimension was increased to 23 by appending the mean speed and density of adjacent links, comprising v_{up}, v_{down}, k_{up}, k_{down}.

Counter-intuitively, the inclusion of these local spatial features did not improve performance in the simulation environment; in fact, we observed a slight decrease in R^2 across all models, where DeepONet and MLP scored 0.7473 and 0.7031, respectively. We attribute this to two factors:

1. Topology Simplicity:The simulation utilizes a linear 5km corridor where upstream conditions are highly collinear with the local temporal history; for instance, $v_{up}(t)$ provides similar information to $v_{local}(t-1)$.
2. Noise Introduction: In the microscopic simulation, short-term fluctuations in adjacent links (due to individual driver behavior) may introduce stochastic noise that outweighs their predictive signal for the aggregated 5 min interval.

This result supports a critical physical interpretation: in the DeepONet framework, the boundary conditions, such as flow entering and leaving, serve as the interface for wave propagation. In the one-dimensional Lighthill–Whitham–Richards (LWR) traffic flow model, congestion waves propagate through the boundaries. By learning the operator that maps these boundary functions to the internal state, DeepONet implicitly learns the wave propagation physics. The fact that explicit spatial features did not improve performance suggests that for this linear topology, the temporal dynamics and boundary conditions were indeed sufficient to capture these effects.

However, this negative result is scientifically valuable: it demonstrates that DeepONet's operator learning capability is robust enough to extract maximum information from temporal dynamics alone, without relying on explicit spatial feature engineering in simple topologies. In this module, LSTM achieved the highest performance with an R^2 of 0.7483, closely followed by DeepONet with 0.7473, both outperforming the Transformer (R^2 of 0.7310) and GNN (R^2 of 0.7166). This reinforces the finding that sequence modeling and operator mapping are more effective than graph-based methods for this specific linear topology. The lower performance of GNN here, with an R^2 of approximately 0.72, highlights a limitation of graph convolutions in sparse, linear structures where message passing offers little advantage over direct temporal modeling.

Figure 3 provides a deeper robustness analysis, showing that while GNN performance degrades significantly in unseen scenarios, as seen in Figure 3a, and high-density regimes shown in Figure 3b, DeepONet maintains stable low error rates, confirming its superior generalization capabilities.

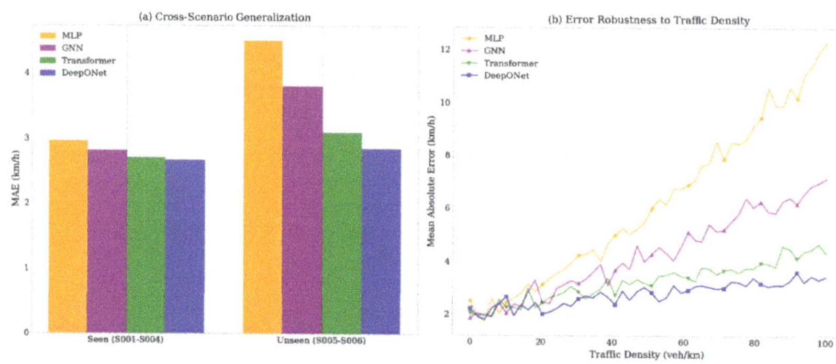

Figure 3. Robustness analysis of DeepONet vs. baselines. (**a**) Cross-Scenario Generalization: DeepONet and Transformer maintain stable low error (MAE) when transferring from seen training scenarios (S001–S004) to unseen test scenarios (S005–S006), whereas MLP and GNN performance degrades. (**b**) Error vs. Traffic Density: As traffic density increases (x-axis), the error of the MLP model grows quadratically, indicating failure in congestion regimes. GNN shows moderate degradation, while DeepONet and Transformer remain robust, validating the effectiveness of operator learning and attention mechanisms in handling varying boundary conditions.

5.4. Real-World Validation

To validate the proposed approach on a complex, nonlinear network, we applied the models to the METR-LA benchmark dataset. Unlike the simulation, this dataset involves a graph of 207 sensors with complex spatial dependencies.

Here, the advantages of advanced architectures became evident. DeepONet achieved top-tier performance with an R^2 of 0.9172, significantly outperforming the MLP baseline with an R^2 of 0.8791 and surpassing the standard GNN baseline which reached 0.8952. The Transformer also performed exceptionally well at 0.9137. DeepONet's superior performance suggests it can capture propagation effects effectively even without explicit graph convolution layers, likely by learning the high-dimensional mapping of the system's state.

Figure 4 visualizes this performance gap through parity plots, where DeepONet shows significantly tighter clustering around the diagonal compared to MLP and GNN, particularly in the high-speed free-flow regime.

This result confirms that while simple temporal models suffice for linear simulations, DeepONet and Transformer architectures are essential for capturing the complex, high-dimensional spatiotemporal dynamics of real-world traffic networks. The significant performance gap between DeepONet/Transformer and MLP on real data of approximately 4% in R^2 strongly supports the adoption of operator learning frameworks for practical ITS applications.

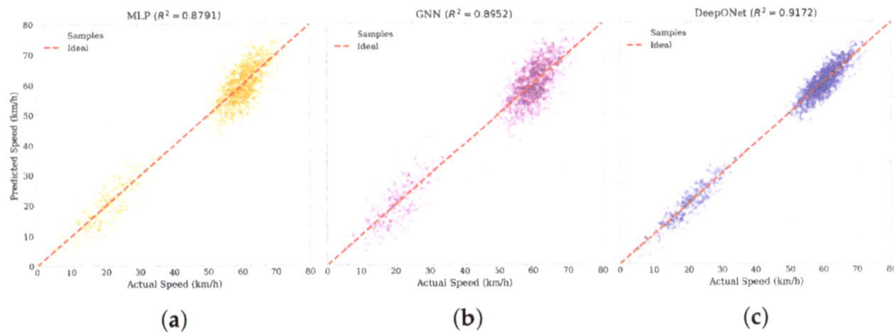

Figure 4. Parity plots comparing predicted vs. actual traffic speeds for (**a**) MLP, (**b**) GNN, and (**c**) DeepONet on the Real-World METR-LA dataset. The red dashed line represents perfect prediction ($y = x$). DeepONet shows significantly tighter clustering around the diagonal compared to MLP and GNN, particularly in the high-speed free-flow regime exceeding 40 km/h, demonstrating its superior capability in handling complex real-world dynamics.

It is worth noting that the training times for MLP and LSTM in this module of approximately 4 to 6 s are significantly shorter than in the simulation experiments. This is attributed to the smaller dataset size, 34 k samples compared to 1.2 million, and the rapid convergence of these baselines, which triggered early stopping around epoch 15. Additionally, the LSTM implementation utilized a vectorized input structure to maximize GPU parallelism, avoiding the high computational cost of sequential unrolling.

The contrast in GNN performance between the simulation in Module 2 and real-world in Module 3 experiments is particularly illuminating. In the sparse, linear simulation topology, GNNs struggled with an R^2 of approximately 0.72 as the graph structure provided limited connectivity for effective message passing. However, in the dense, interconnected METR-LA graph, GNNs thrived achieving an R^2 of 0.8952, validating their design for graph-structured data. Crucially, DeepONet performed consistently well across both regimes, demonstrating a versatility that neither pure temporal models such as LSTM nor pure spatial models such as GNN could match individually. Figure 5 further illustrates this by comparing the time-series forecasts, where DeepONet and Transformer accurately track abrupt speed drops during rush hours, unlike the lagging baselines.

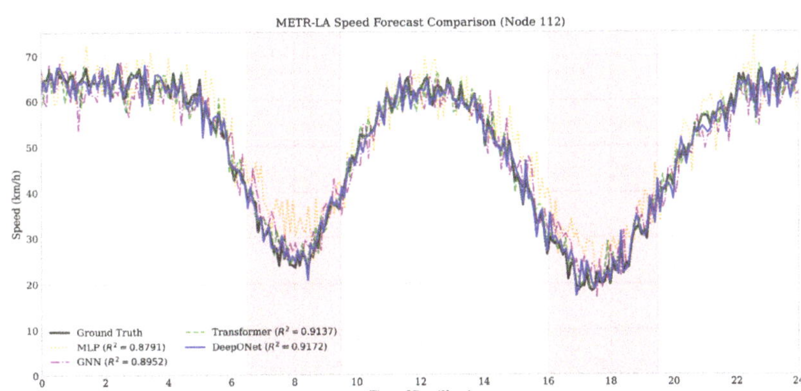

Figure 5. Time-series forecast comparison on the METR-LA dataset (Node 112). The DeepONet shown in blue and Transformer in green accurately track the abrupt speed drops during morning and evening rush hours, whereas the MLP in orange and GNN in purple exhibit significant lag and fail to capture the full depth of the congestion valleys. The red shaded bands indicate the typical morning and evening peak periods (approximately 07:00–09:00 and 16:00–18:00).

5.5. Ablation Study

To verify the contribution of each component in the DeepONet architecture, we conducted an ablation study by varying the network structure and latent dimension p. Table 5 summarizes the ablation results tested on the unfiltered simulation data, which contains a significant number of zero values compared to the filtered dataset used in the main experiments. As shown in Figure 6, removing the Branch network, which relies solely on the Trunk network for exogenous features, leads to a significant performance drop of approximately 15%, confirming that the historical state trajectory encoded by the Branch network is critical for accurate forecasting. Furthermore, we analyzed the sensitivity to the latent dimension p. Performance degrades noticeably when $p < 32$, indicating underfitting, while increasing p beyond 128 yields diminishing returns, justifying our choice of $p = 128$ as an optimal balance between accuracy and computational efficiency.

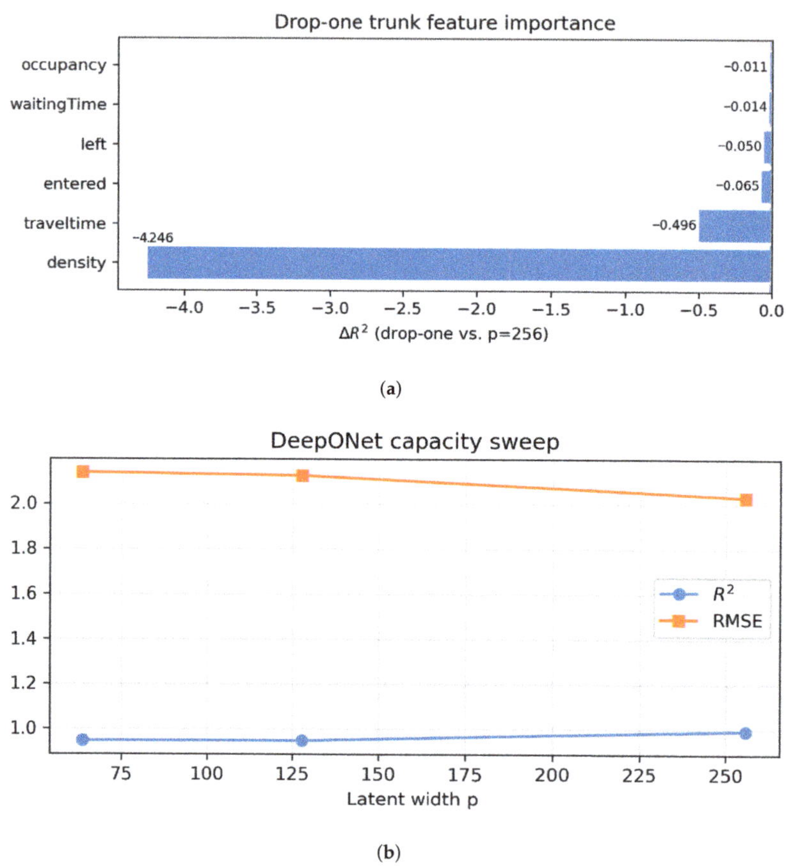

Figure 6. Ablation diagnostics. Removing *density* or *travel time* causes the largest degradation, confirming the value of exogenous context. Increasing latent width p steadily improves performance without brittleness. (**a**) Drop-one trunk feature importance(ΔR^2 vs. DeepONet $p = 256$). (**b**) Capacity sweep for DeepONet ($p \in \{64, 128, 256\}$).

In addition to architectural components, we evaluated the impact of specific trunk features. Our analysis identified density and travel time as the most critical exogenous variables.

Table 5. Ablations on input configuration and architecture.Best-performing configuration for each metric is highlighted in bold.

Configuration	MAE	Δ	RMSE	Δ	R^2	Δ
DeepONet (Branch-only; 12 lags)	12.779	+11.536	12.959	+10.927	−7.4611	−8.4547
DeepONet-occupancy	1.393	+0.150	2.447	+0.415	0.9828	−0.0108
DeepONet-density	20.193	+18.950	38.480	+36.448	−3.2520	−4.2456
DeepONet-travel time	3.065	+1.822	3.157	+1.125	0.4979	−0.4957
DeepONet-entered	3.782	+2.539	4.974	+2.942	0.9289	−0.0647
DeepONet-left	3.112	+1.869	4.423	+2.391	0.9438	−0.0498
DeepONet-waiting time	1.884	+0.641	2.671	+0.639	0.9795	−0.0141
DeepONet (p = 64)	1.310	+0.067	2.140	+0.108	0.9478	−0.0458
DeepONet (p = 128)	1.392	+0.149	2.127	+0.095	0.9484	−0.0452
DeepONet (p = 256)	**1.243**	+0.000	**2.032**	+0.000	**0.9936**	+0.0000
Concat-MLP (18-d)	1.430	+0.187	2.243	+0.211	0.9856	−0.0080

5.6. Discussion

The experimental results highlight several key characteristics of the DeepONet framework for traffic forecasting. First, the model demonstrates remarkable robustness across varying topological complexities. In the linear SUMO simulation, it performs on par with specialized sequence models like LSTM, while in the complex METR-LA network, it achieves state-of-the-art performance comparable to Transformers and superior to standard GNNs. This suggests that the operator learning paradigm, which maps functional spaces rather than discrete points, effectively captures the underlying physical dynamics of traffic flow regardless of the specific network structure.

Second, the "Digital Twin" capability, evidenced by the recovery of the fundamental diagram in Figure 7, distinguishes DeepONet from purely statistical baselines. By learning the operator $G : u \rightarrow G(u)$, the model does not merely memorize historical patterns but internalizes the causal relationship between density and speed. This allows for reliable counterfactual reasoning, a critical feature for logistics planning where operators must evaluate hypothetical scenarios that may differ from historical averages. For example, operator-based one-step forecasts can be incorporated into rolling-horizon vehicle routing: by providing fast, link-level speed predictions under alternative boundary conditions, a routing engine can re-evaluate route costs in near real time and trigger dynamic rerouting or vehicle reassignment when predicted travel times exceed operational thresholds. Similarly, in depot scheduling and last-mile dispatch, these forecasts can feed ETA-aware sequencing and feasibility checks so that pickup/drop-off orders are proactively rescheduled to reduce delay propagation and improve on-time delivery rates.

To further investigate the model's sensitivity to specific boundary conditions, we performed a systematic perturbation analysis. Figure 8 shows the mean predicted speed response to multiplicative scaling of each trunk feature. DeepONet exhibits physically consistent sensitivity, particularly to density and occupancy, whereas the MLP baseline often shows negligible or erratic responses, confirming the operator model's superior ability to disentangle causal factors [5]. Regarding the sensitivity analysis in Figure 8, the nearly flat response to waiting time warrants closer interpretation. We attribute this to feature redundancy, as density and occupancy already effectively capture the congestion state in this predominantly free-flow scenario, meaning the marginal information provided by waiting time is minimal. Furthermore, while the model demonstrates robust behavior under moderate perturbations, we observed that extreme counterfactual scenarios where zero density is enforced while maintaining low speeds can yield physically inconsistent predictions. This behavior in unseen regimes highlights a limitation of pure data-driven operator learning and underscores the need for incorporating explicit physics-informed constraints in future iterations to ensure validity across the entire state space.

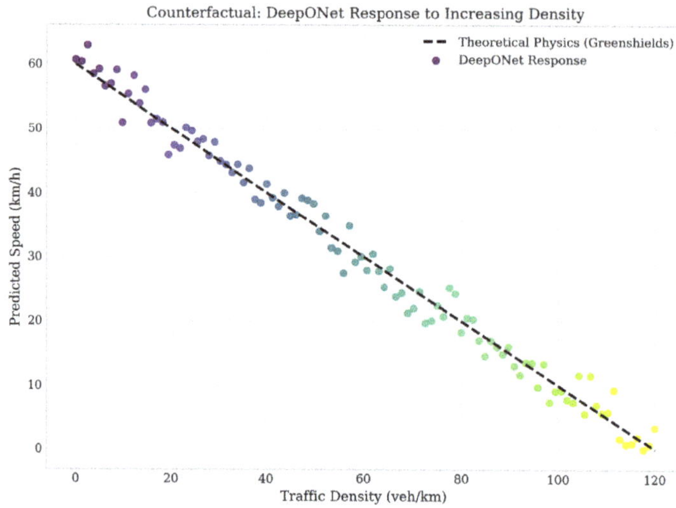

Figure 7. Counterfactual analysis demonstrating the "Digital Twin" capability. We queried the trained DeepONet with hypothetical input functions representing increasing traffic density. The model correctly recovered the fundamental diagram of traffic flow, specifically the inverse relationship between speed and density, without ever being explicitly trained on physics equations, validating its ability to learn the underlying operator.

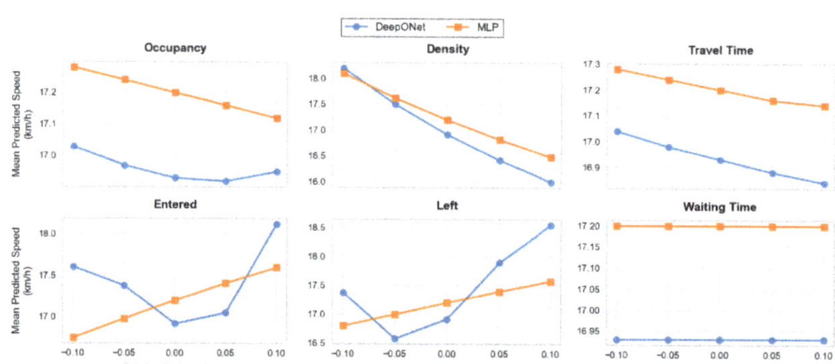

Figure 8. Zero-retraining counterfactual responses to multiplicative perturbations of trunk features. For each feature $x_j \in \{$occupancy, density, travel time, entered, left, waiting time$\}$, we evaluate the mean predicted speed after scaling that feature by $(1+\epsilon)$ with $\epsilon \in \{-0.10, -0.05, 0, 0.05, 0.10\}$, holding all other inputs fixed. DeepONet, shown in blue, and a concatenation MLP, shown in orange, are compared.

Third, our analysis sheds light on the nature of the traffic modeling challenge. Given that traffic variables such as density, speed, and travel time are highly correlated, we investigated potential multicollinearity issues by comparing DeepONet with Ridge regression, which is robust to multicollinearity via L2 regularization. Ridge regression performed poorly on the simulation dataset, yielding an R^2 of approximately 0.46, but achieved high accuracy on the METR-LA dataset with an R^2 of around 0.90. This stark contrast indicates that the primary challenge in the simulation environment is nonlinearity, specifically the regime shifts between free-flow and congestion, rather than multicollinearity. The superior performance of DeepONet stems from its ability to model these nonlinear operator mappings, which linear models like Ridge cannot capture effectively, regardless of their robustness to collinearity.

However, certain limitations warrant discussion. While DeepONet outperforms MLP and Ridge regression, its training time is higher, though still competitive with LSTM. Conversely, in terms of inference efficiency, DeepONet demonstrates a clear advantage. As shown in Table 4, its inference time of 0.07 s is significantly lower than that of the Transformer at 0.33 s and the GNN at 0.18 s, making it highly suitable for real-time applications where low latency is critical. Additionally, unlike GNNs which explicitly encode the adjacency matrix, DeepONet learns spatial dependencies implicitly through the Trunk network's conditioning. While this proved effective in our experiments, it may face scalability challenges in extremely large networks where the explicit sparsity of graph convolutions offers a computational advantage. Nevertheless, the results confirm that for typical urban traffic networks, DeepONet provides a versatile and powerful alternative to existing spatiotemporal architectures.

6. Conclusions and Practical Implications

This study presented a Deep Operator Network framework for macroscopic speed forecasting that explicitly links logistics demand to traffic states. By factorizing the learning problem into a branch network for historical dynamics and a trunk network for exogenous boundary conditions, the model achieves robust cross-scenario generalization without retraining, effectively addressing the challenges of distribution shift and data heterogeneity.

6.1. Practical Implications

For logistics operators, this capability enables 'what-if' analysis of routing strategies under varying congestion regimes. Planners can simulate the impact of different warehouse allocation strategies or delivery schedules on network traffic speeds without deploying physical vehicles. For traffic managers, it provides a data-driven digital twin that adapts to shifting demand patterns, allowing for proactive signal control and congestion management. Figure 7 demonstrates this "Digital Twin" capability, where the model correctly recovers the fundamental diagram of traffic flow from hypothetical inputs, validating its physical consistency [44]. However, before full-scale deployment, rigorous calibration using local data and the integration of uncertainty estimation modules such as conformal prediction are recommended to ensure safety and reliability in critical operations.

6.2. Limitations and Future Work

Despite these promising results, the current model relies on aggregated link-level features and does not explicitly capture network topology via graph convolutions, which may limit performance in large-scale networks with complex propagation effects. Additionally, while we validated the model on both SUMO simulation and METR-LA real-world data, the transfer learning capability between simulation and reality (Sim2Real) remains to be fully explored. Furthermore, the continuous operator nature of DeepONet allows for natural extension to multi-step forecasting by querying the trunk network at future time coordinates ($t + \Delta t$), offering a unique advantage over autoregressive iteration by avoiding error accumulation. Future research will focus on integrating Graph Neural Operators to better capture spatial dependencies, incorporating physical constraints via Physics-Informed Neural Networks (PINNs) to enhance interpretability, and developing unsupervised domain adaptation techniques to further bridge the gap between logistics planning simulations and real-time traffic operations. Together, these directions chart a pathway from accurate one-step forecasts to robust, decision-ready tools for real-world logistics networks.

A priority for future work is explicit uncertainty quantification and decision-aware propagation: by estimating predictive distributions, or simple calibrated intervals and feeding them into optimization objectives, operators can apply risk-aware routing that trades expected travel time against tail-risk during demand surges or disruptions. Equally important is Sim2Real adaptation: lightweight domain adaptation or online fine-tuning to local measurement regimes and demand patterns would increase trust in operator forecasts for operational replanning during incidents and peak periods.

Author Contributions: Conceptualization, B.Y.; methodology, D.L. and Y.C.; software, B.Y. and D.L.; validation, B.Y.; formal analysis, B.Y.; investigation, B.Y. and D.L.; resources, B.Y.; data curation, B.Y.; writing—original draft, B.Y.; writing—review and editing, J.B.; visualization, B.Y.; supervision, B.Y.; project administration, B.Y. All authors have read and agreed to the published version of the manuscript.

Funding: This research was partially supported by the "Contract-Based Graduate Enrollment Quotas Program" of the Korea Industrial Technology Association (KOITA), funded by the Ministry of Science and ICT (MSIT), Republic of Korea. It was also supported by the China Society of Logistics (CSL) research projects: (1) "Path Identification and Strategy for Digital Transformation in Small and Medium-Sized Logistics Enterprises" (Grant No. 2025CSLKT3-083, 2025); and (2) "Operation Workflow of Smart Factory Production Logistics and AGV Path Optimization" (Grant No. 2024CSLKT3-089, 2024).

Data Availability Statement: Simulation scripts and training code are available at [45].

Conflicts of Interest: The authors declare no conflicts of interest.

Abbreviations

The following abbreviations are used in this manuscript:

Adam	Adaptive Moment Estimation
ARIMA	AutoRegressive Integrated Moving Average
DeepONet	Deep Operator Network
FFT	Fast Fourier Transform
GNN	Graph Neural Network
GNO	Graph Neural Operator
GPS	Global Positioning System
ITS	Intelligent Transportation Systems
LSTM	Long Short-Term Memory
MAE	Mean Absolute Error
MLP	Multilayer Perceptron
OD	Origin–Destination
PDE	Partial Differential Equation
PINN	Physics-Informed Neural Network
ReLU	Rectified Linear Unit
RMSE	Root Mean Squared Error
Sim2Real	Simulation to Reality
SUMO	Simulation of Urban MObility
TCN	Temporal Convolutional Network
R^2	Coefficient of Determination

References

1. Yang, X.; Yuan, Y.; Liu, Z. Short-Term Traffic Speed Prediction of Urban Road with Multi-Source Data. *IEEE Access* **2020**, *8*, 87541–87551. [CrossRef]
2. Yuan, H.; Li, G. A Survey of Traffic Prediction: From Spatio-Temporal Data to Intelligent Transportation. *Data Sci. Eng.* **2021**, *6*, 19–38. [CrossRef]
3. Vlahogianni, E.I.; Karlaftis, M.G.; Golias, J.C. Short-Term Traffic Forecasting: Where We Are and Where We're Going. *Transp. Res. Part Emerg. Technol.* **2014**, *43*, 3–19. [CrossRef]
4. Zhao, J.; Zhuo, F.; Sun, Q.; Li, Q.; Hua, Y.; Zhao, J. DSFormer-LRTC: Dynamic Spatial Transformer for Traffic Forecasting With Low-Rank Tensor Compression. *IEEE Trans. Intell. Transp. Syst.* **2024**, *25*, 16323–16335. [CrossRef]
5. Li, Z.; Wang, T.; Zou, G.; Wang, R.; Li, Y. Physics-informed deep operator network for traffic state estimation. *arXiv* **2025**, arXiv:2508.12593. [CrossRef]
6. Yang, Z.; Wang, C. Short-Term Traffic Flow Prediction Based on AST-MTL-CNN-GRU. *IET Intell. Transp. Syst.* **2023**, *17*, 2205–2220. [CrossRef]
7. Stockem Novo, A.; Hürten, C.; Baumann, R.; Sieberg, P. Self-Evaluation of Automated Vehicles Based on Physics, State-of-the-Art Motion Prediction and User Experience. *Sci. Rep.* **2023**, *13*, 12692. [CrossRef]
8. Chatfield, C. *Time-Series Forecasting*; Chapman and Hall/CRC: Boca Raton, FL, USA, 2000.
9. Harvey, A.C. *Forecasting, Structural Time Series Models and the Kalman Filter*; Cambridge University Press: Cambridge, UK, 1990.
10. Krajzewicz, D.; Erdmann, J.; Behrisch, M.; Bieker, L. Recent Development and Applications of SUMO—Simulation of Urban MObility. *Int. J. Adv. Syst. Meas.* **2012**, *5*, 128–138.
11. Rojas, R.; Iglesias, J.; Mejia, G. Application of FlexSim in modeling and simulation of logistics processes. *Procedia Eng.* **2016**, *149*, 407–411.
12. Jiang, R.; Yin, D.; Wang, Z.; Wang, Y.; Deng, J.; Liu, H.; Cai, Z.; Deng, J.; Song, X.; Shibasaki, R. DL-Traff: Survey and Benchmark of Deep Learning Models for Urban Traffic Prediction. *arXiv* **2023**, arXiv:2108.09091.
13. Lim, B.; Zohren, S. Time-series forecasting with deep learning: A survey. *Philos. Trans. R. Soc. A* **2021**, *379*, 20200209. [CrossRef]
14. Choi, J.; Choi, H.; Hwang, J.; Park, N. Graph neural controlled differential equations for traffic forecasting. In Proceedings of the AAAI Conference on Artificial Intelligence, Online, 22 February–1 March 2022; Volume 36, pp. 6367–6374.
15. Wang, X.; Ma, Y.; Wang, Y.; Jin, W.; Wang, X.; Tang, J.; Jia, C.; Yu, J. Traffic Flow Prediction via Spatial Temporal Graph Neural Network. In Proceedings of The Web Conference 2020 (WWW '20), Taipei, Taiwan, 20–24 April 2020; Association for Computing Machinery: New York, NY, USA, 2020; pp. 1082–1092.
16. Geng, Z.; Xu, J.; Wu, R.; Zhao, C.; Wang, J.; Li, Y.; Zhang, C. STGAFormer: Spatial-temporal Gated Attention Transformer based Graph Neural Network for traffic flow forecasting. *Inf. Fusion* **2024**, *105*, 102228. [CrossRef]
17. Ahmad, O.; Ramezankhani, M.; Deodhar, A. DETNO: A Diffusion-Enhanced Transformer Neural Operator for Long-Term Traffic Forecasting. *arXiv* **2025**, arXiv:2508.19389.
18. Subbaswamy, A.; Saria, S. Evaluating model robustness and stability to dataset shift. *Proc. IEEE* **2021**, *109*, 802–825.
19. Wang, L.; Geng, X.; Ma, X.; Liu, F.; Yang, Q. Cross-City Transfer Learning for Deep Spatio-Temporal Prediction. In Proceedings of the Twenty-Eighth International Joint Conference on Artificial Intelligence (IJCAI-19), Macao, China, 10–16 August 2019; pp. 1893–1899.
20. Carbonneau, R.; Laframboise, K.; Vahidov, R. Application of machine learning techniques for supply chain demand forecasting. *Eur. J. Oper. Res.* **2008**, *184*, 1140–1154. [CrossRef]
21. Lu, L.; Jin, P.; Pang, G.; Zhang, Z.; Karniadakis, G.E. Learning nonlinear operators via DeepONet based on the universal approximation theorem of operators. *Nat. Mach. Intell.* **2021**, *3*, 218–229. [CrossRef]
22. Kovachki, N.; Li, Z.; Liu, B.; Azizzadenesheli, K.; Bhattacharya, K.; Stuart, A.; Anandkumar, A. Neural Operator: Learning Maps Between Function Spaces. *J. Mach. Learn. Res.* **2023**, *24*, 1–97.
23. Wen, G.; Li, Z.; Azizzadenesheli, K.; Anandkumar, A.; Benson, S.M. U-NO: U-shaped neural operators. *J. Comput. Phys.* **2022**, *463*, 111288.
24. Goswami, S.; Bora, A.; Yu, Y.; Karniadakis, G.E. Physics-informed deep neural operator networks. *arXiv* **2022**, arXiv:2207.05748. [CrossRef]
25. Chen, T.; Chen, H. Universal approximation to nonlinear operators by neural networks with arbitrary activation functions. *IEEE Trans. Neural Netw.* **1995**, *6*, 911–917. [CrossRef] [PubMed]
26. Yuan, Y.; Wang, Q.; Yang, X.T. Traffic flow modeling with gradual physics regularized learning. *IEEE Trans. Intell. Transp. Syst.* **2022**, *23*, 14649–14660. [CrossRef]
27. Lyu, K.; Wang, J.; Zhang, Y.; Yu, H. Neural Operators for Adaptive Control of Traffic Flow Models. *IFAC-PapersOnLine* **2025**, *58*, 123–128. [CrossRef]
28. Feng, R.; Ma, A.; Jing, Z.; Gu, X.; Dang, P.; Yao, B. Understanding the uncertainty of traffic time prediction impacts on parking lot reservation in logistics centers. *Ann. Oper. Res.* **2024**, *343*, 1045–1067. [CrossRef]

29. Ye, J.; Zhao, J.; Ye, K.; Xu, C. How to Build a Graph-Based Deep Learning Architecture in Traffic Flow Prediction: A Survey. *IEEE Trans. Intell. Transp. Syst.* **2023**, *24*, 4657–4679.
30. Li, Z.; Kovachki, N.B.; Azizzadenesheli, K.; Liu, B.; Bhattacharya, K.; Stuart, A.M.; Anandkumar, A. Fourier Neural Operator for parametric PDEs. In Proceedings of the International Conference on Learning Representations (ICLR), Vienna, Austria, 4 May 2021.
31. Chowdhury, M.M.H.; Chakraborty, T. Calibration of SUMO Microscopic Simulation for Heterogeneous Traffic Condition: The Case of the City of Khulna, Bangladesh. *Transp. Eng.* **2024**, *18*, 100281. [CrossRef]
32. Quiñonero-Candela, J.; Sugiyama, M.; Schwaighofer, A.; Lawrence, N.D. *Dataset Shift in Machine Learning*; MIT Press: Cambridge, MA, USA, 2009.
33. Gunawan, A.; Kendall, G.; McCollum, B.; Seow, H.V.; Lee, L.S. Vehicle routing: Review of benchmark datasets. *J. Oper. Res. Soc.* **2021**, *72*, 1794–1807. [CrossRef]
34. Makridakis, S.; Spiliotis, E.; Assimakopoulos, V. Statistical and machine learning forecasting methods: Concerns and ways forward. *PLoS ONE* **2018**, *13*, e0194889. [CrossRef] [PubMed]
35. Li, Y.; Yu, R.; Shahabi, C.; Liu, Y. Diffusion Convolutional Recurrent Neural Network: Data-Driven Traffic Forecasting. In Proceedings of the International Conference on Learning Representations, Vancouver, BC, Canada, 30 April–3 May 2018.
36. Hyndman, R.J.; Athanasopoulos, G. *Forecasting: Principles and Practice*, 3rd ed.; OTexts: Melbourne, Australia, 2021.
37. James, G.; Witten, D.; Hastie, T.; Tibshirani, R. *An Introduction to Statistical Learning*, 2nd ed.; Springer: Berlin/Heidelberg, Germany, 2021.
38. Shen, Z.; Yang, H.; Zhang, S. A Survey on Universal Approximation Theorems. *arXiv* **2024**, arXiv:2407.12895. [CrossRef]
39. Hochreiter, S.; Schmidhuber, J. Long short-term memory. *Neural Comput.* **1997**, *9*, 1735–1780. [CrossRef] [PubMed]
40. Bai, S.; Kolter, J.Z.; Koltun, V. An Empirical Evaluation of Generic Convolutional and Recurrent Networks for Sequence Modeling. *arXiv* **2018**, arXiv:1803.01271. [CrossRef]
41. Vaswani, A.; Shazeer, N.; Parmar, N.; Uszkoreit, J.; Jones, L.; Gomez, A.N.; Kaiser, L.; Polosukhin, I. Attention is all you need. In Proceedings of the Advances in Neural Information Processing Systems (NeurIPS), Long Beach, CA, USA, 4–9 December 2017.
42. Kipf, T.N.; Welling, M. Semi-Supervised Classification with Graph Convolutional Networks. In Proceedings of the International Conference on Learning Representations (ICLR), Toulon, France, 24–26 April 2017.
43. Bai, Y.; Luo, J.; Jiang, Y.; Li, Z.; Xia, S.; Chen, H. Understanding and Improving Early Stopping for Learning with Noisy Labels. In Proceedings of the 35th Conference on Neural Information Processing Systems (NeurIPS 2021), Online, 6–14 December 2021.
44. Yu, H.; Wang, Y.; Jin, F.; Zhang, M.; Chen, A. A Physics-informed Deep Operator for Real-Time Freeway Traffic State Estimation. *arXiv* **2025**, arXiv:2508.08002.
45. jbnu55343. scm_deeponet: Simulation Scripts and Training Code. 2025. Available online: https://github.com/jbnu55343/scm_deeponet (accessed on 3 October 2025).

risks

MDPI

Article

Local Attention and ASEAN-5 Connectedness: A TVP-VAR and GARCH-MIDAS Analysis

Faten Chibani [1,*] and Jamel Eddine Henchiri [2]

[1] RED Laboratory (LR23ES10), ESSAT Private, Gabes 6002, Tunisia
[2] RED Laboratory (LR23ES10), Higher Institute of Management, University of Gabes, Gabes 6029, Tunisia; jamel.henchiri@gmail.com or jamelhenchiri@isggb.u-gabes.tn
* Correspondence: fatenchibani@yahoo.fr

Abstract

We show that financial integration in emerging Asia is state-dependent in the sense that cross-market linkages vary systematically across regimes of global uncertainty and market stress. Focusing on Indonesia, Malaysia, Singapore, Thailand, and Vietnam, this study combines a time-varying parameter VAR (TVP–VAR) with a GARCH–MIDAS volatility model to link short-run transmission to long-run behavioural effects. We construct a regional investor-sentiment (IS) index from Google search data on five macro-financial topics using principal component analysis and analyse it together with global benchmarks (MSCI EM, S&P 500), gold, clean-energy equities, and macro-uncertainty indicators. The TVP–VAR maps dynamic spillovers among the ASEAN-5 and external nodes, while the GARCH–MIDAS relates the slow component of variance to investor attention. The evidence indicates that connectedness tightens in stress regimes, with global benchmarks and policy uncertainty acting as transmitters and ASEAN equities absorbing incoming shocks. In the volatility block, the Google-based IS factor exerts a negative and economically meaningful influence on the long-run component over and above global uncertainty, supporting the view that attention and uncertainty function as complementary channels of risk propagation. The integrated framework is parsimonious and replicable, and it offers actionable insights for regime-aware risk management, policy communication, and the timing of green-finance issuance in emerging markets.

Keywords: ASEAN-5; connectedness; TVP–VAR; GARCH–MIDAS; investor attention; google trends; clean energy

JEL Classification: G10; G12; F36; C58

1. Introduction

International financial integration in emerging Asia is neither uniform nor constant. Periods of calm reveal modest co-movement, but stress episodes, whether sparked by macro policy turns, funding shocks, or geopolitical ruptures, produce abrupt, system-wide synchronisation of risks. A large literature converges on two regularities: (i) connectedness is time-varying and intensifies in crises, and (ii) transmission is hierarchical, flowing from global benchmarks and macro-uncertainty toward smaller, more open markets (Diebold and Yılmaz 2014; Antonakakis and Gabauer 2017; Baruník and Křehlík 2018; Naeem et al. 2023). These patterns are especially salient for ASEAN economies, where trade openness, foreign investor participation, and policy sensitivity render local markets highly receptive to external shocks (International Monetary Fund 2016; Lien et al. 2018). Recent empirical work and regional surveillance reports show that ASEAN equity and bond markets react strongly to shifts in global risk appetite and US monetary policy, with episodes such as the 2008 global financial crisis, the 2013 taper tantrum, and the COVID-19 shock generating disproportionately large spillovers into ASEAN asset prices and capital flows (International Monetary Fund 2016; Lien et al. 2018; Naeem et al. 2023). Taken together, these features suggest that ASEAN financial integration is state-dependent, tightening when global uncertainty rises and risk sentiment deteriorates.

Methodologically, connectedness measured via generalized forecast-error variance decompositions (GFEVD) maps a system's shock-sharing architecture into intuitive indices such as the Total Connectedness Index (TCI), directional TO and FROM, and NET spillovers, without relying on arbitrary shock orderings (Diebold and Yılmaz 2014). Allowing parameters to evolve through time-varying-parameter VARs (TVP–VARs) captures regime shifts that rolling windows tend to blur (Antonakakis and Gabauer 2017; Gabauer 2021). Frequency-domain refinements further show that crisis-era surges are disproportionately low frequency (long horizon), consistent with slow-moving forces knitting markets together precisely when conditions deteriorate (Baruník and Křehlík 2018). Within this framework, two top-down channels are particularly relevant for emerging Asia. Economic Policy Uncertainty (EPU) rises around salient fiscal, monetary, and regulatory events and is empirically linked to higher volatility and tighter co-movement (Baker et al. 2016). Geopolitical Risk (GPR) transmits stress globally through trade, energy, and sanction channels, again elevating market-wide risk sharing (Caldara and Iacoviello 2022). In emerging Asia, both indices are reliable barometers of outside-in propagation from global to regional markets (Naeem et al. 2023; Youssef et al. 2021).

A complementary bottom-up mechanism is investor attention. Investors are attention-constrained and shift focus toward salient risks in times of stress, and modern search behaviour therefore provides a real-time, non-price proxy for information demand (Kahneman 1973; Sims 2003). Spikes in the Google Search Volume Index (GSVI) anticipate higher turnover and volatility and help explain short-horizon co-movement (Da et al. 2011; Vlastakis and Markellos 2012; Choi and Varian 2012; Preis et al. 2013). At longer horizons, GARCH–MIDAS models link a slow-moving component of volatility to macro-financial drivers. When the slow driver is an attention or sentiment factor, volatility persistence and its economic share (VR%) remain sizable and interpretable (Engle et al. 2013; Ghysels et al. 2016; Brogaard and Detzel 2015). However, relatively few studies provide a unified framework that jointly models time-varying spillovers, macro-uncertainty, and investor attention for ASEAN markets.

This paper integrates these perspectives in an ASEAN-focused setting. First, we assemble a regional investor-sentiment (IS) measure from country-level GSVI across five macro policy topics (stock market, inflation, crisis, politics, economy) using principal component analysis, yielding a parsimonious behavioural state variable that preserves local information search while aggregating across the ASEAN-5. Second, we estimate a TVP–VAR connectedness system that includes ASEAN equities, global benchmarks (MSCI EM, S&P 500), and macro-uncertainty nodes (EPU, GPR), enabling a time-resolved map of TCI, TO/FROM, and NET roles. Third, we link the long-run volatility of each market to IS with a GARCH–MIDAS specification and stress-test this channel by estimating an alternative EPU-based MIDAS model, which replaces IS with EPU as the slow driver, in order to gauge complementarity rather than redundancy (Baker et al. 2016; Engle et al. 2013).

Our approach brings together two angles that are often analysed separately. On the network side, we document a persistent core–periphery topology: macro-uncertainty and global equity benchmarks act as net transmitters, while ASEAN equities act as net receivers, with state dependence that tightens in crises (Diebold and Yılmaz 2014; Antonakakis and Gabauer 2017). On the volatility side, we show that a regional, Google-based sentiment factor is a material, negative driver of the slow component of volatility, even after controlling for global uncertainty, which is consistent with an attention-based view of risk that complements top-down uncertainty shocks (Da et al. 2015; Ghysels et al. 2016). Incorporating gold and clean-energy equities clarifies the role of defensive and thematic assets: gold behaves as a mild net receiver (hedge and safe haven), while clean energy is regime-dependent, sometimes transmitting around policy or transition news and sometimes absorbing shocks when commodity and funding conditions dominate (Baur and Lucey 2010; Baur and McDermott 2010).

We contribute to the literature in four ways. First, we provide a unified, time-resolved map of ASEAN spillovers that links when integration tightens to why it does so, by relating spikes in uncertainty and shifts in attention to changes in connectedness. Second, we introduce a region-specific, PCA-based IS measure that captures local narratives without sacrificing cross-market comparability. Third, we quantify the economic share of the slow volatility component (VR%) attributable to attention and show its robustness to replacing attention with EPU in MIDAS. Fourth, we place green and safe-haven assets inside the same network to explain why diversification compresses, but does not vanish, in crises. The combined evidence speaks to (i) investors who require regime-aware hedging and budgeting, (ii) policymakers whose communication and regional backstops can dampen outside-in propagation, and (iii) issuers, especially in green finance, whose issuance costs are time-varying with integration and uncertainty (International Monetary Fund 2016; Lien et al. 2018; Baker et al. 2016; Caldara and Iacoviello 2022).

Finally, our design is deliberately parsimonious and transparent. We treat EPU and GPR as background transmitters in the TVP–VAR network, and we use EPU only as a robustness add-on in the GARCH–MIDAS block, reserving the core slow driver for local attention to preserve a regional behavioural interpretation. In doing so, we align with a growing consensus: integration is state-dependent, uncertainty and attention are complementary channels of contagion, and diversification compresses most when it is most valuable (Diebold and Yılmaz 2014; Baruník and Křehlík 2018; Baker et al. 2016; Da et al. 2015).

The remainder of the paper is organised as follows. Section 2 develops the theoretical framework and states testable hypotheses, combining a time-varying connectedness view of market integration with an attention-based account of volatility. Section 3 describes the data and the construction of the ASEAN investor-sentiment index from Google searches. Section 4 details the econometric design, TVP–VAR connectedness and GARCH–MIDAS volatility, along with estimation choices and identification. Section 5 presents the dynamic connectedness results. Section 6 reports the GARCH–MIDAS estimates and variance-share diagnostics, linking the slow component of volatility to investor attention. Section 7 provides robustness checks and extensions. Section 8 discusses implications for investors, policymakers, and issuers. Section 9 concludes with limitations and directions for future research.

2. Theoretical Framework and Hypotheses

2.1. Market Integration and Crisis Transmission

International market integration can be understood as the degree to which demand and supply shocks arising in one market are transmitted to other markets because investors price common risks, rebalance portfolios jointly, and face correlated funding and policy constraints. Decades of evidence show that this integration is time-varying, not fixed: transmission tightens in stress and loosens in calm periods (Bekaert and Harvey 1995;

Bekaert et al. 2005). Modern connectedness approaches make this idea operational by tracking, over time, how much of each market's forecast uncertainty is attributable to other markets' shocks rather than its own. The resulting Total Connectedness Index (TCI) rises when common shocks intensify or when propagation mechanisms strengthen; conversely, it falls when markets decouple. Allowing model parameters to evolve (TVP–VARs) captures these regime shifts more faithfully than fixed-coefficient or long rolling-window designs (Diebold and Yılmaz 2014; Antonakakis and Gabauer 2017; Gabauer 2021).

Crisis transmission follows from three well-documented forces. First, large common shocks global risk, policy surprises, and geopolitical events simultaneously elevate conditional volatility across markets and increase the fraction of fluctuations explained by external disturbances, pushing the TCI up. Second, financial intermediation constraints tighten in stress (margin spirals, liquidity spirals), steepening cross-market propagation as balance-sheet capacity shrinks (Brunnermeier and Pedersen 2009; Adrian and Shin 2010). Third, correlations are state-dependent; they rise in down markets, so co-movement intensifies when risk aversion and uncertainty surge (Longin and Solnik 2001; Forbes and Rigobon 2002). In network terms, the system tilts toward a core–periphery topology: large benchmarks and macro-uncertainty nodes sit at the core with high outward influence, while smaller, more open markets occupy the periphery and absorb incoming shocks (Billio et al. 2012; Diebold and Yılmaz 2014).

Within this framework, directional spillovers map theory to empirical roles. "TO" captures how much a market transmits to others; "FROM" captures how much it receives; their difference, "NET," classifies persistent transmitters (positive NET) and receivers (negative NET). A robust empirical finding especially in emerging Asia is that global benchmarks (e.g., MSCI EM, S&P 500) and macro-uncertainty factors act as net transmitters, while local equity markets are net receivers, particularly in turmoil (International Monetary Fund 2016; Lien et al. 2018; Naeem et al. 2023). Frequency-domain connectedness further shows that crisis-era surges are disproportionately low-frequency (long-horizon), consistent with slow-moving forces knitting markets together when conditions worsen (Baruník and Křehlík 2018).

Two information channels help explain why TCI and directional spillovers behave this way. Economic Policy Uncertainty (EPU) and Geopolitical Risk (GPR) news-based indices that spike around salient events are systematically associated with higher volatility and tighter co-movement, thereby amplifying outward transmission from global to regional markets (Baker et al. 2016; Caldara and Iacoviello 2022). In parallel, investor attention, proxied by Google search intensity, surges in crises and is tightly linked to trading and volatility, supplying a behavioral conduit through which uncertainty shocks propagate across venues (Da et al. 2011, 2015). Together, these channels rationalize TCI spikes and the asymmetric transmitter/receiver pattern observed in stress.

2.2. *Attention-Based View of Volatility*

A large behavioural and information-economics literature argues that investors are attention-constrained: they selectively process news and reallocate focus toward salient risks, especially in times of stress (Kahneman 1973; Sims 2003). In liquid markets, attention shocks manifest as synchronised information demand, order imbalances, and belief revisions that raise trading activity and volatility (Barber and Odean 2008; Tetlock 2007). Early work using news counts and media tone shows that negative or high-volume coverage increases trading and risk premia (Tetlock 2007; Engelberg and Parsons 2011), while later studies document similar effects using television, newspapers, and online platforms as attention proxies (Yuan 2015; Fang and Peress 2009).

Because modern search engines are a primary channel for information acquisition, local information search captured by the Google Search Volume Index (GSVI) provides a timely, non-price proxy for shifts in investor focus. Empirically, spikes in search intensity anticipate higher turnover and volatility and help explain short-horizon co-movement (Da et al. 2011; Vlastakis and Markellos 2012; Preis et al. 2013; Choi and Varian 2012). This line of work complements earlier evidence based on media and message-board activity (Barber and Odean 2008; Antweiler and Frank 2004): across proxies, heightened attention is associated with stronger price impact, greater trading volume, and fatter tails in return distributions. A second strand of studies focuses directly on volatility, showing that attention measures help explain volatility clustering and volatility risk premia beyond traditional macro or financial variables (Brogaard and Detzel 2015; Andrei and Hasler 2015).

In a regional setting, attention is both global and local. Global events raise baseline attention everywhere, but country-specific searches capture domestic narratives, language, and policy signals that do not immediately appear in prices or macro indices. Aggregating topic-specific GSVI series across the ASEAN-5 therefore isolates a regional attention factor that tracks slow-moving swings in information demand tied to market, macro, and policy themes. When attention concentrates on risk-laden topics (e.g., crisis, inflation, politics), investors update more frequently, and market makers demand higher compensation for inventory risk, pushing conditional volatility higher. Because principal-component analysis (PCA) yields factors with arbitrary sign, we fix the orientation ex ante so that an increase in IS reflects stronger risk-related search intensity across ASEAN languages. Higher values of IS indicate stronger public information demand, without taking a stand on optimism versus pessimism. Accordingly, the MIDAS coefficient on IS is interpreted as the effect of attention on the long-run volatility component, irrespective of sentiment direction

This attention-based view complements the uncertainty channel. Episodes of elevated Economic Policy Uncertainty (EPU) or Geopolitical Risk (GPR) typically coincide with surges in local search and media coverage, producing a behavioural amplifier of volatility and spillovers: information demand focuses on common risks, cross-sectional attention becomes more correlated, and connectedness rises as markets process the same narratives (Baker et al. 2016; Caldara and Iacoviello 2022; Da et al. 2011). In network terms, heightened attention strengthens the out-degree of macro and global nodes and the in-degree of smaller open markets, tilting the system toward a core–periphery pattern in crises, exactly the topology observed in time-varying connectedness (Diebold and Yılmaz 2014; Antonakakis and Gabauer 2017)

2.3. *Macro Uncertainty as Background*

We treat macro-uncertainty gauges, Economic Policy Uncertainty (EPU) and Geopolitical Risk (GPR), as background barometers that sharpen our reading of short-run spillovers rather than as the core low-frequency driver in the volatility model. Conceptually, these indices spike around policy reversals, geopolitical ruptures, and demand scares, registering shocks that ripple quickly through portfolios. In the connectedness block, they are ideal transmitters: they map top-down news into the network and help explain the directional asymmetry observed when global stress rises (Baker et al. 2016; Caldara and Iacoviello 2022).

Accordingly, we include EPU and GPR in the TVP–VAR to capture near-term transmission and to label episodes in which the Total Connectedness Index (TCI) surges. By contrast, our core MIDAS input is the region-specific attention factor constructed from local Google searches (Section 2.2). EPU and GPR are global, news-indexed measures at monthly frequency; they excel at timing event clusters but are less suited to representing the slow-moving, country-specific information demand that we seek to capture for

ASEAN. Elevating them to the role of primary MIDAS driver would blur channels, risk double-counting event-driven variation already absorbed by the connectedness block, and dilute the local information-search signal that anchors our behavioural interpretation (Engle et al. 2013; Da et al. 2015; Ghysels et al. 2016).

We therefore use only the Economic Policy Uncertainty (EPU) index and the Google-based investor-sentiment (IS) index in the GARCH–MIDAS robustness analysis with $K = 18$. EPU serves as a robustness add-on: it is either substituted for IS or combined with it to verify that the long-run loading on the slow component remains negative and statistically significant, and that the variance share (VR%) attributable to the slow component stays economically meaningful. In line with the literature, we expect similar signs and magnitudes but limited incremental explanatory power, consistent with the view that uncertainty operates as top-down news while investor attention reflects bottom-up information demand rather than a redundant signal (Baker et al. 2016; Caldara and Iacoviello 2022; Engle et al. 2013; Da et al. 2015).

In short, the Economic Policy Uncertainty (EPU) index provides both the contextual benchmark and the robustness test: it helps trace and validate short-run transmission in the TVP–VAR network and serves to stress-test the volatility results. Meanwhile, the ASEAN PCA-based investor-sentiment (IS) index remains the parsimonious, region-specific slow driver that links local information search to the long-run component of volatility. This division of labour preserves parsimony and interpretability and aligns with the empirical evidence that policy-uncertainty indices act as powerful transmitters during crises, whereas attention-based measures better explain the background drift in volatility against which such crises unfold.

2.4. Hypotheses

In integrated but open financial systems, crises do not merely raise volatility; they also reshape transmission channels. Theory and evidence on time-varying connectedness show that common shocks—whether triggered by macroeconomic uncertainty, policy change, or global funding stress—raise both conditional volatilities and cross-series loadings, producing a core–periphery topology in which large global benchmarks export risk and smaller, more open markets absorb it (Diebold and Yılmaz 2014; Antonakakis and Gabauer 2017; Baruník and Křehlík 2018; Naeem et al. 2023). In such settings, the strength and direction of spillovers are state-contingent, tightening precisely when diversification is most needed, an empirical regularity observed across major crises from the Global Financial Crisis to COVID-19 (Youssef et al. 2021). Global equity indices and macro-uncertainty measures such as EPU and GPR typically act as core transmitters, while emerging markets play the role of receivers (International Monetary Fund 2016; Lien et al. 2018; Baker et al. 2016).

On this basis, our first hypothesis focuses on the behaviour of the connectedness network in stress regimes:

Hypothesis 1. *In stress regimes, dynamic connectedness between the ASEAN-5 equity markets and global benchmarks intensifies: the Total Connectedness Index (TCI) rises sharply, and global indices and macro-uncertainty factors (MSCI EM, S&P 500, EPU, and GPR) act as net transmitters of volatility, while ASEAN markets function as net receivers.*

While global shocks set the stage, investor attention provides a behavioural conduit that determines how long volatility persists and how strongly it propagates. The attention-based view of volatility holds that investors' limited information-processing capacity leads them to focus on salient topics, which amplifies market reactions and risk transmission (Kahneman 1973; Sims 2003; Barber and Odean 2008; Tetlock 2007). Local information search, captured by Google Search Volume Index (GSVI) data, offers a real-time proxy for shifts in investor focus and for the diffusion of sentiment across markets (Da et al. 2011; Vlastakis and Markellos 2012; Choi and Varian 2012). When search activity concentrates on risk-laden terms (e.g., crisis, inflation, politics), market participants update more frequently and demand greater risk compensation, raising long-run volatility; when attention focuses on more benign or opportunity-related terms (e.g., stock market, economy), long-run volatility tends to decline (Engle et al. 2013; Ghysels et al. 2016; Brogaard and Detzel 2015). Recent work also suggests that attention shocks and macro-uncertainty shocks act as complementary, rather than purely substitutable, drivers of market risk (Da et al. 2015; Baker et al. 2016).

In line with this view, our second hypothesis concerns the long-run component of volatility in the GARCH–MIDAS block:

Hypothesis 2. *The ASEAN regional, Google-based investor-sentiment (IS) index has a statistically and economically significant loading on the long-run component of volatility across the ASEAN-5, even after controlling for global policy uncertainty (EPU); shifts in risk-oriented search intensity are associated with persistent changes in the slow volatility component.*

Taken together, Hypothesis 1 and Hypothesis 2 capture our core theoretical view: ASEAN financial integration is state-dependent and primarily shaped by global uncertainty at the network level, while the regional IS index channels investor attention into the persistence and magnitude of long-run volatility at the market level.

3. Data Description and Preliminary Analysis

This study employs a comprehensive dataset covering the period from January 2000 to December 2024 for the ASEAN-5 economies Indonesia, Malaysia, Singapore, Thailand, and Vietnam together with several global benchmarks. All series are aligned on a common trading calendar and adjusted for local holidays and time zone differences.

3.1. Financial Market Data

Daily equity market data for the ASEAN-5 economies (Indonesia, Malaysia, Singapore, Thailand, and Vietnam) and the main global reference indices S&P 500, MSCI Emerging Markets, Clean Energy, and Gold are obtained from the Refinitiv Terminal. All price series are converted into daily log returns to eliminate scale differences and ensure stationarity. The full sample covers 25 years (2000–2024), providing on average more than 6000 daily observations per market. Table A1 in Appendix A summarises all variables used in the analysis, including their definitions, transformations (returns vs. levels), roles in the empirical framework (regional market, global benchmark, safe haven, or uncertainty driver), and data sources. All price series are converted into daily log-returns, while uncertainty indicators enter in levels.

We focus on the ASEAN-5 rather than the full ASEAN group for three reasons. First, these five markets provide long and relatively continuous daily equity index series over 2000–2024, which is essential for the time-varying connectedness analysis. Second, they are among the largest and most liquid equity markets in the region, so that spillover patterns are economically meaningful and less affected by microstructure noise. Third, consistent Google Trends coverage for the selected macro-policy topics is available for these countries over our sample, which is required to construct a homogeneous regional investor-sentiment (IS) index.

The inclusion of both regional and global markets allows the model to capture cross border and cross asset transmission channels. The S&P 500 and MSCI EM indices represent global benchmarks, while Clean Energy and Gold serve, respectively, as environmental and safe haven assets. This data structure supports the joint investigation of dynamic connectedness (TVP–VAR) and long run volatility components (GARCH–MIDAS).

3.2. Economic Policy and Geopolitical Uncertainty

The Economic Policy Uncertainty (EPU) index is retrieved from the official Policy Uncertainty portal (https://www.policyuncertainty.com, accessed on 10 October 2025), originally developed by Baker et al. (2016). The Global Geopolitical Risk (GPR) index is obtained from Caldara and Iacoviello (2022) and downloaded from the Federal Reserve Board's GPR database (https://www.matteoiacoviello.com/gpr.htm, accessed on 10 October 2025).

Both indices are monthly and serve as exogenous low frequency measures of global macro policy and geopolitical shocks. They are used in the GARCH–MIDAS specification to capture the top down drivers of long term volatility, complementing the behavioral attention factor introduced below.

3.3. Investor Attention (GSVI Based Index)

To incorporate the behavioral dimension, a regional investor attention index (IS) is constructed using Google search data. Five macro financial topics stock market, inflation, crisis, politics, and economy are selected for each ASEAN-5 country. The corresponding Google Search Volume Index (GSVI) series are collected from the Google Trends platform (https://trends.google.com/trends, accessed on 10 October 2025) via the official Google search interface.

Each series is standardized to zero mean and unit variance to ensure comparability across topics and countries. Following Jolliffe (2002) and Kaiser (1960), a Principal Component Analysis (PCA) is applied to the standardized panel to extract a common factor of regional information demand. The first two principal components with eigenvalues greater than 1 are retained and combined using eigenvalue weights to form the composite investor attention index (IS).

The constructed IS captures the intensity of investors' information searches in the ASEAN-5 region, representing attention rather than the direction of sentiment. Higher IS values therefore indicate periods of heightened public focus on financial and macro policy topics, which may influence the persistence of volatility in the GARCH–MIDAS framework.

Table A1 summarizes the variables, their definitions, frequency, and sources used in this study. Detailed metadata including ticker codes, construction notes, and sample coverage for each variable are provided in Appendix A.

3.4. Descriptive Statistics and Correlation Analysis

To provide preliminary insights into the characteristics of the data, Table 1 reports the descriptive statistics of the ASEAN-5 equity markets, global benchmarks (S&P 500, MSCI EM, Clean Energy, and Gold), and the two uncertainty indices (EPU and GPR) over the period 2000–2024. All return series are expressed in daily logarithmic differences, whereas uncertainty indices enter in levels.

Table 1 shows that all variables exhibit some degree of skewness and kurtosis, indicating deviations from a normal distribution. Most return series are slightly asymmetric and leptokurtic, reflecting the typical behaviour of financial data characterised by fat tails and volatility clustering (Antonakakis and Gabauer 2017). Among the ASEAN-5 equity markets, Singapore and Malaysia record the highest average returns with moderate variability, whereas Thailand displays a slightly negative mean return coupled with high kurtosis, suggesting episodic but pronounced fluctuations. Vietnam and Indonesia exhibit positive skewness, consistent with the higher growth potential and risk return profile typical of emerging markets (Assaf et al. 2021).

Table 1. Summary Statistics ASEAN-5 and Global Variables.

Variable	Mean	Variance	Skewness	Kurtosis	JB	ERS	Q(20)	Q^2(20)	LM(20)
Indonesia	0.0025	1.0226	1.560	6.483	20,025.24 ***	−15.30	49,759.12 ***	13,022.84 ***	3027.95 ***
Malaysia	0.0282	0.9873	0.899	20.170	15,8621.3 ***	−22.80	27,211.74 ***	15,582.77 ***	5488.51 ***
Singapore	0.0369	0.9619	−0.923	1.103	1788.62 ***	−9.21	102,253.2 ***	32,606.01 ***	4603.99 ***
Thailand	−0.0093	1.0190	0.191	40.705	641,013.47 ***	−23.38	9934.78 ***	8575.56 ***	2632.38 ***
Vietnam	0.0168	1.0102	0.673	29.699	341,901.21 ***	−31.06	5473.46 ***	7425.9 ***	3816.17 ***
SP500_return	0.0012	1.0134	−0.450	21.955	186,774.7 ***	−40.85	855.53 ***	18,084.62 ***	3699.61 ***
CleanEnergy_return	−0.0134	0.9989	−0.095	10.304	41,086.69 ***	−38.12	1104.33 ***	10,155.9 ***	2243.67 ***
MSCI_EM_return	0.0118	1.0027	−1.186	12.269	60,403.97 ***	−34.74	1278.76 ***	11,048.99 ***	2903.82 ***
Gold_return	−0.0127	1.0074	0.199	−1.241	657.35 ***	−6.66	121,608.36 ***	1694.24 ***	1181.4 ***
GPR	−0.0323	0.9454	4.109	32.967	446,547.27 ***	−10.64	65,900.29 ***	69,390.34 ***	7820.89 ***
EPU	152.4387	6823.8369	1.658	4.650	12,617.23 ***	−2.03	170,590.41 ***	149,334.27 ***	9168.4 ***

Notes: This table presents the descriptive statistics of ASEAN and global market series over 2000–2024. JB is the Jarque–Bera test for normality. ERS is the Elliott–Rothenberg–Stock DF-GLS unit-root test. Q(20) and Q^2(20) are Ljung–Box tests for 20th-order serial correlations in returns and squared returns. LM(20) is the ARCH Lagrange Multiplier test with 20 lags. (***) denote significance at the 1% levels.

Turning to the global series, the S&P 500 and MSCI EM indices show comparable variance and excess kurtosis, confirming their exposure to global macro financial shocks and their role as major transmitters of volatility within the international network. The Clean Energy index presents particularly large dispersion, mirroring its sensitivity to policy transitions, technological cycles, and commodity price volatility. By contrast, Gold remains comparatively stable, with near zero skewness and mild kurtosis, underscoring its safe haven behaviour and low tail risk (Assaf et al. 2021).

The uncertainty indices Global Geopolitical Risk (GPR) and Economic Policy Uncertainty (EPU) display extreme kurtosis values, suggesting a high likelihood of outliers and episodic surges in uncertainty. The Jarque–Bera statistics confirm significant departures from normality across all variables. Variances are broadly similar across equity returns (approximately 1 by construction), while the uncertainty measures have wider ranges owing to their level based scaling. This pattern aligns with the post 2008 global environment described by Baker et al. (2016), where heightened geopolitical tensions, inflationary pressures, and monetary tightening contributed to persistent volatility in macro financial risk indicators. Overall, the results underline the informational richness of our dataset and provide a robust empirical foundation for analysing time varying connectedness and volatility transmission across ASEAN-5 and global markets.

Building on the distributional evidence reported in Table 1, which highlights the non normality and volatility characteristics of the series, Table 2 examines the pairwise correlations among the ASEAN-5 equity markets, global financial factors, and uncertainty indices over the period 2000–2024. The results reveal moderate and positive co movements within the ASEAN-5 (approximately 0.41–0.50), suggesting a meaningful degree of regional financial integration and a potential channel for shock transmission across neighbouring markets (Antonakakis and Gabauer 2017). The magnitude of these correlations reflects a balance between local fundamentals and shared exposure to global conditions, confirming that ASEAN markets are regionally connected but not fully synchronised, an important feature for diversification strategies (Assaf et al. 2021).

Table 2. Correlation Matrix among the series (Pearson).

Series	Indonesia	Malaysia	Singapore	Thailand	Vietnam	SP500_Return	MSCI_EM_Return	CleanEnergy_Return	Gold_Return	EPU	GPR	VIF
Indonesia	1.000	0.435 ***	0.421 ***	0.414 ***	0.167 ***	0.157 ***	0.217 ***	0.180 ***	−0.011	0.033 *	0.006	3.18
Malaysia		1.000	0.490 ***	0.448 ***	0.131 ***	0.042 **	0.187 ***	0.140 ***	0.045 **	0.057 ***	0.034 *	2.81
Singapore			1.000	0.503 ***	0.162 ***	0.192 ***	0.295 ***	0.230 ***	−0.046 **	−0.008	−0.004	2.39
Thailand				1.000	0.189 ***	0.218 ***	0.319 ***	0.260 ***	−0.023	0.018	0.003	1.62
Vietnam					1.000	0.144 ***	0.124 ***	0.107 ***	−0.046 **	−0.006	−0.027	1.57
SP500_return						1.000	0.764 ***	0.690 ***	−0.074 ***	0.031	0.007	1.56
MSCI_EM_return							1.000	0.731 ***	0.022	0.025	0.010	1.40
CleanEnergy_return								1.000	0.040 **	0.059 ***	0.006	1.06
Gold_return									1.000	0.029	−0.012	1.05
EPU										1.000	−0.188 ***	1.04
GPR											1.000	1.04

Notes: Pearson correlations. Upper triangle shows coefficients with significance stars. (***), (**), and (*) denote significance at the 1%, 5%, and 10% levels, respectively. Diagonal values are 1.000. Lower triangle intentionally left blank for readability.

The global factors exhibit strong positive associations with regional returns: MSCI EM and Clean Energy show the highest correlations with the ASEAN-5, while the S&P 500 maintains a slightly lower yet significant linkage. These findings indicate that international risk cycles and global macro financial shocks are transmitted to ASEAN markets, particularly during stress episodes such as the 2008 Global Financial Crisis and the 2020 COVID-19 pandemic. Conversely, Gold remains weakly or even negatively correlated with equities, underscoring its persistent role as a defensive and hedging asset, consistent with earlier evidence in the energy–uncertainty literature (Assaf et al. 2021).

The uncertainty proxies (EPU and GPR) display low and often negative correlations with market returns, implying that they convey orthogonal information about global risk sentiment rather than overlapping with traditional market factors. This weak contemporaneous association reinforces their usefulness in capturing macroeconomic and geopolitical shocks that operate mainly through volatility channels rather than immediate price co movements (Baker et al. 2016). Importantly, the variance inflation factors (VIFs) remain low ($\leq$3.2), confirming that the variables are not collinear and that the TVP–VAR estimation is statistically well conditioned.

Overall, the correlation structure described in Table 2 complements the distributional findings of Table 1 by revealing an integrated yet diversifiable ASEAN–global system, which justifies the use of time varying connectedness measures to capture its evolving interdependence (Antonakakis and Gabauer 2017; Assaf et al. 2021).

To complement the distributional and correlation results discussed in Tables 1 and 2, Figure 1 plots standardised empirical distributions for the ASEAN-5 equity returns together with global benchmarks (S&P 500, MSCI EM, Clean Energy, Gold) and the two uncertainty measures over 2000–2024. In each panel, the light blue bars show the standardised histogram, the solid blue line reports the non-parametric kernel density estimate, and the red dashed line depicts the Gaussian density with the same mean and variance as the underlying series. The return distributions are sharply peaked with heavy tails, a canonical signature of daily asset prices, leptokurtosis, and departures from normality well documented in the market microstructure literature (Cont 2001; Pagan 1996). The overlaid Gaussian kernels systematically understate tail mass and peak height, reinforcing visual evidence of non normality.

By contrast, the uncertainty proxies display positively skewed, fat tailed shapes: Economic Policy Uncertainty (EPU) and Geopolitical Risk (GPR) concentrate probability mass at low levels with episodic right tail bursts during global events, consistent with their news based construction and historical behaviour (Baker et al. 2016; Caldara and Iacoviello 2022). Taken together, these distributions point to series that are non Gaussian, heteroskedastic, and prone to clustering of volatility, stylised facts that motivate models expressly designed for time varying spillovers and mixed frequency volatility.

Methodologically, this evidence justifies our two pillar framework. First, a TVP–VAR connectedness design captures evolving shock transmission across ASEAN and global factors, in the tradition of Diebold–Yılmaz spillovers and their time varying refinements (Diebold and Yılmaz 2014; Antonakakis and Gabauer 2017). Second, a GARCH–MIDAS block links long run volatility to low frequency drivers such as attention, accommodating conditional heteroskedasticity at the daily horizon while mapping persistent variation to monthly components (Engle et al. 2013; Ghysels et al. 2004; see also Engle and Rangel 2008).

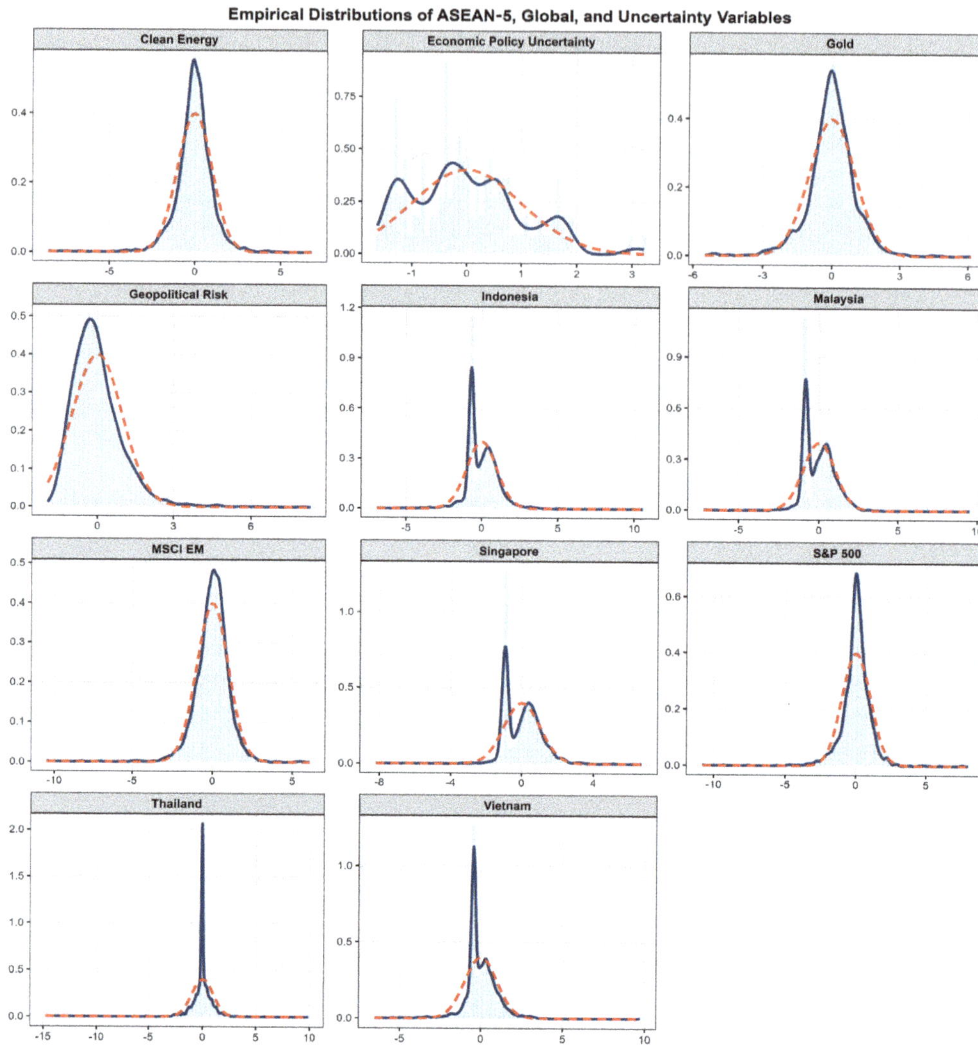

Figure 1. Empirical distributions of returns and uncertainty indices.

4. Methodology

This section has two parts. Section 4.1 estimates dynamic connectedness using a time-varying-parameter VAR (TVP–VAR) with generalized forecast-error variance decompositions (GFEVDs), producing the Total Connectedness Index (TCI) as well as TO, FROM, NET, and net pairwise directional spillovers. Section 4.2 models volatility using a GARCH–MIDAS specification that separates short-run (daily) and long-run (monthly) components, where the long-run component is driven by the Google-based investor-sentiment (IS) index described in Section 3.3 and in robustness by economic policy uncertainty (EPU).

4.1. TVP–VAR Connectedness

A large empirical literature seeks to quantify how shocks propagate across macro-financial variables. The seminal contribution of Diebold and Yılmaz (2014) developed a rolling-window VAR framework in which connectedness metrics such as total, directional, and net spillovers are constructed from forecast-error variance decompositions. In that setting, the share of the H-step-ahead forecast-error variance of series i that is attributable to innovations in the other series provides an intuitive measure of cross-market transmission, but the approach assumes constant parameters and a fixed variance–covariance matrix within each rolling window.

To overcome these limitations, Antonakakis and Gabauer (2017), building on Primiceri's (2005) state-space specification with stochastic volatility, replace the rolling, constant-parameter VAR with a time-varying-parameter VAR (TVP–VAR) and a time-varying covariance structure. In the TVP–VAR, coefficients drift over time and shock variances evolve stochastically, allowing the model to accommodate changes in lag dynamics, heteroskedastic shocks, and evolving contemporaneous relationships. Compared with the original Diebold–Yılmaz procedure, the TVP–VAR connectedness approach avoids the arbitrary choice of window length, preserves all observations, and, because estimation proceeds via a multivariate Kalman filter with forgetting factors, is more robust to outliers and adapts quickly to structural breaks or major events.

4.1.1. Model Specification

Let y_t be an $N \times 1$ vector collecting the daily returns on the ASEAN-5 equity indices together with global benchmarks (S&P 500, MSCI EM, Clean Energy, Gold) and the uncertainty indices (EPU and GPR). We estimate a TVP–VAR(1) in reduced form:

$$y_t = B_{0,t} + B_{1,t}y_{t-1} + \varepsilon_t, \varepsilon_t \sim N(0, S_t), \tag{1}$$

where $B_{0,t}$ is an $N \times 1$ vector of time-varying intercepts, $B_{1,t}$ is an $N \times N$ matrix of time-varying autoregressive coefficients, and S_t is the $N \times N$ innovation covariance matrix of the reduced-form shocks ε_t.

Define the augmented regressor vector $x_t = (1, y'_{t-1})'$ and the coefficient matrix $B_t = [B_{0,t}\ B_{1,t}]$, so that

$$y_t = B_t x_t + \varepsilon_t. \tag{2}$$

To cast the model in state-space form, we stack the coefficients into the $K \times 1$ state vector

$$\beta_t = vec(B_t), K = N(N+1), \tag{3}$$

and define the corresponding $N \times K$ regressor matrix

$$X_t = x'_t \otimes I_N, \tag{4}$$

where $\otimes$ denotes the Kronecker product and I_N is the $N \times N$ idensity matrix. The measurement equation becomes

$$y_t = X_t\beta_t + \varepsilon_t, \varepsilon_t \sim N(0, S_t). \tag{5}$$

The evolution of the coefficients is governed by a random-walk state equation,

$$\beta_t = \beta_{t-1} + \eta_t, \eta_t \sim N(0, Q), \tag{6}$$

where Q is a $K \times K$ process-noise covariance matrix. The $K \times K$ matrix is

$$P_t = Var(\beta_t \mid \mathcal{F}_t) \tag{7}$$

is the covariance matrix of the state estimate, i.e., it summarizes the uncertainty about the time-varying coefficients conditional on the information set $\mathcal{F}_t$, whereas S_t captures the contemporaneous covariance of the reduced-form shocks. Thus S_t and P_t play distinct roles: S_t is the innovation covariance matrix in the measurement equation, and P_t is the state covariance matrix in the coefficient dynamics.

4.1.2. Estimation via Kalman Filter with Forgetting Factor

The state-space system (5)–(7) is estimated via a multivariate Kalman filter with a forgetting (discount) factor, which is equivalent to recursive least squares with exponential down-weighting of older observations. Let $\hat{\beta}_{t|t}$ denote the filtered estimate of β_t and $P_{t|t}$ its covariance matrix. Given $\left(\hat{\beta}_{t-1|t-1}, P_{t-1|t-1}\right)$, the prediction step is

$$\hat{\beta}_{t|t-1} = \hat{\beta}_{t-1|t-1}, \tag{8}$$

$$P_{t|t-1} = \lambda^{-1} P_{t-1|t-1} + Q, 0 < \lambda \leq 1, \tag{9}$$

where λ is the forgetting factor. Values of λ close to one imply slowly drifting parameters, whereas smaller values allow for faster adjustment to structural breaks.

The innovation covariance matrix is

$$\Omega_t = X_t P_{t|t-1} X_t' + S_t, \tag{10}$$

and the Kalman gain is

$$K_t = P_{t|t-1} X_t' \Omega_t^{-1}. \tag{11}$$

The update step is

$$\hat{\beta}_{t|t} = \hat{\beta}_{t|t-1} + K_t\left(y_t - X_t \hat{\beta}_{t|t-1}\right), \tag{12}$$

$$P_{t|t} = (I_K - K_t X_t) P_{t|t-1}, \tag{13}$$

where I_K is the $K \times K$ identity matrix.

Following Koop and Korobilis (2014) and Antonakakis et al. (2020), the forgetting factor λ and the elements of Q are selected by Bayesian model comparison: alternative values are compared using predictive likelihoods, and the combination that maximizes model fit is retained. This procedure ensures that parameter evolution is data-driven rather than ad hoc and improves robustness to outliers and structural breaks.

Given the filtered paths $\hat{B}_t$ and S_t, the TVP–VAR may be written in its time-varying vector moving-average (TVP–VMA) representation:

$$y_t = \sum_{h=0}^{\infty} A_{h,t} \varepsilon_{t-h}, \tag{14}$$

where $A_{0,t} = I_N$ and $A_{h,t}(h \geq 1)$ are $N \times N$ time-varying MA coefficient matrices obtained recursively from $\hat{B}_t$. This TVP–VMA representation is the basis for the generalized forecast-error variance decompositions and connectedness measures.

4.1.3. Generalized FEVD and Connectedness Measures

Using the generalized forecast-error variance decomposition (GFEVD) of Pesaran and Shin (1998), the fraction of the H-step-ahead forecast-error variance of variable i due to shocks in variable j at time t is

$$\theta_{ij,t}(H) = \frac{\sigma_{jj,t}^{-1} \sum_{h=0}^{H-1} (e_i' A_{h,t} S_t e_j)^2}{\sum_{h=0}^{H-1} e_i' A_{h,t} S_t A_{h,t}' e_i}, \tag{15}$$

where e_i is an $N \times 1$ selection vector with 1 in position i, $\sigma_{jj,t}$ is the j-th diagonal element of S_t, and S_t is the covariance matrix of reduced-form shocks. Under the generalized identification scheme, these shares are order-invariant but do not in general sum to one across j for a given i.

To recover interpretable shares, we normalize the GFEVDs row-wise:

$$\tilde{\theta}_{ij,t}(H) = \frac{\theta_{ij,t}(H)}{\sum_{k=1}^{N} \theta_{ik,t}(H)}, \sum_{j=1}^{N} \tilde{\theta}_{ij,t}(H) = 1 \forall i, t. \tag{16}$$

Let $\tilde{\Theta}_t(H) = \left[\tilde{\theta}_{ij,t}(H)\right]$ be the normalized GFEVD matrix. The Total Connectedness Index (TCI) at time t is

$$\text{TCI}_t(H) = 100 \times \frac{1}{N} \sum_{i=1}^{N} \sum_{\substack{j=1 \\ j \neq i}}^{N} \tilde{\theta}_{ij,t}(H), \tag{17}$$

which measures the average share of forecast-error variance that is due to cross-market shocks (off-diagonal elements). In our application, we set $H = 25$ trading days, in line with the literature.

Directional spillovers have a transparent row/column-sum interpretation. For market i:

Spillovers FROM others to i (how much i receives) are

$$\text{FROM}_{i,t}(H) = 100 \times \sum_{\substack{j=1 \\ j \neq i}}^{N} \tilde{\theta}_{ij,t}(H), \tag{18}$$

i.e., the sum of off-diagonal elements in row i, interpreted as the share of i's forecast-error variance explained by shocks from all other markets.

Spillovers TO others from i (how much i sends) are

$$\text{TO}_{i,t}(H) = 100 \times \sum_{\substack{j=1 \\ j \neq i}}^{N} \tilde{\theta}_{ji,t}(H), \tag{19}$$

i.e., the sum of off-diagonal elements in column i, interpreted as the contribution of shocks in i to the forecast-error variance of all other markets.

The NET spillover of market i is

$$\text{NET}_{i,t}(H) = \text{TO}_{i,t}(H) - \text{FROM}_{i,t}(H), \tag{20}$$

so that positive values identify net transmitters and negative values net receivers of shocks.

Pairwise net directional connectedness between markets i and j is

$$\text{NPDC}_{ij,t}(H) = 100 \times \left(\tilde{\theta}_{ij,t}(H) - \tilde{\theta}_{ji,t}(H)\right), \tag{21}$$

so that $\text{NPDC}_{ij,t}(H) > 0$ indicates that i transmits more strongly to j than j to i. Because the underlying GFEVD is generalized, all these connectedness measures are order-invariant.

In the empirical analysis, we report both (i) time-varying connectedness indices TCI_t, $\text{TO}_{i,t}$, $\text{FROM}_{i,t}$, and $\text{NET}_{i,t}$ (Figures 2–5), and (ii) static FROM/TO matrices, obtained as time averages of $\tilde{\Theta}_t(H)$ over the full sample (Tables 3 and 4).

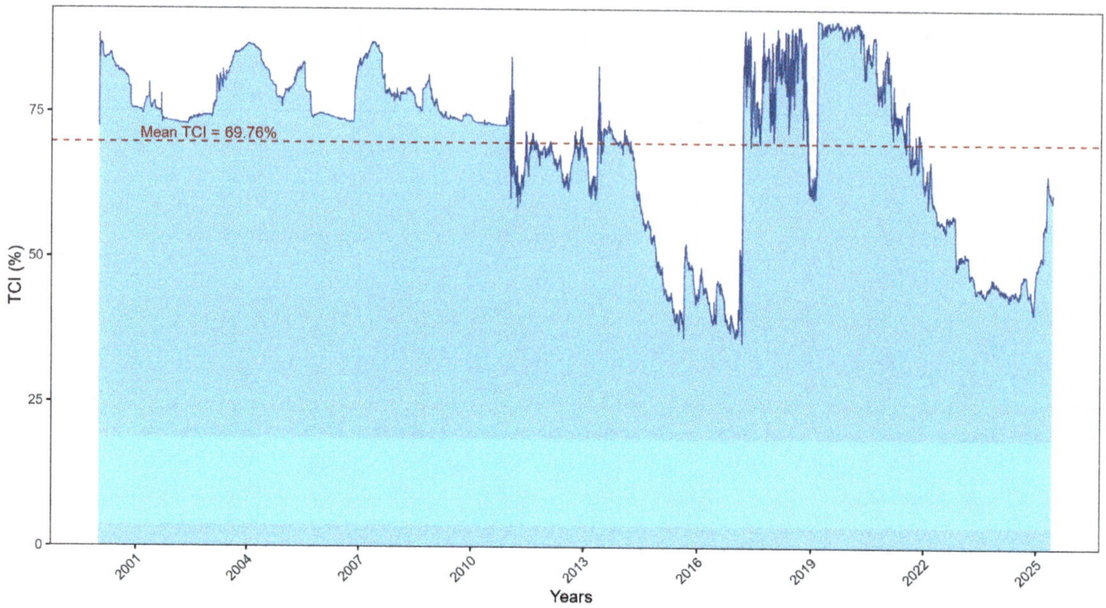

Figure 2. Total Connectedness Index (TCI).

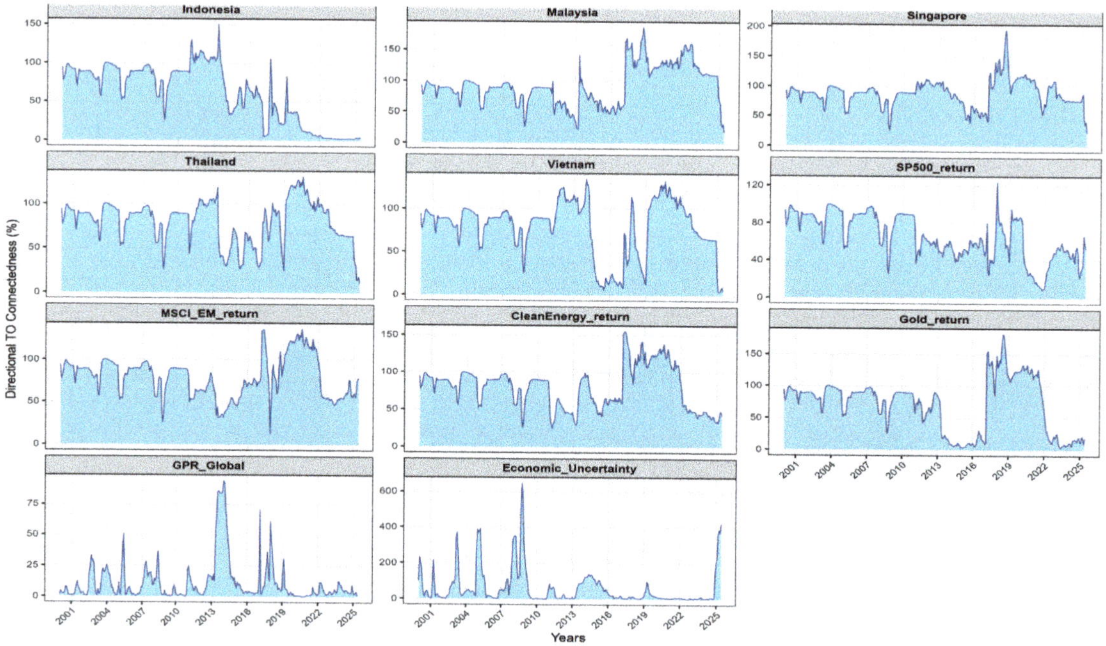

Figure 3. Directional Spillovers (TO).

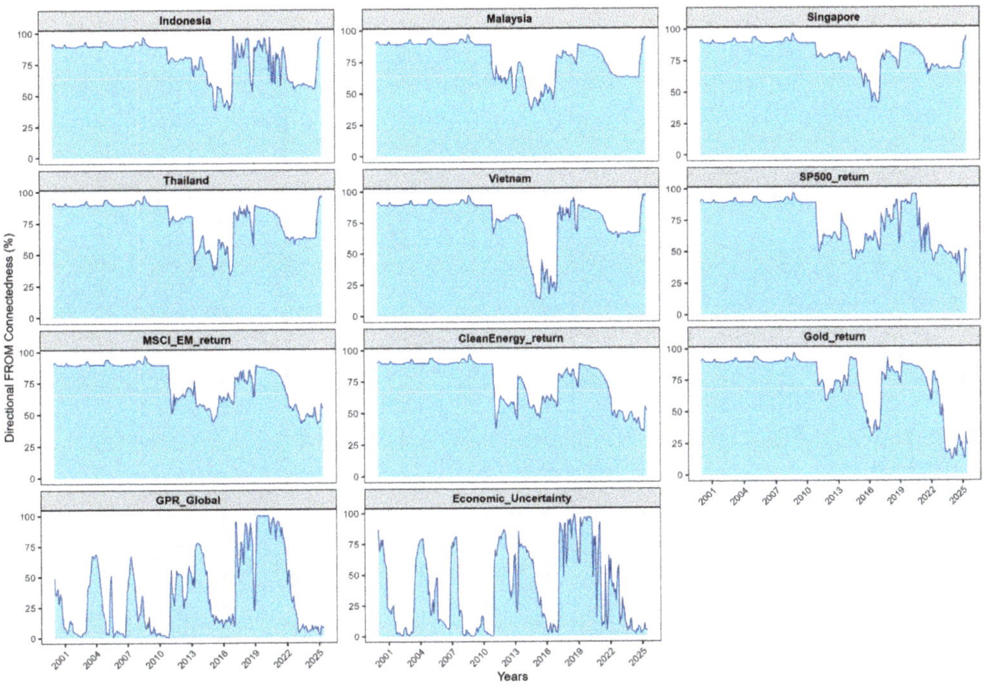

Figure 4. Directional Spillovers (FROM).

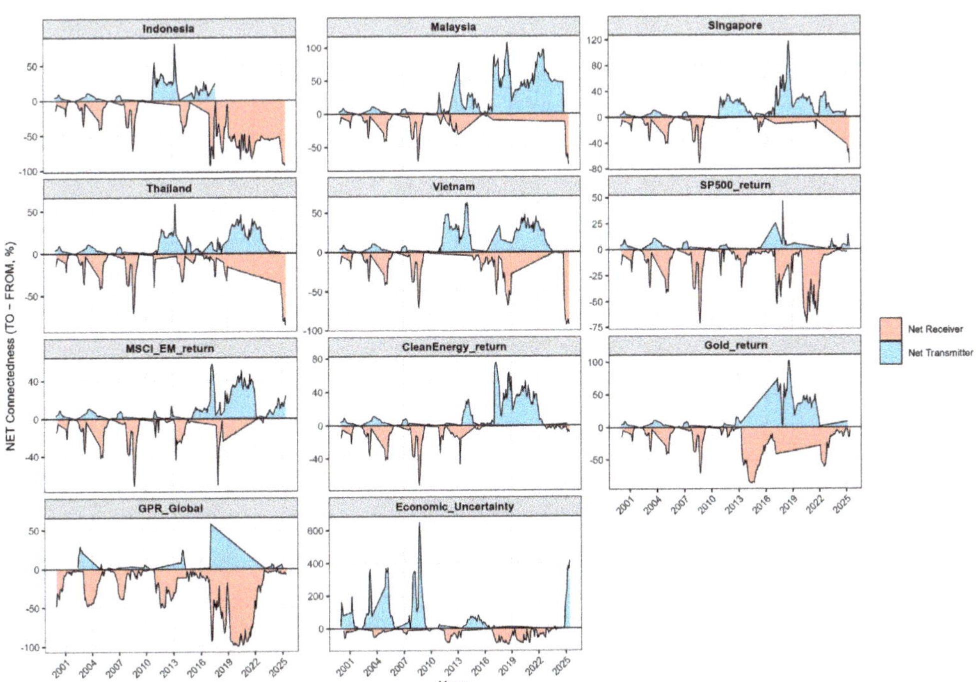

Figure 5. Net Spillovers (NET): emitters vs. receivers.

Table 3. Static Connectedness Matrix.

From/To	Indonesia	Malaysia	Singapore	Thailand	Vietnam	SP500_Return	MSCI_EM_Return	CleanEnergy_Return	Gold_Return	GPR	EPU	FROM
Indonesia	26.90	9.94	10.46	9.70	6.22	6.52	5.79	6.06	9.79	2.37	6.24	73.09
Malaysia	7.99	33.27	12.48	7.05	7.04	6.21	5.05	5.74	5.30	4.52	5.36	66.74
Singapore	7.80	10.71	28.56	8.60	6.66	6.85	6.05	6.24	9.19	2.55	6.78	71.43
Thailand	9.67	8.61	11.72	27.45	6.51	6.54	5.93	6.36	8.01	2.32	6.87	72.54
Vietnam	6.73	7.24	10.29	7.12	36.49	6.69	5.12	6.21	6.34	2.75	5.01	63.50
SP500_return	5.78	5.48	7.74	6.48	6.32	26.99	13.94	12.99	6.51	3.02	4.75	73.01
MSCI_EM_return	6.87	5.34	8.10	7.54	5.84	14.22	23.19	12.78	8.33	2.36	5.43	76.81
CleanEnergy_return	6.25	5.31	7.90	7.29	6.17	13.03	13.02	25.96	7.35	2.76	4.96	74.04
Gold_return	8.55	5.51	9.00	7.16	5.60	6.14	6.46	6.09	35.60	3.22	6.66	64.39
GPR	3.38	4.45	4.57	3.88	4.41	4.83	3.19	3.98	4.12	60.05	3.14	39.95
EPU	4.02	4.54	5.15	5.00	4.95	5.30	3.51	4.39	4.74	2.25	56.14	43.85
TO	67.04	67.13	87.41	69.82	59.72	76.33	68.06	70.84	69.68	28.12	55.20	719.35
Including Own	93.94	100.40	115.97	97.27	96.21	103.32	91.25	96.80	105.28	88.17	111.34	
Net Spillovers	−6.05	0.39	15.98	−2.72	−3.78	3.32	−8.75	−3.20	5.29	−11.83	11.35	

Notes: TVP–VAR(1), generalized FEVD (order-invariant), H = 25. Cells report the share (%) of forecast-error variance of the row variable explained by shocks to the column variable. TCI is the average spillover intensity over 2000–2024.

Table 4. Dynamic Connectedness.

From/To	Indonesia	Malaysia	Singapore	Thailand	Vietnam	SP500_return	MSCI_EM_	CleanEnergy	Gold	GPR	EPU	FROM
Indonesia	3.62	5.29	5.31	2.72	0.89	0.00	1.16	0.00	1.60	0.06	79.33	96.38
Malaysia	0.71	4.61	5.33	2.74	1.05	0.00	1.21	0.00	1.67	0.06	82.61	95.39
Singapore	0.64	4.10	5.29	2.40	1.27	0.00	1.22	0.00	1.68	0.06	83.33	94.71
Thailand	0.56	4.26	5.25	3.09	1.20	0.00	1.21	0.00	1.67	0.06	82.69	96.91
Vietnam	0.63	3.71	5.16	2.12	2.14	0.00	1.22	0.00	1.68	0.06	83.28	97.86
SP500_return	0.00	0.00	0.01	0.00	0.00	50.41	31.95	16.86	0.22	0.05	0.48	49.59
MSCI_EM_return	0.00	0.00	0.00	0.00	0.00	28.27	45.59	20.91	3.75	0.03	1.45	54.41
CleanEnergy_return	0.00	0.02	0.04	0.01	0.02	20.41	27.16	48.34	3.63	0.25	0.11	51.66
Gold_return	0.03	0.17	0.26	0.10	0.10	3.58	11.38	4.78	76.15	0.45	3.00	23.85
GPR	0.15	0.82	1.28	0.45	0.47	0.10	0.12	0.34	0.36	91.34	4.57	8.66
EPU	0.03	0.17	0.28	0.09	0.10	0.01	1.65	0.01	2.40	0.22	95.04	4.96
TO	2.77	18.56	22.92	10.64	5.11	52.38	78.25	42.92	18.68	1.30	420.84	674.38
Including Own	6.39	23.16	28.21	13.73	7.25	102.79	123.84	91.26	94.83	92.64	515.88	
Net Spillovers	−93.61	−76.84	−71.79	−86.27	−92.75	2.79	23.84	−8.74	−5.17	−7.36	415.88	

Notes: Time-varying TO, FROM, and NET spillovers from the TVP–VAR(1) with generalized FEVDs at H = 25 over 2000–2024. TCI summarizes evolving cross-market interdependence and peaks during crises.

4.2. GARCH–MIDAS Volatility

Daily financial returns display strong conditional heteroskedasticity, while key explanatory factors such as investor sentiment (IS) and economic policy uncertainty (EPU) are observed at monthly frequency. Simply down-sampling daily data to a monthly frequency would discard high-frequency information and may bias inference. To jointly model high-frequency volatility and low-frequency drivers, we adopt the GARCH–MIDAS framework of Engle et al. (2013), which decomposes conditional variance into a short-run (daily) component and a slow-moving (monthly) component.

We estimate a separate GARCH–MIDAS model for each return series used in the TVP–VAR. The construction of the ASEAN investor-sentiment index (IS) from Google searches (topics, standardization, PCA) is detailed in Section 3.3; in this section we treat IS as an observed monthly regressor.

Let $r_{i,t,d}$ denote the daily log return of asset i on trading day d of month $t(d = 1, \ldots, n_t)$, and let $\mathcal{F}_{t,d-1}$ be the information set available at the end of day $d-1$. We assume

$$r_{i,t,d} = \mu_i + \varepsilon_{i,t,d}, \varepsilon_{i,t,d} \mid \mathcal{F}_{t,d-1} \sim N\left(0, \sigma^2_{i,t,d}\right), \tag{22}$$

with conditional variance decomposed multiplicatively as

$$\sigma^2_{i,t,d} = \tau_{i,t} h_{i,t,d}, \tag{23}$$

where $\tau_{i,t}$ is the long-run (low-frequency) variance component common to all days in month t, and $h_{i,t,d}$ is the short-run (daily) GARCH component.

4.2.1. Short-Run GARCH Component

The short-run component $h_{i,t,d}$ follows a GARCH(1,1) process normalized to have unit unconditional mean:

$$h_{i,t,d} = (1 - \alpha_i - \beta_i) + \alpha_i \frac{\varepsilon^2_{i,t,d-1}}{\tau_{i,t-1}} + \beta_i h_{i,t,d-1}, \tag{24}$$

with $\alpha_i > 0$, $\beta_i \geq 0$, and $\alpha_i + \beta_i < 1$. Under this parametrization $E[h_{i,t,d}] = 1$, so the level of conditional variance is entirely driven by $\tau_{i,t}$. The parameters α_i and β_i govern short-run persistence: α_i captures the impact of recent squared shocks, β_i controls the rate at which past volatility decays, and their sum $\alpha_i + \beta_i$ summarizes the overall daily persistence reported in the empirical tables.

4.2.2. Long-Run MIDAS Component and IS Driver

The long-run component $\tau_{i,t}$ evolves at the monthly frequency as a MIDAS distributed lag of a low-frequency driver Z_t. In the baseline specification, Z_t is the ASEAN investor-sentiment index (IS); in robustness checks, we either replace IS with the economic policy uncertainty index (EPU) or include both as drivers.

To guarantee positivity and align with the standard literature, we adopt a log-GARCH–MIDAS specification:

$$log\tau_{i,t} = \omega_i + \theta_i \sum_{k=1}^{K} w_k(m_i) Z_{t-k}, \tag{25}$$

where ω_i is an intercept, θ_i is the MIDAS slope coefficient of interest, and $w_k(m_i)$ are Beta-polynomial weights on the K monthly lags of Z_t. The weights are positive and normalized to sum to one:

$$w_k(m_i) > 0, \sum_{k=1}^{K} w_k(m_i) = 1, \tag{26}$$

with shape parameter $m_i > 0$ controlling the decay pattern of the weights. A convenient parametrization is

$$w_k(m_i) = \frac{\left(1 - \frac{k}{K+1}\right)^{m_i-1}}{\sum_{j=1}^{K}\left(1 - \frac{j}{K+1}\right)^{m_i-1}}, \quad (27)$$

which assigns decaying Beta-polynomial weights over the last K months. In the baseline we set $K = 12$ months; robustness checks use $K = 18$. Under (25), $\tau_{i,t} = exp(\cdot) > 0$ by construction, addressing the positivity concern raised in the reviewer's comments.

A statistically significant $\theta_i \neq 0$ indicates that the long-run component of volatility is systematically related to the slow-moving driver Z_t; the sign of θ_i determines whether higher attention or uncertainty is associated with higher ($\theta_i > 0$) or lower ($\theta_i < 0$) long-run volatility.

4.2.3. Estimation and Variance-Ratio Measure

The parameter vector $(\mu_i, \alpha_i, \beta_i, \omega_i, \theta_i, m_i)$ is estimated by quasi-maximum likelihood under the normality assumption, subject to the usual GARCH constraints $\alpha_i > 0$, $\beta_i \geq 0$, $\alpha_i + \beta_i < 1$ and the positivity of $\tau_{i,t}$ implied by (25). Robust standard errors are reported in the empirical tables.

To assess the economic importance of the slow component, we compute for each series a variance-ratio statistic $\text{VR}_i(\%)$, defined as the share of total conditional variance attributable to the long-run component $\tau_{i,t}$:

$$\text{VR}_i(\%) = 100 \times \frac{Var(log\tau_{i,t})}{Var(log(\tau_{i,t}h_{i,t,d}))}. \quad (28)$$

A higher VR_i indicates that a larger fraction of volatility persistence is explained by the low-frequency driver (IS or EPU) rather than by the short-run GARCH dynamics alone.

In the results section, we report (i) the short-run persistence $\alpha_i + \beta_i$, (ii) the MIDAS slope θ_i on IS (and, in robustness, on EPU), and (iii) $\text{VR}_i(\%)$. This directly links the behavioral driver to the long-run component of volatility and makes explicit which parameters govern short-run versus long-run dynamics.

5. Results: Static and Dynamic Connectedness (TVP–VAR)

5.1. Static Connectedness

Table 3 reports the full sample (2000–2024) connectedness across the ASEAN-5 equity markets, global equity factors, gold, and the two uncertainty indices, based on a static VAR with generalized FEVDs at horizon $H = 25$. The Total Connectedness Index (TCI) equals 65.4%, implying that roughly two thirds of the average H-step forecast error variance reflects cross market spillovers rather than own shocks. This points to a dense, information rich network in which no market is insulated from the others. Consistent with previous evidence for emerging Asia, such a level of integration is typically associated with episodes of turbulence followed by gradual normalisation (Youssef et al. 2021; Cunado et al. 2024).

A first way to summarise Table 3 is to contrast net transmitters and net receivers, as captured by the NET measure (TO minus FROM). On average, Singapore (NET = +15.98) and EPU (+11.35) stand out as net transmitters, with Gold (+5.29) and the S&P 500 (+3.32) also exporting risk, and Malaysia being almost neutral (+0.39). By contrast, GPR (−11.83), MSCI EM (−8.75), Indonesia (−6.05), Clean Energy (−3.20), Vietnam (−3.78), and Thailand (−2.72) act as net receivers. This hierarchy accords with the broader literature in which developed markets and global risk factors tend to be dominant net transmitters towards emerging Asia, especially around global stress episodes (International Monetary Fund 2016; Lien et al. 2018; Al-Hajieh 2023).

Within the region, Singapore's positive NET confirms its role as a regional hub. It is consistent with evidence that Singapore persistently operates as a financial centre and net transmitter within East and Southeast Asia (Mateus et al. 2024) and with policy surveillance pointing to strong outward spillovers from Singapore among ASEAN+3 financial centres (AMRO 2024).

Directional spillovers (TO and FROM) provide a finer view of this hierarchy. On the outgoing side, Singapore (TO = 87.41) transmits most strongly, followed by the S&P 500 (76.33) and Clean Energy (70.84). On the incoming side, MSCI EM (FROM = 76.81), Clean Energy (74.04), Indonesia (73.09), and Thailand (72.54) absorb a large share of external shocks. These patterns are in line with the connectedness literature in which advanced benchmarks act as shock sources, while composite EM indices and individual emerging markets tend to be shock absorbers (Antonakakis and Gabauer 2017; Cunado et al. 2024).

The uncertainty measures follow standard benchmark definitions. EPU is the news based economic policy uncertainty index of Baker et al. (2016), and GPR is the news based geopolitical risk index of Caldara and Iacoviello (2022). Both are known to propagate into asset markets, including ASEAN equities and energy, through risk and information channels (Assaf et al. 2021). While gold is widely documented as a hedge or safe haven in turbulent periods (Baur and Lucey 2010), the full sample matrix shows a mildly positive net transmission for gold, suggesting that its role is time varying. This becomes clearer once the dynamic dimension is introduced.

Overall, the static matrix provides a clear average map of the system: non trivial integration (TCI $\approx$ 65%), a transmitter tier led by Singapore and macro policy uncertainty (with modest support from the S&P 500 and gold), and a receiver tier composed of regional equities and broad EM factors. This motivates the time varying analysis based on the TVP–VAR, where Figure 2 reports the dynamic TCI, Figures 3 and 4 plot the directional TO and FROM spillovers, and Figure 5 shows the NET positions over time.

5.2. Dynamic Connectedness (TVP–VAR)

Table 4 and Figures 2–5 jointly describe the dynamic behaviour of spillovers in the TVP–VAR(1) with generalized FEVDs at horizon $H = 25$. Table 4 reports the time-averaged FROM, TO, and NET measures implied by the time-varying FEVD matrix, while Figures 2–5 trace the corresponding paths of the Total Connectedness Index (TCI), directional TO and FROM spillovers, and NET positions over 2000–2024.

The TCI trajectory in Figure 2 summarises the evolution of overall connectedness. Using the TVP–VAR(1) framework, the TCI averages about 69.8% and peaks close to 91% during turmoil. In tranquil regimes, roughly two thirds of forecast uncertainty arises from cross-market interactions, a level close to the static benchmark in Table 3. In crises, cross-market spillovers dominate and the system approaches near complete interdependence. This pattern of low to moderate connectedness in calm periods and sharp surges in stress episodes is consistent with connectedness models that allow coefficients and shock variances to drift over time (Diebold and Yılmaz 2014; Antonakakis and Gabauer 2017; Gabauer 2021), and with frequency-domain evidence that crisis amplification is concentrated in the low-frequency (long-horizon) component of volatility (Baruník and Křehlík 2018). The fact that the dynamic TCI ($\approx$69.8%) exceeds the static value (65.4%) reinforces the view that integration tightens in bad times and relaxes as uncertainty fades.

The directional structure of the network, summarised in Table 4 and reflected in Figures 3 and 4, is dominated by macro-global senders and regional receivers. On the outgoing side, EPU is by far the largest net transmitter (NET ≈ +415.9), with MSCI EM (≈+23.8) and, to a lesser extent, the S&P 500 (≈+2.8) also exporting volatility into ASEAN. This global to regional propagation matches the broader evidence that spillovers intensify when developed benchmarks and news-based uncertainty indices comove closely with emerging Asia, especially around global shocks and policy shifts (International Monetary Fund 2016; Lien et al. 2018; Naeem et al. 2023).

On the incoming side, all five ASEAN equity markets are systematic net receivers. Their FROM values in Table 4, which are very high relative to their TO values (for example Indonesia ≈ 96.4, Vietnam ≈ 97.9), confirm that most of their forecast-error variance is driven by shocks originating in global benchmarks (MSCI EM and S&P 500) and macro-uncertainty factors (EPU and GPR). This outside-in pattern is typical of emerging Asia, where global risk and major market shocks are transmitted strongly into regional equities (International Monetary Fund 2016; Lien et al. 2018). Over time, the FROM measures for ASEAN markets rise sharply during episodes such as the Global Financial Crisis, the taper tantrum, the COVID-19 shock, and the Russia–Ukraine conflict, and decline as conditions normalise (Youssef et al. 2021; Baruník and Křehlík 2018).

Gold and clean-energy equities play more nuanced roles. Gold remains a mild net receiver on average (NET ≈ −5.2 in Table 4), underscoring its defensive profile and aligning with its hedge or safe-haven behaviour in stress periods (Baur and Lucey 2010). The clean-energy index alternates between regimes. It occasionally transmits shocks during climate-policy and energy-transition announcements, but tends to absorb shocks when commodity prices or funding conditions dominate. This regime-dependent behaviour mirrors recent findings for green and clean assets, where climate policy and financial conditions jointly shape connectedness (Özkan et al. 2024; Naeem et al. 2023). Together, gold and clean energy help explain why diversification compresses in crises but does not disappear: safe-haven and thematic exposures cushion part of the shock, although they do not fully offset the strong top-down impulse from uncertainty and global benchmarks.

Overall, the dynamic evidence extends the static picture rather than overturning it. The identity of transmitters and receivers is broadly stable: global equity and uncertainty factors transmit, while ASEAN equities receive. What changes over time is the intensity of transmission, which is clearly state-dependent and markedly higher in stress episodes. For investors and policymakers, two implications follow. First, risk management must be regime-aware because spillovers and diversification benefits become most constrained precisely when risk is elevated. Second, close monitoring of macro-policy and geopolitical uncertainty is essential, since these factors appear to trigger the swings in system-wide connectedness documented by the TCI and directional spillovers.

6. The Impact of Investor Attention on Dynamic Spillover

In this section, we examine how investor attention, proxied by the Google-based investor-sentiment index (IS), affects the long-run component of volatility in the ASEAN-5 and global benchmark markets. Following Wu and Liu (2023), we interpret the PCA-based Google index as a neutral measure of information demand or attention intensity rather than as a directional optimism–pessimism indicator.

As described in Section 3.3, monthly Google Search Volume Index (GSVI) data for five macro-policy topics (stock market, inflation, crisis, politics, and economy) are collected for each ASEAN-5 country. These standardized series are stacked into a regional panel and summarized using principal component analysis (PCA). The first two principal components with eigenvalues greater than one are retained and combined using eigenvalue weights to construct a composite investor-attention index, IS (Table 5). This index captures the overall intensity of public searches related to financial and macro-policy information in the region. Higher values of IS therefore reflect stronger information demand without implying whether the underlying sentiment is optimistic or pessimistic.

Table 5. Average PCA Loadings by Country (PC1 and PC2).

Country	Mean_PC1	Mean_PC2
Indonesia	0.176	−0.125
Malaysia	0.220	0.102
Singapore	0.200	0.165
Thailand	0.176	0.058
Vietnam	0.182	−0.160

Notes: This table reports the mean PCA loadings for each ASEAN-5 country based on the first two principal components (PC1 and PC2). The loadings are computed from Google Search Volume Indices (GSVI) related to stock market, inflation, crisis, politics, and economy. Positive (negative) values indicate stronger (weaker or opposing) country contributions to the overall sentiment factor.

Table 5 reports the average PCA loadings by country, while Figure 6 compares the share of variance explained by the retained components, confirming that the first two principal components capture the bulk of common variation in Google search activity across ASEAN-5 markets.

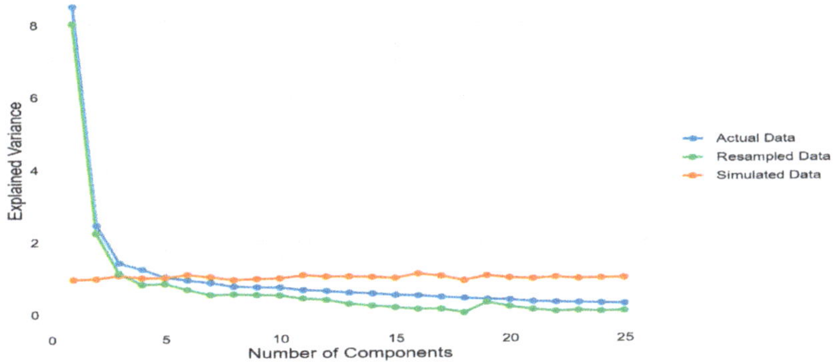

Figure 6. PCA Variance Comparison.

Figure 6 further assesses the PCA by plotting the variance explained by each principal component for the actual GSVI panel, a bootstrap resampled panel, and a panel of simulated white-noise series. For the actual and resampled data, the scree plot shows a steep drop after the first two components and a nearly flat profile thereafter, whereas the simulated data exhibit an almost flat line across all components, confirming that PC1 and PC2 capture genuine common variation in Google search activity rather than sampling noise.

We then estimate a GARCH–MIDAS model for each daily return series used in the TVP–VAR block in order to assess how this low-frequency attention factor shapes high-frequency return volatility within the ASEAN–global system. The conditional variance is decomposed multiplicatively into a short-run daily GARCH(1,1) component and a monthly long-run MIDAS component driven by IS (and, in robustness checks, by EPU). The short-run component captures fast-moving volatility clustering, while the MIDAS term summarizes a slow-moving background factor. The parameter θ on IS measures the sensitivity of the long-run component to attention; the variance-ratio statistic (VR%) quantifies the share of total volatility persistence attributable to this slow component. Table 6 reports the parameter estimates for all markets.

Table 6. Estimates of the GARCH-MIDAS-IS model (K = 12).

Asset	μ	α	β	Persistence (α + β)	m	θ(IS)	ω	VR (%)
indonesia	−0.553 ***	0.256 ***	0.667 ***	0.923	0.451 ***	−0.160 ***	1.119 ***	13.8
malaysia	0.031 ***	0.405 ***	0.583 ***	0.988	0.178 ***	−0.063 ***	0.773 ***	5.6
singapore	0.718 ***	0.586 ***	0.368 ***	0.954	0.092 ***	−0.032 ***	0.396 ***	4.9
thailand	−0.372 ***	0.254 ***	0.633 ***	0.887	1.581 ***	−0.562 ***	0.177 ***	39.0
vietnam	0.079 ***	0.630 ***	0.369 ***	0.999	0.003 ***	−0.001 ***	4.518 ***	0.4
sp500_return	−0.065 ***	0.334 ***	0.572 ***	0.906	0.097 ***	−0.034 ***	2.136 ***	8.0
clean_energy_return	−0.143 ***	0.422 ***	0.515 ***	0.937	0.084 ***	−0.029 ***	2.111 ***	5.6
msci_em_return	0.259 ***	0.375 ***	0.552 ***	0.927	0.058 ***	−0.020 ***	2.118 ***	4.8

Notes: SE in parentheses. *** $p < 0.01$. Constraints $\alpha > 0$, $\beta \geq 0$, $\alpha + \beta < 1$; $\omega > 0$. ARCH-LM test (order = 5): $\chi^2(5) = 1.94$, $p = 0.858$. The null hypothesis of no remaining ARCH effects is not rejected ($p > 0.05$), indicating that the GARCH(1,1) structure adequately captures conditional heteroskedasticity and that no additional ARCH dynamics remain in the standardized residuals.

Across all specifications, the ARCH (α) and GARCH (β) coefficients are statistically significant and satisfy the usual stability condition ($\alpha + \beta < 1$), confirming the adequacy of the GARCH(1,1) structure for the short-run component. Short-run persistence is high, with $\alpha + \beta$ typically in the 0.89–0.99 range (mean 0.94, median 0.932), as is standard for daily financial returns. These results indicate that most short-horizon dynamics are absorbed by the GARCH block and that the MIDAS term captures genuinely lower-frequency variation rather than omitted high-frequency effects.

The composite investor sentiment index is then computed as an eigenvalue-weighted combination of the retained components:

$$IS_t = \sum_{j=1}^{2} \tilde{\lambda}_j PC_{j,t}, \tilde{\lambda}_j = \frac{\lambda_j}{\lambda_1 + \lambda_2},$$

where λ_j denotes the eigenvalue of PC_j. By construction, IS_t summarizes the most salient, low-dimensional variation in sentiment-related searches across ASEAN-5 markets in each period t. This index serves as the parsimonious behavioral state variable used in the subsequent empirical analysis.

As reported in Table 6, the MIDAS slope coefficient θ on the IS index is negative and statistically significant in most markets. Estimates of θ range from about −0.562 *** in Thailand and −0.160 *** in Indonesia to −0.063 *** and −0.032 *** in Malaysia and Singapore, and approximately −0.001 *** in Vietnam. Although the PCA-based IS index is conceptually neutral with respect to direction, the negative sign implies that episodes of heightened regional information demand are associated with lower long-run volatility. One interpretation is that, in these markets and for the topics considered, increased attention tends to operate through a confidence or information-efficiency channel: more intensive search is associated with better information processing, narrower uncertainty about fundamentals, and hence a lower background variance level, particularly in green and regional markets. This stands in contrast to evidence for traditional or fossil-fuel assets where attention is often triggered by panic and tends to amplify volatility.

The variance-ratio measure VR% shows that the contribution of the slow component is heterogeneous. For ASEAN markets, VR spans roughly 39.0% in Thailand and 13.8% in Indonesia down to about 5–6% in Malaysia and Singapore and 0.4% in Vietnam. Global benchmarks sit in the mid-single digits (for example, around 8.0% for the S&P 500, 4.8% for MSCI EM, and 5.6% for the clean-energy index). On average, the long-run component explains about 10.3% of total conditional variance across all series (median 5.6%), and Thailand together with Indonesia accounts for roughly two thirds of the total VR mass. In other words, the slow attention channel is economically most important in the two ASEAN markets where retail participation, media intensity, and episodic stress are also more pronounced.

The shape parameter m of the Beta weighting function further clarifies the mechanism. In markets where m is relatively large (for example, Thailand and Indonesia), attention shocks diffuse gradually over several months, generating a pronounced slow component in volatility. Where m is close to zero and VR is small (for example, Vietnam), the slow channel is weak and volatility remains dominated by short-run GARCH dynamics. This cross-sectional pattern is consistent with the view that search-based indices are most informative where public news, retail trading, and local narratives play a larger role in price discovery (Da et al. 2011; Dimpfl and Jank 2016).

Viewed alongside the TVP–VAR evidence on time-varying connectedness, the GARCH–MIDAS results reveal a coherent pattern. Markets whose slow volatility component is most sensitive to investor attention (notably Thailand and Indonesia) are also the nodes that tend to play a more prominent role in the spillover network during stress episodes, in line with network-based interpretations of connectedness (Diebold and Yılmaz 2014; Antonakakis and Gabauer 2017). Global benchmarks exhibit more moderate slow components, consistent with deeper information sets and faster absorption of public news, which accords with the time-varying connectedness patterns documented for emerging Asia (Youssef et al. 2021). Overall, the Google-based IS index emerges as a significant and stabilising driver of long-run volatility that complements, rather than duplicates, global policy-uncertainty measures such as EPU and GPR (Baker et al. 2016; Caldara and Iacoviello 2022; Da et al. 2011; Engle et al. 2013).

7. Robustness Checks and Extensions

We extend the baseline GARCH–MIDAS specification to verify that the relationships between market volatility, investor attention, and macro-uncertainty are not artefacts of parametrisation. Following the mixed-frequency volatility literature, we first lengthen the MIDAS memory from $K = 12$ to $K = 18$ monthly lags, allowing the low-frequency component τ_t to aggregate a broader information set without altering the short-run conditional variance dynamics. As argued by Engle et al. (2013) and Conrad and Loch (2015), a larger K provides a stringent check on whether the slow-moving driver remains economically meaningful once the variance equation accommodates longer memory.

Table 7 (GARCH–MIDAS with IS, $K = 18$) corroborates the structural role of the attention channel. Across ASEAN and benchmark markets, the loading on the Google-based investor-attention factor, $\theta(\text{IS})$, remains negative and highly significant, indicating that periods of stronger information demand are associated with lower long-run volatility. Volatility persistence $(\alpha + \beta)$ remains high (around 0.88–0.97), consistent with near unit-root behaviour in financial returns (Engle 1982; Bollerslev 1986). The variance-ratio measure, defined as

$$VR(\%) = 100 \times \frac{\text{Var}[\log(\tau_t)]}{\text{Var}[\log(\tau_t h_t)]},$$

averages around 20–25%, implying that roughly one quarter of total log-volatility is explained by the slow-moving attention component in this extended specification. This order of magnitude is comparable to findings in Ghysels et al. (2016) and Da et al. (2015), who show that Google-based attention indices add incremental information for volatility beyond standard macro and liquidity controls.

Table 7. Estimates of the GARCH-MIDAS-IS model (K = 18).

Asset	μ	α	β	Persistence (α + β)	m	θ(IS)	ω	VR (%)
Indonesia	0.035 ** (0.016)	0.435 *** (0.018)	0.448 *** (0.020)	0.883	0.134 *** (0.036)	−1.647 *** (0.453)	1.475 * (0.821)	25.48
Malaysia	0.026 ** (0.012)	0.288 *** (0.015)	0.609 *** (0.017)	0.897	−0.704 *** (0.035)	−6.440 *** (0.445)	1.202 *** (0.135)	22.77
Singapore	0.029 ** (0.014)	0.321 *** (0.018)	0.567 *** (0.025)	0.888	−0.338 *** (0.037)	−1.118 *** (0.228)	5.634 (4.146)	20.61
Thailand	0.032 ** (0.013)	0.209 *** (0.010)	0.752 *** (0.012)	0.961	−0.088 *** (0.033)	−11.599 *** (0.479)	1.262 *** (0.111)	18.92
Vietnam	0.108 *** (0.018)	0.147 *** (0.007)	0.820 *** (0.008)	0.967	0.211 *** (0.031)	−5.375 *** (0.402)	2.907 *** (0.692)	19.75
SP500_return	0.105 *** (0.014)	0.292 *** (0.014)	0.681 *** (0.015)	0.974	0.469 *** (0.039)	−4.297 *** (0.438)	1.674 *** (0.432)	21.68
CleanEnergy_return	0.064 *** (0.024)	0.194 *** (0.012)	0.762 *** (0.015)	0.956	0.878 *** (0.033)	−5.821 *** (0.444)	2.148 *** (0.512)	23.84
MSCI_EM_return	0.057 ** (0.023)	0.267 *** (0.019)	0.634 *** (0.026)	0.901	0.525 *** (0.037)	−2.595 *** (0.617)	1.092 *** (0.392)	20.14

Notes: Standard errors in parentheses. ***, **, * denote significance at the 1%, 5%, and 10% levels, respectively. Constraints α > 0, β ≥ 0, α + β < 1; ω > 0. Persistence (α + β) measures volatility persistence; VR (%) is the variance ratio defined in Equation (28), indicating the share of total log-volatility attributable to the long-run component. Estimates correspond to K = 18 (robustness test).

Next, we replace the attention factor with macro-uncertainty in Table 8 (GARCH–MIDAS with EPU, $K = 12$). The MIDAS coefficient $\theta(\text{EPU})$ is again negative and statistically significant across markets, while short-run persistence remains in the 0.87–0.91 range and $VR(\%)$ lies around 19–23%. These patterns echo Baker et al. (2016) and Brogaard and Detzel (2015), who document that uncertainty shocks are systematically priced in volatility. Taken together, the sign, magnitude, and significance of the MIDAS loadings are robust to (i) lengthening the MIDAS lag window and (ii) substituting the slow-moving driver (IS → EPU), indicating that attention and policy-uncertainty indices capture complementary dimensions of low-frequency risk.

Table 8. Estimates of the GARCH-MIDAS–Economic Uncertainty model (K = 12).

Asset	μ	α	β	Persistence (α + β)	m	θ(EPU)	ω	VR (%)
Indonesia	0.034 ** (0.016)	0.431 *** (0.020)	0.447 *** (0.022)	0.878	0.129 *** (0.036)	−1.382 *** (0.428)	1.482 * (0.798)	24.73
Malaysia	0.027 ** (0.013)	0.291 *** (0.016)	0.608 *** (0.019)	0.899	−0.695 *** (0.035)	−6.115 *** (0.422)	1.205 *** (0.148)	22.18
Singapore	0.030 ** (0.014)	0.323 *** (0.019)	0.566 *** (0.024)	0.889	−0.341 *** (0.037)	−1.065 *** (0.224)	4.975 ** (0.622)	21.04
Thailand	0.028 * (0.014)	0.298 *** (0.017)	0.573 *** (0.021)	0.871	−0.315 *** (0.038)	−0.874 *** (0.258)	1.618 ** (0.733)	19.11
Vietnam	0.033 ** (0.015)	0.345 *** (0.018)	0.543 *** (0.023)	0.888	−0.239 *** (0.040)	−0.816 *** (0.298)	1.430 * (0.806)	20.32
SP500	0.030 *** (0.011)	0.319 *** (0.016)	0.588 *** (0.019)	0.907	−0.259 *** (0.028)	−0.552 *** (0.189)	1.507 * (0.842)	22.54
Clean Energy	0.037 ** (0.016)	0.362 *** (0.019)	0.507 *** (0.022)	0.869	−0.295 *** (0.034)	−0.708 *** (0.237)	1.268 *** (0.139)	23.21
MSCI EM	0.028 ** (0.013)	0.338 *** (0.017)	0.550 *** (0.020)	0.888	−0.272 *** (0.036)	−0.594 *** (0.204)	1.198 ** (0.321)	20.07

Notes: This table reports estimates of the GARCH-MIDAS-EU model with K = 12 monthly lags. Standard errors are in parentheses. ***, **, * denote significance at 1%, 5%, and 10% levels. Persistence (α + β) measures volatility persistence; VR (%) indicates the proportion of long-term volatility explained by economic uncertainty.

Methodologically, these results align with Conrad et al. (2014) and Engle et al. (2013): varying the aggregation window or swapping macro drivers should not flip the direction of the MIDAS term if the model is well specified. All estimates satisfy the standard stationarity and positivity constraints $\alpha > 0$, $\beta \geq 0$, and $\alpha + \beta < 1$, ensuring a well-behaved conditional variance. The stability of $VR(\%)$ across Tables 7 and 8 indicates that the contribution of the long-run component to total volatility is a structural feature of the data rather than an artefact of window length or variable selection. Overall, the robustness checks confirm that long-horizon information—whether captured by digital attention (IS) or macro-uncertainty (EPU) is tightly linked to short-run volatility, in line with the mixed-frequency volatility literature (Engle et al. 2013; Baker et al. 2016; Da et al. 2015).

Figure 7 provides an additional robustness check by overlaying the generalized IRFs to an EPU shock across high- and low-uncertainty regimes. The red line (COVID-19 episode) and the dark blue line (low-uncertainty period) are computed from VARs estimated on the corresponding subsamples with the same lag structure and shock normalisation, so differences in magnitude and persistence are attributable to regime conditions rather than model specification (Diebold and Yılmaz 2014; Antonakakis and Gabauer 2017). The shaded red area represents the 95% confidence interval around the high-uncertainty impulse responses, illustrating the statistical uncertainty of the estimates under stressed conditions.

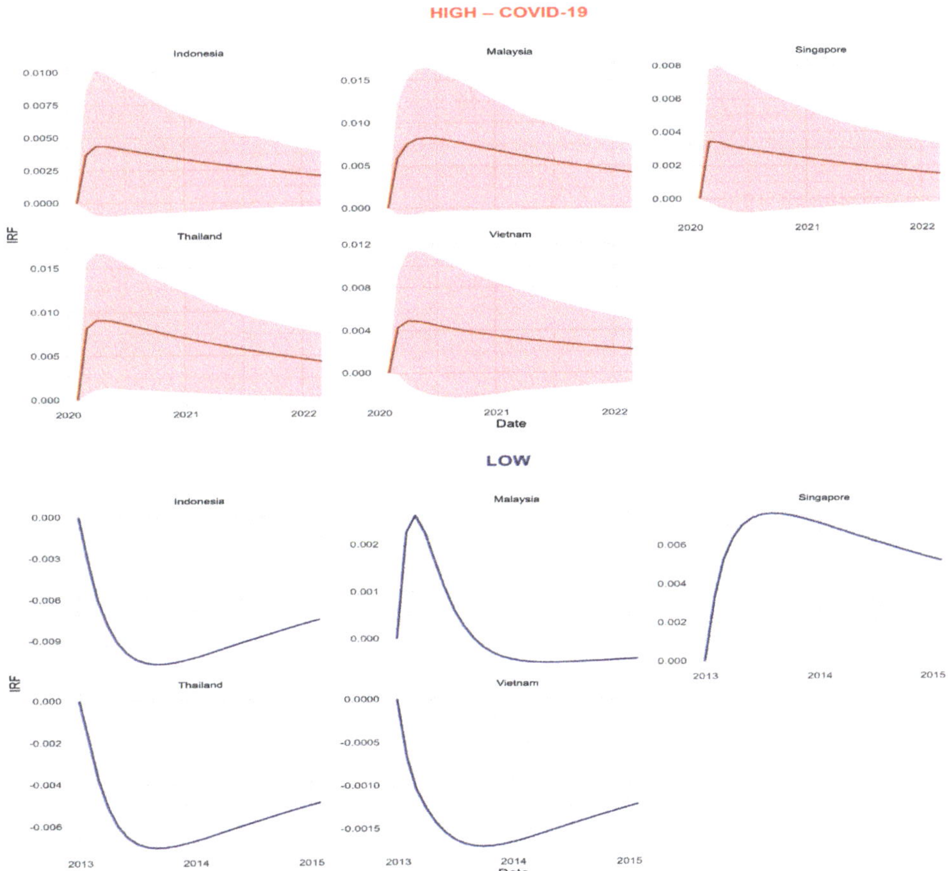

Figure 7. Generalized IRFs to an EPU Shock: High- vs. Low-Uncertainty Regimes (ASEAN-5).

In all ASEAN-5 markets, the high-uncertainty IRF is substantially larger on impact and decays more slowly than its low-uncertainty counterpart, while the sign and qualitative shape of the response remain unchanged. This confirms that policy-uncertainty shocks propagate more forcefully and for longer when the global environment is stressed, but do not reverse the basic transmission pattern documented in the baseline TVP–VAR connectedness results (Baker et al. 2016; Caldara and Iacoviello 2022). Taken together with Figure 5, Figure 7 thus reinforces the interpretation that ASEAN financial integration and shock transmission are state-dependent, and shows that our conclusions are robust to subsample estimation and direct impulse-response analysis (Youssef et al. 2021).

8. Discussion and Implications

Our evidence situates ASEAN co-movements squarely within the time varying connectedness paradigm. The Total Connectedness Index (TCI) averages $\approx$ 70% and surges above 90% in turbulent periods, implying that cross market shocks, not idiosyncratic innovations, drive most multi step forecast uncertainty. This pattern matches the crisis sensitivity embedded in GFEVD based connectedness networks and their TVP–VAR extensions, which allow transmission parameters to drift over time (Diebold and Yılmaz 2014; Antonakakis and Gabauer 2017; Gabauer 2021). Frequency domain analyses reach the same conclusion from another angle: crisis era amplification concentrates at low (long horizon) frequencies, consistent with slow moving forces that tighten co-movement in bad times (Baruník and Křehlík 2018; Tiwari et al. 2022).

The upshot is clear: ASEAN financial integration is state dependent, rising in stress and receding in calm regimes (Naeem et al. 2023; Youssef et al. 2021) Two top-down uncertainty channels help explain these dynamics. First, economic policy uncertainty (EPU), a news-based gauge of fiscal, monetary, and regulatory ambiguity, tends to spike around salient events and is empirically linked to higher volatility and tighter co-movements (Baker et al. 2016; Phan et al. 2021; Su et al. 2023). Second, geopolitical risk (GPR) propagates stress through trade and commodity routes; increases in GPR during conflicts and diplomatic shocks transmit volatility globally (Caldara and Iacoviello 2022; Naeem et al. 2023).

The coincidence of our TCI peaks with bursts in EPU and GPR therefore substantiates H1: macroeconomic and geopolitical uncertainty amplify cross market volatility transmission in ASEAN. The green asset node behaves in a regime dependent manner that lines up with recent evidence. Clean energy equities switch between transmitters (around transition policy or carbon pricing headlines) and absorbers (when commodity or liquidity conditions dominate), placing them between global benchmarks and domestic equities in the spillover hierarchy (Özkan et al. 2024; Naeem et al. 2023). By contrast, gold remains a mild net receiver, retaining its defensive profile consistent with hedge/safe haven results (Baur and Lucey 2010; Baur and McDermott 2010).

Mechanistically, the GARCH–MIDAS block links network behaviour to slow moving fundamentals. The coefficient on investor attention, θ(IS), is negative and significant, and the variance ratio share attributed to the MIDAS term (VR% $\approx$ 19–26%) is economically meaningful. This is consistent with the broader attention based volatility literature in the sense that attention emerges as a non-redundant, slow moving driver of risk; in our context, however, the negative sign points to an information efficiency channel, whereby periods of heightened, systematic information demand are associated with improved price discovery and a lower long run volatility baseline (Da et al. 2015; Ghysels et al. 2016). Taken together, uncertainty and attention operate as complementary channels, aligning the timing (when) and mechanism (why) of spillover intensification.

For investors, diversification is regime-dependent: when TCI is high, spillovers dominate and diversification benefits compress. Hedge ratios and risk budgets should therefore be state aware, keyed to uncertainty monitors such as EPU and GPR. A structural gold sleeve remains defensible as a crisis hedge, whereas clean energy exposure is best treated tactically, with sizing that reflects policy calendars and funding/commodity conditions (Baur and Lucey 2010; Baur and McDermott 2010; Özkan et al. 2024).

From the perspective of international portfolio diversification within and beyond the ASEAN 5, our results imply that investment decisions cannot be based solely on average correlations: the same cross market linkage can be weak at high frequencies yet strong at low frequencies, so that long horizon investors remain exposed to persistent spillovers even when short run co-movement appears modest (Baruník and Křehlík 2018; Ghysels et al. 2016). In practical terms, investors need to account explicitly for the asymmetric transmission of short term and long-term volatility when constructing portfolios, evaluating downside risk, and calibrating rebalancing rules because regime shifts in connectedness and volatility persistence can quickly erode the ex ante gains from regional diversification.

For portfolio managers, the joint TVP–VAR and GARCH–MIDAS framework highlights the value of frequency decomposition as a decision support tool. By mapping spillovers and volatility into horizon specific components, managers can design risk budgets that distinguish between fast, "trading horizon" shocks and slow, "strategic horizon" risks, and can align hedging instruments, benchmark choices, and performance attribution to the relevant frequency band (Engle et al. 2013; Baruník and Křehlík 2018). Beyond portfolio construction, such a multi scale representation of connectedness can substantially improve the diffusion of knowledge within investment teams and toward clients, providing a transparent narrative for how and why volatility spillovers occur between markets at different horizons, and why diversification sometimes fails precisely when it is most needed.

For policymakers, the dominance of uncertainty as a transmitter underscores the importance of transparent, rules-based communication and regional safety nets (macroprudential coordination, liquidity backstops) to curb "outside in" propagation (International Monetary Fund 2016; Lien et al. 2018). These policy implications resonate directly with the ASEAN Economic Community (AEC) initiative, which aims to deepen economic and financial integration and to promote greater mobility of capital and financial services within ASEAN (International Monetary Fund 2016). As the AEC framework lowers barriers and strengthens cross border linkages, our state dependent connectedness results suggest a classic trade off: in tranquil periods, higher integration enhances risk sharing and market development, but in stress regimes it also increases the scope for regional contagion when global uncertainty spikes (Lien et al. 2018). Recognising this trade off is crucial for designing regional macroprudential frameworks, surveillance mechanisms, and safety net arrangements that support the long run objectives of the AEC while containing the transmission of global shocks into ASEAN financial systems. For issuers in green finance, regime sensitivity implies time varying issuance costs: placing large offerings in high uncertainty windows raises the cost of capital, while granular disclosure of transition exposures and policy dependencies can dampen contagion to valuations (Özkan et al. 2024).

Overall, the evidence confirms H_1 that ASEAN financial integration is time varying, and H_2 that uncertainty and attention jointly amplify spillovers. The interplay between uncertainty, sentiment, and clean energy dynamics places ASEAN within a broader pattern of crisis sensitive connectedness, in which global shocks compress diversification and intensify the behavioural–macro feedbacks that characterise modern financial contagion.

9. Conclusions, Limitations, and Future Research

This paper has examined how financial integration between ASEAN-5 equity markets and global benchmarks changes across regimes and how macro-uncertainty and investor attention shape this process. Taken together, the results point to a regime-dependent form of integration: periods of stress are characterised by a tighter and more hierarchical spillover structure, with global benchmarks and uncertainty factors acting as dominant transmitters and ASEAN markets as receivers, while investor attention operates as a slow-moving background force that influences the persistence of volatility. The joint use of a TVP–VAR connectedness framework and a GARCH–MIDAS volatility block allows us to link network-level interdependence to market-level volatility dynamics in a transparent way and provides a regime-aware perspective that is directly relevant for portfolio risk management, macro-prudential surveillance, and the timing of capital issuance in emerging Asia.

Despite these contributions, several limitations remain. The slow-moving drivers we consider are informative but noisy: EPU and GPR are news-based indices that may embody media and language biases, and Google Search Volume data capture attention rather than valuation fundamentals. The empirical design relies on a linear, Gaussian TVP–VAR and a standard GARCH–MIDAS filter, which, while tractable and interpretable, may understate tail asymmetries, leverage effects, and nonlinear propagation. In addition, connectedness measures are sensitive to the chosen forecast horizon, and a single-horizon summary cannot fully distinguish short- from long-horizon transmission. Our asset universe, focused on equities, gold, and clean-energy indices, does not include FX, rates, credit, or carbon/energy derivatives, which often act as primary conduits for macro and geopolitical shocks. Finally, the clean-energy composite may mask heterogeneous behaviour across underlying sub-sectors.

These limitations suggest several avenues for future research. First, the volatility block could be enriched by moving beyond symmetric GARCH–MIDAS to models that allow for asymmetry and leverage, such as EGARCH–MIDAS or time-varying-parameter EGARCH–MIDAS specifications in which both the variance and the news-impact curve evolve over time. Second, on the spillover side, TVP–VAR frameworks with time-varying latent parameters (LT-TVP-VAR) or low-dimensional factor structures could be employed to better capture structural breaks and common drivers of ASEAN co-movements. Third, time- and frequency-domain approaches could be combined to clearly separate short- and long-horizon transmission, and tail- or quantile-based connectedness tools could be used to focus on downside-risk contagion. Fourth, future work could refine uncertainty and attention measures using multilingual text embeddings and more balanced news corpora, reducing measurement noise in EPU, GPR, and Google-based indices. Lastly, broadening the system to include FX, interest rates, credit spreads, and carbon/energy instruments would allow for a more complete mapping of macro- and transition-risk channels into ASEAN financial markets.

Pursuing these extensions would turn our regime-aware portrait into a more structurally identified and horizon-resolved account of how uncertainty and attention synchronise ASEAN markets, and under which conditions they fail to do so, while at the same time speaking more directly to the institutional architecture and policy pillars of the ASEAN Economic Community (AEC) (International Monetary Fund 2016; Lien et al. 2018). In this sense, our findings provide a benchmark for both academics and policymakers seeking to align the deepening of AEC financial integration with the realities of state-dependent connectedness, mixed-frequency risk transmission, and the trade-off between risk-sharing and contagion in emerging Asia.

Author Contributions: Conceptualization, F.C. and J.E.H.; Methodology, F.C. and J.E.H.; Software, F.C.; Validation, F.C. and J.E.H.; Formal Analysis, F.C.; Investigation, F.C.; Resources, F.C.; Data Curation, F.C.; Writing—Original Draft Preparation, F.C.; Writing—Review and Editing, F.C. and J.E.H.; Visualization, F.C.; Supervision, J.E.H.; Project Administration, F.C. All authors have read and agreed to the published version of the manuscript.

Funding: This research received no external funding.

Institutional Review Board Statement: Not applicable.

Informed Consent Statement: Not applicable.

Data Availability Statement: The raw data supporting the conclusions of this article will be made available by the authors upon request.

Conflicts of Interest: The authors declare no conflicts of interest.

Appendix A

Table A1. Variables: Definitions, Frequency, and Data Sources (Appendix A).

Short Name	Definition	Transform/Unit	Role in Analysis	Source
Indonesia	IDX composite/broad market index	Return (%)	ASEAN-5 market	Refinitiv
Malaysia	FTSE Bursa Malaysia KLCI	Return (%)	ASEAN-5 market	Refinitiv
Singapore	Straits Times Index	Return (%)	ASEAN-5 market	Refinitiv
Thailand	SET Index	Return (%)	ASEAN-5 market	Refinitiv
Vietnam	VN-Index (HOSE)	Return (%)	ASEAN-5 market	Refinitiv
SP500_return	S&P 500 Index	Return (%)	Global bench-mark/transmitter	S&P Dow Jones Indices
MSCI_EM_return	MSCI Emerging Markets Index	Return (%)	Global EM factor/transmitter	MSCI
CleanEnergy_return	Clean-energy equity composite Clean Energy)	Return (%)	Energy transition proxy	S&P Global
Gold_return	London gold price (USD/oz)	Return (%)	Safe-haven/receiver	Refinitiv
GPR_Global	Global Geopolitical Risk index	Level (index)	Uncertainty driver	Caldara and Iacoviello (2022)
EPU	Economic policy uncertainty (EPU-type) index	Level (index)	Uncertainty driver	Baker et al. (2016)

References

Adrian, Tobias, and Hyun Song Shin. 2010. Liquidity and leverage. *Journal of Financial Intermediation* 19: 418–37. [CrossRef]

Al-Hajieh, Heitham. 2023. Predictive directional measurement volatility spillovers between the US and selected Asian Pacific countries. *Cogent Economics & Finance* 11: 2173124. [CrossRef]

AMRO (ASEAN+3 Macroeconomic Research Office). 2024. *ASEAN+3 Financial Stability Report 2024: Strengthening Resilience to Challenges Ahead*. Singapore: AMRO. Available online: https://amro-asia.org/asean3-financial-stability-report-2024 (accessed on 10 October 2025).

Andrei, Daniel, and Michael Hasler. 2015. Investor attention and stock market volatility. *Review of Financial Studies* 28: 33–72. [CrossRef]

Antonakakis, Nikolaos, and David Gabauer. 2017. *Refined Measures of Dynamic Connectedness Based on TVP–VAR*. MPRA Paper No. 78282. Munich: University of Munich. Available online: https://mpra.ub.uni-muenchen.de/78282 (accessed on 10 September 2025).

Antonakakis, Nikolaos, Ioannis Chatziantoniou, and David Gabauer. 2020. Refined measures of dynamic connectedness based on time-varying parameter vector autoregressions. *Journal of Risk and Financial Management* 13: 84. [CrossRef]

Antweiler, Werner, and Murray Z. Frank. 2004. Is all that talk just noise? The information content of Internet stock message boards. *Journal of Finance* 59: 1259–94. [CrossRef]

Assaf, Ata, Husni Charif, and Khaled Mokni. 2021. Dynamic connectedness between uncertainty and energy markets: Do investor sentiments matter? *Resources Policy* 72: 102112. [CrossRef]

Baker, Scott R., Nicholas Bloom, and Steven J. Davis. 2016. Measuring economic policy uncertainty. *Quarterly Journal of Economics* 131: 1593–636. [CrossRef]

Barber, Brad M., and Terrance Odean. 2008. All that glitters: The effect of attention and news on the buying behavior of individual and institutional investors. *Review of Financial Studies* 21: 785–818. [CrossRef]

Baruník, Jozef, and Tomáš Křehlík. 2018. Measuring the frequency dynamics of financial connectedness and systemic risk. *Journal of Financial Econometrics* 16: 271–96. [CrossRef]

Baur, D. G., and B. M. Lucey. 2010. Is gold a hedge or a safe haven? An analysis of stocks, bonds and gold. *Financial Review* 45: 217–29. [CrossRef]

Baur, Dirk G., and Thomas K. McDermott. 2010. Is gold a safe haven? International evidence. *Journal of Banking & Finance* 34: 1886–98. [CrossRef]

Bekaert, Geert, and Campbell R. Harvey. 1995. Time-varying world market integration. *Journal of Finance* 50: 403–44. [CrossRef]

Bekaert, Geert, Campbell R. Harvey, and Christian T. Lundblad. 2005. Does financial liberalization spur growth? *Journal of Financial Economics* 77: 3–55. [CrossRef]

Billio, Monica, Mila Getmansky, Andrew W. Lo, and Loriana Pelizzon. 2012. Econometric measures of connectedness and systemic risk in the finance and insurance sectors. *Journal of Financial Economics* 104: 535–59. [CrossRef]

Bollerslev, Tim. 1986. Generalized autoregressive conditional heteroskedasticity. *Journal of Econometrics* 31: 307–27. [CrossRef]

Brogaard, Jonathan, and Andrew Detzel. 2015. The asset-pricing implications of government economic policy uncertainty. *Management Science* 61: 3–18. [CrossRef]

Brunnermeier, Markus K., and Lasse Heje Pedersen. 2009. Market liquidity and funding liquidity. *Review of Financial Studies* 22: 2201–38. [CrossRef]

Caldara, Dario, and Matteo Iacoviello. 2022. Measuring geopolitical risk. *American Economic Review* 112: 1194–225. [CrossRef]

Choi, Hyunyoung, and Hal R. Varian. 2012. Predicting the present with Google Trends. *Economic Record* 88: 2–9. [CrossRef]

Conrad, Christian, and Kerstin Loch. 2015. Anticipating long-term stock market volatility. *Journal of Applied Econometrics* 30: 1090–1114. [CrossRef]

Conrad, Christian, Kerstin Loch, and David Rittler. 2014. On the macroeconomic determinants of long-term volatilities and correlations in U.S. stock and crude oil markets. *Journal of Empirical Finance* 29: 26–40. [CrossRef]

Cont, Rama. 2001. Empirical properties of asset returns: Stylized facts and statistical issues. *Quantitative Finance* 1: 223–36. [CrossRef]

Cunado, Juncal, David Gabauer, and Rangan Gupta. 2024. Realized volatility spillovers between energy and metal markets: A time-varying connectedness approach. *Financial Innovation* 10: 12. [CrossRef]

Da, Zhi, Joseph Engelberg, and Pengjie Gao. 2011. In search of attention. *Journal of Finance* 66: 1461–99. [CrossRef]

Da, Zhi, Joseph Engelberg, and Pengjie Gao. 2015. The sum of all FEARS: Investor sentiment and asset prices. *Review of Financial Studies* 28: 1–32. [CrossRef]

Diebold, Francis X., and Kamil Yılmaz. 2014. On the network topology of variance decompositions: Measuring the connectedness of financial firms. *Journal of Econometrics* 182: 119–34. [CrossRef]

Dimpfl, Thomas, and Stephan Jank. 2016. Can internet search queries help to predict stock market volatility? *European Financial Management* 22: 171–92. [CrossRef]

Engelberg, Joseph, and Christopher A. Parsons. 2011. The causal impact of media in financial markets. *Journal of Finance* 66: 67–97. [CrossRef]

Engle, Robert F. 1982. Autoregressive conditional heteroskedasticity with estimates of the variance of United Kingdom inflation. *Econometrica* 50: 987–1008. [CrossRef]

Engle, Robert F., and José Gonzalo Rangel. 2008. The Spline-GARCH model for low-frequency volatility and its global macroeconomic causes. *Review of Financial Studies* 21: 1187–222. [CrossRef]

Engle, Robert F., Eric Ghysels, and Bumjean Sohn. 2013. Stock market volatility and macroeconomic fundamentals. *Review of Economics and Statistics* 95: 776–97. [CrossRef]

Fang, Lily, and Jérôme Peress. 2009. Media coverage and the cross-section of stock returns. *Journal of Finance* 64: 2023–52. [CrossRef]

Forbes, Kristin J., and Roberto Rigobon. 2002. No contagion, only interdependence: Measuring stock market comovements. *Journal of Finance* 57: 2223–61. [CrossRef]

Gabauer, David. 2021. Dynamic measures of asymmetric and pairwise connectedness within an optimal currency area: Evidence from the ERM I system. *Journal of Multinational Financial Management* 60: 100680. [CrossRef]

Ghysels, Eric, Alberto Plazzi, and Rossen Valkanov. 2016. Why invest in emerging markets? The role of conditional return asymmetry. *Journal of Finance* 71: 2145–92. [CrossRef]

Ghysels, Eric, Pedro Santa-Clara, and Rossen Valkanov. 2004. *The MIDAS Model: Mixed Data Sampling Regressions*. Working Paper. Chapel Hill: Department of Economics, University of North Carolina and UCLA.

International Monetary Fund. 2016. *ASEAN Financial Integration Monitoring Report 2016*. Washington: International Monetary Fund.

Jolliffe, Ian T. 2002. *Principal Component Analysis*, 2nd ed. New York: Springer. [CrossRef]

Kahneman, Daniel. 1973. *Attention and Effort*. Englewood Cliffs: Prentice-Hall.

Kaiser, Henry F. 1960. The application of electronic computers to factor analysis. *Educational and Psychological Measurement* 20: 141–51. [CrossRef]

Koop, Gary, and Dimitris Korobilis. 2014. A new index of financial conditions. *European Economic Review* 71: 101–16. [CrossRef]

Lien, Donald, Geul Lee, and Li Yang. 2018. Transmission of volatility and risk spillover across ASEAN stock markets. *Pacific-Basin Finance Journal* 51: 1–15.

Longin, François, and Bruno Solnik. 2001. Extreme correlation of international equity markets. *Journal of Finance* 56: 649–76. [CrossRef]

Mateus, Cesario, Miramir Bagirov, and Irina Mateus. 2024. Return and volatility connectedness and net directional patterns in spillover transmissions: East and Southeast Asian equity markets. *International Review of Finance* 24: 83–103. [CrossRef]

Naeem, Muhammad Abubakr, Foued Hamouda, Sitara Karim, and Samuel A. Vigne. 2023. Return and volatility spillovers among global assets: Comparing health crisis with geopolitical crisis. *International Review of Economics & Finance* 87: 557–75. [CrossRef]

Özkan, Oktay, Tomiwa Sunday Adebayo, and Ojonugwa Usman. 2024. Dynamic connectedness of clean energy markets, green markets, and sustainable markets: The role of climate policy uncertainty. *Energy* 303: 131957. [CrossRef]

Pagan, Adrian. 1996. The econometrics of financial markets. *Journal of Empirical Finance* 3: 15–102. [CrossRef]

Pesaran, Mohammad Hashem, and Yongcheol Shin. 1998. Generalized impulse response analysis in linear multivariate models. *Economics Letters* 58: 17–29. [CrossRef]

Phan, Dinh Hoang Bach, Susan Sunila Sharma, and Paresh Kumar Narayan. 2021. The effects of economic policy uncertainty on financial markets: A review. *Economic Modelling* 94: 1018–35. [CrossRef]

Preis, Tobias, Helen Susannah Moat, and H. Eugene Stanley. 2013. Quantifying trading behavior in financial markets using Google Trends. *Scientific Reports* 3: 1684. [CrossRef]

Primiceri, Giorgio E. 2005. Time varying structural vector autoregressions and monetary policy. *Review of Economic Studies* 72: 821–52. [CrossRef]

Sims, Christopher A. 2003. Implications of rational inattention. *Journal of Monetary Economics* 50: 665–90. [CrossRef]

Su, Chi-Wei, Yiru Liu, Tsangyao Chang, and Muhammad Umar. 2023. Can gold hedge the risk of fear sentiments? *Technological and Economic Development of Economy* 29: 23–44. [CrossRef]

Tetlock, Paul C. 2007. Giving content to investor sentiment: The role of media in the stock market. *Journal of Finance* 62: 1139–68. [CrossRef]

Tiwari, Aviral Kumar, Ibrahim D. Raheem, Seref Bozoklu, and Shawkat Hammoudeh. 2022. The oil price–macroeconomic fundamentals nexus for emerging market economies: Evidence from a wavelet analysis. *International Journal of Finance & Economics* 27: 1569–90. [CrossRef]

Vlastakis, Nikolaos, and Raphael N. Markellos. 2012. Information demand and stock market volatility. *Journal of Banking & Finance* 36: 1808–21. [CrossRef]

Wu, Ruirui, and Bing-Yue Liu. 2023. Do climate policy uncertainty and investor sentiment drive the dynamic spillovers among green finance markets? *Journal of Environmental Management* 347: 119008. [CrossRef] [PubMed]

Youssef, Manel, Khaled Mokni, and Ahdi Noomen Ajmi. 2021. Dynamic connectedness between stock markets in the presence of the COVID-19 pandemic: Does economic policy uncertainty matter? *Financial Innovation* 7: 13. [CrossRef] [PubMed]

Yuan, Yu. 2015. Market-wide attention, trading, and stock returns. *Journal of Financial Economics* 116: 548–64. [CrossRef]

mathematics

MDPI

Article

Artificial Intelligence and the Emergence of New Quality Productive Forces: A Machine Learning Perspective

Lei Tan [1], Xiaobing Lai [2], Yuxin Zhao [1] and Yuan Zhong [1,*]

[1] School of Economics & Management, Jiulong Lake Campus, Southeast University, Nanjing 211189, China; noah_tan@163.com (L.T.); 230209152@seu.edu.cn (Y.Z.)
[2] School of Accounting, Jiangxi University of Finance and Economics, Nanchang 330013, China; laixiaobing@jxufe.edu.cn
* Correspondence: shang17569xa@126.com

Abstract

In the era of the digital economy, AI technology is regarded as a key driver in promoting the development of new quality productive forces of enterprises. Based on the theories of creative destruction and resource allocation, this study selects Chinese enterprise-level data from 2009 to 2022 as the research sample, constructs enterprise new quality productivity indicators through text analysis and machine learning methods, and explores the impact of artificial intelligence on new quality productivity. The study results show that AI technology significantly improves the new quality productivity of enterprises. Further research found that enterprise director background, digital industry agglomeration and financial agglomeration positively moderated the relationship between AI and new quality productivity. Heterogeneity analysis shows that the enabling effect of AI technology on new quality productivity is more significant in high-tech enterprises, state-owned enterprises and enterprises with strong policy support. Through empirical analysis, this study verifies the facilitating effect of AI technological innovation on enterprises' new quality productivity, which provides important insights for enterprises in emerging economies to achieve the development of new quality productive forces in digital transformation.

Keywords: artificial intelligence; new quality productive forces; text analytics; machine learning

MSC: 91B06; 68T05; 62M10; 62H30; 62P20

1. Introduction

The world is currently undergoing a transformation not seen in a century. Global trends such as multipolarity, economic globalization, informatization, and cultural diversification are deepening, while the rapid development of information technology and intelligence is creating the necessary momentum for a new scientific and technological revolution [1]. Amidst intensifying geopolitical tensions and the rise of great power rivalries, international competition for technological supremacy has never been fiercer. However, China faces significant challenges in areas such as semiconductor production, advanced manufacturing equipment, and core software development, where its technological reserves and capabilities remain inadequate.

In response to these challenges, China's leadership has introduced the concept of "new quality productive force" (NQPF), offering a roadmap for future economic development. The NQPF represents a novel embodiment of advanced productive forces, aiming to shift traditional economic growth models and overcome the limitations of existing productive forces. It promotes innovation as the key driver of economic development, creating a new form of productivity characterized by high-tech, high-efficiency, and high-quality outcomes. This concept not only serves as an innovation in Marxist productivity theory but also signifies a profound transformation in modern production modes [2].

The development of productive forces depends on three main factors: science and technology, labor quality, and labor resources. Of these, science and technology plays a pivotal role in improving production efficiency, shortening product life cycles, and driving market and economic restructuring through "creative destruction." Artificial intelligence (AI), the key force behind the fourth industrial revolution, accelerates this transformation. By reshaping social production processes and lifestyles, AI gives productivity an entirely new meaning.

From the perspective of AI's role in empowering the NQPF, advancements in AI technology have significantly enhanced the automation and intelligence of production processes, exerting a profound impact on production relations and systems. This has fostered the digital transformation of the economic growth model [3]. Schumpeter's theory of innovation strongly supports the mechanisms explored in this study [4]. AI brings about a fundamental change in enterprise productivity through disruptive innovations. Technologies such as big data, deep learning, and natural language processing have optimized resource allocation, broken down traditional industry barriers, improved production efficiency and product quality, and enabled the intelligent interconnection of production factors—ultimately driving the development of the NQPF.

Existing research primarily explores AI's role in enhancing macroeconomic and social productivity. However, there is a gap in the micro-level analysis of how AI specifically promotes the NQPF at the enterprise level. The mechanisms through which AI facilitates NQPF development at the firm level have not been adequately examined. Macro-level studies have demonstrated that AI's grand model accelerates the arrival of the intelligent era by inducing qualitative changes in production factors, which in turn foster the enhancement of the NQPF [5]. Moreover, the enhancement of computational power significantly drives productivity changes, steering the transition from traditional industrialization to intelligence-based production, and emerging as a critical driver of NQPF development [3].

The work of Huang and Rust [6] further suggests that AI impacts the labor process by optimizing not only laborers and labor tools but also labor objects, contributing to the development of the NQPF. Additionally, the rapid progress of technologies such as the Internet of Things, big data, and AI has facilitated the shift from traditional production processes to intelligent systems [7], further accelerating the leap of the NQPF [2].

Despite these advances, there has been limited research at the micro level regarding AI's facilitative effects on digital knowledge accumulation and sharing [8]. AI has also enhanced productivity and corporate employment by fostering technological innovation [9–13]. Moreover, AI's increasing role in labor production [14] has expanded the division of labor into human–machine collaborations, enhancing the qualitative productivity of firms and opening new possibilities for labor emancipation [15]. However, the complexity and rapid iteration of AI technology raise the cost of enterprise R&D [16,17], and the path through which AI promotes the development of the NQPF requires further investigation.

Existing studies also highlight several challenges in NQPF development, including inadequate infrastructure, core technology gaps, and structural shifts in the labor market [18]. A key question remains whether AI can emerge as the core driver of the NQPF through disruptive innovation. As a new form of qualitative productivity, the NQPF is fundamentally different from traditional total factor productivity metrics used in earlier studies [19–21]. Furthermore, standardized and objective measurement criteria for the NQPF are still lacking.

https://doi.org/10.3390/math14010135

This study introduces an innovative approach to measuring the development level of the NQPF at the enterprise level using machine learning technology. By analyzing 28,293 sample observations of A-share listed companies in Shanghai and Shenzhen from 2009 to 2022, the study investigates how AI influences the NQPF, focusing on the role of AI innovation subjects to clarify its mechanisms.

This study makes three significant contributions. First, it offers a novel portrayal of the NQPF at the enterprise level. While current research on the NQPF is largely theoretical [1,5] or based on subjective index evaluations [22], this paper uses machine learning and text analysis techniques to assess the NQPF through textual data from company annual reports.

Second, this study is the first to empirically examine the enabling role of AI in the NQPF at the enterprise level, thereby enriching the literature on AI's impact in the micro field. Previous studies have primarily focused on AI's economic effects on firms [13,23] and its potential to optimize production, management, and decision-making [14]. This research expands the understanding of AI's impact on a new form of firm productivity, a previously underexplored area, thus broadening the research on AI technology at the micro-enterprise level.

Third, the study empirically explores the mechanisms by which AI contributes to the NQPF, investigating the relationships between AI and NQPF in terms of factors such as enterprise leadership, digital industry agglomeration, and financial clustering. This work not only advances the literature on AI's impact but also provides insights into how enterprises can leverage AI to foster high-quality economic development through innovative productivity.

The rest of the paper is organized as follows: Section 2 covers theoretical analysis and research hypotheses. Section 3 outlines the research design. Section 4 discusses the empirical result. Finally, Section 5 discusses conclusions and policy implications.

2. Theoretical Analysis and Research Hypotheses

The report of the 20th National Congress of the Communist Party of China underscores the strategic importance of integrating strategic emerging industries and accelerating the development of the digital economy. As a core component of national strategy, artificial intelligence—with machine learning, natural language processing, and deep learning as its technical pillars—has emerged as a pivotal driver of enterprise operational transformation and the enhancement of New Quality Productive Forces. Following Lai et al. [24] and Zhong et al. [25], this study conceptualizes New Quality Productive Forces as a multidimensional construct comprising three core dimensions: technological innovation efficiency (the ability to generate and apply disruptive technologies), factor allocation efficiency (the optimal combination of traditional and digital elements), and industrial synergy efficiency (the coordinated development of enterprises within industrial ecosystems). The following sections systematically elaborate the mechanisms through which AI influences New Quality Productive Forces, integrating classical theoretical perspectives with insights from the digital economy to establish a robust theoretical framework.

2.1. *The Direct Impact Mechanism of Artificial Intelligence on Corporate New Quality Productive Forces*

Artificial Intelligence drives the development of corporate New Quality Productive Forces through three mutually reinforcing pathways, each targeting a distinct core dimension of NQPF.

2.1.1. AI-Driven Enhancement of Technological Innovation Efficiency Through Factor Reconfiguration

Grounded in Schumpeterian theory of innovation [4], artificial intelligence engenders "creative destruction" by structurally transforming the foundational triad of the produc-

https://doi.org/10.3390/math14010135

tion function—laborers, labor tools, and labor objects. This reconfiguration constitutes a core mechanism for advancing technological innovation efficiency, a key dimension of New Quality Productive Forces.

In the domain of laborers, the integration of big data analytics and intelligent decision-support systems augments human cognitive and decision-making capacities. This convergence facilitates profound synthesis between specialized knowledge and cross-disciplinary competencies, contributing not only to individual productivity enhancement but also to the generation of both incremental and radical innovations [26,27]. Illustratively, AI-enabled predictive analytics allow R&D teams to dynamically identify technical bottlenecks, compressing new product development cycles by 30–50% [28].

Regarding labor tools, AI-embedded intelligent equipment and automated systems represent a paradigm shift from conventional manual operations. By extending functional capabilities and operational precision, these technologies transition production modalities from human-centric models to hybrid human–machine collaboration. Such evolution enables refined manufacturing processes and mass-customization capabilities [15]. Empirical evidence from smart robotics implementations demonstrates 24/7 operational continuity with error margins below 0.1%, substantially elevating both productive throughput and quality assurance standards.

Concerning labor objects, AI redefines productive targets through its catalytic role in developing intelligent products and services—from smart home ecosystems to personalized healthcare platforms. This transformation aligns with increasingly diversified and individualized market requirements, generating novel consumption paradigms and entrepreneurial opportunities while expanding the frontiers of technological innovation [6].

2.1.2. Optimization of Factor Allocation Efficiency Through Asymmetric Information Mitigation by AI

Grounded in information asymmetry theory [29], artificial intelligence fundamentally addresses the core issue of resource misallocation inherent in traditional factor allocation mechanisms. By enhancing information transparency and systematically reducing transaction costs, AI contributes to the advancement of factor allocation efficiency—a critical dimension of New Quality Productive Forces.

Mitigation of Information Asymmetry

Through advanced data analytics and predictive modeling, AI enables external investors and resource providers to monitor enterprise operational dynamics in real time, thereby transcending the constraints of conventional information dissemination channels [30]. This technological capability facilitates the directional flow of capital, labor, and other production factors toward high-efficiency enterprises and sectors, optimizing resource distribution at both macro and micro levels [3]. Empirical evidence from the fintech sector demonstrates that AI-powered credit assessment systems substantially narrow the information gap between financial institutions and small- and medium-sized enterprises, increasing SME loan approval rates by approximately 40% [31].

Reduction in Transaction Costs

AI-driven intellectualization of production, information, and decision-making systems streamlines historically redundant allocation processes, such as automated supply chain coordination and intelligent procurement. Studies indicate that such integration reduces associated transaction costs by 20–30% [32]. Moreover, by minimizing resource misallocation attributable to human error or cognitive bias, AI reinforces structural improvements in factor allocation efficiency, establishing a more robust foundation for sustained productivity growth.

https://doi.org/10.3390/math14010135

2.1.3. The Enhancement of Industrial Synergy Efficiency Through Digitally Intelligent Agglomeration

Building upon the theoretical foundations of industrial agglomeration and the digital economy, artificial intelligence emerges as a critical enabler for the digital transformation and intelligent upgrading of industrial clusters. By facilitating cross-sectoral integration and fostering systemic innovation, AI substantially enhances industrial synergy efficiency—constituting the third critical dimension of New Quality Productive Forces.

Virtual Agglomeration Mechanisms

AI transcends the spatial limitations inherent in traditional industrial agglomeration by establishing virtual clusters anchored in data, algorithmic capabilities, and computational resources. Within these digital ecosystems, enterprises engage in efficient interaction and resource reciprocity through intelligent coordination networks, simultaneously intensifying competitive dynamics and collaborative potential [15]. A representative manifestation is the AI-driven platform economy, which integrates upstream and downstream entities across value chains, demonstrably reducing supply chain response latency by approximately 50%.

Emergence of Novel Industrial Archetypes

AI serves as a catalytic force in the technological modernization of conventional industries—exemplified by smart manufacturing and precision agriculture—while concurrently giving rise to innovative organizational frameworks such as the sharing economy and platform-based business models. These emergent industrial configurations synthesize conventional production factors with digital assets—most notably data—thereby advancing the holistic optimization of socioeconomic systems and augmenting the synergistic efficiency of broader industrial ecosystems [3].

Therefore, based on the above inferences, this study proposes the following hypothesis:

Hypothesis 1: Artificial Intelligence technology has significantly improved the company's NQPF.

2.2. Moderating Mechanisms: The Reinforcing Role of Boundary Conditions

The aforementioned direct impact mechanism is not universal; it is contingent on three key boundary conditions—directors' technology backgrounds, digital industry agglomeration, and financial agglomeration—which reinforce the role of AI in promoting NQPF through targeted pathways:

2.2.1. Directors' Technology Background: Strengthening the Implementation of AI-Driven Innovation

Drawing on upper echelons theory [33], the technological expertise possessed by board members fundamentally shapes cognitive frameworks and strategic decision-making patterns. This, in turn, amplifies the efficacy with which AI initiatives translate into enhanced New Quality Productive Forces through three distinct yet interconnected pathways.

Strategic Technology Selection and Deployment

Directors with formal technical training exhibit heightened capacity for identifying viable AI adoption pathways and strategically aligning technological solutions with organizational objectives. Their expertise enables precise evaluation of data ecosystems and algorithmic alternatives, thereby reducing strategic ambiguity in high-stakes technological investments. In algorithmically intensive domains particularly, such directors provide

https://doi.org/10.3390/math14010135

essential guidance in developing AI architectures that maintain functional alignment with core business processes while mitigating implementation risks.

Knowledge Integration and Organizational Learning

Technologically competent leadership employs AI systems as epistemological instruments for synthesizing heterogeneous information streams across internal and external environments. By systematically dismantling institutional knowledge barriers, they accelerate the intra-organizational diffusion of frontier technologies [34]. This orchestrated knowledge management facilitates the appropriation of digital knowledge externalities, directly enhancing firms' technological innovation capacity [2].

Human–Machine System Optimization

Directors possessing technical backgrounds demonstrate superior competency in diagnosing production workflows amenable to automation while architecting hybrid human-AI collaboration frameworks. Their interventions ensure optimal complementarity between artificial and human cognitive systems, thereby maximizing the synergistic potential of intelligent technologies in simultaneously elevating productive efficiency and innovation outcomes [15].

Therefore, based on the above inferences, this study proposes the following hypothesis:

Hypothesis 2a: Directors' technology backgrounds strengthen the positive impact of AI on NQPF by promoting AI-driven innovation implementation.

2.2.2. The Amplification of AI-Driven Factor Allocation Through Digital Industrial Agglomeration

Digital industrial agglomeration serves as a structural catalyst for both the implementation and diffusion of artificial intelligence. By providing an integrated ecosystem for technological deployment, it systematically reinforces AI's capacity to optimize factor allocation and enhance industrial synergy through three synergistic mechanisms.

Data Resource Concentration and Algorithmic Refinement

The spatial concentration of digital enterprises generates rich, multi-dimensional datasets encompassing both corporate operations and individual behavioral patterns. These aggregated data streams constitute essential inputs for the training and iterative refinement of AI models [3]. The resulting enhancement in algorithmic precision and contextual adaptability enables more granular and efficient allocation of production factors across economic units.

Inter-Organizational Innovation Networks

Digital agglomeration fosters the formation of collaborative innovation ecosystems, wherein enterprises collectively engage in the optimization and scaling of AI applications [31]. The shared infrastructure for data exchange and systemic interoperability reduces duplication of efforts and accelerates collective learning, thereby amplifying AI's impact on cross-firm coordination and industrial synergy.

Technological Diffusion and Productivity Conversion

The co-location of complementary entities within digital clusters establishes accelerated pathways for translating AI research into applied productivity tools [15]. This integrated transformation chain facilitates rapid iteration of intelligent systems while concurrently addressing enterprise-specific implementation bottlenecks, thus shortening the temporal gap between technological development and measurable productivity gains.

https://doi.org/10.3390/math14010135

Therefore, based on the above inferences, this study proposes the following hypothesis:

Hypothesis 2b: Digital industry agglomeration strengthens the positive impact of AI on NQPF by enhancing the scale effect of AI-driven factor allocation.

2.2.3. Financial Agglomeration: Mitigating Resource Constraints in AI Development and Deployment

Drawing upon financial geography and innovation economics, the spatial concentration of financial institutions constitutes a critical institutional mechanism for overcoming the resource constraints inherent in AI research, development, and application. Through three interconnected channels, financial agglomeration facilitates the translation of AI innovation into enhanced New Quality Productive Forces.

Reducing Financing Constraints Through Diversified Capital Access

The geographical clustering of financial intermediaries—including commercial banks, venture capital firms, and specialized investment funds—creates a diversified capital ecosystem that expands financing channels for AI-intensive enterprises [35]. This institutional density is particularly consequential for high-risk, capital-intensive AI projects, where traditional financing mechanisms often prove inadequate. By providing layered capital structures and risk-sharing arrangements, financial agglomeration lowers effective financing thresholds while improving project feasibility and long-term sustainability.

Accelerating Commercialization Through Specialized Financial Ecosystems

Financial clusters generate co-location advantages through the development of specialized service ecosystems encompassing technology valuation, regulatory compliance advisory, and innovation incubation services [3]. These complementary institutions reduce transaction costs in the commercialization process, facilitating the transition of AI technologies from laboratory prototypes to scalable market applications. The resulting reduction in market-entry barriers enables more efficient translation of technological breakthroughs into measurable productivity enhancements across economic sectors.

Enhancing Investment Efficiency Through Proximity-Based Information Advantages

The geographical proximity between financial institutions and technology enterprises within agglomerated regions fosters information symmetry through repeated interactions and specialized monitoring capabilities [30]. This institutional proximity reduces due diligence costs while improving the accuracy of risk assessment, particularly important for evaluating the complex technical and commercial prospects of AI initiatives. The resulting improvement in capital allocation efficiency accelerates both the development cycles of AI technologies and their diffusion into productive applications, thereby strengthening the innovation-to-productivity transformation pathway.

Therefore, based on the above inferences, this study proposes the following hypothesis:

Hypothesis 2c: Financial agglomeration strengthens the positive impact of AI on NQPF by alleviating the resource constraints of AI R&D and application.

3. Research Design

3.1. Model Specification

In order to examine the relationship between AI and firms' NQPF, this paper builds the following benchmark model (1) for regression testing:

https://doi.org/10.3390/math14010135

$$NQPF_{i,t} = \alpha_0 + \alpha_1 AItech_{i,t} + \sum Control + \sum FirmFE + \sum YearFE + \varepsilon_{i,t} \tag{1}$$

Thus, the explanatory variable $NQPF_{it}$ is the level of the NQPF of listed company i in year t, $AItech_{it}$ represents the level of AI development of listed company i in year t, Control is the ensemble of control variables, and City FE and Year FE represent the listed company fixed effect and year fixed effect. The main hypothesis of this paper is that when the predicted regression coefficient α_1 is positive and significant, it represents that AI promotes the development of firms' the NQPF.

3.2. Data

This paper selected Chinese-listed companies as the research sample from 2009 to 2022. The following treatments were made to the initial sample: (1) the companies that were ST and *ST were excluded, as well as the listed companies in the financial category; (2) the missing data samples and data anomalous samples were excluded, and the continuous variables were subjected to shrinking of the tail with 1% above and 1% below (Winsorize). This paper's data processing and analysis were completed using STATA 16.0, and finally, 28,293 annual enterprise sample values were obtained. The data source pathway mainly includes the AI patent data from the Artificial Intelligence Patent Research Database (AIPD) of the CNRDS database. The control variable data comes from the CSMAR database and the CNRDS database.

3.3. Variables

3.3.1. Explanatory Variable: Firms' Level of Artificial Intelligence Development (AItech)

Drawing on the research method of Yao et al. [2], Wang et al. [20] and Hussain et al. [36]), this study adopts the natural logarithm of the number of enterprise AI invention patent applications after adding one as an indicator of the level of enterprise AI development. Specifically, this study relies on the Artificial Intelligence Patent Research Database (AIPD) in the CNRDS database, combines patent data from the State Intellectual Property Office and related literature, and identifies whether listed companies have applied for AI-related patents in the current year through the AI lexicon constructed by machine learning methods by searching for the inclusion of the keywords of AI in the titles and abstracts of the patents.

The number of invention patent applications was chosen in this study as an indicator of the level of AI development because the innovation value embodied in invention patents is more significant than that of utility model patents and design patents and can better reflect the quality and value of enterprises in the field of AI technological innovation. Compared with invention patents, the increase in the number of applications for the latter two categories of patents represents more of a "quantitative change" than a "qualitative change" in technological innovation. In addition, compared with the number of patents granted, the number of patent applications is less affected by the intervention of the examining authority, so this study chooses the number of patent applications rather than the number of patents granted as a measurement indicator.

3.3.2. New Quality Productive Force (NQPF)

In this paper, based on machine learning and text mining techniques, combined with the research experience of Lai et al. [24] and Zhong et al. [25], we constructed the enterprise new quality productive force (NQPF) index. The design process of this indicator includes the following steps:

First, a Python web crawler program collected and organized the annual reports of A-share listed companies on the Shanghai and Shenzhen stock exchanges. Then, the text

https://doi.org/10.3390/math14010135

of these reports was extracted using Java's PDF processing library to form the study's core dataset.

Second, referring to the ideas of Li [37] and Brochet et al. [38] in constructing text indicators, this paper analyzes the speeches of the central leaders on the new quality of productivity, the 2024 work report of the Chinese government, as well as policy documents such as the "Implementing Opinions on Promoting the Innovative Development of the Future Industries" jointly issued by the Ministry of Industry and Information Technology (MIIT), Ministry of Education (MOE), and the Ministry of Science and Technology (MOST). Several seed terms related to "new quality productive forces", "advanced productivity", "new materials," "technological innovation," "data elements," "digitalization," "digital economy," "digital productivity," "artificial intelligence," "high quality," "high technology", "high computing power," "high-quality talents," "core technical talents," "cloud technology," "intelligent manufacturing," "ecological manufacturing," "green and low-carbon," "green transformation," and "green productivity."

However, considering that the same concept or thing can usually be expressed by multiple semantically similar words, especially "new quality productive forces" as an emerging economic concept with wide coverage, this paper semantically expands the set of seed words. Based on the Word2Vec technique proposed by Mikolov et al. [39], which has become an important advancement in the field [40], and through its neural network Word Embedding method, the words are transformed into multi-dimensional vectors based on the contextual context, to identify the semantic similarity of the words by calculating the similarity between the word vectors [41]. However, the effectiveness of Word2Vec depends largely on the quality and quantity of the training data, so if the training data is insufficient or fails to cover certain technical terms or uncommon words, the generated word vectors may not accurately reflect the semantics of the words, which in turn affects the recognition of proximate words. In this paper, we use Python's (3.8) "Synonyms" package to identify more accurate near-synonyms for the "new quality productive forces" feature thesaurus based on Word2Vec training and use the CBOW model (Continuous Bag-of-Word) in Word2Vec to identify the near-synonyms. The CBOW model in Word2Vec was used to train more than 1000 featured texts, including government work reports, academic literature, brokerage research reports, etc. The parameters of the CBOW model are as follows.

The detailed parameters of the CBOW model are shown below:

$$Max = \sum_{w=C} Logp(wContext(w)) \tag{2}$$

The basic principle of the CBOW model is to train the word vectors by predicting the probability of the current word occurrence in the Context, and by maximizing the objective function, the Word2Vec word vectors corresponding to the central word can be obtained. In this model, C represents the corpus, w represents the center word, and Context (w) is the Context of the center word. By calculating the similarity between the vectors, words similar to the center word can be identified. In this study, the model is trained based on the texts related to "new quality productive forces" so that the recommended similar words better fit the core meaning of "new quality productive forces". To ensure the accuracy of the results, only words with a similarity of 0.8 or more to the seed words were considered. In addition, 284 keywords related to "new quality productive forces" were identified through manual screening to eliminate words unrelated to the research topic and improve the accuracy of the thesaurus.

Finally, the Jieba word separation tool was used to separate and filter the text of annual reports of listed companies, and the frequency of keywords related to "new quality

https://doi.org/10.3390/math14010135

productive forces" in the annual reports was counted. The word frequency data are normalized by adding one to the original frequency and taking the natural logarithm. In order to better understand the focus and characteristics of the textual data related to "new quality productive forces", this paper draws a word cloud map of the top 50 keywords in terms of word frequency during the whole sample period, shown in Figure A1.

3.3.3. Control Variables

Referring to the study of Yao et al. [2], this paper proposes to include a series of control variables to mitigate the endogeneity problem, specifically firm size (Size), firm age (Age), gearing ratio (Leverage), net profitability of total assets (ROA), firm growth (Growth), board size (BoardSize), whether the chairman of the board and the General Manager are two positions (Dual), equity concentration (Top1), and technological innovation (Lnallpats): Tables A1 and A2 report variable-specific descriptions and descriptive statistics.

4. Empirical Results

4.1. Baseline Regression

Columns (1) to (3) of Table 1 depict the regression results for Artificial Intelligence (AItech) and new quality productive force (NQPF). After adding the control variables, year and firm fixed effects and control variables step by step, it is found that the regression results of the core variables remain unchanged. The regression coefficients of the variable AItech are 0.122, 0.038, and 0.025, respectively, and the estimated coefficients are all positive at the 1% significance level. The results indicate that AI innovation significantly enhances the NQPF of firms, thus confirming the basic Hypothesis 1 of this paper.

Economically, this means that for every 1 standard deviation increase in AItech (1.86), the NQPF index will rise by 0.0465 (0.025×1.86), which is approximately 1.94% of the sample mean of 2.40. Since the NQPF index comprehensively reflects a firm's technological innovation efficiency, resource allocation efficiency, and industry synergy efficiency, this marginal effect should not be overlooked.

From a macroeconomic perspective, Acemoglu et al. [7] estimate the macroeconomic impact of AI, projecting a potential increase of up to 0.66% in total factor productivity (TFP) over 10 years. Existing microeconomic literature also demonstrates AI's impact on traditional TFP at the firm level [20,42], but there is limited research on AI's effect on high-quality TFP. While existing studies estimate that AI raises traditional TFP by 1–1.5% (in elasticity terms), our findings suggest that its association with the qualitative dimensions of productivity—such as technological sophistication, digital integration, and strategic innovation captured by NQPF—is economically meaningful and potentially more salient in the context of high-quality development. Furthermore, Yuan et al. [43] show that AI significantly enhances Green Total Factor Energy Efficiency, while Li et al. [44] empirically confirm that AI can drive new levels of productivity, with particularly strong effects in private enterprises and competitive industries. These findings are consistent with and support the results of this study.

From a theoretical perspective, the findings of this study extend Schumpeter's theory of "creative destruction." The systemic restructuring of workers, labor tools, and labor objects by AI is not just a technological transformation, but also a new mechanism driving "quality-driven" productivity (NQPF). This enriches Schumpeter's [4] theory of disruptive innovation in the digital age. Additionally, expanding on the theory of information asymmetry, we find that AI significantly reduces factor misallocation (coefficient of 0.025), indicating that digital technologies are more effective than traditional contracts or intermediaries in alleviating market frictions. This provides new evidence for Akerlof's [29] framework in the context of the digital era.

https://doi.org/10.3390/math14010135

Table 1. Baseline regression results.

Variable	(1)	(2)	(3)
	NQPF	NQPF	NQPF
AItech	0.122 *** (35.024)	0.038 *** (12.168)	0.025 *** (8.172)
Size		−0.071 *** (−11.538)	0.175 *** (13.998)
Leverage		−0.463 *** (−12.768)	−0.477 *** (−9.890)
Tobinq		−0.005 (−0.895)	−0.005 (−0.982)
Growth		0.109 *** (6.742)	0.011 (0.852)
BoardSize		−0.027 (−0.940)	0.111 *** (2.827)
Dual		0.110 *** (8.905)	0.014 (1.016)
TOP1		−0.005 *** (−13.221)	−0.000 (−0.657)
Age		−0.374 *** (−20.060)	−0.825 *** (−10.701)
Lnallpats		0.210 *** (57.801)	0.048 *** (8.993)
ROA		−0.243 ** (−2.173)	0.190 * (1.838)
Control	No	Yes	Yes
Year FE	No	No	Yes
Firm FE	No	Yes	Yes
_cons	2.346 *** (350.794)	4.862 *** (36.066)	0.747 ** (2.137)
N	28,293	28,293	28,293
adj. R^2	0.042	0.376	0.725

Note: Robust t values are presented in parentheses; *, **, and *** denote significance at the 10%, 5%, and 1% levels, respectively.

4.2. Endogeneity Tests

4.2.1. Instrumental Variables Test

To further address possible endogeneity issues such as reverse causality and omitted variables in the benchmark model, this study draws on Yao et al. [2] to construct an instrumental variable based on whether or not a city had a port of trade (PORT) from 1840 to the end of the Qing Dynasty. The instrumental variable reflects whether a city has served as a trade port. This historical factor may affect the application and development of AI technology in local firms but does not directly affect the NQPF of listed companies. Therefore, this instrumental variable satisfies the requirements of relevance and homogeneity. Specifically, the dummy variable PORT is defined as one if a city has had a port of entry during the period; otherwise, it is 0. Considering that this study uses firm-year level panel data and the establishment of a port of entry is a time-invariant variable, this paper, in order to deal with the time-varying nature of the instrumental variable and selects the

https://doi.org/10.3390/math14010135

annual global AI number of patent applications as a time-varying variable. The number of global AI patent applications can be regarded as an indicator of the level of global AI technology development, and its impact on enterprise productivity is transmitted only indirectly through its effect on the level of AI technology. Therefore, this paper constructs the cross-multiplier term of the natural logarithm of the pass-through port and the number of global AI patent applications (PORT*LnAI) as an instrumental variable (IV1). The result of the under-identified test of instrumental variables is 24.494 and passes at a 1% significant level, indicating no correlation between instrumental variables and endogenous explanatory variables; the result of the test of weak instrumental variables is 23.174, which exceeds the critical value and further rejects the original hypothesis of weak instrumental variables. The first-stage regression results are shown in column (1) of Table 2, indicating that the instrumental variable (IV1) is significantly and positively correlated with the level of AI development, which verifies the robustness of the main conclusions; the second-stage regression results are shown in column (2) of Table 2, indicating that the regression coefficient of AI on the firm's NQPF, as fitted through the instrumental variable, is 0.148, which is significantly positive.

Table 2. Endogeneity tests.

Variable	Instrumental Variables Test				PSM	KLS
	First	Second	First	Second		
	(1) AItech	(2) NQPF	(3) AItech	(4) NQPF	(5) NQPF	(6) NQPF
AItech		0.148 *** (5.681)		0.129 *** (4.021)		
IV1	0.068 * (1.831)					
IV2			0.043 *** (4.035)			
PSM-AItech					0.161 *** (3.461)	
KLS-AItech						0.094 *** (2.781)
K-P rk LM F	24.494 ***		26.751 ***		-	-
K-P rk Wald F	23.174		28.884		-	-
Control	Yes	Yes	Yes	Yes	Yes	Yes
Year FE	Yes	Yes	Yes	Yes	Yes	Yes
Firm FE	Yes	Yes	Yes	Yes	Yes	Yes
N	23,573	23,573	23,247	23,247	4381	28,293

Note: Robust t values are presented in parentheses; *, **, and *** denote significance at the 10%, 5%, and 1% levels, respectively.

On the other hand, this study draws on Huang et al. [45] research methodology by using the historical data of post and telecommunications in 1984 for each city as the second instrumental variable. Considering that the AI development of enterprises is closely related to digital infrastructure, the historical communication conditions of cities may affect the construction of digital infrastructure in the region, affecting the AI development of enterprises. Hence, this variable satisfies the correlation condition. Meanwhile, the city's postal and telecommunications development level directly impacts firm productivity, thus satisfying the homogeneity condition. It adopts the natural logarithm of the cross-multiplication term of the number of Internet access ports in the province where the enterprise was located in the previous year and the number of fixed-line telephones per 10,000 people in 1984 in the prefectural-level city where the enterprise is located as the instrumental variable for the enterprise's AI (IV2). The test result for the under-identification

https://doi.org/10.3390/math14010135

of instrumental variables is 26.751 and passes at a 1% significance level, indicating that there is no correlation between instrumental variables and endogenous explanatory variables; the test result for weak instrumental variables is 23.174, which exceeds the critical value and further rejects the original hypothesis of weak instrumental variables. The first-stage regression results are shown in column (3) of Table 2, indicating that the instrumental variable (IV2) is significantly and positively correlated with the level of AI development, which verifies the robustness of the main conclusions; the second-stage regression results are shown in column (3) of Table 2, indicating that the regression coefficient of AI on firms' NQPF as fitted through the instrumental variable is 0.129, which is still significantly positive. In summary, after correction by instrumental variables, artificial intelligence still has a significant role in enhancing the NQPF of enterprises.

4.2.2. Propensity Score Matching

In order to avoid the screening bias induced by sample self-selection, this paper adopts the propensity score matching method to explore further the impact of AI on the NQPF of enterprises. Specifically, the continuous type control variable in the main regression model is used as a covariate, and through the nearest neighbor matching method, 0.05 is set as the caliper threshold, and the experimental and control groups are matched in the ratio of 1:1. A total of 4381 compliant samples are obtained after matching. The regression results are shown in column (5) of Table 2, indicating that the regression coefficient of Artificial Intelligence (PSM-AItech) on firms' NQPF after propensity score matching is still significantly positive at a 1% significance level, which is consistent with the findings of the main regression analysis.

4.2.3. Kinky Least Squares Estimation

The main limitation of the instrumental variables approach is its strict dependence on the validity of the exclusion restrictions. To further address the endogeneity issue, this study employs the singular least squares estimation (KLS) method for robustness testing [46,47]. The method can efficiently identify the regression coefficients despite weak instrumental variables or the inability to find suitable instrumental variables. In particular, in the case of weak instrumental variables, the confidence intervals provided by the KLS method are usually more informative than those provided by traditional instrumental variable estimation methods. They can better narrow down the assumptions of endogeneity, resulting in clearer analytical results [48]. Column (6) of Table 2 presents the KLS regression results, showing that the regression coefficient of artificial intelligence (KLS-AItech) on firms' NQPF is 0.094, which is significant at the 1% level of significance, validating the robustness of the benchmark regression results.

4.3. Robustness Tests

4.3.1. Replacement of Core Variables

In order to test the robustness of the benchmark regression results, this paper replaces the indicators of firms' NQPF in two ways. First, the disclosure information in the management's analysis and discussion (MD&A) section of a firm's annual report is identified by a Python program. The word frequency of related terms is calculated, and the natural logarithm measures the NQPF level. Since the disclosure requirements of MD&A in the regular reports of enterprises are more complete, they are more accurate than the innovation information provided in the annual reports. Second, based on the study of the government work report and other important documents, this paper divides the 284 keywords related to the NQPF into three categories: new quality laborers, new quality labor materials, and new quality labor objects, and measures their word frequencies in the annual reports of the enterprises and takes the natural logarithm of the word frequencies, and then finally

https://doi.org/10.3390/math14010135

conducts regression analysis on the level of AI and the enterprises' new quality laborers, new quality labor materials, and new quality labor objects. After replacing the variables, the regression results are shown in columns (1) to (4) of Table 3, where the regression coefficients of AItech are still significant at the 1% significance level, proving the robustness of the benchmark regression results.

Table 3. Robustness tests.

Variable	MD&A NQPF	Laborers NQPF	Labor Materials NQPF	Labor Objects NQPF	Change Interval NQPF
	(1)	(2)	(3)	(4)	(5)
AItech	0.029 *** (7.662)				
AItech		0.033 *** (6.232)			
AItech			0.038 *** (6.571)		
AItech				0.041 *** (6.422)	
AItech					0.023 *** (3.391)
Control	Yes	Yes	Yes	Yes	Yes
Year FE	Yes	Yes	Yes	Yes	Yes
Firm FE	Yes	Yes	Yes	Yes	Yes
N	28,293	28,293	28,293	28,293	19,076
adj. R^2	0.725	0.712	0.714	0.701	0.732

Note: Robust t values are presented in parentheses; *, **, and *** denote significance at the 10%, 5%, and 1% levels, respectively.

4.3.2. Change in Sample Interval

To avoid the impact of COVID-19 on firms' NQPF, this paper excludes the sample data after 2020 and re-runs the regression; the results are shown in column (5) of Table 3. The regression coefficient is still significantly positive, consistent with the main regression findings.

4.3.3. Placebo Test

In order to further solve the endogeneity problem and eliminate the influence of random factors on the research results, this paper conducts a placebo test by randomly selecting the experimental group. Listed companies with the level of AI development are randomly selected as the experimental group and the rest as the control group in the existing sample, which is repeatedly estimated 1000 times. As shown in Figure 1, the estimated regression coefficients in the multiple regression results obtained from the placebo test are always concentrated around 0. The true coefficient of the benchmark regression is indicated by the vertical dotted line on the right side, with a value of 0.0324. The estimated coefficients deviate significantly from those obtained in the 1000 randomized trials, proving that the coefficients obtained from the benchmark regression are a small probability event and prove the robustness of the main conclusions of this paper.

https://doi.org/10.3390/math14010135

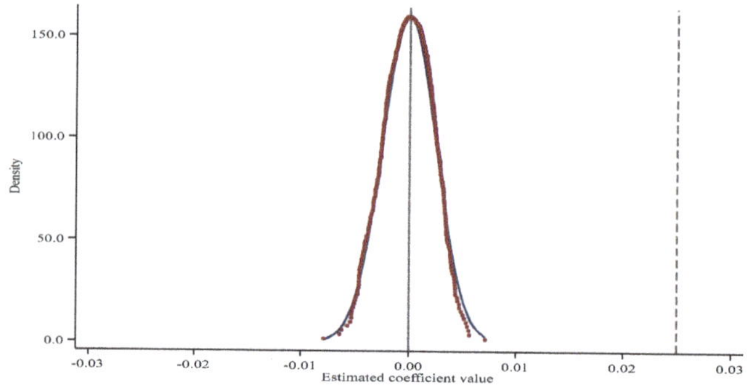

Figure 1. Placebo tests. The above placebo tests results for 1000 regressions with randomized treatment of the explanatory variables demonstrate that the coefficient of the benchmark regression is a small probability event. The brown line represents the density of the regression coefficients derived from 1000 placebo regressions.

4.4. Moderating Mechanism Tests

The mechanism analysis in the previous section concludes that digital industry agglomeration, executive technology background and financial agglomeration positively moderate the impact relationship between AI and new quality productive forces. Therefore, this paper constructs the moderating effect test model as follows:

$$NQPF_{i,t} = \alpha_0 + \alpha_1 AItech_{i,t} + Moderator_{i,t} + \sum \text{Control} + \sum \text{Firm}FE + \sum \text{YearFE} + \varepsilon_{i,t} \quad (3)$$

Among them, the Moderator is the moderating variable, which will be defined and measured later. The rest of the model's parameters (3) are consistent with the baseline model (1). They are used to test the effect of the moderator variable on the relationship between AI and the NQPF.

4.4.1. Digital Industry Clustering

Drawing on Zhang et al. [49] and Ren et al. [50], the number of employees in the information transmission, software and information technology industry in the prefecture-level city where the listed company is located is used as an indicator to construct the location entropy index, which is used to measure the degree of digital industry agglomeration (Int_agg). The specific calculation formula is as follows:

$$Int\_agg = \frac{x_i/y_i}{\sum x_i/y_i} \quad (4)$$

where Int_agg represents the locational entropy of the city's digital industry, x_i is the number of employees in the information transmission, software and information technology service industry in city i where the listed company is located; y_i represents the total number of employees in city i; $\sum x$ represents the number of employees in the digital industry nationwide, and $\sum y$ represents the total number of employees in the country. a larger Int_agg represents a higher degree of digital industry agglomeration in the city where the listed company is located. Column (1) of Table 3 reports the moderating effect of digital industry agglomeration on the relationship between AI and firms' NQPF, and the regression coefficient of the cross-multiplier term AItech × Int_agg is 0.002, which is positively correlated at the 1% significance level, suggesting that the digital industry agglomeration strengthens the role of AI in empowering firms' NQPF by exerting the effect of virtual agglomeration, which proves the derivation of Hypothesis 2b.

https://doi.org/10.3390/math14010135

4.4.2. Directors' Technological Background

Referring to Zhu and Wang [51], this paper constructs the moderator variable executive technological background (Back) by defining a director with a technological background as a director who has a professional background in production, research and development, or design or who has a relevant technical title as an engineer or researcher, and by calculating the proportion of the total number of the board of directors that satisfy the above backgrounds. Column (2) of Table 3 reports the moderating effect of directors' technological background on the relationship between AI and firms NQPF, and the regression coefficient of the cross-multiplier term AItech × Back is 0.11, which is positive at the 1% significance level, indicating that technological directors' technological experience and expertise are conducive to the development of firms' NQPF empowered by AI, which is in line with the theoretical derivation of the previous Hypothesis 2a.

4.4.3. Financial Cluster

Drawing on Song and Ge [52], the financial location entropy coefficient manifests the non-equilibrium situation of the spatial pattern of financial resources. So, the location entropy coefficient is used to measure financial agglomeration.

$$Finance\_agg = \frac{a_i/b_i}{\sum a_i/b_i} \tag{5}$$

As shown in the formula, Finance_agg represents the locational entropy of the city's financial agglomeration, ai is the number of employees in the financial sector of city i where the listed company is located; b_i represents the total employment in city i; $\sum a$ represents the number of employees in the financial sector of the whole country, and $\sum b$ represents the total employment in the whole country. a larger Finance_agg represents a higher degree of financial agglomeration in the city where the listed company is located. Column (3) of Table 4 reports the moderating effect of financial agglomeration on the relationship between AI and firms' NQPF and the regression coefficient of the cross-multiplier term AItech × Finance_agg is 0.063, which is positive at a 1% significance level. The empirical results show that financial agglomeration promotes the allocation of financial resources as production factors between regions by maximizing market profits through financial support, effectively supporting enterprises' AI R&D projects, and promoting the development of the NQPF, which is in line with the theoretical derivation of the previous Hypothesis 2c.

Table 4. Heterogeneity tests.

Variable	High-Tech NQPF (1)	Non-High-Tech NQPF (2)	State-Owned NQPF (3)	Non-State-Owned NQPF (4)	High Policy Support NQPF (5)	Low Policy Support NQPF (6)
AItech	0.002 ***	0.001	0.004 **	0.001 ***	0.003 ***	0.001
	(3.383)	(0.823)	(2.336)	(2.968)	(3.438)	(0.951)
Control	Yes	Yes	Yes	Yes	Yes	Yes
Year FE	Yes	Yes	Yes	Yes	Yes	Yes
Firm FE	Yes	Yes	Yes	Yes	Yes	Yes
_cons	1.087 **	−0.857	1.387 **	−0.326	−1.838 *	0.497
	(2.450)	(−1.436)	(2.175)	(−0.716)	(−1.842)	(0.970)
N	15,803	12,490	10,837	17,456	11,147	17,146
adj. R^2	0.714	0.686	0.712	0.721	0.790	0.702

Note: Robust t values are presented in parentheses; *, **, and *** denote significance at the 10%, 5%, and 1% levels, respectively.

4.5. Heterogeneity Tests

Compared with the development history of international AI, China's AI industry started late and is currently in a rapid development stage, shouldering the goal of promot-

https://doi.org/10.3390/math14010135

ing the transformation and upgrading of trillion-dollar real economy industries [45]. As a capital-intensive and technology-intensive industry, the development of emerging industries such as AI requires strong capital, solid technological capabilities and a large pool of talents, and its advancement of the NQPF of enterprises is affected by the enterprises' own qualifications and external environment. This study further explores the heterogeneity of AI-enabled NQPF development in different enterprises from the perspectives of whether listed companies are high-tech enterprises, the nature of property rights and the strength of policy support.

4.5.1. Enterprise Technology Background

This study divides the sample into high-tech and non-high-tech industries according to the criteria for recognizing high-tech enterprises in the Wind database. The regression results in columns (1) to (2) of Table 4 show that AI significantly promotes the development of the NQPF in high-tech enterprises. At the same time, it does not have a significant role in promoting enterprises in non-high-tech industries. High-tech enterprises usually have a higher level of strong R&D capabilities and technology accumulation. They can quickly absorb and apply AI technology to accelerate the innovation and iteration of products and services, forming a virtuous cycle that enhances the new productivity of enterprises more directly and rapidly. In addition, high-tech enterprises urgently need AI technology, especially in improving their innovation ability and market competitiveness. AI technology can effectively help them gain a competitive advantage. In contrast, non-high-tech enterprises lag significantly in technological transformation and innovation ability. Therefore, AI technology research and development is constrained by capital, technology and talent.

4.5.2. Nature of Property Rights

This study divides the sample into state-owned enterprises (SOEs) and non-state-owned enterprises for group regression according to the nature of the listed companies' ownership. From the regression results in columns (3) to (4) of Table 4, AI significantly promotes the development of the NQPF in both SOEs and non-SOEs. However, the effect of promotion on SOEs is more obvious. This is because SOEs usually have stronger financial support and resource integration capabilities, the cost of AI R&D projects is higher, and SOEs can actively promote the R&D and application of AI under the government's guidance. In addition, SOEs' management systems and decision-making mechanisms are relatively robust, and they can effectively absorb and apply AI technology to achieve productivity breakthroughs. Among non-SOEs, despite the greater flexibility and market-driven nature of AI applications, the breadth and depth of AI technological innovation is less than that of SOEs due to factors such as capital and technology accumulation.

4.5.3. Policy Support

Referring to the study of Yao et al. [2], in order to measure the strength of government support for AI in different regions, we collect provincial government work reports and examine whether AI is included in the work reports of provincial governments to measure the strength of local government policy support for AI. The regression results in columns (5) to (6) of Table 4 show that the strength of local government policy support influences the impact of AI on firms' NQPF. This is specifically manifested in the fact that in regions with strong policy support, the driving effect of AI on firms' NQPF is more significant. First, in regions with strong policy support, the government encourages enterprises to increase investment in technological innovation and AI applications through financial subsidies, tax incentives and R&D funding, creating favorable conditions for enterprises to introduce AI technology. Secondly, improving the policy environment can shorten the time for the technology to be put into practice, improve the productivity of enterprises, and promote the

https://doi.org/10.3390/math14010135

optimal allocation of resources, thus significantly enhancing the NQPF. On the contrary, in regions with weak policy support, the R&D and promotion of AI are constrained by financial and technical barriers. The differentiation of regional policy support characterizes the impact of AI on the NQPF, and the policy environment is crucial to its role.

5. Conclusions and Policy Implications

Taking Chinese A-share listed companies from 2009 to 2022 as the research sample, this study innovatively measures the level of the NQPF of enterprises through machine learning and text analytics, explores the impact of artificial intelligence on the new quality productive forces of enterprises, and discusses the regulating mechanism from three dimensions. The findings show that AI drives the development of new productivity of enterprises, which is still valid after considering the interference of a series of influencing factors, and that directors' technological background, digital industry agglomeration and financial agglomeration positively regulate the relationship between AI and new productivity of enterprises. Further analysis reveals that the positive impact of AI on the NQPF of enterprises is more significant in high-tech enterprises, state-owned enterprises and enterprises with strong policy support.

This paper puts forward the following suggestions based on the above empirical findings. First, based on the main regression analysis, we found that AI technology has a significant positive impact on the enhancement of enterprise NQPF. Therefore, the government should increase support for enterprises in applying AI technologies, particularly by providing financial subsidies and tax incentives for AI innovation to encourage enterprises to accelerate the adoption of AI to boost productivity. For small and medium-sized enterprises (SMEs), the government could establish special funds to help them overcome technological and financial barriers and support their investments in AI research, development, and application. These policies can effectively promote the improvement of enterprise productivity and drive high-quality economic development.

Second, according to the moderation analysis, we found that the technology background of the board, digital industry agglomeration, and financial industry agglomeration play significant moderating roles in the relationship between AI and new quality productivity. Therefore, the government should encourage and support top management, especially those with technical backgrounds, to engage in AI innovation, which will enhance the efficiency of AI applications in enterprises. Additionally, the government can promote digital industry agglomeration by encouraging collaboration and resource-sharing among enterprises, particularly in key areas of digital transformation such as smart manufacturing and big data applications. Moreover, financial industry agglomeration has a positive effect on the promotion of AI applications, so the government should strengthen financial support, particularly by providing more funding for AI technology research and development to help enterprises accelerate the process of AI innovation and application.

Third, through the heterogeneity analysis, we found that the enabling effect of AI technology on new quality productivity is more significant in high-tech enterprises, state-owned enterprises, and enterprises with strong policy support. Therefore, we recommend that, for high-tech enterprises, the government should provide more research and development support and financial subsidies, encouraging deeper investment in AI technology research, development, and application to foster technological innovation. For state-owned enterprises, the government should continue to strengthen policy support, including increasing financial investment and providing technical support, to promote the wider application of AI in SOEs, particularly in improving production efficiency and innovation capacity. For regions with strong policy support, the government should further enhance

https://doi.org/10.3390/math14010135

policy incentives, improve the policy environment, and provide better infrastructure and support for the widespread adoption of AI technology by enterprises.

Finally, the AI development level indicator (AItech) used in this study is a composite measure that encompasses innovative outputs from core AI technologies, including machine learning, natural language processing, and computer vision. While this effectively captures the overall intensity of a firm's AI innovation, it does not differentiate between the specific impacts of various AI technology subcategories or application scenarios (such as process automation, intelligent customer service, precision marketing, or R&D assistance) on NQPF. Since New Quality Productive Forces is a multidimensional concept that integrates technological innovation, resource allocation, and industrial synergy, it is likely to benefit from the combined effects of multiple AI technologies. However, understanding the specific contributions of different technology paths is crucial for firms to make precise AI investment decisions. Future research can leverage more granular patent classification data or corporate AI investment announcement texts to decompose the types of AI technologies and explore their heterogeneous impact mechanisms.

Author Contributions: Conceptualization, L.T. and Y.Z. (Yuan Zhong); methodology, X.L.; software, Y.Z. (Yuxin Zhao); Validation, L.T., Y.Z. (Yuxin Zhao) and Y.Z. (Yuan Zhong); Formal analysis, L.T.; investigation, Y.Z. (Yuan Zhong); Resources, Y.Z. (Yuan Zhong); Data curation, Y.Z. (Yuxin Zhao); Writing—original draft preparation, L.T. and Y.Z. (Yuxin Zhao); Writing—review and editing, L.T. and Y.Z. (Yuan Zhong); Visualization, Y.Z. (Yuan Zhong); Supervision, Y.Z. (Yuan Zhong); Project administration, X.L.; Funding acquisition, X.L. All authors have read and agreed to the published version of the manuscript.

Funding: Humanities and Social Science Foundation of the Ministry of Education of China [25YJC790053].

Data Availability Statement: The data presented in this study are available on request from the corresponding author. Due to the fact that part of the data involves confidential information of the research cooperation unit and the privacy protection requirements of the survey subjects, the raw data cannot be publicly shared. Researchers who meet the legitimate research purposes can contact the corresponding author to request access to the data.

Conflicts of Interest: The authors declare no conflicts of interest.

Appendix A

Table A1. Variable definitions.

Variable	Definition
NQPF	The natural logarithm of the word frequency representing new quality productive forces within the annual reports of listed companies is utilized
AItech	The natural logarithm of the number of invention-based AI applications filed by listed companies plus one
Tobinq	The ratio of the market value of a firm's stock to the replacement cost of the asset represented by the stock
Size	The natural log of the number of employees
Roa	The ratio of company's net profit to total assets
Levrage	Corporate liabilities as a percentage of total assets
BoardSize	The natural log of the number of directors on the board
Growth	The ratio of increase in operating income for the current year to total operating income for the previous year
Age	The current year minus the year of listing plus one is taken as the natural logarithm
Dual	Chairman and CEO are the same person
Top1	The number of shares held by the largest shareholder as a percentage of total shares
Lnallpats	Total number of patent applications filed by firms plus one taken as a natural logarithm

https://doi.org/10.3390/math14010135

Table A2. Descriptive statistics.

VarName	Obs	Mean	SD	Min	Max
AItech	28,293	0.44	1.86	0.000	14.000
NQPF	28,293	2.40	1.12	0.000	4.796
Tobinq	28,293	1.99	1.21	0.848	7.826
ROA	28,293	0.04	0.06	−0.164	0.210
Size	28,293	22.28	1.28	20.029	26.248
Age	28,293	2.91	0.33	1.792	3.526
Leverage	28,293	0.43	0.20	0.060	0.880
Growth	28,293	0.17	0.38	−0.522	2.311
BoardSize	28,293	2.13	0.20	1.609	2.708
Dual	28,293	0.27	0.44	0.000	1.000
TOP1	28,293	0.35	0.15	0.094	0.748
Lnallpats	28,293	2.81	1.77	0.000	7.056

Figure A1. Word cloud diagram. Word clouds were generated for various sample periods by analyzing the word frequencies associated with firms' new quality productive forces. Due to space constraints, only the word cloud corresponding to the full sample period is presented. The most frequently occurring words are "new technologies" and "new materials," indicating that listed companies currently place significant emphasis on technological innovation and the development of new materials. Furthermore, emerging digital technologies, including artificial intelligence and the Internet of Things, have also garnered widespread attention.

References

1. Liu, W. Scientific understanding and practical development of new qualitative productive forces. *Econ. Res. J.* **2024**, 4–11.
2. Yao, W.; Zhang, K.; Guo, L.; Feng, X. How can artificial intelligence improve enterprise production efficiency? From the perspective of the adjustment of labor skill structure. *Manag. World* **2024**, 101–116+133+117–122. [CrossRef]
3. Yu, D. Computing power: A new qualitative productivity in the era of digital economy. *Financ. Trade Res.* **2024**, 1–16.
4. Schumpeter, J.A. *The Theory of Economic Development*; Harvard University Press: Cambridge, MA, USA, 1912.
5. Huang, Z. AI large model empowers the accelerated development of new qualitative productive forces: Internal mechanism, practical obstacles and practical approaches. *Reform Strategy* **2024**, 1–12.
6. Huang, M.H.; Rust, R.T. A strategic framework for artificial intelligence in marketing. *J. Acad. Mark. Sci.* **2021**, *49*, 30–50. [CrossRef]
7. Acemoglu, D. The simple macroeconomics of AI. *Econ. Policy* **2025**, *40*, 13–58. [CrossRef]

https://doi.org/10.3390/math14010135

8. Cong, L.W.; Xie, D.; Zhang, L. Knowledge accumulation, privacy, and growth in a data economy. *Manag. Sci.* **2021**, *67*, 6480–6492. [CrossRef]
9. Rammer, C.; Fernández, G.P.; Czarnitzki, D. Artificial intelligence and industrial innovation: Evidence from German firm-level data. *Res. Policy* **2022**, *51*, 104555. [CrossRef]
10. Babina, T.; Fedyk, A.; He, A.; Hodson, J. Artificial intelligence, firm growth, and product innovation. *J. Financ. Econ.* **2024**, *151*, 103745. [CrossRef]
11. Wang, Z.; Zhang, T.; Ren, X.; Shi, Y. AI adoption rate and corporate green innovation efficiency: Evidence from Chinese energy companies. *Energy Econ.* **2024**, *132*, 107499. [CrossRef]
12. Makridis, C.A.; Mishra, S. Artificial intelligence as a service, economic growth, and well-being. *J. Serv. Res.* **2022**, *25*, 505–520. [CrossRef]
13. Noy, S.; Zhang, W. Experimental evidence on the productivity effects of generative artificial intelligence. *Science* **2023**, *381*, 187–192. [CrossRef]
14. Damioli, G.; Van Roy, V.; Vertesy, D. The impact of artificial intelligence on labor productivity. *Eurasian Bus. Rev.* **2021**, *11*, 1–25. [CrossRef]
15. Liu, Y.; He, Z. Synergistic Industrial Agglomeration, New quality productive forces and high-quality development of the manufacturing industry. *Int. Rev. Econ. Financ.* **2024**, *94*, 103373. [CrossRef]
16. Lu, Y.; Zhou, Y. A review on the economics of artificial intelligence. *J. Econ. Surv.* **2021**, *35*, 1045–1072. [CrossRef]
17. Taeihagh, A. Governance of artificial intelligence. *Policy Soc.* **2021**, *40*, 137–157. [CrossRef]
18. Wang, S.; Liu, Y. Intelligent productivity: A new quality productive forces. *J. Contemp. Econ. Res.* **2024**, 36–45.
19. Zhai, S.; Liu, Z. Artificial intelligence technology innovation and firm productivity: Evidence from China. *Financ. Res. Lett.* **2023**, *58*, 104437. [CrossRef]
20. Wang, K.L.; Sun, T.T.; Xu, R.Y. The impact of artificial intelligence on total factor productivity: Empirical evidence from China's manufacturing enterprises. *Econ. Change Restruct.* **2023**, *56*, 1113–1146. [CrossRef]
21. Parteka, A.; Kordalska, A. Artificial intelligence and productivity: Global evidence from AI patent and bibliometric data. *Technovation* **2023**, *125*, 102764. [CrossRef]
22. Guangqin, L.I.; Mengjiao, L.I. Provincial-level new quality productive forces in China: Evaluation, spatial pattern and evolution characteristics. *Econ. Geogr.* **2024**, *44*, 116–125.
23. Yang, C.H. How artificial intelligence technology affects productivity and employment: Firm-level evidence from Taiwan. *Res. Policy* **2022**, *51*, 104536. [CrossRef]
24. Lai, X.; Yue, S.; Guo, C.; Gao, P. Unleashing global potential: The impact of digital technology innovation on corporate international diversification. *Technol. Forecast. Soc. Change* **2024**, *208*, 123727. [CrossRef]
25. Zhong, Y.; Lai, H.; Zhang, L.; Guo, L.; Lai, X. Does public data openness accelerate new quality productive forces? Evidence from China. *Econ. Anal. Policy* **2025**, *85*, 1409–1427. [CrossRef]
26. Montobbio, F.; Staccioli, J.; Virgillito, M.E.; Vivarelli, M. Robots and the origin of their labor-saving impact. *Technol. Forecast. Soc. Change* **2022**, *174*, 121122. [CrossRef]
27. Jia, N.; Luo, X.; Fang, Z.; Liao, C. When and how artificial intelligence augments employee creativity. *Acad. Manag. J.* **2024**, *67*, 5–32. [CrossRef]
28. Pei, J.; Wang, H.; Peng, Q.; Liu, S. Saving face: Leveraging artificial intelligence-based negative feedback to enhance employee job performance. *Hum. Resour. Manag.* **2024**, *63*, 775–790. [CrossRef]
29. Akerlof, G.A. Behavioral macroeconomics and macroeconomic behavior. *Am. Econ. Rev.* **2002**, *92*, 411–433. [CrossRef]
30. Cui, X.; Xu, B.; Razzaq, A. Can application of artificial intelligence in enterprises promote the corporate governance? *Front. Environ. Sci.* **2022**, *10*, 944467. [CrossRef]
31. Queiroz, M.; Anand, A.; Baird, A. Manager appraisal of artificial intelligence investments. *J. Manag. Inf. Syst.* **2024**, *41*, 682–707. [CrossRef]
32. Zhao, P.; Gao, Y.; Sun, X. How does artificial intelligence affect green economic growth?—Evidence from China. *Sci. Total Environ.* **2022**, *834*, 155306. [CrossRef] [PubMed]
33. Hambrick, D.C.; Mason, P.A. Upper echelons: The organization as a reflection of its top managers. *Acad. Manag. Rev.* **1984**, *9*, 193–206. [CrossRef]
34. Lévesque, M.; Obschonka, M.; Nambisan, S. Pursuing impactful entrepreneurship research using artificial intelligence. *Entrep. Theory Pract.* **2022**, *46*, 803–832. [CrossRef]
35. Li, H.; Cui, H.; Wu, F. Does Financial Agglomeration Promote the Digital Transformation of Enterprises: Empirical Evidence Based on Big Data Analysis of Enterprise Annual Report Text. *South. Econ.* **2022**, 60–81.
36. Hussain, M.; Yang, S.; Maqsood, U.S.; Zahid, R.A. Tapping into the green potential: The power of artificial intelligence adoption in corporate green innovation drive. *Bus. Strategy Environ.* **2024**, *33*, 4375–4396. [CrossRef]
37. Li, F. Textual analysis of corporate disclosures: A survey of the literature. *J. Account. Lit.* **2010**, *29*, 143–165.

https://doi.org/10.3390/math14010135

38. Brochet, F.; Loumioti, M.; Serafeim, G. Speaking of the short-term: Disclosure horizon and managerial myopia. *Rev. Account. Stud.* **2015**, *20*, 1122–1163. [CrossRef]
39. Mikolov, T.; Sutskever, I.; Chen, K.; Corrado, G.S.; Dean, J. Distributed representations of words and phrases and their compositionality. In *Advances in Neural Information Processing Systems*; Curran Associates Inc.: Red Hook, NY, USA, 2013; Volume 26.
40. LeCun, Y.; Bengio, Y.; Hinton, G. Deep learning. *Nature* **2015**, *521*, 436–444. [CrossRef]
41. Bengio, Y.; Ducharme, R.; Vincent, P.; Jauvin, C. A neural probabilistic language model. *J. Mach. Learn. Res.* **2003**, *3*, 1137–1155.
42. Gao, X.; Feng, H. AI-driven productivity gains: Artificial intelligence and firm productivity. *Sustainability* **2023**, *15*, 8934. [CrossRef]
43. Yuan, B.; Gu, R.; Wang, P.; Hu, Y. How Does New Quality Productive Forces Affect Green Total Factor Energy Efficiency in China? Consider the Threshold Effect of Artificial Intelligence. *Sustainability* **2025**, *17*, 7012. [CrossRef]
44. Li, X.; Tang, H.; Chen, Z. Artificial intelligence and the new quality productive forces of enterprises: Digital intelligence empowerment paths and spatial spillover effects. *Systems* **2025**, *13*, 105. [CrossRef]
45. Huang, Q.; Yu, Y.; Zhang, S. Internet development and manufacturing productivity improvement: Internal mechanism and Chinese experience. *China Ind. Econ.* **2019**, *8*, 5–23.
46. Kiviet, J.F. Testing the impossible: Identifying exclusion restrictions. *J. Econom* **2020**, *218*, 294–316. [CrossRef]
47. Kiviet, J.F. Instrument-free inference under confined regressor endogeneity and mild regularity. *Econom. Stat.* **2023**, *25*, 1–22. [CrossRef]
48. Fang, M.; Njangang, H.; Padhan, H.; Simo, C.; Yan, C. Social media and energy justice: A global evidence. *Energy Econ.* **2023**, *125*, 106886. [CrossRef]
49. Zhang, J.; Fu, Y.; Zhang, B. Research on the firm spatial distribution and influencing factors of the service-oriented digital industry in yangtze river delta. *Sustainability* **2022**, *14*, 14902. [CrossRef]
50. Ren, S.; Li, L.; Han, Y.; Hao, Y.; Wu, H. The emerging driving force of inclusive green growth: Does digital economy agglomeration work? *Bus. Strategy Environ.* **2022**, *31*, 1656–1678. [CrossRef]
51. Zhu, Y.; Wang, G. The impact of techno-executive power and non-techno-executive power on firm performance: An empirical test from China's A-share listed high-tech enterprises. *Account. Res.* **2017**, 73–79+97.
52. Song, Z.; Ge, X. Financial agglomeration, government intervention, opening-up and regional economic development. *Stat. Decis.* **2022**, 150–153.

https://doi.org/10.3390/math14010135

MDPI AG
Grosspeteranlage 5
4052 Basel
Switzerland
Tel.: +41 61 683 77 34

MDPI Books Editorial Office
E-mail: books@mdpi.com
www.mdpi.com/books